1000
MICROWAVE
RECIPE
COOKBOOK

1000
MICROWAVE
RECIPE
COOKBOOK

EDITED BY CAROL BOWEN

OCTOPUS BOOKS

Before you begin:

★ All the timings in this book have been tested using ovens with a maximum output of 650–700 watts. Food will need to be cooked for a little longer in a cooker with a lower output.

★ Cooking times may also vary slightly depending on the type and shape of the container used and the temperature of the food, therefore *always observe your manufacturer's instructions*.

★ For all recipes, quantities are given in both metric and imperial measures. Follow one set of measures only, as they are not interchangeable.

★ Standard spoon measurements are used in all recipes:
1 tablespoon = 15 ml
1 teaspoon = 5 ml

All spoon measurements are level.

★ All food is cooked uncovered, unless otherwise stated.

★ Eggs are size 3, unless otherwise stated.

★ Water is cold, unless otherwise stated.

First published 1988 by Octopus Books Limited
a division of the Octopus Publishing Group
Michelin House
81 Fulham Road
London SW3 6RB

© 1988 Octopus Books Limited

ISBN 0 7064 3327 0

Printed in Austria

CONTENTS

MICROWAVE KNOW-HOW

WHAT IS MICROWAVE ENERGY?

Microwave energy is a type of high frequency radio wave positioned at the top end of the radio band. The electromagnetic waves are of very short length and high frequency – hence the name 'microwaves'.

Inside the microwave oven is the magnetron vacuum tube – the so-called 'heart' of the cooker. This converts ordinary household electrical energy into high-frequency microwaves. These are passed, via a wave guide, into the stirrer fan, which distributes the microwave evenly in the oven.

Once in the oven the microwaves can then do three things:

• They can pass through a substance without changing it. Glass, pottery, china and most plastics allow microwaves to pass through them and therefore make ideal cooking utensils.

• They can be reflected from a surface. Metals reflect microwaves, which is why they are safely contained within the metal cavity of the oven, and why cooking utensils must be non-metallic.

• They can be absorbed by a substance. Microwaves are absorbed by the moisture molecules in food, causing them to vibrate rapidly, producing heat to cook the food. The rate at which these molecules vibrate is many thousands of times per second.

THE MICROWAVE OVEN

All ovens consist of a basic unit comprising a door, a magnetron, wave guide, wave stirrer, power supply, power cord and controls. Some have additional features, but the basics upon which they work remain the same.

The plug (a) is inserted into the socket and the electricity flows to the power transformer (b) which increases the ordinary household voltage. This passes into a high-voltage rectifier and capacitor (c) which changes the high alternating voltage to indirectional voltage. The indirectional voltage is applied to the magnetron (d) which converts the electrical energy into electromagnetic or microwave energy.

This energy is then passed through to the wave guide (e) which directs the microwave energy into the oven

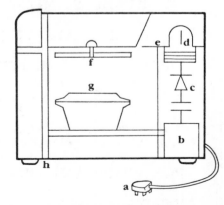

Cross-section diagram of a microwave oven

cavity. As the microwaves enter the oven the wave stirrer **(f)** turns slowly to distribute the microwaves in an even pattern around the oven.

The oven cavity **(g)**, made of metal, contains the microwaves safely and deflects the waves from the walls and base of the oven to be absorbed by the food.

The oven door and the door frame **(h)** are fitted with special seals to ensure that the microwaves are kept safely within the oven. Usually at least one cut–out device is incorporated so that the micro-wave energy is automatically switched off when the door is open.

FEATURES OF MICROWAVE OVENS

The features and controls on modern microwave ovens are numerous and, with increasing sophistication, become more tailored to individual needs.

The very simplest controls on a microwave oven are likely to be a timer and a 'cook' button or switch. To operate them, you simply put the food in the oven, close the door, set the timer for the cooking time required and start the microwave energy by depressing the 'cook' control. The microwave will cook with microwave energy until the timer moves to the 'off' position, when it will automatically stop the microwave energy.

Exactly the same would happen if the door were opened during the cooking period. Restarting can take place only when the door is closed and the 'cook' button depressed again.

Timer Control: Most microwave ovens have at least one timer, which generally is up to 30 minutes. Gradua-tions of a second are usually incorpor-ated at the lower end of the scale for short cooking times where timing is very critical, whereas half-minute – and sometimes minute – graduations are given at the higher end of the scale. Often the control is in the form of a sliding device, rather than a dial, and care should be taken to set the timer accurately.

Cook Control: This is sometimes called the start control since it simply switches on the microwave power whether you are thawing, reheating or prime cooking.

On/Off Control: As well as begin-ning the cooking operation, in many types of microwave oven the on/off control also switches on the cooling fan and the interior oven light. Some ovens have a delay of about ten seconds after being switched on, to allow the power source to warm up. An oven without an on/off control will be oper-ated automatically when it is switched on at the power supply. (If the door has inadvertently been left open, the oven will not switch on.)

Power Control Dial: This is discus-sed in greater detail later but, very simply, it enables you to decrease the microwave energy, introducing a 'slower' cooking rate for items that require it. Basic microwave ovens with on/off controls operate the power on a constant full or high power, whereas variable control microwave ovens have a control that enables the power to be reduced to low, medium or high, graduated in numbers from, say, 1-6, or expressed verbally as 'simmer', 'roast', 'reheat', and so on.

Indicator Lights: These are very useful as a reminder that a cooking operation has been set, is in progress or has finished.

Audible Reminders: Usually in the form of a bell or buzzer, audible reminders tell you that a cooking operation is complete.

Cooking Guide: A panel incorporated into the front of the oven giving basic cooking information and times needed for various cooking operations (not on all ovens).

Thermometers: These may only be used if the manufacturer specifically states that it is possible. Some manufacturers supply integral thermometers specially designed for use in their ovens in conjunction with a control for cooking meats and roasts.

Turntable: Some ovens incorporate a turntable instead of, or as an extra to, the wave stirrer; the turntable's purpose is to distribute the microwaves evenly through the food. The revolving turntable can often be removed but, if it can't, then the size and shape of dishes that can be used in that microwave are restricted.

'Off' Indicator: This tells you when cooking time is complete.

Interior Oven Light: This generally lights up as soon as the oven is turned n.

Splash Guard: Sometimes the wave stirrer has a special protective guard to protect it from food splashing.

Removable Floor or Base: Made of special glass or plastic, a removable floor or base acts as a spillage plate and positions the food to best advantage in the oven.

Other features which may be found in microwave ovens include:

Automatic Defrost: Foods may be defrosted in the microwave oven by giving them short bursts of energy followed by rest periods until the food is evenly thawed. (For timings see pages 326–332.) An automatic defrost button will automatically turn the energy on and off at regular intervals.

Browning Element: Rather like an electric grill, this is sometimes incorporated into the top of the microwave oven and can be used to pre-brown food, or to brown it after or during microwave cooking.

Slow Cook Control: This enables the microwave output to be reduced or the power to be 'pulsed', thereby slowing down the cooking time.

Keep Warm/Stay Hot Control: Based on a very low power pulse, this enables you to keep food warm for up to one hour without further cooking.

Two Power-level Cooking: A recent innovation, in which the microwaves enter from the sides rather than from the top of the oven. This means two cooking levels or more may be used simultaneously with different power ratings.

OVEN CONTROL SETTINGS

The simplest form of microwave oven has an on/off control whereby energy is either switched on or off. The energy that is turned on operates on FULL POWER.

Greater control over energy has now been made possible with the introduction of the variable or multiple controls described previously. The variable control dial 'pulses' the energy into the microwave cavity, thereby allowing different speeds of microwave cooking. The pulse control turns the microwave power on and off automatically every so many seconds so that the food receives a quick burst of energy with rests in between to enable the heat to

GUIDE TO COMPARATIVE MICROWAVE OVEN CONTROL SETTINGS

	DEFROST	LOW	MEDIUM		FULL		
Descriptions of settings used in this book	1	2	3	4	5	6	7
Descriptions of settings available on popular microwave ovens	keep warm low 2	simmer 3	stew medium/low 4	defrost medium 5	bake medium 6	roast high 7–8	full/high normal 10
Approximate % power input	20%	30%	40%	50%	60%	70%	100%
Approximate power output in watts	120–150W	200W	250W	300W	400W	500–550W	650–700W
Cooking time in minutes (for times greater than 10 minutes simply add the figures in the appropriate columns)	4	3¼	2½	2	1¾	1¼	1
	8	6¾	5	4	3¼	2¾	2
	12	10	7½	6	5	4	3
	16	13¼	10	8	6¾	5¼	4
	20	16¾	12½	10	8¼	6¾	5
	24	20	15	12	10	8	6
	28	23¼	17½	14	12	9¼	7
	32	26¾	20	16	13¼	10¾	8
	36	30	22½	18	15	12	9
	40	33¼	25	20	16½	13¼	10

distribute itself evenly. This is especially useful when defrosting foods and cooking dishes that need slower cooking, such as less tender cuts of meat and delicate dishes like home-made egg custards.

Use of Power Control Dial

Note: It is important to use the power control settings outlined here in conjunction with the chart on page 9, showing comparable descriptions of variable control power settings for popular microwave ovens and giving a guide to adjusting the cooking time for the different foods.

Defrost (1, Keep Warm, Low or 2): Energy on for about 20 per cent of the time. Use for keeping foods warm for up to half an hour, softening butter, cream cheese and chocolate, proving yeast mixtures, and for slow defrosting of meat, fish and dairy foods or dishes made with rice or pasta.

Low (2, Simmer or 3): Energy on for about 30 per cent of the time. Use for quick defrosting of meat, poultry and fish, finishing slow-cooking casseroles and stews or for cooking delicate egg dishes.

Medium (4, Defrost, Medium or 5): Energy on for about 50 per cent of the time. Use for roasting meats and poultry, cooking fish, yeast doughs, pâtés, rice and pasta.

Full (7, Full/High or 10): Energy on 100 per cent of the time. The only setting on basic on/off models. Use for most prime cooking, quick reheating of shallow dishes of food and fast-speed dishes. Made-up meat products (casseroles with vegetables), soups, sauces and stock can be defrosted on this setting as well.

FACTORS AFFECTING COOKING

Starting Temperature of Food

The colder the temperature of a food the longer it will take to cook, so you should adjust the times in the recipes according to whether your ingredients are at room temperature, chilled or frozen. *All the times given in the recipes in this book refer to foods cooked from room temperature unless otherwise stated.*

For best results, defrost frozen foods first, then cook them.

Density of Food

The denser the food, the longer it will take to cook. A fairly small but dense piece of steak may be similar in size to a hamburger but the hamburger's looser texture means it will cook faster in the microwave. Defrosting and reheating times will also be longer for denser foods like meat than for light, foods.

Remember that when cooking both a dense and a light porous substance together, you should take care to apply more energy to the denser mass of food. In most cases this can be done by arranging the denser food to the outside of the dish where it receives more energy. Where this is not possible, such as when cooking a pie, insert a rolled-up piece of brown paper about 2.5 cm (1 inch) in length into the centre of the pie to direct the energy and encourage microwaves to the dense filling rather than the light crust.

Shape of Food

In both conventional and microwave cooking, thin areas of food cook faster than thick areas. To compensate for this in microwave cooking, thicker pieces of food should be placed to the outer edges of the dish where they receive most energy, and thinner pieces kept to the centre.

Wherever possible, try to secure foods into regular shapes – bone and roll a rib of beef, for example.

When cooking unstuffed poultry or game birds in a microwave oven, tuck the wings, legs and any tail end into the body shape of the bird to prevent overheating and dehydration in these areas. Alternatively these parts of the bird may be wrapped in lightweight aluminium foil which can be removed for the last 10-15 minutes' cooking time. Protecting small areas of a food is the only purpose for which foil may be used in the microwave.

Size of Food
Larger pieces of food take longer to cook than smaller pieces because microwaves only penetrate to a depth of about 5 cm (2 inches), the heat penetrating right to the centre by induction. For best results, cook portions similar in size and shape together.

Quantity of Food
Timings in the microwave oven are directly related to the quantity of food being cooked. For example, two jacket potatoes will take almost twice as long to cook as a single jacket potato.

As a general guideline, if you double the amount of food being cooked in the microwave you should increase the cooking time by 50-75 per cent. Err on the side of safety by increasing at the lower end of this percentage scale to begin with.

Composition of Food
Fats and sugars absorb microwave energy at a greater rate than liquids and other components. Therefore foods like bacon and jams will cook faster than foods like vegetables and meats.

Foods with a low water content like breads and cakes will also cook faster than those with a high water content like soups and vegetables.

Height of Food in the Oven
Any food that is positioned near to the energy source will cook faster than food further away, whether cooked conventionally or in the microwave oven. In some microwave ovens the energy source may be near the roof of the oven, in others it may be near the base; check your instruction manual for details and advice.

For best results, turn over, rearrange or stir foods during cooking to take this action into account.

Bones in Meat
Bone always conducts heat into a food. Wherever possible, for even cooking, remove the bone and roll the meat into a regular shape.

If you do not choose to do this, then remember the meat next to the bone will cook faster, and you should shield this area with a little foil to prevent overcooking for about half of the overall cooking time.

MICROWAVE COOKING TECHNIQUES

Most of the techniques used in microwave cooking are the same as those employed in conventional cooking but, because of the speed at which foods cook, they have to be followed carefully and employed at regular intervals for good cooking results. The following techniques speed up cooking or promote even heating.

Turning Over: We turn foods over in conventional cooking and this is also important in microwave cooking to ensure even results. Turning is often used with the three techniques of stirring, rotating and rearranging.

Stirring: This helps to distribute the heat evenly through the food throughout the cooking time. Always stir from the outside of the dish where the food cooks first.

Rotating: When the food cannot be stirred or turned over the dish should be rotated in the oven. This is necessary when the microwave oven does not have a turntable and is particularly important when cooking cakes and large items such as meat roasts.

Rearranging: To ensure even cooking, foods can be rearranged in the dish during cooking or defrosting. In most cases this is generally only necessary once during the cooking or defrosting time.

Covering Foods: Covering foods during cooking can speed up the cooking and retain the moisture. A loose cover will also prevent spattering on the oven walls, especially from fatty foods like bacon, sausages and chops.

A tight-fitting lid on a dish, microwave cling film, greaseproof paper, roasting bags without the metal ties (use an elastic band or a piece of string to secure), absorbent kitchen paper, or an inverted plate all make suitable covers in the oven.

Arranging Foods: Careful arranging of foods in the microwave oven can help them to cook evenly. If you are cooking several items of the same food, arrange them in a ring shape, leaving the centre empty for even heating. The centre of a dish receives less microwave energy while the sides receive equal amounts.

Irregular-shaped foods like chicken pieces, whole fish, chops and many vegetables should be placed with the thinner parts to the centre where they will receive less energy.

Shielding: This means protecting vulnerable parts of the food from overcooking. This is the only time when small pieces of foil should be used in the microwave oven. Make sure that the area uncovered is greater than the area covered with foil or the microwaves may arc (see page 17). The foil will reflect the microwaves from sensitive areas including the tips of legs and wings of poultry and game, the heads and tails of fish, the breast bone of poultry and the bone ends of chops.

Releasing Pressure in Foods: Any foods that have a tight-fitting skin or membrane must be pricked prior to cooking in the microwave. If you do not do this they will burst or explode as the pressure from the production of steam mounts during cooking. Such foods include sausages and jacket potatoes. The same procedure must be used with cook-in bags, boil-in-the-bag pouches and roasting bags. Always prick microwave cling film or pierce it in a couple of places if it is being used as a cover for a dish.

The yolk of an egg must also be pricked since microwave energy is attracted to the fats in the yolk, causing it to cook faster and risk exploding. Pricking the yolk carefully with a cocktail stick or the tip of a knife so it does not run will prevent this happening.

Drying Techniques: In many ways the microwave simulates a steam cabinet and does not produce dry and crisp results. Absorbent kitchen paper is one of the most useful materials that you can use to overcome this. Place jacket potatoes on a double-thickness of absorbent kitchen paper and they will cook dry and crisp. Bacon, covered with or placed between two sheets of absorbent kitchen paper, will also cook crisp rather than greasy and soggy. The same technique can also be used to dry herbs or flowers in the microwave. Place the herbs or flowers between two sheets of absorbent kitchen paper and cook until they are dry enough to crumble; this should take about five minutes on FULL POWER, but do check constantly.

Removing Excess Cooking Juices: Any juices that are produced during microwave cooking will continue to attract microwave energy and can, in effect, slow down the cooking process. Remove any juices with a bulb baster at regular intervals during cooking. If the food starts to dry out the juices can always be re-introduced later.

Observing Standing Times: Foods cooked in the microwave will continue to cook after the microwave energy has been turned off because of the conduction of heat within the food. You should take account of this to make the best use of the microwave energy by ensuring that you do not cook the foods too much, otherwise the foods may overcook while standing.

You should usually allow between 5 and 20 minutes for standing time. For most foods 5 minutes is sufficient, but for larger or denser pieces, like meat and roasts, 15-20 minutes is usually recommended after the energy is switched off.

For foods that need to be served hot this standing time is best carried out under foil. The foil traps the heat inside the food, so it can be served without reheating.

MICROWAVE COOKING LIMITATIONS

Among the limitations to cooking in microwave are:

Browning: Since there is no applied surface heat, food does not brown readily in the microwave with short cooking times. See below.

Metals: These cannot be used in the microwave oven as they may cause arcing (see page 17).

Some Foods Cannot Be Cooked in a Microwave: *Eggs in shells* are liable to explode due to the build-up of pressure within the shell. *Batter* items like Yorkshire puddings, soufflés, pancakes and crêpes need conventional cooking to become crisp or firm. *Conventional meringues* should be cooked in the conventional oven. *Deep fat frying* is not recommended; since it requires prolonged heating, it is difficult to control the fat temperature and food may burn.

Liquids in Bottles: Check that bottles do not have too narrow necks or they may shatter.

Very Large Food Loads: Any time advantage over the conventional cooker may be quickly eroded if you try to cook very large loads of food. Calculate the microwave cooking times and compare them for efficiency with conventional cooking.

Tips on Browning

The most obvious disadvantage of microwave cooking is the lack of browning. Since there is no applied surface heat, food does not brown readily on the outside when cooking times are short. A large turkey cooked in the microwave will brown without any special treatment because of its long cooking time, but steaks, chops and small roasts may well look unappetizingly grey.

There are, though, numerous ways you may overcome this problem.

MEAT, POULTRY AND FISH

• Manufacturers have now produced microwave models with integral browning elements or grills incorporated in the roof of the oven. These can be used in some cases prior to cooking, after cooking, or, in special cases, during cooking, depending upon the type. You should check the individual manufacturer's instructions. The same effect can be achieved by using a conventional grill, after cooking.

• There are several microwave browning dishes on the market which all assist with prebrowning meat, poultry and fish prior to microwave cooking (see page 16). The same browning dish can also be used to brown and 'fry' sandwiches and eggs.

• Some manufacturers have introduced special browning agents and mixes to coat meat, fish and poultry prior to cooking. These are usually dark-coloured marinade-type sauces which you brush on the food; there are also dark-coloured spicy mixtures to coat the food.

• Home-made browning agents that work very well include coating foods with browned breadcrumbs, dusting with ground paprika pepper, coating with a colourful dry soup mix, brushing with tomato or brown sauce, coating with crushed crisps or brushing with soy sauce.

CAKES, BISCUITS AND BREADS

Choosing a dark coloured mixture, like chocolate, ginger, coffee or spice, helps but if you wish to have a plain cake or biscuit mixture then the following tips to overcome the pale appearance may prove useful:

• Try sprinkling cakes and biscuits with chopped nuts, a mixture of cinnamon and sugar, mixed chopped glacé fruits, toasted coconut, hundreds and thousands or chocolate vermicelli before cooking.

• A colourful frosting or icing on a cake after cooking will quickly hide any pale, uncooked-looking crust.

• Quickly brown a microwave-baked bread under a preheated hot grill after cooking.

• Try sprinkling bread loaves and rolls with poppy seeds, cracked wheat, buckwheat, grated cheese, toasted sesame seeds, chopped nuts, caraway seeds or dried herbs prior to cooking, as these all give an interesting crust to the bread.

MICROWAVE COOKING UTENSILS

The range of cooking utensils that can be used in the microwave is greater than the range that can be used in the conventional oven since, as well as materials like plastic and glass, paper, basketware and linen may all be used in the microwave.

The following basic household equipment is ideal for use since microwaves pass through it, rather than acting as a barrier, enabling quick cooking, defrosting and reheating.

Glass, Pottery and China: Ovenproof and plain glass, pottery and china are all suitable for use in the microwave oven. They must not have any metallic trim, screws or handles and pottery must be nonporous.

Paper: For low heat and short cooking times, such as thawing, reheating or very short prime cooking, and for foods with a low fat, sugar or water content, paper is excellent in the microwave oven. Napkins, paper towels, cups, cartons, paper freeze wrap and paper pulp board often used for meat packaging are all suitable. Paper towels are especially useful for cooking fatty foods since they absorb excess fats and oils and can be used to prevent splattering on the walls of the oven.

Wax-coated paper cups and plates should be avoided since the high temperature of the food will cause the wax to melt; they can, however, be used for defrosting cold items like frozen cakes and desserts.

Plastics: The 'Dishwasher Safe' label is a useful indicator as to whether or not a plastic is suitable for use in the microwave. Plastic dishes and containers, unless made of a thermoplastic material, should not be used for cooking food with a high fat or sugar content, since the heat of the food may cause them to melt or lose their shape.

Plastic film and products like boil-in-the-bags work well in the microwave. Pierce the film or bag before cooking to allow the steam to escape. Government guidelines now recommend that ordinary cling film with plasticizers, i.e. pvc film, should not be used as a covering or lining for foods cooked in the microwave. All cling film referred to in this book is of the 'polythene' film type without plasticizers and can be found under such brand names as Purecling, Saran Wrap and Glad Wrap. This type of film does not cling as well as standard pvc film, but can often be more manageable when pulling back to stir during microwave cooking. If you do not wish to use cling film as a covering then use an upturned plate, saucer, special microwave plate cover or baking parchment instead.

Do not attempt to cook in thin plastic storage bags as they will not withstand the heat of the food. Thicker storage bags are acceptable. Use elastic bands, string or non-metal ties to secure the bags loosely before cooking.

Melamine is not recommended for microwave cooking since it absorbs enough microwave energy to char.

Cotton and Linen: Napkins can be used for short reheating purposes, such as reheating bread rolls, but the material should be 100 per cent cotton or linen and should not contain any synthetic fibres.

Wooden Bowls and Basketware: These are only suitable for short reheating purposes, since the wood or wicker tends to char, dry out or crack if in the oven too long.

Roasting Bags: These provide a clean, convenient way of cooking many foods. This is particularly true of meats, since browning takes place more readily within them than in other plastic bags. However, the metal ties must be replaced with elastic bands or string. Snip a couple of holes in the bag to help the steam escape.

Microwave Containers: Several ranges of cookware manufactured from polythene, polystyrene and thermoplastic specially for microwave ovens are now widely available in a comprehensive range of shapes and sizes.

Thermometers: Ones made specially for microwave ovens are available, but these may be used in an oven only when specified by that oven's manufacturer. To take the temperature reading with a standard meat thermometer, remove the food from the oven, insert the thermometer into the thickest portion of food and let it stand for about 10 minutes to register the internal temperature. If more cooking is needed, remove the thermometer and return the meat to the oven.

Browning Dishes: These help the oven duplicate the conventional browning and searing processes of conventional cooking. Especially useful for pre-browning meat, poultry and fish, they can also be used for 'frying' eggs and sandwiches, and browning vegetables.

THE MICROWAVE AND FREEZER

The microwave has often been given the title 'the unfreezer' since it efficiently and safely defrosts foods in a fraction of the time it normally takes at room temperature. Most microwave ovens have a DEFROST POWER facility on the control dial. If your oven does not have a DEFROST POWER button then you can simulate this by turning the oven on and off at regular intervals – one minute on FULL POWER followed by ten minutes' resting, repeated as necessary – until the frozen food is defrosted. The DEFROST POWER facility automates this switching on and off.

When defrosting foods, refer to the times in the charts on pages 326–332. Err on the side of safety by under- rather than over-timing until you can judge the cooking or defrosting speeds of your microwave.

The following hints will ensure good even defrosting:

- Pierce any skins, membranes or pouches before defrosting.
- Remove any metal containers, ties or dishes before defrosting.
- Turn foods over during defrosting.
- If turning foods over is not possible, rotate the dish to ensure even heating.
- Flex any pouches that cannot be broken up or stirred during the defrosting time and rotate on a regular basis.
- Place any foods like cakes, bread rolls, sausage rolls and pastry items on a double sheet of absorbent kitchen paper when defrosting to absorb any excess moisture.
- Any blocks of frozen food should be broken up with a fork during defrosting.
- Separate any blocks of frozen meats like hamburgers, sausages and steaks as they defrost.
- Remove any giblets from the cavity of chickens and other game or poultry meats as they defrost.
- Open all cartons and remove any lids before defrosting.
- Remove any thaw juices or drips from frozen foods during the defrosting time with a bulb baster.
- With items like meat joints, whole poultry, game birds and whole fish, defrost until they appear 'frosty' then leave to defrost completely at room temperature.
- If any parts of the food start to defrost at too fast a rate or even start to cook or become warm, then shield or protect these areas with small strips of foil attached with wooden cocktail sticks.
- Always observe a standing time action as foods will continue to thaw with the heat produced via conduction.

SAFETY

Microwave ovens have been carefully designed to be totally safe in use. To ensure complete safety, follow these guidelines:

• Keep the door seals free from food, dust or grease.

• Do not use or operate the oven if it has been damaged in any way, or if the door catch seems loose.

• Do not operate the oven when it is empty.

Arcing

The most noticeable problem that could occur in your oven is arcing, when you will see sparks inside the oven cavity. It is a sign that the microwave patterns have been disturbed, usually because a large amount of metal has inadvertently been introduced into the oven.

ADAPTING RECIPES

Many recipes can be converted for use in the microwave simply by adjusting, and often shortening, the recipe cooking time. Check that all the foods included in the recipe microwave well. The following guidelines should help:

• In general terms, microwave foods cook in about one-quarter to one-third of the time they take conventionally. Allow for standing times (see page 13).

• Check the cooking process regularly. Stir and rearrange foods if necessary.

• Use less liquid when cooking stews, casseroles, soups and vegetables.

• Foods rise higher during microwave cooking so use larger containers.

• Reduce flavourings like herbs and spices by one-third since these concentrate with microwave cooking.

RECIPE GUIDELINES BEFORE YOU BEGIN

All the recipes in this book were created and tested using microwave ovens with a power output of 650–700 watts on FULL POWER. The ovens also had variable power ranging from 150–700 watts for greater flexibility. If your microwave has a power output higher than 700 watts, reduce the cooking time accordingly; if your microwave has a power output lower than 700 watts then you should increase the cooking time accordingly.

Checking if Food is Cooked

Since appearances differ between microwave cooked food and conventionally cooked food, the usual procedures for checking if a food is cooked are not always appropriate.

Cakes and Sponge Puddings: These will often appear wet on the surface when cooked but will dry out with the residual heat during standing time. The best check is with a wooden cocktail stick at the minimum time. The food is cooked if the stick when inserted comes out clean.

Jacket Potatoes: Check that they give a little under thumb pressure.

Meat: This should be fork-tender when cooked.

Chicken: Juices should run clear when pricked and the flesh should be soft to the pinch when cooked.

Fish: The flesh will flake easily when cooked.

Vegetables: These should be only fork-tender, not soft, when cooked.

Reheated Meals: These are generally hot when the plate base feels warm.

Pastries: When cooked, the base of pastries should be dry and opaque.

SOUPS

LENTIL AND ORANGE SOUP

METRIC/IMPERIAL
25 g/1 oz butter
100 g/4 oz split red lentils
1 onion, finely chopped
1 celery stick, finely sliced
½ medium carrot, grated
¼ teaspoon dried thyme
900 ml/1½ pints hot chicken stock
150 ml/¼ pint orange juice
grated rind of ½ orange
1 bay leaf
salt
freshly ground black pepper
orange rind, to garnish

Place the butter and lentils in a large bowl. Cover and cook on FULL (100%) for 2 minutes, stirring halfway through.

Stir in the onion, celery, carrot and thyme. Cover and cook on FULL (100%) for 7 minutes, stirring once.

Stir in 600 ml/1 pint of the hot stock with the orange juice, rind, bay leaf, salt and pepper. Cover and cook on FULL (100%) for 10 minutes, stirring once. Remove the bay leaf and stir in the remaining hot stock. Cool slightly.

Pour the soup into a blender or food processor and blend until smooth. Return to the bowl and reheat on FULL (100%) for 8 minutes, stirring once. Adjust the seasoning and garnish with orange.
SERVES 4

FRENCH ONION SOUP

METRIC/IMPERIAL
450 g/1 lb large Spanish onions, thinly sliced
1 clove garlic, crushed
½ teaspoon sugar
40 g/1½ oz butter
2 tablespoons flour
pinch of powdered mustard
1 beef stock cube, crumbled
600 ml/1 pint boiling water
300 ml/½ pint canned beef consommé
½ teaspoon Worcestershire sauce
salt
freshly ground black pepper
6 thick slices of French bread, toasted
50 g/2 oz Cheddar cheese, grated

Combine the onions, garlic, sugar and butter in a large bowl and cook on FULL (100%) for 6 to 8 minutes until the onions are golden, stirring occasionally during cooking.

Stir in the flour, mustard, stock cube, boiling water, consommé and Worcestershire sauce. Partially cover and cook on FULL (100%) for 20 minutes, stirring occasionally. Leave to STAND for 5 minutes, then add salt and pepper to taste.

Sprinkle the toast with cheese and brown under a preheated grill. Pour the soup into individual bowls, add a slice of toast to each one and serve immediately.
SERVES 6

GOLDEN CARROT SOUP

METRIC/IMPERIAL
25 g/1 oz butter
1 onion, chopped
1 × 225 g/8 oz packet frozen diced carrots
600 ml/1 pint hot chicken stock
salt
freshly ground black pepper
1 teaspoon sugar
Garnish:
4 tablespoons single cream
1 tablespoon chopped fresh parsley

Place the butter in a bowl and heat on FULL (100%) for ½ minute or until melted. Add the onion, cover and cook on FULL (100%) for 3 minutes, stirring once.

Stir in the carrots, stock, salt and pepper to taste and the sugar, blending well. Cover and cook on FULL (100%) for 10 minutes, stirring

18

once. Leave to STAND for 5 minutes.

Pour into a blender or food processor and blend until smooth. Pour into a serving bowl and cook on FULL (100%) for a further 2 minutes to reheat.

Serve garnished with a swirl of cream and sprinkled with parsley.
SERVES 2

SWEETCORN SOUP

METRIC/IMPERIAL
15 g/½ oz butter
1 onion, finely chopped
50 g/2 oz bacon, chopped
15 g/½ oz cornflour
300 ml/½ pint milk
2 × 175 g/6 oz packets frozen sweetcorn, thawed
300 ml/½ pint hot chicken stock
salt
freshly ground black pepper

Place the butter, onion and bacon in a large bowl and cook on FULL (100%) for 1 minute. Blend the cornflour and milk together and pour on to the bacon and onion. Cook on FULL (100%) for 3 minutes, stirring twice during cooking.

Whisk the sauce and add the sweetcorn (reserving a little for garnish) and the stock. Return to the oven and cook on FULL (100%) for a further 2½ minutes.

Allow to cool slightly, then place in a blender or food processor and purée until smooth. Adjust the seasoning and reheat, if necessary. Garnish with the reserved sweetcorn.
SERVES 4

TOMATO SOUP

METRIC/IMPERIAL
675 g/1½ lb firm, ripe tomatoes
25 g/1 oz butter
1 small onion, finely chopped
1 carrot, finely chopped
1 streaky bacon rasher, derinded and chopped
2 cloves garlic, finely chopped
25 g/1 oz flour
1 litre/1¾ pints hot chicken stock
salt
freshly ground black pepper
Garnish:
Toasted Crumbs (see page 314)
chopped fresh parsley

Prick each tomato with a fork and arrange on a large plate. Cook on FULL (100%) for 3 minutes or until the skins split. (The timing will vary according to the size and ripeness of the tomatoes.) Skin the tomatoes and roughly chop the flesh. Set aside.

Place the butter in a medium bowl and heat on FULL (100%) for 1 minute or until melted. Add the onion, carrot, bacon and garlic, and cook on FULL (100%) for 2½ minutes.

Add the flour to the onion and bacon mixture and blend. Stir in the tomatoes, hot stock, salt and pepper to taste. Cook on FULL (100%) for 8 minutes, then stir. Allow to STAND, covered, for 10 minutes, then purée in a blender or food processor or pass through a sieve. Sprinkle with toasted crumbs and parsley before serving.
SERVES 4

'PHILLY' ONION SOUP

METRIC/IMPERIAL
450 g/1 lb onions, finely chopped
2 potatoes (about 275 g/10 oz), peeled and chopped
900 ml/1½ pints boiling chicken stock
salt
freshly ground black pepper
150 g/5 oz Philadelphia soft cheese

Place the onions in a large bowl with the potatoes, boiling stock and salt and pepper to taste. Cover and cook on FULL (100%) for 10 minutes, stirring once. Pour into a blender or food processor and blend until smooth.

Cream the cheese with a little of the soup, beating well to prevent lumps. Stir into the soup and cook on FULL (100%) for 10 minutes, stirring once. Serve hot with French bread.
SERVES 4

CREAM OF CELERY SOUP

METRIC/IMPERIAL
1 head of celery, chopped
1 onion, chopped
25 g/1 oz butter
25 g/1 oz flour
½ teaspoon salt
¼ teaspoon freshly ground black pepper
¼ teaspoon grated nutmeg

19

900 ml/1½ pints hot chicken stock
150 ml/¼ pint creamy milk
2 tablespoons soured cream
2 bacon rashers, cooked and finely chopped

Combine the celery, onion and butter in a large bowl and cook on FULL (100%) for 10 minutes, stirring occasionally.

Stir in the flour, salt, pepper and nutmeg, then add the stock. Partially cover and cook on FULL (100%) for 10 minutes. Purée in a blender or food processor, or press through a sieve.

Stir in the milk and cream. Adjust the seasoning, if necessary, and cook on FULL (100%) for 2 minutes. Serve the soup either hot or chilled, garnished with the chopped bacon.
SERVES 6 to 8

ORANGE TOMATO SOUP

METRIC/IMPERIAL
2 large onions, chopped
15 g/½ oz butter
1 orange
½ small red pepper, cored, seeded and chopped
3 mint sprigs
600 ml/1 pint hot water
1 chicken stock cube, crumbled
1 × 450 g/1 lb can tomatoes
salt
freshly ground black pepper
2 teaspoons cornflour
1 tablespoon lemon juice
1 teaspoon Worcestershire sauce
mint sprigs, to garnish

Combine the onions and butter in a large bowl. Cook on FULL (100%) for 5 minutes, stirring once.

Peel the orange, remove the pith and pips and chop the flesh. Add to the onions with the chopped pepper, mint, water, stock cube, tomatoes with their juice, and a light sprinkling of salt and pepper. Partially cover and cook on FULL (100%) for 15 minutes.

Without removing the mint, purée the soup in a blender or food processor, or press through a sieve. Blend the cornflour, lemon juice and Worcestershire sauce with 1 tablespoon of cold water. Stir into the soup and cook on FULL (100%) for 5 minutes, stirring once.

Stir briskly and adjust the seasoning before serving hot, garnished with mint sprigs.
SERVES 4 to 6

CAULIFLOWER SOUP

METRIC/IMPERIAL
50 g/2 oz butter
1 onion, finely diced
2 tablespoons flour
750 ml/1¼ pints hot chicken stock
1 × 350 g/12 oz packet frozen cauliflower florets
salt
freshly ground black pepper
2 tablespoons single cream
1 tablespoon chopped fresh parsley

Place the butter and onion in a large bowl and cook on FULL (100%) for 2 minutes. Blend in the flour, then gradually stir in the stock. Cook on FULL (100%) for 2½ minutes.

Place the frozen cauliflower in a dish, cover and cook on FULL (100%) for 7½ minutes, stirring once. Add the cauliflower florets to the sauce and cook on FULL (100%) for 2 minutes.

Allow to cool slightly, then purée in a blender or food processor. Reheat, and stir in the seasoning, cream and parsley before serving.
SERVES 4

COURGETTE SOUP

METRIC/IMPERIAL
350 g/12 oz firm courgettes, cut into chunks
2 medium tomatoes, skinned and quartered
450 ml/¾ pint milk
½ teaspoon snipped chives
rosemary sprig
salt
freshly ground black pepper
2 tablespoons single cream

Put the courgettes into a large bowl. Partially cover and cook on FULL (100%) for 3½ minutes or until the courgettes are just tender (do not overcook or they will become spongy).

Purée the courgettes in a blender or food processor with the tomatoes and milk. Return to the bowl and add the chives and rosemary. Cook on FULL (100%) for 4 minutes, stirring once. Reduce the setting to LOW (30%) and cook for a further 12 to 13 minutes, stirring once during cooking.

Add salt and pepper to taste, then pass through a sieve. Reheat on FULL (100%) for 3 to 4 minutes. Pour the hot soup into individual soup cups and add a swirl of cream.
SERVES 4

STILTON SOUP

METRIC/IMPERIAL
1 tablespoon vegetable oil
1 small onion, finely chopped
1 tablespoon flour
300 ml/½ pint milk
600 ml/1 pint hot chicken stock
salt
freshly ground black pepper
1 bay leaf
pinch of ground mace, nutmeg and cayenne
pepper
225 g/8 oz Stilton cheese, crumbled
150 ml/¼ pint single cream

Place the oil and onion in a large bowl and cook on FULL (100%) for 2 minutes. Stir in the flour, then add all the remaining ingredients, except the Stilton cheese and cream. Cook on FULL (100%) for 4 minutes, stirring once.

Add the cheese, reserving a little for garnish. Return to the oven and cook on FULL (100%) for a further 1 minute. Allow to cool slightly, then purée in a blender or food processor. Reheat, if necessary, then stir in the cream and sprinkle with the reserved Stilton before serving.
SERVES 4

BROCCOLI SOUP

METRIC/IMPERIAL
1 small onion, finely chopped
25 g/1 oz butter
25 g/1 oz flour
600 ml/1 pint hot chicken stock
1 × 225 g/8 oz packet frozen broccoli, thawed
and roughly chopped
pinch of freshly grated nutmeg
salt
freshly ground black pepper
300 ml/½ pint milk

Place the onion and butter in a large bowl and cook on FULL (100%) for 2 minutes. Stir in the flour, then gradually add the stock, chopped broccoli (reserving a little for the garnish), nutmeg, and salt and pepper to taste. Cook on FULL (100%) for 6 minutes, stirring twice during cooking.

Allow to cool slightly, then purée in a blender or food processor. Adjust the seasoning and pour

in the milk. Cook on FULL (100%) for 2 to 3 minutes, stirring once. Allow to STAND for a few minutes before serving. Garnish with the reserved broccoli.
SERVES 4

TOMATO AND HORSERADISH SOUP

METRIC/IMPERIAL
25 g/1 oz butter
100 g/4 oz onion, finely chopped
25 g/1 oz flour
450 g/1 lb tomatoes, skinned and chopped
600 ml/1 pint hot chicken stock
salt
freshly ground black pepper
3 teaspoons creamed horseradish
3 tablespoons tomato purée
pinch of ground mace
Garnish:
4 tablespoons double cream
1 teaspoon creamed horseradish

Place the butter in a large bowl and heat on FULL (100%) for ½ minute or until melted. Add the onion and cook on FULL (100%) for 2 minutes, then stir in the flour and tomatoes.

Gradually add the chicken stock, salt and pepper to taste, creamed horseradish, tomato purée and mace. Cook on FULL (100%) for 10 minutes, stirring once.

Allow to cool slightly, then purée in a blender or food processor. Garnish with swirls of double cream mixed with the creamed horseradish.
SERVES 4

ARTICHOKE SOUP

METRIC/IMPERIAL
450 g/1 lb Jerusalem artichokes, sliced
1 small onion, finely chopped
2 tablespoons lemon juice
25 g/1 oz butter
2 tablespoons flour
600 ml/1 pint hot chicken stock
300 ml/½ pint milk
salt
freshly ground black pepper

Place the artichokes, onion, lemon juice and butter in a bowl. Cover and cook on FULL (100%) for 8 minutes, stirring once.

Add the flour and stir in the stock. Cook on FULL (100%) for 9 minutes, stirring four times during cooking.

Allow to cool slightly, then purée in a blender or food processor. Pour the milk into a jug and cook on FULL (100%) for 2 minutes. Stir the milk into the soup and add salt and pepper to taste before serving.

SERVES 4

BORTSCH

METRIC/IMPERIAL
575–675 g/1¼–1½ lb raw beetroot, peeled and coarsely grated
900 ml/1½ pints water
1½ teaspoons salt
¼ teaspoon freshly ground black pepper
25 g/1 oz sugar
4½ tablespoons lemon juice
150 ml/¼ pint soured cream

Place the beetroot, water, salt, pepper, sugar and lemon juice in a large bowl. Cook on FULL (100%) for 12 minutes, stirring twice, or until the beetroot is tender.

Cover and leave to cool, then chill for 4 to 6 hours or overnight.

Spoon into serving bowls and top with a swirl of the soured cream. Serve cold.

SERVES 6 to 8

SPINACH SOUP

METRIC/IMPERIAL
25 g/1 oz butter
25 g/1 oz flour
450 ml/¾ pint milk
300 ml/½ pint hot chicken stock
½ teaspoon grated nutmeg
1 tablespoon grated onion
salt
freshly ground black pepper
1 × 225 g/8 oz packet frozen chopped spinach, thawed
double cream, to serve

Place the butter in a large bowl and heat on FULL (100%) for ½ minute or until melted. Stir in the flour until well mixed, then gradually add the milk, stock, nutmeg, onion and salt and pepper to taste, whisking well.

Cook on FULL (100%) for 6 minutes, whisk-ing three times during cooking to prevent lumps forming. Add the spinach and mix well. Cook on FULL (100%) for a further 3 minutes.

Allow to cool slightly, then purée in a blender or food processor. Reheat, if necessary. Swirl cream into the soup just before serving.

SERVES 4

LETTUCE SOUP WITH CROÛTONS

METRIC/IMPERIAL
1 onion, finely chopped
50 g/2 oz butter
25 g/1 oz plain flour
450 ml/¾ pint hot chicken stock
300 ml/½ pint milk
225 g/8 oz lettuce leaves, chopped
¼ teaspoon grated nutmeg
¼ teaspoon caster sugar
salt
freshly ground black pepper
1 egg yolk
Croûtons:
2 slices fresh white bread, cut into cubes
4 tablespoons oil

Place the onion and butter in a large bowl. Cover and cook on FULL (100%) for 4 minutes.

Stir in the flour, hot stock, milk, lettuce, nutmeg, sugar, salt and pepper. Cover and cook on FULL (100%) for 9 minutes, stirring twice. Cool slightly.

Pour the soup and the egg yolk into a blender or food processor and blend until smooth. Return the soup to the bowl. Reheat on FULL (100%) for 2 minutes. Taste and adjust the seasoning, then serve garnished with croûtons.

To make the croûtons, toss the pieces of bread in the oil. Spread the cubes over a plate. Cook on FULL (100%) for 2 minutes. Stir and cook on FULL (100%) for a further 2 minutes, checking and stirring the croûtons frequently until browned. Drain on absorbent kitchen paper.

SERVES 4

POTATO SOUP

METRIC/IMPERIAL
100 g/4 oz peeled potato
1 small onion, peeled
2 tablespoons frozen peas
¼ teaspoon powdered bay leaves
½ chicken stock cube, crumbled
300 ml/½ pint water
4 tablespoons milk
¼ teaspoon salt
freshly ground black pepper

Cut the potato and onion into thin slices and place in a large bowl. Add the remaining ingredients and stir well. Partially cover and cook on FULL (100%) for 10 minutes, stirring once during cooking.

Purée the soup in a blender or food processor, or press through a sieve. Adjust the seasoning and serve hot.
SERVES 2

For 4 or more servings: increase the ingredients accordingly and combine all ingredients in the bowl, except the milk; stir well. Cook on FULL (100%) for 15 minutes, stirring twice during cooking, then purée as above. Add the milk to the purée, then cook on FULL (100%) for 3 to 4 minutes to reheat before serving.

LENTIL AND BACON SOUP

METRIC/IMPERIAL
100 g/4 oz lentils, soaked overnight
900 ml/1½ pints hot ham stock
4 lean bacon rashers, derinded and chopped
1 onion, finely chopped
2 celery sticks, chopped
salt
freshly ground black pepper
pinch of cayenne pepper
2 tablespoons chopped fresh parsley

Place the drained lentils, stock, bacon, onion, celery, salt, black pepper and cayenne in a large mixing bowl. Cook on FULL (100%) for 20 to 25 minutes, stirring twice during cooking, until the lentils are tender.

Allow to cool slightly, then purée in a blender or food processor. Adjust the seasoning and stir in the chopped parsley. Reheat, if necessary, before serving.
SERVES 4

BEETROOT AND CELERY SOUP

METRIC/IMPERIAL
1 small onion, finely chopped
½ stick celery, finely chopped
1 teaspoon butter
1 teaspoon flour
150 ml/¼ pint water
2 tablespoons red wine
1 chicken stock cube, crumbled
pinch of mustard powder
pinch of powdered bay leaves
100 g/4 oz cooked beetroot, finely chopped
salt
freshly ground black pepper
4 tablespoons 'top of the milk'
1 tablespoon chopped chives, to garnish

Combine the onion, celery and butter in a bowl and cook on FULL (100%) for 3 minutes, stirring once during cooking.

Mix in the flour, then gradually stir in the water and wine. Add the crumbled stock cube, mustard, bay leaves, beetroot, salt and pepper to taste. Cook on FULL (100%) for 10 minutes, stirring once during cooking.

Purée the soup in a blender or press through a sieve. Return to the bowl, add the milk and cook on FULL (100%) for 1 to 1¼ minutes until hot.

Sprinkle with chopped chives and serve with crusty bread.
SERVES 2

ASPARAGUS SOUP

METRIC/IMPERIAL
50 g/2 oz butter
450 g/1 lb asparagus, trimmed and sliced
1 onion, finely chopped
50 g/2 oz cornflour
900 ml/1½ pints milk
1 bouquet garni
salt
freshly ground white pepper
150 ml/¼ pint double cream
cooked asparagus tips, to garnish

Place the butter, asparagus and onion in a large bowl. Cover and cook on FULL (100%) for 9 minutes, stirring halfway through cooking.

Mix the cornflour with a little of the milk to make a smooth paste. Stir in the remaining milk and pour over the asparagus. Add the bouquet garni and salt and pepper to taste. Cover and cook on FULL (100%) for 9 minutes, stirring after 2, 4, and 6 minutes.

Remove and discard the bouquet garni. Purée the soup in a blender or food processor. Stir in the cream and reheat, if necessary, but do not boil. Garnish with cooked asparagus tips.
SERVES 6

CREAM OF CHICKEN SOUP

METRIC/IMPERIAL
25 g/1 oz butter
25 g/1 oz flour
450 ml/¾ pint water
1 chicken stock cube, crumbled
salt
freshly ground black pepper
100 g/4 oz cooked chicken
1 tablespoon snipped chives
2 tablespoons double cream

Put the butter and flour in a large bowl and cook on FULL (100%) for 1½ minutes. Gradually stir in the water and cook on FULL (100%) for 4 minutes, stirring occasionally.

Add the crumbled stock cube, salt and pepper to taste, and the chicken. Cook on FULL (100%) for 10 minutes, stirring once during cooking. Sprinkle with the chives and cook on FULL (100%) for 1 minute.

Stir in the cream just before serving.
SERVES 2 to 3

COUNTRY-STYLE CHICKEN SOUP

METRIC/IMPERIAL
1.2 litres/2 pints hot chicken stock
1 chicken breast
100 g/4 oz fresh leaf spinach, washed and drained
2 tablespoons grated Parmesan cheese
salt
freshly ground black pepper
1 egg, beaten

Pour the stock into a large bowl and add the chicken. Cover and cook on FULL (100%) for 15 minutes. Take out the chicken, remove the skin and bone and shred the flesh. Discard the thick stem from the spinach, roll up the leaves and slice finely.

Add the shredded chicken and spinach to the stock and cook on FULL (100%) for 5 minutes. Stir in the cheese and season to taste with salt and pepper. Cook on FULL (100%) for 2 minutes or until boiling.

Pour the soup into a hot serving tureen and quickly strain the beaten egg over the soup. Serve immediately.
SERVES 4

MULLIGATAWNY SOUP

METRIC/IMPERIAL
25 g/1 oz butter
1 onion, chopped
1 carrot, chopped
2 celery sticks, chopped
½ green pepper, cored, seeded and chopped
225 g/8 oz tomatoes, skinned and chopped
1 apple, peeled, cored and chopped
900 ml/1½ pints boiling stock
1 tablespoon curry powder
2 cloves
1 tablespoon chopped fresh parsley
1 tablespoon sugar
salt
freshly ground black pepper
2 tablespoons cornflour
150 ml/¼ pint milk
75–100 g/3–4 oz cooked lamb, beef or chicken, finely chopped
25 g/1 oz long-grain rice

Place the butter in a large bowl and heat on FULL (100%) for ½ minute or until melted. Add the onion, carrot, celery and pepper and cook on FULL (100%) for 3 minutes, stirring once.

Add the tomatoes and apple, blending well. Cook on FULL (100%) for a further 2 minutes.

Add the boiling stock, curry powder, cloves, parsley, sugar, and salt and pepper to taste, blending well. Cook on FULL (100%) for 10 minutes, stirring once.

Blend the cornflour with a little of the milk, then stir in the remaining milk. Stir the milk mixture into the soup with the meat and rice. Stir well to blend.

Cook on FULL (100%) for 5 minutes, stirring twice. Cover and leave to STAND for 5 minutes or until the rice is cooked.

Reheat by cooking on FULL (100%) for 2 minutes. Serve hot.
SERVES 4 to 6

CHICKEN AND CORN SOUP WITH CROÛTONS

METRIC/IMPERIAL
50 g/2 oz butter
50 g/2 oz plain flour
300 ml/½ pint hot chicken stock
450 ml/¾ pint milk
salt
freshly ground black pepper
½ × 350 g/12 oz can sweetcorn kernels, drained
100 g/4 oz cooked chicken meat, chopped
2 tablespoons 'top of the milk'
Croûtons, to serve (see page 314)

Place the butter in a large mixing bowl and heat on FULL (100%) for 1½ minutes or until melted.

Stir in the flour, mixing well. Gradually stir in the stock and milk, and season with salt and pepper to taste.

Cook on FULL (100%) for 7 minutes, stirring once halfway through cooking. Whisk well.

Stir in the sweetcorn and chicken with the top of the milk. Serve immediately, sprinkled with croûtons.
SERVES 4

MUSSEL CHOWDER

METRIC/IMPERIAL
100 g/4 oz green streaky bacon, derinded and chopped
1 onion, chopped
1 celery stick, chopped
1 small green pepper, cored, seeded and chopped
2 small potatoes, peeled and chopped
450 ml/¾ pint boiling water
1 bay leaf
salt
freshly ground black pepper
40 g/1½ oz plain flour
600 ml/1 pint milk
1 × 275 g/10 oz can mussels, drained
chopped fresh parsley, to garnish

Place the bacon in a large bowl. Cook on FULL (100%) for 2 minutes. Add the onion, celery and green pepper and cook on FULL (100%) for 3 minutes, stirring once.

Add the potatoes, boiling water, bay leaf and salt and pepper to taste. Cook on FULL (100%) for 6 minutes, stirring once. Remove and discard the bay leaf.

Blend the flour with a little of the milk, then add the remaining milk. Whisk this mixture into the soup.

Cook on FULL (100%) for 10 minutes, whisking every 2 minutes. Add the mussels, blending well and cook for a further 3 minutes, stirring once. Serve hot, garnished with chopped parsley.
SERVES 4 to 6

MINESTRONE

METRIC/IMPERIAL
1 × 275 g/10 oz can condensed consommé
450 ml/¾ pint boiling water
1 × 150 g/5 oz can baked beans in tomato sauce
1 medium carrot, finely diced
1 medium leek, cut into 5 cm/2 inch lengths and shredded
50 g/2 oz quick-cook macaroni
1 × 225 g/8 oz can tomatoes
1 small clove garlic, crushed
1 celery stick, finely sliced
1 small onion, finely chopped
25 g/1 oz ham, diced (optional)
salt
freshly ground black pepper
about 2 tablespoons grated Parmesan cheese

Combine the consommé, boiling water, beans, carrot, leek, macaroni, tomatoes with their juice, garlic, celery, onion, ham, salt and pepper to taste and 2 teaspoons of the Parmesan cheese in a large bowl. Three-quarters cover and cook on FULL (100%) for 20 minutes, stirring twice during cooking. Leave to STAND for 5 minutes before carefully removing the cover.

Serve the soup hot, allowing about 200 ml/⅓ pint per person. Sprinkle over the remaining Parmesan cheese to serve.
SERVES 6

WARMING WINTER SOUP

METRIC/IMPERIAL
50 g/2 oz butter
1 large leek, finely sliced
2 large carrots, thinly sliced
1 × 225 g/8 oz potato, cubed
1 small cauliflower, divided into florets
2 celery sticks, finely chopped
1 onion, finely chopped
2 streaky bacon rashers, derinded and chopped

1 teaspoon mixed herbs
1 litre/1¾ pints well-flavoured, boiling beef or
chicken stock
freshly ground black pepper

Put the butter into a large mixing bowl and heat on FULL (100%) for 1½ minutes or until melted. Stir in the leek, carrots, potato, cauliflower, celery, onion and bacon. Mix well.

Cover and cook on FULL (100%) for 4 minutes. Stir in the herbs, stock and pepper to taste. Cover and cook on FULL (100%) for 17 minutes, stirring once halfway through cooking.

Leave to STAND, covered, for 6 minutes before serving with grated cheese and French bread.

SERVES 6

CRAB BISQUE

METRIC/IMPERIAL
15 g/½ oz butter
1 small piece fennel, finely chopped
1 clove garlic, crushed
1 medium onion, finely chopped
50 g/2 oz fresh white breadcrumbs
450 g/1 lb crabmeat, half white and half dark
meat
salt
freshly ground black pepper
750 ml/1¼ pints hot fish stock
1 bay leaf
150 ml/¼ pint double cream
flakes of white crabmeat, to garnish

Place the butter, fennel, garlic and onion in a large bowl. Cover and cook on FULL (100%) for 4 minutes, stirring halfway through cooking. Stir in the breadcrumbs, crabmeat and salt and pepper to taste. Cover and cook on FULL (100%) for 4 minutes, stirring halfway through cooking.

Stir in the stock and bay leaf, then cover and cook on FULL (100%) for a further 8 minutes, stirring halfway through cooking. Remove the bay leaf, pour the soup into a blender or food processor and blend until smooth. Cool slightly.

Stir in the cream; check and adjust the seasoning. If necessary, reheat in the microwave for a minute or so, but do not boil. Garnish with pieces of white crabmeat and serve.

SERVES 4

BEEF AND VEGETABLE SOUP

METRIC/IMPERIAL
225 g/8 oz minced beef
1 large onion, finely chopped
1 small green pepper, cored, seeded and chopped
1 large potato, peeled and diced
1 × 450 g/1 lb can tomatoes
4 tablespoons tomato purée
750 ml/1¼ pints hot beef stock
1 tablespoon paprika
½ teaspoon freshly ground black pepper
salt

Preheat a large browning dish on FULL (100%) for 5 minutes (or according to the manufacturer's instructions). Add the meat, stir briskly and cook on FULL (100%) for 3 minutes. Add the onion and green pepper and cook on FULL (100%) for 4 minutes.

Cover and leave to STAND for 5 minutes. Using a slotted spoon, transfer the mixture to a large bowl. Add the potato, tomatoes with their juice, tomato purée, stock, paprika and pepper. Partially cover and cook on FULL (100%) for 25 minutes, stirring occasionally.

Add salt to taste and crush the soup with a potato masher to break up the tomatoes. Serve hot.

SERVES 4 to 6

FISH SOUP WITH BEAN CURD

METRIC/IMPERIAL
1 tablespoon vegetable oil
1 celery stick, finely sliced
1 shallot, thinly sliced
½ medium carrot, sliced diagonally, paper thin
3 thin slices root ginger
900 ml/1½ pints hot chicken stock
1 bunch watercress, washed and sorted
1 tablespoon soy sauce
salt
freshly ground black pepper
225 g/8 oz fresh haddock fillets, skinned and
boned and cut into 1 cm/½ inch cubes
1 × 100 g/4 oz block bean curd

Combine the oil, celery, shallot, carrot and ginger in a large bowl and cook on FULL (100%) for 5 minutes, stirring once.

Stir in the stock and watercress leaves (without

stalks) and cook on FULL (100%) for about 10 minutes, until boiling.

Add the soy sauce and salt and pepper to taste. Stir in the fish and cook on FULL (100%) for 5 minutes, stirring once.

While the fish is cooking, carefully cut the bean curd into 1.5 cm/½ inch cubes. Gently put the bean curd into the soup and cook on FULL (100%) for 2 minutes before serving.
SERVES 6

CURRIED PARSNIP SOUP

METRIC/IMPERIAL
1 tablespoon mild curry powder
1 large onion, chopped
1 celery stick, finely chopped
675 g/1½ lb parsnips, thinly sliced
1 tablespoon white wine vinegar
25 g/1 oz butter
15 g/½ oz plain flour
600 ml/1 pint milk
300 ml/½ pint hot vegetable stock
salt
freshly ground black pepper
2 tablespoons double cream
Croûtons, to garnish (see page 314)

Place the curry powder, onion, celery, parsnips, vinegar and butter in a large bowl. Cover and cook on FULL (100%) for 13 minutes, stirring halfway through cooking.

Blend in the flour, then gradually stir in the milk. Cover and cook on FULL (100%) for 6 minutes, stirring halfway through cooking.

Add the hot stock and season to taste with salt and pepper. Place the mixture in a blender or food processor and blend until the mixture is smooth. Stir in the cream. Pour into warm bowls, garnish with croûtons and serve with hot toast.
SERVES 4

CORN AND CRAB SOUP

METRIC/IMPERIAL
1 small onion, finely chopped
1 celery stick, finely chopped
1 lean bacon rasher, derinded and finely chopped
15 g/½ oz butter
25 g/1 oz flour
600 ml/1 pint milk
450 ml/¾ pint hot water
1 bay leaf

1 × 225 g/8 oz can creamed sweetcorn, drained
225 g/8 oz fresh or canned crabmeat
salt
freshly ground black pepper

Place the onion, celery and bacon in a large bowl and add the butter. Cook on FULL (100%) for 4 minutes, stirring once during cooking.

Stir in the flour, blending well, then gradually add the milk, water and bay leaf. Cook on FULL (100%) for 8 minutes, stirring occasionally. Strain into another bowl.

Lightly mash the sweetcorn and flake the crabmeat. Add to the soup and cook on FULL (100%) for 4 minutes until hot. Add salt and pepper to taste. Serve hot.
SERVES 4 to 6

CONSOMMÉ WITH TAGLIATELLE

METRIC/IMPERIAL
1 × 275 g/10 oz can condensed beef consommé
hot water, to mix
1 teaspoon tomato ketchup
25 g/1 oz dried tagliatelle
25 g/1 oz Edam cheese, finely diced
freshly ground black pepper

Pour the consommé into a large bowl. Add the required quantity of water (according to the can instructions) and the tomato ketchup; stir well. Cook on FULL (100%) for 5 to 5½ minutes until boiling.

Add the pasta, cover and cook on FULL (100%) for 6 minutes, stirring once during cooking. Add the cheese and sprinkle liberally with black pepper.

Leave to STAND for 1 minute to allow the cheese to soften. Serve hot with crusty bread.
SERVES 2 to 3

Note: If only one portion of soup is required, just add cheese and pepper to this serving. The rest of the consommé may be reheated later with the cheese and pepper added just before serving.

VICHYSSOISE

METRIC/IMPERIAL
25 g/1 oz butter
3 medium leeks, coarsely sliced
1 onion, chopped
2 large potatoes, peeled and chopped

27

900 ml/1½ pints hot chicken stock
150 ml/¼ pint double cream
salt
freshly ground white pepper
snipped chives, to garnish

Place the butter in a large bowl and heat on FULL (100%) for ½ minute or until melted. Add the leeks and onion. Cover and cook on FULL (100%) for 3 minutes, stirring once.

Add the potatoes and chicken stock. Cover and cook on FULL (100%) for 15 to 18 minutes, or until the potatoes are tender, stirring twice.

Pour into a blender or food processor and blend until smooth.

Return to the bowl and stir in the cream and salt and pepper to taste. Cover and cook on FULL (100%) for a further 4 minutes, stirring once.

Serve hot or chilled, sprinkled with snipped chives.

SERVES 4 to 6

PRAWN AND WATERCRESS SOUP

METRIC/IMPERIAL
25 g/1 oz butter
1 large bunch watercress, washed and sorted
1 onion, thinly sliced
225 g/8 oz fresh or frozen peas
600 ml/1 pint milk
salt
freshly ground black pepper
150 ml/¼ pint single cream
100 g/4 oz peeled prawns, chopped
Garnish:
watercress sprigs
4 whole prawns

Place the butter in a large casserole dish and heat on FULL (100%) for ½ minute or until melted. Stir in the watercress and onion. Cook on FULL (100%) for 2½ minutes, stirring once.

Add the peas and half of the milk. Cover and cook on FULL (100%) for 10 minutes, stirring once.

Pour into a blender or food processor with the remaining milk and blend until smooth. Season to taste with salt and pepper. Chill thoroughly.

Whisk the cream into the soup mixture and stir in the prawns. Serve chilled, garnished with watercress sprigs and whole prawns.

SERVES 4

ICED AVOCADO SOUP

METRIC/IMPERIAL
25 g/1 oz butter
1 small onion, finely chopped
15 g/½ oz plain flour
450 ml/¾ pint hot chicken stock
300 ml/½ pint milk
1 egg yolk
3 tablespoons double cream
2 ripe avocados
2 teaspoons fresh lemon juice
salt
freshly ground black pepper

Put the butter and onion into a medium bowl and cook on FULL (100%) for 3 minutes, stirring once.

Mix in the flour, then add the chicken stock and milk and cook on FULL (100%) for 5 minutes, stirring twice during cooking. (The liquid will be very thin at this stage.)

Beat the egg yolk and cream together and strain into the liquid in the bowl. Cook on FULL (100%) for ¼ minute until the soup is hot but not boiling (overheating will cause the soup to curdle).

Peel the avocados, remove the stones and cut into chunks. Sprinkle with the lemon juice, then purée in a blender or food processor with the soup (this can be done in two batches if the blender goblet is not big enough).

Add salt and pepper to taste, then cover the soup and chill for several hours before serving.

SERVES 4

COOL CUCUMBER AND CORIANDER SOUP

METRIC/IMPERIAL
2 cucumbers, cut into 2.5 cm/1 inch cubes
1 large onion, finely chopped
1 celery stick, thinly sliced
600 ml/1 pint hot vegetable or chicken stock
salt
freshly ground black pepper
1 × 150 g/5 oz carton natural yogurt
2 tablespoons chopped fresh coriander
1 tablespoon chopped fresh parsley

Place the vegetables in a large bowl or casserole with 150 ml/¼ pint of the hot stock. Cover and cook on FULL (100%) for 3¼ minutes, stirring once during cooking.

Stir in the remainder of the hot stock and season with salt and pepper to taste. Cook on FULL (100%) for a further 3¼ minutes. Leave to STAND, covered, for 5 minutes. Pour the soup into a blender or food processor and blend until smooth. Transfer to a soup tureen and leave to cool completely.

Stir in the yogurt and coriander. Chill before serving and garnish with parsley.

SERVES 4 to 6

CHILLED MELON SOUP

METRIC/IMPERIAL
1 large canteloupe melon
20 g/¾ oz butter
1 tablespoon sugar
grated rind and juice of ½ lemon
pinch of ground ginger
pinch of ground mace
pinch of salt
450 ml/¾ pint water
150 ml/¼ pint sweet white wine
freshly ground black pepper (optional)
few mint sprigs, to garnish

Cut the melon in half and scoop out and discard the seeds. Scoop a few melon balls from the flesh, using a melon baller or teaspoon, and set aside for garnish.

Remove and dice all the remaining melon flesh and place in a large deep dish. Add the butter, sugar, lemon rind and juice, ginger, mace and salt. Cook on FULL (100%) for 5 minutes, stirring twice.

Purée the mixture in a blender or food processor, or pass through a sieve. Stir in the water and wine and chill in the refrigerator for 2 to 3 hours.

Adjust the seasoning, adding pepper to taste, if desired. Turn into a serving tureen or individual soup bowls. Serve chilled, garnished with the melon balls and sprigs of mint.

SERVES 4

ICED TOMATO AND FENNEL SOUP

METRIC/IMPERIAL
575 g/1¼ lb ripe tomatoes, quartered
1 potato, peeled and cubed
1 large onion, finely chopped
1 head of fennel, thinly sliced, fronds reserved

2 teaspoons brown sugar
600 ml/1 pint hot vegetable stock
2 tablespoons tomato purée
pinch of salt
freshly ground black pepper

Place the prepared vegetables and sugar in a large bowl or casserole. Add 150 ml/¼ pint of the hot stock. Cover and cook on FULL (100%) for 7½ minutes, stirring twice.

Add the remaining hot stock, stir in the tomato purée and cook on FULL (100%) for a further 3½ minutes, stirring once during cooking. Season with salt and pepper and allow to STAND, covered, for 10 minutes.

Pour the soup into a blender or food processor and blend until smooth. Transfer to a soup tureen and leave to cool completely before chilling in the refrigerator. Chop the fennel fronds and use to garnish the soup.

SERVES 4 to 6

CHILLED CARROT AND ORANGE SOUP

METRIC/IMPERIAL
750 g/1½ lb carrots, sliced
1 potato, peeled and cubed
1 small leek, white part only, sliced
1 large onion, finely chopped
1 clove garlic, crushed
150 ml/¼ pint skimmed milk
750 ml/1¼ pints hot vegetable stock
pinch of salt
freshly ground black pepper
grated rind and juice of 1 large orange
1 tablespoon chopped chervil, to garnish

Place the vegetables in a large bowl or casserole with the skimmed milk. Cover and cook on FULL (100%) for 7½ minutes, stirring twice during cooking. Add the hot stock, seasoning and orange rind. Cover and cook on FULL (100%) for a further 3½ minutes. Leave to STAND, covered, for 5 minutes.

Pour the soup into a blender or food processor and blend until smooth. Transfer to a serving dish and leave to cool completely. Stir in the orange juice and chill in the refrigerator. Sprinkle with chopped chervil before serving.

SERVES 4 to 6

APPETIZERS AND FIRST COURSES

BACON-WRAPPED CHIPOLATAS

METRIC/IMPERIAL
8 pork chipolata sausages
8 long streaky bacon rashers, derinded

Prick the sausages with a fork. Wrap a rasher of bacon around each sausage and secure with a wooden cocktail stick.

Place on a roasting rack or plate and cook on FULL (100%) for 8 to 10 minutes, turning over once and rearranging once. Serve hot.
SERVES 8

DEVILS ON HORSEBACK

METRIC/IMPERIAL
2 slices of bread, toasted and buttered
8 streaky bacon rashers, derinded
8 large prunes, soaked, drained and stoned
8 anchovies
parsley sprigs, to garnish

Cut the toast into 5 × 8 cm/2 × 3 inch fingers. Trim the bacon rashers to fit the toast. Place between sheets of absorbent kitchen paper. Stuff the prunes with the anchovies.

Cook the bacon and prunes, simultaneously, on FULL (100%) for 6 minutes or until the bacon is crisp. Lay the bacon on the toast and arrange the prunes on top.

Place on individual plates and cook on FULL (100%) for 2 minutes. Serve immediately, garnished with parsley.
SERVES 4

ROQUEFORT CANAPÉS

METRIC/IMPERIAL
100 g/4 oz curd cheese
2 tablespoons Roquefort cheese
1 tablespoon ground hazelnuts
¼ teaspoon made mustard
½ teaspoon Worcestershire sauce
1 teaspoon chutney
freshly ground black pepper
20 crisp crackers

Mix the cheeses, hazelnuts, mustard, Worcestershire sauce, chutney and pepper to taste, blending well. Cook on FULL (100%) for ½ minute, then spread on to the crackers. Serve at once.
MAKES 20

SOURED CREAM AND CAVIAR TARTLETS

METRIC/IMPERIAL
6 thin slices of bread
25 g/1 oz butter
4 tablespoons soured cream
1 × 50 g/2 oz jar caviar
Garnish:
parsley sprigs
lemon wedges

Using an upturned cup or pastry cutter, cut out a large round from each slice of bread. Butter each piece on both sides and press firmly into a six-holed bun or muffin dish. Cook on FULL (100%) for 2½ to 3 minutes until crisp.

Put the soured cream in a jug and cook on LOW (30%) for 1 minute. Arrange the tartlets on a heated serving platter, fill with the soured cream and top with caviar. Garnish with parsley sprigs and lemon wedges.
SERVES 4 to 6

BACON ROLLS

METRIC/IMPERIAL
50 g/2 oz red Leicester cheese, grated
½ × 75 g/3 oz packet thyme and parsley stuffing,
made up according to instructions
12 streaky bacon rashers, derinded
100 g/4 oz chicken livers, finely chopped
1 small onion, finely chopped

Mix the cheese into the prepared stuffing.

Stretch the bacon slices on a chopping board, using the back of a knife, then cut each in half to provide 24 short lengths of bacon. Spread a little of the stuffing mix on to half of the bacon slices. Roll up and secure with wooden cocktail sticks.

On the remaining bacon halves put a piece of chicken liver and a little chopped onion. Roll up and secure.

Arrange the bacon rolls on a double thickness of absorbent kitchen paper on a plate, leaving a space in the centre. Cook on FULL (100%) for 7 to 9 minutes. Serve warm.
SERVES 6 to 8

SESAME BALLS

METRIC/IMPERIAL
50 g/2 oz Cheddar cheese, grated
1 small onion, finely chopped
1 small strip of green pepper, finely chopped
2 tablespoons mayonnaise
2 drops of Tabasco
100 g/4 oz fresh soft breadcrumbs
1 egg, beaten
50 g/2 oz sesame seeds
25 g/1 oz butter

Mix the cheese, onion, green pepper, mayonnaise, Tabasco and breadcrumbs together. Add the egg and stir with a fork to form a stiff paste.

Put the sesame seeds in a small bowl. Form the mixture into 2 cm/¾ inch balls and toss, one at a time, in the sesame seeds.

Preheat a large browning dish on FULL (100%) for 4 minutes (or according to the manufacturer's instructions). Add the butter and cook on FULL (100%) for 1 minute. Quickly add the sesame balls and cook on FULL (100%) for 3 minutes, turning them over after 1½ minutes. Drain on absorbent kitchen paper, then transfer to a warm serving dish.
MAKES about 30

SALTED ALMONDS

METRIC/IMPERIAL
225 g/8 oz shelled almonds, skinned
50 g/2 oz butter
salt

Put the almonds and butter in a large shallow dish and cook on FULL (100%) for 5 minutes, stirring occasionally. Turn on to absorbent kitchen paper and sprinkle liberally with salt while still hot.
MAKES 225 g/8 oz

Note: These may be stored in a screwtop jar for up to 6 weeks.

HOT CRAB CANAPÉS

METRIC/IMPERIAL
1 small onion, finely chopped
15 g/½ oz butter
15 g/½ oz flour
2 tablespoons milk
4 tablespoons single cream
175 g/6 oz cooked fresh or canned crabmeat,
flaked
½ teaspoon lemon juice
salt
freshly ground black pepper
24 small cracker biscuits
Garnish:
paprika
mustard and cress

Combine the onion and butter in a bowl and cook on FULL (100%) for 1½ to 2 minutes until the onion is soft. Stir in the flour, milk and cream and cook on FULL (100%) for 2 minutes, stirring halfway through cooking.

Mix in the crabmeat and lemon juice and season with salt and pepper to taste. Cook on MEDIUM (50%) for 2 minutes, stirring after 1 minute.

Spread the crackers on the oven base or turntable and cook on FULL (100%) for 1½ to 2 minutes, rearranging the crackers twice during cooking. Spread each cracker with a little of the hot crab paste and sprinkle with paprika and cress.

Arrange the canapés on a large serving platter and serve hot.
MAKES 24

CHEDDAR PUFFS

METRIC/IMPERIAL
25 g/1 oz butter, softened
5 tablespoons water
pinch of salt
40 g/1½ oz plain flour, sifted
1 egg, beaten
25 g/1 oz Cheddar cheese, grated

Place the butter, water and salt in a large jug. Cook on FULL (100%) for 1½ to 2 minutes until the water is boiling fast.

Remove from the oven, quickly toss in the flour and beat vigorously. Leave to cool for a few minutes, then gradually add the egg, beating thoroughly until the mixture is thick and shiny. Stir in the cheese.

Using two teaspoons, place small mounds of mixture on the oven base or turntable, lined with greaseproof paper. Cook on FULL (100%) for 6 to 8 minutes until crisp, giving the paper a half-turn after 3 minutes. Leave to cool, then pile into a serving bowl.
MAKES 35 to 45

COUNTRY-STYLE TERRINE

METRIC/IMPERIAL
450 g/1 lb streaky bacon, derinded
225 g/8 oz pork fillet, minced
100 g/4 oz belly of pork, minced
100 g/4 oz lamb's or pig's liver, minced
1 small onion, grated
50 ml/2 fl oz brandy
50 ml/2 fl oz dry red wine
salt
freshly ground black pepper
1 teaspoon grated nutmeg
1 teaspoon dried mixed herbs
1 clove garic, crushed
50 g/2 oz fresh white breadcrumbs
2 bay leaves
2 cloves

Line a 1 kg/2 lb glass loaf dish or a glazed pottery terrine dish with about three-quarters of the bacon.

Mix the pork fillet with the belly of pork, liver, onion, brandy, wine, salt and pepper to taste, nutmeg, herbs, garlic and breadcrumbs, blending well.

Spoon into the bacon-lined dish, pressing down well. Cover with the remaining bacon slices and top with the bay leaves and cloves.

Place in a dish filled with warm water, so that the water comes halfway up the sides of the pâté loaf dish or terrine. Cook on FULL (100%) for 40 minutes or until the pâté is cooked.

Drain off any excess fat and cover with greaseproof paper. Place a heavy weight on top and chill overnight or for about 6 to 8 hours.

To serve, remove and discard the bay leaves and cloves. Turn out on to a serving dish and serve with toast, crackers or French bread.
SERVES 8 to 10

PÂTÉ MAISON

METRIC/IMPERIAL
100 g/4 oz streaky bacon, derinded and stretched
175 g/6 oz chicken livers, trimmed
1 egg, beaten
1 clove garlic, crushed
1 onion, chopped
2 tablespoons brandy
2 tablespoons chopped fresh thyme or marjoram
½ teaspoon ground mixed spice
pinch of grated nutmeg
freshly ground black pepper
225 g/8 oz lean pork, minced
175 g/6 oz pork fat, minced
100 g/4 oz ham or tongue, minced
2 tablespoons red wine

Line a 13 × 23 cm/5 × 9 inch glass loaf dish or earthenware pâté dish with the bacon rashers, allowing them to hang over the edge by about 2.5 cm/1 inch.

Mix the chicken livers with the egg, garlic, onion, brandy, thyme or marjoram, mixed spice, nutmeg and pepper to taste, blending well.

In a separate bowl mix the pork with the pork fat, ham or tongue and red wine, blending well. Spoon a quarter of this mixture into the base of the prepared loaf dish. Top with the chicken liver mixture. Cover with the remaining pork mixture. Fold the bacon ends over the top of the pâté.

Pour 450 ml/¾ pint water into a large dish. Stand the pâté in this dish, cover and cook on FULL (100%) for 30 minutes, turning the dish twice. Remove from the waterbath. Weight the pâté and chill to set.

Invert on to a serving plate and to serve cut into slices.
SERVES 8

SMOKED HADDOCK PÂTÉ

METRIC/IMPERIAL
450 g/1 lb smoked haddock fillets, skinned
2 tablespoons finely chopped onion
225 g/8 oz cream cheese
salt
freshly ground black pepper
Garnish:
lemon wedges
parsley sprigs

Cut the fish into chunks and place in a bowl with the onion. Cover and cook on FULL (100%) for 4 minutes, stirring twice. Leave to STAND for 5 minutes.
Cool the fish, then place in a blender or food processor with the cream cheese and purée until smooth. Add salt and pepper to taste before pressing into individual ramekin dishes or a large serving dish. Chill until firm and garnish with lemon wedges and parsley before serving.
SERVES 4

TARRAGON PÂTÉ

METRIC/IMPERIAL
1 small onion, finely chopped
1 clove garlic, crushed
4 tablespoons chicken stock
350 g/12 oz calf's liver, cut into strips
50 g/2 oz butter
1 tablespoon brandy
1 tablespoon double cream
1 teaspoon chopped fresh tarragon
salt
freshly ground black pepper
tarragon sprigs to garnish

Place the onion, garlic and stock in a large bowl. Cover and cook on FULL (100%) for 3 minutes. Stir in the liver and cook on FULL (100%) for a further 3½ minutes, stirring halfway through cooking.
Add the butter, brandy, cream, tarragon and salt and pepper to taste. Pour the mixture into four ramekin dishes and refrigerate until firm.
Garnish with sprigs of tarragon just before serving. Serve with Melba toast.
SERVES 4

Note: You can pour a little melted butter over the pâté about 1 hour before serving. Leave to set before garnishing.

CHICKEN LIVER PÂTÉ

METRIC/IMPERIAL
75 g/3 oz butter
1 onion, chopped
1 clove garlic, crushed
2 tablespoons chicken stock
225 g/8 oz chicken livers, trimmed
1 egg, beaten
1 tablespoon cornflour
4 tablespoons double cream
1 tablespoon sherry
salt
freshly ground black pepper

Place 25 g/1 oz of the butter, the onion, garlic and stock in a cooking dish. Cover and cook on FULL (100%) for 5 minutes, stirring once.
Add the chicken livers, blending well. Cover and cook on FULL (100%) for 4 minutes, stirring once. Place in a blender or food processor and blend until smooth.
Mix the egg with the cornflour and stir into the liver mixture, blending well. Add the cream, sherry and salt and pepper to taste.
Spoon into a 600 ml/1 pint serving dish. Cover and cook on FULL (100%) for 5 to 5½ minutes, turning the dish twice.
Place the remaining butter in a bowl and cook on FULL (100%) for 1 to 1½ minutes or until melted.
Pour over the pâté and chill. Serve with fingers of toast or crusty bread.
SERVES 4 to 6

SMOOTH LIVER PÂTÉ

METRIC/IMPERIAL
15 g/½ oz butter
1 small onion, chopped
1 bacon rasher, derinded and chopped
150 g/5 oz lamb's liver, chopped
2 hard-boiled eggs, shelled
4 tablespoons soured cream
3 tablespoons sherry
salt
freshly ground black pepper
1 lettuce heart, shredded

Combine the butter, onion and bacon in a large shallow dish. Cook on FULL (100%) for 3 minutes. Stir in the liver and cook on FULL (100%) for 4 to 5 minutes until the liver is no longer pink, stirring occasionally.

Add the eggs to the liver mixture and purée in a blender or food processor or press through a sieve. Return to the dish and mix in the cream, sherry, and salt and pepper to taste. Cover loosely and cool rapidly. Chill in the refrigerator for 3 to 4 hours.

Line individual serving plates with shredded lettuce, and scoop or pile the pâté on top. Serve accompanied by thin slices of toast.

SERVES 4

EXOTIC KIPPER PÂTÉ

METRIC/IMPERIAL
2 kippers
juice of ½ lemon
225 g/8 oz cream cheese
50 g/2 oz canned pineapple chunks
pinch of ground mace
pineapple juice, to flavour
salt
freshly ground black pepper

Place the kippers in a shallow dish and sprinkle with a little of the lemon juice. Cover and cook on FULL (100%) for 5 minutes.

Allow to cool slightly, then flake into a blender or food processor, removing any skin and as many bones as possible.

Add the cream cheese, remaining lemon juice, pineapple chunks, mace, a little pineapple juice to flavour and salt and pepper to taste. Purée until smooth.

Spoon into a serving dish and chill until firm.

SERVES 4

KIPPER AND CREAM CHEESE PÂTÉ

METRIC/IMPERIAL
1 × 200 g/7 oz packet frozen kipper fillets
75 g/3 oz butter
1 × 75 g/3 oz packet Philadelphia soft cheese
1 teaspoon Worcestershire sauce
salt
freshly ground black pepper
lemon slices, to garnish

Pierce the bag of kipper fillets and place on a plate. Cook on FULL (100%) for 6 minutes, turning over once. Allow to cool slightly, then flake the fillets into a blender or food processor.

Place the butter in a bowl and heat on FULL

(100%) for 1 minute or until melted. Add two-thirds of the butter to the kippers with the cheese, Worcestershire sauce and salt and pepper to taste. Blend until smooth then turn into a small terrine or serving dish.

Pour the remaining butter over the pâté and chill to set. Garnish with lemon slices and serve with hot buttered toast.

SERVES 4

SMOKED MACKEREL PÂTÉ

METRIC/IMPERIAL
350 g/12 oz smoked mackerel fillet
50 g/2 oz butter
100 g/4 oz curd cheese
1 tablespoon lemon juice
1 tablespoon mild creamed horseradish
salt (optional)
freshly ground black pepper
4–6 tablespoons single cream or 'top of the milk'
lemon slices, to garnish

Remove the skin and bones from the mackerel and put the flaked fish into a bowl. Cook on FULL (100%) for 1½ minutes or until the fish is warm.

Stir in the butter and pound until pulped, then work in the remaining ingredients, adding salt to taste, if liked, and pepper. Add sufficient cream to mix to a spreading consistency. (For a smoother pâté, purée the mixture in a blender or food processor.)

Pile the pâté into a dish or individual ramekins and garnish with slices of fresh lemon. Chill lightly before serving with Melba or hot buttered toast.

SERVES 6

Variation
For a less rich-tasting pâté, use cottage cheese instead of curd.

TUNA PÂTÉ

METRIC/IMPERIAL
100 g/4 oz butter
2 onions, finely chopped
75 g/3 oz plain flour
300 ml/½ pint milk
salt
freshly ground black pepper
2 teaspoons chopped fresh parsley

1 × 200 g/7 oz can tuna fish, drained
3 tablespoons soured cream or natural yogurt
2 teaspoons lemon juice
lemon slices, to garnish
To serve:
toast
carrot slices
cucumber slices

Place half the butter in a large jug and cook on FULL (100%) for 1½ minutes to melt. Stir in the onion and cook on FULL (100%) for 2 minutes.

Stir in the flour, then gradually stir in the milk. Cook on FULL (100%) for 4 minutes. Beat well with a whisk (the sauce will be very thick). Beat in salt and pepper to taste, parsley and the remaining butter. Cover with a damp tea towel and leave to STAND for 10 minutes.

Flake the fish into a blender or food processor. Add the soured cream or yogurt, lemon juice and cooled sauce and blend until smooth. Pour into a serving dish and refrigerate.

Garnish with lemon slices and serve with fresh, warm toast and sliced, raw carrots and cucumber.
SERVES 6

SPINACH AND ANCHOVY PÂTÉ

METRIC/IMPERIAL
350 g/12 oz fresh spinach leaves (bought weight 675 g/1½ lb)
1 × 50 g/1¾ oz can anchovy fillets
1 tablespoon oil from anchovy fillets
1 small onion, finely chopped
¼ teaspoon freshly ground black pepper
3 eggs
100 g/4 oz fresh breadcrumbs
cucumber slices, to garnish

Wash the spinach leaves and put in a roasting bag with only the water clinging to the leaves. Seal with an elastic band, leaving a gap in the top for the steam to escape. Cook on FULL (100%) for 5 minutes. Drain thoroughly.

Place the anchovy oil and onion in a bowl and cook on FULL (100%) for 3 minutes, stirring once.

Purée all the ingredients in a blender or food processor until smooth, adding the breadcrumbs last.

Divide the mixture equally between 6 individual ramekins. Cover and cook on LOW (30%) for 7 to 8 minutes. Give each dish a half-turn and cook on LOW (30%) for a further 7 to 8 minutes or until the mixture is set. Leave to STAND for 20 minutes. Garnish with cucumber and serve warm with hot buttered toast.
SERVES 6

COUNTRY HERB PÂTÉ

METRIC/IMPERIAL
6 bacon rashers, derinded
225 g/8 oz belly pork, derinded and boned
225 g/8 oz calf's liver
1 onion, chopped
2 cloves garlic, crushed
225 g/8 oz stewing steak
2 teaspoons anchovy essence
¼ teaspoon chopped fresh parsley
¼ teaspoon chopped fresh thyme
¼ teaspoon chopped fresh sage
¼ teaspoon chopped fresh rosemary
65 g/2½ oz fresh white breadcrumbs
salt
freshly ground black pepper
2 large eggs, lightly beaten
bay leaves, to garnish

Line a 1.75 litre/3 pint soufflé dish with the bacon and set aside.

Mince or process together the pork, liver, onion, garlic, beef, anchovy essence, herbs, breadcrumbs, and salt and pepper to taste. Bind the mixture with the eggs.

Spread into the bacon-lined dish. Cover and cook on FULL (100%) for 15 minutes, giving the dish a half-turn halfway through cooking. Leave to STAND, covered, for 10 minutes.

Remove the cover and replace it with grease-proof paper. Place a weighted plate on top. Leave to cool and set.

Unmould for serving and garnish with bay leaves.
SERVES 4

POPPADOM SURPRISES

METRIC/IMPERIAL
4 poppadoms
5 streaky bacon rashers, derinded
3 hard-boiled eggs, finely chopped
50 g/2 oz red Leicester cheese, grated
chopped fresh parsley, to garnish
yogurt dressing or mayonnaise, to serve

35

Put one poppadom in each of the 4 cereal or soup bowls. Arrange in the microwave oven, leaving a small space in the centre. Cook on FULL (100%) for 2 minutes, until the poppadoms puff up. Set aside.

Arrange the bacon on a double thickness of absorbent kitchen paper on a plate. Leave the centre of the plate clear. Cook on FULL (100%) for 3 to 4 minutes; then cool and crumble or chop.

Mix together the eggs, cheese and bacon, and divide the mixture between the cooked poppadoms. Garnish with parsley and offer a bowl of yogurt dressing or mayonnaise separately. Serve at once.
SERVES 4

BEEF SHAMI

METRIC/IMPERIAL
225 g/8 oz lean minced beef
1 onion, grated
2 teaspoons curry paste
½ teaspoon cumin powder
½ teaspoon salt
1 tablespoon flour
1 tablespoon vegetable oil

Combine all the ingredients, except the oil, and mix well. Divide into eight equal-size pieces and, with floured hands, shape into rolls about 1.5 cm/¾ inch thick.

Preheat a browning dish on FULL (100%) for 5 minutes (or according to the manufacturer's instructions). Immediately add the oil and the beef rolls. Cook on FULL (100%) for 4 minutes, turning the meat over after 2 minutes. Serve hot.
SERVES 4

SNAILS WITH GARLIC BUTTER

METRIC/IMPERIAL
40 g/1½ oz butter
1 teaspoon finely grated onion
2 cloves garlic, crushed
pinch of salt
pinch of grated nutmeg
1 teaspoon chopped fresh parsley
freshly ground black pepper
12 canned snails with shells
coarse salt (see method)

Cream together the butter, onion, garlic, salt, nutmeg, parsley and pepper to taste. Push some of the butter mixture into each shell. Place the snails in the shells and cover with the remaining butter.

Arrange the shells, with the open ends uppermost, in a circle on a plate covered with coarse salt to hold them steady.

Cook on FULL (100%) for 1½ to 2 minutes. Serve hot with plenty of brown bread fingers or French bread so that your guests can use it to soak up the butter.
SERVES 2

MUSHROOMS IN GARLIC BUTTER

METRIC/IMPERIAL
100 g/4 oz butter
2 cloves garlic, crushed
1 tablespoon lemon juice
freshly ground black pepper
450 g/1 lb button mushrooms, trimmed

Place the butter in a bowl and heat on FULL (100%) for 1 to 1½ minutes or until melted. Add the garlic, lemon juice and pepper to taste, blending well. Cook on FULL (100%) for 1 minute.

Add the mushrooms, stirring well to coat in the butter. Cover and leave to marinate for 1 to 2 hours.

Cook, covered, on FULL (100%) for 5 to 6 minutes, stirring once.

Serve the mushrooms hot with chunks of wholemeal bread.
SERVES 4

STUFFED MUSHROOMS

METRIC/IMPERIAL
2 large flat mushrooms, at least 7.5 cm/3 inches in diameter
15 g/½ oz butter
1 small onion, finely chopped
salt
freshly ground black pepper
4 tablespoons fresh brown breadcrumbs
1 teaspoon mixed dried herbs
½ teaspoon Worcestershire sauce
1 tablespoon sherry
½ beaten egg
15 g/½ oz slivered flaked almonds

Wipe the mushrooms, remove and chop the stems. Set the caps aside.

Put the butter in a medium bowl and cook on FULL (100%) for ½ minute or until melted. Add the chopped stems and the onion and cook on FULL (100%) for 2 minutes or until the onions are soft. Season to taste with salt and pepper.

Mix in the breadcrumbs, herbs, Worcestershire sauce and sherry. Bind with the beaten egg. Stir in the almonds.

Pile the mixture on to the dark side of the mushrooms and cook on FULL (100%) for 1 minute. Turn the dish and cook for a further 1 minute. Serve hot or cold with lettuce and watercress.
SERVES 2

HOT BUTTERED GRAPEFRUIT

METRIC/IMPERIAL
1 large grapefruit
25 g/1 oz butter, softened
25 g/1 oz soft brown sugar
1 glacé cherry, halved, to decorate

Cut the grapefruit in half and loosen the segments. Put each half into a sundae dish.

Mix together the butter and sugar and divide between the grapefruit halves. Cook on FULL (100%) for 2 minutes. Serve immediately, decorated with half a cherry.
SERVES 2

PASTA SALAD ITALIENNE

METRIC/IMPERIAL
100 g/4 oz pasta twists
600 ml/1 pint boiling water
1 teaspoon vegetable oil
100 g/4 oz frozen sliced green beans
2 tablespoons cold water
½ cucumber, chopped
5 tomatoes, skinned and cut into wedges
50 g/2 oz salami, cut into thin strips
6 black olives
3 tablespoons Italian garlic or French dressing

Place the pasta in a bowl with the boiling water and oil. Cover and cook on FULL (100%) for 10 minutes, stirring once. Leave to STAND while cooking the beans.

Place the beans in a bowl with the cold water.

Cover and cook on FULL (100%) for 4 minutes, stirring once. Drain and rinse in cold water.

Drain and rinse the pasta in cold water and place in a salad bowl with the beans, cucumber, tomatoes, salami and olives, blending well.

Pour over the dressing and toss well to mix.
SERVES 4

CHEESE AND MUSHROOM SAVOURIES

METRIC/IMPERIAL
1–2 tablespoons grated Parmesan cheese
100 g/4 oz mushrooms, finely chopped
1 small onion, finely chopped
1 tablespoon chopped fresh parsley
1 tablespoon fresh wholemeal breadcrumbs
25 g/1 oz Edam cheese, grated
salt
freshly ground black pepper
25 g/1 oz butter
1 tablespoon wholemeal flour
150 ml/¼ pint skimmed milk
2 eggs, separated
½ teaspoon cream of tartar

Lightly oil 4 ramekins and dust them with the Parmesan cheese.

Place the mushrooms and onion in a bowl. Cover and cook on FULL (100%) for 2½ minutes, stirring halfway through the cooking time. Using a slotted spoon, transfer the cooked vegetables to a large mixing bowl. Stir in the chopped parsley, breadcrumbs and grated Edam cheese; season with salt and pepper and set aside.

Place the butter in a medium-sized bowl and heat on FULL (100%) for ½ minute or until melted. Stir in the flour and gradually blend in the milk. Cook on FULL (100%) for 2½ minutes to thicken, stirring every 1 minute. Whisk vigorously to break down any lumps. Cover and leave to STAND for 3 minutes, stirring frequently. Beat in the egg yolks, one at a time, then stir the sauce into the reserved mushroom mixture. Mix thoroughly.

In a medium-sized clean bowl, whisk the egg whites with the cream of tartar to firm peaks. Fold into the mushroom mixture.

Divide between the prepared ramekins. Place in a circle in the oven and cook on LOW (30%) for 3 minutes. Give the ramekins a half-turn and cook on LOW (30%) for a further 6 minutes. Serve immediately.
SERVES 4

CHEESY MUSHROOMS AND PRAWNS

METRIC/IMPERIAL
50 g/2 oz savoury butter with black pepper
1 small onion, chopped
100 g/4 oz button mushrooms, sliced
225 g/8 oz peeled prawns
150 ml/¼ pint double cream
50 g/2 oz Cheddar cheese, grated
1 tablespoon chopped fresh parsley, to garnish

Place the savoury butter, onion and mushrooms in a bowl. Cover and cook on FULL (100%) for 3 minutes, stirring once.

Add the prawns, blending well. Cover and cook on FULL (100%) for 3 minutes, stirring once.

Add the double cream, blending well. Spoon equally into 4 ramekin dishes and sprinkle with the cheese. Cook on FULL (100%) for 2 minutes.

If wished, brown under a preheated hot grill before serving. Sprinkle with the chopped parsley and serve with brown bread and butter.
SERVES 4

VEGETABLES À LA GRECQUE

METRIC/IMPERIAL
2 tablespoons vegetable oil
1 clove garlic, crushed
1 small onion, thinly sliced
2 tablespoons white wine vinegar
150 ml/¼ pint dry white vermouth
3 tablespoons tomato purée
2 tablespoons soft brown sugar
3 tablespoons chopped fresh marjoram or parsley
salt
freshly ground black pepper
225 g/8 oz button mushrooms, trimmed
225 g/8 oz cauliflower, broken into small florets

Place the oil, garlic and onion in a bowl. Cook on FULL (100%) for 2 minutes, stirring once.

Add the vinegar, vermouth, tomato purée, sugar, herbs and salt and pepper to taste, blending well. Add the vegetables and stir well to coat in the marinade. Cover and cook on FULL (100%) for 5 minutes, stirring once.

Allow to cool, then chill thoroughly. Serve chilled with crusty bread as a starter.
SERVES 4

DEVIL'S DIP

METRIC/IMPERIAL
25 g/1 oz butter
3 tablespoons plain flour
½ teaspoon curry powder (medium strength)
300 ml/½ pint milk
1 green pepper, cored, seeded and chopped
50 g/2 oz walnuts, chopped
50 g/2 oz raisins
2 tablespoons wine vinegar
1 tablespoon lemon juice
pinch of cayenne pepper
150 ml/¼ pint double cream

Place the butter in a bowl and heat on FULL (100%) for ½ minute or until melted. Add the flour and curry powder, blending well. Gradually add the milk and cook on FULL (100%) for 3 minutes, stirring every 1 minute until smooth and thickened.

Add the pepper, walnuts, raisins, wine vinegar, lemon juice and cayenne pepper, blending well. Finally add the double cream and stir well to blend.

Serve hot or chilled with crisps, crackers or salad crudités.
SERVES 4

AUBERGINE DIP

METRIC/IMPERIAL
1 × 225 g/8 oz aubergine
3 tablespoons soured cream
1 clove garlic, crushed
1 teaspoon salt
¼ teaspoon freshly ground black pepper
2 tablespoons lemon juice
1 small onion, chopped
1 tablespoon chopped fresh parsley
3 tablespoons olive oil

Wash the aubergine, score around the middle with a sharp knife and cook on FULL (100%) for 5 minutes, turning over once.

Cut in half, scoop out the flesh and place in a blender or food processor. Add the soured cream, garlic, salt, pepper, lemon juice, onion and parsley. Purée until smooth.

Gradually blend in the olive oil and pour into a serving dish. Chill thoroughly.

Serve chilled with chunks of wholemeal bread.
SERVES 4

GUACAMOLE

METRIC/IMPERIAL
1 medium tomato
2 teaspoons fresh lemon juice
1 teaspoon olive oil
1 slice of onion
shake of garlic salt
pinch of ground coriander
pinch of chilli powder
1 × 175 g/6 oz ripe avocado
salt
freshly ground black pepper

Prick the tomato skin with a sharp knife and place on a plate. Cook on FULL (100%) for 1 minute, then peel away the skin. Cut the tomato into quarters, discarding the seeds.

Put the tomato, lemon juice, olive oil, onion, garlic salt and spices in the blender or food processor and purée until smooth.

Halve the avocado and remove the stone. Peel the avocado halves and cut into slices. Add to the blender or food processor and blend until smooth. Season to taste and serve as a dip.
SERVES 4

POTTED SHRIMPS

METRIC/IMPERIAL
175 g/6 oz butter, cut into small pieces
350 g/12 oz peeled shrimps
salt
cayenne pepper

Place the butter in a bowl and heat on FULL (100%) for 2 to 2½ minutes or until melted.

Add the shrimps and salt and cayenne pepper to taste, blending well. Pour into a serving bowl or individual ramekin dishes and chill to set.

Serve with warm wholemeal toast and lemon wedges.
SERVES 4

MARINATED MUSHROOMS

METRIC/IMPERIAL
25 g/1 oz butter
1 small onion, finely chopped
1 clove garlic, crushed
450 g/1 lb button mushrooms, trimmed
½ teaspoon dried mixed herbs

150 ml/¼ pint dry white wine
1 bay leaf
1 teaspoon chopped fresh parsley
salt
freshly ground black pepper

Place the butter in a bowl and heat on FULL (100%) for ½ minute or until melted. Add the onion and garlic. Cover and cook on FULL (100%) for 1 minute.

Add the mushrooms, blending well. Cover and cook on FULL (100%) for 3 minutes, stirring once.

Stir in the herbs, wine, bay leaf, parsley and salt and pepper to taste. Cook on LOW (30%) for 8 to 10 minutes, stirring once.

Leave to cool, then chill lightly. Remove and discard the bay leaf. Serve chilled with French bread.
SERVES 4

POTTED TURKEY

METRIC/IMPERIAL
50 g/2 oz savoury butter with black pepper
1 onion, finely chopped
350 g/12 oz cooked turkey, finely chopped
75 g/3 oz cooked ham, finely chopped
2 tablespoons sherry
75 g/3 oz butter

Place the savoury butter and the onion in a bowl. Cover and cook on FULL (100%) for 4 minutes, stirring once.

Add the turkey, ham and sherry, blending well. Spoon into a small terrine or serving dish and press down well.

Dice the butter and place in a small bowl. Cook on FULL (100%) for 1½ minutes or until melted. Pour over the potted turkey and chill to set. Serve chilled with fingers of warm toast.
SERVES 4 to 6

TOMATOES STUFFED WITH MUSHROOM PÂTÉ

METRIC/IMPERIAL
4 firm medium tomatoes
salt
50 g/2 oz button mushrooms, finely chopped
15 g/½ oz butter
4 spring onions, finely chopped
2 teaspoons chopped fresh parsley

¼ teaspoon dried basil
¼ teaspoon pepper
1 teaspoon cornflour, blended with 2 teaspoons medium sherry
4 tablespoons soured cream

Slice the caps from the tomatoes and set aside. Scoop the pulp and seeds from the tomato shells and reserve for use in another recipe. Sprinkle the insides of the shells with salt, then turn upside down to drain.

Place the mushrooms, butter and spring onions in a medium bowl and cook on FULL (100%) for 1½ minutes. Stir, then cook for a further 1½ minutes or until the mushrooms are soft.

Mix in the parsley, basil, ¼ teaspoon salt, the pepper and the cornflour mixed with the sherry. Cook on FULL (100%) for ½ minute, then stir and cook for a further ¼ minute or until thick. Stir in the soured cream; cover and leave to cool.

Fill the tomato shells with the mushroom stuffing and top with the reserved caps. Arrange on a bed of lettuce leaves and serve cold.
SERVES 4

TAGLIATELLE WITH WALNUT SAUCE

METRIC/IMPERIAL
350 g/12 oz tagliatelle verdi
900 ml/1½ pints boiling water
salt
1 teaspoon vegetable oil
50 g/2 oz butter
4 tablespoons soured cream
Walnut sauce:
6 tablespoons olive oil
2 cloves garlic, crushed
100 g/4 oz walnuts, chopped
75 g/3 oz grated Parmesan cheese

Place the pasta in a deep bowl with the boiling water, a little salt and the oil. Partially cover and cook on FULL (100%) for 6 minutes. Leave to STAND for 3 minutes.

Make the walnut sauce. Place the olive oil in a bowl and cook on FULL (100%) for 1 to 2 minutes until hot. Add the garlic and walnuts and cook on FULL (100%) for a further 2 to 4 minutes or until the mixture browns slightly. Stir in the Parmesan cheese. Keep hot while finishing the tagliatelle.

Place the butter in a bowl and heat on FULL

(100%) for 1 minute or until melted. Drain the cooked tagliatelle and toss in the melted butter.

Spoon the tagliatelle into a hot serving dish and top with the soured cream. Serve as a starter with the hot walnut sauce.
SERVES 4

SPINACH ROULADE

METRIC/IMPERIAL
2 tablespoons grated Parmesan cheese
225 g/8 oz frozen leaf spinach, defrosted, drained and finely chopped
25 g/1 oz Edam cheese, finely grated
freshly ground black pepper
3 eggs, separated
½ teaspoon cream of tartar
Filling:
1 onion, finely chopped
225 g/8 oz firm button mushrooms, thinly sliced
1 × 200 g/7 oz can tomatoes, drained
3 tablespoons tomato purée
½ teaspoon demerara sugar
1 tablespoon chopped fresh basil or 1 teaspoon dried basil
½ tablespoon wholemeal flour blended with 3 tablespoons water

Line a 30 × 20 cm/12 × 8 inch shallow baking dish with greaseproof paper, leaving some paper overlapping at each end. Lightly oil the paper and sprinkle it with an even layer of half the grated Parmesan. Reserve the remaining Parmesan cheese.

To make the filling, place the onion and mushrooms in a bowl; cover and cook on FULL (100%) for 2½ minutes. Stir in the tomatoes, tomato purée, sugar and basil, cover as before and cook on FULL (100%) for a further 3¼ minutes, stirring halfway through the cooking time. Stir in the flour mixture and season with pepper to taste. Cover again and cook on FULL (100%) for 2½ minutes, stirring twice during cooking. Keep the sauce warm while making the roulade.

Place the spinach in a large bowl. Add the grated Edam cheese and season with pepper to taste. Beat in the egg yolks, one at a time.

In a clean bowl, whisk the egg whites and cream of tartar to firm peaks and fold into the spinach mixture. Spread in the prepared dish and cook on LOW (30%) for 6½ minutes. Turn the dish and cook on LOW (30%) for a further 6½ minutes.

Meanwhile, dust a large piece of greaseproof paper with the remaining grated Parmesan cheese. Turn the roulade out on to this and carefully peel off the paper in which it was cooked.

Spread with the filling and roll up. Transfer to a warmed serving dish and serve immediately.
SERVES 4

Note: If your microwave cooker has a turntable, use a 25 cm/10 inch square dish.

SALMON VOL-AU-VENT

METRIC/IMPERIAL
1 × 375 g/13 oz packet frozen puff pastry, just thawed
a little milk for brushing
Filling:
25 g/1 oz butter
25 g/1 oz plain flour
salt
freshly ground black pepper
1 × 215 g/7½ oz can red salmon, drained and flaked
1 tablespoon chopped fresh parsley
1 teaspoon fresh lemon juice

Roll the pastry out on a floured surface to a round 23 cm/9 inches in diameter. Place the circle of pastry upside down on a suitable container.

Place an 18 cm/7 inch plate gently on top of the pastry and mark round it with a sharp knife, but do not cut right through. On the inner circle, mark an attractive lattice pattern. Brush the pastry with a little milk.

Put the vol-au-vent into the refrigerator for 10 minutes. Cook on FULL (100%) for 9 to 10 minutes, turning the plate once during this time. Allow to STAND for 3 minutes, then carefully remove the vol-au-vent 'lid' with a sharp knife.

To prepare the filling, place the butter in a large jug and cook on FULL (100%) for 1 minute until melted.

Stir in the flour and salt and pepper. Gradually stir in the milk. Cook on FULL (100%) for 3½ minutes, then beat well. Beat in the salmon, parsley and lemon juice.

Put the 'lid' of the vol-au-vent under a preheated very hot grill. It will brown beautifully in a few seconds. Put the vol-au-vent base on a serving dish. Fill with the sauce, then top with the 'lid'. Serve with a green salad.
SERVES 4

HOT SMOKED MACKEREL FILLETS

METRIC/IMPERIAL
2 smoked mackerel fillets
1 tablespoon cottage cheese
½ teaspoon dried tarragon
6 mushroom caps, finely chopped
salt
freshly ground black pepper
a little garlic seasoning or minced garlic (optional)
Garnish:
paprika
lemon slices

Lay the mackerel fillets on an oval dish, tails to the centre. Mix together the cottage cheese, tarragon, mushrooms, salt, pepper and the garlic, if using. Arrange this mixture down the centre of each fillet.

Cover loosely and cook on MEDIUM (50%) for 4 to 4½ minutes. Drain, if necessary, and garnish with paprika and lemon slices. Serve immediately.
SERVES 2

HIGHLAND PRAWNS

METRIC/IMPERIAL
50 g/2 oz butter
1 small onion, chopped
350 g/12 oz peeled prawns
4 tablespoons double cream
2 tablespoons whisky or brandy
salt
freshly ground black pepper
100 g/4 oz Cheddar cheese, grated

Place the butter in a bowl and heat on FULL (100%) for 1 minute or until melted. Add the onion, cover and cook on FULL (100%) for 3 minutes, stirring once.

Stir in the prawns, blending well. Cover and cook on FULL (100%) for 2 minutes. Divide the mixture between 4 small ramekin dishes.

Place the cream and whisky or brandy in a bowl and cook on FULL (100%) for ½ minute. Season with salt and pepper to taste. Stir well and spoon evenly over the prawns.

Sprinkle with the cheese and brown under a preheated hot grill. Serve hot with fingers of toast.
SERVES 4

SMOKED HADDOCK MOUSSE

METRIC/IMPERIAL
225 g/8 oz smoked haddock fillet
1 tablespoon water
15 g/½ oz powdered gelatine
150 ml/¼ pint chicken stock
1½ tablespoons lemon juice
75 g/3 oz Gouda cheese, grated
freshly ground black pepper
75 g/3 oz butter
1 tablespoon chopped fresh parsley
Garnish:
lemon wedges
cucumber slices
tomato slices
mustard and cress

Place the haddock in a dish with the water. Cover and cook on FULL (100%) for 3 to 3½ minutes. Allow to cool slightly, then skin and flake the haddock into a blender or food processor.

Meanwhile, mix the gelatine with the stock and leave to soften for 2 minutes. Cook on FULL (100%) for 1 minute until the gelatine is clear and dissolved. Add to the blender or food processor.

Add the lemon juice, cheese and pepper to taste. Purée until smooth.

Place the butter in a bowl and heat on FULL (100%) for 1¼ minutes or until melted. Stir into the haddock mixture with the parsley, blending well. Pour into a small greased ring mould and chill until set.

To serve, dip the mould briefly into hot water and turn the mousse on to a serving plate. Garnish with lemon wedges, cucumber and tomato slices and small bunches of mustard and cress in the centre. Serve as a starter.
SERVES 4 to 6

HAM AND MUSHROOM COCOTTES

METRIC/IMPERIAL
Cocottes:
25 g/1 oz butter
1 onion, chopped
25 g/1 oz plain flour
300 ml/½ pint ham stock
2 tablespoons single cream
salt
freshly ground black pepper
100 g/4 oz button mushrooms, very finely sliced
225 g/8 oz cooked ham, cubed
Croûtons:
50 g/2 oz butter
75 g/3 oz bread, crusts removed, cut into cubes
Garnish:
parsley sprigs

Place the butter in a bowl and heat on FULL (100%) for 1 minute or until melted. Add the onion, cover and cook on FULL (100%) for a further 3 minutes.

Stir in the flour, mixing well. Gradually add the stock and cook on FULL (100%) for 3½ to 4 minutes, stirring every 1 minute, until smooth and thickened.

Stir in the cream and salt and pepper to taste, blending well. Fold in the mushrooms and ham.

Spoon into 4 cocotte dishes, cover and cook on FULL (100%) for 2 minutes.

Place the butter for the croûtons in a large bowl. Heat on FULL (100%) for ¾ to 1 minute until melted. Add the bread cubes and toss to coat. Cook on FULL (100%) for 1½ minutes; stir, and cook on FULL (100%) for a further 1½ minutes. Sprinkle the croûtons over the cocottes and serve as a starter, garnished with parsley.
SERVES 4

HOT SMOKED BACON AND SPINACH SALAD

METRIC/IMPERIAL
225 g/8 oz spinach, trimmed
100 g/4 oz smoked bacon rashers, derinded
5 spring onions, chopped
4 tablespoons grapeseed or sunflower oil
2 tablespoons white wine vinegar
1 teaspoon honey
freshly ground black pepper
1 tablespoon sesame seeds, toasted

Shred the spinach leaves and place in a large bowl. Place the bacon slices on several thicknesses of absorbent kitchen paper and cook on FULL (100%) for 3¼ minutes. Leave to STAND for 2 minutes.

Combine the spring onions, oil, vinegar, honey and pepper in a bowl. Cook on FULL (100%) for 1 to 1½ minutes or until boiling.

Crumble the bacon slices over the spinach and pour in the hot dressing. Toss the salad and mix well, then sprinkle with the toasted sesame seeds.
SERVES 4

EGG MOUSSE

METRIC/IMPERIAL
25 g/1 oz butter
1 clove garlic, crushed
3 tablespoons flour
300 ml/½ pint milk
4 hard-boiled eggs, chopped
2 eggs, separated
15 g/½ oz powdered gelatine
2 tablespoons hot water
Garnish:
2 hard-boiled eggs, quartered
watercress sprigs

Place the butter in a large bowl and heat on FULL (100%) for ½ minute or until melted. Add the garlic and stir in the flour. Gradually add the milk, whisking well. Cook on FULL (100%) for 3½ to 4 minutes, stirring every 1 minute.

Add the chopped hard-boiled eggs and egg yolks to the sauce and cool slightly. Dissolve the gelatine in the hot water, add to the sauce and leave in a cool place until half set. Whisk the egg whites until they form stiff peaks then, using a metal spoon, fold into the half-set mixture. Pour into a lightly oiled 1.5 litre/2½ pint mould and leave to set in a cool place.

Turn out on to a serving dish and garnish with quartered hard-boiled eggs and sprigs of watercress. Serve with Melba toast.
SERVES 4

ASPARAGUS MOUSSE

METRIC/IMPERIAL
1 × 350 g/12 oz can green asparagus spears
15 g/½ oz butter, softened
15 g/½ oz flour
2 eggs, separated
15 g/½ oz powdered gelatine
150 ml/¼ pint chicken stock
salt
freshly ground black pepper
pinch of cayenne pepper
1 teaspoon lemon juice
150 ml/¼ pint double cream, whipped
Garnish:
lemon slices
cucumber slices

Drain the juice from the asparagus into a jug and mix with the butter and flour. Cook on FULL (100%) for 2 to 2½ minutes, whisking once

during cooking. Remove from the oven and whisk well to remove any lumps. Allow to cool slightly, then stir in the egg yolks.

Sprinkle the gelatine over the chicken stock and leave to soften. Cook on FULL (100%) for 1 minute until clear and dissolved. Stir into the sauce. Chop the asparagus and stir into the sauce, adding salt and pepper to taste and the lemon juice.

When on the point of setting, whisk the egg whites and fold into the sauce with the whipped cream. Pour into a wetted 1 litre/2 pint mould and chill until set.

When required, dip the mould quickly into hot water and turn out. Garnish with lemon and cucumber slices.
SERVES 4 to 6

FRESH ASPARAGUS WITH BEURRE MALTAISE

METRIC/IMPERIAL
675 g/1½ lb asparagus
150 ml/¼ pint water
Beurre Maltaise:
100 g/4 oz butter
4 tablespoons double cream
3 egg yolks
juice of ½ lemon
juice and grated rind of 1 small sweet orange
¼ teaspoon salt
¼ teaspoon freshly ground black pepper

Break off and discard the thick fibrous ends of the asparagus. Rinse under cold running water. Arrange in a large shallow dish with the asparagus tips towards the centre. Sprinkle the water over the top.

Cover the dish loosely and cook on FULL (100%) for 14 to 16 minutes, giving the dish a half-turn once during cooking. The asparagus tips should be just tender when pierced with the tip of a knife. Leave to STAND, covered, while preparing the sauce.

Put the butter in a bowl and cook on FULL (100%) for 2 minutes until melted. Add all the remaining sauce ingredients and whisk until smooth. Cook on LOW (30%) for 2 to 3 minutes until the sauce thickens, beating vigorously every ½ minute during cooking.

Carefully transfer the drained asparagus to a heated serving dish. Pour the sauce into a sauceboat and hand separately.
SERVES 4

JELLIED HAM AND CHICKEN

METRIC/IMPERIAL
100 g/4 oz cooked chicken meat, finely diced
100 g/4 oz cooked ham, finely chopped
15 g/½ oz powdered gelatine
450 ml/¾ pint well-flavoured chicken stock
½ teaspoon meat extract
2 teaspoons chopped fresh parsley
freshly ground black pepper
4 cucumber slices, to garnish

Mix together the chicken and ham and divide between 4 pots.

Place the gelatine in a jug and slowly stir in half the stock. Cook on FULL (100%) for 2½ minutes or until the gelatine has dissolved, stirring after each minute.

Stir in the meat extract, parsley and remaining chicken stock. Season to taste with pepper. Cool, then pour over the chicken and ham. Chill until set.

Garnish each pot with a slice of cucumber.
SERVES 4

ARTICHOKES WITH BUTTER SAUCE

METRIC/IMPERIAL
4 globe artichokes
1 tablespoon lemon juice
½ teaspoon salt
300 ml/½ pint water
½ teaspoon butter
Sauce:
100 g/4 oz butter
½ teaspoon salt
½ teaspoon freshly ground black pepper

Using kitchen scissors, trim the tips of the outer artichoke leaves. Wash the artichokes under cold running water.

Combine the lemon juice, salt and water in a large dish and add the butter. Cook on FULL (100%) for 3 to 4 minutes until boiling. Place the artichokes upright in the dish, cover and cook on FULL (100%) for 15 to 18 minutes until the lower leaves can be pulled away from the stem easily. Leave to STAND, covered, while preparing the sauce.

Place the butter, salt and pepper in a small serving jug and cook on FULL (100%) for 2 minutes or until melted.

Transfer the drained artichokes to heated serving plates. Serve each one on a small plate standing on a larger plate, so there is ample place for the discarded leaves. Hand the sauce round separately.
SERVES 4

VEGETABLE TERRINE

METRIC/IMPERIAL
6–8 large spinach leaves, trimmed and blanched
350 g/12 oz carrots, sliced
1 onion, finely chopped
1 clove garlic, crushed
2 potatoes, peeled and cubed
6 tablespoons skimmed milk
salt
freshly ground black pepper
1 egg, lightly beaten
2 courgettes, cut into sticks and blanched
225 g/8 oz green beans, blanched
2 small egg whites

Lightly oil a 1.5 litre/2½ pint loaf dish and line with 4 or 5 of the blanched spinach leaves, making sure that the leaves slightly overlap the edge of the dish.

Place the carrots, onion, garlic and potatoes in a large bowl with the skimmed milk. Cover and cook on FULL (100%) for 10 minutes, or until the vegetables are tender, stirring two or three times during cooking.

Purée in a blender or food processor. Transfer to a bowl, season with salt and pepper and stir in the beaten egg, mixing together well. Drain the blanched vegetables thoroughly and pat dry on absorbent kitchen paper.

Whisk the egg whites to soft peaks and fold into the vegetable purée. Arrange alternate layers of the purée and blanched vegetables in the spinach-lined loaf dish; starting and ending with a layer of vegetable purée. Fold over the overlapping spinach and cover with the remaining leaves of spinach. Cover the dish with greaseproof paper and cook on FULL (100%) for 5 minutes. Turn the dish around and cook on FULL (100%) for a further 4 minutes.

Allow to cool completely before chilling in the refrigerator for several hours. Unmould the terrine and serve in thick slices with a fresh tomato sauce.
SERVES 4 to 6

VINE LEAVES WITH MUSHROOM STUFFING

METRIC/IMPERIAL

12 fresh, packed or canned vine leaves
50 g/2 oz butter
1 onion, chopped
225 g/8 oz mushrooms, chopped
175 g/6 oz cooked long-grain rice
1 tablespoon chopped fresh parsley
salt
freshly ground black pepper
1 × 350 g/12 oz can ready-to-use meat sauce

If using fresh vine leaves, place them in a deep dish. Add just sufficient cold water to cover and cook on FULL (100%) for 10 minutes. Drain and set aside.

Place the butter in a large shallow dish and heat on FULL (100%) for 1 minute or until melted. Stir in the onion and cook on FULL (100%) for 3 minutes. Add the mushrooms and cook on FULL (100%) for 6 minutes, stirring occasionally.

Stir in the rice, parsley and a little salt and pepper. Mix thoroughly. Spread a little of the mixture along one edge of each vine leaf and roll up, enclosing the filling and tucking in the sides to form a packet.

Arrange the stuffed vine leaves, with the seams underneath, round the edge of the dish. Pour over the sauce. Cover and cook on FULL (100%) for 6 to 8 minutes. Serve hot.

SERVES 4

ARTICHOKE MOUSSE

METRIC/IMPERIAL

150 ml/¼ pint chicken stock
15 g/½ oz powdered gelatine
15 g/½ oz butter
15 g/½ oz plain flour
1 × 400 g/14 oz can artichoke hearts
1 teaspoon lemon juice
2 large eggs, separated
salt
freshly ground black pepper
150 ml/¼ pint double cream, whipped
Garnish:
parsley sprigs
lemon twists

Place the stock in a jug and cook on FULL (100%) for 1 minute or until hot. Sprinkle in the gelatine and stir briskly until the gelatine has dissolved. Set aside.

Place the butter in a medium bowl and cook on FULL (100%) for ¼ minute or until melted. Stir in the flour, then gradually blend in the liquid from the can of artichoke hearts and the lemon juice. Cook on FULL (100%) for 2 minutes. Stir after 1 and 1½ minutes.

Whisk the egg yolks into the sauce. Chop the artichokes and stir these in. Cook on FULL (100%) for 1 minute.

Pour the sauce into a blender or food processor and add the stock, gelatine liquid and salt and pepper to taste. Purée until smooth, then pour into a bowl and chill until almost set.

Fold in the whipped cream. Whisk the egg whites until stiff and fold in gently. Spoon into a 750 ml/1¼ pint soufflé dish. Chill until set.

Serve garnished with sprigs of parsley and lemon twists.

SERVES 6

CHEESE AND SALMON RING MOULD

METRIC/IMPERIAL

25 g/1 oz butter
25 g/1 oz plain flour
salt
freshly ground black pepper
1 tablespoon tomato purée
300 ml/½ pint milk
7 g/¼ oz powdered gelatine
75 g/3 oz Edam cheese, grated
1 × 200 g/7 oz can salmon
cucumber slices, to garnish

First make the sauce. Place the butter in a large jug and heat on FULL (100%) for 1 minute until melted. Stir in the flour, salt and pepper. Blend in the tomato purée and milk.

Cook on FULL (100%) for 3 minutes. Beat well until smooth, then cool slightly for 5 minutes. Add the gelatine and beat until dissolved. Beat in the cheese.

Drain the salmon and discard the bones. Flake the fish into the sauce and mix well. Pour into a wetted 900 ml/1½ pint ring mould. Cool, then chill until firm.

Turn out on to a plate and garnish, if liked, with sliced cucumber. Serve with brown bread and butter.

SERVES 6

ANCHOVY EGGS

METRIC/IMPERIAL
4 eggs
2 tablespoons cream cheese
250 ml/8 fl oz whipping cream
2 teaspoons lemon juice
½ × 45 g/1¾ oz can anchovy fillets, drained and chopped
salt
freshly ground black pepper
paprika, to garnish

Lightly butter 4 ramekin dishes. Break an egg into each dish and prick the yolk with a cocktail stick.

Place the cream cheese in a jug and cook on LOW (30%) for 2 minutes, to soften. Beat the cream and lemon juice into the cream cheese. Fold in the chopped anchovy fillets and season with salt and pepper to taste.

Divide the cream cheese mixture between the ramekins and sprinkle a little paprika on top of each.

Cook on LOW (30%) for 7 to 8 minutes, rearranging the dishes twice during cooking, if necessary, until the eggs are just set. Allow to STAND for 3 minutes before serving.
SERVES 4

COQUILLES ST JACQUES

METRIC/IMPERIAL
450 g/1 lb potatoes, peeled and roughly diced into 2.5 cm/1 inch cubes
3 tablespoons water
salt
100 g/4 oz button mushrooms, sliced
1 clove garlic, crushed
50 g/2 oz butter
25 g/1 oz plain flour
150 ml/¼ pint dry white wine
1 egg yolk
4 large scallops, cleaned and sliced, with shells
2 tablespoons double cream
freshly ground black pepper
1 tablespoon milk
Garnish:
4 parsley sprigs
1 scallop, cooked and sliced

Place the potatoes in a medium bowl with the water and a pinch of salt. Cover and cook on FULL (100%) for 8 minutes, stirring halfway through cooking. Leave to STAND, covered, while making the sauce.

Place the mushrooms, garlic and 25 g/1 oz of the butter in a medium bowl. Cover and cook on FULL (100%) for 3 minutes.

Stir in the flour and then the wine. Cook, uncovered, on FULL (100%) for 2 minutes. Beat in the egg yolk, then stir in the scallops, cream and salt and pepper to taste. Cook, uncovered, on FULL (100%) for 2 minutes.

Meanwhile, mash the potatoes with the remaining butter, the milk and salt and pepper to taste. Place in a piping bag fitted with a large star nozzle and pipe around the edges of 4 scallop shells.

Spoon the sauce into the centre. Reheat, if necessary. Serve garnished with parsley and scallop slices.
SERVES 4

HOT CRAB

METRIC/IMPERIAL
50 g/2 oz fresh white breadcrumbs
2 teaspoons oil
1 tablespoon anchovy essence
1 tablespoon lemon juice
1 tablespoon Worcestershire sauce
150 ml/¼ pint double cream
175 g/6 oz crabmeat (see note)
salt
freshly ground black pepper
4 pieces fried bread
Garnish:
mild paprika
parsley sprigs

Place the breadcrumbs, oil, anchovy essence, lemon juice, Worcestershire sauce, cream, crabmeat, salt and pepper in a bowl and mix them all together.

Cook on FULL (100%) for 3 minutes, stirring every 1 minute. Taste and adjust the seasoning.

Spoon on to the fried bread and serve garnished with paprika and a sprig of parsley.
SERVES 4

Note: Frozen crabmeat, thawed and drained, may be used.

AVOCADO WITH SHRIMPS

METRIC/IMPERIAL
25 g/1 oz butter
50 g/2 oz fresh brown breadcrumbs
1 tablespoon grated lemon rind
100 g/4 oz peeled shrimps
5 tablespoons single cream
salt
freshly ground black pepper
2 large ripe avocados
1 tablespoon lemon juice

Place the butter in a bowl and heat on FULL (100%) for ½ minute or until melted.

Stir in the breadcrumbs and cook on FULL (100%) for 1 minute. Stir in the lemon rind, shrimps, cream, salt and pepper.

Cut the avocados in half. Remove and discard the stones, then sprinkle the flesh with lemon juice. Pile the shrimp mixture into each of the avocado halves. Arrange on a plate and cook on FULL (100%) for a further 3½ minutes.
SERVES 4

TOMATO PASTA BOWS

METRIC/IMPERIAL
1.8 litres/3 pints boiling water
1 tablespoon oil
salt
225 g/8 oz pasta bows
Sauce:
1 onion, finely chopped
2 cloves garlic, crushed
1 teaspoon cornflour
1 × 225 g/8 oz can tomatoes, chopped
1 teaspoon dried mixed herbs
2 tablespoons tomato purée
freshly ground black pepper
15 g/½ oz butter
2 tablespoons grated Parmesan cheese

Place the boiling water, oil, salt and pasta in a large bowl. Cover and cook on FULL (100%) for 8 minutes. STAND, covered, for 10 minutes.

Place the onion and garlic in a small bowl. Cover and cook on FULL (100%) for 3 minutes. Stir in the cornflour, undrained tomatoes, herbs, tomato purée and salt and pepper to taste. Cook on FULL (100%) for 3 minutes, stirring halfway through. Drain the pasta and stir in the sauce and butter. Serve sprinkled with Parmesan cheese.
SERVES 4

SCAMPI IN BRANDY SAUCE

METRIC/IMPERIAL
2 cloves garlic, crushed
1 onion, finely chopped
25 g/1 oz butter
25 g/1 oz cornflour
scant 300 ml/½ pint milk
2 teaspoons tomato purée
2 tablespoons brandy
1 tablespoon double cream
450 g/1 lb peeled scampi
salt
freshly ground black pepper

Place the garlic, onion and butter in a large bowl. Cover and cook on FULL (100%) for 4 minutes, stirring once.

Stir in the cornflour, then blend in the milk, tomato purée, brandy, cream and scampi. Season to taste with salt and pepper. Cook on FULL (100%) for 8 minutes, stirring halfway through cooking. Serve with lemon wedges.
SERVES 4

SCALLOP APPETIZER

METRIC/IMPERIAL
8 large or 12 small scallops, defrosted if frozen
2.5 cm/1 inch piece fresh ginger, peeled and finely shredded
1 clove garlic, crushed
1 tablespoon tomato purée
2 tablespoons dry white wine
3 spring onions, trimmed and sliced
pinch of salt
pinch of cayenne pepper

Rinse the scallops then drain well. If using large scallops, cut them in half.

Place the scallops in a shallow dish with the ginger and garlic. Mix the tomato purée with the wine and stir into the scallop mixture. Sprinkle with the sliced spring onions, cover loosely with dampened kitchen paper towels and cook on FULL (100%) for 2 to 2½ minutes, stirring once during cooking. *Do not overcook the scallops as they will toughen.*

Season with salt and cayenne, cover with foil and allow to STAND for 3 minutes.

Divide the scallops between 4 individual serving dishes and serve immediately.
SERVES 4

SNACKS AND LIGHT MEALS

TOAST

METRIC/IMPERIAL
25 g/1 oz butter
2 slices bread, crusts removed

Butter the bread generously on both sides. Preheat a large browning dish on FULL (100%) for 5 minutes (or according to the manufacturer's instructions). Quickly place the bread in the dish and cook on FULL (100%) for ½ minute. Immediately turn the bread over and cook on FULL (100%) for ½ to ¾ minute until lightly browned.
SERVES 1 to 2

Note: If triangles of toast are required, cut the buttered bread before microwaving. Move the triangles in the centre to the outside edges of the dish before the second cooking period.

GRANOLA

METRIC/IMPERIAL
2 tablespoons clear honey
1 tablespoon vegetable oil
100 g/4 oz rolled oats
2 tablespoons wheatgerm
25 g/1 oz hazelnuts, chopped
2 tablespoons desiccated coconut
25 g/1 oz stoned dates, chopped
25 g/1 oz raisins
To serve:
2–3 bananas, apples or oranges, peeled and chopped
150 ml/¼ pint natural yogurt, single or soured cream, or milk

Put the honey and oil in a large bowl and cook on FULL (100%) for ½ minute. Gently mix in the oats, wheatgerm, hazelnuts and coconut. Turn on to a sheet of greaseproof paper, then carefully lift on to the oven turntable or base.
Cook on FULL (100%) for 3 minutes until lightly browned, stirring frequently during cooking to prevent the centre of the mixture

from burning. Granola continues to brown after the oven is switched off, so do not overcook.
Add the dates and raisins, stir well, then leave to STAND, covered, for 1 minute. Divide the granola between cereal bowls, allowing 1 to 2 tablespoons per person. Serve sprinkled over chopped banana, apple or orange. Top each portion with a little yogurt, cream or milk.
SERVES 6 to 8

Note: If your oven is fitted with a turntable, make sure that the greaseproof paper does not overlap the shelf.

HOT SOUTHERN MUESLI

METRIC/IMPERIAL
50 g/2 oz porridge oats
25 g/1 oz brown sugar
25 g/1 oz flaked peanuts or almonds, toasted
¼ teaspoon grated nutmeg
1 orange
25 g/1 oz sultanas
½ sharp dessert apple, cored and cut into chunks
150 ml/¼ pint natural yogurt

Combine the oats, sugar, peanuts or almonds, and nutmeg in a dish. Cook on FULL (100%) for 2 minutes, stirring occasionally.
Peel the orange, then carefully cut out the segments with a sharp knife, removing all pith. Chop the flesh roughly.
Add the chopped orange to the oats, and squeeze over the juice from the pithy membrane. Add the sultanas and the apple chunks. Cook on FULL (100%) for 1½ minutes, stirring occasionally, until the fruit is hot but not soft.
Stir in the yogurt, cover and leave to STAND for 1 minute, then spoon into cereal bowls and serve at once.
SERVES 4

Note: For a refreshing summer breakfast, top cereals with sliced peaches, strawberries, raspberries or other seasonal fruits of your choice.

POACHED EGG

METRIC/IMPERIAL
5 tablespoons hot water
¼ teaspoon white wine vinegar
1 egg
pinch of salt

Pour the water and vinegar into a ceramic cereal bowl or a 10 cm/4 inch custard cup. Cook on FULL (100%) for ½ minute or until boiling. Carefully break the egg into the water. Prick the yolk, add salt and cover loosely.

Cook on MEDIUM (50%) for ¾ to 1 minute or cook on FULL (100%) for ½ minute until the yolk just starts to change colour. Leave to STAND, covered, for 1 to 2 minutes, then cook on FULL (100%) for ¼ to ½ minute, according to taste. Remove the egg with a slotted spoon, allowing the water to drain off, then transfer to a serving plate.
SERVES 1

To cook 2 poached eggs: combine 450 ml/¾ pint boiling water, ½ teaspoon white wine vinegar and ½ teaspoon salt in a large deep dish and cook on FULL (100%) for 1 to 1½ minutes, until fast boiling. Break the eggs into the water, one at a time. Prick the yolks, cover and cook on MEDIUM (50%) for 1 to 1½ minutes or cook on FULL (100%) for ¾ to 1 minute. Leave to STAND, covered, for 2 minutes before serving.

To cook 4 poached eggs: combine 600 ml/1 pint boiling water, 1 tablespoon white vinegar and 1 teaspoon salt in a large deep dish. Cook on FULL (100%) for 3 to 4 minutes until fast boiling. Break the eggs into the water, one at a time. Prick the yolks, cover and cook on MEDIUM (50%) for 3½ to 4 minutes or cook on FULL (100%) for 1¾ to 2 minutes.

CRUNCHY EGG FRIES

METRIC/IMPERIAL
2 slices of bread
40 g/1½ oz butter (at room temperature)
¼ teaspoon salt
2 eggs

Remove the crusts and cut the bread into small cubes. Preheat a large browning dish on FULL (100%) for 5 minutes (or according to the manufacturer's instructions), adding the butter

after 4 minutes. Immediately toss in the bread, turning over quickly with a wooden spoon, to brown on all sides.

Cook on FULL (100%) for ½ minute then sprinkle with the salt, stir and cook on FULL (100%) for ½ minute.

Divide the croûtons in half and move to opposite corners of the browning dish. Break an egg over each pile of croûtons. Prick the yolks and cook on FULL (100%) for ½ minute.

Partially cover and leave to STAND for ½ minute before serving.
SERVES 2

To cook 4 portions: double the ingredients and increase the microwave cooking times to ¾ minute at each stage. Cook each egg on one quarter of the croûtons at each corner of the browning dish.

BACON, EGG AND TOMATO

METRIC/IMPERIAL
2 bacon rashers
1 medium firm tomato, halved
1 egg

Snip the bacon rind with kitchen scissors in two or three places or trim away. Put the bacon on a plate and cook on FULL (100%) for ½ minute. Place the tomato halves on the plate, cut side up.

Break the egg into a greased cup and prick the yolk with the tip of a sharp knife. Cover loosely and put on the plate with the bacon and tomato. Cook on FULL (100%) for 1½ minutes, giving the plate a quarter-turn every ¼ minute.
SERVES 1

To cook 4 portions: preheat a large browning dish on FULL (100%) for 5 minutes (or according to the manufacturer's instructions). Arrange the bacon rashers, side by side, on the dish and cook on FULL (100%) for 3 minutes. Remove the bacon and keep warm.

Reheat the browning dish on FULL (100%) for 2 minutes, then break an egg into each corner. Prick the yolks, cover and cook on FULL (100%) for 1½ to 2 minutes, giving the dish a half-turn once during cooking. Leave to STAND while cooking the tomatoes.

Arrange the tomatoes on a plate, cover and cook on FULL (100%) for 2½ to 3 minutes, giving the dish a quarter-turn every ½ minute.

CRISP-FRIED EGGS

METRIC/IMPERIAL
15 g/½ oz butter
2 eggs

Preheat a large browning dish on FULL (100%) for 5 minutes (or according to the manufacturer's instructions). Add the butter and break the eggs into opposite corners. Prick the yolks, cover and cook on FULL (100%) for 1½ to 2 minutes until cooked to taste. Remove with a slotted spoon and transfer to a serving plate.
SERVES 1 or 2

For each additional crisp-fried egg: allow an extra 7 g/¼ oz butter and increase the cooking times by ½ to ¾ minute.

BREAKFAST OMELETTE

METRIC/IMPERIAL
15 g/½ oz butter
2 eggs
3 tablespoons milk
salt
freshly ground black pepper

Put the butter in a shallow dish. Cook on FULL (100%) for ½ minute until melted, then swirl to completely coat the dish.

Beat the eggs and milk together with salt and pepper to taste, until thoroughly blended. Pour into the prepared dish. Cook on MEDIUM (50%) for 2½ minutes until almost set, drawing the cooked edges towards the middle three times during cooking.

Serve the omelette in the dish, or fold in half and transfer to a heated plate. Place under a preheated hot grill for a few seconds to brown the top, if liked.
SERVES 1

CODDLED EGG

METRIC/IMPERIAL
150 ml/¼ pint water
1 egg (at room temperature)

Pour the water into a glass or jug, then cook on FULL (100%) for 1¾ minutes until the water is boiling. Break the egg on to a spoon and carefully lower into the water. Cover and leave

to STAND for 5 minutes, then lift out the egg and serve immediately.
SERVES 1

Note: If the eggs have been stored in the refrigerator, place them, one at a time, on the oven turntable or base and cook on FULL (100%) for 5 seconds before cooking as above.

To cook 2 coddled eggs: pour 150 ml/¼ pint water into each of two glasses, place both in the oven and cook on FULL (100%) for 3 minutes. As soon as the water boils, carefully lower an egg into each glass, cover and leave to STAND for 5 minutes before serving.

CHEESY STUFFED BAKED POTATO

METRIC/IMPERIAL
1 × 200 g/7 oz potato (unblemished)
1 teaspoon butter
3 tablespoons milk
2 tablespoons grated Cheddar cheese
salt
freshly ground black pepper
parsley sprig, to garnish

Scrub and dry the potato; prick thoroughly and place on a double thickness of absorbent kitchen paper. Cook on FULL (100%) for 4 to 6 minutes until just tender, turning the potato over halfway through cooking.

Leave to STAND for 3 to 4 minutes then cut in half and scoop out the centre of the potato, leaving the skins intact. Mash the potato with the butter, milk, cheese and salt and pepper to taste. Pile the stuffing into the potato shells.

To reheat, cook on FULL (100%) for 1 minute. Garnish with parsley and serve hot.
SERVES 1

To cook 2 potatoes: double the quantities and proceed as above. Cook on FULL (100%) for 8 to 10 minutes. Reheat on FULL (100%) for 1½ minutes.

Stuffing variations
1. 2 tablespoons soured cream, mixed with 1 tablespoon snipped chives, butter, salt and pepper to taste.
2. 15 g/½ oz cream cheese, mixed with ¼ teaspoon nutmeg, salt and pepper to taste.
3. 1 small chopped onion, mixed with a little

butter and cooked on FULL (100%) for 2 minutes, then drained and mixed with ¼ teaspoon curry powder.

4. Chopped cooked ham, mixed with 2 tablespoons milk, butter, salt and pepper to taste.

5. Chopped canned pimiento mixed with 1 tablespoon finely chopped nuts, butter, salt and pepper.

6. Sardines mashed with salt and pepper to taste.

SAUSAGES

Choose fat pork or beef sausages. Prick them thoroughly and arrange in a circle on a plate. Cover with a piece of absorbent kitchen paper.

To cook 2 sausages: cook on FULL (100%) for 1½ to 2½ minutes.

To cook 4 sausages: cook on FULL (100%) for 3 to 4 minutes.

Give the plate a half-turn halfway through cooking and leave to STAND for 3 minutes before serving.

Sausages should not be overcooked in the microwave oven because cooking continues after the oven is switched off. Pork sausages must be cooked until they are no longer pink inside.

Note: A browner appearance can be achieved by dipping the sausages into gravy browning, dissolved in a little water, before cooking.

CRISPY SAUSAGES

Prick fat pork or beef sausages all over. Preheat a large browning dish on FULL (100%) for 5 minutes (or according to the manufacturer's instructions). Quickly add a knob of butter, then immediately put in the sausages, turning quickly to brown on all sides.

To cook 2 crispy sausages: cook on FULL (100%) for 2½ minutes.

To cook 4 crispy sausages: cook on FULL (100%) for 4 minutes.

Move the sausages to the sides of the dish and turn them over halfway through cooking. Remove and drain on absorbent kitchen paper. Leave to STAND for 3 minutes before serving.

KEDGEREE

METRIC/IMPERIAL
175 g/6 oz smoked haddock
20 g/¾ oz butter
1 hard-boiled egg, chopped
225 g/8 oz cooked, long-grain rice
2 tablespoons single cream
1 tablespoon chopped fresh parsley
pinch of cayenne pepper
¼ teaspoon paprika

Place the smoked haddock in a deep pie dish. Cover loosely and cook on FULL (100%) for 2½ to 3½ minutes until the flesh is tender. Remove any skin and flake the fish. Drain the residual juices from the dish.

Put the butter into the hot dish and swirl around until melted. Stir in the flaked fish, chopped egg and rice. Cook on FULL (100%) for 3 to 3½ minutes until the rice is hot.

Stir in the cream and sprinkle the kedgeree with the parsley, cayenne and paprika before serving.
SERVES 2

SMOKED SALMON WITH SCRAMBLED EGGS

METRIC/IMPERIAL
4 eggs
2 tablespoons double cream
salt
freshly ground black pepper
25 g/1 oz butter
4 large, thin slices smoked salmon
lime slices, to garnish
To serve:
150 ml/¼ pint soured cream
Melba toast

Place the eggs, cream, and salt and pepper to taste in a medium bowl. Whisk well and add the butter. Cook on FULL (100%) for 2½ to 3 minutes or until the mixture is cooked. Using a fork, break up and stir the mixture after 1 and 2 minutes.

Spread out the salmon slices and cut them in half. Spoon a little scrambled egg over each slice and roll them up. Garnish with lime slices and serve immediately.

Hand soured cream and Melba toast separately.
SERVES 4

QUICK STUFFED TOMATOES WITH BACON

METRIC/IMPERIAL
2 large tomatoes
2 eggs
2 lean bacon rashers, derinded

Cut a slice from the top of each tomato and set aside. Scoop out half the pulp. Arrange the tomato shells, side by side, on a serving plate and carefully break an egg into each one.

Wrap a slice of bacon around each tomato to form a collar, about 1 cm/½ inch taller than the tomato. Spoon the remaining tomato pulp over the egg and top with the tomato lid.

Cover with a piece of absorbent kitchen paper and cook on MEDIUM (50%) for 4½ to 5 minutes, or cook on FULL (100%) for 2½ to 3½ minutes, giving the dish a half-turn once during cooking, until the egg white just begins to thicken.

Leave to STAND for 1 minute before removing the paper and serving.
SERVES 1 to 2

To cook 4 stuffed tomatoes: double the quantities. Cook on MEDIUM (50%) for 7½ to 9 minutes, or cook on FULL (100%) for 4 to 6 minutes, giving the dish a half-turn once during cooking.

FRIED LIVER AND BACON

METRIC/IMPERIAL
1 teaspoon butter
2 bacon rashers, derinded
175 g/6 oz lamb's liver, sliced

Preheat a large browning dish on FULL (100%) for 5 minutes (or according to the manufacturer's instructions). Add the butter and bacon. Turn the bacon over immediately and move the slices towards opposite sides of the dish. Arrange the liver in the centre.

Cook on FULL (100%) for 2½ to 3 minutes until the liver is still just pink inside, turning the liver slices over halfway through cooking. Take care not to overcook or the liver will toughen.

Serve immediately with mushrooms and baked tomatoes or other vegetables of your choice.
SERVES 2

KIPPERS

METRIC/IMPERIAL
2 kippers
cayenne pepper

Using kitchen scissors, remove the heads and tails from the kippers. Place the kippers, skin side down, on a plate. Cover loosely and cook on FULL (100%) for 3 to 4 minutes, giving the dish a half-turn once during cooking. Remove the cover and sprinkle the kippers with cayenne pepper before serving.
SERVES 1 to 2

Note: Boil-in-the-bag kipper fillets will take less time to cook. Place the kippers in their bags on a plate. Prick the top of the bag and cook for half the time specified on the packet.

To cook 4 or 8 kippers: arrange the kippers, either individually or in pairs, on individual serving plates. Using stacking rings, place these one above the other. Cover the top plate only. Cook on FULL (100%) for 6 to 10 minutes, depending on the thickness and the number of kippers being cooked. There is no need to turn the kippers during cooking.

EGG IN THE MIDDLE

METRIC/IMPERIAL
2 thin slices of bread or toast
7 g/¼ oz butter
7 g/¼ oz anchovy paste
1 egg

Using an upturned cup, cut a large circle of bread from the centre of one slice. Spread the whole slice of bread with butter and anchovy paste and place the cut-out slice on top. Spread with the remaining butter and anchovy paste.

Put the sandwich on a plate and break an egg into the hole. Prick the yolk gently with the tip of a sharp knife. Cover with the circle of bread and cook on FULL (100%) for 1 to 1½ minutes. Leave to STAND for 1 minute and remove the circle of bread before serving.
SERVES 1

To cook 2 or 4 eggs: increase the quantities accordingly. Two eggs will take 2 to 2½ minutes to cook. Four eggs will take 3½ to 4 minutes to cook.

SCRAMBLED EGGS

METRIC/IMPERIAL
2 eggs
2 tablespoons milk
pinch of salt
freshly ground black pepper
2 teaspoons butter

Lightly beat the eggs, milk, salt, and pepper to taste in a jug. Add the butter and cook on FULL (100%) for 2 to 2¼ minutes until almost set, stirring with a fork once or twice during cooking. Leave to STAND for 1 minute before serving.

To cook 4, 6, or 8 scrambled eggs: increase the quantities accordingly and cook on FULL (100%), allowing an additional ½ minute for each extra egg.

SMOKED HADDOCK

METRIC/IMPERIAL
450 g/1 lb smoked haddock fillet
15 g/½ oz butter
cayenne pepper

Place the smoked haddock, skin side down, in a large shallow dish. Cover loosely and cook on FULL (100%) for 5 to 6 minutes, giving the dish a half-turn once during cooking. Leave to STAND for 2 minutes.

Use a fork to test whether the haddock is cooked; the flesh should be creamy white and flake easily. Dot with butter and sprinkle with cayenne pepper before serving.
SERVES 2

TOMATOES

Tomatoes must either be pricked thoroughly or halved before cooking. Arrange in a circle, cut sides up, in a shallow dish. Dot with butter, season with salt and pepper to taste and cook on FULL (100%). Microwave cooking timings vary, depending upon the size and ripeness of the tomatoes. One small ripe tomato will be softened in ¼ to ½ minute; 4 large under-ripe tomatoes will take 3 to 4 minutes to cook. Each tomato should be removed from the oven as soon as it is cooked.

BACON

Avoid salty bacon rashers as these are inclined to become brittle.

To cook up to 4 bacon rashers: place between folded sheets of absorbent kitchen paper. To reduce shrinkage, press down well before cooking.
Cook on FULL (100%), allowing approximately 1 minute for each bacon rasher. Remove the bacon rashers from the paper the moment they are cooked.

To cook up to 450 g/1 lb bacon rashers: arrange the bacon rashers either on a bacon rack or in a large shallow dish, overlapping so that the fat parts lay over the lean. Cover with a piece of absorbent kitchen paper to prevent splattering.
Cook on FULL (100%), allowing approximately 12 to 14 minutes for 450 g/1 lb bacon, turning the slices over halfway through cooking and removing each one as soon as it is cooked.
The use of a bacon rack will enable excess fat to drain away, avoiding the need to drain the bacon on absorbent kitchen paper before serving.

Note: Bacon may also be cooked in a preheated browning dish without using additional fat.

EGG AND BACON ROLLS

METRIC/IMPERIAL
4 crispy bread rolls
2 bacon rashers, derinded and finely chopped
50 g/2 oz mushrooms, finely chopped
4 eggs
salt
freshly ground black pepper

Slice the tops off the rolls and scoop out the centres (use for breadcrumbs for another dish). Reserve the tops.
Place the bacon and mushrooms in a bowl and cook on FULL (100%) for 2½ to 3 minutes. Drain thoroughly, then divide evenly between the bread roll shells. Break an egg into each roll, prick the yolk carefully and season with salt and pepper to taste. Cover with the bread roll tops and cook on FULL (100%) for 2½ to 3 minutes.
Leave to STAND for 1 minute before serving.
SERVES 4

QUICK BEEF SAVOURY

METRIC/IMPERIAL
225 g/8 oz minced lean beef
1 teaspoon salt
¼ teaspoon freshly ground black pepper
2 teaspoons flour
150 ml/¼ pint canned cream of celery soup

Spread the beef in a small shallow dish. Sprinkle with the salt, pepper and flour. Using the blade of a knife, chop the mixture until the flour is thoroughly incorporated.

Pour the soup over the meat. Cook on FULL (100%) for 5 minutes, giving the dish a half-turn after 2½ minutes.

Serve hot, with crusty French bread, potatoes or boiled rice.
SERVES 2

MUSHROOMS

Mushrooms cook very quickly in the microwave oven. A little butter should be added before cooking. Sprinkle the mushrooms with salt and pepper just before serving.

To cook 3 or 4 small mushrooms: arrange on a plate and dot with a little butter. Cover and cook on FULL (100%) for ½ minute.

To cook 100 g/4 oz mushrooms: place in a dish and dot with 15 g/½ oz butter. Cover and cook on FULL (100%) for 2 minutes, stirring once during cooking.

SCALLOPED MINCE BAKE

METRIC/IMPERIAL
450 g/1 lb minced lean beef
1 onion, finely chopped
1 beef stock cube, crumbled
1 × 215 g/7½ oz can baked beans
3 tablespoons water or tomato juice
salt
freshly ground black pepper
450 g/1 lb potatoes, peeled and thinly sliced
a little grated cheese

Place the beef and onion in a medium casserole. Stir well and cook on FULL (100%) for 3 minutes.

Stir and pour off excess fat. Add the crumbled stock cube, beans and water or tomato juice. Add salt and pepper to taste and stir. Arrange the potato slices over the surface, to cover thinly. Cover and cook on MEDIUM (50%) for 25 to 28 minutes.

Sprinkle a little cheese over the potato and return to the oven and cook on FULL (100%) for 2 minutes to melt, then brown under a preheated conventional grill.
SERVES 4

FRANKFURTER RISOTTO

METRIC/IMPERIAL
100 g/4 oz long-grain rice
4 tablespoons frozen peas
1 × 40 g/1½ oz packet instant soup (any variety)
15 g/½ oz butter
600 ml/1 pint water
2–3 frankfurters, sliced

Combine the rice, peas, soup mix, butter and water in a large bowl. Cover loosely and cook on FULL (100%) for 3 minutes. Reduce the power to MEDIUM (50%) and cook for a further 12 minutes, stirring twice, until most of the liquid is absorbed. Add the frankfurters and cook on FULL (100%) for 2 to 3 minutes until the rice is cooked and the frankfurters are hot. Serve immediately.
SERVES 2

FRANKFURTERS, EGG AND BEANS

METRIC/IMPERIAL
2 frankfurters
4 tablespoons baked beans
1 egg

Make four or five slits along one side of each frankfurter. Bend each one into a curve and arrange on a suitable plate to form a circle. Surround with a border of baked beans and break the egg into the centre of the frankfurters.

Cover the plate loosely with greaseproof paper and cook on FULL (100%) for 2½ minutes, giving a ¼ minute rest halfway through cooking. Leave to STAND, covered, for 1 to 2 minutes until the egg white has set.
SERVES 2

POACHED EGGS WITH PEAS AND POTATOES

METRIC/IMPERIAL
450 g/1 lb old potatoes, peeled and diced
3 tablespoons milk
salt
4 eggs
1 × 225 g/8 oz packet frozen peas
extra milk for mashing
25 g/1 oz butter

Put the potatoes into a mixing bowl. Add the milk and salt to taste. Cover and cook on FULL (100%) for 7 to 9 minutes, stirring once. Stir well and leave to STAND, covered.

Put 1 tablespoon water into each of 4 holes in a microwave egg poacher, 6-holed bun or muffin dish, or into each of 4 cocotte dishes. Cook on FULL (100%) for 1½ minutes, until the water is boiling.

Crack an egg into each dish or hole. Prick the yolks with a cocktail stick and cook on MEDIUM (50%) for 3½ to 4 minutes. Set aside.

Place the peas in their packet in a small dish and prick the packet. Cook on FULL (100%) for 3 minutes.

Meanwhile, mash the potatoes, adding the extra milk, as necessary, and the butter. Serve the potato and eggs with the peas.
SERVES 4

BRUNCH

METRIC/IMPERIAL
1 onion, finely chopped
100 g/4 oz streaky bacon, derinded and chopped
225 g/8 oz cooked potatoes, sliced
4 eggs, beaten
150 ml/¼ pint milk
salt
freshly ground black pepper

Place the onion and bacon in a serving dish. Cover and cook on FULL (100%) for 3 minutes, stirring once.

Add the potatoes, blending well. Mix the eggs with the milk and salt and pepper to taste. Pour over the potato mixture. Cover and cook on MEDIUM (50%) for 10 minutes, turning the potatoes over twice.

Serve at once, straight from the dish.
SERVES 2

HERB, CHEESE AND GARLIC BREAD

METRIC/IMPERIAL
1 Vienna loaf, about 30 cm/12 inches long
1 × 100 g/4 oz roll of savoury butter with herbs and garlic
75 g/3 oz Double Gloucester cheese, grated

Check that the loaf will fit inside the microwave and turn freely. If not, cut in half to prepare.

Make diagonal slits in the loaf almost to the base but not quite through, about 4 cm/1½ inches apart. Slice the savoury butter into rounds and place a round in each slit with some of the cheese.

Loosely wrap the loaf in absorbent kitchen paper and place, cut side uppermost, in the oven. Cook on FULL (100%) for 1½ to 2 minutes or until the butter has melted and the bread is warm.

Serve at once, perhaps as an accompaniment to soups or vegetable starters.
SERVES 4

CHEESE AND HAM TOASTIES

METRIC/IMPERIAL
8 small slices thin white bread, crusts removed
1–2 teaspoons wholegrain mustard
4 slices quick-melting processed cheese
4 slices of cooked ham
40 g/1½ oz butter

Spread half the bread slices with mustard to taste. Top each with a slice of cheese and ham. Cover with the remaining bread slices, pressing down well.

Place the butter in a bowl and heat on FULL (100%) for 1 minute or until melted.

Preheat a large browning dish on FULL (100%) for 5 minutes (or according to the manufacturer's instructions).

Brush one side of each sandwich with half the butter. Place in the browning dish, buttered-side down, and allow to brown on the underside, about 1 to 2 minutes on FULL (100%).

Quickly brush the second side of each sandwich with the remaining butter, turn over with tongs and cook on FULL (100%) for a further 2 minutes, turning the dish once. Cut each sandwich in half diagonally and serve with napkins.
SERVES 4

SAUSAGE, BACON AND EGG

METRIC/IMPERIAL
7 g/¼ oz butter
2 × 50 g/2 oz sausages, well-pricked
1 bacon rasher
1 egg

Preheat a large browning dish on FULL (100%) for 5 minutes (or according to the manufacturer's instructions). Quickly add the butter and sausages, turning the sausages over once to brown on both sides. Cook on FULL (100%) for 2 minutes, then add the bacon and cook on FULL (100%) for 1 minute.

Finally, break in the egg, prick the yolk and cook on FULL (100%) for 1 minute. Cover and leave to STAND for 2 minutes. Using a slotted spoon, transfer to a heated plate and serve immediately.
SERVES 1

To cook 2 portions: double the quantities. Follow the above method, but add the butter to the browning dish after just 4 minutes. Cook the sausages on FULL (100%) for 3½ minutes, then add the bacon and cook on FULL (100%) for 1½ minutes. Add the eggs, prick the yolks and cook on FULL (100%) for 1½ minutes. Leave to STAND for 2 minutes before serving.

WELSH RAREBIT

METRIC/IMPERIAL
100 g/4 oz Cheddar, Gouda or Gruyère cheese, finely grated
1 teaspoon mustard powder
1 egg, lightly beaten
2 teaspoons tomato ketchup
4 slices white or brown bread

Preheat a large browning dish on FULL (100%) for 5 minutes (or according to the manufacturer's instructions).

Mix the cheese with the mustard, egg and tomato ketchup, blending well. Spoon evenly on to the bread slices.

Place on the browning dish and cook on MEDIUM (50%) for 4 minutes or until the cheese starts to bubble.

Serve at once.
SERVES 4

SAUSAGES AND BAKED BEANS

METRIC/IMPERIAL
2 × 50 g/2 oz pork or beef sausages, well-pricked
4–5 tablespoons baked beans

Arrange the sausages on a plate. Cover with absorbent kitchen paper. Cook on FULL (100%) for 1½ to 2½ minutes. Leave to STAND while cooking the beans.

Pile the baked beans on to a suitable warmed serving plate. Cover loosely and cook on FULL (100%) for 1 minute. Add the sausages and serve immediately.
SERVES 1

To cook 3 or 4 portions: arrange 8 sausages on a plate. Cover with absorbent kitchen paper. Cook on FULL (100%) for 5 minutes, rearranging once. Use a 225 g/8 oz can baked beans and divide between the serving plates. Stack the plates so that the piles of beans are staggered. Cover the top plate only and cook on FULL (100%) for 2½ to 3 minutes. Serve with the sausages.

CHEESEBURGERS IN A BUN

METRIC/IMPERIAL
225 g/8 oz minced lean beef
salt
freshly ground black pepper
2 slices processed cheese
2 teaspoons tomato ketchup
2 baps, halved and toasted, to serve

Divide the meat into 4 equal portions and roll each into a ball, then flatten into rounds, about 3 mm/¼ inch thick. Sprinkle liberally with salt and pepper. Sandwich the burgers together in pairs, with a slice of cheese in the middle. Press the meat around the edges to seal in the cheese.

Place the cheeseburgers on a large plate, lined with absorbent kitchen paper. Cook on FULL (100%) for 3½ to 4 minutes, giving the plate a half-turn once during cooking. Brush the tops with tomato ketchup, then place in the baps. Cook on FULL (100%) for ¼ to ½ minute to reheat before serving.
SERVES 2

MACARONI CHEESE WITH BACON

METRIC/IMPERIAL
100 g/4 oz dried macaroni
600 ml/1 pint boiling water
1 teaspoon salt
15 g/½ oz butter
2 bacon rashers, derinded and chopped
25 g/1 oz flour
½ teaspoon mustard powder
300 ml/½ pint milk
100 g/4 oz Cheddar cheese. grated
freshly ground black pepper
tomato slices, to garnish

Place the macaroni in a deep dish and stir in the boiling water and salt. Cook on FULL (100%) for 10 minutes, then cover and leave to STAND while preparing the sauce.

Combine the butter and bacon in a large bowl and cook on FULL (100%) for 1 to 1½ minutes until the bacon is lightly cooked. Add the flour and mustard, then gradually stir in the milk. Cook on FULL (100%) for 3 to 4 minutes, whisking frequently, until the sauce thickens.

Drain the macaroni and stir into the sauce with the cheese. Add salt and pepper to taste and garnish with tomato slices.
SERVES 2

CHEESE AND HAM QUICHE

METRIC/IMPERIAL
Pastry:
100 g/4 oz plain flour
pinch of salt
100 g/4 oz butter
100 g/4 oz rolled oats
about 3 tablespoons water
Filling:
1 tablespoon vegetable oil
1 large onion, sliced
2 eggs, beaten
150 ml/¼ pint milk
100 g/4 oz Cheddar cheese, grated
50 g/2 oz cooked ham, chopped
4 mushrooms, sliced
salt
freshly ground black pepper

Sift the flour and salt into a bowl. Rub in the butter until the mixture resembles fine bread-crumbs. Stir in the oats, then add enough cold water to bind to a soft dough.

Roll out the pastry on a lightly floured surface to a round large enough to line a 20 cm/8 inch flan dish plus a little extra. Press in firmly, taking care not to stretch the pastry. Cut the pastry away leaving a 5 mm/¼ inch 'collar' above the dish (this allows for any shrinkage that may occur). Prick the base well with a fork.

Line the inside, upright edge of the pastry with a long strip of foil, about 4 cm/1½ inches wide. (This prevents the outer edges from overcooking.) Place a double thickness of absorbent kitchen paper over the base, easing it into position around the edges to keep the foil in place.

Cook on FULL (100%) for 4 to 4½ minutes, giving the dish a quarter-turn every 1 minute. Remove the paper and foil and cook on FULL (100%) for 1 to 2 minutes. Allow to cool.

Meanwhile, place the oil and onion in a bowl and cook on FULL (100%) for 3 to 4 minutes until tender, stirring once.

Lightly beat the eggs with the milk. Add the cheese, ham, mushrooms, onion and salt and pepper to taste, blending well. Pour into the pastry case. Cook on LOW (30%) for 16 to 18 minutes, giving the dish a quarter-turn every 3 minutes. Leave to STAND, covered, for 15 to 20 minutes. The quiche should set completely in this time. Serve hot or cold.
SERVES 4 to 6

SPICY CHEDDAR RAREBIT

METRIC/IMPERIAL
15 g/½ oz butter
250 g/9 oz Cheddar cheese, grated
½ teaspoon Worcestershire sauce
dash of hot chilli sauce
pinch of cayenne pepper
3 tablespoons double cream
1 egg yolk, beaten
4 slices bread, toasted and buttered

Place the butter and cheese in a bowl. Cook on FULL (100%) for 2 to 3 minutes, stirring twice, until smooth and creamy.

Add the Worcestershire sauce, chilli sauce, cayenne, cream and egg yolk, blending well. Cook on MEDIUM (50%) for 5 to 7 minutes, stirring every 1 minute until hot, smooth and thickened. Spoon over the toast slices to serve.
SERVES 4

SPANISH OMELETTE

METRIC/IMPERIAL
25 g/1 oz butter
½ onion, chopped
1 tomato, skinned and chopped
¼ green pepper, cored, seeded and chopped
2 tablespoons cooked, long-grain rice
2 eggs, beaten
salt
freshly ground black pepper

Place the butter in a shallow glass pie dish and heat on FULL (100%) for ½ minute or until melted. Swirl to coat the dish.

Add the onion and cook on FULL (100%) for 1 minute. Add the tomato, pepper and rice, blending well. Cook on FULL (100%) for 1½ to 2 minutes.

Add the eggs and salt and pepper to taste. Cover and cook on FULL (100%) for 1½ minutes. Using a fork, move the cooked egg from the edge of the dish to the centre. Cover and cook for a further ¾ minute.

Uncover and cook on FULL (100%) for ¼ minute. Leave to STAND for ¼ minute, then fold in half. Serve with a green salad.
SERVES 1

MEDITERRANEAN OMELETTE

METRIC/IMPERIAL
Filling:
15 g/½ oz butter
1 onion, chopped
1 small red pepper, cored, seeded and chopped
1 clove garlic, crushed
50 g/2 oz mushrooms, sliced
2 tomatoes, skinned, seeded and chopped
Omelette:
4 eggs, beaten
3 tablespoons milk
1 teaspoon dried mixed herbs
salt
freshly ground black pepper
15 g/½ oz butter
25 g/1 oz grated Parmesan cheese

To make the filling, place the butter, onion, pepper and garlic in a bowl. Cook on FULL (100%) for 4 minutes, stirring once. Add the mushrooms and tomatoes, blending well. Cook on FULL (100%) for 3 minutes, stirring once.

Leave to STAND, covered, while preparing the omelette.

To make the omelette, beat the eggs with the milk, herbs and salt and pepper to taste. Place the butter in a 25 cm/10 inch pie plate and heat on FULL (100%) for ½ minute or until melted. Swirl over the plate to coat. Pour in the egg mixture, cover and cook on FULL (100%) for 1½ minutes. Using a fork, move the cooked egg from the edge of the dish to the centre. Cover and cook for a further 1¼ to 1½ minutes, then allow to STAND for 1½ to 2 minutes.

Loosen the omelette with a spatula. Spoon the vegetable mixture over the omelette. Fold in half and sprinkle with the Parmesan cheese. Cut in half to serve.
SERVES 2

CHEESE AND ONION BAKE

METRIC/IMPERIAL
25 g/1 oz butter
2 onions, cut into rings
50 g/2 oz mushrooms, finely chopped
600 ml/1 pint milk
100 g/4 oz fresh brown breadcrumbs
100 g/4 oz Cheddar cheese, finely grated
salt
freshly ground black pepper
3 large eggs (size 1 or 2), beaten
1 teaspoon dried dill
paprika pepper
Garnish (optional):
tomato slices
parsley sprigs

Put the butter in a medium heatproof dish and heat on FULL (100%) for ½ minute. Stir in the onions and cook on FULL (100%) for 2 minutes. Stir in the mushrooms and set aside.

Place the milk in a large jug and cook on FULL (100%) for 6 minutes. Place the breadcrumbs, cheese and salt and pepper in a mixing bowl. Pour over the hot milk and stir well. Stir in the eggs and dill.

Pour on to the onions and mushrooms. Cook on MEDIUM (50%) for 13 to 15 minutes, giving the dish a half-turn, twice, during cooking.

Sprinkle with paprika and garnish with tomato slices and parsley, if using. Leave to STAND fo 5 minutes before serving.
SERVES 4

SPICY EGG SUPPER

METRIC/IMPERIAL
1 tablespoon vegetable oil
1 small onion, finely chopped
1 clove garlic, crushed
1 teaspoon ground coriander
1 teaspoon ground cumin
½ teaspoon chilli powder
freshly ground black pepper
2 tablespoons sesame seeds
½ teaspoon salt
150 ml/¼ pint natural yogurt
1 tablespoon lemon juice
4 hard-boiled eggs, cooled and halved

Place the oil, onion and garlic in a bowl. Cook on FULL (100%) for 2 minutes, stirring once. Add the coriander, cumin, chilli power, pepper to taste and sesame seeds. Cook on FULL (100%) for 1 minute, stirring once.

Add the salt, yogurt and lemon juice, blending well. Cook on FULL (100%) for 1½ to 2 minutes until hot but *not* boiling.

Add the eggs, blending well. Cook on FULL (100%) for 1 to 2 minutes until hot.

Serve at once with boiled rice or lentils and a green salad.
SERVES 2

EGGS BENEDICT

METRIC/IMPERIAL
4 slices of cooked ham
4 thick slices of buttered white toast, cut to the size of the ham
Poached eggs:
250 ml/8 fl oz water
4 tablespoons white vinegar
4 eggs
Hollandaise sauce:
2 egg yolks
1 tablespoon lemon juice
100 g/4 oz butter, cut into 8 pieces
pinch of cayenne pepper
½ teaspoon dry mustard

Place a piece of ham on each slice of toast. Keep warm.

Divide the water and vinegar equally between 4 ramekin dishes. Cook on FULL (100%) for 2 minutes or until boiling. Break an egg into each dish.

To make the sauce, prick the egg yolks and place with the lemon juice in a small bowl. Cook on FULL (100%) for ½ minute. Beat hard until smooth.

Prick the eggs for poaching, place in the oven and cook on FULL (100%) for 2 minutes. STAND for 1 minute before draining.

Meanwhile, beat a piece of butter at a time into the sauce, until all 8 pieces are incorporated. Beat in the cayenne pepper and mustard.

Place the poached eggs on the ham and toast and top with a large spoonful of sauce. Serve at once.
SERVES 4

QUICHE LORRAINE

METRIC/IMPERIAL
Pastry:
100 g/4 oz plain flour
pinch of salt
25 g/1 oz butter
15 g/½ oz lard
2½–3 tablespoons cold water
Filling:
6 bacon rashers, microwaved and crumbled
50 g/2 oz Gruyère cheese, grated
3 spring onions, thinly sliced
¼ teaspoon salt
¼ teaspoon grated nutmeg
pinch of cayenne pepper
1½ tablespoons flour
450 ml/¾ pint single cream
4 eggs, lightly beaten
Garnish:
1 tablespoon fried breadcrumbs
1 bacon rasher, microwaved and crumbled
1 tablespoon chopped fresh parsley

To make the pastry, sift the flour and salt into a mixing bowl. Rub in the butter and lard until the mixture resembles fine breadcrumbs. Mix in sufficient water to form a firm dough. Cover and chill for 30 minutes.

Roll out the pastry thinly and use to line a 23 cm/9 inch round dish. Place a double thickness of absorbent kitchen paper over the base and cook on FULL (100%) for 3½ minutes, giving the dish a half-turn once during cooking. Remove the paper and cook on FULL (100%) for 1½ minutes, giving the dish a half-turn once during cooking. Sprinkle the bacon, cheese and onion into the pastry case.

Combine the salt, nutmeg, cayenne pepper, flour and cream in a large bowl. Cook on

MEDIUM (50%) for 7 minutes, stirring frequently. Stir into the beaten eggs, then pour into the pastry case. Cook on MEDIUM (50%) for 4 minutes.

Sprinkle with the garnish ingredients. Give the dish a half-turn, then cook on MEDIUM (50%) for 2 minutes or until almost set. Leave to STAND for 5 minutes before serving hot, or serve cold.

SERVES 4 to 6

SCOTCH EGGS IN HERBY CHEESE SAUCE

METRIC/IMPERIAL
225 g/8 oz sausagemeat
75 g/3 oz onion, grated
4 hard-boiled eggs
50 g/2 oz fresh brown breadcrumbs
1 tablespoon flour
300 ml/½ pint milk
100 g/4 oz cheese, finely grated
1 teaspoon mixed herbs
salt
freshly ground black pepper
Garnish:
tomato wedges
watercress sprigs

Mix the sausagemeat with the grated onion and divide into 4 pieces. On a floured board, wrap each egg evenly in the sausagemeat. Roll the Scotch eggs in the breadcrumbs and place, as far apart as possible, in a round dish. Cook on FULL (100%) for 2½ minutes, turning the dish and eggs round three or four times during cooking.

In a measuring jug, blend the flour with a little of the milk and gradually whisk in the rest of the milk. Stir in the cheese and herbs and cook on FULL (100%) for 2½ minutes, whisking twice during cooking and at the end of the cooking time.

Add salt and pepper to taste, then pour the sauce over the Scotch eggs. Garnish with wedges of tomatoes and sprigs of watercress before serving.

SERVES 4

Note: Eggs must NOT be boiled in the microwave oven as steam builds up within the shell and causes the egg to explode.

Coating with egg and breadcrumbs in the traditional manner is unsuccessful in the microwave oven.

COTTAGE CHEESE AND WATERCRESS FLAN

METRIC/IMPERIAL
175 g/6 oz frozen wholemeal shortcrust pastry, defrosted
350 g/12 oz cottage cheese
1 onion, very finely chopped
2 eggs, beaten
salt
freshly ground black pepper
¼ teaspoon paprika
1 bunch watercress, trimmed and chopped
2 tablespoons sesame seeds, toasted

Lightly oil and flour a 20 cm/8 inch flan dish. Roll out the pastry on a floured board and line the dish. Prick the pastry with a fork and cook on FULL (100%) for 3¼ minutes or until crisp.

Mix together the cottage cheese, onion and eggs in a bowl and season with salt and pepper. Sprinkle with the paprika and cook on FULL (100%) for 2½ minutes, stirring halfway through the cooking time. Stir in the watercress and transfer the filling to the pastry case.

Sprinkle with sesame seeds and cook on FULL (100%) for 4 minutes, then STAND for 5 minutes. Serve with a crisp green salad.

SERVES 4

MUSHROOM AND EGG RAMEKINS

METRIC/IMPERIAL
225 g/8 oz small button mushrooms, trimmed
1 clove garlic, crushed
150 ml/¼ pint beef stock
4 eggs
1 tablespoon chopped fresh parsley
salt
freshly ground black pepper

Place the mushrooms, garlic and stock in a bowl. Cook on FULL (100%) for 4 minutes, stirring once.

Meanwhile, break an egg into each of 4 greased ramekins. Prick the egg yolks carefully to prevent them bursting. Cover and cook on MEDIUM (50%) for 3½ to 4 minutes, rearranging once.

Stir the parsley and salt and pepper to taste into the mushroom mixture. Spoon on top of the eggs and serve at once.

SERVES 4

SWISS FONDUE

METRIC/IMPERIAL
1 clove garlic, peeled
150 ml/¼ pint dry white wine
1 tablespoon lemon juice
450 g/1 lb Gruyère or Emmenthal cheese, grated
1 tablespoon cornflour
2 tablespoons Kirsch
salt
freshly ground white pepper

Cut the garlic clove in half and rub around the inside of a fondue or casserole dish. Add the wine and lemon juice, blending well. Cook on FULL (100%) for 1 to 2 minutes until very hot.

Add half the cheese and stir well to blend. Add the remaining cheese and cook on FULL (100%) for 1 minute.

Blend the cornflour with the Kirsch and stir into the fondue mixture. Add salt and pepper to taste, then cook on FULL (100%) for 3 to 4 minutes, stirring every 1 minute until the mixture is smooth and completely melted.

Serve hot with cubes of French bread for dipping.
SERVES 4

SPANISH BAKED EGGS

METRIC/IMPERIAL
50 g/2 oz butter
1 clove garlic, crushed
100 g/4 oz sliced chorizo sausage or salami
1 green pepper, cored, seeded and finely chopped
4 eggs
salt
freshly ground black pepper
4 tablespoons single cream

Place the butter in a shallow dish and heat on FULL (100%) for 1 minute or until melted. Add the garlic, chorizo or salami and pepper, blending well. Cover and cook on FULL (100%) for 4 minutes, stirring once.

Spoon equally into 4 large individual ramekins. Carefully break an egg over each and quickly prick the yolks with the pointed end of a knife. Season with salt and pepper to taste and spoon over the cream.

Cover and cook on MEDIUM (50%) for 3½ to 4½ minutes or until the eggs are just lightly set, rearranging the dishes twice.
SERVES 4

CURRIED EGGS

METRIC/IMPERIAL
1 onion, finely chopped
1 clove garlic, crushed
1 tablespoon tomato purée
1 tablespoon lemon juice
1 tablespoon medium curry powder
1 teaspoon mild chilli powder
2 tablespoons white wine vinegar
15 g/½ oz butter
15 g/½ oz flour
300 ml/½ pint hot chicken stock
4 hard-boiled eggs
4 lemon slices, to garnish

Place the onion, garlic, tomato purée, lemon juice, curry powder, chilli powder and vinegar in a medium bowl. Cover and cook on FULL (100%) for 5 minutes, stirring halfway through cooking.

Stir in the butter until melted. Stir in the flour and blend in the stock. Cook on FULL (100%) for 3½ to 4 minutes, stirring every 1 minute until smooth and thickened.

Cut each egg in half and arrange, cut sides down, on a serving dish. Strain the sauce and pour over the eggs. Garnish with lemon slices.

Serve with boiled rice, sliced tomatoes and desiccated coconut.
SERVES 4

PUFFY OMELETTE

METRIC/IMPERIAL
15 g/½ oz butter
3 eggs, separated
3 tablespoons milk
¼ teaspoon salt
¼ teaspoon freshly ground black pepper

Put the butter in a 23 cm/9 inch round pie dish and heat on FULL (100%) for ¼ minute or until melted. Beat the egg whites until stiff peaks form.

In a separate bowl, whisk together the egg yolks, milk and salt and pepper to taste. Gently fold the whisked egg whites into the egg yolk mixture. Turn into the pie dish and cook on LOW (30%) for 5 to 6 minutes until the middle of the omelette has just set.

Leave to STAND for ¼ minute, then fold in

half and turn out on to a serving dish. If desired, place under a preheated hot grill to brown. Serve with baked potatoes and a green salad, if liked.
SERVES 2 to 3

Note: Alternatively, the omelette can be cooked on FULL (100%) for 2 to 3 minutes, giving the dish a quarter-turn every ½ minute.

Variations
Add 1 tablespoon snipped chives or parsley to the egg yolk mixture, before folding in the egg whites.

Sprinkle grated cheese, chopped cooked ham, finely chopped green pepper, diced cooked bacon or flaked smoked haddock over the omelette, before folding and browning.

PIPERANDA

METRIC/IMPERIAL
50 g/2 oz butter
1 small onion, finely chopped
1 small green pepper, cored, seeded and finely chopped
75 g/3 oz tomatoes, chopped
75 g/3 oz cooked ham, chopped
4 eggs, beaten
salt
freshly ground black pepper

Place the butter, onion and pepper in a bowl. Cover and cook on FULL (100%) for 3 minutes, stirring once.

Add the tomatoes, ham, eggs, and salt and pepper to taste, blending well. Cover and cook on MEDIUM (50%) for 12 to 15 minutes, stirring three times, until lightly cooked.

Leave to STAND, covered, for 2 minutes, before serving.
SERVES 4

SPICED EGGS AND CAULIFLOWER

METRIC/IMPERIAL
2 tablespoons vegetable oil
1 teaspoon ground ginger
1 teaspoon ground coriander
1 teaspoon ground turmeric
1 small cauliflower, broken into florets
2 carrots, sliced
2 celery sticks, chopped
1 onion, sliced
100 ml/4 fl oz vegetable or chicken stock
4 hard-boiled eggs, halved
1 tablespoon chopped fresh parsley
225 g/8 oz long-grain rice
600 ml/1 pint boiling water
1 teaspoon salt
150 ml/¼ pint natural yogurt

Place the oil in a large bowl and heat on FULL (100%) for 1 minute. Add the ginger, coriander and turmeric, blending well. Cook on FULL (100%) for 1 minute, stirring once.

Add the cauliflower, carrots, celery, onion and stock, blending well. Cover and cook on FULL (100%) for 10 minutes, stirring once.

Add the eggs and parsley, cover and leave to STAND while cooking the rice.

Place the rice, boiling water and salt in a bowl. Cover and cook on FULL (100%) for 3 minutes. Reduce the power setting to MEDIUM (50%) and cook for a further 12 minutes, stirring twice. Leave to STAND, covered, for 5 minutes.

Reheat the spiced cauliflower and egg mixture by cooking on FULL (100%) for 2 minutes. Stir in the yogurt, blending well.

Spoon the rice on to a warmed serving dish and top with the spiced cauliflower and egg mixture. Serve at once.
SERVES 4

CHEESE AND PRAWN MOUSSELINE

METRIC/IMPERIAL
100 g/4 oz Edam cheese, grated
75 g/3 oz peeled prawns, finely chopped
75 g/3 oz fresh wholemeal breadcrumbs
1 teaspoon Dijon mustard
pinch of mace (optional)
salt
freshly ground black pepper
2 eggs, lightly beaten
300 ml/½ pint skimmed milk
fresh dill, to garnish
4 slices wholemeal toast, to serve

Lightly oil a 600 ml/1 pint soufflé or loaf dish. Line the base with a piece of lightly oiled grease-proof paper.

Place the cheese, prawns, breadcrumbs, mustard, mace (if using) and salt and pepper to taste in a mixing bowl. Stir in the eggs and milk and mix thoroughly with a fork.

Pour into the prepared dish and cook on FULL (100%) for 4 minutes. Give the dish a half-turn, and continue cooking on LOW (30%) for 7½ minutes (or on DEFROST/20% for 10 minutes). Unmould on to a serving platter and remove the lining paper. Garnish with fresh dill, and serve immediately with slices of hot wholemeal toast cut into fingers or triangles.
SERVES 4

EGGS WITH CUCUMBER SAUCE

METRIC/IMPERIAL
40 g/1½ oz butter
½ cucumber, peeled and coarsely chopped
1 tablespoon plain flour
150 ml/¼ pint hot chicken stock
½ tablespoon chopped fresh dill
salt
freshly ground black pepper
4 tablespoons double cream
2 hard-boiled eggs, halved

Place the butter in a bowl with the cucumber. Cover and cook on FULL (100%) for 2½ to 3 minutes until tender, stirring once.

Add the flour, blending well. Gradually add the stock and cook on FULL (100%) for 2 to 3 minutes, stirring every 1 minute until smooth and thickened. Add the dill, salt and pepper to taste and cream, blending well.

Place the egg halves on a serving plate and spoon the cucumber sauce over them. Serve hot with chunks of crusty bread.
SERVES 2

WENSLEYDALE AND CIDER FONDUE

METRIC/IMPERIAL
½ clove garlic, crushed
150 ml/¼ pint dry cider
1 teaspoon lemon juice
1½ tablespoons gin or Kirsch
400 g/14 oz Wensleydale cheese, grated
1 tablespoon cornflour
pinch of dried mixed herbs or nutmeg
freshly ground black pepper
cubes of French bread, to serve

Place the garlic, cider, lemon juice and gin or Kirsch in a fondue dish or casserole. Cook on

FULL (100%) for 3½ to 4 minutes until very hot.

Toss the cheese with the cornflour, herbs or nutmeg and pepper to taste until well blended. Quickly stir or whisk the cheese into the hot liquid.

Cover and cook on MEDIUM (50%) for 2½ to 3½ minutes, stirring every 1 minute until the cheese has just melted.

Serve at once with cubes of French bread for dipping.
SERVES 4

BEAN LASAGNE

METRIC/IMPERIAL
175 g/6 oz dried lasagne
1 teaspoon vegetable oil
900 ml/1½ pints boiling water
salt
Beef and bean sauce:
1 tablespoon vegetable oil
1 large onion, chopped
225 g/8 oz minced lean beef
1 × 450 g/1 lb can baked beans in tomato sauce
2 tablespoons tomato purée
½ teaspoon ground nutmeg
freshly ground black pepper
100 g/4 oz Cheddar cheese, grated

Place the lasagne in a deep rectangular casserole. Add the oil, water and a pinch of salt. Cover and cook on FULL (100%) for 9 minutes. Leave to STAND while preparing the sauce, then drain thoroughly.

To make the sauce, place the oil in a bowl with the onion, cover and cook on FULL (100%) for 3 minutes. Add the beef and cook on FULL (100%) for 3 minutes, breaking up the beef and stirring twice.

Add the beans, tomato purée, nutmeg, and salt and pepper to taste, blending well. Cook on FULL (100%) for 10 minutes, stirring once.

Layer the lasagne and beef and bean sauce in the casserole, finishing with a layer of sauce.

Sprinkle with the cheese and cook on FULL (100%) for a further 2 to 4 minutes until heated through. Alternatively, place under a preheated grill until golden, if wished.
SERVES 4

HAM AND CHEESE PUDDING

METRIC/IMPERIAL
50 g/2 oz cooked ham, finely chopped
175 g/6 oz mature Cheddar cheese, grated
225 g/8 oz fresh brown breadcrumbs
1 teaspoon dried mixed herbs
pinch of mustard powder
salt
freshly ground black pepper
3 eggs, beaten
600 ml/1 pint milk
chopped fresh parsley, to garnish

Mix the ham with the cheese, breadcrumbs, herbs, mustard, and salt and pepper to taste, blending well. Add the eggs and milk and stir well to blend.

Pour into a 1.8 litre/3 pint soufflé dish and leave to STAND for 10 minutes.

Cook on FULL (100%) for 12 to 14 minutes, stirring once. Sprinkle with the parsley and serve at once.
SERVES 4

SURPRISE PATTIES

METRIC/IMPERIAL
100 g/4 oz cold boiled potatoes
25 g/1 oz flour
15 g/½ oz butter, softened
50 g/2 oz cheese, grated
50 g/2 oz cooked chicken, beef, ham or fish
salt
freshly ground black pepper
beaten egg for binding
6–8 tablespoons golden breadcrumbs
4 tablespoons vegetable oil

Mash the potatoes and mix with the flour, butter, cheese and meat or fish. Season with salt and pepper to taste and bind with the egg. Shape into 6 to 8 patties and coat with the breadcrumbs, pressing them on with a palette knife.

Put the oil in a large shallow dish and cook on FULL (100%) for 2 minutes. Using a palette knife, carefully transfer the patties to the oil and cook on FULL (100%) for 2 minutes. Turn over and rearrange the patties. Cook on FULL (100%) for 2 to 3 minutes until thoroughly hot.

Drain on absorbent kitchen paper. Serve hot with bottled fruit sauce.
SERVES 4 to 6

SCRAMBLED EGGS AND SHRIMPS

METRIC/IMPERIAL
20 g/¾ oz butter
4 eggs
4 tablespoons milk
salt
freshly ground black pepper
50 g/2 oz cooked, peeled shrimps
2 slices hot buttered toast
paprika

Put the butter in a round shallow dish and heat on FULL (100%) for ½ minute to melt. Swirl the melted butter round the dish.

Break in the eggs, add the milk and salt and pepper to taste, and mix with a fork. Stir in the shrimps. Cook on FULL (100%) for 3 to 3½ minutes, stirring frequently, until the eggs are soft and just set. Leave to STAND for 1 to 2 minutes.

Pile the scrambled egg and shrimps on top of the toast and sprinkle with paprika before serving.
SERVES 2

TOASTED CHEESE SANDWICH

METRIC/IMPERIAL
2 slices processed cheese
¼ teaspoon English mustard
2 slices buttered toast

Preheat a small browning dish on FULL (100%) for 4 minutes (or according to the manufacturer's instructions). Meanwhile, sandwich the cheese slices together with mustard and place between the slices of toast, buttered side out. Put into the hot browning dish and cook on FULL (100%) for ¾ minute, turning over after ¼ minute.
SERVES 1

Note: Before making a second sandwich, reheat the dish on FULL (100%) for 2 minutes.

Filling variations
1. Chopped hard-boiled egg, mixed with mayonnaise.
2. Chopped ham, cream cheese and pickle.
3. Sardine, mashed with tomato ketchup.
4. Crushed sugared raspberries.
5. Mashed banana.

WHOLEWHEAT TOMATO PIZZA

METRIC/IMPERIAL
Pizza dough:
150–200 ml/5–7 fl oz cold water
¼ teaspoon sugar
225 g/8 oz wholewheat flour
½ teaspoon salt
1 teaspoon quick active yeast
1 tablespoon vegetable oil
Topping:
25 g/1 oz butter or margarine
1 onion, finely chopped
2 teaspoons cornflour
1 teaspoon dried marjoram
1 × 400 g/14 oz can tomatoes
salt
freshly ground black pepper
225 g/8 oz Cheddar cheese, grated
8 bacon rashers, cooked and cut into thin strips
16 black olives, stoned and halved

To make the dough, put 150 ml/¼ pint cold water in a jug and cook on FULL (100%) for 1 minute or until warm to the touch. Stir in the sugar.

Put the flour into a large bowl, stir in the salt and cook on FULL (100%) for 1 minute or until the flour is warm.

Mix the yeast into the flour, then stir in the sweetened warm water, mixing to a soft dough and adding more warm water, if necessary. Knead the dough lightly and shape into a ball. Replace in the bowl and cover with cling film.

Put about 450 ml/¾ pint water into a jug and bring to the boil on FULL (100%) for about 4 to 6 minutes. Push the jug towards the back of the oven, then put in the bowl of dough beside it. Close the door but do not switch on the oven. Leave for 20 minutes or until the dough rises (wholewheat dough does not rise very much).

Divide the dough in half, and shape each half into a round large enough to fit into a large browning dish. Brush the tops with oil.

Put the butter or margarine in a large bowl and cook on FULL (100%) for ½ minute or until melted. Stir in the onion and cook on FULL (100%) for a further 5 minutes, stirring occasionally.

Add the cornflour, marjoram, the tomatoes and their juice and salt and pepper to taste and cook on FULL (100%) for a further 6 minutes, stirring occasionally.

Preheat a large browning dish on FULL (100%) for 5 minutes (or according to the manufacturer's instructions). Lightly brush with oil and immediately press in one piece of dough, then turn it over and cook on FULL (100%) for 1 minute. Cover with half the topping, then add half of the cheese. Arrange half the bacon on top and fill the centre with half of the olives. Cook on FULL (100%) for 2 minutes. Remove the pizza.

To cook the remaining pizza, brush the browning dish with oil and reheat on FULL (100%) for 2 to 3 minutes, depending on how cool it has become, then cook the remaining pizza as above.
SERVES 4

Note: Quick active yeast is always mixed with the flour and never with the water. For this recipe, you can substitute 4 teaspoons dried yeast which should be dissolved in the warm water and left for 10 minutes to froth up.

POTATO PIZZA

METRIC/IMPERIAL
350 g/12 oz Creamed Potato (see page 184)
25 g/1 oz fine dried white breadcrumbs
1 teaspoon dried mixed herbs
salt
freshly ground black pepper
100 g/4 oz onion, chopped
50 g/2 oz green pepper, cored, seeded and chopped
100 g/4 oz streaky bacon, derinded and chopped
1 × 400 g/14 oz can tomatoes, drained
175 g/6 oz mozzarella cheese, grated
1 × 50 g/2 oz can anchovy fillets, drained
few black olives

Mix together the potato, breadcrumbs and herbs. Season with salt and pepper to taste and press into the base and slightly up the sides of a round shallow dish

Mix together the onion, pepper and bacon in a bowl and cook on FULL (100%) for 4 minutes. Arrange this mixture on the potato base. Top with the drained tomatoes and grated cheese.

Arrange the anchovy fillets in a lattice pattern on top of the pizza and cook on FULL (100%) for 3½ minutes, turning the dish four times during cooking. Place an olive in each square of the lattice before serving.
SERVES 4

QUICK PIZZA BAPS

METRIC/IMPERIAL
1 small onion, finely chopped
1 green pepper, seeded and finely chopped
3 tablespoons water
4 tablespoons tomato purée
1 teaspoon brown sugar (optional)
½ teaspoon dried mixed herbs
freshly ground black pepper
4 wholemeal baps
4 slices lean ham, cut in half
2 tomatoes, very thinly sliced
175 g/6 oz Mozzarella cheese, sliced
1 teaspoon dried oregano

Place the onion and green pepper in a bowl with the water and cook on FULL (100%) for 3½ to 4 minutes, stirring halfway through the cooking time. Stir in the tomato purée, brown sugar, if using, and the dried herbs and pepper to taste.

Cut each bap in half horizontally and toast the cut sides. Divide the tomato mixture between the halves. Top each half with a slice of ham and divide the tomato slices and cheese between the baps to make 8 miniature pizzas. Sprinkle them with oregano and arrange on absorbent kitchen paper on the turntable or base of the oven.

Cook on FULL (100%) for 4 minutes, re-arranging the baps halfway through the cooking time. Cook under a preheated hot grill until lightly browned, if liked. Serve immediately.
SERVES 4

MUFFIN PIZZAS

METRIC/IMPERIAL
1 × 225 g/8 oz can tomatoes, drained and chopped
1 small clove garlic, crushed
½ teaspoon dried oregano
salt
freshly ground black pepper
2 muffins, split and toasted on one side
50 g/2 oz Cheddar cheese, grated
50 g/2 oz salami, sliced
2 tablespoons grated Parmesan cheese

Place the tomatoes, garlic, oregano and salt and pepper to taste in a bowl. Cover and cook on FULL (100%) for 2½ minutes, stirring once.

Preheat a small browning dish on FULL (100%) for 3 minutes (or according to the manufacturer's instructions).

Spread the tomato mixture evenly over the muffins, then top with the Cheddar cheese and salami. Sprinkle with the Parmesan cheese, place in the browning dish and press down firmly. Cook on FULL (100%) for 2 to 3 minutes until the cheese has just melted.

Serve at once with a green salad, if liked.
SERVES 2

TOMATO AND ONION PIZZA

METRIC/IMPERIAL
Pizza dough:
50 ml/2 fl oz milk
7 g/¼ oz fresh yeast
pinch of caster sugar
175 g/6 oz plain wholewheat flour
pinch of salt
25 g/1 oz butter
1 egg, lightly beaten
Topping:
350 g/12 oz onions, sliced
1 tablespoon olive oil
1 clove garlic, crushed
225 g/8 oz tomatoes, skinned and chopped
1 tablespoon tomato purée
salt
freshly ground black pepper
1 × 50 g/2 oz can anchovies, drained and chopped
2 cloves garlic, chopped
8 black olives, stoned and halved
1 tablespoon chopped fresh basil

Place the milk in a small jug and cook on FULL (100%) for 15 seconds. Sprinkle in the yeast and sugar and STAND for 10 minutes or until the mixture is frothy. Place the butter in a small bowl and cook on FULL (100%) for ½ minute or until melted.

Sift the flour with the salt. Pour the yeast mixture, butter and egg into the flour. Mix to a soft dough, then knead for 10 minutes or until smooth. Place in a lightly oiled bowl, cover and cook on FULL (100%) for ½ minute, then STAND, covered, for 10 minutes. Set the dough aside in a warm place to double in size.

Make the topping while the dough is proving. Place the onions, oil and garlic in a large bowl. Cover and cook on FULL (100%) for 7 minutes or until the onions are soft, stirring once. Stir in the tomatoes and tomato purée and add salt and pepper to taste. Cover and cook on FULL (100%) for 5 minutes, stirring once.

Preheat a large browning dish on FULL (100%) for 5 minutes (or according to the manufacturer's instructions).

Meanwhile, knead the dough and roll it out to make a 23 cm/9 inch diameter circle. Lightly brush the top with oil and place the dough, oiled side down, in the browning dish. Cook on FULL (100%) for 2½ minutes.

Spread the onion and tomato mixture over the pizza base and arrange the anchovies, chopped garlic and olives on top. Sprinkle with the basil and cook on FULL (100%) for a further 3 minutes. Serve immediately.
SERVES 2

Note: If you do not have a browning dish, use a non-metallic plate and do not oil the dough.

LEEK AND HAM ROLL-UPS

METRIC/IMPERIAL
450 g/1 lb leeks (two thick leeks), each cut in half widthways
2 tablespoons water
25 g/1 oz butter
25 g/1 oz plain flour
salt
freshly ground black pepper
1 teaspoon made mustard
300 ml/½ pint milk
50 g/2 oz red Leicester cheese, finely grated
4 slices cooked ham
Toasted Crumbs (see page 314)
tomato slices, to garnish (optional)

Arrange the leeks in an ovenproof pie dish. Add the water, cover and cook on FULL (100%) for 7 minutes. Remove from the oven and set aside.

To make the sauce, place the butter in a large jug and cook on FULL (100%) for ½ minute. Stir in the flour, salt and pepper and mustard, then gradually add the milk, stirring well. Cook on FULL (100%) for 3 to 4 minutes, stirring every 1 minute until smooth and thickened. Beat in the grated cheese.

Drain the leeks and roll one slice of ham around each half. Pour the sauce over the leeks and ham, sprinkle with toasted crumbs and arrange a few tomato slices on top, if liked. Cook on MEDIUM (50%) for 5 to 7 minutes and serve immediately.
SERVES 4

PASTA SCALLOPS

METRIC/IMPERIAL
175 g/6 oz dried pasta shells
750 ml/1¼ pints boiling water
1 tablespoon vegetable oil
salt
6 streaky bacon rashers, derinded
20 g/¾ oz butter
20 g/¾ oz plain flour
300 ml/½ pint milk
freshly ground black pepper
75 g/3 oz cheese, grated
2 hard-boiled eggs

Place the pasta in a deep dish with the water, oil and salt to taste. Cover and cook on FULL (100%) for 12 to 14 minutes, stirring once. Leave to STAND while cooking the bacon and sauce.

Place the bacon rashers on a plate, cover with absorbent kitchen paper and cook on FULL (100%) for 3 minutes until crisp.

Place the butter in a jug and heat on FULL (100%) for ½ minute or until melted. Add the flour, blending well. Gradually add the milk and cook for 3½ to 4 minutes, stirring every 1 minute until smooth and thickened. Add salt and pepper to taste. Stir in two-thirds of the cheese until melted.

Chop the eggs coarsely and mix with the hot drained pasta and salt and pepper to taste.

Arrange the pasta mixture in 4 deep scallop shells. Spoon over the sauce. Crumble the bacon coarsely and sprinkle it over the sauce.

Cook on FULL (100%) for 2 to 3 minutes, rearranging the shells twice.

Brown under a preheated hot grill, if wished, before serving.
SERVES 4

SPEEDY STIR-FRIED CHICKEN

METRIC/IMPERIAL
350 g/12 oz boneless chicken breasts, skinned and sliced into thin strips
2 tablespoons dry sherry
1 tablespoon soy sauce
1 teaspoon Chinese 5-spice powder
2 carrots, cut into thin strips
1 red pepper, cored, seeded and cut into thin strips
1 green pepper, cored, seeded and cut into thin strips

50 g/2 oz mini corn on the cob
100 g/4 oz Chinese leaves, thickly shredded
2 canned pineapple slices, chopped
salt
freshly ground black pepper
25 g/1 oz cashew nuts

Place the chicken in a bowl with the sherry, soy sauce and Chinese 5-spice powder, mix well. Cover and leave to marinate for 30 minutes. Meanwhile prepare the other ingredients.

Place the carrots and peppers in a bowl. Cover and cook on FULL (100%) for 2 minutes.

Mix the mini corn with the chicken. Cover and cook on FULL (100%) for 4 minutes, stirring once. Remove the cover and cook for a further 2 minutes.

Add the carrot and pepper mixture, Chinese leaves and pineapple pieces, blending well. Add salt and pepper to taste. Cook on FULL (100%) for 4 minutes, stirring twice. Transfer to a serving dish, sprinkle with the nuts and serve with boiled rice.
SERVES 4

BROCCOLI AND CHICKEN BAKE

METRIC/IMPERIAL
350 g/12 oz broccoli spears, trimmed
4 tablespoons water
salt
225 g/8 oz cooked chicken, cut into thin strips
Béchamel sauce:
1 small onion, peeled and halved
1 carrot, sliced
1 bay leaf
12 peppercorns
few parsley sprigs
300 ml/½ pint milk
25 g/1 oz butter
25 g/1 oz plain flour
freshly ground black pepper
Garnish:
50 g/2 oz toasted flaked almonds

Place the broccoli spears in a shallow flameproof dish with the water and a pinch of salt, arranging the stalks to the outside of the dish and the florets to the centre. Cover and cook on FULL (100%) for 6 minutes. Drain thoroughly, then add the chicken and mix well.

Meanwhile, place the onion, carrot, bay leaf, peppercorns, parsley and milk in a large jug.

Cook on LOW (30%) for 10 to 11 minutes until hot. Strain.

Place the butter in another jug and heat on FULL (100%) for ½ minute or until melted. Stir in the flour and salt and pepper to taste.

Gradually add the strained milk and cook on FULL (100%) for 1½ to 2 minutes, stirring every ½ minute until smooth and thickened. Pour over the broccoli and chicken mixture.

Cover and cook on FULL (100%) for 3 to 4 minutes, turning the dish twice. Sprinkle with the almonds and serve at once.
SERVES 4

HAM AND POTATO SUPPER

METRIC/IMPERIAL
50 g/2 oz butter
2 onions, chopped
2 teaspoons Meaux mustard
2 teaspoons chopped fresh tarragon or 1 teaspoon dried tarragon
3 tablespoons plain flour
300 ml/½ pint milk
300 ml/½ pint white meat stock
675 g/1½ lb cooked ham, cubed
1 kg/2 lb potatoes, cubed
8 tablespoons water
2 tablespoons milk
pinch of ground nutmeg
salt
freshly ground black pepper

Place half the butter in a bowl with the onion. Cover and cook on FULL (100%) for 4 minutes.

Stir in the mustard, tarragon and flour, blending well. Gradually add the 300 ml/½ pint milk and stock. Cook on FULL (100%) for 8 to 9 minutes, stirring every 2 minutes, until smooth and thickened. Fold in the cubed ham.

Place the potatoes in a bowl with the water. Cover and cook on FULL (100%) for 16 to 18 minutes until tender. Drain and mash with the remaining butter, 2 tablespoons milk, nutmeg and salt and pepper to taste.

Spoon the ham mixture into a large dish. Spoon the potato mixture into a piping bag fitted with a large star-shaped nozzle and pipe round the edge to make a border.

Cook on FULL (100%) for a further 4 minutes, turning the dish every 1 minute.

Brown under a preheated hot grill, if wished.
SERVES 4

QUICK RICE SUPPER

METRIC/IMPERIAL
225 g/8 oz long-grain rice
600 ml/1 pint boiling water
50 g/2 oz butter
salt
freshly ground black pepper
100 g/4 oz frozen peas
4 gammon steaks (each weighing about 100 g/
4 oz)
2 hard-boiled eggs, chopped
½ red pepper, seeded and chopped

Place the rice, boiling water, half the butter, and salt in a mixing bowl. Cover and cook on FULL (100%) for 3 minutes. Reduce the power to MEDIUM (50%) and cook for a further 12 minutes. Stir, cover and leave to STAND.

Place the peas in a small dish and add the remaining butter. Cover and cook on FULL (100%) for 2 minutes. Set aside.

Arrange the gammon on a double thickness of absorbent kitchen paper in a circular fashion, with the fat side to the outside. Cook on FULL (100%) for 5 minutes, turning the steaks over once, halfway through cooking. Cool and chop.

Combine the rice, eggs, peas, red pepper and bacon and serve.
SERVES 4

QUICK-COOK PLAICE FILLETS

METRIC/IMPERIAL
2–3 plaice fillets
15–25 g/½–1 oz butter
squeeze of lemon juice
salt
freshly ground black pepper

Arrange the fish fillets, skin side down and with the thinner parts towards the middle, in a single layer on a plate or serving dish. Spread the butter around the outside edges of the fillets. Sprinkle with lemon juice, salt and pepper to taste.

Cover the dish loosely and cook on FULL (100%) for 3½ to 6 minutes, depending on the number and size of the fillets, until the flesh is opaque and flakes when tested with a fork. Leave to STAND, covered, for 5 minutes before serving.
SERVES 2 to 3

FISH IN CHEESE SAUCE

METRIC/IMPERIAL
225 g/8 oz frozen fish steaks
1 egg
300 ml/½ pint milk
25 g/1 oz Cheddar cheese, grated
salt
freshly ground black pepper

Arrange the fish steaks in a large shallow dish and cook on FULL (100%) for 2 minutes. Beat the egg, milk, cheese and salt and pepper to taste together. Pour over the fish and cook on FULL (100%) for 6 to 8 minutes, stirring occasionally during cooking, and breaking the fish into pieces as it becomes tender.

Serve the fish with baked tomatoes, peas or other vegetables of your choice.
SERVES 2

NUTTY DRUMSTICKS

METRIC/IMPERIAL
8 chicken drumsticks, skinned
2 tablespoons tomato purée
¼ teaspoon Worcestershire sauce
1 teaspoon clear honey
2 teaspoons peanut butter, crunchy or smooth
75 g/3 oz roasted unsalted peanuts, crushed
To serve:
lettuce leaves
cucumber slices
tomato slices

Pat the drumsticks dry on absorbent kitchen paper. In a small bowl, mix together the tomato purée, Worcestershire sauce, honey and peanut butter. Spread this mixture all over the chicken drumsticks. Sprinkle the crushed peanuts on a plate and roll to coat each drumstick.

Arrange the drumsticks in a single layer on a large dish, with their thin ends pointing towards the centre, and cook on FULL (100%) for 8 minutes. Turn the drumsticks over, rearrange them and cook on FULL (100%) for a further 8 minutes.

Wrap the drumsticks in foil and leave to STAND for 2 to 5 minutes before serving.
SERVES 4

Note: The drumsticks may be too hot for small fingers to hold. Remove the foil and allow them to cool for several minutes before serving.

TUNA SNACKS

METRIC/IMPERIAL
1 × 200 g/7 oz can tuna fish
1½ teaspoons lemon juice
2 tablespoons mayonnaise
½ small green pepper, cored, seeded and finely
chopped
cayenne pepper
butter for spreading
6 slices wholemeal bread
6 black olives (optional)

Place the fish, lemon juice, mayonnaise, chopped green pepper and cayenne pepper in a bowl and mash well.

Butter the bread generously on both sides; remove the crusts and cut each slice in half. Arrange in a circle on a piece of greaseproof paper on the oven base or turntable. Cook on FULL (100%) until the bread is crisp, giving the paper a half-turn after 1 minute.

Pile the tuna mixture in a pyramid on each slice and cook on FULL (100%) for 1 minute. Garnish with olives, if liked, and serve hot.
SERVES 4 to 6

SARDINE AND RICE SNACK

METRIC/IMPERIAL
1 large tomato
1 × 120 g/4¼ oz can sardines, drained
1 small egg (size 4 or 5)
4 tablespoons milk
salt
freshly ground black pepper
25 g/1 oz cheese, grated
250 g/9 oz cooked long-grain rice
15 g/½ oz butter

Prick the tomato skin with a sharp knife and place on a plate. Cook on FULL (100%) for 1 minute, then peel away the skin. Cut into thin slices.

Arrange the tomato slices and sardines in one half of a two-section microwave dish. Mix the egg with the milk, salt and pepper to taste and the cheese, blending well. Pour over the sardines and cook on FULL (100%) for 1 minute.

Place the rice in the other half of the dish with the butter and cook on FULL (100%) for 1½ minutes to heat through. Serve hot.
SERVES 2

SALMON FISH CAKES

METRIC/IMPERIAL
1 × 100 g/4 oz can pink salmon
100 g/4 oz mashed potato (see note)
1 teaspoon softened butter
1 teaspoon lemon juice
1 tablespoon chopped fresh parsley
salt
freshly ground black pepper
1 small egg, beaten
4–5 tablespoons golden crumbs
3 tablespoons vegetable oil

Drain and flake the salmon. Mix thoroughly with the potato, butter, lemon juice and parsley. Add salt and pepper to taste. Bind the mixture with the beaten egg.

Divide the mixture into four equal portions and shape each one into a round cake, about 1 cm/½ inch thick. Coat with the crumbs, pressing them on firmly with a palette knife.

Put the oil in a round dish and cook on FULL (100%) for 1 minute. Arrange the fish cakes in the dish and cook on FULL (100%) for 3 to 4 minutes until thoroughly hot, turning the fish cakes over once during cooking. Drain on absorbent kitchen paper.

Serve the salmon fish cakes, either hot or cold, with a mixed salad.
SERVES 2

Note: Either mashed boiled potatoes or reconstituted instant dried potato may be used for these fish cakes.

SOFT FISH ROES ON TOAST

METRIC/IMPERIAL
15 g/½ oz butter
100 g/4 oz soft herring roes
lemon juice
salt
freshly ground black pepper
1–2 slices of bread
cayenne pepper

Put the butter in a small shallow dish and heat on FULL (100%) for ¼ minute or until melted.

Wash the herring roes and drain thoroughly. Sprinkle with lemon juice and season with salt and pepper to taste.

Add the herring roes to the butter, turning

them until thoroughly coated. Arrange in a single layer, cover the dish loosely and cook on LOW (30%) for 4 to 4½ minutes.

Leave to STAND, covered, for 2 minutes or while toasting the bread. Pile the herring roes onto the unbuttered toast and sprinkle with cayenne pepper before serving.
SERVES 1 to 2

TUNA-STUFFED PEPPERS

METRIC/IMPERIAL
3 large even-sized peppers (about 225 g/8 oz each)
2 tablespoons water
1 × 200 g/7 oz can tuna fish, drained
50 g/2 oz Edam cheese, grated
1 tablespoon drained, canned sweetcorn
2 tablespoons cooked rice
2 tablespoons mayonnaise
salt
freshly ground black pepper

Cut the tops off the peppers and reserve. Scrape out the core and seeds, and discard. Stand the peppers in a casserole and add the water. Cover and cook on FULL (100%) for 3 minutes. Drain the peppers and set aside.

To make the filling, combine all the remaining ingredients and mix well. Stuff the peppers with the filling and replace the tops. Cover and cook on FULL (100%) for 7 to 8 minutes, then leave to STAND for 1 minute.
SERVES 3

BEAN-STUFFED PEPPERS

METRIC/IMPERIAL
1 tablespoon oil
1 onion, chopped
450 g/1 lb minced lean beef
5 tablespoons beef stock
1 tablespoon tomato purée
100 g/4 oz button mushrooms, chopped
salt
freshly ground black pepper
2 medium red peppers
2 medium green peppers
2 medium yellow peppers
1 × 450 g/1 lb can baked beans in tomato sauce
1 × 225 g/8 oz can chopped tomatoes
1 clove garlic, crushed
1 teaspoon dried mixed herbs
rosemary sprigs, to garnish

Place the oil and onion in a large bowl. Cover and cook on FULL (100%) for 3 minutes. Add the beef, blending well. Cook on FULL (100%) for 9 minutes, stirring and breaking up the beef twice.

Add the stock, tomato purée, mushrooms and salt and pepper to taste. Cover and cook on FULL (100%) for 8 minutes, stirring once.

Meanwhile, cut a slice from the top of each pepper. Remove and discard the core and seeds. Place the peppers in a bowl, cover and cook on FULL (100%) for 4½ minutes; turn over and cook for a further 4½ minutes.

Blend the meat mixture with the beans. Stand the peppers upright in a shallow dish and fill with the bean and beef mixture. Mix the tomatoes with the garlic and herbs and spoon around the peppers. Cover and cook on FULL (100%) for 8 to 10 minutes. Garnish with rosemary and serve.
SERVES 6

TUNA AND SWEETCORN BURGERS

METRIC/IMPERIAL
1 onion, finely chopped
100 g/4 oz frozen sweetcorn
2 tablespoons water
1 × 200 g/7 oz can tuna in brine, well drained
1 tablespoon wholemeal flour
6 tablespoons fresh wholemeal breadcrumbs
1 small egg, lightly beaten
pinch of salt
freshly ground black pepper
6 tablespoons fresh wholemeal breadcrumbs, toasted, to coat

Place the onion and sweetcorn in a large bowl with the water. Cover and cook on FULL (100%) for 2½ minutes, stirring after 1½ minutes. Add all the remaining ingredients, except the toasted breadcrumbs. Mix well with a fork to mash the tuna.

Form into 4 large or 8 small fish shapes and roll each of them in the toasted breadcrumbs to coat thoroughly. Place on a plate lined with absorbent kitchen paper and cook on FULL (100%) for 1½ to 2 minutes. Turn each burger over and rearrange them on the plate. Cook on FULL (100%) for a further 1½ to 2 minutes.

Cover with foil and leave to STAND for 3 to 5 minutes before serving.
SERVES 4

STUFFED PORK CHOPS

METRIC/IMPERIAL
4 × 100 g/4 oz pork chops, trimmed
2 teaspoons gravy browning
25 g/1 oz butter
2 tablespoons sage and onion stuffing mix
3–4 tablespoons milk
salt
freshly ground black pepper
1 small dessert apple, peeled, cored and thinly
sliced

Sprinkle one side of each chop with gravy powder. Place the chops, coated side down, in a large shallow dish.

Put the butter in a bowl and heat on FULL (100%) for ½ minute to melt. Stir in the dry stuffing mix and sufficient milk to form a soft mixture. Season with salt and pepper to taste.

Spread the stuffing over the chops. Cover loosely with greaseproof paper and cook on FULL (100%) for 5 to 6 minutes until the chops are no longer pink inside, giving the dish a half-turn once during cooking.

Arrange the apple slices on top of the pork chops and baste with the meat juices. Cover loosely and cook on FULL (100%) for 2 minutes.

Serve hot with vegetables of your choice.
SERVES 2

LIVER AND ONION CHARLOTTE

METRIC/IMPERIAL
175 g/6 oz calf's liver, sliced
salt
freshly ground black pepper
1 onion, chopped
2 tablespoons vegetable oil
2 teaspoons gravy powder
6 tablespoons water
2 tablespoons shredded suet
8 tablespoons soft fresh breadcrumbs
1 small beetroot, thinly sliced (optional)

Rinse and dry the liver slices and sprinkle both sides with salt and pepper to taste. Combine the onion and oil in a pie dish and cook on FULL (100%) for 3 minutes, stirring once. Stir in the gravy powder and water and cook on FULL (100%) for 2 minutes, stirring once during cooking.

Add the liver and baste thoroughly with the sauce. Mix the suet and breadcrumbs together, spread evenly over the liver and cook on FULL (100%) for 3 minutes. Give the dish a half-turn, lightly press the crumbs into the sauce and cook on FULL (100%) for 2½ to 3 minutes until the liver is tender.

Serve immediately or, if preferred, cover the top with overlapping beetroot slices and cook on FULL (100%) for 1 minute before serving.
SERVES 2

GAMMON AND APPLE

METRIC/IMPERIAL
2 × 175 g/6 oz gammon steaks
1 dessert apple
¼ teaspoon ground allspice
2 tablespoons brown sugar

Remove the rind from the gammon steaks and snip the fat at 2.5 cm/1 inch intervals, with kitchen scissors, to prevent the meat curling up during cooking. Peel and core the apple, cut into rings and spread in a large shallow dish. Sprinkle with the allspice.

Arrange the gammon steaks on top of the apples and sprinkle with sugar. Cover loosely with greaseproof paper and cook on FULL (100%) for 5 minutes, giving the dish a half-turn after 2½ minutes. Carefully remove the covering and test the meat with the tip of a sharp knife. If it is not quite tender, cook on FULL (100%) for a further 2 to 3 minutes.
SERVES 2

HOT DOGS

METRIC/IMPERIAL
25 g/1 oz butter
1 onion, chopped
4 frankfurter sausages
4 soft finger bread rolls
relish, to serve (optional)

Place the butter and onion in a bowl. Cover and cook on FULL (100%) for 3 minutes, stirring once.

Place the frankfurters on a plate and cook on FULL (100%) for 1 minute.

Slit the rolls and fill with the onion mixture. Top each with a frankfurter and a little relish, if liked. Serve at once in paper napkins.
SERVES 4

SAUSAGES WITH HORSERADISH SAUCE

METRIC/IMPERIAL
3 pork sausages
2 tablespoons French dressing
Sauce:
75 ml/3 fl oz mayonnaise
2 tablespoons whipped cream
1 teaspoon creamed horseradish
1 small celery stick, chopped
½ dessert apple, cored and chopped
1 small dill pickle, chopped

Prick the sausages thoroughly and arrange on a plate. Cover with absorbent kitchen paper and cook on FULL (100%) for 1½ minutes. Turn over and cook on FULL (100%) for a further 1 minute. Place in a shallow dish, pour over the French dressing and chill for 2 hours.

Meanwhile, to make the sauce, mix the mayonnaise with the cream, horseradish, celery, apple and dill pickle. Chill lightly.

Serve the sausages with the sauce.
SERVES 1

MINIATURE SAUSAGE KEBABS

METRIC/IMPERIAL
2 tablespoons tomato purée
½ teaspoon Worcestershire sauce
1 teaspoon clear honey
16 cocktail frankfurters
1 × 275 g/10 oz can pineapple cubes in fruit juice, drained
8 cherry tomatoes or 4 very small tomatoes, halved

In a bowl, mix together the tomato purée, Worcestershire sauce and honey. Prick the sausages in several places and stir them into the tomato mixture so that they are evenly coated.

Thread the sausages and pineapple cubes on to 4 bamboo or wooden skewers, starting and ending with a cherry tomato or tomato half.

Place in a single layer on a plate and cook on FULL (100%) for 2½ minutes. Turn the kebabs over and rearrange them on the plate. Cook on FULL (100%) for a further 2½ minutes. Leave to STAND, covered with foil, for 3 to 5 minutes before serving.
MAKES 4

MEATLOAF WITH PEPPER SAUCE

METRIC/IMPERIAL
1 tablespoon vegetable oil
1 large onion, chopped
225 g/8 oz minced lean beef
225 g/8 oz minced lean pork
6 tablespoons fresh brown breadcrumbs
1 clove garlic, crushed
1 tablespoon tomato purée
salt
freshly ground black pepper
1 egg, beaten
Sauce:
25 g/1 oz butter
100 g/4 oz green pepper, cored, seeded and chopped
1 tablespoon flour
300 ml/½ pint boiling water
1 beef stock cube, crumbled
1 tablespoon tomato purée
50 g/2 oz button mushrooms
Garnish:
tomato wedges
watercress sprigs

Place the oil in a large mixing bowl and heat on FULL (100%) for 1½ minutes. Add the onion and cook on FULL (100%) for 3 minutes, stirring once. Stir in the meats, breadcrumbs, garlic and tomato purée. Season with salt and pepper to taste, then bind with the beaten egg.

Mix well and press into a 1 litre/1¾ pint pie dish. Cook on FULL (100%) for 4 minutes, turning the dish twice during cooking. Wrap completely in foil, placing the shiny side inside, and leave to STAND for 15 minutes. Remove the foil and return to the oven on FULL (100%) for a further 2½ minutes. Wrap in foil again and STAND for a further 5 minutes.

Place the butter for the sauce in a jug and heat on FULL (100%) for ½ minute or until melted. Add the green pepper and stir well. Cover and cook on FULL (100%) for 2½ minutes. Stir in the flour until blended, and carefully add the water and crumbled stock cube, tomato purée and mushrooms. Cook on FULL (100%) for 2 minutes, stirring once. Add salt and pepper to taste.

Turn out the meatloaf and serve with some of the sauce poured over. Garnish with tomato wedges and watercress. Serve the remaining sauce in a sauceboat.
SERVES 4

ONE-POT CASSOULET

METRIC/IMPERIAL
25 g/1 oz streaky bacon, derinded and chopped
50 g/2 oz garlic sausage, cubed
2 small tomatoes, skinned, seeded and chopped
100 g/4 oz baked beans in tomato sauce
salt
freshly ground black pepper
pinch of mixed dried herbs
25 g/1 oz fresh wholemeal breadcrumbs

Place the bacon and garlic sausage in a small heatproof serving dish. Cook on FULL (100%) for 2 minutes, stirring once.

Add the tomatoes, beans, salt and pepper to taste and herbs, blending well. Cover and cook on FULL (100%) for 3 minutes, stirring once.

Sprinkle with the breadcrumbs and brown under a preheated hot grill until bubbly, if liked. Serve hot.
SERVES 1

BEEF AND BRAN BURGERS

METRIC/IMPERIAL
1 small onion, finely chopped
1 clove garlic, crushed (optional)
1 tablespoon water
675 g/1½ lb minced lean beef
1 tablespoon bran
pinch of salt
freshly ground black pepper
2 tablespoons sunflower or grapeseed oil
4 soft wholemeal rolls
4 teaspoons wholegrain mustard
2 tomatoes, thinly sliced
spring onions, to garnish

Place the onion and garlic, if using, in a large bowl with the water and cook on FULL (100%) for 3 minutes, stirring halfway through the cooking time. Set aside to cool slightly.

When the mixture is cool enough to handle, add the beef and bran and season with salt and pepper to taste. Mix together thoroughly. Divide the mixture into 4 portions and knead into firm balls. Flatten each one into a burger shape, about 2 cm/¾ inch thick.

Preheat a large browning dish on FULL (100%) for 5 minutes (or according to the manufacturer's instructions). Without removing it from the oven, add the oil and burgers, pressing each one lightly with a spatula. Cook on FULL (100%) for 1½ to 2 minutes on each side for medium rare burgers, or 3¼ minutes on each side for well done burgers. Remove the burgers from the browning dish, drain them on absorbent kitchen paper, then wrap them in foil. Set aside.

Meanwhile, cut the rolls in half and toast the cut sides. Spread 4 halves generously with mustard and place a burger on each. Top with tomato slices and replace the remaining roll halves. Garnish with spring onions and serve with baked potatoes, a selection of relishes and a salad, for a substantial and nourishing meal.
SERVES 4

MEATY MOUTHFULS

METRIC/IMPERIAL
350 g/12 oz minced lean beef
225 g/8 oz pork sausage meat
1 teaspoon mixed herbs
50 g/2 oz fresh white breadcrumbs
salt
freshly ground black pepper
1 meat stock cube, crumbled
1 egg, beaten
1 × 115 g/4½ oz packet powdered potato
1 × 300 g/11 oz can tomato soup
freshly grated Parmesan cheese
thyme or rosemary sprigs, to garnish

First prepare the meatballs. Combine the minced beef with the sausage meat. Mix in the herbs, breadcrumbs, salt, pepper and stock cube. Bind together with the beaten egg.

Roll into 12 meatballs and arrange on a 30 × 20 × 5 cm/12 × 8 × 2 inch ovenproof glass dish. Cover and cook on MEDIUM (50%) for 16 minutes.

Make up the potato as directed on the packet. Pipe a border of potato around a serving dish, and arrange the meatballs in the centre of the dish.

Place the soup in a jug and cook on FULL (100%) for 3 minutes. Pour the soup over the meatballs and sprinkle with Parmesan cheese.

Return the dish to the oven and cook on FULL (100%) for 2 minutes before serving. Alternatively brown the potato under a preheated hot grill, if preferred. Garnish with thyme or rosemary.
SERVES 4

SAUSAGE AND KIDNEY SUPPER DISH

METRIC/IMPERIAL
25 g/1 oz butter
1 onion, chopped
6 lambs' kidneys, skinned, halved and cored
225 g/8 oz skinless pork sausages, cut into 5 cm/
2 inch pieces
25 g/1 oz plain flour
1 tablespoon tomato purée
300 ml/½ pint meat stock
1 teaspoon French mustard
salt
freshly ground black pepper
chopped fresh parsley, to garnish

Place the butter in a mixing bowl and heat on FULL (100%) for ½ minute. Stir in the onion and kidneys, and cook on FULL (100%) for 2 minutes.

Stir in the sausages, then cover and cook on MEDIUM (50%) for 7 minutes. Leave to STAND for 3 minutes.

Using a slotted spoon, transfer the sausages and kidneys to a warm ovenproof glass dish and cover with foil.

Add the flour and tomato purée to the onion and stir well to mix. Gradually stir in the stock and season with mustard, salt and pepper. Cook on FULL (100%) for 4 minutes, stirring once.

Beat well and pour over the sausages and kidneys. Serve garnished with chopped parsley.
SERVES 3 to 4

SAUSAGE CASTLES

METRIC/IMPERIAL
450 g/1 lb pork sausage meat, formed into a roll
about 5 cm/2 inches in diameter
1 egg
50 g/2 oz seasoned plain flour
1 tablespoon oil
Sauce:
1 × 400 g/14 oz can chopped tomatoes
1 small onion, roughly chopped
1 tablespoon tomato purée
1 teaspoon soft brown sugar

Cut the sausage meat into 6 thick slices. Pat into rounds and coat with egg and seasoned flour.

Preheat a large browning dish on FULL (100%) for 5 minutes (or according to the manufacturer's instructions). Pour the oil into the dish and swirl to coat, then add all the sausage meat rounds. Cook on FULL (100%) for 2 minutes. Turn the rounds over and cook on MEDIUM (50%) for 6 minutes.

Transfer to a warmed 30 × 20 × 5 cm/ 12 × 8 × 2 inch ovenproof glass dish. Cover and set aside.

To make the sauce, put all the ingredients into a blender or food processor. Blend until smooth. Pour into a jug and cook on FULL (100%) for 3 minutes. Pass through a sieve on to the sausage meat rounds.

Serve with jacket potatoes and peas.
SERVES 4

SAVOURY MUFFIN TOPPERS

METRIC/IMPERIAL
1 × 100 g/4 oz jar tomato paste with basil or
1 × 141 g/5 oz can tomato purée and 2 teaspoons
dried basil
100 g/4 oz garlic sausage, cubed
1 clove garlic, crushed
1 small onion, grated
4 large muffins, halved and toasted
175 g/6 oz Cheddar cheese, grated
1 × 50 g/2 oz can anchovy fillets, drained
black olives, to garnish

Place the tomato paste with basil, or purée and dried basil, in a bowl with the garlic sausage, garlic and onion. Cover and cook on FULL (100%) for 4 minutes, stirring once.

Place the muffin slices, cut side up on paper towels, on a large microwave baking tray and spread evenly with the tomato mixture. Top with the grated cheese. Arrange a lattice of anchovy fillets on top and garnish with black olives.

Cook on FULL (100%) for 4 minutes, re-arranging the muffins twice so that they cook evenly.
SERVES 4

PORK AND PEANUT LOAF

METRIC/IMPERIAL
225 g/8 oz pork sausage meat
225 g/8 oz lean pork, minced
100 g/4 oz salted peanuts, minced or roughly ground
1 × 50 g/2 oz packet stuffing mix
1 eating apple, peeled, cored and finely chopped
1 onion, finely chopped
freshly ground black pepper
1 large egg (size 1 or 2)
redcurrant jelly, to glaze
slices of green and red-skinned apples, dipped in lemon juice, to garnish

Mix together the sausage meat and minced pork, and add the nuts. Add the stuffing mix, apple, onion and pepper, and mix well. Add sufficient egg to bind.

Press into a 1 kg/2 lb loaf dish and cook on MEDIUM (50%) for 10 to 18 minutes. Allow to STAND for 5 minutes before turning out.

Glaze with a little redcurrant jelly and garnish with apples. Serve hot or cold with a green salad.

This makes an excellent picnic dish.

SERVES 6

CHEESE AND TOMATO LAYER

METRIC/IMPERIAL
50 g/2 oz lightly cooked brown rice
3 large beefsteak tomatoes, thinly sliced
1 teaspoon dried oregano
3 tablespoons fresh wholemeal breadcrumbs
100 g/4 oz Edam cheese, coarsely grated
3 eggs
150 ml/¼ pint skimmed milk
pinch of salt
freshly ground black pepper

Lightly oil a large baking dish and spread the rice over the base. Arrange one third of the tomato slices in a single layer over the rice. Sprinkle with a little oregano, 1 tablespoon of breadcrumbs and one third of the cheese. Repeat this procedure twice more.

Beat the eggs and milk together and season with salt and pepper. Carefully pour the mixture into the dish and cook on FULL (100%) for 9 minutes, turning the dish around halfway through. Allow to STAND for 5 minutes before serving. Brown the topping under a preheated conventional grill, if liked.

SERVES 4 to 6

CHEESE AND POTATO CAKES

METRIC/IMPERIAL
50 g/2 oz Edam cheese, finely grated
225 g/8 oz cooked potato, mashed
1 egg, lightly beaten
1 tablespoon chopped fresh parsley and chives or
1 teaspoon dried mixed herbs
2 tablespoons wholemeal flour
pinch of salt
freshly ground black pepper
2 tablespoons grapeseed or sunflower oil

Place the cheese, mashed potato, egg, herbs and 1 tablespoon of the flour in a bowl. Season with salt and pepper and mix thoroughly.

Shape into 4 × 2.5 cm/1 inch thick round cakes. Dust each cake with the remaining flour, shaking off any excess.

Heat a large browning dish for 5 minutes (or according to the manufacturer's instructions). Without removing it from the microwave cooker, add the oil and the potato cakes and cook on FULL (100%) for 1½ minutes. Turn the cakes and cook on FULL (100%) for a further 1½ minutes. Transfer to a warmed serving dish.

MAKES 4

GARLIC BACON STICKS

METRIC/IMPERIAL
1 clove garlic
8 streaky bacon rashers, derinded and stretched
8 grissini (bread sticks)
25 g/1 oz Cheddar cheese, finely grated

Rub the garlic over each rasher of bacon. Twist a rasher of bacon around the top half of each bread stick. Place the sticks on a piece of absorbent kitchen paper on a plate. Cook on FULL (100%) for 5½ minutes or until the bacon is cooked.

Twirl the hot bacon in the cheese to coat on all sides. Serve hot or cold with drinks.

SERVES 4

LEEKS MIMOSA

METRIC/IMPERIAL
6 leeks, cut into 7.5 cm/3 inch lengths
6 tablespoons water
2 hard-boiled eggs
Dressing:
1 teaspoon Dijon mustard
1 tablespoon lemon juice or cider vinegar
freshly ground black pepper
4 tablespoons grapeseed or sunflower oil

Arrange the leeks in a single layer in a shallow dish and add the water. Cover and cook on FULL (100%) for 5 minutes. Carefully turn the leeks over and cook on FULL (100%) for a further 5 minutes. Drain the leeks and leave to cool.

Halve the hard-boiled eggs, reserve one of the yolks and chop the whites and remaining yolk very finely. Set aside.

Prepare the dressing. Place the mustard in a small bowl. Add the lemon juice or vinegar, season with black pepper, and mix well. Gradually add the oil, beating well with a fork or whisk. Stir in the reserved finely chopped egg yolk and whites.

Divide the leeks between 4 small plates and pour some of the dressing over each portion. Rub the reserved egg yolk through a sieve and sprinkle over the dressed leeks, to garnish.
SERVES 4

Note: Do not overcook the leeks. They should be *al dente*, i.e., cooked but still slightly firm.

SALAMI AND CHEESE FLAN

METRIC/IMPERIAL
175 g/6 oz prepared shortcrust pastry
125 ml/4 fl oz milk
3 eggs
75 g/3 oz salami, finely diced
salt
freshly ground black pepper
50 g/2 oz Samsoe or Cheddar cheese, finely grated
parsley sprig, to garnish

Roll out the pastry and line a 17 cm/6½ inch base diameter, 22 cm/8½ inch top diameter plate tart dish. Prick the sides and base with a fork. Cook on FULL (100%) for 3½ minutes or until the pastry looks dry. Set aside.

Place the milk, eggs, salami, salt and pepper in a jug. Lightly beat together. Cook on FULL (100%) for 2 minutes, beating with a fork every ½ minute. Pour the mixture into the pastry case and cook for 3 minutes, stirring gently after 1 and 2 minutes.

Sprinkle the cheese over the egg and brown under a preheated conventional grill for about 5 minutes. Serve garnished with a sprig of parsley.
SERVES 4

Note: The results of this flan may not be quite the same as if cooked by the conventional method. However, the flavour is excellent and it is a speedy dish to make. The egg mixture will still be wet in the centre after microwave cooking, but it sets during grilling.

SMOKED HADDOCK WITH EGG SAUCE

METRIC/IMPERIAL
300 ml/½ pint milk
1 bay leaf
1 onion slice
8 smoked haddock fillets
50 g/2 oz butter
25 g/1 oz plain flour
salt
freshly ground black pepper
2 hard-boiled eggs, finely chopped
2 tablespoons snipped fresh chives

Place the milk in a jug with the bay leaf and onion slice and cook for 2 minutes. Leave for 15 minutes.

Place the haddock fillets in a shallow dish and dot with 25 g/1 oz of the butter. Cover and cook on FULL (100%) for 2 minutes. Turn the dish round and cook for a further 2 minutes. Keep warm while making the sauce.

Place the remaining butter in a 600 ml/1 pint jug. Cook on FULL (100%) for 1 minute or until melted. Blend in the flour. Strain the hot milk, discarding the bay leaf and onion, and stir it into the roux. Add salt and pepper to taste. Cook on FULL (100%) for 2 minutes, stirring every 1 minute. Stir in the chopped hard-boiled eggs and chives.

Pour the sauce over the fish and reheat on FULL (100%) for 2 minutes before serving.
SERVES 4

FISH

SOLE WITH BUTTER

METRIC/IMPERIAL
4 × 350 g/12 oz fresh or frozen sole, cleaned and
skinned
25 g/1 oz butter, softened
salt
freshly ground black pepper

If using frozen fish, thaw before cooking.

Place two fish side by side and head to tail in a
large shallow dish. Dot with butter and sprinkle
with salt and pepper to taste. Cover loosely and
cook on FULL (100%) for 6 minutes, giving the
dish a quarter-turn every 1½ minutes.

Set aside while cooking the remaining sole in
the same way. To reheat, cook on FULL (100%)
for 2 minutes. Do not overcook.

SERVES 4

FILLETS OF SOLE WITH TOMATO SAUCE

METRIC/IMPERIAL
12–16 sole fillets (total weight about 675 g/
1½ lb), skinned
fresh basil, to garnish
Tomato sauce:
20 g/¾ oz butter
3 shallots, finely chopped
1 clove garlic, crushed
1 teaspoon caster sugar
1 teaspoon chopped fresh basil
2 tablespoons tomato purée
20 g/¾ oz plain flour
350 g/12 oz tomatoes, skinned and chopped
scant 150 ml/¼ pint hot chicken stock
salt
freshly ground black pepper
1 tablespoon cream

Roll up the sole fillets and arrange in one layer in
a shallow dish. If required, secure each fillet with
a wooden cocktail stick. Cover and cook on
FULL (100%) for 3½ minutes. Rearrange, then

cover and cook on FULL (100%) for a further 1
to 2 minutes. Set aside, covered.

Place the butter, shallots, garlic, sugar, basil
and tomato purée in a medium bowl. Cover and
cook on FULL (100%) for 4½ minutes. Stir in
the flour, tomatoes and hot stock. Cover and
cook on FULL (100%) for 5 minutes, stirring
after 2 and 4 minutes.

Sieve the sauce, if liked, and season to taste
with salt and pepper. Stir in the cream.

Drain excess liquid from the sole, if necessary,
then pour over the sauce. Cook on FULL (100%)
for 2 minutes to reheat. Serve garnished with
fresh basil.

SERVES 6

SALMON STEAKS WITH LEMON

METRIC/IMPERIAL
4 × 175 g/6 oz salmon steaks
1 tablespoon lemon juice
salt
freshly ground black pepper
2 tablespoons flour
25 g/1 oz butter
lemon slices, to garnish

Preheat a large browning dish on FULL (100%)
for 5 minutes (or according to the manufacturer's
instructions). Rinse and dry the salmon steaks.
Sprinkle with lemon juice and salt and pepper to
taste. Coat with flour.

As soon as the dish is hot, and without
removing from the microwave oven, toss in the
butter. Quickly put in the salmon steaks, arranging them so that the thickest parts are towards
the outside of the dish.

Cook on FULL (100%) for 3 minutes. Turn
the salmon over and cook on FULL (100%) for 2
to 3 minutes until the fish flakes easily, giving the
dish a half-turn after 1 minute. Cover and leave
to STAND for 5 minutes.

Garnish with lemon slices before serving.

SERVES 4

HALIBUT WITH PRAWN SAUCE

METRIC/IMPERIAL
4 halibut steaks, about 2.5 cm/1 inch thick
15 g/½ oz butter, softened
salt
freshly ground black pepper
100 g/4 oz peeled prawns
150 ml/¼ pint double cream
2 tablespoons tomato ketchup

Arrange the halibut steaks in a large shallow dish, with the thickest part towards the edge of the dish. Spread with butter and season with salt and pepper to taste. Cover and cook on FULL (100%) for 6 to 7 minutes until the fish is opaque in colour.

Mix together the prawns, cream and tomato ketchup. Spoon a little of the sauce over each fish steak. Cover and cook on LOW (30%) for 2 minutes until hot. Serve immediately.
SERVES 4

STUFFED TROUT WITH ORANGE SAUCE

METRIC/IMPERIAL
4 × 175 g/6 oz trout, cleaned
Stuffing:
25 g/1 oz butter
1 small onion, chopped
50 g/2 oz mushrooms, chopped
6 tablespoons fresh white breadcrumbs
2 tablespoons chopped fresh parsley
salt
freshly ground black pepper
1 egg, beaten
Orange sauce:
25 g/1 oz butter
pinch of caster sugar
1 orange, thinly sliced
8 tablespoons orange juice
1½ tablespoons lemon juice
Garnish:
dill or parsley sprigs

Remove the heads from the trout and bone, if preferred.

Place the butter in a bowl and heat on FULL (100%) for ½ minute or until melted. Add the onion, cover and cook on FULL (100%) for 2 minutes. Stir in the mushrooms, cover and cook on FULL (100%) for 1 minute.

Stir in the breadcrumbs, parsley and salt and pepper to taste. Bind together with the beaten egg. Use to stuff the trout and place in a shallow oblong dish, head end next to tail, and stuffing pockets uppermost.

Cover and cook on FULL (100%) for 5 minutes. Turn the dish and cook on FULL (100%) for a further 5 minutes. Leave to STAND, covered, while preparing the orange sauce.

Preheat a large browning dish on FULL (100%) for 5 minutes (or according to the manufacturer's instructions). Add the butter and sugar and swirl to coat. Add the orange slices and turn quickly on all sides to brown lightly. Add the orange juice and lemon juice and cook on FULL (100%) for 2 minutes.

Garnish the trout with the orange slices and dill or parsley and spoon over the orange sauce.
SERVES 4

FISH PIE

METRIC/IMPERIAL
450 g/1 lb cod or haddock fillets
2 tablespoons water
25 g/1 oz butter
25 g/1 oz plain flour
300 ml/½ pint hot milk
2 hard-boiled eggs, chopped
100 g/4 oz cooked peas
celery salt
freshly ground white pepper
450 g/1 lb Creamed Potatoes (see page 184)

Place the fish in a shallow dish with the water. Cover and cook on FULL (100%) for 4 minutes, turning the dish once. Drain and flake the fish, discarding any skin and bones.

Place the butter in a bowl and cook on FULL (100%) for ½ minute or until melted. Stir in the flour, blending well. Gradually add the milk and cook on FULL (100%) for 3½ to 4 minutes, stirring every 1 minute until smooth and thickened.

Add the eggs, flaked fish, peas and celery salt and pepper to taste, blending well.

Line a serving dish with the creamed potatoes. Spoon the fish mixture into the centre. Cook on FULL (100%) for 5 minutes, turning the dish once. Brown under a preheated hot grill before serving, if liked.
SERVES 4

BAKED COD WITH ORANGE AND WALNUT TOPPING

METRIC/IMPERIAL
25 g/1 oz butter
50 g/2 oz onion, chopped
450 g/1 lb cod fillet, skinned
salt
freshly ground black pepper
juice and grated rind of 1 orange
25 g/1 oz fresh brown breadcrumbs
50 g/2 oz walnuts, roughly chopped
Garnish:
orange segments
watercress sprigs

Place the butter in a casserole dish and heat on FULL (100%) for ½ minute or until melted. Add the onion and cook on FULL (100%) for 2½ minutes.

Place the fish in the dish, season lightly with salt and pepper and pour over the orange juice. Cook on FULL (100%) for 3¼ minutes, turning the fish once.

Mix together the orange rind, breadcrumbs and walnuts. Season lightly and sprinkle on top of the fish. Cook on FULL (100%) for 1½ to 2 minutes. Garnish with orange segments and watercress before serving.
SERVES 4

POACHED SALMON STEAKS

METRIC/IMPERIAL
150 ml/¼ pint chicken stock
1 bay leaf
salt
freshly ground black pepper
1 teaspoon lemon juice
4 salmon steaks (total weight about 675 g/1½ lb),
formed into uniform shapes and secured with
wooden cocktail sticks
50 g/2 oz butter
Garnish:
lemon quarters
parsley sprigs or fresh bay leaves

Place the stock, bay leaf, salt, pepper and lemon juice in a small jug. Cook on FULL (100%) for 1½ minutes.

Arrange the salmon steaks in a 30 × 20 × 5 cm/ 12 × 8 × 2 inch ovenproof glass dish. Pour the stock over, and put 15 g/½ oz of the butter on top of each salmon steak. Cover and cook on FULL (100%) for 5 to 6 minutes, turning the steaks over once, halfway through cooking.

STAND for 2 minutes before transferring the salmon to a serving dish. Remove the cocktail sticks and serve garnished with lemon and parsley or bay leaves.
SERVES 4

Note: The salmon can also be allowed to cool completely in the stock and then drained and served cold.

Use the stock as the base for a sauce or serve with the fish.

NEAPOLITAN HADDOCK

METRIC/IMPERIAL
450 g/1 lb courgettes, sliced
salt
1 × 400 g/14 oz can chopped tomatoes
freshly ground black pepper
1 teaspoon chopped fresh parsley
4 × 90 g/3½ oz haddock steaks
25 g/1 oz butter
25 g/1 oz Cheddar cheese, grated
4 black olives, to garnish

Arrange the courgettes in a colander, layered with a little salt. Cover with a plate and place a weight on top. Leave for 30 minutes to extract the bitter juice.

Rinse the courgettes well and place in a 30 × 20 × 5 cm/12 × 8 × 2 inch ovenproof glass dish or a shallow 28 cm/11 inch round dish. Pour over the tomatoes and mix in salt and pepper to taste and the chopped parsley. Cover and cook on FULL (100%) for 9 minutes, stirring once, halfway through cooking. Set aside.

Arrange the haddock steaks on a plate, towards the outer edge. Put a little butter on each and sprinkle with salt and pepper. Cover tightly and cook on FULL (100%) for 3 to 3½ minutes, then drain.

Drain most of the liquid from the vegetables and reserve to use in a sauce or soup recipe. Arrange the haddock on top of the vegetables. Sprinkle with cheese and garnish with olives.

Cook on FULL (100%) for 1 to 2 minutes, until the cheese has melted.
SERVES 4

FISH IN WINE SAUCE

METRIC/IMPERIAL
25 g/1 oz butter
25 g/1 oz plain flour
salt
freshly ground black pepper
150 ml/¼ pint white wine
150 ml/¼ pint chicken stock
50 g/2 oz mushrooms, thinly sliced
350 g/12 oz white fish fillets, skinned, cooked
and flaked
50 g/2 oz peeled prawns
1 tomato, sliced

Place the butter in a large jug and heat on FULL (100%) for 1 minute. Stir in the flour and salt and pepper to taste. Gradually add the wine and the stock, stirring until the ingredients are well mixed. Cook on FULL (100%) for 3½ minutes, stirring twice until smooth and glossy.

Stir the mushrooms, flaked fish and prawns into the sauce. Divide the mixture between individual dishes, or place in a 900 ml/1½ pint casserole dish. Garnish with tomato slices. Cover and cook on MEDIUM (50%) for 6 minutes, giving the dish a half-turn once.
SERVES 3 to 4

SAVOURY FISH CRUMBLE

METRIC/IMPERIAL
50 g/2 oz butter
1 onion, chopped
1 tablespoon chopped green pepper
450 g/1 lb cod fillet, skinned and chopped
salt
freshly ground black pepper
75 g/3 oz fresh brown breadcrumbs
grated rind of 1 lemon
50 g/2 oz red Leicester cheese, grated
2 tablespoons chopped fresh parsley

Place the butter in a casserole dish and heat on FULL (100%) for 1 minute or until melted. Add the onion and green pepper and cook on FULL (100%) for 3½ to 4 minutes, stirring twice. Add the fish and season lightly with salt and pepper. Cook on FULL (100%) for a further 3½ minutes, stirring every 1 minute.

Mix together the remaining ingredients and cover the fish with the mixture. Cook on FULL (100%) for 3¼ to 3½ minutes, turning twice.
SERVES 4

SMOKED HADDOCK WITH NOODLES

METRIC/IMPERIAL
1 small onion, peeled
6 cloves
1 bay leaf
6 peppercorns
1 small carrot, peeled
300 ml/½ pint milk
2 × 200 g/7 oz packets frozen buttered smoked
haddock
40 g/1½ oz butter
40 g/1½ oz plain flour
2 teaspoons chopped fresh parsley
75 g/3 oz grated cheese
225 g/8 oz dried noodles or tagliatelle
600 ml/1 pint boiling water
1 tablespoon vegetable oil
Garnish:
lemon slices
tomato slices
parsley sprigs

Stud the onion with cloves and place in a bowl with the bay leaf, peppercorns, carrot and milk. Cook on LOW (30%) for 10 to 11 minutes until hot. Leave to STAND while cooking the haddock.

Pierce the packets of smoked haddock and place on a plate. Cook on FULL (100%) for 10 minutes, shaking the packets gently after 6 minutes.

Place the butter in a jug and heat on FULL (100%) for ½ minute or until melted. Add the flour, mixing well. Gradually add the strained milk and cook on FULL (100%) for 2 to 2½ minutes, stirring every 1 minute until the sauce is smooth and thickened. Stir in the parsley and the cheese until melted.

Place the noodles, water and oil in a deep dish. Cover and cook on FULL (100%) for 6 minutes. Leave to STAND for 3 minutes, then drain.

Flake the haddock into bite-sized pieces, removing and discarding any skin. Stir into the sauce, tossing gently to mix.

To serve, arrange the noodles round the edge of a shallow serving dish. Spoon the haddock mixture into the centre. Garnish with lemon slices, tomato slices and parsley sprigs.
SERVES 4

SIMPLE MUSTARD HERRINGS

METRIC/IMPERIAL
15 g/½ oz butter
1 tablespoon lemon juice
½ teaspoon salt
3 teaspoons whole-grain or Dijon mustard
2 herrings, cleaned
1 tablespoon flour

Put the butter into a dish in which the herrings will fit snugly. Cook on FULL (100%) for ¼ minute until melted. Stir in the lemon juice, salt and mustard.

Coat the herrings with the flour, then place in the dish and turn over so that they are completely coated with butter. Arrange them head to tail.

Cover and cook on FULL (100%) for 3 to 4 minutes until the fish is tender, turning the herrings over once during cooking. Leave to STAND, covered, for 2 to 3 minutes before serving.
SERVES 1 to 2

SWEET AND SOUR MONKFISH

METRIC/IMPERIAL
575 g/1¼ lb monkfish, skinned and boned, cut into 2.5 cm/1 inch cubes
1 onion, cut into wedges
1 cm/½ inch piece fresh ginger, finely grated
1 carrot, cut into fine matchstick strips
150 ml/¼ pint hot water
3 tablespoons tomato purée
2 tablespoons clear honey
2 tablespoons cider vinegar
1 tablespoon cornflour, blended with 3 tablespoons water
50 g/2 oz frozen peas, defrosted

Place the fish cubes in a single layer in a shallow dish. Cover and cook on FULL (100%) for 3¼ minutes, stirring halfway through the cooking time. Drain thoroughly, cover with foil and set aside.

Place the onion, ginger and carrot in a medium-sized bowl, and add 3 tablespoons of the hot water. Cover and cook on FULL (100%) for 3¼ minutes, stirring halfway through the cooking time.

Mix together the tomato purée, honey, vinegar and remaining hot water and stir into the vegetables. Cover and cook on FULL (100%) for

1½ to 2 minutes, stirring halfway through the cooking time.

Stir the cornflour mixture into the sauce. Return the fish to the bowl, together with the peas. Cover and cook on FULL (100%) for 2½ minutes, stirring twice during the cooking time. Serve with brown rice or green noodles.
SERVES 4

SEAFOOD SCALLOPS

METRIC/IMPERIAL
175 g/6 oz haddock fillet, skinned
150 ml/¼ pint dry white wine
small piece of onion
2 parsley sprigs
1 bay leaf
40 g/1½ oz butter
50 g/2 oz button mushrooms, sliced
3 tablespoons plain flour
200 ml/7 fl oz milk
50 g/2 oz Cheddar cheese, grated
50 g/2 oz potted shrimps
salt
freshly ground black pepper
350 g/12 oz Creamed Potatoes (see page 184)

Place the haddock in a cooking dish with the wine, onion, parsley and bay leaf. Cover and cook on FULL (100%) for 2 to 3 minutes, until tender.

Drain, reserving the stock. Remove and discard the onion, parsley and bay leaf. Flake the fish.

Place 15 g/½ oz of the butter in a bowl with the mushrooms. Cover and cook on FULL (100%) for 2 minutes. Set aside.

Place the remaining butter in a bowl and heat on FULL (100%) for ½ minute or until melted. Stir in the flour, blending well. Gradually add the reserved stock and milk, blending well. Cook on FULL (100%) for 3 to 4 minutes, stirring every 1 minute until smooth and thickened.

Add the flaked fish, mushrooms, cheese, potted shrimps and salt and pepper to taste, blending well.

Pipe creamed potatoes around the edge of 4 scallop shells. Spoon the fish mixture into the centre. Cook on FULL (100%) for 3 to 4 minutes, rearranging the shells once. Brown under a preheated hot grill, if liked. Serve at once.
SERVES 4

RICH FISH STEW

METRIC/IMPERIAL
750 g/1½ lb assorted white fish fillets, skinned
225 g/8 oz assorted cooked shellfish (shrimps,
prawns, crabmeat, lobster meat, for example)
1 onion, finely chopped
1 leek, thinly sliced
1 clove garlic, crushed
2 tablespoons olive oil
2 tomatoes, skinned, seeded and chopped
1 tablespoon finely chopped fresh parsley
¼ teaspoon powdered saffron
1 bay leaf
1 bouquet garni
1 teaspoon lemon juice
1.2 litres/2 pints boiling water
salt
freshly ground black pepper
6 slices French bread

Cut the fish into 5 cm/2 inch slices. Shell the
shrimps and prawns, if necessary; chop the crab
and lobster meat.

Combine the onion, leek, garlic and olive oil
in a large deep dish and cook on FULL (100%)
for 3 minutes. Add the fish, shellfish, tomatoes,
parsley, saffron, bay leaf, bouquet garni and
lemon juice. Pour in the water and add salt and
pepper to taste.

Cover and cook on FULL (100%) for 10 to 12
minutes, or until the fish is tender, stirring gently
several times during cooking. Discard the bay
leaf and the bouquet garni. Adjust the seasoning.

Place a slice of French bread in each warmed
soup bowl and ladle the soup over the top.
SERVES 6

HERRINGS WITH MUSTARD SAUCE

METRIC/IMPERIAL
1 small onion, chopped
½ teaspoon dried thyme
½ teaspoon dried marjoram
grated rind of ½ lemon
50 g/2 oz fresh brown breadcrumbs
salt
freshly ground black pepper
1 small egg (size 4)
4 herrings, cleaned (total weight 350 g/12 oz)
Sauce:
40 g/1½ oz butter

25 g/1 oz plain flour
450 ml/¾ pint milk
1 tablespoon dry English mustard
1 tablespoon white wine vinegar
1 teaspoon caster sugar
salt
freshly ground black pepper
chopped fresh parsley, to garnish

Place the onion in a small bowl, cover and cook
on FULL (100%) for 2 minutes. Stir in the
thyme, marjoram, lemon rind, breadcrumbs,
salt and pepper, and bind with the egg.

Fill the herrings with the stuffing. Close and
secure with wooden cocktail sticks. Place the
herrings in a shallow casserole dish, cover and
cook on FULL (100%) for 5 minutes, rearranging halfway through cooking. Set aside, covered,
whilst making the sauce.

Place the butter in a large jug and heat on
FULL (100%) for ½ minute or until melted. Stir
in the flour. Gradually blend in the milk, mustard, vinegar, sugar, and salt and pepper to taste.
Cook on FULL (100%) for 4 to 6 minutes,
stirring every 1 minute until smooth and thickened.

Remove the cocktail sticks from the herrings
and pour over the sauce. Sprinkle with the
chopped parsley to garnish and serve with new
potatoes.
SERVES 4

POACHED TURBOT WITH HOLLANDAISE SAUCE

METRIC/IMPERIAL
8 turbot fillets, skinned (total weight about
1.25 kg/2½ lb)
25 g/1 oz butter, cut into 4 pieces
salt
freshly ground black pepper
4 stuffed olives, sliced, to garnish
Hollandaise sauce:
2 egg yolks
1 tablespoon lemon juice
100 g/4 oz butter, cut into 8 pieces
pinch of cayenne pepper
½ teaspoon dry mustard

Dot each turbot fillet with a knob of butter and
sprinkle with salt and pepper. Roll up each fillet
and secure with a wooden cocktail stick.

Place the fillets in a shallow dish. Cover and
cook on FULL (100%) for 7½ minutes,

rearranging once. Set aside the fillets, covered, while making the sauce.

Mix together the egg yolks and lemon juice in a small jug and cook on FULL (100%) for ½ minute. Beat the mixture until it is smooth, then beat in the butter, one piece at a time. Finally beat in the pepper and the mustard.

Lift the fish on to a warm serving dish. Pour over the sauce and garnish with slices of stuffed olive. Serve immediately with parsleyed potatoes and mangetout.

SERVES 4

SOLE NORMANDE

METRIC/IMPERIAL
12 sole fillets, skinned (total weight about 675 g/ 1½ lb)
salt
freshly ground black pepper
2 tablespoons chopped fresh parsley
Sauce:
grated rind of 1 lemon
1 clove garlic, finely chopped
50 g/2 oz button mushrooms, sliced
25 g/1 oz butter
50 g/2 oz peeled prawns
50 g/2 oz mussels, cooked
2 teaspoons brandy
lemon slices, to garnish

Season the skinned side of the fillets with salt, pepper and parsley. Roll up with the skinned side inwards and secure with wooden cocktail sticks. Place the fish rolls in a shallow dish, cover and cook on FULL (100%) for 6 minutes, rearranging once. Set aside, covered

Place the lemon rind, garlic, button mushrooms and butter in a medium bowl. Cover and cook on FULL (100%) for 2 minutes. Stir in the prawns and the mussels, then cover and cook for a further 2 minutes.

Stir in the brandy and season to taste with salt and pepper. Arrange the sole on a warm serving dish, remove the cocktail sticks and spoon over the sauce. Garnish with slices of lemon and serve with creamed potatoes and fried courgettes or another green vegetable.

SERVES 4 to 6

Note: Do not be tempted to use plastic cocktail sticks instead of wooden ones as they could melt during cooking.

LEAFY TROUT

METRIC/IMPERIAL
3 large lettuce or spinach leaves
3 mushrooms, chopped
2 teaspoons chopped onion
2–3 tablespoons low-fat natural yogurt
salt
freshly ground black pepper
1 × 225 g/8 oz trout, cleaned and boned
1 leek, sliced
2 tablespoons water

Place the lettuce or spinach leaves in a bowl and cook on FULL (100%) for 1 minute to soften.

Mix the mushrooms with the onion, yogurt and salt and pepper to taste, blending well. Use to stuff the trout, then wrap in the spinach or lettuce leaves.

Place the leek and water in a cooking dish. Cover and cook on FULL (100%) for 2 minutes. Top with the stuffed trout and cook on FULL (100%) for 7 to 9 minutes, turning the dish once. Leave to STAND for 2 minutes before serving.

SERVES 1

SOUSED MACKEREL

METRIC/IMPERIAL
100 g/4 oz onion, sliced
150 ml/¼ pint vinegar
150 ml/¼ pint water
2 bay leaves
¼ teaspoon salt
freshly ground black pepper
4 mackerel, cleaned and boned
Garnish:
lemon wedges
watercress sprigs

Place the onion in a casserole dish and pour over the vinegar and water. Add the bay leaves, salt and freshly ground black pepper.

Place 2 mackerel in the liquid and cook on FULL (100%) for 6½ minutes, turning the fish four times during cooking. Remove the fish from the cooking liquid and cook the second pair of mackerel on FULL (100%) for approximately 5 to 6½ mintes. (The second pair of fish may not take quite as long as the first pair since the cooking liquid will already have been heated.) Serve the fish cold, garnished with lemon wedges and watercress.

SERVES 4

HADDOCK WITH DILL SAUCE

METRIC/IMPERIAL
1 × 800 g/1¾ lb haddock fillet
juice of 1 lemon
salt
freshly ground black pepper
3 streaky bacon rashers, derinded
25 g/1 oz butter
1 rounded tablespoon plain flour
1 teaspoon dried dill
150 ml/¼ pint double cream

Season the haddock fillet with the lemon juice and salt and pepper to taste. Place in a greased cooking dish. Lay the bacon rashers on top. Cover and cook on FULL (100%) for 12 to 14 minutes, turning the dish once.

Remove the fish and bacon with a slotted spoon and arrange on a warmed serving plate. Keep warm.

Strain the cooking juices into a measuring jug and make up to 300 ml/½ pint with hot water. Gradually add the butter, blended with the flour and dill, whisking well. Cook on FULL (100%) for 5 minutes, stirring three times.

Add the cream, blending well. Check and adjust the seasoning, if necessary. Pour over the fish to serve.
SERVES 4

CRISPY HADDOCK

METRIC/IMPERIAL
1 × 675 g/1½ lb haddock fillet
salt
freshly ground black pepper
1 large egg (size 1 or 2), beaten
6–8 tablespoons golden breadcrumbs
4 tablespoons vegetable oil

Cut the fish into 4 to 6 serving pieces and season with salt and pepper. Dip into the beaten egg and coat with breadcrumbs. Put the oil into a large shallow dish and cook on FULL (100%) for 3 minutes.

Arrange the fish in the dish in a single layer. Cover with a piece of greaseproof paper and cook on FULL (100%) for 4 to 6 minutes until the fish is cooked through.

Drain on absorbent kitchen paper. Serve hot or cold.
SERVES 4 to 6

PICKLED HERRING, SWEDISH STYLE

METRIC/IMPERIAL
1 kg/2 lb herring fillets, cut into bite-sized pieces
¾ tablespoon salt
2 bay leaves
8 white peppercorns
1 tablespoon fresh dill
600 ml/1 pint hot water
150 ml/¼ pint white wine vinegar

Place the herrings, salt, bay leaves, peppercorns, dill, hot water and white wine vinegar in a large bowl. Cover and cook on FULL (100%) for 4 minutes.

Stir, reduce the setting to LOW (30%), cover and cook for 15 minutes. STAND, covered, until cool, then chill in the refrigerator.

Spoon the herrings into a shallow serving dish and pour over enough of the cooking liquid to cover. Serve as a starter with dark rye bread and add a green salad for a lunch dish.
SERVES 4

CIDER-SOUSED MACKEREL

METRIC/IMPERIAL
2 × 450 g/1 lb mackerel, cleaned, with heads and fins removed
freshly ground black pepper
finely pared rind of ½ lemon
1 onion, sliced into rings
few thyme and rosemary sprigs
2 large bay leaves
300 ml/½ pint dry cider
150 ml/¼ pint water
2 teaspoons arrowroot
salt

Season the inside of each mackerel with pepper to taste. Place in a cooking dish with the lemon rind, onion and herbs. Pour over the cider and water. Cover and cook on FULL (100%) for 6 to 7 minutes, turning the dish once.

When cooked, drain off and reserve 300 ml/½ pint of the cooking liquid. Remove the fish, onion and herbs and arrange on a serving dish.

Blend the arrowroot with a little water and stir into the reserved hot cooking liquid. Cook on FULL (100%) for 4 minutes, stirring twice. Season to taste and pour over the fish.
SERVES 2

TROUT WITH BACON

METRIC/IMPERIAL
8 streaky bacon rashers, derinded
4 trout, cleaned
1 onion, finely chopped
2 tablespoons chopped fresh parsley
salt
freshly ground black pepper
watercress sprigs, to garnish

Wrap 2 rashers of bacon neatly round each trout. Arrange the fish, compactly, head to tail in an oblong casserole. Make two slight incisions in the side of each fish. Sprinkle the onion and parsley over the fish and season to taste.

Cover and cook on FULL (100%) for 7 minutes, turning the trout over once during cooking. STAND for 3 minutes before serving. Garnish with watercress.

SERVES 4

SOLE WITH SHERRY SAUCE AND MUSHROOMS

METRIC/IMPERIAL
1 × 575 g/1¼ lb Dover sole fillet, skinned
120 ml/4 fl oz water
1 tablespoon vinegar
½ teaspoon salt
¼ teaspoon freshly ground black pepper
¼ onion, chopped
Sauce:
50 g/2 oz butter
40 g/1½ oz flour
400 ml/¾ pint milk
½ teaspoon salt
¼ teaspoon freshly ground black pepper
100 g/4 oz Cheddar cheese, grated
2 egg yolks
2 tablespoons single cream
2 tablespoons dry sherry
Topping:
225 g/8 oz mushrooms, finely chopped
7 g/¼ oz butter
To flambé:
2 tablespoons brandy

Place the fish in a large shallow dish and pour over the water, vinegar, salt, pepper and onion. Cover and cook on FULL (100%) for 6 to 8 minutes until the fish is opaque, giving the dish a quarter-turn every 2 minutes. Leave to STAND, covered, while preparing the sauce and topping.

To prepare the sauce, put the butter in a deep bowl and cook on FULL (100%) for 1 minute. Stir in the flour and cook on FULL (100%) for 1 minute. Add the milk, salt and pepper and whisk until smooth. Cook on FULL (100%) for 5 minutes, whisking every 1½ minutes. Beat in the cheese.

Blend the egg yolks and cream together; stir into the sauce and cook on LOW (30%) for 2 minutes. Stir in the sherry, then cover and leave to STAND while preparing the topping.

For the topping, place the mushrooms and butter in a bowl, cover and cook on FULL (100%) for 3 minutes, stirring once.

To assemble the dish, drain the fish and place in a serving dish. Spoon the sauce over the fish and arrange the mushrooms on top. Dot with the butter.

To reheat, cook on FULL (100%) for 2 minutes. Pour the brandy into a small glass and cook on FULL (100%) for ¼ minute. Ignite the brandy, pour over the mushrooms and serve immediately.

SERVES 4

HADDOCK MORNAY

METRIC/IMPERIAL
350 g/12 oz haddock, cleaned
2 tablespoons milk
15 g/½ oz butter
2 hard-boiled eggs, chopped
3 tomatoes, skinned and sliced
300 ml/½ pint hot Parsley Sauce (see page 306)
salt
freshly ground black pepper
50 g/2 oz cheese, grated
25 g/1 oz fresh breadcrumbs
Garnish:
stuffed olives
watercress sprigs

Place the haddock, milk and butter in an oblong flameproof dish and cook on FULL (100%) for 2½ minutes. Remove the fish and flake. Return to the dish with the hard-boiled eggs, tomatoes, hot parsley sauce and salt and pepper to taste. Mix well and sprinkle with the cheese and breadcrumbs.

Cook on FULL (100%) for 1 to 2 minutes or until the cheese has melted. Alternatively, brown under a preheated grill. Garnish with the olives and watercress.

SERVES 4

SALMON TROUT WITH CHIVE DRESSING

METRIC/IMPERIAL
1 × 1.75 kg/4 lb salmon trout, cleaned
2 tablespoons lemon juice
4 tablespoons boiling water
Dressing:
8 tablespoons soured cream
8 tablespoons mayonnaise
3 tablespoons snipped chives
salt
freshly ground black pepper
Garnish:
watercress sprigs
cucumber slices
lemon slices

Place the salmon trout in a shallow cooking dish with the lemon juice and boiling water. Prick the fish in several places to prevent it from bursting during cooking. Cover and cook on FULL (100%) for 28 minutes, giving the dish a quarter-turn ever 7 minutes. Leave to cool.

Meanwhile, blend the soured cream with the mayonnaise, chives and salt and pepper to taste. Spoon into a small serving bowl and chill lightly.

Skin the salmon trout and place on a serving plate. Garnish with watercress sprigs and cucumber and lemon slices. Serve with the dressing.
SERVES 8 to 10

MARINATED COD STEAKS

METRIC/IMPERIAL
25 g/1 oz butter
4 spring onions, thinly sliced
4 × 100 g/4 oz frozen cod steaks
6 tablespoons white wine
1 tablespoon medium sherry
1 tablespoon brandy
½ teaspoon dried mixed herbs
½-1 teaspoon salt
½ teaspoon freshly ground black pepper
100 g/4 oz mushrooms, sliced
2 tablespoons double cream
parsley sprigs, to garnish

Place the butter and spring onions in a large shallow dish and cook on FULL (100%) for 3 minutes. Arrange the fish steaks in the dish, in a single layer, and baste thoroughly.

Mix the wine, sherry, brandy, herbs, salt and pepper together and pour over the fish. Cover and leave in the refrigerator for 24 hours, basting the fish occasionally.

Add the mushrooms to the fish and cook on FULL (100%) for 8 to 10 minutes, giving the dish a half-turn and basting after 4 minutes.

Transfer the fish to a heated serving dish. Blend the cream into the liquid. Taste and adjust the seasoning, then pour the sauce over the fish. Garnish with parsley before serving.
SERVES 4

TURBOT WITH CREAM SAUCE AND OYSTERS

METRIC/IMPERIAL
4 × 175 g/6 oz turbot steaks
salt
Sauce:
40 g/1½ oz flour
3 tablespoons vegetable oil
450 ml/¾ pint milk
1 egg yolk
3 tablespoons double cream
freshly ground black pepper
Garnish:
12 oysters
50 g/2 oz grated Cheddar cheese

Arrange the fish steaks in a single layer in a large shallow dish. Sprinkle with salt and cover loosely. Cook on FULL (100%) for 5 minutes. Turn the fish slices over and give the dish a half-turn. Cover and cook on FULL (100%) for 4 to 6 minutes until the flesh is opaque. Leave to stand, covered, while preparing the sauce.

Combine the flour, oil and milk in a large bowl and stir thoroughly. Cook on FULL (100%) for 4 minutes, stirring every 1 minute.

Beat together the egg yolk and cream, then add a few spoonfuls of the hot sauce and mix thoroughly. Stir this mixture into the sauce and cook on FULL (100%) for ¼ minute. Add salt and pepper to taste.

Place the oysters on a plate, cover with damp absorbent kitchen paper and cook on FULL (100%) for 2 to 3 minutes until opaque, giving the dish a half-turn after 1 minute.

Transfer the turbot to a flameproof serving platter, coat with the sauce and arrange the oysters on top. Sprinkle with the cheese and place under a preheated hot grill to brown the top. Serve immediately.
SERVES 4

SKATE WITH BLACK BUTTER

METRIC/IMPERIAL
2 skate wings (total weight about 1 kg/2 lb)
4 tablespoons water
175 g/6 oz unsalted butter
2 tablespoons white wine vinegar
2 tablespoons chopped fresh parsley

Cut each skate wing into two. Place the skate in a large bowl with the thin ends facing the centre. Add the water, cover and cook on FULL (100%) for 9 minutes, rearranging the skate once.

Meanwhile place the butter in a frying pan and cook on a conventional hob until it is brown but not scorched. Stir in the vinegar and parsley.

Drain the skate. Pull off the skin and discard. Place the fish on a warm serving platter. Pour over the hot butter and serve immediately with buttered boiled potatoes and green beans or a salad.
SERVES 4

SEAFOOD TERRINE WITH SPINACH

METRIC/IMPERIAL
225 g/8 oz fresh salmon, skinned and boned
4 egg whites
225 g/8 oz Greek-style (strained) yogurt
120 ml/4 fl oz skimmed milk
salt
freshly ground white pepper
1 teaspoon dried dill
225 g/8 oz sole fillets, skinned
75 g/3 oz peeled prawns
8–10 spinach leaves, trimmed and blanched

Place the salmon and two of the egg whites in a blender or food processor and blend until smooth. Transfer to a bowl and beat in half of the yogurt and half of the skimmed milk. Season with salt and pepper to taste and stir in the dill. Cover with cling film and chill in the refrigerator.

Repeat this process with the sole fillets and remaining egg whites, yogurt and milk. Stir the prawns into the sole mixture, cover and chill.

Lightly oil a 1.2 litre/2 pint terrine or loaf dish. Drain the spinach leaves thoroughly and pat them dry on absorbent kitchen paper. Set aside two of the larger leaves. Use the remainder to line the terrine, ensuring that the tops of the leaves overlap the edge. Spoon the salmon mixture into the bottom of the terrine and carefully spoon the sole mixture on top. Fold over the spinach leaves and use the reserved leaves to cover the top.

Cover loosely with greaseproof paper and cook on FULL (100%) for 2½ minutes. Continue cooking on LOW (30%) for 10 minutes (or on DEFROST/20% for 12½ minutes), turning the dish around halfway through the cooking time.

Leave to STAND, covered, until cool. Carefully pour off any liquid. Cover again and set aside until completely cold. Chill before unmoulding.
SERVES 6

PLAICE AND ASPARAGUS

METRIC/IMPERIAL
4 plaice fillets, skinned
salt
freshly ground black pepper
about 20 canned asparagus spears, drained, or frozen ones, thawed
150 ml/¼ pint dry white wine
150 ml/¼ pint water
1 tablespoon lemon juice
25 g/1 oz butter
25 g/1 oz plain flour
1 bunch watercress, washed and sorted
whole prawns, to garnish

Season the fish fillets with salt and pepper to taste. Wrap each fillet around about 5 asparagus spears. Arrange 'spoke' fashion in a cooking dish. Add the wine, water and lemon juice. Cover and cook on FULL (100%) for 5 minutes, turning the dish once.

Drain the fish with a slotted spoon and place on a warmed serving plate. Keep warm. Reserve the stock.

Place the butter in a bowl and heat on FULL (100%) for ½ minute or until melted. Add the flour, blending well. Gradually add the reserved stock. Cook on FULL (100%) for 3½ to 4 minutes, stirring ever 1 minute until smooth and thickened.

Pour the sauce into a blender or food processor and add half of the watercress. Process until finely chopped. Pour over the fish. Garnish with the whole prawns and remaining watercresss. Serve at once.
SERVES 2

ST CLEMENT'S PLAICE

METRIC/IMPERIAL
3 oranges
6 plaice fillets, skinned
juice of 1 lemon
salt
freshly ground white pepper

Peel, remove the pith and coarsely chop the flesh of 2 of the oranges, reserving any juice. Thickly slice the remaining orange.

Spoon the chopped orange flesh over the plaice fillets and roll up to enclose. Place in a cooking dish. Spoon over any reserved orange juice and the lemon juice. Season with salt and pepper to taste.

Cover and cook on FULL (100%) for 4 minutes, turning the dish twice.

Serve hot, garnished with the orange slices.
SERVES 3 to 4

SPICY FISH SUPPER

METRIC/IMPERIAL
25 g/1 oz butter
1 onion, sliced
1 teaspoon ground cumin
1 teaspoon chilli powder
½ teaspoon ground turmeric
½ teaspoon dried basil
1 clove garlic, crushed
2 tablespoons cornflour
2 tomatoes, skinned and chopped
1 tablespoon creamed coconut
300 ml/½ pint water
pinch of sugar
juice of ½ lemon
salt
freshly ground black pepper
275 g/10 oz peeled prawns
175 g/6 oz cooked white fish (cod, haddock, coley or sole, for example)

Place the butter in a bowl and heat on FULL (100%) for ½ minute or until melted. Add the onion, blending well. Cover and cook on FULL (100%) for 3 minutes, stirring once.

Meanwhile, blend the cumin with the chilli powder, turmeric, basil, garlic, cornflour, and a little water to make a paste.

Gradually add the paste to the onion with the tomatoes, coconut, water, sugar, lemon juice, and salt and pepper to taste, blending well.

Cover and cook on FULL (100%) for 3 to 4 minutes, stirring every 1 minute, until smooth and thickened.

Add the prawns and fish and cook on FULL (100%) for 2 minutes, stirring once, until hot. Serve hot with boiled rice.
SERVES 4

MONKFISH IN TOMATO AND COGNAC SAUCE

METRIC/IMPERIAL
1 kg/2 lb monkfish tails
25 g/1 oz butter
1 carrot, very finely chopped
1 small onion, very finely chopped
2 shallots, very finely chopped
1 clove garlic, crushed
150 ml/¼ pint dry white wine
2 tablespoons cognac
225 g/8 oz tomatoes, skinned, seeded and chopped
1 teaspoon tomato purée
120–150 ml/4–5 fl oz fish stock or dry white wine
2 teaspoons cornflour
salt
freshly ground black pepper
lemon juice
fresh dill, to garnish

Prepare the monkfish tails by removing the flesh, in two pieces, from the central bone and slice into bite-sized pieces.

Place the butter in a large bowl and heat on FULL (100%) for ½ minute or until melted. Add the monkfish pieces, cover and cook on FULL (100%) for 8 minutes, stirring twice. Remove the monkfish with a slotted spoon and reserve.

Add the carrot, onion, shallots and garlic to the juices. Cover and cook on FULL (100%) for 5 minutes, stirring once.

Add the wine, cognac, tomatoes and tomato purée, blending well. Cover and cook on FULL (100%) for 4 minutes.

Mix the fish stock or wine with the cornflour, according to the required consistency, and stir into the tomato mixture with salt, pepper and lemon juice to taste. Cover and cook on FULL (100%) for 2 to 3 minutes, stirring twice. Add the monkfish pieces.

Cook on FULL (100%) for a further 2 minutes to reheat. Garnish with fresh dill and serve with boiled rice.
SERVES 4

DEVONSHIRE COD

METRIC/IMPERIAL
2 × 225 g/8 oz cod steaks
150 ml/¼ pint dry cider
salt
freshly ground black pepper
1 tomato, skinned and sliced
25 g/1 oz mushrooms, chopped
25 g/1 oz butter
15 g/½ oz cornflour
50 g/2 oz cheese, grated
450 g/1 lb Creamed Potatoes (see page 184)

Place the cod in a casserole dish. Pour over the cider and season with salt and pepper to taste. Top with the tomato and mushrooms and dot with half of the butter. Cover and cook on FULL (100%) for 5 minutes, turning the dish once.

Carefully strain the juices from the fish and make up to 150 ml/¼ pint with extra cider, if necessary.

Place the remaining butter in a jug and heat on FULL (100%) for ½ minute or until melted. Gradually add the cornflour and reserved juices, blending well. Cook on FULL (100%) for 3 minutes, stirring twice. Pour over the fish and sprinkle with the cheese.

Pipe the creamed potatoes in a decorative border around the fish. Cook on FULL (100%) for 2 minutes, turning the dish once. Serve hot.
SERVES 2

MONKFISH PROVENÇALE

METRIC/IMPERIAL
575 g/1¼ lb monkfish, skinned and boned
1 large onion, finely chopped
2 cloves garlic, crushed
1 small green pepper, cored, seeded and finely chopped
3 tablespoons dry white wine or water
1 × 400 g/14 oz can chopped tomatoes
2 tablespoons tomato purée
½ teaspoon paprika
pinch of cayenne pepper (optional)
1 bouquet garni or 1 teaspoon dried mixed herbs
salt
freshly ground black pepper

Place the fish in a bowl, cover and cook on FULL (100%) for 2½ minutes, stirring halfway through. Remove and set aside.

Place the onion, garlic and green pepper in a large bowl or casserole. Add the wine or water. Cover and cook on FULL (100%) for 3¼ minutes, stirring halfway through the cooking time.

Stir in the tomatoes with their juice, tomato purée, paprika and cayenne, if using. Cover and cook on FULL (100%) for 5 minutes, stirring halfway through.

Stir in the fish, add the bouquet garni or mixed herbs, cover again and cook on FULL (100%) for 3¼ minutes. Stir in salt and pepper to taste, cover again and cook on FULL (100%) for a further 3¼ minutes, stirring twice during cooking. Leave to STAND, covered, for 5 minutes. Remove the bouquet garni, if used, before serving.
SERVES 4

PLAICE IN WHITE WINE SAUCE

METRIC/IMPERIAL
50 g/2 oz button mushrooms, finely sliced
1 onion, finely chopped
100 g/4 oz butter
300 ml/½ pint dry white wine
1 kg/2 lb plaice fillets
50 g/2 oz plain flour
300 ml/½ pint milk
salt
freshly ground black pepper
100 g/4 oz white grapes, peeled, halved and seeded
4 lemon slices, to garnish

Place the mushrooms, onion, 50 g/2 oz of the butter and the wine in a shallow casserole. Cover and cook on FULL (100%) for 4 minutes or until the onion is translucent.

Roll up the plaice fillets and place them in the casserole. Cover and cook on FULL (100%) for 4 minutes. Turn the casserole round and cook on FULL (100%) for a further 5 minutes. Drain the fish, reserving the liquid, and keep hot.

Place the remaining butter in a 1 litre/1¾ pint jug. Cook on FULL (100%) for 1 minute or until the butter has melted. Blend in the flour, fish liquid, milk, salt and pepper. Cook on FULL (100%) for 7½ minutes, stirring every 1 minute.

Stir in the grapes, then pour the sauce over the fish. Cover and cook on FULL (100%) for a further 1 minute. Garnish with lemon slices before serving.
SERVES 4

BAKED TROUT

METRIC/IMPERIAL
1 lemon, sliced
4 parsley sprigs
4 × 225–275 g/8–10 oz trout, cleaned
grated rind of 2 lemons
50 g/2 oz butter
Garnish:
lemon twists
parsley sprigs

Place a few lemon slices and one of the sprigs of parsley inside each trout. Place the fish on a shallow dish, cover and cook on FULL (100%) for 4 minutes.

Rearrange the trout, sprinkle with the lemon rind and dot with butter. Cover and cook on FULL (100%) for a further 3 to 5 minutes, basting the fish with the juices halfway through cooking.

Leave to STAND, covered, for 5 minutes. Serve garnished with the lemon twists and parsley.
SERVES 4

SMOKED MACKEREL CRUMBLE

METRIC/IMPERIAL
100 g/4 oz smoked mackerel fillets, skinned
2 tablespoons roughly chopped onion
2 eggs
150 ml/¼ pint milk
50 g/2 oz Double Gloucester cheese, grated
1 tablespoon chopped fresh mixed herbs
75 g/3 oz crunchy peanut butter
100 g/4 oz crisps and savoury biscuits, crushed
Garnish:
lemon slices
parsley sprigs

Place the mackerel, onion, eggs, milk and cheese in a blender or food processor and purée until smooth. Stir in the herbs and divide the mixture between four 11 cm/4½ inch quiche dishes. Cook, two at a time, on FULL (100%), allowing each pair 1½ to 2 minutes.

Place the peanut butter in a bowl and cook on FULL (100%) for 1½ to 2 minutes, or until melted. Add the crumbs and mix well. Top the cooked fish with the crumb mixture and garnish with the lemon slices and parsley sprigs.
SERVES 4

MACKEREL WITH YOGURT SAUCE

METRIC/IMPERIAL
4 mackerel fillets (total weight about 675 g/
1½ lb)
50 g/2 oz butter
salt
freshly ground black pepper
1 teaspoon dried tarragon
juice of ½ lemon
Sauce:
1 teaspoon tomato purée
1 teaspoon lemon juice
150 ml/¼ pint natural yogurt
1 teaspoon dried tarragon
a few capers

Arrange the fish, skin side down, in a 30 × 20 × 5 cm/12 × 8 × 2 inch ovenproof glass dish. Flake the butter evenly over the fish. Add salt and pepper to taste and sprinkle over the tarragon. Sprinkle with the lemon juice. Cover and cook on FULL (100%) for 8 minutes, giving the dish a half-turn, halfway through cooking. Cover and set aside.

Meanwhile, prepare the sauce. Blend the tomato purée and lemon juice together, then gradually beat in the yogurt. Add salt and pepper to taste and fold in the tarragon and capers.

Serve the fish with a selection of fresh vegetables and hand the cold sauce separately.
SERVES 4

HADDOCK IN PERNOD SAUCE

METRIC/IMPERIAL
4 haddock steaks (total weight about 1 kg/2 lb)
300 ml/½ pint single cream, less 2 tablespoons
2 tablespoons Pernod
salt
freshly ground black pepper
20 g/¾ oz cornflour
dill sprigs, to garnish

Arrange the haddock steaks in a shallow dish with the thin ends facing the centre. Mix together the cream, Pernod, salt and pepper and pour over the fish. Cover and cook on FULL (100%) for 11 minutes or until the fish is opaque and cooked, rearranging once. Remove the fish and place on a warm serving dish.

Blend the cornflour with a little water to make

a smooth paste and stir into the cream mixture. Pour the cream mixture into a large jug and cook on FULL (100%) for 3 minutes or until thickened, stirring every 1 minute.

Pour the sauce over the fish and garnish with fresh dill. Serve immediately with creamed potatoes, buttered carrots and petit pois.

SERVES 4

Variation
This recipe can also be made with salmon steaks instead of haddock, and whisky can be substituted for the Pernod.

SOLE IN TOMATO AND MUSHROOM SAUCE

METRIC/IMPERIAL
4 × 350 g/12 oz Dover sole, skinned and trimmed
Sauce:
1 small bunch spring onions, thinly sliced
25 g/1 oz butter
225 g/8 oz mushrooms, sliced
450 g/1 lb tomatoes, skinned and quartered
2 tablespoons chopped fresh parsley
2 teaspoons chopped fresh basil
pinch of sugar
½ teaspoon salt
¼ teaspoon freshly ground black pepper

To prepare the sauce, combine the spring onions and butter in a large shallow dish. Cook on FULL (100%) for 3 minutes, stirring once during cooking. Add the mushrooms and cook on FULL (100%) for 3 minutes, stirring once.

Stir in the remaining ingredients, cover loosely and cook on LOW (30%) for 15 minutes, stirring twice. Leave to STAND while cooking the fish.

Place each fish on a suitable serving plate. Season with salt and pepper to taste and cover. Cook, one at a time, on FULL (100%) for 4 minutes.

Meanwhile, break up the vegetables in the sauce with a potato masher. Spoon the sauce on top of the fish before serving.

SERVES 4

Note: Alternatively, to cook the fish, stack the plates and cook on FULL (100%) for 12 to 14 minutes, altering the position of each plate occasionally during cooking.

COLD POACHED SALMON

METRIC/IMPERIAL
450 g/1 lb piece of fresh salmon
300 ml/½ pint water
2 tablespoons red wine
1 small onion, quartered
¼ teaspoon freshly ground black pepper
1 teaspoon salt
6 white peppercorns, crushed
1 bay leaf
pinch of dried dill, tarragon or mixed herbs
¼ cucumber, peeled and thinly sliced

Lay the salmon, cut side up, in a deep dish into which it fits snugly. Combine the water, wine, onion, seasoning and herbs. Pour over the fish.

Cover and cook on MEDIUM (50%) for 6 to 8 minutes, turning the salmon over halfway through cooking. The fish is cooked when the flesh can easily be separated from the bone. Leave the fish to cool in the liquor.

Remove the skin from the salmon by inserting the prongs of a fork between the skin and flesh and pulling it away from the sides. Using a fish slice, carefully transfer the salmon to a serving dish. Garnish with the cucumber slices and serve accompanied by mayonnaise.

SERVES 3 to 4

SEA BASS WITH FENNEL

METRIC/IMPERIAL
1.25 kg/2½ lb sea bass, cleaned
1 teaspoon fennel seeds
salt
freshly ground black pepper
2 heads fennel, thinly sliced, fronds reserved
2 tablespoons water
2 tablespoons lemon juice

Open out the fish and sprinkle the cavity with the fennel seeds and season with salt and pepper.

Place the sliced fennel in a large baking dish, sprinkle with the water and lemon juice and season with pepper. Cover and cook on FULL (100%) for 2½ minutes. Stir the fennel and lay the fish on top.

Cover and cook on FULL (100%) for 8¼ minutes, turning the fish over halfway through the cooking time. Leave to STAND, covered, for 5 minutes. Serve garnished with the reserved fennel fronds.

SERVES 4

TROUT NIÇOISE

METRIC/IMPERIAL
2 tablespoons olive oil
1 × 400 g/14 oz can tomatoes, drained and
chopped
1 small onion, finely sliced
2 cloves garlic, crushed
2 tablespoons tomato purée
2 tablespoons dry vermouth
3 tablespoons chopped fresh parsley
sugar
salt
freshly ground black pepper
2 × 225 g/8 oz trout, cleaned and boned
1 × 50 g/2 oz can anchovy fillets in oil, drained
black olives
parsley sprigs, to garnish

Place the oil, tomatoes, onion, garlic, tomato
purée, dry vermouth, parsley, sugar and salt and
pepper to taste in a bowl. Cover and cook on
FULL (100%) for 5 minutes, stirring twice.

Slash the trout in two or three places, to
prevent the skin from bursting, and place in a
cooking dish. Spoon over the sauce. Top with a
lattice of anchovy fillets and black olives. Cook
on FULL (100%) for 6 minutes, turning the dish
twice. Leave to cool, then chill thoroughly.

Serve lightly chilled and garnished with parsley sprigs.
SERVES 2 to 4

SALMON QUICHE

METRIC/IMPERIAL
100 g/4 oz plain savoury biscuits
100 g/4 oz butter
50 g/2 oz cheese, finely grated
Filling:
25 g/1 oz butter
50 g/2 oz onion, finely chopped
1 tablespoon flour
1 × 200 g/7 oz can red salmon
3 tablespoons milk
grated rind of ½ lemon
1 tablespoon chopped fresh parsley
Garnish:
tomato slices
watercress sprigs

Place the biscuits in a polythene bag and crush
with a rolling pin. Place the butter in a bowl and
heat on FULL (100%) for 2 minutes or until

melted, then stir in the biscuits and grated
cheese. Press this mixture into the base and sides
of an 18 cm/7 inch quiche dish. Chill thoroughly.

Place the butter for the filling in a bowl and
heat on FULL (100%) for ½ minute or until
melted. Add the onion and cook on FULL
(100%) for 1½ to 2 minutes. Stir in the flour,
then carefully add the liquid from the can of
salmon, the milk, lemon rind and parsley. Cook
on FULL (100%) for a further 2½ minutes,
stirring once during cooking. Stir in the flaked
salmon, mix well and fill the prepared quiche
dish. Smooth the top and garnish with slices of
tomato and sprigs of watercress. Serve chilled.
SERVES 4

MONKFISH,
MEDITERRANEAN STYLE

METRIC/IMPERIAL
1 clove garlic, crushed
½ green pepper, cored, seeded and diced
½ yellow pepper, cored, seeded and diced
1 onion, chopped
350 g/12 oz tomatoes, skinned and chopped
150 ml/¼ pint dry white wine
1 teaspoon dried oregano
2 tablespoons tomato purée
1 teaspoon caster sugar
salt
freshly ground black pepper
2 teaspoons cornflour
3 tablespoons brandy
1 kg/2 lb monkfish, boned and cut into bite-sized
pieces
2 tablespoons double or whipping cream

Place the garlic, peppers and onion in a large
bowl. Cover and cook on FULL (100%) for 6
minutes, stirring once. Stir in the tomatoes,
wine, oregano, tomato purée and sugar and add
salt and pepper to taste. Cover and cook on
FULL (100%) for 4 minutes.

Mix the cornflour with the brandy to make a
smooth paste. Stir into the sauce and cook on
FULL (100%) for 4 minutes, stirring every 1
minute. Set aside.

Place the monkfish in a large bowl. Cover and
cook on FULL (100%) for 4 minutes, stirring
once. Add the tomato sauce and cook for a
further 3 minutes or until hot, stirring once.

Stir in the cream and pile on to a warm serving
dish. Serve hot with boiled rice.
SERVES 4

SMOKED SALMON MOUSSE

METRIC/IMPERIAL
25 g/1 oz butter
25 g/1 oz plain flour
300 ml/½ pint cold chicken stock
¼ teaspoon ground cumin
4 tablespoons dry white wine
15 g/½ oz powdered gelatine
300 ml/½ pint mayonnaise
2 teaspoons anchovy essence
400 g/14 oz smoked salmon, chopped
salt
freshly ground black pepper
150 ml/¼ pint double cream, whipped
Garnish:
lemon slices

Place the butter in a large jug and heat on FULL (100%) for ½ minute or until melted. Stir in the flour, then gradually incorporate the stock. Add the cumin and cook on FULL (100%) for a further 3½ to 4 minutes, stirring every 1 minute.

Place the wine in a small bowl. Stir in the gelatine and cook on FULL (100%) for ¼ minute. Stir briskly until the gelatine has dissolved. Beat the gelatine mixture into the sauce. Put to one side and allow the mixture to cool.

Fold the mayonnaise, anchovy essence, salmon, salt and pepper to taste and the cream into the sauce. Spoon the mixture into a 1.2 litre/2 pint mould and chill until set.

To serve, unmould the mousse and garnish with lemon slices.
SERVES 4

Variation
Smoked meat mousse: use 400 g/14 oz diced smoked ham or beef in place of the smoked salmon and add 2 teaspoons of drained capers instead of the cumin. Omit the anchovy essence.

TUNA MOUSSE

METRIC/IMPERIAL
25 g/1 oz butter
25 g/1 oz plain flour
300 ml/½ pint cold chicken stock
¼ teaspoon ground mace
15 g/½ oz powdered gelatine
4 tablespoons dry sherry
300 ml/½ pint mayonnaise
2 teaspoons anchovy essence

2 × 200 g/7 oz cans tuna fish, drained and flaked
salt
freshly ground black pepper
150 ml/¼ pint double or whipping cream, whipped
Garnish:
lemon slices
parsley sprigs

Place the butter in a jug and heat on FULL (100%) for ½ minute or until melted. Blend in the flour, stock and mace. Cook on FULL (100%) for a further 3½ minutes and set aside.

Place the gelatine in a small bowl and stir in the sherry. Cook on FULL (100%) for ¼ minute until dissolved. Stir to dissolve the gelatine completely. Beat the sherry gelatine liquid into the sauce. Set aside to cool slightly.

Stir the mayonnaise, anchovy essence, tuna fish, salt and pepper into the sauce, then fold in the cream. Gently pour the mixture into a 1.2 litre/2 pint serving dish. Place in the refrigerator and chill for at least 4 hours or until set.

Turn out and garnish with lemon and parsley before serving.
SERVES 4

STUFFED TROUT IN RIESLING SAUCE

METRIC/IMPERIAL
200 g/7 oz mushrooms, chopped
25 g/1 oz butter
½ teaspoon dried sage
salt
freshly ground black pepper
4 trout (total weight about 675 g/1½ lb), cleaned, with heads left on
150 ml/¼ pint dry Riesling
4 teaspoons cornflour
150 ml/¼ pint single cream
2 egg yolks
Garnish:
1–2 mushrooms, sliced
1 stuffed olive, cut into 4 slices

Place the mushrooms, butter and sage in a large jug. Cover and cook on FULL (100%) for 3 minutes, stirring once. Season with salt and pepper to taste.

Stuff each trout with one quarter of the mushroom mixture and place them, head to tail, in a shallow dish. Cover and cook on FULL

(100%) for 12 minutes, rearranging them once. Set aside to STAND, covered, for 5 minutes.

Place the wine in a small jug and cook on FULL (100%) for 2 minutes. Meanwhile, blend the cornflour with the cream

Beat the egg yolks into the wine and then beat in the cream. Cook on FULL (100%) for 2 minutes or until the sauce is thick, beating every ½ minute. Season with salt and pepper to taste.

Arrange the trout on a warm serving platter. Spoon a little sauce over each one and garnish with a sliced mushroom and place a slice of stuffed olive over the eye of each trout. Serve with buttered boiled potatoes, a green salad and the remaining sauce.
SERVES 4

Variation
For a less rich sauce you can substitute the same quantity of milk for the wine and the cream.

SCAMPI IN WHITE WINE SAUCE

METRIC/IMPERIAL
1 onion, finely chopped
25 g/1 oz butter
25 g/1 oz cornflour
150 ml/¼ pint milk
150 ml/¼ pint dry or medium white wine
450 g/1 lb peeled fresh or thawed scampi (see note)
salt
freshly ground black pepper
1 tablespoon double cream (optional)
chopped spring onions or fresh parsley, to garnish

Place the onion and butter in a large bowl. Cover and cook on FULL (100%) for 3 minutes. Stir in the cornflour.

Gradually blend in the milk and wine. Cook on FULL (100%) for 8½ minutes. Add the scampi halfway through cooking and stir well.

Season with the salt and pepper to taste. Stir in the cream, if using. Pile into warm serving dishes. Garnish with chopped spring onions or parsley.
SERVES 4

Note: If using frozen scampi, increase the cooking time by 3 to 4 minutes and use an extra teaspoon of cornflour to compensate for the extra liquid from the frozen shellfish.

MARINATED TROUT FILLETS

METRIC/IMPERIAL
4 medium trout, cleaned and boned
1 large onion, thinly sliced
150 ml/¼ pint cold water
150 ml/¼ pint white wine vinegar
¼ teaspoon ground mace
pinch of salt
12 black peppercorns
4 bay leaves

Roll up the trout fillets with the skin outside and place them in a shallow dish. Arrange the onion over the trout.

Mix together the water, vinegar, mace, salt, peppercorns and bay leaves. Pour over the trout and onions. Cover and cook on FULL (100%) for 9 minutes. Rearrange halfway through cooking.

Leave to cool, then marinate in the refrigerator for at least 24 hours.

Serve the trout fillets with brown bread and a tossed green salad.
SERVES 4

Note: Herring or mackerel fillets can be used in place of trout fillets.

RED MULLET WITH TOMATOES

METRIC/IMPERIAL
15 g/½ oz butter
½ onion, chopped
2 red mullet, cleaned
1 × 225 g/8 oz can tomatoes
1 teaspoon lemon juice
garlic salt
chopped fresh parsley, to garnish

Place the butter in a shallow cooking dish and heat on FULL (100%) for ½ minute or until melted. Add the onion, cover and cook on FULL (100%) for 2½ minutes, stirring once.

Place the red mullet on the onion and add the tomatoes with their juice, the lemon juice, and garlic salt to taste. Cover and cook on FULL (100%) for 6 to 7 minutes, turning the dish once.

Serve hot or chilled, garnished with chopped parsley.
SERVES 2

SCALLOPS WITH CIDER AND CREAM

METRIC/IMPERIAL
50 g/2 oz butter
2 shallots, finely chopped
40 g/1½ oz plain flour
5 tablespoons dry cider
5 tablespoons milk
100 g/4 oz mushrooms, sliced
450 g/1 lb scallops, cleaned
salt
freshly ground white pepper
2 tablespoons double cream
25 g/1 oz cheese, grated
chopped fresh parsley, to garnish

Place the butter and shallots in a large cooking dish. Cover and cook on FULL (100%) for 3 minutes, stirring once. Add the flour, blending well. Cook on FULL (100%) for 1 minute, stirring once.

Gradually add the cider and milk, blending well. Stir in the mushrooms, scallops, and salt and pepper to taste. Cover and cook on FULL (100%) for 5 to 6 minutes, stirring three times, until the scallops are cooked and coated in sauce.

Add the cream and cheese, blending well. Cover and cook on FULL (100%) for 2 to 3 minutes, stirring once.

Serve hot in individual scallop shells or small dishes, garnished with chopped parsley.
SERVES 4

SEAFOOD TURBAN

METRIC/IMPERIAL
175 g/6 oz fresh salmon, skinned and chopped
225 g/8 oz scallops, cleaned and chopped
2 eggs, separated
100 g/4 oz Greek-style (strained) yogurt
50 ml/2 fl oz skimmed milk
salt
freshly ground black pepper
50 g/2 oz shelled pistachio nuts, roughly chopped
8 sole fillets, skinned and lightly flattened
dill or fennel sprigs, to garnish

Place the salmon and scallops in a blender or food processor and blend until smooth. Transfer the mixture to a mixing bowl. With a fork or whisk, beat in the egg yolks, yogurt and skimmed milk. Season with salt and pepper to taste and stir in the pistachio nuts.

Lightly oil a 1 litre/1¾ pint ring mould, and line with six of the sole fillets.

Whisk the egg whites to soft peaks and fold into the salmon mixture. Spoon into the mould. Fold over any overlapping sole fillets and seal in the salmon mixture with the remaining two fillets.

Cover loosely with greaseproof paper and cook on FULL (100%) for 2½ minutes. Continue cooking on LOW (30%) for 7½ minutes (or on DEFROST/20% for 10 minutes).

Leave to STAND, covered, for 10 minutes. Carefully pour off any liquid and unmould the ring on to a serving dish. Garnish with the dill or fennel.
SERVES 4

HOT CRAB WITH TARRAGON

METRIC/IMPERIAL
2 × 1 kg/2 lb cooked crabs
100 g/4 oz butter
1 teaspoon chopped fresh tarragon
3 cloves garlic, crushed
100 g/4 oz fresh white breadcrumbs
6 tablespoons double cream
salt
freshly ground black pepper
Garnish:
2 hard-boiled eggs, yolks and whites sieved separately
parsley sprigs
lemon and lime wedges

Twist the claws and legs off the crab and crack them with a heavy weight. Using a skewer, scrape out all the white meat and set it aside. Place the crabs on their backs and pull the body away from the shell. Remove and discard the greyish white stomach sac and the grey feathered gills. Using a fork, scrape out the light and dark meat and mix with the meat from the claws. Scrub and rinse the shells.

Place the butter, tarragon and garlic in a large bowl. Cover and cook on FULL (100%) for 2 to 3 minutes. Stir in the breadcrumbs, crabmeat, cream, and salt and pepper to taste. Cover and cook on FULL (100%) for 7 minutes, stirring halfway through cooking.

Spoon the mixture into the shells. Garnish with sieved egg yolk and white, sprigs of parsley and lemon and lime wedges.
SERVES 2

SCAMPI WITH LEEKS AND TOMATO SAUCE

METRIC/IMPERIAL
450 g/1 lb leeks, sliced
25 g/1 oz butter
1 lemon
2 tablespoons dry cider
50 g/2 oz mushrooms, sliced
1 × 400 g/14 oz can chopped tomatoes
2 teaspoons cornflour
225 g/8 oz peeled scampi
1 teaspoon chopped fresh parsley
salt
freshly ground black pepper

Put the leeks into a 23 cm/9 inch pie dish. Do not add any extra water. Cover and cook on FULL (100%) for 6 minutes. Set to one side.

To make the sauce, place the butter in a bowl and cook on FULL (100%) for 1 minute. Add the juice of half the lemon, the cider, mushrooms and tomatoes, and stir well. Cover and cook on FULL (100%) for 3 minutes.

Mix the cornflour to a smooth paste with 1 tablespoon cold water. Stir into the tomato mixture. Add the scampi, parsley and salt and pepper to taste. Cook on FULL (100%) for 1 to 2 minutes, until the scampi are heated through and the sauce has thickened.

Pour over the prepared leeks and garnish with lemon slices cut from the remaining half lemon.
SERVES 2

SQUID IN TOMATO SAUCE

METRIC/IMPERIAL
1 kg/2 lb squid
1 onion, chopped
25 g/1 oz butter, cut into pieces
2 cloves garlic, crushed
25 g/1 oz plain flour
325 ml/11 fl oz passata (Italian sieved tomatoes)
2 tablespoons dry vermouth or water
1 tablespoon double or whipping cream
salt
freshly ground black pepper
1 teaspoon caster sugar
1 teaspoon mixed dried herbs

To prepare the squid, pull the head away from the body. Attached to the head are the entrails. Pull out the transparent bone. Cut the tentacles from the head. Discard the head, entrails and

bone. Peel the skin from the body and tentacles. Wash the squid in cold water and pat dry; then cut the bodies into rings and chop the tentacles.

Place the onion, butter and garlic in a large bowl. Cover and cook on FULL (100%) for 5 minutes, stirring once.

Stir in the flour. Gradually blend in the passata, dry vermouth and cream. Stir in salt and pepper to taste, the sugar, dried herbs and squid pieces. Cover and cook on FULL (100%) for 10 minutes, stirring after 2 and 4 minutes.

Stir the squid mixture. Reduce the power setting to LOW (30%) and cook for 25 minutes, stirring halfway through cooking. Spoon on to a warm serving dish and serve hot.
SERVES 4

FISH AND MUSSEL CASSEROLE WITH CIDER

METRIC/IMPERIAL
1 tablespoon vegetable oil
1 onion, finely chopped
½ red pepper, cored, seeded and finely sliced
1 small aubergine, finely sliced
few drops of lemon juice
450 g/1 lb cod or haddock fillets, cut into bite-sized pieces
1 × 150 g/5 oz can mussels, drained
300 ml/½ pint dry cider
salt
freshly ground black pepper
1 teaspoon fresh marjoram
2 tablespoons chopped fresh parsley
25 g/1 oz butter
25 g/1 oz flour
Garnish:
lemon slices
watercress sprigs

Place the oil, onion, pepper and aubergine in a bowl. Cover and cook on FULL (100%) for 3 minutes, rearranging the vegetables halfway through the cooking time. Add the lemon juice, fish, mussels, cider, salt and pepper and herbs. Cover and cook on FULL (100%) for 4 minutes, stirring once. Allow to STAND for 2 minutes.

Place the butter and flour in a jug and mix well together. Strain the fish liquor into the jug, stirring well. Cook on FULL (100%) for 2 to 2½ minutes until thickened, stirring twice. Pour over the fish and reheat, if necessary. Garnish with lemon slices and watercress.
SERVES 4

CRAB MOUSSE

METRIC/IMPERIAL
25 g/1 oz butter
25 g/1 oz flour
300 ml/½ pint light chicken stock
5 tablespoons white wine
3 teaspoons powdered gelatine
300 ml/½ pint mayonnaise
450 g/1 lb cooked crabmeat, flaked
150 ml/¼ pint double cream, whipped
salt
freshly ground black pepper
cucumber slices, to garnish

Place the butter in a bowl and heat on FULL (100%) for ½ minute or until melted. Add the flour, blending well. Gradually add the stock, blending well. Cook on FULL (100%) for 3½ to 4 minutes, stirring every 1 minute until smooth and thickened.

Place the wine in a bowl and cook on FULL (100%) for ½ minute. Sprinkle in the gelatine, stirring well to dissolve.

Stir the gelatine mixture into the sauce with the mayonnaise, blending well. Fold in the crabmeat, cream and salt and pepper to taste.

Spoon into individual ramekins or a large serving dish and chill to set.

Garnish with cucumber slices and serve lightly chilled with thin slices of brown bread and butter.
SERVES 6 to 8

CRAB GRATINÉE DIABLE

METRIC/IMPERIAL
25 g/1 oz butter
350 g/12 oz canned or frozen crabmeat, thawed
25 g/1 oz cheese, grated
2 tablespoons fresh white breadcrumbs
1 tablespoon single cream
pinch of mustard powder
pinch of cayenne pepper
salt
freshly ground black pepper
dash of anchovy essence
1 firm banana
lemon juice
chopped fresh parsley, to garnish

Place the butter in a bowl and heat on FULL (100%) for ½ minute or until melted. Add the crabmeat, cheese, breadcrumbs, cream, mustard, cayenne, salt and pepper to taste and the anchovy essence, blending well. Spoon into a small serving dish.

Cook on FULL (100%) for 2 minutes. Leave to STAND for 5 minutes. Turn the dish and cook on FULL (100%) for a further 2 minutes.

Peel and slice the banana and toss in the lemon juice to prevent discoloration. Place around the edge of the crab dish. Cook on FULL (100%) for 1 minute.

Sprinkle with the chopped parsley and serve at once with fingers of toast or crisp dry crackers.
SERVES 4

STEAMED PRAWNS WITH NOODLES

METRIC/IMPERIAL
450 g/1 lb uncooked prawns, peeled and deveined
3 tablespoons water
salt
1 cm/½ inch piece fresh ginger, finely grated
1 tablespoon soy sauce
150 ml/¼ pint hot fish stock
75 g/3 oz Chinese egg noodles
2 spring onions, sliced
100 g/4 oz mangetout peas, blanched
1 teaspoon cornflour, blended with 1 tablespoon water

Place the prawns in a large bowl with the water and sprinkle lightly with salt. Cover and cook on FULL (100%) for 3¼ minutes, stirring halfway through the cooking time. Using a slotted spoon, transfer the prawns to a plate, cover with foil and set aside.

Place the ginger, soy sauce and stock in a large bowl or casserole. Cover and cook on FULL (100%) for 1½ to 2 minutes. Stir in the noodles and cook on FULL (100%) for 3¼ minutes, stirring once. Stir in the spring onions and mangetout peas.

Pour in the cornflour mixture and add the reserved prawns. Cover and cook on FULL (100%) for 1½ to 2 minutes, stirring halfway through the cooking time.
SERVES 4 to 6

Note: Most good fishmongers sell uncooked prawns. You can use ready-cooked prawns, although the taste will not be quite the same. Add them towards the end of the cooking time, with the noodles.

MOULES MARINIÈRE

METRIC/IMPERIAL
1.2 litres/2 pints mussels, scrubbed
1 small onion, finely chopped
25 g/1 oz butter
175 ml/6 fl oz dry white wine
1 shallot, chopped
2 cloves garlic, finely chopped
1 tablespoon chopped fresh parsley
salt
freshly ground black pepper

Rinse the mussels in plenty of cold water until all the grit is washed away. Discard any mussels that are not tightly closed. Set aside.

Place the chopped onion and the butter in a large bowl. Cover and cook on FULL (100%) for 3 minutes. Stir in the wine, shallot, garlic and parsley and season with salt and pepper to taste. Cover and cook on FULL (100%) for 2 minutes.

Toss the mussels into the bowl. Cover and cook on FULL (100%) for a further 5 minutes or until the shells open (discard any that do not open). Toss the mussels again halfway through cooking.

Pile the mussels on to two warmed serving dishes. Pour over the cooking liquid and serve immediately with lots of French bread.
SERVES 2

BOUILLABAISSE

METRIC/IMPERIAL
2 tablespoons olive oil
1 onion, sliced
100 g/4 oz leeks, finely sliced
3 cloves garlic, crushed
1 fennel sprig
1 thyme sprig
1 sliver of fresh orange peel
2 bay leaves
2 small tomatoes, skinned, seeded and chopped
225 g/8 oz cod fillets, skinned and cut into pieces
225 g/8 oz monkfish, cut into pieces
600 ml/1 pint cold water
450 ml/¾ pint hot fish stock
175 g/6 oz peeled prawns
175 g/6 oz cooked mussels
salt
freshly ground black pepper
½ teaspoon powdered saffron
small slices of hot toast, to serve

Rouille:
1 small red pepper, cored, seeded and chopped
1 clove garlic, chopped
pinch of powdered saffron
25 g/1 oz crustless white bread
1 egg yolk, beaten
100–120 ml/3½–4 fl oz olive oil

Place the oil, onion, leeks, garlic, fennel, thyme and orange peel in a large bowl. Cover and cook on FULL (100%) for 8 minutes or until the vegetables are tender, stirring once.

Stir in the bay leaves, tomatoes, cod, monkfish and water. Cover and cook on FULL (100%) for 6 minutes, stirring once.

Meanwhile, make the rouille. Using a pestle and mortar, crush the red pepper and garlic to a paste. Add the saffron and salt and pepper to taste. Moisten the bread with a little of the cooking liquid from the bouillabaisse and the egg yolk, then work it into the pepper and garlic mixture until it is thoroughly incorporated. Add the oil a little at a time to begin with, as if making mayonnaise, then as the rouille thickens, pour it in in a thin steady stream. Spoon the rouille into a sauceboat.

Stir the hot fish stock, prawns and mussels into the bouillabaisse and season with salt and pepper. Cover and cook on FULL (100%) for 5 minutes, stirring once.

Remove the bay leaves and stir in the powdered saffron. Taste the bouillabaisse and adjust the seasoning if necessary, then transfer it to a warm soup tureen.

To serve, place a few slices of hot toast in each soup bowl and pour over enough soup to moisten generously, then let guests help themselves to some pieces of fish. Hand the rouille separately.
SERVES 4

MIXED SEAFOOD PASTA

METRIC/IMPERIAL
225 g/8 oz cod fillet, skinned
1 onion, finely chopped
1 clove garlic, crushed
2 tablespoons dry white wine or water
1 tablespoon wholemeal flour
150 ml/¼ pint hot fish stock
1 × 90 g/3½ oz can tuna in brine, well drained and roughly flaked
100 g/4 oz cooked mussels
75 g/3 oz peeled prawns

freshly ground black pepper
For the pasta:
1.2 litres/2 pints boiling water
1 tablespoon sunflower or grapeseed oil
225 g/8 oz dried wholewheat spaghetti or spinach
noodles
grated Parmesan cheese, to garnish

Place the cod fillet on a large plate, tail end to the centre. Cover loosely with greaseproof paper and cook on FULL (100%) for 2½ minutes. Drain the fish on absorbent kitchen paper. Flake it coarsely, transfer to a bowl and reserve.

Place the onion and garlic in a large bowl or casserole. Add the wine or water. Cover and cook on FULL (100%) for 2½ minutes, stirring halfway through the cooking time.

Blend the flour with a little of the stock and stir into the onion mixture with the remainder of the stock. Cover and cook on FULL (100%) for 1½ to 2 minutes, stirring after 1 minute.

Stir in the tuna, together with the mussels, prawns and the reserved cod. Season with plenty of pepper, cover and cook on FULL (100%) for 2½ minutes, stirring halfway through the cooking time. Leave to STAND, covered, while cooking the pasta.

Place the boiling water and oil in a large bowl. Add the noodles or spaghetti (softening in the water until completely immersed) and cook on FULL (100%) for 6 minutes, if using thin egg noodles, or 10 to 12 minutes for spaghetti, stirring once. Cover and allow to STAND for 5 minutes. Drain well.

Mix the cooked pasta and fish together thoroughly. Cover and cook on FULL (100%) for 1½ to 2 minutes. Sprinkle with the Parmesan cheese and serve immediately.
SERVES 4 to 6

Note: Frozen prawns can be thawed easily in the microwave oven. Slit the bag and put it on a plate. Cook on DEFROST (20%) for 3½ to 5½ minutes if thawing 225 g/8 oz; 7 to 8 minutes for 450 g/1 lb.

PRAWN FRIED RICE

METRIC/IMPERIAL
1 tablespoon vegetable oil
2 onions, chopped
350 g/12 oz frozen mixed vegetables, thawed
225 g/8 oz cooked brown rice
2 tablespoons soy sauce

350 g/12 oz peeled prawns
75 g/3 oz salted peanuts
4 eggs, beaten
salt
freshly ground black pepper

Place the oil and onion in a shallow cooking dish. Cover and cook on FULL (100%) for 4 minutes, stirring once.

Add the vegetables, blending well. Cook on FULL (100%) for 2 minutes, stirring once.

Add the rice, soy sauce, prawns and peanuts. Cook on FULL (100%) for 4 minutes, stirring once.

Pour the egg over the rice mixture. Cook for a further 1 to 2 minutes until lightly set. Toss the rice mixture well with a fork to distribute the cooked egg. Season to taste with salt and pepper and serve at once.
SERVES 4

SEAFOOD SALAD PLATTER

METRIC/IMPERIAL
12 thawed scallops (total weight about 225 g/
8 oz)
12 shelled uncooked scampi (total weight about
200 g/7 oz)
7 g/¼ oz butter
2 tablespoons sherry
about 300 ml/½ pint dry white wine
2 slices onion
freshly ground black pepper
24 fresh mussels (total weight about 450 g/1 lb)
dressed crabmeat from 1 large crab
50 g/2 oz peeled cooked prawns
1 tablespoon plain flour
1 tablespoon cold water
Garnish:
coriander sprigs
4 lemon wedges

Rinse the scallops in cold water, removing any black parts or beard that may be attached but leaving the white and coral parts. Put on a small shallow dish with the scampi. Dot the scallops with butter and spoon the sherry over the scampi.

Cover and cook on FULL (100%) for 1½ to 2 minutes or until the scampi are opaque (take care not to overcook or the scallops will become tough).

Put 3 scallops and 3 scampi on each of 4 dinner

plates. Pour the juices into a measuring jug and add enough white wine to make it up to 300 ml/½ pint. Pour the wine mixture into a 2 litre/3½ pint bowl and add the onion and a shake of pepper.

Scrub the mussels under cold water, removing the beards, then wash in three or four changes of cold water. Discard any mussels that do not close when tapped.

Cook the wine mixture on FULL (100%) for 2 minutes or until boiling, then cook on FULL (100%) for a further 2 minutes. Add the mussels in their shells and cook on FULL (100%) for 4 minutes, shaking the bowl and stirring the mussels occasionally. Remove any cooked mussels as soon as they are ready (when the shells open to reveal a gap the size of your little finger). Discard any that do not open. As the mussels are cooked, drain them and put on to the dinner plates, allowing 6 per person.

Divide the crabmeat and the prawns between the servings and garnish with the coriander and lemon wedges. Serve cold with a sauce made from the mussel liquor, mayonnaise or a piquant sauce.

To make a sauce from the mussel liquor, strain it into a clean bowl. Blend the flour and water together, then stir into the liquor in the bowl. Cook on FULL (100%) for 2½ minutes until the mixture boils and thickens, stirring twice. Leave to cool.

SERVES 4

MIXED SEAFOOD CURRY

METRIC/IMPERIAL
1 tablespoon vegetable oil
1 onion, chopped
2 tablespoons curry powder
2 tablespoons flour
300 ml/½ pint water
225 g/8 oz cod fillet, skinned and cut into chunks
50 g/2 oz button mushrooms, sliced
salt
freshly ground black pepper
150 ml/¼ pint soured cream
225 g/8 oz peeled prawns

Place the oil in a 1.5 litre/2½ pint dish and heat on FULL (100%) for 2 minutes. Add the onion and curry powder, stir well and cook on FULL (100%) for 3¼ minutes.

Add the flour and carefully stir in the water. Add the cod and mushrooms, mix well and season with salt and pepper to taste. Cook on FULL (100%) for 3 minutes, stirring every 1 minute.

Stir in the soured cream and prawns and cook on FULL (100%) for 1 minute before serving with boiled rice.

SERVES 4

SOLE AND PRAWNS IN CREAM SAUCE

METRIC/IMPERIAL
225 g/8 oz sole fillets, skinned
salt
freshly ground black pepper
75 g/3 oz butter
150 ml/¼ pint milk plus 1 tablespoon
1 onion, finely chopped
100 g/4 oz button mushrooms, chopped
25 g/1 oz plain flour
150 ml/¼ pint dry vermouth
150 ml/¼ pint single cream
225 g/8 oz peeled prawns
Garnish:
mint sprigs
whole prawns

Place the sole in a bowl and season with salt and pepper. Dot with 25 g/1 oz butter and pour over 1 tablespoon of the milk. Cover and cook on FULL (100%) for 2 minutes. Set aside.

Put 25 g/1 oz butter and the onion in a small bowl. Cook on FULL (100%) for 1 minute. Stir in the mushrooms.

To make the sauce, place the remaining butter in a large jug and heat on FULL (100%) for 1 minute. Stir in the flour to make a roux. Gradually stir in the dry vermouth, cream and 150 ml/¼ pint milk. Stir well. Cook on FULL (100%) for 3½ minutes, until the sauce rises nearly to the top of the jug, stirring twice. Season with salt and pepper to taste.

Add the white fish and the prawns to the mushroom mixture, and stir to combine them evenly. Turn into an oval serving dish and cover with the sauce. Cook on FULL (100%) for 2 minutes.

Garnish with mint and prawns, and serve with boiled potatoes and a green salad.

SERVES 4

FISH QUENELLES IN CHEESE SAUCE

METRIC/IMPERIAL
450 g/1 lb halibut fillet, skinned
2 tablespoons chopped fresh parsley
25 g/1 oz flour
25 g/1 oz butter
5 tablespoons milk
1 teaspoon salt
½ teaspoon freshly ground black pepper
Court bouillon:
600 ml/1 pint boiling water
1 tablespoon wine vinegar
⅓ teaspoon powdered bay leaves
small piece of onion
Sauce:
40 g/1½ oz butter
40 g/1½ oz flour
600 ml/1 pint milk
¼ teaspoon salt
½ teaspoon freshly ground black pepper
2 tablespoons anchovy essence
25 g/1 oz grated Cheddar cheese
Garnish:
8 canned anchovy fillets, drained and cut into
thin strips

Mince the fish and parsley together. Blend in the flour.

Put the butter in a small bowl and heat on FULL (100%) for ½ minute or until melted. Add the milk, salt, pepper and melted butter to the fish and mix thoroughly until smooth.

To prepare the court bouillon, combine the boiling water, vinegar, powdered bay leaves and onion in a jug. Cook on FULL (100%) for 1 to 2 minutes to bring back to the boil. Pour into a large shallow dish.

Divide the fish mixture into 12 equal portions. Form each one into an oval-shaped quenelle, using two tablespoons. Arrange half the quenelles around the edge of the dish and cook on FULL (100%) for 4 minutes. Move these into the centre of the dish and arrange the remaining quenelles around the edge. Cook on FULL (100%) for 2 minutes. Cover and set aside.

To prepare the sauce, put the butter in a deep bowl and heat on FULL (100%) for 1 minute or until melted. Blend in the flour and cook on FULL (100%) for 1 minute. Whisk in the milk, salt and pepper and cook on FULL (100%) for 4 minutes, whisking thoroughly every minute. Stir in the anchovy essence and the cheese.

Drain the quenelles, cover and cook on FULL (100%) for 2 minutes to reheat, rearranging once. Transfer to a heated serving platter and coat with the sauce. Arrange the anchovy strips in a lattice pattern on top. Serve immediately.
SERVES 4

Note: This dish also makes a tasty starter; the above quantities will serve 6 people as a first course.

CRAB CREOLE

METRIC/IMPERIAL
2 tablespoons desiccated coconut
6 tablespoons fresh wholemeal breadcrumbs
6 tablespoons skimmed milk
4 shallots or 1 onion, very finely chopped
50 g/2 oz firm button mushrooms, finely
chopped
1 tablespoon lemon juice
2 slices lean ham, finely chopped
275 g/10 oz white crabmeat
1 egg, lightly beaten
pinch of salt
freshly ground black pepper
1 tablespoon chopped fresh parsley
1 tablespoon grated Parmesan cheese
chopped fresh parsley, to garnish

Place the coconut in a small bowl with 4 tablespoons of the breadcrumbs. Stir in the milk and leave to soak for 15 minutes.

Place the shallots or onion and mushrooms in a large bowl or casserole. Sprinkle with the lemon juice and cook on FULL (100%) for 2½ minutes, stirring halfway through the cooking time.

Stir in the ham, crabmeat, soaked breadcrumb and coconut mixture and the egg. Season with salt and pepper and stir in the chopped parsley. Cover and cook on FULL (100%) for 2½ minutes.

Stir well and divide the mixture between 4 individual baking dishes or scallop shells. Mix the Parmesan cheese with the remaining breadcrumbs and sprinkle a little over the top of each dish. Cook under a preheated hot grill until lightly browned. Leave to STAND for 3 minutes before serving, garnished with more parsley.
SERVES 4

Variation
Cooked and flaked white fish can be used instead of crabmeat.

FISH RISOTTO

METRIC/IMPERIAL
50 g/2 oz butter
1 large onion, finely chopped
½ green pepper, cored, seeded and finely diced
½ red pepper, cored, seeded and finely diced
2 tablespoons tomato purée
1 clove garlic, crushed
1 teaspoon dried mixed herbs
50 g/2 oz mushrooms, finely chopped
350 g/12 oz long-grain rice
750 ml/1¼ pints hot chicken stock
salt
¼ teaspoon vegetable oil
675 g/1½ lb cod fillets, rinsed in cold water
freshly ground black pepper

Place the butter, onion, peppers, tomato purée, garlic, herbs and mushrooms in a large bowl. Cover and cook on FULL (100%) for 10 minutes, stirring halfway through cooking.

Stir in the rice, stock, salt and oil. Cover and cook on FULL (100%) for 3 minutes. Reduce the power setting to MEDIUM (50%) and cook for a further 12 minutes, stirring twice. Set aside, covered.

Place the cod fillets in a shallow dish. Cover and cook on FULL (100%) for 7 minutes, rearranging halfway through cooking. Leave to STAND for 4 minutes, covered.

Flake the fish, removing the skin. Stir the fish into the rice mixture and season to taste with pepper before serving.
SERVES 4

MIXED SEAFOOD IN WINE SAUCE

METRIC/IMPERIAL
1 small onion, chopped
40 g/1½ oz butter
4 scallops, cleaned and halved
225 g/8 oz hake fillet, skinned and cut into
2.5 cm/1 inch chunks
100 g/4 oz shelled scampi
150 ml/¼ pint dry white wine
2 teaspoons lemon juice
1 bay leaf
½–1 teaspoon salt
½ teaspoon freshly ground black pepper
25 g/1 oz flour
150 ml/¼ pint water
100 g/4 oz button mushrooms, trimmed

100 g/4 oz peeled shrimps
1 × 100 g/4 oz can tuna fish, flaked
1 × 150 g/5 oz jar mussels, drained
450 g/1 lb Creamed Potatoes (see page 184)
Garnish:
50 g/2 oz black grapes, skinned and pipped
lemon slices

Combine the onion and one third of the butter in a large deep dish and cook on FULL (100%) for 3 minutes. Add the scallops, hake, scampi, wine, lemon juice, bay leaf, salt and pepper. Cook on FULL (100%) for 5 minutes, basting occasionally. Carefully transfer the fish to a plate and set aside; strain the liquor into a small bowl.

Put the remaining butter in the dish, stir in the flour and cook on FULL (100%) for 1 minute. Stir in the reserved liquor and the water and cook on FULL (100%) for 4 minutes, stirring occasionally.

Add the mushrooms to the sauce and cook on FULL (100%) for 3 minutes. Fold in the shrimps, flaked tuna and mussels. Add the scallops, hake and scampi. Cover and cook on LOW (30%) for 15 to 18 minutes or until all the fish is cooked, stirring gently several times during cooking.

Pipe a deep border of creamed potato around the edges of a flameproof serving dish. Place under a preheated hot grill until crisp and lightly browned. Spoon the fish mixture into the centre.

Put the grapes on a saucer and cook on FULL (100%) for ½ minute. Garnish the dish with the grapes and lemon slices before serving.
SERVES 6

Note: If only 4 servings are required, reduce the amount of fish but leave the remaining quantities as stated above.

FISH MOULD

METRIC/IMPERIAL
50 g/2 oz butter, cut into pieces
2 cloves garlic, crushed
25 g/1 oz plain flour
120 ml/4 fl oz cold fish stock
50 ml/2 fl oz double cream
¼ teaspoon anchovy essence
300 g/11 oz cod fillets, skinned and cut into bite-
sized pieces
50 g/2 oz fresh white breadcrumbs
1 large egg (size 1), lightly beaten
175 g/6 oz crabmeat

75 g/3 oz peeled prawns
1 tablespoon lemon juice
½ teaspoon dried oregano
salt
freshly ground black pepper
Garnish:
fresh prawns
lemon slices
parsley sprigs

Place the butter and garlic in a large jug. Heat on FULL (100%) for 1 minute or until melted.

Stir in the flour, then gradually blend in the fish stock, cream and anchovy essence. Cook on FULL (100%) for 2 minutes, stirring once.

Place the pieces of fish in a small bowl, cover and cook on FULL (100%) for 3 minutes, stirring once.

Meanwhile, beat the breadcrumbs into the sauce and then beat in the egg. Gently stir in the crab, prawns, lemon juice, oregano, the cooked fish and the fish liquid, and add salt and pepper to taste.

Spoon the mixture into a 750 ml/1½ pint soufflé dish. Cover and cook on FULL (100%) for 6 minutes, stirring after 2 and 4 minutes.

Remove the dish from the microwave oven and cover tightly with foil. Set aside to cool, then chill in the refrigerator for several hours until firm.

Loosen the edges of the dish and turn out the fish mould on to a serving dish. Garnish with fresh prawns, lemon slices and sprigs of parsley and serve with a mixed salad as a main course or by itself as a starter.
SERVES 4 to 6

SCAMPI PROVENÇALE

METRIC/IMPERIAL
25 g/1 oz butter
1 onion, chopped
1 clove garlic, chopped
1 × 400 g/14 oz can tomatoes, drained
5 tablespoons dry white wine
pinch of sugar
1 tablespoon chopped fresh parsley
salt
freshly ground black pepper
225 g/8 oz frozen scampi, thawed

Place the butter in a bowl and heat on FULL (100%) for ½ minute or until melted. Add the onion and garlic, blending well. Cover and cook

on FULL (100%) for 3 minutes, stirring once.

Add the tomatoes, wine, sugar, parsley, and salt and pepper to taste, blending well. Cover and cook on FULL (100%) for 3 minutes, stirring once.

Add the scampi, blending well. Cover and cook on FULL (100%) for 2 to 4 minutes, stirring once, until just cooked.

Serve hot with boiled rice and a crisp green salad.
SERVES 4

FISH FILLETS WITH ALMONDS

METRIC/IMPERIAL
1 kg/2 lb plaice fillets
25 g/1 oz button mushrooms, thinly sliced (optional)
1 onion, finely chopped
1 clove garlic, crushed
100 g/4 oz butter, cut into pieces
300 ml/½ pint dry white wine
300 ml/½ pint milk
50 g/2 oz plain flour
salt
freshly ground black pepper
1 tablespoon double cream
75 g/3 oz flaked almonds, lightly toasted

Roll up the fish fillets and secure with wooden cocktail sticks, if required. Set aside.

Place the mushrooms (if using), onion, garlic, half of the butter and the wine in a shallow dish. Cover and cook on FULL (100%) for 4 minutes or until the onion is tender, stirring halfway through cooking.

Place the fish rolls in the dish and baste with the wine sauce. Cover and cook on FULL (100%) for 9 minutes. Rearrange halfway through cooking. Drain off the liquid and reserve. Cover the fish and set aside.

Mix together the fish liquid and milk. Place the remaining butter in a large jug. Heat on FULL (100%) for 1 minute or until melted. Blend in the flour, then add the liquid, and salt and pepper to taste. Cook on FULL (100%) for 7 minutes or until thick. Stir after 4 minutes and every subsequent minute. Stir in the cream.

Arrange the fish rolls on a warm serving platter, removing the cocktail sticks, if used. Spoon over the sauce and scatter the almonds on top.
SERVES 4 to 6

WHITE FISH WITH CRISP TOPPING

METRIC/IMPERIAL
½ red pepper, seeded and finely chopped
25 g/1 oz butter
1 tablespoon frozen peas
450 g/1 lb sole fillets, skinned and flaked
salt
freshly ground black pepper
2 large, firm tomatoes, skinned and sliced
75 g/3 oz plain crisps, crushed

Place the pepper (reserving a little for garnish) and butter in a bowl. Cook on FULL (100%) for 1 minute. Add the peas, fish, salt and pepper to taste, and stir.

Arrange the tomato slices over the base of a serving dish. Season with a little salt and pepper. Spoon the fish mixture evenly over the tomatoes. Cover and cook on FULL (100%) for 4 minutes. Remove the cover and drain off any surplus liquid.

Sprinkle the crisps over the fish, and cook, uncovered, on FULL (100%) for 2 minutes. Serve immediately, garnished with the reserved pepper.
SERVES 4

FISH IN SOURED CREAM SAUCE

METRIC/IMPERIAL
4 whiting fillets (total weight about 450 g/1 lb)
50 g/2 oz butter
2 tablespoons milk
salt
freshly ground black pepper
½ red pepper, seeded and chopped
150 ml/¼ pint soured cream
50 g/2 oz peeled prawns
fresh dill, to garnish

Lay the fish fillets in a shallow dish, keeping the tails to the centre. Flake half the butter over the fish, add the milk and season with salt and pepper.

Cover and cook on FULL (100%) for 4 to 5 minutes, giving the dish a half-turn once during this time. Allow to STAND for 5 minutes.

Place the remaining butter and the pepper in a small jug and cook on FULL (100%) for ½ to 1 minute, depending on the size of the pepper, until barely tender. Stir in the soured cream and

prawns. Cook on LOW (30%) for 3 to 4 minutes, stirring once. Add the juices from the fish, blending well.

Arrange the fish on a serving dish, pour over the soured cream sauce and garnish with dill.
SERVES 2

RUSSIAN FISH BALLS

METRIC/IMPERIAL
1 × 675 g/1½ lb haddock fillet, skinned
1 large onion, peeled
1 large carrot, peeled
1¼ teaspoons salt
¾ teaspoon freshly ground black pepper
40 g/1½ oz fresh white breadcrumbs
40 g/1½ oz ground almonds
150 ml/¼ pint milk
150 ml/¼ pint water
2 bay leaves

Finely mince the fish with the onion and the carrot. Stir in the salt, pepper, breadcrumbs and almonds. Divide into 18 to 20 even-sized pieces and roll into balls.

Combine the milk, water and bay leaves in a large shallow dish and cook on FULL (100%) for 2½ minutes until boiling. Arrange the fish balls around the edge of the dish. Cook on LOW (30%) for 12 to 13 minutes, turning the fish balls over halfway through cooking. Discard the bay leaves.

Serve hot or cold, moistened with the cooking liquor, if liked.
SERVES 3 to 4

Note: The fish balls can be reheated successfully: leave in the liquid, cover loosely and cook on FULL (100%) for 5 minutes, giving the dish a half-turn after 2½ minutes.

SAVOURY PANCAKES

METRIC/IMPERIAL
1 small onion, finely chopped
25 g/1 oz butter
1 × 275 g/10 oz packet frozen rice, peas and mushrooms
75 ml/3 fl oz water
2 tablespoons wholegrain mustard
1 × 200 g/7 oz can tuna in brine, drained and flaked
150 ml/¼ pint whipping cream

salt
freshly ground black pepper
12 small (15 cm/6 inch) cooked pancakes
1 tablespoon chopped fresh parsley
3 tablespoons grated Cheddar cheese

Place the onion, butter, rice, peas and mushrooms and water in a small casserole dish. Cover and cook on FULL (100%) for 12 minutes, stirring once, until tender. Leave to STAND for 5 minutes.

Add the mustard, tuna, 2 tablespoons of the cream, and salt and pepper to taste, blending well. Divide the mixture between the pancakes, roll up and arrange in a shallow dish.

Stir the parsley into the remaining cream with salt and pepper to taste. Pour over the pancakes. Sprinkle with the cheese and cook on FULL (100%) for 5 minutes, turning the dish twice.

Serve hot with vegetables in season.
SERVES 4

SEAFOOD SUPPER

METRIC/IMPERIAL
4 plaice fillets, skinned
fish seasoning
lemon pepper
50 g/2 oz butter, cut into 4 pieces
2 teaspoons cornflour
150 ml/¼ pint milk
100 g/4 oz peeled prawns
150 ml/¼ pint soured cream
1 teaspoon lemon juice
1 teaspoon chopped fresh parsley
Garnish:
lemon twists
whole prawns
parsley sprigs

Sprinkle each plaice fillet with fish seasoning and lemon pepper to taste. Wrap each fillet around a piece of the butter and place in a cooking dish.

Blend the cornflour with 2 tablespoons of the milk. Pour the remaining milk over the fish, cover and cook on FULL (100%) for 7 minutes, turning the dish twice. Drain the milk from the fish and mix with the cornflour mixture, blending well. Cook on FULL (100%) for 1 minute, stirring once.

Add the prawns, soured cream, lemon juice and chopped parsley to the sauce, blending well.

Pour over the fish to coat. Cook on FULL (100%) for 1 minute.

Serve hot, garnished with lemon twists, whole prawns and parsley sprigs.
SERVES 4

SCALLOPS WITH VERMOUTH AND CREAM SAUCE

METRIC/IMPERIAL
450 g/1 lb potatoes, peeled and cut into 2.5 cm/
1 inch cubes
3 tablespoons water
salt
1 clove garlic, finely chopped
50 g/2 oz butter
25 g/1 oz plain flour
150 ml/¼ pint dry vermouth
1 egg yolk, lightly beaten
8 large scallops, cleaned and sliced
3 tablespoons double cream
freshly ground black pepper
1½ tablespoons tomato purée

Place the potatoes, water and salt in a medium bowl and cook on FULL (100%) for 8 minutes, stirring once. Cover and set aside.

Place the garlic and 25 g/1 oz of the butter in a medium bowl. Cover and cook on FULL (100%) for 1 minute or until the butter has melted. Stir in the flour and gradually add the vermouth and cook on FULL (100%) for 2 minutes. Beat in the egg yolk. Stir in the scallops and cream and add salt and pepper to taste. Cook on FULL (100%) for 2 minutes.

Rub the potatoes through a sieve and beat in the remaining butter and the tomato purée. Add salt and pepper to taste. Place the potato in a forcing bag fitted with a large star potato nozzle. Pipe around the edges of 4 scallop shells and spoon the sauce into the centre Cook on FULL (100%) for 2 minutes to reheat, if necessary.
SERVES 4

PRAWN VOL-AU-VENTS

METRIC/IMPERIAL
50 g/2 oz butter, cut into pieces
50 g/2 oz plain flour
450 ml/¾ pint milk
150 ml/¼ pint single cream

1 egg yolk
salt
freshly ground black pepper
100 g/4 oz peeled prawns
4 vol-au-vent cases, about 7.5 cm/3 inches in
diameter, cooked
Garnish:
4 whole prawns
4 parsley sprigs

Place the butter in a large jug and heat on FULL (100%) for 1 minute or until melted. Stir in the flour, then gradually stir in the milk and the cream. Cook on FULL (100%) for 5½ minutes or until thick, stirring every 1 minute.

Beat in the egg yolk and season to taste with salt and pepper. Stir in the prawns and cook on FULL (100%) for 1 minute. Keep warm.

Arrange the vol-au-vent cases in a circle on a paper towel. Heat on FULL (100%) for ½ minute. Using a sharp knife, remove the centre lid from each vol-au-vent case and retain. Scrape out the inside pastry and discard. Fill each case with the hot sauce and top with the pastry lids. Garnish each one with a whole prawn and a sprig of parsley and serve hot as a starter.
SERVES 4

SMOKED FISH PIE

METRIC/IMPERIAL
250 ml/8 fl oz skimmed milk
1 onion, sliced
1 bay leaf
5 black peppercorns
450 g/1 lb cod fillet, skinned
100 g/4 oz smoked cod fillet, skinned
1 tablespoon wholemeal flour
freshly ground black pepper
100 g/4 oz frozen sweetcorn kernels
2 tablespoons chopped fresh parsley
2 large potatoes, scrubbed and thinly sliced
2 tablespoons grated Parmesan cheese

Place the milk in a medium-sized bowl with the onion, bay leaf and peppercorns. Cook on FULL (100%) for 2 minutes. Leave to infuse for 10 minutes. Pour into a large shallow baking dish.

Place the fish in a single layer in the milk cover and cook on FULL (100%) for 3½ to 4 minutes. Transfer the fish to a plate with a slotted spoon, flake it roughly and reserve.

Blend the flour with a little of the cooking liquid and pour into the baking dish. Cook on

FULL (100%) for 1½ minutes, stirring well after 1 minute to prevent the formation of lumps. Add plenty of pepper to taste.

Stir in the reserved flaked fish, with the sweetcorn and parsley and top with the potato slices. Cover and cook on FULL (100%) for 9 minutes, or until the potatoes are tender. Allow to STAND, covered, for 5 minutes.

Before serving, sprinkle with the Parmesan cheese and brown under a conventional grill preheated to hot.
SERVES 4

CURRIED COD

METRIC/IMPERIAL
750 g/1½ lb cod fillets, skinned and cut into large
pieces
1 clove garlic, finely chopped
1 small cooking apple, peeled, cored and
chopped
1 small carrot, sliced
1 onion, finely chopped
65 g/2½ oz butter
1½ tablespoons plain flour
450 g/1 lb tomatoes, skinned and chopped
2 tablespoons tomato purée
50 ml/2 fl oz coconut cream
300 ml/½ pint hot fish stock
1 tablespoon lemon juice
½ teaspoon ground coriander
½ teaspoon ground turmeric
½ teaspoon ground mustard seeds
3 teaspoons mild curry powder
1 tablespoon chutney
40 g/1½ oz long-grain rice
1 tablespoon chopped fresh coriander, to garnish

Place the fish in a medium bowl, cover and cook on FULL (100%) for 4½ minutes. Set aside.

Place the garlic, apple, carrot, onion and butter in a large bowl. Cover and cook on FULL (100%) for 6 minutes. Stir in the flour. Gradually stir in the tomatoes, tomato purée, coconut cream, stock, lemon juice, coriander, turmeric, mustard, curry power, chutney and rice. Cover and cook on FULL (100%) for 13 minutes, stirring after 6½ minutes.

Add the fish and its cooking liquid, cover and cook on FULL (100%) for 5 minutes. Spoon the curry on to a warm serving dish, garnish with the fresh coriander and serve with sliced tomatoes, poppadoms and mango chutney.
SERVES 4

BEEF

STEAK AND KIDNEY PUDDING

METRIC/IMPERIAL
25 g/1 oz butter or margarine
25 g/1 oz flour
1 beef stock cube, crumbled
1 teaspoon salt
¼ teaspoon freshly ground black pepper
200 ml/⅓ pint hot water
225 g/8 oz ox kidney, trimmed and chopped
450 g/1 lb chuck steak, trimmed and finely
chopped or minced
2 onions, grated or puréed
parsley sprig, to garnish
Suet crust pastry:
225 g/8 oz plain flour
2 teaspoons baking powder
1 teaspoon salt
100 g/4 oz shredded suet
8–10 tablespoons cold water

Steak and kidney pudding is made more quickly in the microwave than in a conventional oven but the texture of the filling will be firmer than the traditional recipe.

Put the butter or margarine in a 2 litre/3½ pint bowl and heat on FULL (100%) for ½ minute or until it has just melted.

Stir in the flour, then add all the remaining filling ingredients. Stir thoroughly, then three-quarters cover and cook on FULL (100%) for 20 minutes, stirring every 5 minutes. Reduce the setting to LOW (30%) and cook for a further 20 minutes, stirring once during cooking.

Meanwhile prepare the suet pastry. Sift the flour, baking powder and salt into a mixing bowl. Stir in the suet and gently mix in sufficient cold water to form a soft but manageable dough.

Gather the dough into a ball with the hands and shape on a lightly floured work surface. Cut off one-quarter of the dough, cover with cling film and set aside.

Roll or press the remaining pastry into a circle and fit into a well-greased 1.2 litre/2 pint pudding basin, coaxing the pastry so that it reaches about 2.5 cm/1 inch above the rim of the basin. (If the filling is not yet cooked, cover the basin and pastry with cling film until needed.)

Spoon the filling into the basin, shape the reserved pastry quarter into a lid and lightly place on top of the meat. Dampen the edges of the protruding pastry and fold over the lid to form a seal.

Slit the pastry lid with a sharp knife, then cover the basin loosely with greaseproof paper and string so that there is plenty of room for the pudding to rise. Cook on LOW (30%) for 20 minutes, giving the dish a quarter-turn every 5 minutes. Release the greaseproof paper covering at one corner and leave the pudding to STAND for 10 minutes before turning out on to a hot dish. Garnish with the parsley.
SERVES 4

BEEF AND APRICOT CURRY

METRIC/IMPERIAL
25 g/1 oz butter
1 large onion, chopped
1 clove garlic, crushed
1 tablespoon plain flour
2 tablespoons curry powder
1 × 400 g/14 oz can stewed steak in gravy
1 × 275 g/10 oz can apricots in their juice

Place the butter in a casserole dish and heat on FULL (100%) for ½ minute or until melted. Add the onion and garlic, cover and cook on FULL (100%) for 2 minutes.

Stir in the flour and curry powder and cook on FULL (100%) for ½ minute. Add the stewed steak and juice from the apricots, blending well. Cover and cook on FULL (100%) for 3½ minutes, stirring once.

Add the apricots, blending well. Cover and cook on FULL (100%) for a further ½ minute. Serve hot with boiled rice.
SERVES 4

GARLIC ROAST BEEF

METRIC/IMPERIAL
1.5 kg/3 lb topside of beef
vegetable oil for coating
3 cloves garlic, peeled
salt
freshly ground black pepper

Rub the beef with the oil, 1 clove of garlic and salt and pepper. Stand on an upturned saucer in a shallow container and cook on FULL (100%) for 10 minutes.

With a sharp knife, cut the remaining garlic cloves into slivers. Make incisions in the meat and insert the slivers of garlic.

Cook on FULL (100%) for 10 minutes, then remove the meat and wrap tightly in foil, with the shiny side inside. Leave the meat to STAND for 20 minutes. Brown under a preheated conventional grill before carving.
SERVES 4

CHILLI CON CARNE

METRIC/IMPERIAL
1 onion, chopped
2 streaky bacon rashers, derinded and chopped
450 g/1 lb minced lean beef
1 tablespoon chilli powder
1 beef stock cube, crumbled
50 g/2 oz mushrooms, chopped
1 teaspoon chopped fresh parsley
1 tablespoon chutney
1 × 200 g/7 oz can kidney beans, drained
2 tablespoons tomato purée
salt
freshly ground black pepper
chopped fresh parsley, to garnish

Preheat a large browning dish on FULL (100%) for 5 minutes (or according to the manufacturer's instructions).

Put the onion and bacon in the dish, cover and cook on FULL (100%) for 1 minute. Add the beef and stir. Cook on FULL (100%) for 3 minutes.

Add all the remaining ingredients and stir well. Cover and cook on MEDIUM (50%) for 25 minutes. Garnish with a little chopped parsley, and serve with a green salad and French bread, rice or jacket potatoes.
SERVES 3 to 4

STROGANOFF SUPERB

METRIC/IMPERIAL
40 g/1½ oz butter
450 g/1 lb beef topside, cut into thin strips
1 small onion, chopped
100 g/4 oz mushrooms, sliced
¼ teaspoon mustard powder
salt
freshly ground black pepper
150 ml/¼ pint soured cream
4 tablespoons milk

Place the butter in a cooking dish and heat on FULL (100%) for 1 minute or until melted. Stir in the beef and cook on FULL (100%) for 10 minutes, stirring twice.

Add the onion, mushrooms, mustard, and salt and pepper to taste, blending well. Cook on FULL (100%) for 4 minutes, stirring once.

Add the soured cream and milk, blending well. Cook on FULL (100%) for a further 4 minutes, stirring once.

Serve hot with noodles and a green salad.
SERVES 4

STIR-FRIED BEEF WITH GREEN PEPPERS

METRIC/IMPERIAL
75 g/3 oz rump steak, thinly sliced
½ teaspoon salt
½ teaspoon caster sugar
1 teaspoon dry sherry
1 teaspoon cornflour
dash of chilli sauce
freshly ground black pepper
1 tablespoon vegetable oil
1 small green pepper, cored, seeded and thinly sliced
1 small tomato, cut into wedges
1 spring onion, chopped
pinch of ground ginger
1 teaspoon soy sauce

Place the steak in a bowl with half of the salt, the sugar, sherry, cornflour, chilli sauce and pepper to taste. Mix well and leave to marinate for about 20 minutes.

Preheat a small browning dish on FULL (100%) for 3 minutes (or according to the manufacturer's instructions). Add the oil and heat on FULL (100%) for 1 minute. Add the green pepper, tomato, spring onion, ginger and remaining salt. Cook on FULL (100%) for 1 minute, stirring once. Remove from the dish with a slotted spoon.

Add the steak mixture and cook on FULL (100%) for 1½ minutes, stirring once. Add the green pepper mixture and soy sauce. Cook for a further 1 minute, stirring once.

Serve at once straight from the dish.
SERVES 1

BEEF AND BACON MEATLOAF

METRIC/IMPERIAL
450 g/1 lb minced lean beef
225 g/8 oz lean bacon, derinded and chopped
50 g/2 oz fresh breadcrumbs
1 onion, finely chopped
1 teaspoon dried parsley
1 teaspoon dry mustard
1 tablespoon tomato sauce
1 beef stock cube, crumbled
salt
freshly ground black pepper
2 teaspoons dried peppers
1 large egg, beaten
1 tablespoon tomato sauce, mixed with 1 teaspoon yeast extract, to glaze
Garnish:
parsley sprig
red pepper

Place the beef and bacon in a bowl and work together to combine. Add all the remaining ingredients, except the egg, glaze and garnish, and stir well to combine.

Add the egg and mix well. Press the mixture evenly into a 23 × 13 × 10 cm/9 × 5 × 4 inch loaf dish. Cook on MEDIUM (50%) for 15 minutes, turning twice during cooking. STAND, covered loosely with foil, for 5 minutes.

Turn out and brush the glaze over the surface to add colour. Garnish with parsley and red pepper.
SERVES 6

Variation
Slice 50 g/2 oz cheese thinly and arrange over the surface of the cooked loaf, after the standing time. Return to the oven and cook on FULL (100%) for 1½ minutes until the cheese has melted. Serve immediately.

BEEF AND WALNUT CASSEROLE

METRIC/IMPERIAL
25 g/1 oz butter
2 tablespoons flour
675 g/1½ lb chuck steak, cut into 2.5 cm/1 inch cubes
1 onion, finely chopped
4 celery sticks, thinly sliced
100 g/4 oz shelled walnuts, chopped
300 ml/½ pint hot water
1 beef stock cube, crumbled
300 ml/½ pint brown ale
1 teaspoon salt
freshly ground black pepper

Put the butter in a large deep dish and heat on FULL (100%) for ½ minute to melt. Blend in the flour and cook on FULL (100%) for 5 minutes or until just turning colour.

Add the meat, onion, celery and walnuts. Stir in the water and stock cube. Cover and cook on LOW (30%) for 30 minutes, stirring occasionally.

Add the brown ale and salt and pepper to taste. Cover and cook on LOW (30%) for 20 to 30 minutes, stirring occasionally, then cook on FULL (100%) for 15 minutes. Leave to STAND, covered, for 10 minutes before serving.
SERVES 4

COUNTRY CASSEROLE

METRIC/IMPERIAL
2 large leeks, cut into 1 cm/½ inch slices
1 turnip, chopped
1 carrot, sliced
1 celery stick, chopped
450 g/1 lb minced lean beef
1 teaspoon dried mixed herbs
1 tablespoon tomato purée
300 ml/½ pint hot beef stock
salt
freshly ground black pepper

Place the leeks, turnip, carrot and celery in a casserole dish. Cover and cook on FULL (100%) for 10 minutes, stirring once.

Stir in the beef, herbs, tomato purée, stock and salt and pepper to taste, blending well. Cover and cook on FULL (100%) for 7 minutes, stirring twice. Serve hot.
SERVES 4

STUFFED BEEF ROLL

METRIC/IMPERIAL
450 g/1 lb minced lean beef
2 teaspoons Worcestershire sauce
1 teaspoon salt
½ teaspoon freshly ground black pepper
1 egg, beaten
1–2 tablespoons flour
4 tablespoons sage and onion stuffing mix
about 8 tablespoons water
1 teaspoon gravy powder

Mix the beef, Worcestershire sauce, salt, pepper and egg together. Roll out on a floured surface to a rectangle about 15 × 20 cm/6 × 8 inches.

Make up the stuffing according to the directions on the packet, and bind the mixture with the water. Form into a sausage shape, the same width as the meat, and place along one edge. Roll up, enclosing the stuffing, and press the edges of the meat together to seal.

Transfer the meat roll to a shallow dish into which it fits snugly. Sprinkle with the gravy powder and cook on FULL (100%) for 10 minutes, turning the meat over halfway through cooking. Leave to STAND, covered, for 5 minutes before serving.
SERVES 3 to 4

BEEF AND BACON CRUMBLE

METRIC/IMPERIAL
4 lean bacon rashers, derinded and finely chopped
450 g/1 lb minced lean beef
1 beef stock cube, crumbled
150 ml/¼ pint hot water
1 teaspoon turmeric
1 teaspoon cornflour
150 ml/¼ pint cold water
Topping:
175 g/6 oz self-raising flour
pinch of salt
1 teaspoon baking powder
75 g/3 oz butter

Put the bacon into a large shallow dish. Cook on FULL (100%) for 4 minutes, stirring occasionally.

Add the beef and cook on FULL (100%) for 5 minutes, breaking up the meat with a fork halfway through cooking.

Add the crumbled stock cube to the hot water and stir in the turmeric. Pour over the meat and stir well. Blend the cornflour with the cold water and stir into the meat mixture. Cover and cook on FULL (100%) for 2 minutes, stirring twice.

To prepare the topping, sift the flour, salt and baking powder into a mixing bowl. Rub in the butter until the mixture resembles coarse breadcrumbs.

Uncover the meat, stir, then spread the crumble evenly on top. Cook on FULL (100%) for 8 minutes, giving the dish a half-turn after 4 minutes. Place under a preheated grill to brown the top before serving.
SERVES 4 to 6

MEATLOAF WITH MUSHROOM TOPPING

METRIC/IMPERIAL
450 g/1 lb minced lean beef
75 g/3 oz fresh wholemeal breadcrumbs
1 onion, finely chopped
1 teaspoon dried parsley
1 beef stock cube, crumbled
1 tablespoon tomato purée
1 egg, lightly beaten
Topping:
25 g/1 oz butter
75 g/3 oz mushrooms, sliced
2 spring onions, chopped
3 tablespoons double cream
1 tablespoon lemon juice

Mix the beef with the breadcrumbs, onion, parsley, crumbled stock cube, tomato purée and egg, blending well. Place in a 450 g/1 lb loaf dish and cook on FULL (100%) for 7 minutes, turning the dish twice.

Cover with foil, shiny side inside, and leave to STAND for 5 minutes.

Meanwhile, make the topping. Place the butter in a bowl and heat on FULL (100%) for ½ minute or until melted. Add the mushrooms and spring onions. Cover and cook on FULL (100%) for 3 minutes.

Stir in the cream and lemon juice and cook on FULL (100%) for ½ to 1 minute until hot and thickened.

To serve, invert the meatloaf on to a warmed serving dish and spoon over the mushroom topping. Cut into slices to serve.
SERVES 4

BEEF OLIVES

METRIC/IMPERIAL
50 g/2 oz mushrooms, trimmed
1 onion, quartered
1 tablespoon orange juice
3 tablespoons beef stock
grated rind of 1 lemon
½ teaspoon dried mixed herbs
salt
freshly ground black pepper
25 g/1 oz fresh white breadcrumbs
450 g/1 lb topside of beef, cut into 4 thin slices
and lightly beaten
½ green pepper, cored, seeded and chopped
100 g/4 oz mushrooms, chopped
40 g/1½ oz butter, diced
2 tablespoons plain flour
150 ml/¼ pint white wine
1 teaspoon soy sauce

Purée the whole mushrooms, onion, orange juice, stock, lemon rind, herbs, and salt and pepper to taste in a blender or food processor. Stir in the breadcrumbs.

Divide the mixture between the slices of beef and roll up. Secure with string. Cook on FULL (100%) for 6 minutes, turning over halfway through. Set aside, covered.

Place the green pepper and chopped mushrooms in a large jug. Cover and cook on FULL (100%) for 4 minutes. Stir in the butter until melted. Stir in the flour, wine, soy sauce and meat juices. Season with salt and pepper, and pour over the beef. Cook on FULL (100%) for a further 3 minutes.
SERVES 4

FILLET OF BEEF WITH MUSHROOMS AND CREAM SAUCE

METRIC/IMPERIAL
450 g/1 lb fillet steak
2 tablespoons vegetable oil
25 g/1 oz butter
1 small onion, chopped
2 tablespoons flour
225 g/8 oz button mushrooms, trimmed
150 ml/¼ pint medium dry white wine
150 ml/¼ pint condensed beef consommé
5 tablespoons water
1 teaspoon lemon thyme

1 teaspoon salt
¼ teaspoon freshly ground black pepper
1 teaspoon paprika
½ teaspoon sugar
3 tablespoons double cream
Garnish:
lemon thyme sprigs
Pommes Parisiennes (see page 195)

Slice the fillet steak thinly and brush with the oil.

Combine the butter and onion in a large shallow dish and cook on FULL (100%) for 4 to 5 minutes until the onion begins to brown. Stir in the mushrooms and cook on FULL (100%) for 3 minutes, stirring once.

Sprinkle the flour over the mushrooms, turning them with a spoon to coat evenly. Stir in the wine, consommé, water, thyme, salt, pepper, paprika and sugar. Cook on FULL (100%) for 7 minutes, stirring twice. Stir in the cream, cover and set aside.

Preheat a large browning dish on FULL (100%) for 5 minutes (or according to the manufacturer's instructions). Add the steak and toss quickly. Cook on FULL (100%) for 3 to 4 minutes, stirring occasionally.

Add the steak to the sauce, stir well, and cook on LOW (30%) for 2 to 3 minutes until thoroughly reheated. Transfer to a large serving platter and garnish with sprigs of lemon thyme and clusters of potato balls.
SERVES 4

BEEF IN GINGER WINE

METRIC/IMPERIAL
1 kg/2 lb lean braising steak, cut into large cubes
50 g/2 oz seasoned flour
2 tablespoons vegetable oil
6 carrots, cut into thick strips
5 celery sticks, cut into thick strips
1 bunch watercress, coarsely chopped
salt
freshly ground black pepper
300 ml/½ pint ginger wine
1–2 teaspoons cornflour (optional)
watercress sprigs, to garnish

Preheat a large browning dish on FULL (100%) for 5 minutes (or according to the manufacturer's instructions).

Brush the dish with oil and cook on FULL (100%) for 1 minute. Toss the beef in the seasoned flour, then add to the dish, turning

112

quickly on all sides to brown evenly. Cook on FULL (100%) for 5 minutes, stirring once.

Place the vegetables in a large casserole. Sprinkle with salt and pepper. Add the meat and pour over the ginger wine. Cover and cook on FULL (100%) for 10 minutes.

Reduce the setting to MEDIUM (50%) and cook for 40 to 50 minutes, stirring once, until fork-tender.

Thicken with the cornflour dissolved in a little water, if using. Leave to STAND for 5 minutes. Serve garnished with watercress.

SERVES 4

ROAST BEEF WITH ONION RICE

METRIC/IMPERIAL
25 g/1 oz butter
2 cloves garlic, crushed
freshly ground black pepper
1 × 1.6 kg/3½ lb boned and rolled rib of beef
2 onions, sliced
2 tablespoons vegetable oil
350 g/12 oz long-grain rice
900 ml/1½ pints boiling beef stock

Place the butter in a bowl and cook on FULL (100%) for ½ minute or until melted. Add the garlic and pepper to taste, blending well. Brush the beef with the garlic butter and place on a roasting rack set in a shallow dish. Cook on FULL (100%) for 12 to 13 minutes, turning the dish twice.

Turn the beef over and brush with any remaining garlic butter. Cover with greaseproof paper and cook on FULL (100%) for a further 12 to 14 minutes, turning the dish twice. Wrap the beef in foil, shiny side inside, and leave to STAND while preparing the onion rice.

Place the onion, oil and rice in a bowl, blending well. Cook on FULL (100%) for 2 to 3 minutes, stirring once. Add the boiling stock, cover and cook on FULL (100%) for 3 minutes. Reduce the power setting to MEDIUM (50%) and cook for a further 12 minutes, stirring twice. Leave to STAND, covered, for 5 minutes.

Serve the beef carved into thin slices with the onion rice.

SERVES 6

BEEF HOT POT WITH DUMPLINGS

METRIC/IMPERIAL
450 g/1 lb beef skirt, cut into 2.5 cm/1 inch cubes
1½ tablespoons seasoned flour
2 onions, sliced
225 g/8 oz carrots, sliced
2 celery sticks, sliced
600 ml/1 pint beef stock
Dumplings:
225 g/8 oz plain flour
1 teaspoon salt
2½ teaspoons baking powder
100 g/4 oz shredded suet
7 tablespoons water

Toss the beef in the flour to coat. Place in a casserole dish with the onions, carrots, celery and stock. Cover and cook on FULL (100%) for 25 minutes, stirring three times.

Meanwhile, to make the dumplings, sift the flour into a bowl with the salt and baking powder. Add the suet, blending well. Stir in the water to make a fairly stiff dough. Divide and shape into 12 dumplings.

Add the dumplings to the hot pot, cover and cook on FULL (100%) for 7 minutes, turning the dish twice. Leave to STAND, covered, for 5 minutes.

Serve hot with green vegetables.

SERVES 4

PEPPERED STEAKS WITH MADEIRA

METRIC/IMPERIAL
50 g/2 oz butter
1 clove garlic, crushed
2 large onions, sliced
1 green pepper, cored, seeded and sliced
1 red pepper, cored, seeded and sliced
5 tablespoons Madeira
salt
2 teaspoons Marmite
4 × 175 g/6 oz rump steaks
20 black peppercorns, crushed
watercress, to garnish

Place the butter in an oblong dish and heat on FULL (100%) for 1½ to 2 minutes or until melted. Add the garlic, onions and green and red pepper. Toss well, cover and cook on FULL (100%) for 4 minutes.

113

Stir the vegetables and add 4 tablespoons of the Madeira. Season lightly with salt, cover and cook on FULL (100%) for 4 minutes.

Mix the Marmite with the remaining Madeira and brush the steaks on both sides with this mixture. Place them on the bed of vegetables and sprinkle the crushed peppercorns over the top. Return to the oven and cook on FULL (100%) for 3¼ minutes, turning and rearranging the steaks once during cooking. (If the steaks are not cooked to your liking after 3¼ minutes, cook for a little longer.) Garnish with watercress before serving.
SERVES 4

BEEF AND TOMATO CASSEROLE

METRIC/IMPERIAL
25 g/1 oz butter
1 large onion, sliced
2 tablespoons flour
100 g/4 oz tomato purée
300 ml/½ pint hot beef stock
1 tablespoon paprika
450 g/1 lb good-quality topside, cut into 2.5 cm/
1 inch cubes
225 g/8 oz tomatoes, skinned and chopped
salt
freshly ground black pepper

Place the butter in a casserole and heat on FULL (100%) for ½ minute or until melted. Add the onion and cook on FULL (100%) for 4 minutes. Stir in the flour and gradually add the tomato purée, stock and paprika. Add the meat, stir well, and cook on FULL (100%) for 15 minutes, stirring every 5 minutes.

Stir in the tomatoes, cover and leave to STAND for 10 minutes. Add salt and pepper to taste before serving.
SERVES 4

SLIMMER'S CHILLI CON CARNE

METRIC/IMPERIAL
75 g/3 oz minced lean beef
1 small onion, chopped
½ green pepper, cored, seeded and chopped
100 g/4 oz canned tomatoes with their juice
5 tablespoons tomato juice
½–1 teaspoon chilli powder

¾ teaspoon vinegar
2 teaspoons tomato purée
salt
freshly ground black pepper
75 g/3 oz cooked red kidney beans
2 bran crispbreads

Place the beef, onion and pepper in a small casserole dish. Cover and cook on FULL (100%) for 5 minutes, stirring twice to break up the meat.

Add the tomatoes, tomato juice, chilli powder, vinegar, tomato purée and salt and pepper to taste, blending well. Cover and cook on FULL (100%) for 5 minutes, stirring once.

Stir in the kidney beans and leave to STAND, covered, for 5 minutes before serving. Serve hot with the crispbreads.
SERVES 1

FILLET STEAK IN RED WINE SAUCE

METRIC/IMPERIAL
4 × 175 g/6 oz fillet steaks
25 g/1 oz butter
2 teaspoons Worcestershire sauce
Sauce:
1 small onion, chopped
2 tablespoons vegetable oil
1 tablespoon flour
5 tablespoons canned beef consommé
5 tablespoons water
150 ml/¼ pint red wine
1 tablespoon brandy

Spread the steaks with butter and brush with the Worcestershire sauce. Cover and set aside.

To prepare the sauce, combine the onion and oil in a large shallow dish and cook on FULL (100%) for 3 to 4 minutes until the onion is lightly browned. Stir in the flour and cook on FULL (100%) for 2 minutes, stirring once. Gradually stir in the consommé, water, wine and brandy and cook on FULL (100%) for 3 minutes, stirring occasionally. Cover and set aside.

Preheat a large browning dish on FULL (100%) for 5 minutes (or according to the manufacturer's instructions). Quickly add two steaks, turning them over almost immediately. Cook on FULL (100%) for 2 minutes, then turn the steaks over and cook on FULL (100%) for 2 to 3 minutes until cooked according to taste. Add to the sauce.

Wipe the browning dish with absorbent kitchen paper. Reheat on FULL (100%) for 4 minutes. Cook the remaining steaks as above. Add to the sauce and cook on FULL (100%) for 3 minutes to reheat. Serve immediately.
SERVES 4

Note: Alternatively, cook the steaks simultaneously: cook on FULL (100%) for 6 to 10 minutes, until cooked according to taste. This method will not give the same crisp browned finish to the steaks.

BEEF KEBAB

METRIC/IMPERIAL
100 g/4 oz rump steak, cut into cubes
100 g/4 oz mushrooms, trimmed
2 tablespoons lemon juice
1 tablespoon chopped fresh parsley
1 small clove garlic, crushed (optional)
freshly ground black pepper
2 small tomatoes
½ green pepper, cored, seeded and cut into large pieces
sunflower oil for brushing

Place the steak, mushrooms, lemon juice, parsley, garlic, if using, and pepper to taste in a bowl. Mix well, cover and leave to marinate for 2 hours.

Thread the meat and mushrooms on to a long wooden skewer with the tomatoes and green pepper. Brush very lightly with sunflower oil.

Preheat a small browning dish on FULL (100%) for 3 minutes (or according to the manufacturer's instructions). Add the kebab and cook on FULL (100%) for 1 minute. Turn over and cook on FULL (100%) for a further ½ minute. Serve at once.
SERVES 1

BEEF AND VEGETABLE CASSEROLE

METRIC/IMPERIAL
4 tablespoons vegetable oil
25 g/1 oz flour
575 g/1¼ lb chuck steak, cut into 2 cm/¾ inch cubes
350 ml/12 fl oz hot beef stock
1 × 400 g/14 oz can tomatoes
225 g/8 oz carrots, thinly sliced

225 g/8 oz onions, thinly sliced
1 clove garlic, crushed
1 bay leaf
1 teaspoon salt
½ teaspoon freshly ground black pepper

Blend the oil and flour in a large deep dish and cook on FULL (100%) for 5 minutes, stirring twice, until just turning colour. Add the meat all at once and stir. Cook on FULL (100%) for 5 minutes, stirring after 2 minutes.

Add all the remaining ingredients. Cover and cook on FULL (100%) for 35 minutes, stirring occasionally during cooking and scraping away any gravy sticking to the sides of the dish.

Leave to STAND, covered, for 15 minutes before serving.
SERVES 4

MEATBALLS IN MUSHROOM AND TOMATO SAUCE

METRIC/IMPERIAL
450 g/1 lb minced lean beef
25 g/1 oz fresh brown breadcrumbs
1 onion, grated
1 teaspoon dried mixed herbs
1 tablespoon tomato purée
salt
freshly ground black pepper
1 egg
Sauce:
40 g/1½ oz butter
100 g/4 oz mushrooms, finely chopped
350 g/12 oz tomatoes, skinned and chopped
1 tablespoon tomato purée
40 g/1½ oz plain flour
450 ml/¾ pint hot beef stock
salt
freshly ground black pepper

Mix the beef, breadcrumbs, onion, herbs, tomato purée, salt and pepper together. Add the egg and mix well. Form the mixture into 16 balls.

Place the meatballs on a plate and cook on FULL (100%) for 2 minutes. Turn the meatballs over, rearrange and turn the plate round. Cook on FULL (100%) for a further 2 minutes.

To make the sauce, place the butter, mushrooms, tomatoes and tomato purée in a medium bowl. Cover and cook on FULL (100%) for

5 minutes. Stir in the flour, then gradually add the hot stock. Cook on FULL (100%) for a further 2 minutes, stirring twice. Cool slightly, then pour into a blender or food processor and blend until smooth. Stir in the salt and pepper to taste.

Place the meatballs in a bowl and pour over the sauce. Cook on FULL (100%) for a further 5 minutes. Serve with noodles and Parmesan cheese.
SERVES 4

HUNGARIAN GOULASH

METRIC/IMPERIAL
25 g/1 oz butter
450 g/1 lb chuck steak, cut into bite-sized pieces
1 large onion, chopped
1 clove garlic, crushed
3 teaspoons paprika
½ teaspoon sugar
pinch of caraway seeds
1 × 225 g/8 oz can tomatoes
2 tablespoons natural yogurt or soured cream
salt

Place the butter in a casserole dish and heat on FULL (100%) for ½ minute or until melted. Add the steak, onion and garlic, blending well. Cover and cook on MEDIUM (50%) for 15 minutes, stirring once.

Add the paprika, sugar, caraway seeds and tomatoes with their juice, blending well. Cover and cook on MEDIUM (50%) for a further 15 minutes.

Add the yogurt or soured cream and salt to taste, blending well. Leave to STAND, covered, for 5 minutes before serving.
SERVES 4

STEAK, KIDNEY AND OYSTER PUDDING

METRIC/IMPERIAL
450 g/1 lb braising steak, cut into 2.5 cm/1 inch cubes
150 ml/¼ pint red wine
1 onion, chopped
1 teaspoon dried mixed herbs
25 g/1 oz plain flour
salt
freshly ground black pepper
175 g/6 oz ox kidney, skinned, cored and chopped

6–8 oysters, fresh or canned
paprika, to garnish
Suet crust pastry:
225 g/8 oz self-raising flour
pinch of salt
100 g/4 oz shredded suet
150–200 ml/5–7 fl oz cold water

Place the steak in a shallow bowl. Pour over the wine and marinate for 24 hours, stirring the mixture occasionally. Drain the wine from the meat and reserve to serve as gravy, if wished.

Place the onion and the mixed herbs in a large bowl. Cover and cook on FULL (100%) for 4 minutes, stirring once. Stir in the meat and cook on FULL (100%) for a further 3 minutes, stirring once.

Stir in the flour and add salt and pepper to taste. Cover and cook on FULL (100%) for 10 minutes, stirring after 5 minutes. Stir in the kidney and reduce the power setting to LOW (30%). Cover and cook for 40 minutes or until the meat is tender. Stir in the oysters.

To make the suet crust pastry, mix together the flour, salt and suet. Add enough water to make a dough. Roll out two-thirds of the dough and use to line a greased 1.2 litre/2 pint pudding basin. Roll out the remainder to make a lid.

Spoon the meat and gravy into the lined basin. Dampen the pastry edges with water and seal on the pastry lid. Cover loosely and cook on FULL (100%) for 9 minutes or until tender.

Remove the cover. Wrap a napkin around the basin, garnish with paprika and serve immediately with boiled potatoes and buttered cabbage.
SERVES 4

Note: It is most important that this pudding is served freshly made as it tends to harden on cooling.

STEAK AU POIVRE

METRIC/IMPERIAL
2 × 225 g/8 oz thick sirloin steaks
20 g/¾ oz butter
1 tablespoon crushed black peppercorns
1 tablespoon brandy
2 tablespoons double cream
salt

Preheat a large browning dish on FULL (100%) for 5 minutes (or according to the manufacturer's instructions).

116

Dry the steaks with absorbent kitchen paper and smear with the butter. Press the peppercorns into the steaks on both sides.

Add the steaks to the browning dish, pressing down well. Cook on FULL (100%) for 1 minute for a rare to medium steak, or 2 minutes for a medium to well-done steak. Turn over and cook for a further 1 minute for a rare to medium steak, or 2 minutes for a medium to well-done steak. Remove from the dish and place on warmed serving plates.

Add the brandy to the dish and cook on FULL (100%) for ½ minute. Stir in tne cream and salt to taste, blending well. Cook for a further ¾ minute.

Pour over the steaks to serve. Serve at once.
SERVES 2

MEXICAN BEEF

METRIC/IMPERIAL
1 medium onion, sliced
1 small carrot, sliced
1 green pepper, cored, seeded and chopped
1 red pepper, cored, seeded and chopped
1 medium potato, peeled and diced
50 g/2 oz butter, cut into pieces
1 teaspoon dried mixed herbs
½ teaspoon chilli powder
½ teaspoon Worcestershire sauce
1 teaspoon dried parsley
1 clove garlic, crushed
575 g/1¼ lb topside of beef, cut into 7.5 × 1 cm/
3 × ½ inch strips
salt
freshly ground black pepper
2 tablespoons plain flour
1 × 400 g/14 oz can tomatoes, chopped with their juice
150 ml/¼ pint hot beef stock

Place the onion, carrot, peppers and potato in a large bowl. Cover and cook on FULL (100%) for 6½ minutes.

Stir in the butter until melted. Stir in the herbs, chilli powder, Worcestershire sauce, parsley, garlic, beef and salt and pepper to taste. Cover and cook on FULL (100%) for 4 minutes, stirring halfway through cooking.

Stir in the flour, tomatoes with their juice, and stock. Cover and cook on FULL (100%) for 5 minutes, stirring halfway through cooking. Leave to STAND, covered, for 5 minutes.
SERVES 4

BEEF AND DRY VEGETABLE CURRY

METRIC/IMPERIAL
4 × 50 g/2 oz frozen beefburgers
225 g/8 oz carrots, thinly sliced
100 g/4 oz French beans, trimmed
2 onions, thinly sliced
6–8 cauliflower florets
1 teaspoon salt
3 tablespoons tomato purée
2 tablespoons curry paste

Arrange the frozen beefburgers on a double thickness of absorbent kitchen paper and cook on FULL (100%) for 4 minutes, giving the paper a half-turn after 2 minutes. Cut into cubes and combine with all the remaining ingredients in a large deep dish.

Cover tightly and cook on FULL (100%) for 10 to 12 minutes, stirring occasionally, adding a little water during cooking if the curry seems too dry. Serve hot.
SERVES 4

Note: Fresh or frozen vegetables are equally suitable for this dish.

SIZZLING BEEF STEAKS WITH TOMATO SAUCE

METRIC/IMPERIAL
4 thin slices blade steak
25 g/1 oz seasoned flour
1 tablespoon vegetable oil
Tomato sauce:
25 g/1 oz butter
1 onion, sliced
1 small clove garlic, crushed
6 tomatoes, skinned, seeded and chopped
¼ teaspoon dried thyme or ½ teaspoon chopped fresh thyme
150 ml/¼ pint beef stock
salt
freshly ground black pepper
Garnish:
thyme sprigs

Place the blade steaks between sheets of cling film and beat with a rolling pin until paper-thin. Coat in the seasoned flour.

Meanwhile, prepare the sauce by placing the butter in a bowl. Heat on FULL (100%) for ½ minute or until melted. Add the onion and garlic;

cover and cook on FULL (100%) for 3 minutes.

Add the tomatoes, thyme, stock and salt and pepper to taste, blending well. Cover and cook on FULL (100%) for 3 minutes, stirring once.

Preheat a large browning dish on FULL (100%) for 5 minutes (or according to the manufacturer's instructions). Brush with the oil and cook on FULL (100%) for a further 1 minute. Add the steaks and turn quickly on all sides to brown evenly.

Spoon over the sauce and cook on FULL (100%) for 3 to 4 minutes. Garnish with thyme and serve with boiled rice.

SERVES 4

TOURNEDOS PROVENÇALE
METRIC/IMPERIAL
1 onion, chopped
25 g/1 oz button mushrooms, trimmed
2 cloves garlic, crushed
2 teaspoons mixed dried herbs
25 g/1 oz butter, cut into pieces
25 g/1 oz plain flour
1 tablespoon tomato purée
150 ml/¼ pint tomato juice
150 ml/¼ pint hot beef stock
½ teaspoon sugar
salt
freshly ground black pepper
4 fillet steaks, 2.5 cm/1 inch thick and 9–10 cm/
3½–4 inches wide (total weight 575 g/1¼ lb)
fresh chervil, to garnish

Place the onion, mushrooms, garlic and dried herbs in a large jug. Cover and cook on FULL (100%) for 3 minutes, stirring once.

Stir in the butter until melted, then stir in the flour, tomato purée and juice, the hot stock, sugar and salt and pepper to taste. Cook on FULL (100%) for 4 minutes, stirring every 1 minute. Keep warm.

Place the steaks in a shallow dish and cook on FULL (100%) for 5 minutes, turning over and rearranging once. Pour the cooking juices into the sauce.

Arrange the steaks on a warm serving platter, pour over the sauce and garnish with the fresh chervil. Serve immediately with baby Brussels sprouts and sauté potatoes.

SERVES 4

BOEUF EN DAUBE
METRIC/IMPERIAL
675 g/1½ lb lean stewing steak, cut into 2.5 cm/
1 inch cubes
100 g/4 oz unsmoked streaky bacon, cut into
small pieces
450 ml/¾ pint red wine
450 g/1 lb carrots, sliced
450 g/1 lb onions, sliced
2 cloves garlic, crushed
25 g/1 oz butter
1 bouquet garni
2 tablespoons tomato purée
1 tablespoon chopped fresh parsley
salt
freshly ground black pepper
20 g/¾ oz cornflour
4 tablespoons single cream or milk
chopped fresh parsley, to garnish

Place the steak, bacon, wine, carrots, onions and garlic in a large bowl and leave to marinate for 3 to 4 hours, stirring occasionally.

Cover and cook on FULL (100%) for 20 minutes, stirring once. Stir in the butter, bouquet garni, tomato purée, parsley and salt and pepper to taste.

Reduce the power setting to LOW (30%), then cover and cook for 1 hour or until the meat is tender, stirring occasionally. Remove the bouquet garni and spoon the meat and vegetables on to a warm serving dish. Keep warm.

Blend the cornflour and cream or milk together to make a smooth paste and stir into the cooking liquid. Cook on FULL (100%) for 3 minutes, stirring every 1 minute. Check and adjust the seasoning, if necessary.

Spoon the sauce over the meat and garnish with chopped parsley. Serve with green beans and boiled potatoes or rice.

SERVES 4

BEEF MOUSSAKA
METRIC/IMPERIAL
450 g/1 lb potatoes, cut into even-sized pieces
2 onions, chopped
2 tablespoons vegetable oil
½ teaspoon garlic powder
450 g/1 lb minced lean beef
1 × 150 g/5 oz can tomato purée
1 teaspoon salt
½ teaspoon freshly ground black pepper

1 teaspoon dried oregano
1 tablespoon chopped fresh parsley
2 aubergines, sliced and par-boiled (optional)
2 eggs
5 tablespoons soured cream
5 tablespoons milk
4 tablespoons grated Parmesan cheese
50 g/2 oz Cheddar cheese, grated

Put the potatoes into a large roasting bag and lay flat on the oven base or turntable, tucking the open end loosely underneath. Cook on FULL (100%) for 10 minutes, shaking the bag once to rearrange the potatoes. Leave to STAND for 5 minutes.

Combine the onions, oil and garlic powder in a large round dish and cook on FULL (100%) for 4 minutes until the onions are soft.

Add the beef, stir and cook on FULL (100%) for 5 minutes, breaking up the meat with a fork halfway through cooking. Stir in the tomato purée, salt, pepper and herbs and cook on FULL (100%) for 2 minutes.

Place the aubergine slices on top, if using. Slice the potatoes thinly and arrange, overlapping, on top. Beat the eggs, soured cream, milk and Parmesan cheese together and pour over the potatoes. Cook on FULL (100%) for 4 minutes, giving the dish a half-turn once during cooking.

Sprinkle the top with the grated cheese and place under a preheated grill to brown before serving.
SERVES 6

Note: If preferred, the aubergine and meat may be layered in the casserole dish.

CHINESE-STYLE BEEF

METRIC/IMPERIAL
1 tablespoon sesame oil
2 onions, sliced
1 red pepper, cored, seeded and thinly sliced
1 clove garlic, crushed
575 g/1¼ lb fillet steak, cut into 7.5 × 1 cm/
3 × ½ inch strips
100 g/4 oz button mushrooms, sliced
1 teaspoon ground ginger
¼ teaspoon ground cumin
¼ teaspoon grated nutmeg
1 teaspoon dried mixed herbs
15 g/½ oz cornflour
1 tablespoon lemon juice
50 ml/2 fl oz dry sherry

175 ml/6 fl oz hot beef stock
1 tablespoon Worcestershire sauce
1 tablespoon soy sauce
salt
freshly ground black pepper
1 × 275 g/10 oz can beansprouts, drained

Place the oil, onions, red pepper and garlic in a large bowl. Cover and cook on FULL (100%) for 5 minutes, stirring halfway through cooking.

Stir in the beef, mushrooms, ginger, cumin, nutmeg and herbs. Cover and cook on FULL (100%) for 3 minutes, stirring once.

Stir in the cornflour, lemon juice, sherry, stock, Worcestershire sauce, soy sauce and salt and pepper to taste. Fold in the beansprouts. Cover and cook on FULL (100%) for a further 4 minutes, stirring halfway through.

Leave to STAND, covered, for 4 minutes before serving. Serve with boiled rice.
SERVES 4

BOEUF À LA BOURGUIGNONNE

METRIC/IMPERIAL
4 bacon rashers, derinded and cut into strips
1 onion, chopped
450 g/1 lb chuck steak, cut into 2.5 cm/1 inch cubes
300 ml/½ pint hot beef stock
150 ml/¼ pint red wine
1 clove garlic, crushed
1 bouquet garni
8 button onions, peeled and left whole
salt
freshly ground black pepper
100 g/4 oz button mushrooms, trimmed
chopped fresh parsley, to garnish

Place the bacon and onion in a large dish and cook on FULL (100%) for 4 minutes, stirring every 1 minute. Add the meat and cook on FULL (100%) for 2 minutes.

Stir in the stock, red wine, garlic, bouquet garni, button onions and salt and pepper to taste. Cook on FULL (100%) for 25 minutes, stirring three times during cooking. Add the mushrooms and cook on FULL (100%) for a further 4 minutes. Allow to STAND for 5 minutes before serving. Garnish with chopped parsley.
SERVES 4

FILLET STEAK TANDOORI

METRIC/IMPERIAL
4 fillet steaks
2 tablespoons oil
Marinade:
275 g/10 oz natural yogurt
1 tablespoon paprika
1 clove garlic, crushed
3 bay leaves
5 peppercorns
1 teaspoon salt
1 tablespoon tomato purée
1 teaspoon lemon juice
fresh bay leaves, to garnish

Prick the steaks well with a fork and place in a shallow dish.

Mix together all the ingredients for the marinade. Pour the marinade over the steaks, ensuring complete coverage. Cover and refrigerate overnight. Remove the bay leaves and peppercorns and discard.

Preheat a large browning dish on FULL (100%) for 5 minutes (or according to the manufacturer's instructions).

Put the oil in the dish, then, using a slotted spoon, arrange the steaks in the dish. Cook on FULL (100%) for 3½ to 4 minutes, turning the steaks over once, halfway through cooking.

Allow to STAND for 4 minutes. Serve garnished with bay leaves, accompanied by Fluffy White Rice (see page 224) and an orange salad.
SERVES 4

BEEF AND MANGO KORMA

METRIC/IMPERIAL
1.25 kg/2½ lb chuck steak, cut into 2.5 cm/1 inch cubes
1 × 425 g/15 oz can medium curry cook-in-sauce
120 ml/4 fl oz beef stock
100 g/4 oz desiccated coconut
150 ml/¼ pint single cream
100 g/4 oz seedless raisins
1 × 425 g/15 oz can mango slices, drained, or 2 large mangoes, stoned and sliced

Place the beef in a large casserole with the curry sauce, stock, coconut, cream and raisins, blending very well. Cover and cook on FULL (100%) for 15 minutes, stirring once.

Reduce the setting to MEDIUM (50%), cover and cook for a further 20 minutes, stirring twice.

Add the mango slices, blending well. Cover and cook on MEDIUM (50%) for a further 15 to 20 minutes until the meat is tender. Leave to STAND for 5 minutes.

Serve with boiled rice, poppadoms, sliced bananas in yogurt (dipped in lemon juice first) and spicy mango chutney.
SERVES 4 to 6

CHILLI-BEEF TACOS

METRIC/IMPERIAL
2 tablespoons vegetable oil
1 onion, chopped
1 teaspoon chilli powder
1 teaspoon salt
350 g/12 oz minced lean beef
1 × 225 g/8 oz can tomatoes, drained
1 × 65 g/2½ oz can tomato purée
1 tablespoon lemon juice
6–8 taco shells
50 g/2 oz Cheddar cheese, grated
1 red pepper, cored, seeded and sliced into rings

Preheat a large browning dish on FULL (100%) for 5 minutes (or according to the manufacturer's instructions). Mix the oil and onion together in a small basin, then quickly stir into the browning dish. Cook on FULL (100%) for 2 minutes.

Mix in the chilli powder and salt and cook on FULL (100%) for 2 minutes. Stir in the meat, breaking it up with a fork. Cook on FULL (100%) for 5 minutes, stirring once during cooking. Drain off any surplus fat.

Add the tomatoes, tomato purée and lemon juice to the meat. Cover and cook on FULL (100%) for 5 minutes. Leave to STAND for 5 minutes.

Arrange the taco shells, open side up, on a serving dish and fill with the beef mixture. Sprinkle the grated cheese over the meat and top with the pepper rings before serving.
SERVES 3 to 4

SPICED-UP BEEF

METRIC/IMPERIAL
1 celery stick (optional)
1 onion, chopped
1 clove garlic, crushed
1 tablespoon mild curry paste
1½ tablespoons plain flour
450 ml/¾ pint hot beef stock

1 tablespoon tomato purée
1 tablespoon chutney
1 × 350 g/12 oz can corned beef, cut into large
cubes

Place the celery, if using, onion, garlic and curry paste in a large bowl. Cover and cook on FULL (100%) for 5 minutes, stirring halfway through cooking.

Stir in the flour. Gradually blend in the stock, tomato purée and chutney. Cook on FULL (100%) for 4 minutes, stirring halfway through cooking.

Stir in the meat. Cook on FULL (100%) for 8 minutes, stirring halfway through cooking. Spoon on to a warm serving dish.
SERVES 4

SWEET AND SOUR MEATBALLS

METRIC/IMPERIAL
2 tablespoons oil
1 onion, finely chopped
450 g/1 lb minced lean beef
50 g/2 oz fresh white or brown breadcrumbs
1 teaspoon Worcestershire sauce
salt
freshly ground black pepper
1 egg, beaten
Sauce:
1 tablespoon oil
1 red pepper, cored, seeded and chopped
1 green pepper, cored, seeded and chopped
2 tablespoons soft brown sugar
2 teaspoons soy sauce
2 tablespoons vinegar
120 ml/4 fl oz orange juice
120 ml/4 fl oz beef stock
2 teaspoons cornflour

Heat the oil in a large dish on FULL (100%) for ½ minute. Add the onion and cook on FULL (100%) for 3 minutes, stirring once.

Meanwhile, mix the beef, breadcrumbs, Worcestershire sauce, salt and pepper to taste and enough egg to bind the mixture. Divide into 8 portions and roll into balls. Place these in a single layer on top of the onion. Cook on FULL (100%) for 5 minutes, turning once. Leave to stand while preparing the sauce.

Place the oil and peppers in a bowl. Cover and cook on FULL (100%) for 4 minutes, stirring once. Stir in the sugar, soy sauce, vinegar,

orange juice, beef stock and cornflour, blending well. Cook on FULL (100%) for 3 minutes, stirring every 1 minute. Pour over the meatballs and cook on FULL (100%) for 5 minutes.
SERVES 4

BEEF WITH CHEESE SAUCE

METRIC/IMPERIAL
1 onion, thinly sliced
1 carrot, sliced
100 g/4 oz potato, peeled and sliced
100 g/4 oz mushrooms, chopped
1 tablespoon tomato purée
350 g/12 oz minced lean beef
1 teaspoon dried mixed herbs
salt
freshly ground black pepper
40 g/1½ oz butter
40 g/1½ oz plain flour
600 ml/1 pint milk
100 g/4 oz Cheddar cheese, finely grated

Place the onion, carrot and potato in a 1.5 litre/ 2½ pint soufflé dish. Cover and cook on FULL (100%) for 4½ minutes, stirring halfway through cooking. Stir in the mushrooms, tomato purée, beef, herbs and salt and pepper to taste. Cover and cook on FULL (100%) for 8 minutes. Break up and stir with a fork halfway through cooking. Set aside, covered.

Place the butter in a large jug and heat on FULL (100%) for ½ minute or until melted. Stir in the flour, then gradually blend in the milk, with salt and pepper to taste. Cook on FULL (100%) for 7 minutes or until thick, stirring every 2 minutes. Stir in the cheese until melted. Pour the sauce over the beef mixture and cook on FULL (100%) for 2 minutes. Brown under a preheated conventional grill, if preferred.
SERVES 4

LAMB

GRIDDLED LAMB CHOPS

METRIC/IMPERIAL
2 lamb chops
15–25 g/½–1 oz butter
salt
freshly ground black pepper

Preheat a large browning dish on FULL (100%) for 5 minutes (or according to the manufacturer's instructions). Meanwhile trim the chops and spread both sides with butter. As soon as the oven switches off, place the chops in the dish with the bones towards the centre.

Cooking times will depend upon the size of the chops: 2 × 100–175 g/4–6 oz loin chops should be cooked on FULL (100%) for 6 to 7 minutes, turning over once; 2 × 100–175 g/4–6 oz chump chops should be cook on FULL (100%) for 6 to 8 minutes, turning over once. Sprinkle with salt and pepper to taste.
SERVES 2

MINTED ROAST SHOULDER OF LAMB

METRIC/IMPERIAL
1.5 kg/3 lb boned and rolled shoulder of lamb
Marinade:
150 ml/¼ pint dry cider
1 teaspoon chopped fresh mint
1 teaspoon brown sugar
3 teaspoons soy sauce
2 tablespoons vinegar
salt
freshly ground black pepper
Garnish:
mint sprigs
spring onion curls

Place the meat in a large dish. Combine the ingredients for the marinade and pour over the meat. Refrigerate overnight, if possible, basting at least twice.

Remove the meat from the marinade and pour off all but about 3 tablespoons of the marinade. Reserve this for the gravy.

Sprinkle a little salt over the fat of the meat and put the meat into a roasting bag. Fold the open end under loosely or tie loosely with string or an elastic band. Snip the bag in two or three places to allow the steam to escape.

Arrange the meat on an upturned saucer or roasting rack in the base of the roasting dish. Cook on FULL (100%) for 10 minutes. Reduce the power to MEDIUM (50%) and cook for a further 32 minutes, turning the dish once, if necessary. Remove from the oven and STAND, covered with foil, for 20 minutes.

Uncover the meat and place under a preheated grill for 10 minutes or until brown and crisp. Garnish with mint and spring onion curls.
SERVES 6

STUFFED LEG OF LAMB

METRIC/IMPERIAL
1 small onion, finely chopped
25 g/1 oz butter
75 g/3 oz fresh white breadcrumbs
1 tablespoon dried mint or 2 tablespoons chopped fresh mint
salt
freshly ground black pepper
1 egg, beaten
1 kg/2 lb boned leg of lamb

Place the onion and butter in a large bowl. Cover and cook on FULL (100%) for 2 minutes. Stir in the breadcrumbs, mint, salt and pepper. Add the egg and mix well.

Lay the boned leg of lamb out flat. Spread the stuffing over the meat, roll up and secure. Wrap in microwave cling film and place on an upturned saucer in a large dish. Cook on FULL (100%) for 16 minutes.

Remove the cling film and wrap the meat in foil, shiny side inside, then leave to STAND for 15 minutes before carving.
SERVES 4

GUARD OF HONOUR

METRIC/IMPERIAL
1 guard of honour, prepared weight 675 g/1½ lb,
each rack comprising 6 chops
25 g/1 oz butter
1 small onion, chopped
¼ teaspoon chopped fresh marjoram
¼ teaspoon chopped fresh rosemary
¼ teaspoon chopped fresh sage
1 tablespoon chopped fresh parsley
75 g/3 oz fresh white breadcrumbs
salt
freshly ground black pepper
1 egg, beaten

With the fat on the outside, ease and push the racks together to interlock the rib bones. Sew or tie the bases.

Place the butter, onion, marjoram, rosemary, sage and parsley in a small bowl. Cover and cook on FULL (100%) for 3 minutes. Stir in the breadcrumbs and salt and pepper to taste. Bind with the egg.

Stuff the guard and place in a shallow dish. Cook on FULL (100%) for 22 minutes, turning round halfway through.

Wrap tightly in foil, shiny side inside, and STAND for 15 to 20 minutes before serving.
SERVES 4

CROWN ROAST WITH MANGO STUFFING

METRIC/IMPERIAL
2 best ends of neck of lamb, each with 6–7 cutlets
1 onion, finely chopped
25 g/1 oz butter, cut into pieces
175 g/6 oz mango, peeled, stoned and puréed
100 g/4 oz fresh white breadcrumbs
1 tablespoon mixed dried herbs
25 g/1 oz hazelnuts, finely chopped
salt
freshly ground black pepper
1 egg, lightly beaten (optional)
vegetable oil for brushing
parsley sprigs, to garnish

To make the crown of lamb, remove the chine bones from the best ends, make a cut across the joints about 2.5 cm/1 inch away from the tops of the bones and scrape away all the fat and meat. Reserve the meat trimmings. Sew one end of each joint together, sewing round the last bone

of each joint. Stand the joints upright and bend them round until the other ends meet. Stitch these together to form a crown. (You can ask your butcher to do this for you.)

Place the meat trimmings, onion and butter in a medium bowl, cover and cook on FULL (100%) for 4 minutes. Stir in the mango, breadcrumbs, herbs, hazelnuts, and salt and pepper to taste. If necessary, mix in sufficient egg to bind the mixture.

Place the lamb on a trivet or upturned plate in a shallow dish and brush with oil. Spoon the stuffing into the centre of the crown. Cook on FULL (100%) for 25 minutes, turning halfway through cooking.

Wrap tightly in foil and STAND for 20 minutes. Alternatively, place the meat, without the foil, in a *conventional oven*, preheated to 190°C/375°F/Gas Mark 5, and cook for 15 to 20 minutes until it has browned.

Transfer to a warm serving dish and place cutlet frills on the bones. Garnish with sprigs of parsley and serve hot with vegetables in season.
SERVES 4

NOISETTES OF LAMB

METRIC/IMPERIAL
8 lamb noisettes
1 small carrot, thinly sliced
1 onion, chopped
1 celery stick, chopped
25 g/1 oz button mushrooms, sliced
1 teaspoon dried mixed herbs
1 teaspoon dried rosemary
25 g/1 oz butter, diced
25 g/1 oz plain flour
about 300 ml/½ pint hot chicken stock
2 tablespoons tomato purée
150 ml/¼ pint red wine
salt
freshly ground black pepper
parsley sprigs, to garnish

Place the noisettes in a shallow 1.5 litre/2½ pint casserole dish. Cover with a piece of absorbent kitchen paper and cook on FULL (100%) for 7 to 8 minutes, turning over and rearranging halfway through cooking. Set aside, covered.

Place the carrot, onion, celery, mushrooms and herbs in a medium bowl. Cover and cook on FULL (100%) for 7 minutes, stirring halfway through cooking.

Stir in the butter until melted, then stir in the

flour. Make up the meat juices to 300 ml/½ pint with the stock, then stir in the tomato purée, wine, and salt and pepper to taste. Cook, uncovered, on FULL (100%) for 3½ to 4 minutes, stirring every 1 minute until smooth and thickened. Pour over the meat and cook on FULL (100%) for a further 3 minutes.

Garnish with the parsley and serve with boiled potatoes and broccoli.

SERVES 4

BARBECUED LAMB CHOPS

METRIC/IMPERIAL
5–6 trimmed lamb chops (total weight 450 g/ 1 lb)
Marinade:
4 tablespoons corn or sunflower oil
8 tablespoons red wine
1 clove garlic, crushed
1 teaspoon grated onion
½ teaspoon salt
1 tablespoon Worcestershire sauce
1 tablespoon tomato purée
½ teaspoon freshly ground black pepper
Garnish:
rosemary sprigs
onion rings

To make the marinade, mix the oil, wine, garlic, onion, salt, Worcestershire sauce, tomato purée and pepper together in a large bowl. Cook on FULL (100%) for 3 minutes or until the onion is tender, stirring once. Put the lamb chops into the liquid in the bowl, cover and marinate for 2 hours, basting occasionally.

To prepare for cooking on the barbecue, put the chops in a shallow dish and cook on FULL (100%) for 2 minutes. Brush with the marinade and barbecue over hot coals.

If not using a barbecue, the dish can be completed in the microwave oven. Remove the lamb from the bowl and drain on absorbent kitchen paper.

Preheat a large browning dish on FULL (100%) for 5 minutes (or according to the manufacturer's instructions.) Quickly add 2 tablespoons of the oil from the surface of the marinade. Immediately add the lamb chops, pressing them down well with a fish slice. Turn them over quickly and press down once more. Cook on FULL (100%) for 4½ minutes or until the chops are tender. Remove from the dish and keep hot.

Pour the marinade into the juices remaining in the browning dish and skim as much of the oil and fat from the surface as possible. Cook, uncovered, on FULL (100%) for 4 minutes, until about 4 tablespoons of the juice and sediment remain. Spoon the sediment over the hot chops and serve at once, garnished with sprigs of rosemary and onion rings.

SERVES 5 to 6

LAMB WITH APRICOTS

METRIC/IMPERIAL
750 g/1½ lb boned leg of lamb, cubed
½ teaspoon ground ginger
75 g/3 oz clarified butter, cut into pieces
2 teaspoons ground coriander
1½ teaspoons garam masala
salt
1–2 teaspoons chilli powder
25 g/1 oz ground almonds
300 ml/½ pint hot lamb or chicken stock
175 g/6 oz dried apricots, soaked overnight
25 g/1 oz pistachio nuts
4 tablespoons double or whipping cream

Place the lamb, ginger, clarified butter, coriander, garam masala, salt and chilli powder in a large bowl. Cover and cook on FULL (100%) for 10 minutes, then stir in the ground almonds and hot stock and cook on FULL (100%) for a further 10 minutes.

Reduce the setting to LOW (30%) and cook for 30 minutes, stirring once. Drain the apricots and stir into the mixture with the pistachio nuts. Cook on LOW (30%) for a further 20 minutes or until the meat is tender, stirring once.

Remove the meat, apricots and nuts. Place on a warm serving dish and keep warm. Stir the cream into the sauce and pour over the meat. Serve with saffron rice.

SERVES 4

RICE-STUFFED BREAST OF LAMB

METRIC/IMPERIAL
25 g/1 oz butter
350 g/12 oz cooked long-grain rice
50 g/2 oz raisins
grated rind and juice of 1 orange
25 g/1 oz walnuts, chopped
salt
freshly ground black pepper
1 egg, beaten
1 breast of lamb, boned
1 clove garlic, cut into slivers

Place the butter in a bowl and heat on FULL (100%) for ½ minute or until melted. Add the rice, raisins, orange rind and juice, walnuts and salt and pepper to taste, blending well. Bind together with the beaten egg.

Lay the breast of lamb flat, skin side down, on a board and spread the stuffing over the flesh, reserving any extra. Roll up and secure neatly with string. Make deep incisions into the meat with a sharp knife and insert the garlic slivers.

Place on a roasting rack, in a shallow dish. Cover and cook on FULL (100%) for 28 minutes, turning the dish four times during cooking.

Spoon any reserved rice mixture on to a serving dish and top with the stuffed breast of lamb. Cook on FULL (100%) for a further 2 minutes.

Brown under a preheated hot grill before serving, if liked.
SERVES 4

LEMON LAMB CHOPS

METRIC/IMPERIAL
1 or 2 medium lamb chump chops
1 tablespoon vegetable oil
grated rind of ½ lemon
1 tablespoon lemon juice
1 teaspoon brown sugar
½ teaspoon ground ginger
salt
freshly ground black pepper

Place the chops in a shallow dish. Mix the oil with the lemon rind, lemon juice, sugar, ginger and salt and pepper to taste. Pour over the chops, cover and leave to marinate for 3 hours, turning the chops occasionally.

Preheat a small browning dish on FULL (100%) for 3 minutes (or according to the manufacturer's instructions). Add the chops and cook on FULL (100%) for 5 to 6 minutes, turning over once. Baste with a little of the marinade halfway through the cooking time.
SERVES 1

LAMB AND LENTIL CRUMBLE

METRIC/IMPERIAL
100 g/4 oz red lentils
150 ml/¼ pint boiling water
1 onion, finely chopped
1 clove garlic, crushed
2 tablespoons cold water
575 g/1¼ lb lean lamb, minced or finely chopped
1 courgette, diced
1 potato, diced
1 tablespoon chopped fresh parsley or 1 teaspoon dried mixed herbs
salt
freshly ground black pepper
300 ml/½ pint hot stock
1 tablespoon fresh wholemeal breadcrumbs
½ tablespoon grated Parmesan cheese

Place the lentils in a large bowl and stir in the boiling water. Cover and cook on FULL (100%) for 3¼ minutes. Stir, then cover and cook on FULL (100%) for a further 4 minutes, stirring halfway through the cooking time. Leave to STAND, covered, while cooking the meat.

Place the onion and garlic in a flameproof dish with the water. Cover and cook on FULL (100%) for 2½ minutes. Stir in the minced lamb, cover as before and cook on FULL (100%) for 4 minutes, stirring halfway through cooking. Stir with a fork to break up the meat.

Add the vegetables, parsley or herbs, salt and pepper to taste and hot stock. Stir to mix well; cover again and cook on FULL (100%) for 4 minutes. Stir, replace the cover and cook on LOW (30%) for 12½ minutes (or on DE-FROST/20% for 16½ minutes), stirring several times during the cooking time to break up the meat.

Spoon the cooked lentils on top of the meat, cover again and cook on FULL (100%) for 4 minutes. Leave to STAND, covered, for 5 minutes. Sprinkle with the breadcrumbs and cheese and cook under a preheated hot grill for a few minutes to brown the topping.
SERVES 4

LAMB FRICASSÉE

METRIC/IMPERIAL
1 × 1.6–2 kg/3½–4 lb leg of lamb, boned and cut
into 2.5 cm/1 inch cubes
2 tablespoons vegetable oil
1 large onion, finely sliced
2 tablespoons plain flour
200 ml/7 fl oz boiling lamb or light stock
200 ml/7 fl oz dry vermouth
1 × 450 g/1 lb packet frozen baby carrots
salt
freshly ground black pepper
2 egg yolks
2 tablespoons lemon juice
finely grated rind of ½ lemon
2 tablespoons chopped fresh parsley

Place the lamb, oil and onion in a large casserole
dish. Cook on FULL (100%) for 5 minutes,
stirring once.

Add the flour, blending well. Gradually add
the boiling stock and vermouth, mixing well to
blend. Stir in the carrots and salt and pepper to
taste. Cover and cook on FULL (100%) for 25 to
30 minutes, stirring twice, until the lamb is
cooked.

Beat the egg yolks with the lemon juice,
lemon rind, parsley and 5 tablespoons of the
cooking juices. Stir into the casserole, blending
well.

Cover and cook on FULL (100%) for 5
minutes, stirring once, until just beginning to
thicken. Leave to STAND for 5 minutes before
serving with noodles, rice or baby new potatoes.
SERVES 6

THIRTY-FIVE MINUTE
IRISH STEW

METRIC/IMPERIAL
2 large onions, peeled
675 g/1½ lb stewing lamb, cut into 2.5 cm/1 inch
cubes
2 large potatoes, scrubbed and pricked
300 ml/½ pint hot chicken stock
½ teaspoon salt
¼ teaspoon freshly ground black pepper
few parsley sprigs

Put the onions into a large deep casserole, cover
and cook on FULL (100%) for 4 minutes. Leave
in the dish and separate the onion layers with a
knife and fork.

Spread the lamb over the onions. Cover and
cook on FULL (100%) for 10 minutes, stirring
occasionally. Set aside while preparing the potatoes.

Put the potatoes on a double thickness of
absorbent kitchen paper on the oven base or
turntable and cook on FULL (100%) for 5
minutes. Slice and arrange on top of the meat.
Season the stock with salt and pepper and pour
over the potatoes. Add the parsley. Cover tightly
and cook on FULL (100%) for 15 minutes,
giving the dish a half-turn during cooking.
Discard the parsley and serve hot.
SERVES 4

SHEPHERDS' PIE

METRIC/IMPERIAL
1 large onion, finely chopped
1 tablespoon tomato purée
1 beef stock cube, crumbled
300 ml/½ pint beef stock
350 g/12 oz cooked minced lamb
1 tablespoon flour
salt
freshly ground black pepper
450 g/1 lb potatoes, peeled and cubed
4 tablespoons water
15 g/½ oz butter
6 tomatoes, pricked

Place the onion, tomato purée, stock cube and
stock in a large shallow dish. Cover and cook on
FULL (100%) for 10 minutes, stirring occasionally.

Toss the meat in the flour, then stir into the
onion mixture. Cover and cook on FULL
(100%) for 10 minutes, stirring occasionally.
Add salt and pepper to taste. Leave to STAND
while cooking the potatoes.

Put the potatoes in a large shallow dish and
add the water. Cover loosely and cook on FULL
(100%) for 7 to 9 minutes until soft, shaking the
dish vigorously two or three times during cooking. Leave to STAND, covered, for 5 minutes.
Drain and mash the potatoes with the butter,
adding salt and pepper to taste.

Arrange the tomatoes on top of the meat
mixture and cover with the mashed potato.
Cook on FULL (100%) for 5 minutes, giving the
dish a quarter-turn every 1 minute. Place under a
preheated hot grill to brown.
SERVES 4 to 6

BAKED LAMB AND VEGETABLES

METRIC/IMPERIAL
6–8 lamb chops
8 small tomatoes, pierced
1 large potato, peeled and diced
2 large onions, sliced
salt
freshly ground black pepper

Trim away the surplus fat and arrange the chops in single layer round the edge of a large deep dish. Pile the tomatoes in the centre. Spread the potato and onions over the chops and sprinkle with salt and pepper to taste.

Cover loosely and cook on LOW (30%) for 45 minutes until the meat is tender, giving the dish a half-turn, halfway through cooking. Leave to STAND, covered, for 10 minutes. Serve hot.
SERVES 4 to 6

STUFFED SHOULDER OF LAMB VALENCIA

METRIC/IMPERIAL
1 tablespoon vegetable oil
1 onion, chopped
175 g/6 oz cooked long-grain rice
2 tablespoons chopped fresh parsley
100 g/4 oz seedless raisins
grated rind and juice of 1 lemon
25 g/1 oz walnuts, chopped
salt
freshly ground black pepper
1 egg, beaten
1 × 1.6 kg/3½ lb shoulder of lamb, boned
1 clove garlic, cut into slivers
2 tablespoons plain flour
300 ml/½ pint meat stock
2 tablespoons single cream
1 tablespoon chopped fresh parsley
lemon wedges, to garnish

Place the oil and onion in a bowl. Cover and cook on FULL (100%) for 3 minutes. Add the rice, parsley, raisins, lemon rind and juice, walnuts, and salt and pepper to taste, blending well. Bind together with the beaten egg.

Stuff the shoulder of lamb with the rice mixture and sew up the opening with fine string. Using a sharp knife, make incisions in the lamb and insert the garlic slivers. Place on a roasting rack in a shallow dish. Cover and cook on

MEDIUM (50%) for 40 to 44 minutes, turning the dish every 10 minutes, until cooked. Remove from the dish, wrap in foil, shiny side inside, and leave to STAND for 15 to 20 minutes.

Remove and discard any excess fat from the cooking juices until just 1 tablespoon remains. Place in a bowl, blend with the flour and cook on FULL (100%) for ¾ minute. Gradually add the stock, blending well. Cook on FULL (100%) for 3½ to 4 minutes, stirring every 1 minute, until smooth and thickened. Stir in the cream, parsley and salt and pepper to taste.

Place the meat on a warmed serving dish and garnish with lemon wedges. Serve the sauce separately.
SERVES 6

LAMB CASSEROLE WITH AUBERGINE AND ARTICHOKES

METRIC/IMPERIAL
1 large aubergine, peeled and cut into cubes
salt
2 tablespoons vegetable oil
675 g/1½ lb boned leg of lamb, cut into 2.5 cm/ 1 inch cubes
4 tablespoons plum jam
8 tablespoons red wine
1 × 400 g/14 oz can artichoke hearts, drained
2 tablespoons chopped gherkins
2 teaspoons cornflour
4 tablespoons cold water

Sprinkle the aubergine with salt and set aside for at least 30 minutes. Rinse and pat dry with absorbent kitchen paper.

Preheat a large browning dish on FULL (100%) for 5 minutes (or according to the manufacturer's instructions). Quickly add the oil, then rapidly stir in the lamb. Cook on FULL (100%) for 5 minutes, stirring once.

Add the aubergine, cover and cook on FULL (100%) for 5 minutes, stirring once. Stir in the jam, wine and 1 teaspoon salt; then add the artichoke hearts and chopped gherkins. Cover and cook on LOW (30%) for 35 minutes, stirring once. Leave to STAND for 10 minutes.

Blend the cornflour with the water, stir into the lamb casserole and cook on FULL (100%) for 3 minutes, stirring occasionally, until the sauce thickens. Serve hot.
SERVES 4

LAMB CHOPS WITH ORANGE AND HONEY

METRIC/IMPERIAL
4 thick lamb cutlets (with 2 rib bones)
2 teaspoons vegetable oil
2 tablespoons flour
2 tablespoons demerara sugar
4 orange slices
7 tablespoons hot chicken stock
2 tablespoons clear honey
½ teaspoon salt
freshly ground black pepper
mint sprigs, to garnish

With a sharp knife, make two horizontal slits through the meat to the bone, but do not completely cut through. Brush both sides of the chops with oil and coat with flour. Sprinkle with the sugar, then insert an orange slice into each chop.

Preheat a browning dish on FULL (100%) for 5 minutes (or according to the manufacturer's instructions). Quickly put the chops into the dish, arranging the thicker parts towards the outside. Cook on FULL (100%) for 4 minutes, turning the chops over after 2 minutes.

Mix together the stock, honey, salt and pepper to taste, then pour into the dish. Cover and cook on LOW (30%) for 8 to 10 minutes or until the meat is tender, giving the dish a half-turn once or twice during cooking.

Leave to STAND, covered, for 5 minutes before serving. Garnish with sprigs of fresh mint and serve hot.
SERVES 4

LAMB KEBABS WITH PINEAPPLE

METRIC/IMPERIAL
9 streaky bacon rashers, derinded
4 × 100 g/4 oz good quality lamb burgers, each cut into 8 pieces
5 firm tomatoes, quartered
18 cubes canned pineapple
18 button mushrooms, trimmed
a few pieces of green pepper

Stretch out the bacon rashers, using the back of a round-bladed knife. Cut each piece in half and make into 18 rolls.

Arrange alternating pieces of the prepared food on 6 wooden kebab sticks; that is, a bacon roll, a piece of burger, a quarter of a tomato, a piece of pineapple, a mushroom, and the occasional piece of pepper, until all 6 sticks are full. Leave a small space at the end of each stick.

Place the kebabs widthways across an oven-proof glass dish. Cook on FULL (100%) for 15 minutes, turning the kebabs and rearranging them twice during cooking.

Leave to STAND for 4 minutes before serving on a bed of rice.
SERVES 6

Note: Metal kebab sticks may be used in this recipe, *provided* almost *all* of the metal is masked by the food. The metal must not come into contact with the sides of the oven.

SUCCULENT LAMB STEW

METRIC/IMPERIAL
675 g/1½ lb stewing lamb, cut into 2.5 cm/1 inch cubes
1 tablespoon gravy powder
2 sticks celery, thinly sliced
225 g/8 oz carrots, thinly sliced
2 large onions, thinly sliced
2 large potatoes, thinly sliced
300 ml/½ pint hot chicken stock
½ teaspoon salt
¼ teaspoon freshly ground black pepper
1 tablespoon chopped fresh parsley
1 teaspoon chopped fresh thyme

Put the lamb into a large deep casserole and sprinkle with the gravy powder. Stir and cook on FULL (100%) for 5 minutes.

Add all the remaining ingredients to the meat. Cover and cook on LOW (30%) for 50 to 60 minutes, stirring occasionally, until the meat and vegetables are tender. Leave to STAND, covered, for 10 minutes before serving.
SERVES 6

SPICED LAMB

METRIC/IMPERIAL
3 tablespoons vegetable oil
1 onion, finely chopped
1 green pepper, cored, seeded and finely chopped
1 green chilli, seeded and finely chopped
3 cloves garlic, finely chopped
450 g/1 lb lean lamb, cut into 2.5 cm/1 inch cubes
1 × 400 g/14 oz can tomatoes, chopped

2 teaspoons ground cumin
1 teaspoon ground coriander
½ teaspoon ground turmeric
½ teaspoon cayenne pepper
1 teaspoon salt
150 ml/¼ pint water

Place the oil, onion, pepper, chilli and garlic in a casserole dish. Cover and cook on FULL (100%) for 4 minutes, stirring once.

Add the lamb, blending well. Cover and cook on FULL (100%) for 4 minutes, stirring once.

Add the tomatoes with their juice, cumin, coriander, turmeric, cayenne pepper, salt and water, blending well. Cook on LOW (30%) for 12 to 14 minutes. Leave to STAND, covered, for 3 minutes before serving.

If the lamb is not tender, cook on LOW (30%) for a further 5 to 10 minutes.
SERVES 4

LAMB PILAFF

METRIC/IMPERIAL
50 g/2 oz butter
225 g/8 oz long-grain rice
1 onion, chopped
1 clove garlic, crushed
350 g/12 oz cooked lamb, cut into bite-sized cubes
50 g/2 oz sultanas
1 small courgette, sliced
1 canned pimiento, sliced
juice of 1 lemon
600 ml/1 pint boiling light meat stock
salt
freshly ground black pepper
Garnish:
25 g/1 oz flaked almonds
thin strips of lemon rind
1 lemon, sliced

Place the butter, rice, onion and garlic in a large casserole dish. Cook on FULL (100%) for 3 minutes until the onion is almost tender.

Add the lamb, sultanas, courgette, pimiento, lemon juice, boiling stock, and salt and pepper to taste. Cover and cook on FULL (100%) for 14 minutes, stirring twice. Leave to STAND, covered, for 5 minutes.

Serve hot, garnished with the almonds, lemon rind and lemon slices.
SERVES 4

QUICK LAMB COUSCOUS

METRIC/IMPERIAL
400 g/14 oz couscous
250 ml/8 fl oz warm water
250 ml/8 fl oz hot vegetable stock
1 tablespoon chopped fresh coriander or parsley, to garnish
For the stew:
100 g/4 oz prunes
2 onions, sliced
1 clove garlic, crushed
2 tablespoons water
675 g/1½ lb lean lamb, cut into 5 cm/2 inch cubes
2 tomatoes, chopped
1 bay leaf
4–5 thyme sprigs or ½ teaspoon dried thyme
4 cm/1½ inch piece of cinnamon stick
½ teaspoon coriander seeds
5 cm/2 inch piece dried orange peel (optional)
300 ml/½ pint hot vegetable or chicken stock
1 × 400 g/14 oz can chickpeas, rinsed and drained
salt
freshly ground black pepper

Place the couscous in a large bowl. Pour over the water and leave to soak.

Meanwhile cook the stew. Place the prunes in a small bowl, cover with warm water and leave them to soak. Place the onions and garlic in a large bowl or casserole with the water and cook on FULL (100%) for 3¼ minutes, stirring halfway through cooking. Stir in the meat, cover and cook on FULL (100%) for 7½ minutes, stirring three or four times during cooking.

Drain the prunes thoroughly and add to the meat, together with the tomatoes, herbs and spices and orange peel, if using. Stir in the hot stock, cover as before and cook on LOW (30%) for 25 minutes (or on DEFROST/20% for 34 to 35 minutes), stirring several times during cooking. Stir in the chickpeas, season with salt and pepper to taste and cook for a further 8¾ minutes on LOW (30%) (or for 12½ minutes on DEFROST/20%). Leave to STAND, covered, while finishing the couscous.

Stir the couscous lightly with a fork, then pour on the stock without stirring. Cover and cook on FULL (100%) for 3¼ minutes. Leave to STAND, covered, for 4 to 5 minutes before stirring with a fork. Garnish with the chopped coriander or parsley and serve with the meat stew.
SERVES 6

KOFTA MEATBALLS

METRIC/IMPERIAL
350 g/12 oz minced lean lamb
½ teaspoon salt
½ teaspoon freshly ground black pepper
¾ teaspoon ground cumin
¾ teaspoon ground coriander
⅛ teaspoon ground nutmeg
⅛ teaspoon ground mixed spice
⅛ teaspoon cayenne pepper
1½ tablespoons gram or besam flour
5 teaspoons natural yogurt
1 tablespoon vegetable oil
lettuce and red pepper rings, to garnish

Mix all the ingredients, except the oil, and form into 12 small balls.

Preheat a large browning dish on FULL (100%) for 5 minutes (or according to the manufacturer's instructions). Add the oil and cook on FULL (100%) for ½ minute.

Quickly add the Kofta balls and toss so that they are brown on all sides. Cook on FULL (100%) for 2½ minutes. Serve at once, garnished with lettuce and red pepper rings.
SERVES 4

KASHMIR LAMB

METRIC/IMPERIAL
1.25 kg/2½ lb leg of lamb
Marinade:
2.5 cm/1 inch piece of fresh ginger, peeled and finely grated
1 clove garlic, crushed
1 tablespoon fresh lime or lemon juice
salt
¼ teaspoon ground turmeric
¼ teaspoon freshly ground black pepper
2 teaspoons garam masala (see note)
1 tablespoon ground almonds or desiccated coconut
1 × 150 g/5 oz carton natural yogurt
2 teaspoons clear honey

Remove the skin and all the fat from the lamb. With the point of a sharp knife, make deep incisions all over the meat.

Place all the marinade ingredients in a large bowl or casserole and mix thoroughly. Add the lamb and turn in the mixture until well coated. Cover and leave to marinate for 24 hours, turning the meat in the mixture several times to keep it well coated.

Drain off half of the marinade, cover the bowl and cook on FULL (100%) for 8¾ minutes, turning the lamb over halfway through cooking. Cover as before and cook on LOW (30%) for 25 minutes (or on DEFROST/20% for 34 to 35 minutes), turning the lamb over several times during cooking.

Cover with foil and leave to STAND for 10 minutes before serving.
SERVES 4 to 6

Note: Garam masala is a blend of Indian spices. It is available ready made, but is very easy to make at home. Simply grind to a fine powder 1 tablespoon cardamom seeds (not pods), 1 teaspoon whole cloves, 1 teaspoon black peppercorns, 1 teaspoon cumin seeds and a 4 cm/1½ inch cinnamon stick (or 1 teaspoon ground cinnamon). You need only make a small quantity at a time and it will keep for up to a month in a small airtight container.

SWEET AND SOUR LAMB

METRIC/IMPERIAL
1 onion, finely chopped
2 celery sticks, finely sliced
1 tablespoon vegetable oil
675 g/1½ lb lean shoulder of lamb, cut into 2.5 cm/1 inch cubes
seasoned flour
1 × 400 g/14 oz can tomatoes
2 tablespoons tomato purée
2 tablespoons wine vinegar
1 tablespoon brown sugar
300 ml/½ pint meat stock
1 tablespoon redcurrant jelly
1 teaspoon dried basil
salt
freshly ground black pepper

Place the onion, celery and oil in a large dish. Cover and cook on FULL (100%) for 4 minutes, stirring twice during cooking. Toss the meat in seasoned flour and add to the vegetables. Cover and cook on FULL (100%) for 1½ to 2 minutes.

Add the remaining ingredients, cover and cook on FULL (100%) for 16 to 17 minutes, stirring twice during cooking. Leave to STAND for 10 minutes before serving.
SERVES 4

LAMB AND CORIANDER KEBABS

METRIC/IMPERIAL
1 onion, finely chopped
1 clove garlic, crushed
2 tablespoons water
350 g/12 oz lean lamb, minced
½ teaspoon ground coriander
1 tablespoon chopped fresh coriander or parsley
2 tablespoons fresh wholemeal breadcrumbs
1 egg
salt
freshly ground black pepper
6 tablespoons sesame seeds, toasted
1 green pepper, cored, seeded and cut into squares
1 yellow pepper, cored, seeded and cut into squares
8 button mushrooms, halved
lemon wedges, to garnish

Place the onion and garlic in a large bowl with the water and cook on FULL (100%) for 2½ minutes, stirring halfway through cooking. Add the lamb, ground coriander, herbs, breadcrumbs and egg, and season with salt and pepper. Mix thoroughly and form into 16 firm small balls. Roll the meatballs in the toasted sesame seeds to coat them.

Thread the meatballs alternately with the green and yellow pepper squares and mushrooms on 8 wooden skewers. Arrange the skewers like the spokes of a wheel on a round plate and cook on FULL (100%) for 2½ minutes. Turn the skewers over and cook on FULL (100%) for a further 2½ minutes.

Wrap the kebabs in foil and leave to STAND for 5 minutes before serving. Garnish with lemon wedges.
SERVES 4

LAMB CURRY

METRIC/IMPERIAL
1 onion, chopped
1 clove garlic, crushed
1 tablespoon ground coriander
1 teaspoon turmeric
½ teaspoon ground cumin
¼ teaspoon chilli powder
¼ teaspoon ground cinnamon
¼ teaspoon ground ginger
¼ teaspoon grated nutmeg
1 tablespoon plain flour
1 tablespoon tomato purée
1 teaspoon lemon juice
1 tablespoon desiccated coconut
¼ teaspoon meat extract
25 g/1 oz sultanas
450 ml/¾ pint hot chicken stock
2 teaspoons curry paste
675 g/1½ lb boneless cooked lamb, finely chopped
salt
freshly ground black pepper

Place the onion, garlic, coriander, turmeric, cumin, chilli powder, cinnamon, ginger and nutmeg in a large bowl. Cover and cook on FULL (100%) for 4 minutes, stirring once.

Stir in the flour, tomato purée, lemon juice, coconut, meat extract, sultanas, stock, curry paste and lamb. Season to taste with salt and pepper. Cover and cook on FULL (100%) for 10 minutes, stirring twice.

Serve with rice, sliced tomatoes, sliced bananas, mango chutney and desiccated coconut.
SERVES 4

MOUSSAKA

METRIC/IMPERIAL
1 large aubergine, cut into 5 mm/¼ inch slices
salt
25 g/1 oz butter
2 onions, finely sliced
2 cloves garlic, crushed
450 g/1 lb lean lamb, minced
3 tablespoons tomato purée
1 teaspoon dried mixed herbs
25 g/1 oz plain flour
150 ml/¼ pint beef stock
freshly ground black pepper
Sauce:
25 g/1 oz butter
25 g/1 oz plain flour
300 ml/½ pint milk
50 g/2 oz Cheddar cheese, grated
1 teaspoon dry mustard
1 egg, beaten

Place the aubergine slices in a colander and sprinkle with salt. Leave for 30 minutes, then rinse under cold water and drain.

Place the aubergine slices in a medium bowl, cover and cook on FULL (100%) for 3 minutes. Set aside.

131

Place the butter, onions and garlic in a large bowl. Cover and cook on FULL (100%) for 3 minutes or until translucent, stirring once.

Stir in the lamb, cover and cook on FULL (100%) for 4 minutes, stirring once. Stir in the tomato purée, herbs, flour, stock, salt and pepper. Cover and cook on FULL (100%) for a further 12 minutes. Set aside.

To make the sauce, place the butter in a 600 ml/1 pint jug. Cook on FULL (100%) for ½ minute or until melted. Blend in the flour and milk. Cook on FULL (100%) for 3½ to 4 minutes, stirring twice. Stir in the cheese, mustard and beaten egg.

Make alternate layers of lamb and aubergine slices in a large shallow oblong casserole. Pour over the sauce and cook on FULL (100%) for a further 5 minutes.

SERVES 4

flat surface, veined side upwards, and put a heaped dessertspoon of the filling on to each vine leaf near to the stem. Fold first the stem end, then both sides of the leaf, over the filling and roll into a cigar shape.

Line the bottom of a shallow container with the remaining vine leaves and pack the stuffed vine leaves tightly over the base. Pour over sufficient hot water to cover them.

Cover and cook on FULL (100%) for 20 minutes. Gently turn over halfway through cooking. Drain, place on a warm serving dish and garnish with lemon slices, if wished. Serve hot with tomato sauce and a green salad.

SERVES 4 to 6

Variation
Blanched cabbage leaves can be used for this recipe instead of vine leaves.

STUFFED VINE LEAVES

METRIC/IMPERIAL
1 × 225 g/8 oz packet vine leaves in brine, drained
1 small onion, chopped
25 g/1 oz butter
1 tablespoon tomato purée
2 cloves garlic, crushed
100 g/4 oz long-grain rice
450 ml/¾ pint hot lamb or chicken stock
225 g/8 oz lean lamb, minced
salt
freshly ground black pepper
lemon slices, to garnish

Place the vine leaves in a shallow dish. Cover with boiling water and leave to soak for 20 minutes. Rinse the vine leaves under cold water and drain.

Meanwhile, place the onion, butter, tomato purée and garlic in a large bowl. Cover and cook on FULL (100%) for 4 minutes. Stir in the rice and hot stock. Cover and cook on FULL (100%) for 3 minutes. Reduce the power setting to MEDIUM (50%) and cook for a further 12 minutes, stirring once. Set aside to STAND, covered, for 5 minutes.

Place the lamb in a small bowl, cover and cook on FULL (100%) for 3 minutes, stirring once. Stir into the rice mixture. Season to taste with salt and pepper.

Select 20 large vine leaves for stuffing and reserve the remainder. Place the vine leaves on a

FRENCH-STYLE LAMB

METRIC/IMPERIAL
575 g/1¼ lb lamb fillet, cubed
40 g/1½ oz butter
1 tablespoon plain flour
Marinade:
250 ml/8 fl oz red wine
2 carrots, sliced
2 onions, roughly cut into chunks
1 teaspoon dried thyme
1 bay leaf
small piece of orange rind
salt
freshly ground black pepper
40 g/1½ oz butter
1 tablespoon plain flour

Place the lamb and marinade ingredients in a bowl. Cover and leave to marinate for 3 hours. When this time has elapsed, drain the wine from the meat mixture and set aside.

Place the butter in a casserole and heat on FULL (100%) for ½ minute to melt. Blend in the flour and cook on FULL (100%) for 1 minute. Gradually add the reserved wine, blending well. Stir in the meat mixture. Cover tightly and cook on FULL (100%) for 15 minutes, stirring twice.

Reduce the power setting to MEDIUM (50%) and cook for a further 8 minutes. Remove and discard the bay leaf and orange rind. Serve hot with baked potatoes and vegetables in season.

SERVES 4

LAMB IN LEMON SAUCE

METRIC/IMPERIAL
25 g/1 oz butter
1 onion, finely chopped
1 celery stick, chopped
50 g/2 oz bacon, derinded and finely chopped
1 kg/2 lb boned shoulder of lamb, cut into
1–2 cm/½–¾ inch cubes
pinch of grated nutmeg
salt
freshly ground black pepper
2 tablespoons dry white wine
300 ml/½ pint hot chicken stock
2 cloves garlic, crushed
1 tablespoon chopped fresh parsley
3 egg yolks
2 tablespoons lemon juice
25 g/1 oz Parmesan cheese, finely grated

Place the butter, onion, celery and bacon in a large bowl and cook on FULL (100%) for 6 minutes. Stir in the lamb, nutmeg, salt and pepper to taste, the wine, stock, garlic and parsley. Cook on FULL (100%) for 10 minutes, stirring once. Stir again, then reduce the setting to LOW (30%) for 45 minutes or until the meat is tender.

Put the egg yolks in a bowl with the lemon juice and Parmesan cheese. Beat well to mix, then stir in a little of the hot cooking liquid.

Transfer the lamb mixture to a saucepan and gradually stir in the egg mixture. Cook very gently on a *conventional hob*, stirring constantly, until the sauce thickens. Do not allow it to boil or the sauce will curdle.
SERVES 4

LAMB AND FETA BAKE

METRIC/IMPERIAL
750 g/1½ lb lean lamb, cut into 2.5 cm/1 inch cubes
1 tablespoon lemon juice
1 tablespoon grapeseed or sunflower oil
1 large onion, thinly sliced
2 large tomatoes, chopped
2 teaspoons brown sugar (optional)
½ teaspoon dried thyme
½ teaspoon dried mint
1 aubergine, cut in 2.5 cm/1 inch cubes
pinch of salt
freshly ground black pepper
100 g/4 oz Feta cheese, crumbled

Place the meat in a large bowl or casserole, sprinkle with the lemon juice and oil, cover with kitchen paper towels and cook on FULL (100%) for 6 minutes, stirring two or three times during the cooking time. Transfer the meat to a plate with a slotted spoon, cover it with foil and set aside. Add the onion, tomatoes, sugar, if using, and herbs to the casserole and cook on FULL (100%) for 4 minutes, stirring once during cooking.

Stir the aubergine cubes into the casserole and cook on FULL (100%) for 3 minutes. Stir in the lamb, cover as before and cook on LOW (30%) for 19 minutes, stirring several times during cooking. Season with salt and plenty of black pepper. Sprinkle on the cheese and cook on FULL (100%) for 10 minutes.

Allow to STAND, covered, for 10 minutes before serving.
SERVES 4 to 6

LAMB CHOP CASSEROLE

METRIC/IMPERIAL
8 lamb loin chops (total weight 1 kg/2 lb)
225 g/8 oz potatoes, peeled and diced
1 large onion, chopped
2 large carrots, thinly sliced
1 small turnip, diced
2 courgettes, sliced
3 tablespoons cold water
25 g/1 oz butter, cut into pieces
25 g/1 oz plain flour
about 450 ml/¾ pint hot chicken stock
½ teaspoon dried thyme
¼ teaspoon gravy browning
salt
freshly ground black pepper

Place the chops over the bottom and sides of a large bowl. Cover and cook on FULL (100%) for 6½–9½ minutes, rearranging halfway through cooking. Set aside, covered.

Place the potatoes, onion, carrot, turnip, courgettes and water in another large bowl. Cover and cook on FULL (100%) for 13 minutes or until tender, stirring halfway through. Stir in the butter until melted. Stir in the flour. Make up the meat juices to 450 ml/¾ pint with the stock, then stir in with the thyme, gravy browning and salt and pepper. Cover and cook on FULL (100%) for 4 minutes, stirring halfway through cooking. Fold in the chops. Cook on FULL (100%) for 4 minutes.
SERVES 4

PORK

SPARE RIBS WITH BARBECUE SAUCE

METRIC/IMPERIAL
15 g/½ oz butter
1 clove garlic, crushed
1 onion, finely chopped
1 × 400 g/14 oz can tomatoes, drained
1 tablespoon dried mixed herbs
2 tablespoons Worcestershire sauce
1 tablespoon clear honey
1 tablespoon soy sauce
1 tablespoon dark brown sugar
salt
freshly ground black pepper
675 g/1½ lb pork spare ribs

Place the butter, garlic and onion in a large shallow bowl. Cover and cook on FULL (100%) for 3½ minutes, stirring once.

Stir in the tomatoes, herbs, Worcestershire sauce, honey, soy sauce, sugar and salt and pepper to taste. Cover and cook on FULL (100%) for 5 minutes, stirring once.

Add the spare ribs. Cover and cook on FULL (100%) for 10 minutes, stirring once. Rearrange the spare ribs and baste with the sauce. Cook on FULL (100%) for a further 10 minutes or to taste.
SERVES 4

PORK FILLETS IN WINE SAUCE

METRIC/IMPERIAL
4 pork fillets (total weight 675 g/1½ lb)
1 onion, chopped
100 g/4 oz button mushrooms, sliced
1 celery stick, sliced
¼ teaspoon dried parsley
¼ teaspoon dried sage
¼ teaspoon dried tarragon
25 g/1 oz butter, diced
25 g/1 oz plain flour
about 150 ml/¼ pint hot chicken stock

150 ml/¼ pint rosé wine
salt
freshly ground black pepper
Garnish:
fried apple rings
parsley sprigs

Place the pork fillets in a shallow dish, cover and cook on FULL (100%) for 6 to 9 minutes, turning over and rearranging halfway through cooking. Set aside, covered.

Place the onion, mushrooms, celery, parsley, sage and tarragon in a medium bowl. Cover and cook on FULL (100%) for 5½ minutes.

Stir in the butter until melted, then stir in the flour. Make up the meat juices to 150 ml/¼ pint with stock. Stir in with the wine and salt and pepper. Cover and cook on FULL (100%) for 2 minutes, stirring after 1 minute.

Add the fillets and turn to coat with the sauce. Cover and cook on FULL (100%) for a further 3 minutes. Garnish with the apple rings and parsley sprigs. Serve with new potatoes and fried courgettes.
SERVES 4

PORK FRICASSÉE WITH RED WINE AND CREAM

METRIC/IMPERIAL
1 kg/2 lb boned loin of pork, cut into 2.5 cm/1 inch cubes
2 large onions, sliced
2 carrots, sliced
3 cloves garlic, crushed
2 bay leaves
2 thyme sprigs
400 ml/14 fl oz red wine
2 tablespoons olive oil
8 black peppercorns
salt
2 tablespoons plain flour
100 ml/3½ fl oz hot chicken stock
25 g/1 oz cornflour
3 tablespoons double or whipping cream

1 tablespoon tomato purée
freshly ground black pepper
Garnish:
fried croûtons (optional)
chopped fresh parsley

Place the pork, onions, carrots, garlic, bay leaves, thyme, wine, oil, peppercorns and salt in a large bowl. Leave to marinate for 12 hours, stirring occasionally.

Remove the pork from the marinade, drain and dry. Strain the marinade and reserve. Discard the vegetables.

Place the pork in a large bowl, cover and cook on FULL (100%) for 5 minutes, stirring once. Stir in the flour, then gradually stir in 200 ml/ ⅓ pint of the marinade and the stock to cover the meat.

Cover and cook on FULL (100%) for 10 minutes, stirring once. Reduce the setting to LOW (30%), cover and cook for 45 minutes or until tender. Remove the meat and place on a warm serving dish; cover and keep warm.

Blend the cornflour with a little water to make a smooth paste and stir into the cooking liquid. Cook on FULL (100%) for 3 minutes, stirring every 1 minute. Stir in the double cream and tomato purée, blending well, and season to taste with salt and pepper. Spoon the sauce over the meat and garnish with fried croûtons, if wished, and chopped parsley. Serve hot with boiled rice and braised celery.
SERVES 4

ROAST PORK WITH PLUMS

METRIC/IMPERIAL
1.5 kg/3 lb boned and rolled loin of pork
Plum sauce:
25 g/1 oz butter
1 onion, sliced
2 tablespoons tomato purée
50 g/2 oz soft, dark brown sugar
1 kg/2 lb plums, stoned
1 tablespoon cornflour
150 ml/¼ pint dry red wine

Shield the ends of the joint with a little foil, then place in a shallow dish and cook on FULL (100%) for 30 minutes. (Do not allow the foil to touch the oven walls.) Remove the foil after 15 minutes.

Transfer the pork to a *conventional oven* preheated to 200°C/400°F/Gas Mark 6 and cook for 15 to 20 minutes or until well browned. Alternatively, wrap the pork tightly in foil and leave to STAND for 15 to 20 minutes.

Place the butter, onion, tomato purée and sugar in a large bowl. Cover and cook on FULL (100%) for 4 minutes, stirring once. Stir in the plums. Blend the cornflour with the wine to make a smooth paste and stir into the plum mixture. Cover and cook on FULL (100%) for 9 minutes, stirring once.

Slice the pork and arrange around the edge of a warm serving dish. Spoon some of the plums into the centre, and drizzle a little plum juice over the meat. Serve with sauté potatoes, Brussels sprouts and the remaining plums.
SERVES 6

Variation
Boned and rolled shoulder of pork may be used for this recipe instead of loin.

SOMERSET PORK WITH CIDER CREAM SAUCE

METRIC/IMPERIAL
25 g/1 oz butter
225 g/8 oz onions, chopped
675 g/1½ lb pork fillet, cut into 2.5 cm/1 inch cubes
100 g/4 oz button mushrooms, sliced
300 ml/½ pint dry cider
salt
freshly ground black pepper
2 tablespoons cornflour
1 tablespoon water
2 tablespoons double cream

Place the butter in a casserole dish and heat on FULL (100%) for ½ minute or until melted. Add the onion and cook on FULL (100%) for 4 minutes. Stir in the cubed pork and cook on FULL (100%) for 6½ minutes, stirring four times.

Add the mushrooms and cider and season lightly with salt and pepper. Cook on FULL (100%) for 8½ to 9 minutes, stirring four times.

Blend the cornflour with the water and stir into the casserole, then return to the oven and cook on FULL (100%) for a further 1½ to 2 minutes. Stir the double cream into the sauce before serving.
SERVES 4

PORK CASSEROLE WITH APPLE

METRIC/IMPERIAL
25 g/1 oz butter
1 large onion, quartered
1 tablespoon flour
675 g/1½ lb lean pork, cut into bite-sized pieces
few sprigs mixed fresh herbs, tied in a bundle
175 ml/6 fl oz dry white wine
salt
freshly ground black pepper
1 large eating apple, cored and sliced
juice of ½ lemon
50 g/2 oz mushrooms, sliced

Place the butter and onion in a casserole dish and cook on FULL (100%) for 4 minutes. Stir in the flour, add the meat and herbs and carefully stir in the wine. Season lightly with salt and pepper and cook on FULL (100%) for 5½ to 6 minutes, stirring three times.

Dip the apple slices in the lemon juice to prevent discoloration. Add to the casserole, together with the mushrooms, and cook on FULL (100%) for a further 4 minutes, stirring once during cooking. Remove the herbs from the casserole before serving.
SERVES 4

SPICY GREEN LENTILS WITH PORK, BACON AND FRANKFURTERS

METRIC/IMPERIAL
1 onion, finely chopped
1 tablespoon vegetable oil
3–5 bacon rashers, derinded
575 g/1¼ lb pork fillet, trimmed and cut into thin strips
1 teaspoon fenugreek seeds
1 teaspoon coriander seeds
1 teaspoon ground turmeric
¼ teaspoon freshly ground black pepper
450 ml/¾ pint water or stock
100 g/4 oz green lentils, soaked overnight
2 frankfurters, cut into 1 cm/½ inch slices
coriander sprig, to garnish

Put the onion and oil in a large deep dish and cook on FULL (100%) for about 3 minutes or until the onions are golden, stirring once.

Cut 3 bacon rashers into thin strips and stir into the onion mixture with the pork and spices. Cook on FULL (100%) for 1½ minutes. Stir and cook on FULL (100%) for a further 1½ minutes.

Add the pepper, water or stock and stir in the drained lentils. Three-quarters cover and cook on FULL (100%) for 20 minutes, stirring twice during cooking.

Stir in the frankfurters and cook on FULL (100%) for a further 6 to 9 minutes or until the lentils are pulpy and the mixture is thick.

If wished, place the extra 2 bacon rashers on absorbent kitchen paper and cook on FULL (100%) for 2 minutes. Arrange the bacon over the lentils just before serving and garnish with coriander.
SERVES 6

TENDER PORK CASSEROLE WITH HERBS

METRIC/IMPERIAL
450 g/1 lb pork fillet, cut into 2.5 cm/1 inch cubes
1 onion, finely chopped
2 carrots, thinly sliced
1 red pepper, cored, seeded and chopped
1 clove garlic, crushed
¼ teaspoon ground mace
¼ teaspoon dried thyme
¼ teaspoon dried sage
¼ teaspoon dried parsley
2 tablespoons tomato purée
25 g/1 oz butter, cut into pieces
25 g/1 oz plain flour
about 300 ml/½ pint chicken stock
1 × 200 g/7 oz can sweetcorn kernels, drained
salt
freshly ground black pepper

Place the pork in a shallow dish, cover and cook on FULL (100%) for 4 to 6 minutes, stirring halfway through cooking. Set aside, covered.

Place the onion, carrot, red pepper, garlic, mace, thyme, sage, parsley and tomato purée in a medium bowl. Cover and cook on FULL (100%) for 8 minutes, stirring halfway through cooking.

Stir in the butter until melted, then stir in the flour. Make up the meat juices to 300 ml/½ pint with stock, then stir in the sweetcorn, pork and salt and pepper. Cook on FULL (100%) for a further 4 minutes, stirring every 1 minute.

Serve with creamed potatoes and mangetout.
SERVES 4

SWEET AND SOUR PORK

METRIC/IMPERIAL
1 onion, sliced
15 g/½ oz butter
675 g/1½ lb lean boned pork
1 × 225 g/8 oz can pineapple cubes
2 tablespoons malt vinegar
4 tablespoons soy sauce
25 g/1 oz cornflour
1 teaspoon salt
½ teaspoon freshly ground black pepper
½ red pepper, cored, seeded and shredded, to garnish

Place the onion and butter in a large dish and cook on FULL (100%) for 3 minutes.

Cut the pork into 2.5 cm/1 inch cubes and add to the dish, spooning the onion over the meat. Cook on FULL (100%) for 7 minutes.

Drain the liquor from the pineapple into a measuring jug. Add the vinegar and soy sauce, then make up to 600 ml/1 pint with water.

Mix the cornflour with the salt and pepper, then blend with a little of the pineapple liquid. Stir in the remaining liquid, then pour over the meat and stir well. Cover and cook on FULL (100%) for 5 minutes, stirring twice, or until the sauce boils.

Stir in the pineapple cubes, re-cover and cook on LOW (30%) for 25 to 30 minutes until the meat is tender, stirring occasionally during cooking.

Garnish with the shredded red pepper and serve with boiled noodles or rice.
SERVES 4 to 6

Note: To cook this dish more quickly, cook on FULL (100%) for 15 to 18 minutes after adding the pineapple, stirring occasionally during cooking.

PORK FILLET WITH ONIONS

METRIC/IMPERIAL
2 onions, cut into rings
1 Bramley cooking apple, peeled, cored and sliced
25 g/1 oz butter
675 g/1½ lb pork fillet, fat removed, cut into 5 × 0.5 cm/2 × ¼ inch strips
300 ml/½ pint boiling chicken stock
½ teaspoon oregano
1 tablespoon tomato purée
50 g/2 oz button mushrooms, sliced
salt
freshly ground black pepper
2 teaspoons cornflour
Garnish (optional):
thin slices of green pepper
matchstick strips of raw carrot

Put the onion and the apple into a mixing bowl. Cover and cook on FULL (100%) for 2 minutes.

Put the butter in a large ovenproof dish. Cook on FULL (100%) for ½ to 1 minute, until the butter has melted and is very hot. Stir in the meat and cook on FULL (100%) for 2 minutes.

Add the apple and onion mixture, stock, oregano, tomato purée, mushrooms, salt and pepper. Stir until all the ingredients are well mixed. Cover and cook on FULL (100%) for 7 minutes, stirring twice during cooking.

Cream the cornflour with a little water and stir into the pork. Cook on FULL (100%) for 1 minute, stirring once.

Remove from the oven, cover with foil, and leave to STAND for 12 minutes. Serve with buttered noodles and garnish with green pepper and carrot, if liked.
SERVES 4

PRUNE-STUFFED PORK FILLET

METRIC/IMPERIAL
150 g/5 oz pitted prunes
1 large or 2 small pork fillets (total weight 450 g/ 1 lb)
freshly ground black pepper
1 tablespoon chopped fresh sage or 1 teaspoon dried sage
1½ tablespoons wholemeal flour
salt
2 tablespoons grapeseed or sunflower oil
1 onion, thinly sliced
1 tablespoon apple and thyme jelly or redcurrant jelly
2 teaspoons cornflour, blended with 2 tablespoons water
fresh sage, to garnish

Place the prunes in a bowl, cover with hot water and leave to soak for 30 minutes.

With a sharp knife, make a deep slit along one side of each fillet and open them out. Flatten slightly with a rolling pin or meat cleaver; season with plenty of black pepper and sprinkle with the sage.

Drain the prunes and reserve the liquid. Arrange a line of prunes down the centre of each fillet, fold up the fillets and secure with wooden cocktail sticks or fine string. Season the flour with salt and pepper. Coat the fillets with the seasoned flour and shake off any excess.

Preheat a large browning dish on FULL (100%) for 5 minutes (or according to the manufacturer's instructions). Without removing it from the oven, add the oil and place the stuffed fillets in the dish. Cook on FULL (100%) for 3¼ minutes on each side. Set aside.

Place the onion in a shallow dish, large enough to hold both stuffed fillets in one layer. Add 85 ml/3 fl oz of the reserved soaking liquid from the prunes. Cook on FULL (100%) for 2½ minutes. Place the meat on top; cover and cook on FULL (100%) for 4 minutes, turning the meat over halfway through cooking.

Cook on LOW (30%) for a further 10 minutes (or on DEFROST/20% for 14 minutes), turning the meat over again halfway through. Remove the fillets, wrap them tightly in foil and leave to STAND for 8 to 10 minutes.

Stir the jelly into the onion and meat juices, and cook on FULL (100%) for 1 minute or until the jelly has melted. Stir in the cornflour mixture and cook on FULL (100%) for 1½ to 2 minutes, stirring halfway through the cooking time.

Slice the meat and arrange it on a warmed serving dish. Pour over a little of the sauce and serve the rest separately. Garnish the pork with fresh sage.
SERVES 4

Note: Pitted prunes are readily available but you can use whole prunes – allow 175–225 g/6–8 oz – and remove the stones after soaking.

CIDER PORK CASSEROLE

METRIC/IMPERIAL
575 g/1¼ lb lean pork shoulder, cut into 2.5 cm/1 inch cubes
300 ml/½ pint cider or 300 ml/½ pint cider and water mixed
1½ tablespoons plain flour
salt
freshly ground black pepper
1 onion, sliced
2 carrots, sliced
2 bay leaves
1 chicken stock cube, crumbled
squeeze of lemon juice
50 g/2 oz mushrooms, sliced
black grapes, halved, to garnish (optional)

Leave the meat to soak in the cider, or cider and water, for ½ hour or overnight.

Drain the meat, and reserve the liquid. Toss the meat in the flour seasoned with salt and pepper.

Arrange the onion and carrots in a 2 litre/3½ pint casserole. Add the meat, bay leaves, stock cube, lemon juice and reserved liquid. Cover and cook on FULL (100%) for 10 minutes.

Stir and cook on MEDIUM (50%) for 30 minutes.

Remove the bay leaves and stir in the mushrooms. STAND for 10 minutes, covered. Garnish with grapes, if liked, before serving.
SERVES 4

THAI HOT-COLD SALAD

METRIC/IMPERIAL
4 large crisp lettuce leaves
2 large navel oranges, peeled, pith removed, and thinly sliced
2 tablespoons vegetable oil
1 clove garlic, crushed
675 g/1½ lb cold cooked pork, minced
2 tablespoons finely chopped peanuts
2 teaspoons sugar
2 tablespoons soy sauce
2 tablespoons water
salt
cayenne pepper
coriander sprigs, to garnish

Line 4 serving plates with the lettuce. Arrange the orange slices on top and chill.

Place the oil in a large bowl and heat on FULL (100%) for 1 minute. Add the garlic and pork, blending well. Cook on FULL (100%) for 3 to 4 minutes, stirring twice, until hot and bubbly.

Add the peanuts, sugar, soy sauce, water, and salt and pepper to taste, blending well. Cook on FULL (100%) for a further 1 minute, stirring once.

Spoon the hot pork mixture over the oranges. Garnish with coriander sprigs. Serve at once.
SERVES 4

ROAST LOIN OF PORK

METRIC/IMPERIAL
1.75 kg/4 lb boned and rolled loin of pork
Marinade:
2 tablespoons wine vinegar
2 tablespoons soy sauce
1 clove garlic, crushed
1 teaspoon French mustard
1 teaspoon mixed herbs
salt
freshly ground black pepper
150 ml/¼ pint apple juice or pure orange juice
1 sherry glass of dry sherry

Mix all the ingredients for the marinade together and pour over the meat. Cover and refrigerate for 8 hours, turning the meat three times during this period.

Place two upturned saucers on the base of an ovenproof glass dish.

Drain the marinade and retain for gravy. Put the meat into a roasting bag and fold the open end under loosely or tie loosely with string or an elastic band. Place in the ovenproof dish and snip the base of the bag in three places.

Cook on FULL (100%) for 11 minutes, then give the dish a half-turn.

Reduce the power setting to MEDIUM (50%) and cook for 36 minutes, giving the dish a half-turn, halfway through cooking.

Remove from the oven and STAND, covered with foil, for 20 minutes. Cook the pork under a preheated hot grill for about 12 minutes to 'crisp' the crackling.

Serve with baked apples with a mincemeat and nut filling and vegetables of your choice.
SERVES 6

PORK ROLLS WITH CABBAGE

METRIC/IMPERIAL
450 g/1 lb pork sausage meat
1 onion, chopped
100 g/4 oz button mushrooms, chopped
1 tablespoon lemon juice
grated rind of ½ lemon
1 teaspoon mustard powder
2 tablespoons chopped fresh parsley
1 egg, beaten
salt
freshly ground black pepper
1 medium cabbage, shredded

4 tablespoons water
1 tablespoon soy sauce
1 tablespoon vegetable oil
Garnish:
tomato wedges
parsley sprig

Mix the sausage meat with the onion, mushrooms, lemon juice, lemon rind, mustard, parsley, egg and salt and pepper to taste, blending well. Divide and shape into 8 rolls.

Place the cabbage in a bowl with the water and salt to taste. Cover and cook on FULL (100%) for 8 minutes, stirring once. Drain and toss with the soy sauce.

Preheat a large browning dish on FULL (100%) for 5 minutes (or according to the manufacturer's instructions). Brush with the oil and cook on FULL (100%) for a further 1 minute.

Add the pork rolls and turn quickly on all sides to brown evenly. Cook on FULL (100%) for 7 to 8 minutes, turning and rearranging the rolls once. Serve on a bed of the seasoned cabbage and garnish with tomato wedges and parsley.
SERVES 4

PORK AND BEANSPROUT STIR-FRY

METRIC/IMPERIAL
450 g/1 lb pork fillet
½ clove garlic, peeled
salt
freshly ground black pepper
2 tablespoons vegetable oil
2 celery sticks, finely sliced
1 onion, finely chopped
1 tablespoon cornflour
½ teaspoon ground ginger
3 tablespoons soy sauce
1 tablespoon sweet sherry
4 tablespoons water
175 g/6 oz fresh beansprouts

Rub the pork fillet with the cut side of the garlic and season with salt and pepper to taste. Cut into thin strips.

Preheat a large browning dish on FULL (100%) for 5 minutes (or according to the manufacturer's instructions). Add the oil and pork and stir well to brown evenly. Cook on FULL (100%) for 3 minutes, stirring once.

Add the celery and onion, cover and cook on

FULL (100%) for 3 minutes, stirring occasionally. Blend the cornflour with the ginger, soy sauce, sherry and water. Stir into the pork, cover and cook on FULL (100%) for 3 minutes, stirring twice.

Stir the beansprouts into the pork mixture with salt to taste. Cook on FULL (100%) for a further 2 minutes. Serve with boiled rice.

SERVES 4

COUNTRY-STYLE PORK

METRIC/IMPERIAL
4 spare rib pork chops
25 g/1 oz seasoned flour
2 tablespoons vegetable oil
1 onion, chopped
1 green pepper, cored, seeded and chopped
2 courgettes, sliced
1 × 400 g/14 oz can tomatoes
25 g/1 oz butter
50 g/2 oz fresh white breadcrumbs
1 cooking apple, peeled, cored and chopped
50 g/2 oz cheese, grated
salt
freshly ground black pepper
beaten egg yolk

Coat the chops in the seasoned flour. Place the oil in a casserole dish and heat on FULL (100%) for 1 minute. Add the chops and cook on FULL (100%) for 4 minutes, turning over once.

Add the onion, pepper and courgettes and cook on FULL (100%) for 3 minutes, stirring once.

Place the tomatoes in a shallow heatproof serving dish. Top with the pork and vegetable mixture.

Place the butter in a bowl and heat on FULL (100%) for ½ minute or until melted. Stir in the breadcrumbs, apple, cheese and salt and pepper to taste. Bind together with the beaten egg yolk. Press the mixture on top of the chops and vegetables.

Cook on FULL (100%) for 15 minutes, turning the dish twice. Brown under a preheated hot grill before serving.

SERVES 4

CARIBBEAN PORK

METRIC/IMPERIAL
4 thick pork chops
1 tablespoon flour
salt
freshly ground black pepper
25 g/1 oz butter
1 small onion, finely chopped
150 ml/¼ pint soured cream
2 bananas, sliced in half lengthways
1 teaspoon paprika

Trim the surplus fat from the chops and coat with flour. Season with salt and pepper to taste. Preheat a large browning dish on FULL (100%) for 5 minutes (or according to the manufacturer's instructions). Add the butter and swirl to coat. Quickly add the chops, turning them to brown on both sides. Remove the chops and set aside.

Return the browning dish to the oven and cook on FULL (100%) for 3 minutes. Add the onion and cook on FULL (100%) for 3 minutes. Replace the chops, cover and cook on FULL (100%) for 10 minutes, giving the dish a quarter-turn every 2 minutes.

Spoon off all surplus fat from the dish. Stir in all but 2 tablespoons of the soured cream. Place a banana half on each chop and baste with the soured cream. Cover and cook on LOW (30%) for 5 minutes, giving the dish a quarter-turn every 1 minute.

Arrange the chops and creamy sauce on a hot serving platter. Spoon the remaining cream over the top and sprinkle with the paprika. Serve immediately.

SERVES 4

PORK CHOPS WITH PINEAPPLE

METRIC/IMPERIAL
1 × 440 g/15½ oz can pineapple slices in natural juice
1 teaspoon made mustard
1 tablespoon soy sauce
freshly ground black pepper
6 loin pork chops (total weight 675 g/1½ lb)
1 tablespoon oil
25 g/1 oz butter
2 teaspoons cornflour

Drain the pineapple slices and reserve the juice. Mix together the mustard, soy sauce and black pepper and gradually stir in the pineapple juice. Pour the mixture over the chops, cover and refrigerate for ½ hour.

Preheat a large browning dish on FULL (100%) for 5 minutes (or according to the manufacturer's instructions). Put the oil, butter and drained chops into the heated dish. Cook on FULL (100%) for 6 minutes. Turn the chops over and cook on FULL (100%) for a further 6 minutes. Arrange the chops on a heated serving dish, cover and set aside.

To complete the dish, pour the juices in which the chops were soaking into a jug and add the meat juices. Cook on FULL (100%) for 1½ minutes.

Cream the cornflour with a little water. Pour the heated juices on to the cornflour, stirring all the time. Cook on FULL (100%) for 2 to 3 minutes, stirring twice. Beat the sauce well and pour it over the chops. Garnish the dish with pineapple rings.
SERVES 6

GAMMON STEAKS WITH PINEAPPLE

METRIC/IMPERIAL
1 tablespoon cooking oil
4 gammon steaks (about 100 g/4 oz each)
1 × 225 g/8 oz packet frozen sweetcorn and peppers
2 slices of cheese (optional)
1 × 225 g/8 oz can pineapple slices, drained
watercress sprigs, to garnish

Preheat a large browning dish on FULL (100%) for 5 minutes (or according to the manufacturer's instructions). Put the oil and gammon steaks on to the browning dish and cook on MEDIUM (50%) for 3 minutes.

Turn the steaks over and cook on FULL (100%) for 3 minutes. Transfer to a warm serving dish and cover with foil.

Pierce the packet of frozen vegetables and cook on FULL (100%) for 4 minutes. Set aside.

If using cheese, cut each slice in half and arrange half a slice on each gammon steak. Top with a pineapple ring and return to the oven on FULL (100%) for 2 minutes.

Drain the vegetables and arrange on the serving dish with the gammon steaks. Garnish with watercress and serve with creamed potatoes.
SERVES 4

QUICK CASSOULET

METRIC/IMPERIAL
4 Toulouse sausages
2 tablespoons grapeseed or sunflower oil
450 g/1 lb piece of unsmoked gammon, covered with cold water and soaked overnight
2 onions, finely chopped
1 clove garlic, crushed
2 tablespoons water
175 g/6 oz dried pinto beans, covered in boiling water and soaked overnight
1 × 400 g/14 oz can tomatoes, chopped
1 bouquet garni or 1 teaspoon dried mixed herbs
2 tablespoons clear honey
150 ml/¼ pint boiling water

Prick the sausages in several places to prevent bursting. Preheat a large browning dish on FULL (100%) for 5 minutes (or according to the manufacturer's instructions). Without removing it from the oven, add the oil and sausages and cook on FULL (100%) for 3¼ minutes on each side. Wrap the sausages in foil.

Drain the gammon and pat dry on absorbent kitchen paper. Remove the rind and fat and cut the meat into large cubes.

Place the onions and garlic in a large bowl or casserole with the water and cook on FULL (100%) for 2½ minutes, stirring halfway through cooking.

Drain the beans and stir into the casserole with the tomatoes and their juice. Add the herbs, cover and cook on FULL (100%) for 16½ minutes, stirring several times during cooking.

Stir in the honey and boiling water. Add the gammon cubes, cover and cook on FULL (100%) for 8¾ minutes. Stir, cover again and cook on LOW (30%) for 16½ minutes (or on DEFROST/20% for 21 minutes), stirring several times during cooking.

Add the reserved sausages, cover and cook on LOW (30%) for a further 16½ minutes, stirring two or three times during cooking. Leave to STAND, covered, for 10 minutes. Remove the bouquet garni before serving.
SERVES 4

Note: Cassoulet is traditionally made with Toulouse sausage, but if this is unavailable, use a good quality pork sausage instead.

Variation
Use haricot beans instead of pinto beans.

CRISPY GAMMON JOINT

METRIC/IMPERIAL
1 × 1.75 kg/4 lb piece middle cut or corner of
green gammon, soaked in water overnight
1 tablespoon honey
75 g/3 oz demerara sugar mixed with 1 teaspoon
dry mustard
cloves (see method)
glacé cherries, halved (optional)

Put the drained gammon into a roasting bag with
the honey. Arrange on an upturned saucer in a
round casserole dish. Seal the roasting bag and
slit at the base to enable the steam to escape, and
cook on FULL (100%) for 10 minutes.

Turn the joint over and cook on MEDIUM
(50%) for 40 minutes, giving the dish a half-turn,
twice, during cooking. Leave to STAND, covered with a foil, for 20 minutes.

Remove the gammon and peel away the skin.
Score the fat into diamond shapes with a sharp
knife and press the sugar and mustard mixture
onto the fat. Press a clove into each diamond.

Place under a preheated hot grill until the
gammon is crisp and brown. If liked, decorate
with cherries and serve with vegetables of your
choice. Delicious hot or cold.
SERVES 6 to 8

Note: If preferred, the skin can be removed and
the fat scored and coated with toasted breadcrumbs. Use the cloves as described.

GAMMON IN CHERRY SAUCE

METRIC/IMPERIAL
1 × 1.75 kg/4 lb gammon joint
1 × 425 g/15 oz can black cherries
about 150 ml/¼ pint red wine
2 teaspoons arrowroot powder
1 teaspoon lemon juice

Preheat a large browning dish on FULL (100%)
for 5 minutes (or according to the manufacturer's
instructions).

Meanwhile, using a sharp knife, peel the rind
from the gammon and score the fat in a diamond
pattern.

Add the gammon joint to the dish and turn
quickly on the fat side to brown evenly. Remove
and place on a roasting rack or on a saucer in a
shallow dish. Cook on MEDIUM (50%) for 38

to 42 minutes, turning the dish occasionally.
Cover with foil and leave to STAND.

Meanwhile, drain the juice from the cherries
into a measuring jug and make up to 300 ml/½
pint with red wine. Cut the cherries in half and
remove and discard the stones.

Mix the arrowroot powder with a little of the
cherry juice mixture and lemon juice, then stir
into the jug. Cook on FULL (100%) for 3 to 4
minutes, stirring every 1 minute. Add the cherries, blending well. (Add a little sugar, if
wished.)

Carve the gammon and spoon over the sauce.
SERVES 6 to 8

GLAZED HAM WITH APRICOT RICE

METRIC/IMPERIAL
1 × 1.75 kg/4 lb ham joint
Glaze:
6 tablespoons made mustard
6 tablespoons clear honey
1 tablespoon dark brown sugar
½ teaspoon ground cloves
Apricot rice:
2 tablespoons vegetable oil
1 large onion, chopped
350 g/12 oz long-grain rice
100 g/4 oz dried apricots, chopped
1 tablespoon lemon juice
1.2 litres/2 pints boiling light stock

Shield the ham shank with a little foil. Place, flat
side down, on a roasting rack in a shallow dish,
ensuring that the foil does not touch the sides of
the oven. Cover and cook on MEDIUM (50%)
for 22 minutes.

Remove the foil, turn the ham flat side up,
cover and cook on MEDIUM (50%) for a
further 7 minutes.

Using a sharp knife, remove the rind and most
of the outer layer of fat from the ham. Cover and
cook on MEDIUM (50%) for a further 10
minutes.

Meanwhile, blend the mustard with the
honey, sugar and cloves. Baste the ham evenly
with the glaze, then cover and cook on
MEDIUM (50%) for a further 5 to 9 minutes,
until cooked. Remove the ham, wrap in foil,
shiny side inside, and leave to STAND while
preparing the apricot rice.

Place the oil in a bowl with the onion and rice.
Cook on FULL (100%) for 2 minutes. Add the

apricots, lemon juice and stock, blending well. Cover and cook on FULL (100%) for 3 minutes. Reduce the power setting to MEDIUM (50%) and cook for a further 12 minutes, stirring once. Leave to STAND for 3 minutes.

Place the ham on a warmed serving dish and serve with the apricot rice.

SERVES 6 to 8

DANISH STROGANOFF

METRIC/IMPERIAL
3 × 175 g/6 oz unsmoked gammon steaks, derinded
50 g/2 oz butter
1 onion, sliced
225 g/8 oz button mushrooms, sliced
25 g/1 oz plain flour
1 tablespoon tomato purée
150 ml/¼ pint ham or light chicken stock or dry white wine
salt
freshly ground black pepper
150 ml/¼ pint soured cream
chopped fresh parsley, to garnish

Cut the gammon into thin strips.

Place the butter in a bowl and heat on FULL (100%) for ½ to 1 minute to melt. Add the gammon and cook on FULL (100%) for 4 minutes.

Add the onion and mushrooms. Cover and cook on FULL (100%) for 4 minutes, stirring once. Remove the gammon and reserve.

Stir in the flour and tomato purée, blending well. Gradually add the stock or wine and reserved gammon. Cook on FULL (100%) for 1½ minutes, stirring once. Add salt and pepper to taste. Stir in the soured cream, sprinkle with chopped parsley and serve hot.

SERVES 4

HERDER'S PIE

METRIC/IMPERIAL
25 g/1 oz butter
1 large onion, chopped
100 g/4 oz button mushrooms, quartered
1 × 175 g/6 oz can pimientos, drained and chopped
1 × 400 g/14 oz can tomatoes, drained
450 g/1 lb cooked bacon or ham, coarsely minced or finely chopped

1 tablespoon plain flour
2 tablespoons tomato ketchup
1 tablespoon Worcestershire sauce
½ teaspoon dried rosemary
freshly ground black pepper
Topping:
675 g/1½ lb potatoes, cubed
1 large carrot, grated
5 tablespoons water
25 g/1 oz butter
50 g/2 oz cheese, grated

Place the butter in a large bowl with the onion and mushrooms. Cover and cook on FULL (100%) for 5 minutes, stirring once.

Add the pimientos, tomatoes, bacon or ham tossed in the flour, tomato ketchup, Worcestershire sauce, rosemary and pepper to taste, blending well. Cover and cook on FULL (100%) for 10 minutes, stirring twice. Spoon into a large shallow dish.

Place the potatoes and carrot in a bowl with the water. Cover and cook on FULL (100%) for 12 to 14 minutes until tender. Drain and mash with the butter and cheese. Pipe or spoon over the meat mixture to cover. If piping the mixture, spoon into a piping bag fitted with a large star-shaped nozzle.

Cook on FULL (100%) for a further 6 minutes, turning the dish every 1½ minutes.

Brown under a preheated hot grill, if preferred.

SERVES 4

BACON AND VEGETABLE CASSEROLE

METRIC/IMPERIAL
½ green pepper, cored, seeded and thinly sliced
225 g/8 oz onion, thinly sliced into rings
275 g/10 oz potato, peeled and diced
1 celery stick, chopped
100 g/4 oz carrot, thinly sliced
100 g/4 oz frozen cauliflower florets
12 streaky bacon rashers, derinded, stretched, rolled and secured with wooden cocktail sticks
25 g/1 oz plain flour
450 ml/¾ pint hot chicken stock
1 teaspoon dried mixed herbs
salt
freshly ground black pepper

Place the green pepper, onion, potato, celery, carrot and cauliflower in a large bowl. Cover and cook on FULL (100%) for 10 minutes, stirring twice during cooking.

Place the bacon rolls on top of the vegetables. Cover and cook on FULL (100%) for 5 minutes.

Remove the bacon. Stir in the flour, stock, herbs and salt and pepper to taste. Cook, uncovered, on FULL (100%) for a further 3 minutes.

Remove the sticks from the bacon rolls. Stir the bacon into the vegetables. Cook for 2 minutes on FULL (100%). Serve immediately as a complete supper dish.
SERVES 4

Variation
Use red or yellow peppers in place of the green pepper, and swedes or turnips in place of the carrots.

Homemade chicken stock will give the casserole a richer flavour.

SLIPPER PUDDING

METRIC/IMPERIAL
Suet pastry:
225 g/8 oz self-raising flour
salt
100 g/4 oz shredded beef suet
150 ml/¼ pint cold water
Filling:
225 g/8 oz lean cooked bacon, chopped
25 g/1 oz plain flour
1 teaspoon dried sage
1 onion, chopped
1 small cooking apple, peeled, cored and grated
100 g/4 oz button mushrooms, sliced
freshly ground black pepper
150 ml/¼ pint chicken stock

Sift the flour and a pinch of salt into a bowl. Stir in the suet and water and mix quickly, using a round-bladed knife, to form a light elastic dough. Knead lightly until smooth and free from cracks.

Roll out the pastry on a lightly floured surface to a round about 5 cm/2 inches larger than the diameter of a 900 ml/1½ pint pudding basin. Cut a quarter section from the pastry round and reserve for a lid.

Lift the remaining piece of pastry and ease it into the basin, pinching the 2 cut edges together to seal, and moulding the pastry on to the base and round the sides of the basin.

Toss the bacon in the flour. Add the sage,

onion, apple, mushrooms and pepper to taste. Spoon into the basin and pour over the stock.

Roll out the remaining pastry to a round large enough to make a lid. Dampen the pastry edges with water and cover with the lid. Pinch the edges together firmly to seal.

Partially cover with greaseproof paper and cook on FULL (100%) for 12 minutes, giving the dish a quarter-turn every 3 minutes. Allow to STAND for 10 minutes. Serve hot with fresh vegetables in season.
SERVES 4

BACON POT-AU-FEU

METRIC/IMPERIAL
1 × 1.5 kg/3¼ lb unsmoked bacon joint, soaked in water overnight
1 onion, cut into wedges
1 bay leaf
450 ml/¾ pint boiling water
3 carrots, scraped, quartered lengthways and blanched
6 small potatoes, scrubbed and halved
3 leeks, trimmed, cut into 6 cm/2½ inch lengths and blanched

Place the bacon joint in a large, deep dish. Add the onion, bay leaf and boiling water, cover and cook on FULL (100%) for 8 minutes. Turn the meat over, cover and cook on FULL (100%) for a further 8 minutes. Turn the meat again, cover again and cook on LOW (30%) for 15 minutes (or on DEFROST/20%) for 19 minutes).

Remove the meat, wrap tightly in foil and set aside. Add the blanched carrots and potatoes to the dish and replace the cover. Cook on FULL (100%) for 5½ minutes, stirring twice during cooking. Add the leeks, cover and cook on FULL (100%) for a further 5½ minutes.

Return the bacon to the middle of the dish and surround with the vegetables. Cover again and cook on FULL (100%) for 4½ minutes. Allow to STAND, covered, for 8 to 10 minutes, and remove the bay leaf before serving.
SERVES 6

DICED HAM WITH BARBECUE SAUCE

METRIC/IMPERIAL
1 onion, chopped
1 red or green pepper, cored, seeded and diced
1 clove garlic, crushed
2 tablespoons tomato purée
2 tablespoons plain flour
1 × 400 g/4 oz can tomatoes, chopped
1 teaspoon dried mixed herbs
scant 300 ml/½ pint hot ham or chicken stock
1 tablespoon soy sauce
3 tablespoons white wine vinegar
3 tablespoons soft, dark brown sugar
1 × 450 g/1 lb can ham, jelly removed, diced

Place the onion, red or green pepper, garlic and tomato purée in a large bowl. Cover and cook on FULL (100%) for 6 minutes, stirring halfway through cooking.

Stir in the flour. Gradually blend in the tomatoes and juice, herbs, hot stock, soy sauce, vinegar, sugar and ham. Cover and cook on FULL (100%) for 10 minutes, stirring halfway through cooking.
SERVES 4

Variation
Cooked chicken can be used in place of the canned ham.

GAMMON IN CIDER

METRIC/IMPERIAL
575 g/1¼ lb gammon, cubed
1 onion, peeled and chopped
1 celery stick, chopped
1 teaspoon dried marjoram
2 red eating apples, cored and sliced
25 g/1 oz butter, cut into pieces
25 g/1 oz cornflour
150 ml/¼ pint hot chicken stock
300 ml/½ pint dry cider
freshly ground black pepper

Place the gammon in a shallow dish, cover and cook on FULL (100%) for 4 minutes, stirring halfway through cooking. Remove the gammon with its juices and set aside, covered.

Add the onion, celery and marjoram to the dish, cover and cook on FULL (100%) for 3 minutes. Stir in the apples, cover and cook on FULL (100%) for 2 minutes. Stir in the butter until melted. Stir in the cornflour, stock, cider and pepper to taste. Cook on FULL (100%) for 3 minutes, until thickened, stirring every 1 minute.

Replace the gammon and its juices and heat through on FULL (100%) for about 3 minutes.

Serve with boiled potatoes and broccoli.
SERVES 4

GAMMON STEAKS WITH APRICOT PURÉE

METRIC/IMPERIAL
75 g/3 oz dried apricots
200 ml/7 fl oz hot water
2 tablespoons grapeseed or sunflower oil
4 gammon steaks (total weight 750 g/1½ lb), covered with cold water, soaked for 2 hours and drained

Place the apricots in a bowl with the hot water and soak for 30 minutes. Transfer the bowl to the microwave oven and cook on FULL (100%) for 2 to 2½ minutes, stirring halfway through the cooking time. Drain the apricots and purée in a blender or food processor. Transfer to a serving bowl.

Heat a large browning dish for 5 minutes (or according to the manufacturer's instructions). Without removing it from the oven, add the oil and gammon and cook on FULL (100%) for 3 minutes on each side.

Arrange the steaks on a serving dish and serve with the apricot purée.
SERVES 4

145

VEAL, LIVER AND KIDNEY

VEAL CONTINENTAL WITH RICE

METRIC/IMPERIAL
675 g/1½ lb stewing veal, cut into 2.5 cm/1 inch cubes
25 g/1 oz seasoned flour
25 g/1 oz butter
300 ml/½ pint beef stock
2 tomatoes, skinned and quartered
100 g/4 oz mushrooms, halved
1 onion, chopped
1 tablespoon tomato purée
salt
freshly ground black pepper
225 g/8 oz long-grain rice
600 ml/1 pint boiling water
1 teaspoon salt

Preheat a large browning dish on FULL (100%) for 5 minutes (or according to the manufacturer's instructions).

Toss the veal in the seasoned flour. Add the butter to the browning dish and swirl to coat. Add the veal and cook on FULL (100%) for 2 minutes, stirring once.

Add any remaining flour and cook on FULL (100%) for a further 1 minute. Gradually add the stock, blending well. Cover and cook on FULL (100%) for 10 minutes, stirring once.

Add the tomatoes, mushrooms, onion, tomato purée and salt and pepper to taste, blending well. Cover and cook on FULL (100%) for 10 minutes, stirring once.

Reduce the setting and cook on MEDIUM (50%) for 25 minutes, stirring twice, or until the veal is tender. Leave to STAND, covered, while cooking the rice.

Place the rice, boiling water and salt in a bowl. Cover and cook on FULL (100%) for 3 minutes. Reduce the power setting to MEDIUM (50%) and cook for a further 12 minutes, stirring twice. Leave to STAND for 5 minutes.

Spoon the rice on to a warmed serving dish and top with the veal. Serve at once.
SERVES 4

VEAL CORDON BLEU

METRIC/IMPERIAL
4 × 100 g/4 oz escalopes of veal
100 g/4 oz cooked ham, thinly sliced
50 g/2 oz Edam cheese, thinly sliced
1 egg, beaten
40 g/1½ oz dried breadcrumbs
4 tablespoons vegetable oil
Garnish:
1 hard-boiled egg, chopped
few parsley sprigs
lemon wedges

Beat the veal with a mallet or rolling pin to flatten. Place a slice of ham and cheese on the centre of each. Fold up, completely enclosing the cheese and ham, to form a parcel. Dip into the beaten egg and coat with crumbs.

Preheat a large browning dish on FULL (100%) for 5 minutes (or according to the manufacturer's instructions). Quickly add the oil, then the veal and cook on FULL (100%) for 1 minute.

Turn over and cook on FULL (100%) for 5 minutes, giving the dish a half-turn after 2½ minutes. Drain on absorbent kitchen paper.

Transfer the veal to a heated serving dish. Garnish with chopped egg, parsley and lemon wedges.
SERVES 4

VEAL SPECIALITY

METRIC/IMPERIAL
8 escalopes of veal (total weight 675 g/1½ lb)
25 g/1 oz fresh breadcrumbs
1 tablespoon chopped fresh parsley
50 g/2 oz button mushrooms, finely chopped
50 g/2 oz Edam cheese, finely grated
2 tablespoons mayonnaise
salt
freshly ground black pepper
1 small egg
50 g/2 oz butter

Sauce:
6 tablespoons white wine
6 tablespoons well-flavoured veal or chicken
stock
3 teaspoons cornflour
50 g/2 oz button mushrooms, sliced
1 egg yolk
3 tablespoons double cream
Garnish:
parsley sprigs

Beat the veal escalopes with a meat hammer until each one is very thin. Mix together the breadcrumbs parsley, mushrooms, cheese, mayonnaise, and salt and pepper to taste. Bind the mixture using the egg. Spread a spoonful of the stuffing on each escalope. Roll up and secure each one with a wooden cocktail stick.

Place the butter in a round pie dish and cook on FULL (100%) for 2 minutes until foaming. Put the veal escalopes into the dish, turning so that all sides are coated with the hot butter.

Cover and cook on FULL (100%) for 6 minutes, turning the escalopes over and around, halfway through cooking. Set aside, covered with foil.

To make the sauce, put the wine and stock into a small jug and cook on FULL (100%) for 2 minutes. Cream the cornflour with a little water until smooth. Beat into the wine mixture with the juices from the meat. Season with salt and pepper.

Cook on FULL (100%) for 1½ minutes, until boiling. Cool slightly, then beat in the mushrooms, egg yolk and cream. Arrange the veal in a serving dish. Pour over the sauce and serve garnished with parsley.
SERVES 4

VEAL WITH MUSHROOMS AND ONIONS

METRIC/IMPERIAL
1 kg/2 lb veal from the leg, shoulder or breast,
cut into 1–2 cm/½–¾ inch cubes
1 onion, peeled and stuck with 4 cloves
1 carrot, quartered
1 celery stick, quartered
1 leek, white part only, quartered
1 bouquet garni
200 ml/⅓ pint dry white wine
salt
freshly ground black pepper
175 g/6 oz button mushrooms, trimmed

3 tablespoons lemon juice
10 pickling onions, peeled
25 g/1 oz butter
3 egg yolks
150 ml/¼ pint double cream
freshly grated nutmeg

Place the veal, onion, carrot, celery, leek, bouquet garni and white wine in a large bowl and add sufficient water to cover the meat. Season with salt and pepper, cover and cook on FULL (100%) for 15 minutes or until boiling. Skim, then reduce the power setting to LOW (30%). Cover and cook for 45 minutes or until the veal is tender, stirring twice.

Meanwhile, place the mushrooms in a bowl and sprinkle with 1½ tablespoons of the lemon juice. Leave to soak.

Using a slotted spoon, transfer the veal to a warm serving dish and keep warm. Strain the liquid into a saucepan and discard the vegetables.

Place the pickling onions and butter in a bowl. Cover and cook on FULL (100%) for 4½ minutes, stirring once. Stir in the mushrooms and the lemon juice in which they were soaking. Cover and cook on FULL (100%) for 3 minutes, stirring once. Sprinkle the onions and mushrooms over the veal. Keep warm.

Place the egg yolks in a small bowl with 1 tablespoon of the hot veal cooking liquid. Pour 350 ml/12 fl oz of the remaining liquid into a saucepan. Bring to the boil on a *conventional hob* and cook over a high heat until reduced to 250 ml/8 fl oz. Stir in the cream and add nutmeg to taste.

Whisk a ladleful of the hot sauce into the egg yolk mixture, then whisk this back into the saucepan. Whisk vigorously for 15 seconds over low heat. (Do not allow the sauce to boil at this stage or it will curdle.) Whisk in the remaining lemon juice, then taste and adjust the seasoning. Pour the sauce over the veal and serve immediately with boiled rice and fried aubergines.
SERVES 4

ROAST VEAL WITH MANDARIN ORANGES

METRIC/IMPERIAL
1 × 1.6 kg/3½ lb veal roast
½ teaspoon dried oregano
½ teaspoon dried basil
1 teaspoon ground paprika
freshly ground black pepper

salt
5 tablespoons dry white wine
Sauce:
150 ml/¼ pint chicken stock
1 × 200 g/7 oz can mandarin oranges
2 teaspoons plain flour
3 tablespoons single cream
3 tablespoons dry white wine

Season the veal with the oregano, basil, paprika, and salt and pepper to taste. Place in a shallow cooking dish with the wine. Cook on MEDIUM (50%) for 18 minutes.

Turn the veal roast over and cook on MEDIUM (50%) for a further 18 to 24 minutes until cooked. Remove from the dish and wrap in foil, shiny side inside. Leave to STAND for 20 minutes.

Meanwhile, stir the chicken stock and mandarin juice into the meat juices, blending well.

Blend the flour with the cream to a smooth paste and stir into the sauce mixture with the wine, blending well. Cook on FULL (100%) for 3 to 5 minutes, stirring three times, until smooth and thickened.

Stir in the mandarins. Cook on FULL (100%) for a further 1 minute, to reheat.

Place the veal on a warmed serving plate and serve with the hot mandarin sauce.

SERVES 6

AUSTRIAN VEAL ESCALOPES

METRIC/IMPERIAL
450 g/1 lb veal fillet
1 large egg (size 1), beaten
7 tablespoons golden crumbs or dark toasted breadcrumbs
1 tablespoon flour
salt
freshly ground black pepper
5 tablespoons vegetable oil
Garnish:
1 tablespoon chopped fresh parsley
6 lemon twists

Cut the veal into slices, about 5 × 10 cm/2 × 4 inches, and beat with a mallet or rolling pin to flatten. Dip the veal slices into the beaten egg and coat with the crumbs, pressing them on with a palette knife. Dust with flour and sprinkle with salt and pepper.

Preheat a large browning dish on FULL (100%) for 5 minutes (or according to the manufacturer's instructions). Add the oil and cook on FULL (100%) for 2 minutes. Quickly add the veal to the dish and cook on FULL (100%) for 5 minutes, turning the slices over after 2 minutes.

Drain on absorbent kitchen paper. Arrange on a heated serving dish and garnish with chopped parsley and twists of lemon to serve.

SERVES 3 to 4

VEAL ESCALOPES WITH HAM, CHEESE AND TOMATO

METRIC/IMPERIAL
½ onion, finely chopped
1 tablespoon olive oil
225 g/8 oz tomatoes, skinned and mashed
salt
freshly ground black pepper
4 × 100 g/4 oz escalopes of veal
plain flour for coating
1 large egg (size 1), lightly beaten
dried breadcrumbs for coating
100 g/4 oz butter
1 tablespoon vegetable oil
4 slices prosciutto or cooked ham
4 slices Gruyère cheese
chopped fresh parsley, to garnish

Place the onion and olive oil in a small bowl, cover and cook on FULL (100%) for 3 minutes or until soft, stirring once. Add the tomatoes and salt and pepper to taste. Cover and cook on FULL (100%) for 2½ minutes, then set aside.

Meanwhile, beat out the veal escalopes and coat lightly with flour. Dip them into the egg and coat with the breadcrumbs, pressing them on with a palette knife.

Heat the butter and the vegetable oil in a frying pan on a *conventional hob*, add the veal and brown quickly on both sides. Transfer to a shallow dish, overlapping the escalopes, if necessary. Place a slice of ham, then a slice of cheese on each one and cook on FULL (100%) for 3 minutes or until the cheese has melted.

Reheat the sauce, covered, on FULL (100%) for 2 minutes or until hot, then pour over the escalopes and sprinkle with chopped parsley. Serve immediately with buttered spaghetti and mushrooms.

SERVES 4

148

BALLOTINE OF VEAL

METRIC/IMPERIAL
450 ml/¾ pint hot vegetable stock
1 onion, sliced
1 carrot, sliced
1 bay leaf
1.25 kg/2½ lb breast of veal, boned
Stuffing:
5 tablespoons fresh wholemeal breadcrumbs
3 tablespoons skimmed milk
100 g/4 oz frozen spinach, defrosted
275 g/10 oz cooked chicken, minced
40 g/1½ oz pistachio nuts
¼ teaspoon grated nutmeg
1 small egg, lightly beaten
salt
freshly ground black pepper

Place the hot stock, onion, carrot and bay leaf in a large bowl. Cover and cook on FULL (100%) for 4 minutes. Leave to infuse while making the stuffing.

Put the breadcrumbs into a mixing bowl, add the skimmed milk and leave to soak. Squeeze the spinach to extract as much water as possible, then shred it finely. Add it to the soaked breadcrumbs, together with the remaining stuffing ingredients and mix thoroughly.

Lay the breast of veal on a board, skinned side down, and spread with the stuffing. Roll the meat, from the short end, and secure with wooden cocktail sticks and string. Wrap the veal in a double layer of muslin, or a thin tea towel, and tie it firmly at both ends with string.

Return the infused stock to the oven and cook on FULL (100%) for 4 minutes to heat. Place the ballotine in the stock, cover and cook on FULL (100%) for 5 minutes. Turn the ballotine over, cover again, and cook on FULL (100%) for a further 5 minutes. Turn the ballotine over again, cover and cook on LOW (30%) for 34 to 35 minutes (or on DEFROST/20% for 42 minutes), turning the ballotine over three or four times during cooking.

To test if the ballotine is cooked, pierce with a skewer; if the juices run clear the meat is cooked. Lift the ballotine out, wrap tightly in foil and leave to cool.

When cool, remove the foil and muslin, wrap in cling film and chill in the refrigerator.
SERVES 4 to 6

VEAL AND TOMATO CASSEROLE

METRIC/IMPERIAL
25 g/1 oz flour
4 tablespoons vegetable oil
1 kg/2 lb boned shoulder or breast of veal, thinly sliced or cut into cubes
2 onions, chopped
1 clove garlic, crushed
1 teaspoon salt
1 teaspoon freshly ground black pepper
450 ml/¾ pint boiling water
1 chicken stock cube, crumbled
1 bouquet garni
1 × 400 g/14 oz can tomatoes

Blend the flour and oil together in a large deep dish and cook on FULL (100%) for 5 minutes, stirring once during cooking, until browned.

Add the veal, onions, garlic and salt and pepper. Cook on FULL (100%) for 5 minutes, stirring once. Add the water, stock cube, bouquet garni and tomatoes with their juice. Cover and cook on FULL (100%) for 20 minutes, stirring once, or cook on MEDIUM (50%) for 35 minutes, stirring occasionally. Remove and discard the bouquet garni.

Leave to STAND for 10 minutes before serving.
SERVES 6

VEAL WITH PIMIENTOS AND SOURED CREAM

METRIC/IMPERIAL
450 g/1 lb veal fillet
1 × 225 g/8 oz can sweet pimientos, drained
2 tablespoons flour
2 tablespoons vegetable oil
1 small onion, chopped
300 ml/½ pint hot chicken stock
salt
freshly ground black pepper
1 egg yolk
150 ml/¼ pint soured cream

Slice the veal thinly and cut into strips, about 1 × 7.5 cm/½ × 3 inches. Cut the pimientos into strips.

Combine the flour and oil in a large deep dish and cook on FULL (100%) for 3 minutes, stirring once. Stir in the chopped onion and cook on FULL (100%) for 3 minutes, stirring

149

occasionally. Add the veal and cook on FULL (100%) for 2 minutes, stirring after 1 minute.

Pour the chicken stock over the veal and season with salt and pepper to taste. Gently stir in the pimientos and cover. Cook on FULL (100%) for 5 minutes. Stir well, then cook on LOW (30%) for 10 minutes until the veal is tender, stirring once.

Beat the egg yolk and soured cream together, then blend in 2 or 3 tablespoons of the hot sauce. Stir this mixture into the dish, then cook on LOW (30%) for 2 to 3 minutes until the sauce has thickened, stirring twice. Leave to STAND, covered, for 5 minutes before serving.

No additional garnish is required for this dish, although it may be served on a heated platter surrounded by a border of boiled rice.
SERVES 4

ORANGE-STUFFED VEAL

METRIC/IMPERIAL
1 × 1.5 kg/3 lb boned shoulder joint of veal
Stuffing:
40 g/1½ oz fresh white breadcrumbs
50 g/2 oz sultanas
grated rind of 2 oranges
1 small onion, grated
1 tablespoon marmalade
1 teaspoon dried rosemary
salt
freshly ground black pepper
1 egg, lightly beaten
Sauce:
25 g/1 oz cornflour
2 tablespoons fresh orange juice
1 tablespoon brandy
about 450 ml/¾ pint cold chicken stock
grated rind of 1 orange
Garnish:
orange slices
watercress

To make the stuffing, mix together the breadcrumbs, sultanas, orange rind, onion, marmalade, rosemary and salt and pepper to taste. Add sufficient egg to bind the ingredients together.

Untie and open the veal. Cut along the meat if there is insufficient space for the stuffing. Stuff the cavity or spread the stuffing over the meat. Reroll and tie securely with string.

Place the veal on a roasting rack in a shallow dish. Cook on FULL (100%) for 25 to 27 minutes, or on MEDIUM (50%) for 33 to 36 minutes, turning the meat over halfway through cooking.

Pour off the juices from the dish and set aside. Wrap the meat tightly in foil and leave to STAND for 20 minutes before serving.

To make the sauce, mix together the cornflour, orange juice and brandy in a large jug. Stir in the juices from the veal and add sufficient stock to make 600 ml/1 pint. Add the orange rind and cook on FULL (100%) for 3 minutes or until thickened. Stir every 1 minute. Add salt and pepper to taste.

Remove the string from the veal and place the meat on a warm serving platter. Garnish with orange slices and watercress, and serve with the sauce.
SERVES 6

Note: To calculate microwave cooking times for a larger piece of veal, when the veal has been stuffed, weigh it and cook for 8½ to 9 minutes per 450 g/1 lb. The standing time remains the same.

Variation
Lemon-stuffed veal: use the grated rind of 2 lemons in place of the orange rind in the stuffing, and use lemon juice and the grated rind of 1 lemon in the sauce. Garnish the veal with lemon slices and watercress or sprigs of fresh parsley and serve as above.

VEAL WITH MUSHROOMS AND WINE SAUCE

METRIC/IMPERIAL
450 g/1 lb escalope of veal, thinly sliced
25 g/1 oz plain flour
1 teaspoon salt
½ teaspoon freshly ground black pepper
50 g/2 oz butter
1 onion, chopped
1 × 225 g/8 oz can button mushrooms
1 teaspoon dried oregano
120 ml/4 fl oz dry red wine
5 tablespoons double cream
chopped fresh parsley, to garnish

Beat the veal slices with a mallet or rolling pin to flatten. Coat with flour, then season with salt and pepper to taste.

Place half of the butter in a large shallow dish and heat on FULL (100%) for ½ minute to melt.

Stir in the onion and cook on FULL (100%) for 4 to 5 minutes until soft and lightly browned, stirring occasionally.

Place the veal slices on top and dot with the remaining butter. Cook on FULL (100%) for 4 minutes, then turn the veal over and add the mushrooms, together with their juice, the oregano and wine. Move the veal towards the sides of the dish, leaving a well in the centre. Cover and cook on LOW (30%) for 30 minutes, stirring once or twice during cooking.

Stir in the cream and cook on LOW (30%) for 3 to 5 minutes until reheated. Serve immediately, garnished with parsley and accompanied by carrots, if liked.

SERVES 4

ORANGE-GLAZED BREAST OF VEAL

METRIC/IMPERIAL
100 g/4 oz fresh breadcrumbs
50 g/2 oz suet, shredded
25 g/1 oz raisins
salt
freshly ground black pepper
1 tablespoon pure orange juice
2 eggs
1.75 kg/4 lb breast of veal, boned and rolled
25 g/1 oz butter
2 tablespoons marmalade
orange slices to garnish

To make up the stuffing, mix together the breadcrumbs, suet, raisins, salt and pepper, orange juice and eggs. Lay the veal flat and spread the stuffing over it. Roll up the veal and tie with thin string at 2.5 cm/1 inch intervals all along the length.

Place the butter in a small bowl and heat on FULL (100%) for ½ minute. Brush the melted butter over the veal and sprinkle over a little salt.

Put the veal into a roasting bag and arrange, on an upturned saucer, in an ovenproof glass dish. Snip the bag at its base in three places and cook on FULL (100%) for 10 minutes. Reduce the setting to MEDIUM (50%) and cook for 32 minutes, turning the joint over and around halfway through cooking.

Leave to STAND, covered with foil, for 15 to 20 minutes. Uncover the meat and place under a preheated hot grill to brown the top.

Place the marmalade in a small jug and cook on FULL (100%) for 1 minute. Sieve and use to glaze the meat. Garnish with orange slices before serving.

SERVES 6

Note: Breast of veal is cooked for 8 to 9 minutes for each 450 g/1 lb. It is a good idea to use a microwave meat thermometer. Insert the thermometer into the centre of the meat before it goes into the roasting bag. Remove the meat from the microwave oven when the thermometer reads 65°C/149°F.

DEVILLED KIDNEY AND SAUSAGE ON RICE

METRIC/IMPERIAL
225 g/8 oz long-grain rice
600 ml/1 pint boiling water
1 teaspoon salt
50 g/2 oz butter
1 onion, chopped
8 pork chipolatas
8 lambs' kidneys, skinned, halved and cored
2 tablespoons dry sherry
2 tablespoons Worcestershire sauce
1 teaspoon mustard powder
1 tablespoon chopped fresh parsley
salt
freshly ground black pepper

Place the rice in a bowl with the boiling water and salt. Cover and cook on FULL (100%) for 3 minutes. Reduce the power to MEDIUM (50%) and cook for a further 12 minutes, stirring twice. Leave to STAND while preparing the kidney and sausage mixture.

Place the butter in a bowl and heat on FULL (100%) for 1 minute or until melted. Add the onion, cover and cook on FULL (100%) for 3 minutes.

Twist each chipolata into two pieces and cut. Add the kidney and sausage pieces to the onion mixture, blending well. Cover and cook on FULL (100%) for 4 minutes, stirring once. Add the sherry, Worcestershire sauce, mustard, parsley, and salt and pepper to taste, blending well. Cover and cook on FULL (100%) for 3 minutes, stirring once.

To serve, spoon the rice into a warmed serving dish and top with the devilled kidney and sausage mixture.

SERVES 4

SHERRIED KIDNEYS

METRIC/IMPERIAL
25 g/1 oz butter
1 small onion, finely chopped
575 g/1¼ lb lambs' kidneys, skinned, halved and cored
120 ml/4 fl oz beef stock
1 teaspoon French mustard
2 tablespoons dry sherry
2 tablespoons smooth liver pâté
salt
freshly ground black pepper

Place the butter in a medium casserole and heat on FULL (100%) for ½ minute or until melted. Add the onion, cover and cook on FULL (100%) for 2 minutes.

Stir in the kidneys, cover and cook on FULL (100%) for 6 to 8 minutes, stirring them once.

Add the stock, mustard, sherry, pâté and salt and pepper to taste, blending well. Cover and cook on FULL (100%) for a further 2 to 3 minutes until hot, bubbly and the kidneys are cooked through. Leave to STAND for 3 to 5 minutes. Serve with boiled rice.

SERVES 4

MEXICAN LIVER

METRIC/IMPERIAL
2 tablespoons vegetable oil
1 onion, sliced
100 g/4 oz green pepper, cored, seeded and sliced
1 clove garlic, crushed
225 g/8 oz lamb's liver, sliced
100 g/4 oz button mushrooms
2 × 400 g/14 oz can tomatoes
3 tablespoons water
salt
freshly ground black pepper

Place the oil in a deep dish and heat on FULL (100%) for 1½ to 2 minutes. Add the onion, pepper and garlic and cook on FULL (100%) for 3 to 3½ minutes, stirring once during cooking.

Add the liver and cook on FULL (100%) for 1 minute before mixing in the remaining ingredients. Add salt and pepper to taste and continue to cook on FULL (100%) for 4 minutes, stirring once during cooking. Leave to STAND for a few minutes before serving.

SERVES 4

LIVER STROGANOFF

METRIC/IMPERIAL
15 g/½ oz butter
100 g/4 oz lamb's or calf's liver, cut into short, narrow strips
½ small onion, thinly sliced
¼ green pepper, cored, seeded and chopped
25 g/1 oz mushrooms, sliced
1 teaspoon plain flour
50 ml/2 fl oz beef stock
1 teaspoon tomato purée
pinch of sugar
salt
freshly ground black pepper
1 tablespoon double or soured cream

Preheat a small browning dish on FULL (100%) for 3 minutes (or according to the manufacturer's instructions). Add the butter and swirl to coat. Heat on FULL (100%) for a further 1 minute.

Add the liver and turn quickly on all sides to brown. Cook on FULL (100%) for 2 minutes, stirring once. Remove from the dish with a slotted spoon and set aside.

Add the onion, pepper and mushrooms to the dish. Cover and cook on FULL (100%) for 3 minutes, stirring once. Stir in the flour, blending well.

Gradually add the stock, tomato purée, sugar and salt and pepper to taste. Cook on FULL (100%) for 1½ minutes, stirring once.

Return the liver to the dish and cook on FULL (100%) for a further 1 minute, stirring once. Stir in the cream and serve at once with noodles or rice.

SERVES 1

LIVER AND BACON CASSEROLE

METRIC/IMPERIAL
4 streaky bacon rashers, derinded and chopped
25 g/1 oz butter
1 carrot, thinly sliced
½ celery stick, finely chopped
1 onion, finely chopped
25 g/1 oz cornflour
300 ml/½ pint hot beef stock
225 g/8 oz tomatoes, skinned and chopped
3 tablespoons tomato purée
1 teaspoon Worcestershire sauce
50 g/2 oz mushrooms, chopped

1 teaspoon dried mixed herbs
2 bay leaves
salt
freshly ground black pepper
450 g/1 lb lamb's liver, thinly sliced
bay leaves, to garnish

Place the bacon, butter, carrot, celery and onion in a large bowl. Cover and cook on FULL (100%) for 6½ minutes, stirring halfway through cooking. Stir in the cornflour, then blend in the hot stock.

Add the tomatoes, tomato purée, Worcestershire sauce, mushrooms, herbs, bay leaves, salt, pepper and liver. Cover and cook on FULL (100%) for 10 minutes, stirring halfway through cooking. Leave to STAND, covered, for 5 minutes. Garnish with bay leaves.
SERVES 4

ORIENTAL LIVER

METRIC/IMPERIAL
350 g/12 oz calf's liver, sliced
50 g/2 oz seasoned wholemeal flour
25 g/1 oz butter
2 onions, sliced
1 red or green pepper, cored, seeded and chopped
2 teaspoons chilli powder
2 tablespoons soy sauce
1 tablespoon tomato purée
2 tomatoes, skinned, seeded and chopped
salt
freshly ground black pepper
250 ml/8 fl oz milk
watercress sprigs, to garnish

Coat the liver in the seasoned flour. Preheat a large browning dish on FULL (100%) for 5 minutes (or according to the manufacturer's instructions). Add the butter and swirl quickly.

Add the liver and turn quickly on both sides to brown evenly. Cook on FULL (100%) for 4 minutes, turning once. Set aside.

Place the onion, pepper and chilli powder in a bowl. Cover and cook on FULL (100%) for 6 minutes, stirring once. Add the soy sauce, tomato purée, tomatoes, and salt and pepper to taste, blending well. Stir into the liver with the milk, blending well. Cover and cook on FULL (100%) for 3 to 4 minutes, stirring twice.

Serve hot, garnished with watercress sprigs.
SERVES 4

KIDNEY CASSEROLE WITH RICE

METRIC/IMPERIAL
1 onion, finely chopped
15 g/½ oz butter
1 tablespoon vegetable oil
10 lambs' kidneys, skinned, halved and cored
1 tablespoon flour
salt
freshly ground black pepper
2 tablespoons tomato purée
300 ml/½ pint hot chicken stock
4 frankfurters, sliced
100 g/4 oz button mushrooms, trimmed
3 tablespoons whisky or sherry
550 ml/18 fl oz boiling water
225 g/8 oz long-grain rice
½ teaspoon salt

Place the onion, butter and oil in a large dish and cook on FULL (100%) for 3 minutes, stirring once. Stir in the kidneys and cook on FULL (100%) for 4 minutes, stirring once during cooking.

Add the flour and mix well, then add salt and pepper to taste, the tomato purée, chicken stock, frankfurters and mushrooms. Cook on FULL (100%) for 6½ minutes. Stir in the whisky or sherry and allow to STAND while cooking the rice.

Place the water, rice and ½ teaspoon salt in a bowl. Cover and cook on FULL (100%) for 3 minutes. Reduce the power setting to MEDIUM (50%) and cook for a further 12 minutes, stirring once. Leave to STAND, covered, for 5 minutes. Stir well, arrange a border around the edge of a warmed serving dish and place the kidneys in the centre.
SERVES 4

KEBABS À LA GRECQUE

METRIC/IMPERIAL
575 g/1¼ lb lean boned leg of lamb
1 aubergine, peeled
1 green pepper, cored and seeded
4 lambs' kidneys, skinned, halved and cored
6 button mushrooms, trimmed
6 small firm tomatoes
Marinade:
4 tablespoons vegetable oil
juice of ½ lemon
1 small onion, chopped

1 clove garlic, quartered
1 teaspoon salt
½ teaspoon freshly ground black pepper
¼ teaspoon mustard powder
1 teaspoon dried oregano
2 bay leaves

Cut the lamb and aubergine into 2.5 cm/1 inch cubes and cut the green pepper into similar-sized squares.

Combine the marinade ingredients in a bowl. Add the kidneys, lamb, aubergine and green pepper, stirring well. Cover and leave to marinate in the refrigerator for at least 12 hours, stirring occasionally.

Strain the marinade and reserve. Thread the lamb, kidneys and vegetables on to 6 wooden kebab skewers, placing a tomato in the centre of each skewer. Arrange in a large shallow dish and spoon over the marinade.

Cook on FULL (100%) for 12 minutes, basting and giving the dish a half-turn occasionally during cooking, until the lamb is tender and cooked. Serve hot, on a bed of rice.
SERVES 4 to 6

SPEEDY LEMON LIVER

METRIC/IMPERIAL
3 onions, peeled and cut into rings
25 g/1 oz butter
350 g/12 oz calf's liver, cut into thin strips
150 ml/¼ pint beef stock
1 teaspoon dried parsley
1 teaspoon French mustard
2 teaspoons lemon juice
salt
freshly ground black pepper
2 teaspoons cornflour
Garnish:
2 lemon slices
chopped fresh parsley

Put the onions in a bowl. Cover and cook on FULL (100%) for 3 minutes. Set aside.

Place the butter in serving dish and cook on FULL (100%) for 1 minute. Stir the liver into the hot butter. Cover and cook on FULL (100%) for 2 minutes. Set aside.

In a large jug, place the stock, parsley, French mustard, lemon juice, and salt and pepper to taste. Cook on FULL (100%) for 2 minutes.

Cream the cornflour with a little water to form a smooth paste. Add the juices from the liver to the heated stock. Beat in the cornflour and cook on FULL (100%) for 1 minute, stirring once.

To assemble the dish: transfer the liver to a heated plate; rinse the dish and arrange the onion rings on the bottom. Top with the cooked liver and pour and gravy over. Garnish with lemon slices (cut into a butterfly shape, if wished), and sprinkle with parsley. Serve with glazed carrots, sweetcorn and jacket potatoes.
SERVES 4

KIDNEY AND BUTTER BEAN CASSEROLE

METRIC/IMPERIAL
675 g/1½ lb ox kidney, rinsed in salted water, skinned, halved and cored
3 lean bacon rashers, derinded and chopped
1 onion, chopped
20 g/¾ oz butter
2 tablespoons flour
150 ml/¼ pint beef stock
150 ml/¼ pint red wine
2 tablespoons tomato purée
1 teaspoon salt
½ teaspoon freshly ground black pepper
1 × 225 g/8 oz can butter beans, drained
Garnish:
triangles of French toast
2 tablespoons chopped fresh parsley

Cut the kidney into small pieces. Combine the bacon, onion and butter in a large deep dish and cook on FULL (100%) for 5 minutes, stirring occasionally. Stir in the flour, then add the stock, wine, tomato purée, salt and pepper. Cover and cook on MEDIUM (50%) for 10 minutes, stirring occasionally.

Add the beans, adjust the seasoning, re-cover and cook on LOW (30%) for 15 to 20 minutes until the kidney is tender, stirring occasionally during cooking. Leave to STAND for 5 minutes.

Arrange triangles of French toast around the edge of the dish, and sprinkle the casserole with chopped parsley.
SERVES 4 to 6

Variation
Peas, mushrooms or carrots can be used instead of butter beans, if preferred.

CALF'S LIVER HELVETIA

METRIC/IMPERIAL
25 g/1 oz butter
1 onion, finely chopped
450 g/1 lb calf's liver, cut into thin strips
150 ml/¼ pint beef stock
3 tablespoons soured cream
3 tablespoons red wine
1 teaspoon chopped fresh basil
1–2 teaspoons plain flour
1–2 tablespoons cold water
salt
freshly ground black pepper

Place the butter in a small casserole dish and heat on FULL (100%) for ½ minute or until melted. Add the onion, cover and cook on FULL (100%) for 3 minutes, stirring once.

Add the liver, blending well. Cover and cook on FULL (100%) for 5 to 6 minutes, stirring twice. Add the stock, soured cream, wine and basil, blending well.

Mix the flour and water to a smooth paste. Stir into the liver mixture with salt and pepper to taste. Cook on FULL (100%) for 2 to 3 minutes, stirring twice, until smooth and thickened.

Serve at once with noodles or creamed potatoes.
SERVES 4

KIDNEYS IN RED WINE

METRIC/IMPERIAL
50 g/2 oz butter
1 onion, chopped
2 streaky bacon rashers, derinded and chopped
10 lambs' kidneys, skinned, halved and cored
1 teaspoon dried tarragon or marjoram
salt
freshly ground black pepper
25 g/1 oz plain flour
50 g/2 oz button mushrooms, chopped
150 ml/¼ pint red wine
1 tablespoon soured cream

Put the butter into a casserole dish and heat on FULL (100%) for 1½ minutes. Stir in the onion and bacon. Cook on FULL (100%) for 1½ minutes.

Stir in the kidneys and tarragon or marjoram, and season with salt and pepper to taste. Cover and cook on FULL (100%) for 4 minutes.

Stir in the flour, mushrooms and wine. Cook

on FULL (100%) for 3 minutes, stirring twice. Leave to STAND, covered, for 5 minutes.

Just before serving, swirl a tablespoon of soured cream into the gravy.
SERVES 4

KIDNEYS IN GRAPE JUICE

METRIC/IMPERIAL
8 lambs' kidneys, skinned, halved and cored
600 ml/1 pint boiling water
2 tablespoons grapeseed or sunflower oil
1 onion, finely chopped
1 tablespoon hot water
150 ml/¼ pint red grape juice
1 tablespoon wholemeal flour
150 ml/¼ pint hot chicken or vegetable stock
100 g/4 oz button mushrooms, thinly sliced
pinch of salt
freshly ground black pepper
2 tablespoons chopped fresh parsley

Place the kidneys on a wooden board, cut side down. With a sharp knife, make deep incisions in a criss-cross pattern on each kidney. Transfer the kidneys to a bowl. Add the boiling water and cook on FULL (100%) for 2 to 2½ minutes, stirring halfway through the cooking time. Drain the kidneys and pat dry on absorbent kitchen paper. Discard the cooking liquid.

Heat a large browning dish for 5 minutes (or according to the manufacturer's instructions). Without removing it from the oven, add the oil and kidneys and cook on FULL (100%) for 2 to 2½ minutes, stirring halfway through. Remove the kidneys with a slotted spoon and drain them on absorbent kitchen paper.

Place the onion and hot water in a large bowl or casserole and cook on FULL (100%) for 2 to 2½ minutes. Stir in the grape juice and cook for a further 1½ minutes. Blend the flour with a little of the stock and stir it into the grape juice with the remaining stock. Stir in the reserved kidneys, cover and cook on FULL (100%) for 3 minutes, stirring every 1 minute to avoid lumps forming.

Stir in the mushrooms and season with salt and pepper. Cover and cook on FULL (100%) for a further 1½ minutes. Stir in the chopped parsley and allow to STAND, covered, for 3 minutes. Serve with brown rice or creamed potatoes.
SERVES 4

Note: Boiling the kidneys first opens them up and helps to remove any impurities.

POULTRY AND GAME

ROAST CHICKEN WITH WALNUT AND ORANGE STUFFING

METRIC/IMPERIAL
1 × 1.75 kg/4 lb oven-ready chicken
25 g/1 oz butter
1 tablespoon plain flour
300 ml/½ pint chicken stock
Stuffing:
50 g/2 oz butter
1 small onion, finely chopped
100 g/4 oz fresh white breadcrumbs
25 g/1 oz chopped fresh parsley
grated rind of 1 orange and 2 tablespoons orange juice
50 g/2 oz walnuts, chopped
salt
freshly ground black pepper
1 egg, beaten
Garnish:
orange slices
parsley sprigs

To make the stuffing, put the butter in a bowl and heat on FULL (100%) for ½ to 1 minute or until melted. Add the onion, cover and cook on FULL (100%) for 2 minutes.

Add the breadcrumbs, three-quarters of the parsley, the orange rind and juice, walnuts, and salt and pepper. Add sufficient beaten egg to bind. Use to stuff the neck end of the chicken. Secure with wooden cocktail sticks. Roll the remaining stuffing into balls.

Shield the tips of the wings with small pieces of aluminium foil, ensuring that the foil does not touch the walls of the oven. Place on a roasting rack or upturned saucer in a dish and dot with butter.

Cook on FULL (100%) for 26 to 34 minutes, giving the dish a half-turn halfway through cooking. Cover with foil and leave to STAND for 15 minutes.

Meanwhile, place the stuffing balls in a ring on a plate or roasting rack and cook on FULL (100%) for 2 to 3 minutes, turning the plate once. Sprinkle with the remaining parsley.

To make the gravy, place 2 tablespoons of the chicken juices in a bowl and stir in the flour. Cook on FULL (100%) for 2 minutes until the flour turns golden. Gradually add the stock, mixing well. Cook for a further 2 to 3 minutes, stirring every 1 minute, until smooth and boiling.

Garnish the chicken with orange and parsley.
SERVES 4

BURGUNDY CHICKEN

METRIC/IMPERIAL
1 × 1.5 kg/3¼ lb oven-ready chicken
1 bay leaf
1 thyme sprig
1 clove garlic, crushed
salt
freshly ground black pepper
600 ml/1 pint full-bodied red wine
3 tablespoons bramble or redcurrant jelly
25 g/1 oz butter
1 thick slice lean bacon, derinded and cut into strips or cubes
12 button onions, peeled
12 black olives
thyme sprig, to garnish

Place the chicken in a deep cooking dish with the bay leaf, thyme, garlic, salt and pepper to taste, wine and bramble or redcurrant jelly. Cook on LOW (30%) for 40 to 45 minutes, turning over two to three times. Remove from the oven, cover the chicken with foil, shiny side inside, and leave to STAND for 20 minutes.

Meanwhile, place the butter, bacon and onions in a shallow cooking dish. Cook on FULL (100%) for 5 minutes, stirring once.

To serve, place the chicken on a warmed serving dish. Surround with the cooked bacon, onions and olives. Spoon over some of the cooking juices and garnish with the thyme.
SERVES 4

ROAST CHICKEN

METRIC/IMPERIAL
25 g/1 oz butter
1.5 kg/3¼ lb oven-ready chicken
chicken seasoning (browning agent)

Place the butter in a small bowl and heat on FULL (100%) for 1 minute. Spread the butter all over the skin of the chicken, then sprinkle liberally with chicken seasoning.

Place the chicken in a roasting bag, neck end first. Fold the bag loosely under the bird and pierce the base. Arrange the chicken on an upturned saucer in an ovenproof dish. Cook on FULL (100%) for 18 to 24 minutes.

Remove from the oven and cover the bird with foil, shiny side inside. Leave to STAND for 20 minutes before carving.
SERVES 4

Note: Chicken is cooked for 7 minutes for each 450 g/1 lb. The bird can be stuffed according to taste, but allow an extra 5 minutes cooking time.

CHICKEN BAKED IN YOGURT

METRIC/IMPERIAL
4 chicken breasts
4 tablespoons lemon juice
1 teaspoon salt
Marinade:
1 onion, coarsely chopped
2 teaspoons ground turmeric
1 clove garlic, peeled
4 slices fresh root ginger, peeled and coarsely chopped
1 tablespoon garam masala
250 ml/8 fl oz natural yogurt
Garnish:
chopped fresh coriander or parsley
lemon wedges

Make three or four diagonal slashes across each chicken breast and rub them on both sides with lemon juice and salt. Place them in a shallow dish and leave in a cool place for 20 minutes.

Place the onion, turmeric, garlic, ginger, garam masala and yogurt in a blender or food processor and blend until smooth.

Rub the marinade into the chicken, then cover and refrigerate for 8 to 12 hours, turning over two or three times.

Place the dish in the microwave oven, cover and cook on FULL (100%) for 12 minutes or until the chicken is cooked, turning the breasts over and rearranging them after 6 minutes.

Drain the marinade and discard. Place the chicken on a warm serving dish, sprinkle with chopped coriander or parsley and garnish with lemon wedges. Serve hot with boiled sweet potato and creamed corn.
SERVES 4

CHICKEN MARENGO

METRIC/IMPERIAL
4 boneless chicken breasts, skinned
2 tablespoons flour
6–8 spring onions, chopped
25 g/1 oz butter, softened
100 g/4 oz mushrooms, sliced
1 × 400 g/14 oz can tomatoes
1 teaspoon finely chopped fresh basil
½ teaspoon finely chopped fresh thyme
2 bay leaves
½ teaspoon freshly ground black pepper
1 teaspoon salt
1 lemon slice
150 ml/¼ pint medium white wine
4 cooked king prawns, to garnish (see note)

Beat the chicken to flatten, then dip in the flour and coat thoroughly. Blend the spring onions and butter together.

Preheat a large browning dish on FULL (100%) for 5 minutes (or according to the manufacturer's instructions). Quickly add the spring onion mixture and cook on FULL (100%) for 2 minutes. Immediately add the chicken breasts and cook on FULL (100%) for 2 minutes. Turn the chicken pieces over and cook on FULL (100%) for 2 minutes.

Stir in the mushrooms and cook on FULL (100%) for 1 minute. Add all the remaining ingredients, crushing the tomatoes slightly. Cover and cook on LOW (30%) for 15 to 20 minutes, or until the chicken is tender. Remove the lemon and bay leaves and serve garnished with the prawns.
SERVES 4

Note: To cook king prawns, place in a dish and cover with water. Add a slice of lemon, a bay leaf and ½ teaspoon salt. Cover and cook on FULL (100%) until boiling. Leave to STAND for 5 minutes before serving.

GLAZED POUSSINS

METRIC/IMPERIAL
25 g/1 oz butter
1 tablespoon soft, dark brown sugar
1 tablespoon Worcestershire sauce
4 bacon rashers, derinded
4 oven-ready poussins (total weight about 1.5 kg/3¼ lb)
watercress sprigs, to garnish

Place the butter, sugar and Worcestershire sauce in a small jug. Cook on FULL (100%) for 1 minute. Set aside.

Push a rasher of bacon into each poussin. Place the poussins, breast sides down, in a shallow casserole dish. Cook on FULL (100%) for 12 minutes.

Turn the poussins over and brush with the sugar glaze. Cook on FULL (100%) for a further 10 minutes. Wrap the casserole in foil and leave to STAND, covered, for 10 minutes. Garnish with watercress before serving.

SERVES 4

CHICKEN WATERZOOI

METRIC/IMPERIAL
1 × 1.5 kg/3¼ lb oven-ready chicken
1 leek, white part only, sliced
1 onion, chopped
4 celery sticks, chopped
2 parsley sprigs
2 cloves garlic, crushed
1 carrot, chopped
¼ teaspoon grated nutmeg
¼ teaspoon dried thyme
3 cloves
salt
freshly ground black pepper
about 1.2 litres/2 pints hot chicken stock
1 lemon, thinly sliced
1 tablespoon chopped fresh parsley
4 egg yolks, beaten with 4 tablespoons double cream

Place the chicken, breast side down, in a large bowl. Cover and cook on FULL (100%) for 15 minutes. Mix together the leek, onion, celery, parsley, garlic, carrot, nutmeg, thyme, cloves and salt and pepper to taste. Place around the chicken and pour over sufficient hot stock to almost cover the chicken.

Cover and cook on FULL (100%) for 5 minutes, then reduce the setting to LOW (30%) and cook for a further 30 minutes.

Remove the chicken from the stock and, when it is cool enough to handle, take the flesh from the bones in large pieces, discarding the skin. Keep the chicken warm.

Strain 750 ml/1¼ pints of the stock into a clean saucepan, add the lemon slices and chopped parsley and heat on a *conventional hob* until almost boiling.

Stir a little hot stock into the egg yolk mixture, then pour back into the saucepan. Continue stirring over a low heat until the sauce has thickened slightly. (Do not allow it to boil.) Remove from the heat and stir in the chicken pieces. Pour into a heated tureen and serve immediately.

SERVES 4

Note: This soup is a great favourite in Holland and Belgium. Another version is made with freshwater fish.

POUSSINS AU PRINTANIER

METRIC/IMPERIAL
50 g/2 oz butter
225 g/8 oz baby onions, peeled
225 g/8 oz courgettes, sliced
225 g/8 oz button mushrooms, trimmed
salt
freshly ground black pepper
1 lemon, quartered
4 × 450 g/1 lb oven-ready poussins
soy sauce for brushing

Place the butter in a large cooking dish and heat on FULL (100%) for 1 minute or until melted. Add the onions, courgettes, mushrooms and salt and pepper to taste, blending well.

Place a lemon quarter inside each poussin. Arrange on top of the vegetables, breast sides down. Brush the skins with soy sauce. Cook on FULL (100%) for 20 minutes, turning the dish twice.

Turn the poussins breast sides up, brush with soy sauce again and cook on FULL (100%) for a further 20 minutes, turning the dish twice. Cover and leave to STAND for 5 minutes.

Serve the poussins, one per person, surrounded with the buttery vegetables.

SERVES 4

CHICKEN CASSEROLE

METRIC/IMPERIAL
1 × 1.5 kg/3¼ lb oven-ready chicken, cut into 8 pieces
25 g/1 oz flour
6 bacon rashers, derinded and chopped
2 onions, finely chopped
1 × 300 g/11 oz can condensed mushroom soup
450 ml/¾ pint chicken stock or water
½ teaspoon salt
¼ teaspoon freshly ground black pepper
1 teaspoon paprika

Dust the chicken pieces with the flour. Place the bacon in a large deep dish and cook on FULL (100%) for 5 minutes, stirring once. Add the onions and cook on FULL (100%) for 4 minutes until they soften.

Stir in the soup, stock and salt and pepper. Add the chicken pieces, arranging them so that the thicker parts are round the outside. Cover and cook on FULL (100%) for 18 to 24 minutes, stirring two or three times during cooking.

Cover and leave to STAND for 10 minutes. Test with the tip of a sharp knife and, if the chicken is not quite cooked, cook on FULL (100%) for a further 3 to 4 minutes before serving, sprinkled with paprika.
SERVES 4

CHICKEN WITH VEGETABLES IN WINE

METRIC/IMPERIAL
1 × 1.5 kg/3¼ lb oven-ready chicken
25 g/1 oz butter
225 g/8 oz baby onions, peeled
225 g/8 oz carrots, thickly sliced
100 g/4 oz streaky bacon, derinded and chopped
1 green pepper, cored, seeded and chopped
2 celery sticks, sliced
100 g/4 oz small button mushrooms, trimmed
1 bay leaf
salt
freshly ground black pepper
2 tablespoons flour
300 ml/½ pint medium dry white wine
300 ml/½ pint chicken stock

Tie the legs of the chicken together firmly to hold them as close to the body of the bird as possible. Place the chicken on a saucer in a shallow dish or on a roasting rack. Cook on FULL (100%) for 18 to 24 minutes, turning over twice during cooking.

Wrap the chicken in a double thickness of foil, with the shiny side inside, and allow to STAND for 10 to 15 minutes before serving.

Place the butter in a shallow dish and heat on FULL (100%) for ½ minute or until melted. Add the onions, carrots, bacon, pepper and celery. Cook on FULL (100%) for 4 minutes before adding the mushrooms and bay leaf. Season with salt and pepper to taste and stir in the flour until well blended. Gradually add the wine and stock and cook on FULL (100%) for 8½ to 9 minutes, stirring twice.

Brown the chicken under a preheated hot grill, if liked, and then place in a serving dish. Arrange the vegetables and sauce round the chicken.
SERVES 4

CHICKEN GOULASH

METRIC/IMPERIAL
2 tablespoons plain flour
1 tablespoon paprika
salt
freshly ground black pepper
8 small or 4 large chicken drumsticks, skinned
25 g/1 oz butter
1 onion, finely chopped
300 ml/½ pint chicken stock
1 tablespoon tomato purée
4 tomatoes, skinned, seeded and chopped
3 tablespoons soured cream

Mix the flour with the paprika and salt and pepper to taste. Coat the chicken drumsticks in the seasoned flour.

Place the butter in a casserole dish and heat on FULL (100%) for 1 minute or until melted. Add the coated drumsticks and cook on FULL (100%) for 2 minutes. Turn over and cook on FULL (100%) for a further 2 minutes. Remove the drumsticks with a slotted spoon and set aside.

Add the onion to the dish juices and cook on FULL (100%) for 3 minutes, stirring once. Stir in any remaining flour mixture, chicken stock, tomato purée and tomatoes, blending well. Cook on FULL (100%) for 3 minutes, stirring once. Return the chicken drumsticks to the casserole. Cover and cook on FULL (100%) for a further 8 minutes, stirring once.

Quickly swirl in the soured cream and serve at once with cooked noodles or rice.
SERVES 4

COQ AU VIN

METRIC/IMPERIAL
25 g/1 oz butter
1 tablespoon vegetable oil
2 × 1 kg/2¼ lb oven-ready chickens, jointed
3 tablespoons seasoned flour
12 baby onions, peeled
3 tablespoons brandy
1 clove garlic, peeled
1 bay leaf
1 celery stick, coarsely chopped
600 ml/1 pint red wine
salt
freshly ground black pepper
225 g/8 oz mushrooms, thinly sliced

Preheat a large browning dish on FULL (100%) for 5 minutes (or according to the manufacturer's instructions). Add the butter and oil and swirl quickly to coat. Cook on FULL (100%) for 1 minute.

Coat the chicken in the seasoned flour and add to the browning dish with the onions. Turn quickly on all sides to brown evenly. Remove with a slotted spoon and place in a large casserole dish.

Stir the brandy into the dish juices, blending well. Pour the brandy liquid over the chicken and onions in the casserole.

Add the garlic, bay leaf, celery, wine and salt and pepper to taste. Cover and cook on FULL (100%) for 12 minutes, stirring twice.

Add the mushrooms, blending well. Cook, uncovered, on FULL (100%) for 8 minutes, until tender, stirring once. Remove and discard the garlic and bay leaf. Serve hot with jacket potatoes.
SERVES 4 to 6

SPINACH-WRAPPED CHICKEN PARCELS

METRIC/IMPERIAL
1 small onion, finely chopped
1 tablespoon water
225 g/8 oz fresh spinach, trimmed, blanched and chopped, or 100 g/4 oz frozen chopped spinach, defrosted
2 tablespoons fresh wholemeal breadcrumbs
pinch of nutmeg
2 tablespoons flaked almonds
salt
freshly ground black pepper

4 chicken breasts, skinned and boned
8 large spinach leaves, trimmed and blanched, for wrapping
a little sunflower oil
radicchio leaves, to garnish

Place the onion in a bowl with the water and cook on FULL (100%) for 2½ minutes.

Drain the spinach thoroughly and squeeze to extract as much water as possible. Add to the onion with the breadcrumbs, nutmeg and flaked almonds. Season with salt and pepper to taste and mix thoroughly.

With a sharp knife, make a deep slit down one side of each chicken breast to form a deep pocket. Spoon some stuffing into each cavity.

Pat excess moisture from the spinach leaves with absorbent kitchen paper. Use the spinach leaves to wrap the chicken breasts – 2 leaves for each parcel. Brush lightly with the oil. Place the parcels in a single layer in a shallow dish, folded sides down. Cover loosely with greaseproof paper and cook on FULL (100%) for 8¾ minutes, rearranging halfway through the cooking time.

Leave to stand, covered, for 5 minutes before serving. Garnish with radicchio leaves and serve with baked potatoes and tomato sauce.
SERVES 4

Note: To blanch spinach, rinse the leaves and place in a large flat dish. Add 2 tablespoons of cold water, cover and cook on FULL (100%) for 2½ minutes for each 450 g/1 lb fresh spinach. Drain the spinach and cool immediately after cooking.

CHICKEN SATAY

METRIC/IMPERIAL
450 g/1 lb boned and skinned chicken breasts, cut into 1 cm/½ inch cubes
2 tablespoons natural yogurt
1 tablespoon garam masala
salt
1 tablespoon clear honey
grated rind of 1 lime or lemon
Satay sauce:
3 tablespoons desiccated coconut
150 ml/¼ pint hot skimmed milk
2 cloves garlic, crushed
1 small onion, chopped
1 tablespoon water
100 g/4 oz roasted peanuts

2 teaspoons dark soy sauce
1 teaspoon mild chilli powder
1 tablespoon tahini or unsweetened peanut butter
1 tablespoon peanut or sunflower oil
fresh coriander leaves, to garnish
1 small cucumber, diced, to serve

Place the chicken cubes in a bowl. Add the yogurt, garam masala, salt to taste, honey and lime or lemon rind. Mix well to coat the meat thoroughly. Leave to marinate for 1 hour, stirring several times to keep the meat well coated.

Meanwhile, prepare the sauce. Place the coconut in a small bowl. Stir in the hot skimmed milk and leave to soak.

Put the garlic and onion in a small bowl with the water and cook on FULL (100%) for 1½ to 2 minutes to soften slightly.

Place the peanuts in a blender or food processor. Add the garlic and onion with the coconut and its soaking liquid. Blend to a paste. Add the remaining ingredients and stir well to incorporate them, then transfer to a serving bowl.

Thread the chicken cubes on to 8 bamboo or wooden skewers. Place the skewers in one layer on a large flat dish and cook on FULL (100%) for 2½ minutes. Turn them over and cook on FULL (100%) for a further 1½ to 2 minutes.

Wrap the skewers in foil and leave to STAND for 3 to 5 minutes. Transfer to a serving platter, garnish with fresh coriander leaves and surround the satay with cucumber cubes. Serve with the satay sauce.
SERVES 4

Note: Cook the satay under a preheated hot grill for 1 minute on each side to brown, if liked, before serving.

ISADORA'S CHICKEN

METRIC/IMPERIAL
4 frozen chicken quarters
salt
freshly ground black pepper
1 × 450 g/1 lb can lentil soup

Arrange the frozen chicken quarters on a double thickness of absorbent kitchen paper and cook on LOW (30%) for 15 minutes until thawed, turning the pieces over after 7 minutes.

Rinse the chicken under cold running water. Drain, then season lightly on both sides with salt and pepper. Place, skin side down, in a large deep casserole. Pour the soup over the chicken, cover and cook on MEDIUM (50%) for 30 to 35 minutes, turning the chicken over and giving the dish a half-turn occasionally.

Leave to STAND, covered, for 10 minutes. Test each chicken quarter with the tip of a sharp knife and, if the juices do not run clear, then cook on FULL (100%) for a further 3 to 4 minutes. The chicken may be served without further standing time.
SERVES 4

POUSSINS WITH GRAPES

METRIC/IMPERIAL
2 tablespoons sunflower or grapeseed oil
2 oven-ready poussins, halved along the breast-bone
120 ml/4 fl oz white grape juice
1 tablespoon chopped fresh tarragon or 1 teaspoon dried tarragon
2 teaspoons cornflour, blended with 2 tablespoons water
225 g/8 oz green or black grapes, halved and pips removed
salt
freshly ground black pepper
fresh tarragon, to garnish

Preheat a large browning dish on FULL (100%) for 5 minutes (or according to the manufacturer's instructions). Without removing it from the oven, add the oil and the poussins, breast sides down. Cook on FULL (100%) for 2½ minutes to brown, rearranging the poussins halfway through the cooking time. Drain on absorbent kitchen paper.

Place the grape juice in a large shallow dish and cook on FULL (100%) for 1½ to 2 minutes. Add the tarragon and poussins and spoon over some juice. Cover and cook on FULL (100%) for 7½ minutes, rearranging halfway through cooking.

Remove the poussins with a slotted spoon, wrap them in foil and leave them to STAND while finishing the sauce.

Stir the cornflour mixture into the sauce with the grapes. Season with salt and pepper to taste and cook on FULL (100%) for 1½ to 2 minutes, stirring halfway through the cooking time.

Arrange the poussin halves on a warmed serving dish and pour the sauce over. Garnish with the fresh tarragon.
SERVES 2 to 4

HUNGARIAN CHICKEN

METRIC/IMPERIAL
4 chicken breasts, skinned and boned
salt
freshly ground black pepper
2 × 400 g/14 oz cans tomatoes
300 ml/½ pint natural yogurt
3 tablespoons paprika
1 green pepper, cored, seeded and thinly sliced
1 red pepper, cored, seeded and thinly sliced
1 onion, thinly sliced into rings

Season the chicken breasts with salt and pepper. Drain the tomatoes, reserving the juice, and set aside. Blend the tomato juice with the yogurt and paprika.

Place the chicken in a large deep dish, cover with the tomatoes, peppers and onion rings and pour the tomato liquid over the top. Cover and cook on FULL (100%) for 30 minutes, turning the dish and rearranging the chicken breasts occasionally. Serve hot.
SERVES 4

CHICKEN ITALIAN STYLE

METRIC/IMPERIAL
50 ml/2 fl oz dry vermouth
1 × 400 g/14 oz can tomatoes, drained and chopped
4 tablespoons tomato purée
1 clove garlic, crushed
1 onion, thinly sliced
1 teaspoon dried oregano
salt
freshly ground black pepper
4 boneless chicken breasts, skinned
black olives, to garnish

Place the vermouth, tomatoes, tomato purée, garlic, onion, oregano and salt and pepper to taste in a cooking dish. Cover and cook on FULL (100%) for 5 minutes, stirring once.

Arrange the chicken breasts, spoke fashion, on top of the sauce, spooning a little over the chicken. Cover and cook on FULL (100%) for 10 minutes, turning the dish once.

Leave to STAND, covered, for 5 minutes. Serve garnished with a few black olives.
SERVES 4

CHICKEN BLANQUETTE

METRIC/IMPERIAL
25 g/1 oz butter
1 onion, sliced
2–3 celery sticks, sliced
100 g/4 oz streaky bacon, derinded and chopped
1 × 275 g/10 oz can condensed cream of chicken soup
150 ml/¼ pint chicken stock or water
salt
freshly ground black pepper
4 chicken breasts, skinned
100 g/4 oz button mushrooms, trimmed
4-6 tablespoons soured or double cream

Place the butter in a casserole dish and heat on FULL (100%) for ½ minute or until melted. Add the onion, celery and bacon. Cover and cook on FULL (100%) for 5 minutes, stirring once.

Add the soup, stock or water, and salt and pepper to taste, blending well. Add the chicken breasts and cook on FULL (100%) for 17 minutes, stirring twice.

Stir in the mushrooms and cook on FULL (100%) for a further 3 minutes. Swirl in the cream and serve at once with rice or noodles.
SERVES 4

CHICKEN BREASTS WITH ASPARAGUS SAUCE

METRIC/IMPERIAL
4 chicken breasts, skinned
5 tablespoons white wine
1 tablespoon dry sherry
1 × 275 g/10 oz can condensed asparagus soup
25 g/1 oz split almonds, toasted
3–4 tablespoons soured cream

Place the chicken breasts in a shallow cooking dish with the wine and sherry. Cover and cook on FULL (100%) for 10 minutes, turning the chicken over once.

Remove the chicken from the cooking juices with a slotted spoon and place on a warmed serving dish. Cover with foil, shiny side inside.

Add the soup and almonds to the cooking juices, blending well. Cook on FULL (100%) for 5 minutes, stirring twice.

Stir in the soured cream and spoon over the chicken breasts to serve.
SERVES 4

DEVILLED CHICKEN PIECES

METRIC/IMPERIAL
4 chicken breasts, skinned and boned
25 g/1 oz butter
1 tablespoon vegetable oil
Marinade:
2 tablespoons soy sauce
1 tablespoon tomato purée
3 tablespoons corn oil
1 clove garlic, crushed
1 teaspoon tarragon

Place the chicken pieces in a large dish. Combine the ingredients for the marinade and pour over the chicken. Cover and refrigerate for 2 hours, turning occasionally.

Preheat a large browning dish on FULL (100%) for 5 minutes (or according to the manufacturer's instructions). Place the butter and oil in the browning dish and cook on FULL (100%) for ½ minute. Using a slotted spoon, drain the chicken pieces, then place in the hot fat. Cover and cook on FULL (100%) for 6 minutes, turning over once, halfway through cooking.

Remove from the oven, cover, and leave to STAND for 5 minutes. Garnish as desired, and serve with rice or ratatouille.
SERVES 4

CHICKEN CORDON BLEU

METRIC/IMPERIAL
4 part-boned chicken breasts, skinned
4 streaky bacon rashers, derinded and finely chopped
50 g/2 oz button mushrooms, finely chopped
1 teaspoon chopped fresh parsley
salt
freshly ground black pepper
25 g/1 oz plain flour
50 g/2 oz butter
4 Gouda cheese slices
fresh parsley, to garnish

Cut a 'pocket' in each piece of chicken.

To prepare the filling, put the bacon in an ovenproof glass bowl and cook on FULL (100%) for 1½ minutes. Stir in the mushrooms and parsley and add salt and pepper to taste. Use the filling to stuff each chicken breast, then coat them with flour seasoned with salt and pepper.

Put the butter in an ovenproof glass dish and heat on FULL (100%) for 1½ minutes. Place the chicken pieces in the dish and brush with the melted butter.

Cover and cook on MEDIUM (50%) for 8 to 8½ minutes. Rearrange the chicken pieces. Baste the chicken, cover again and cook on MEDIUM (50%) for 8 to 8½ minutes.

Remove the chicken and place on a serving dish. Wrap one cheese slice round each piece of chicken. Cook on FULL (100%) for 2 minutes. Serve garnished with parsley.
SERVES 4

SWEET AND SOUR CHICKEN

METRIC/IMPERIAL
1 × 440 g/15½ oz can pineapple pieces
juice of half an orange
2 tablespoons clear honey
3 tablespoons dry white wine or 2 tablespoons dry sherry
2 teaspoons soy sauce
25 g/1 oz raisins
salt
freshly ground black pepper
4 chicken pieces, skinned
50 g/2 oz butter
3 teaspoons cornflour
25 g/1 oz flaked almonds

Combine the juice drained from the pineapple with the orange juice, honey, wine or sherry, soy sauce, raisins, salt and pepper. Stir well.

Arrange the chicken pieces in a large dish. Pour over the sauce and leave, covered, for at least 30 minutes.

Place half the butter in an ovenproof glass dish and cook on FULL (100%) for 1 minute.

Using a slotted spoon, drain the chicken pieces and reserve the marinade. Put the chicken pieces into the hot butter and baste. Cover and cook on MEDIUM (50%) for 18 to 22 minutes, turning the chicken pieces over once, halfway through cooking. Remove from the oven, cover with foil, and leave to STAND.

To finish the sauce, blend the cornflour and a little of the marinade to a smooth paste. Put the remaining marinade into a large jug and cook on FULL (100%) for 2 minutes.

Mix in the prepared cornflour and any juice from the chicken. Cook on FULL (100%) for 2 minutes and beat well. Add the drained pineapple pieces and pour the sauce over the chicken.

To toast the almonds, arrange the nuts and remaining butter in a small bowl, keeping the butter in the centre. Cook on FULL (100%) for 1½ minutes, then stir. Cook on FULL (100%) for 1 minute and stir again. Put the almonds to one side and they will crisp and colour.

Drain on absorbent kitchen paper and use to garnish the chicken.

SERVES 4

CHICKEN BREASTS PARMESAN

METRIC/IMPERIAL
50 g/2 oz fine dry breadcrumbs
75 g/3 oz grated Parmesan cheese
salt
freshly ground black pepper
4 boneless chicken breasts, skinned
1 egg, beaten
2 tablespoons vegetable oil
1 × 225 g/8 oz can tomatoes
25 g/1 oz plain flour
1 teaspoon dried oregano
¼ teaspoon garlic salt
7 tablespoons chicken stock
50 g/2 oz Cheddar cheese, grated
parsley sprigs, to garnish

Mix the breadcrumbs with 25 g/1 oz of the Parmesan cheese and salt and pepper to taste in a shallow dish. Dip the chicken breasts in egg, then in the breadcrumb mixture to coat.

Meanwhile, preheat a large browning dish on FULL (100%) for 5 minutes (or according to the manufacturer's instructions). Add the oil and cook on FULL (100%) for 1 minute.

Add the chicken breasts and turn quickly on both sides to brown evenly. Remove with a slotted spoon and place in a cooking dish.

Mix the tomatoes and their juice with the flour, oregano, garlic salt and stock in a bowl, blending well. Cook on FULL (100%) for 3 minutes, stirring once. Purée in a blender or food processor or pass through a fine sieve.

Spoon the tomato sauce over the chicken and sprinkle with the Cheddar cheese. Cover loosely with greaseproof paper and cook on FULL (100%) for 5 to 6 minutes, turning twice.

Sprinkle with the remaining Parmesan cheese and cook, uncovered, for a further ½ to 1 minute or until the cheese has melted.

Serve at once, garnished with parsley sprigs.

SERVES 4

CHICKEN LIVER MOUSSE

METRIC/IMPERIAL
225 g/8 oz chicken livers
1 clove garlic, crushed
1 tablespoon chopped fresh parsley
salt
freshly ground black pepper
25 g/1 oz butter
25 g/1 oz plain flour
200 ml/7 fl oz milk
2 eggs, lightly beaten
2 teaspoons powdered gelatine
85 ml/3 fl oz double or whipping cream
Garnish:
parsley sprigs
lemon slices

Place the chicken livers, garlic, parsley and salt and pepper to taste in a medium bowl. Cover and cook on FULL (100%) for 4 minutes, stirring after 2 minutes. Set aside.

Place the butter in a large jug and heat on FULL (100%) for ½ minute or until melted. Stir in the flour, then add the milk and cook on FULL (100%) for 2½ minutes, stirring every 1 minute.

Beat in the eggs and cook on FULL (100%) for a further 1½ minutes, beating every ½ minute. Add the gelatine to the hot mixture and stir until dissolved.

Place the sauce and chicken liver mixture in a blender or food processor and blend until smooth. Season with salt and pepper to taste and set aside to cool, stirring occasionally.

Whip the cream until it holds stiff peaks and fold it into the chicken liver purée. Spoon into a 900 ml/1½ pint loaf dish lined with greaseproof paper. Cover and chill overnight in the refrigerator.

Turn out the mousse on to a chilled plate, remove the paper and garnish with parsley and lemon slices. Serve with hot toast.

SERVES 4 to 6

MEDITERRANEAN MEATBALLS

METRIC/IMPERIAL
450 g/1 lb minced raw chicken
1 small onion, grated or finely chopped
1 clove garlic, crushed
salt
freshly ground black pepper
1 tablespoon chopped fresh thyme

25 g/1 oz butter
1 tablespoon olive oil
300 ml/½ pint red wine
1 tablespoon tomato purée
1 red pepper, cored, seeded and finely chopped
2 tablespoons raisins
8 black olives, stoned and coarsely chopped
6 tomatoes, skinned, seeded and chopped
1 tablespoon pine nuts

Mix the chicken with the onion, garlic, salt and pepper to taste and about three-quarters of the thyme, blending well. Divide and shape into small meatballs. Cover and chill for 30 minutes.

Place the butter and oil in a deep cooking dish and heat on FULL (100%) for 1 minute. Add the meatballs, turning quickly in the hot fat to coat. Cook on FULL (100%) for 4 minutes, turning over once.

Add the red wine, tomato purée, red pepper, raisins, olives, tomatoes and pine nuts, blending well. Cover and cook on FULL (100%) for 7 minutes, turning twice.

Sprinkle with the remaining chopped fresh thyme to serve. Serve with hot crusty bread and a green salad.
SERVES 4

CURRIED CHICKEN

METRIC/IMPERIAL
4 tablespoons vegetable oil
4 onions, finely chopped
1 teaspoon ground coriander
1 teaspoon ground cumin
1 teaspoon ground turmeric
1 teaspoon ground cardamom
1 teaspoon salt
½ teaspoon freshly ground black pepper
1 chicken stock cube, crumbled
150 ml/¼ pint boiling water
2 tablespoons lemon juice
5 tablespoons tomato purée
1 × 1.5 kg/3½ lb oven-ready chicken, cut into 8 pieces
4 tomatoes, quartered

Combine the oil, onions, spices, salt and pepper in a large deep dish and cook on FULL (100%) for 10 minutes, stirring occasionally. Dissolve the stock cube in the water and add to the dish with the lemon juice and tomato purée, stirring well.

Arrange the chicken pieces in the sauce, with the boniest parts towards the centre. Add the tomatoes, cover tightly and cook on FULL (100%) for 25 to 30 minutes, stirring and turning the chicken pieces over twice during cooking. Leave to STAND, covered, for 10 minutes before serving.

Serve with Saffron and Paprika Rice (page 226), Dhal (page 230) and cucumber with yogurt.
SERVES 4

Note: Chicken curry may be prepared in advance and stored in the refrigerator or frozen. This will enhance the flavour. Reheat thoroughly before serving.

CHICKEN CHANTILLY

METRIC/IMPERIAL
15 g/½ oz butter
100 g/4 oz long-grain rice
150 ml/¼ pint chicken stock
5 tablespoons white wine
2 teaspoons lemon juice
1 small onion, coarsely chopped
1 bay leaf
450 g/1 lb cooked chicken, half chopped and half cut into small strips
150 ml/¼ pint mayonnaise
5 tablespoons double cream, whipped
salt
freshly ground black pepper
watercress sprigs, to garnish

Place the butter in a bowl and heat on FULL (100%) for ½ minute or until melted. Add the rice and cook on FULL (100%) for 1 minute. Add the stock, wine, lemon juice, onion and bay leaf, blending well. Cover and cook on FULL (100%) for 3 minutes.

Add the chopped chicken, blending well. Cover and cook on MEDIUM (50%) for 12 minutes, stirring once, then leave to STAND, covered, for 5 minutes. Cool quickly and remove and discard the bay leaf.

Mix the mayonnaise with the cream and salt and pepper to taste.

Pack the rice mixture into an oiled ring mould, pressing down firmly. Invert on to a serving dish. Spoon about half of the mayonnaise mixture over the rice ring.

Fold the chicken strips into the remaining mayonnaise mixture and spoon into the centre of the ring. Garnish with watercress sprigs to serve.
SERVES 4

HAWAIIAN CHICKEN

METRIC/IMPERIAL
1 onion, chopped
2 tablespoons curry powder
1 tablespoon oil
1 tablespoon plain flour
450 ml/¾ pint chicken stock
2 tablespoons apricot jam or chutney
salt
freshly ground black pepper
1 apple, cored and chopped
1 banana, sliced
25 g/1 oz sultanas
100 g/4 oz frozen mixed vegetables
450 g/1 lb cooked chicken meat, chopped
100 g/4 oz drained pineapple rings, chopped
To serve:
cooked rice
cucumber slices
desiccated coconut

Place the onion, curry powder and oil in a casserole. Cover and cook on FULL (100%) for 2 minutes.

Stir in the flour and gradually stir in the stock. Add the jam or chutney, salt and pepper to taste, apple, banana and sultanas. Stir well, cover and cook on FULL (100%) for 10 minutes, stirring once, halfway through cooking.

Add the frozen vegetables, chicken meat and pineapple. Cook, covered, on FULL (100%) for 5 minutes. Leave to STAND for 5 minutes. Serve with rice, cucumber and coconut.
SERVES 4

CHICKEN PACKETS

METRIC/IMPERIAL
1 × 225 g/8 oz packet frozen puff pastry
2 thin slices cooked ham
225 g/8 oz boned, cooked chicken, skinned
salt
freshly ground black pepper
1 egg, beaten

To thaw the pastry, heat on DEFROST (20%) for 2½ to 3 minutes, then leave to STAND for 5 minutes, until it is just pliable. Cut in half and roll each piece to an oblong, approximately 13 × 18 cm/5 × 7 inches.

Place a slice of ham on each piece of pastry, leaving a 2.5 cm/1 inch border. Dice the chicken and place on top of the ham. Season lightly with salt and pepper. Brush the edges of the pastry with beaten egg. Fold in half to form packets, enclosing the filling. Press the edges together to seal, trimming them if necessary.

Arrange the packets on a piece of greaseproof paper, pressing the sealed edges underneath. Cut two or three slits in the top of the packets with a sharp knife. Brush with beaten egg and cook on FULL (100%) for 5½ minutes, then turn over and cook on FULL (100%) for 2 minutes.

Immediately place under a preheated hot grill to brown. Serve hot with parsley sauce, if liked, or cold with salad.
SERVES 2

CHICKEN PIMIENTO PIE

METRIC/IMPERIAL
1 × 1.5 kg/3¼ lb oven-ready chicken, cut into 8 pieces
20 g/¾ oz butter
3 tablespoons flour
300 ml/½ pint milk
salt
freshly ground black pepper
1 × 200 g/7 oz can red pimientos, drained and shredded
1 egg, beaten
1 × 225 g/8 oz packet frozen puff pastry, thawed (see recipe above)

Put the chicken into a deep pie dish, cover and cook on FULL (100%) for 18 to 24 minutes, stirring and rearranging occasionally.

Leave to STAND, covered, for 5 minutes. Skin and bone the chicken and replace in the dish.

Put the butter in a large bowl and heat on FULL (100%) for ½ minute until melted. Stir in the flour and cook on FULL (100%) for ½ minute. Whisk in the milk gradually and cook on FULL (100%) for 3 to 4 minutes, stirring occasionally. Add salt and pepper to taste.

Add the pimientos to the chicken and spoon the sauce over the top. Brush the edges of the pie dish with beaten egg.

Roll out the pastry to make a pie lid, 2.5 cm/1 inch larger than the dish. Place over the dish, folding the edges under to form a double thickness. Brush the pastry with the beaten egg. Using a sharp knife, make three slits on top of the pie and vertical cuts 1 cm/½ inch apart around the edges. Decorate with the pastry trimmings.

Cook on FULL (100%) for 6 minutes until the pastry is puffed-up and holding its shape, giving the dish a quarter-turn every 1½ minutes. Immediately place under a preheated hot grill to brown the top. Serve hot.
SERVES 4

CHICKEN À LA KING

METRIC/IMPERIAL
40 g/1½ oz butter
25 g/1 oz flour
150 ml/¼ pint water
150 ml/¼ pint milk
½ chicken stock cube, crumbled
½ teaspoon celery salt
freshly ground black pepper
225 g/8 oz cooked chicken, diced
1 thin slice ham, diced·
100 g/4 oz frozen peas
175–225 g/6–8 oz cooked long-grain rice

Put the butter in a large shallow dish and heat on FULL (100%) for ¾ to 1 minute or until melted. Stir in the flour. Add the water, milk, stock cube, celery salt and pepper to taste. Cook on FULL (100%) for 2 minutes, stirring thoroughly from the sides to the centre of the dish after 1 minute.

Add the chicken, ham and peas to the sauce. Partially cover and cook on FULL (100%) for 10 minutes, stirring occasionally, until the peas are cooked and the chicken is hot.

Remove the cover and arrange the rice in a border around the edge of the dish. Cook on FULL (100%) for 2 minutes or until the rice is hot, giving the dish a half-turn after 1 minute. Serve immediately.
SERVES 2

CHICKEN AND CORN IN CREAMY SAUCE

METRIC/IMPERIAL
50 g/2 oz butter
1 small onion, chopped
50 g/2 oz flour
600 ml/1 pint hot chicken stock
few drops of Tabasco
½ teaspoon salt
¼ teaspoon freshly ground black pepper
1 × 175 g/6 oz can sweetcorn kernels, drained
450 g/1 lb cooked chicken, diced

2 tablespoons double cream
3 hard-boiled eggs, finely chopped
2 teaspoons paprika

Combine the butter and onion in a large deep dish and cook on FULL (100%) for 3 minutes, stirring occasionally.

Stir in the flour, then gradually mix in the hot stock, Tabasco, salt and pepper, corn and chicken. Cook on MEDIUM (50%) for 10 to 12 minutes, stirring occasionally. Stir in the cream and adjust the seasoning.

Combine the chopped egg and paprika, and sprinkle over the top. Cook on LOW (30%) for 3 minutes, giving the dish a half-turn after 1½ minutes.

Serve immediately, with brown rice or baked potatoes and green vegetables of your choice.
SERVES 4

CUCUMBER, CHICKEN AND ORANGE SALAD

METRIC/IMPERIAL
3 large boneless chicken breasts
1 lettuce, shredded
½ cucumber, thinly sliced
3 oranges, peeled, pith removed and sliced
juice of ½ orange
1 tablespoon salad oil
1 tablespoon snipped chives
salt
freshly ground black pepper
75 g/3 oz peanuts
watercress sprigs, to garnish

Place the chicken breasts in a cooking dish, cover and cook on FULL (100%) for 7 to 9 minutes, turning once. Allow to cool, then remove and discard the skin. Slice the chicken into thin strips.

Line a serving dish with the lettuce and top with alternate layers of cucumber, orange and chicken.

Beat the orange juice with the oil, chives and salt and pepper to taste, blending well. Spoon over the salad evenly.

Sprinkle peanuts down the centre of the dish and garnish with watercress sprigs. Serve at once.
SERVES 4

CHICKEN GALANTINE

METRIC/IMPERIAL
50 g/2 oz fresh white breadcrumbs
25 g/1 oz hazelnuts, finely chopped
1 teaspoon dried tarragon
1 teaspoon dried thyme
1 teaspoon dried parsley
salt
freshly ground black pepper
350 g/12 oz pork sausage meat
1 × 1.75 kg/4 lb chicken, boned
100 g/4 oz ham, cut into strips
50 g/2 oz pistachio nuts
6 black olives, stoned and quartered
Aspic jelly:
475 ml/¾ pint cold clarified chicken stock
1 tablespoon powdered gelatine
2 tablespoons dry sherry
1 tablespoon lemon juice
3 peppers (red, green and yellow), cored, seeded
and cut into thin diamond shapes, to garnish

Mix together the breadcrumbs, hazelnuts, tarragon, thyme and parsley and season with salt and pepper. Using hands, work in the sausage meat.

Put the chicken on a board, skin side down, and smooth the flesh into an even layer. Arrange the ham over the chicken and sprinkle over the nuts and olives. Form the stuffing into an oblong and place in the centre of the chicken. Tuck in the ends, then fold the sides of the bird over the stuffing to form a neat roll. Check that the roll is not too long to fit into the oven.

Tie the roll very securely with string and use wooden cocktail sticks to secure, if necessary. Put the chicken roll, seam side down, in a shallow dish and cook on FULL (100%) for 21 minutes. Remove the galantine from the oven and wrap tightly in foil. Place heavy weights on top and leave until cold. When cold, remove the string and cocktail sticks.

To make the aspic jelly, place the stock in a large jug and cook on FULL (100%) for 6 minutes or until very hot. Sprinkle over the gelatine and whisk well to dissolve. Cook on FULL (100%) for ½ minute, then stir in the sherry and lemon juice. Set aside until cool and beginning to set.

Spoon a layer of aspic over the chicken and leave to set. Spoon over a second layer and, when nearly set, garnish with green, yellow and red pepper shapes. Spoon over a further layer of aspic and allow to set.
SERVES 4 to 6

CHICKEN CHASSEUR

METRIC/IMPERIAL
1 × 1.5 kg/3¼ lb oven-ready chicken, cut into 8
pieces
½ clove garlic
50 g/2 oz plain flour
50 g/2 oz butter
1 teaspoon salt
1 small onion, chopped
100 g/4 oz button mushrooms
2 tablespoons tomato purée
1 tablespoon chopped fresh parsley
3 thyme sprigs
2 bay leaves
½ teaspoon freshly ground black pepper
250 ml/8 fl oz brown stock
5 tablespoons rosé wine
2 tablespoons brandy
Garnish:
4–6 parsley sprigs
8 triangles of toast

Skin the chicken pieces, rub with the cut side of the garlic, then dust liberally with the flour. Preheat a large browning dish on FULL (100%) for 5 minutes (or according to the manufacturer's instructions). Toss in 40 g/1½ oz of the butter and the salt and quickly put in half of the chicken pieces. Cook on FULL (100%) for 2 minutes.

Add the remaining chicken and cook on FULL (100%) for 10 minutes, turning the pieces over once or twice during cooking. Remove the browning dish from the oven and spoon away any surplus fat. Cover and leave to STAND while preparing the sauce.

Place the onion and the remaining butter in a large shallow dish and cook on FULL (100%) for 3 to 4 minutes until the onion has softened. Stir in the mushrooms and cook on FULL (100%) for 4 minutes, stirring once. Add the tomato purée, herbs, pepper, stock, wine and brandy. Cook on FULL (100%) for 3 minutes. Taste and add salt, if necessary.

Pour the sauce over the chicken, cover and cook on LOW (30%) for 20 minutes, stirring and rearranging the chicken pieces once. Remove and discard the thyme and bay leaves.

Garnish with parsley sprigs and triangles of toast before serving.
SERVES 4

CHICKEN PAELLA

METRIC/IMPERIAL
1 tablespoon vegetable oil
25 g/1 oz butter
1 small onion, chopped
225 g/8 oz long-grain rice
600 ml/1 pint boiling chicken stock
freshly ground black pepper
1 × 225 g/8 oz packet frozen mixed vegetables
1 × 225 g/8 oz packet boned frozen cod steaks, defrosted
1 × 90 g/3½ can tuna fish, drained
4 tomatoes, skinned and roughly chopped
225 g/8 oz cooked chicken meat, chopped
pinch of saffron
few pimiento-stuffed olives, halved, to garnish

Put the oil and butter into a large bowl and cook on FULL (100%) for 1 minute. Add the onion and rice and stir well. Cook on FULL (100%) for 2 minutes.

Add the boiling stock, stir well, and season with pepper to taste. Cover and cook on FULL (100%) for 10 to 13 minutes. Stir and leave to STAND, covered.

To prepare the frozen vegetables, put the packet on a plate and snip a corner. Cook on FULL (100%) for 4 minutes, then drain.

To cook the cod steaks, place the packet on a plate and snip the corner. Cook on FULL (100%) for 3 minutes. Drain and chop roughly.

Put the rice mixture into a serving dish. Add the tuna fish, cod, tomatoes, chicken, saffron and the mixed vegetables. Toss to mix.

Garnish with the olives. Cover loosely and cook on FULL (100%) for 5 minutes, stirring once, to reheat. Serve immediately with green salad and crusty French bread.
SERVES 4

CHILLI CHICKEN

METRIC/IMPERIAL
1 onion, finely chopped
1 red pepper, cored, seeded and chopped
1 clove garlic, finely chopped
2 tablespoons olive oil
450 g/1 lb minced raw chicken
300 ml/½ pint chicken stock
2 tablespoons tomato purée
2 tablespoons chopped fresh parsley
2 tablespoons raisins
2 tablespoons salted peanuts

6 stuffed olives, sliced
salt
freshly ground black pepper
grated rind and juice of ½ orange
1 tablespoon chilli powder
1 × 440 g/15½ oz can red kidney beans
½ teaspoon chopped dried chillies

Place the onion, pepper, garlic and oil in a shallow cooking dish. Cook on FULL (100%) for 5 minutes, stirring once.

Add the chicken and cook on FULL (100%) for 3 minutes. Add the chicken stock, tomato purée, parsley, raisins, peanuts, olives, salt and pepper to taste, orange rind and juice and chilli powder, blending well. Cover and cook on LOW (30%) for 15 to 20 minutes, stirring twice.

Add the drained kidney beans and cook on LOW (30%) for 3 to 5 minutes.

Serve at once sprinkled with the chopped dried chillies. Serve with boiled rice.
SERVES 4 to 6

TANDOORI CHICKEN

METRIC/IMPERIAL
8 chicken breasts on the bone (about 275 g/10 oz each)
3 tablespoons lemon juice
2 teaspoons salt
150 ml/¼ pint natural yogurt
2 tablespoons salad oil
4 cloves garlic, crushed
2 teaspoons paprika
1 teaspoon ground cumin
1 teaspoon ground coriander
1 teaspoon ground turmeric
½ teaspoon ground ginger
orange and red food colouring (see note)
Garnish:
bay leaves
cucumber slices

Rinse the chicken pieces in cold water, then pat dry with absorbent kitchen paper. Slash the chicken pieces deeply in three or four places.

Mix the remaining ingredients together in a large bowl, adding sufficient colouring to produce a deep orangey-red mixture. Add the chicken pieces one at a time, rubbing the mixture well in. Cover the bowl and marinate for 10 to 12 hours in the refrigerator, turning and basting the chicken pieces occasionally.

Put a roasting rack into a large shallow dish

and stack up the chicken pieces in the same way as toast in a toast rack. Cook on FULL (100%) for 25 to 30 minutes, repositioning halfway through, so that the inside pieces are also moved to the outside and the pieces are also turned over. When cooked, any juices from the chicken will run clear.

Transfer the chicken to a grill pan and brown under a preheated hot grill or on the barbecue grid over hot coals. Serve garnished with bay leaves and cucumber.
SERVES 4 to 8

Note: The length of cooking time will depend upon the starting temperature of the chicken. If the cooking is to be completed on the barbecue, the microwave cooking time can be reduced and the barbecue cooking time increased.

Powdered food colouring is more satisfactory than liquid but is more difficult to obtain. You may need 1 to 2 teaspoons liquid food colouring.

SAFFRON CHICKEN

METRIC/IMPERIAL
¼ teaspoon saffron strands or ground turmeric
1 tablespoon very hot water
2 tablespoons desiccated coconut
4 tablespoons skimmed milk
1 onion, thinly sliced
2 cloves garlic, crushed
300 ml/½ pint hot chicken stock
4 chicken breasts, skinned, boned and cut into thick strips
¼ teaspoon ground ginger
1 tablespoon wholemeal flour
salt
freshly ground black pepper
1 × 400 g/14 oz can baby sweetcorns, rinsed and drained

Place the saffron or turmeric in a small bowl with the very hot water. Stir, pressing the saffron strands (if using) with a spoon to extract the colour and flavour. Set aside.

Place the coconut in a small bowl, stir in the skimmed milk and set aside.

Place the onion and garlic in a large bowl or casserole with 2 tablespoons of the stock and cook on FULL (100%) for 2½ minutes. Stir in the chicken pieces and ginger. Cover and cook on FULL (100%) for 5 minutes, stirring halfway through the cooking time.

Stir in the saffron or turmeric and desiccated

coconut with their respective soaking liquids. Mix the flour with a little of the stock and stir into the chicken. Add the remaining stock, and season with salt and pepper to taste. Cover and cook on LOW (30%) for 12½ minutes (or on DEFROST/20% for 16½ minutes), stirring several times during cooking.

Stir in the baby sweetcorns, cover again and cook on FULL (100%) for 4 minutes. Leave to STAND, covered, for 10 minutes before serving.
SERVES 4 to 6

Variation
Frozen sweetcorn can be substituted for the baby sweetcorns. Add for the last 4 minutes of the cooking time.

FRICASSÉE OF CHICKEN

METRIC/IMPERIAL
25 g/1 oz butter
1 onion, finely chopped
1½ tablespoons plain flour
salt
freshly ground black pepper
300 ml/½ pint milk
1 chicken stock cube, crumbled
2 tablespoons frozen minted peas
50 g/2 oz mushrooms, sliced
2 tablespoons single cream
meat taken from 1 × 1.5 kg/3¼ lb cooked chicken, cut into pieces
2 tablespoons canned sweetcorn
Garnish:
Toasted Crumbs (see page 314)
tomato slices

Place the butter in a large jug and cook on FULL (100%) for 1 minute. Add the onion and cook on FULL (100%) for 1 minute. Stir in the flour and salt and pepper and gradually stir in the milk. Cook on FULL (100%) for 3 minutes, stirring twice.

Whisk well until smooth and glossy. Beat in the crumbled stock cube and peas. Stir in the mushrooms and add the cream.

Put the chicken and corn into a large mixing bowl. Pour over the sauce and mix to coat the chicken. Pour into an ovenproof dish and garnish with the Toasted Crumbs and tomato slices. Reheat on MEDIUM (50%) for 5 minutes. Serve with rice.
SERVES 4

CHICKEN AND SPINACH CANNELLONI

METRIC/IMPERIAL
1 small onion, finely chopped
1 clove garlic, crushed
1 tablespoon water
100 g/4 oz frozen spinach, defrosted
225 g/8 oz cooked chicken, minced
2 tablespoons fresh wholemeal breadcrumbs
1 tablespoon chopped fresh parsley
freshly ground black pepper
8 spinach or wholemeal cannelloni tubes
600 ml/1 pint hot Tomato Sauce (see page 307)
25 g/1 oz Parmesan cheese

Place the onion and garlic in a large bowl with the water and cook on FULL (100%) for 2½ minutes, stirring halfway through the cooking time.

Drain the spinach, squeezing to extract as much water as possible. Chop the spinach and add to the onion and garlic with the chicken, breadcrumbs and parsley. Season with pepper to taste and mix well. Use to stuff the cannelloni tubes.

Place the cannelloni in a baking dish and pour over the tomato sauce. Cover and cook on FULL (100%) for 8¾ minutes. Leave to STAND, covered, for 5 minutes. Sprinkle with the cheese and cook under a preheated hot grill until golden.
SERVES 4

ORIENTAL CHICKEN

METRIC/IMPERIAL
6 tablespoons Hoisin sauce
2 tablespoons sesame oil
½ teaspoon ground ginger
½ teaspoon salt
1 × 1.5 kg/3¼ lb oven-ready chicken
1 tablespoon cornflour
2 teaspoons cold water
4 water chestnuts, finely sliced
Garnish:
spring onions
tomato roses

Combine the Hoisin sauce, sesame oil, ground ginger and salt in a small bowl or jug.

Put the chicken in a shallow dish and rub with the sauce mixture, spooning the remainder into the cavity.

Cover the chicken with a split roasting bag and leave in a cool place to marinate for 2 hours, basting occasionally.

Cook on FULL (100%) for 15 minutes, basting once during cooking. Reduce the setting to LOW (30%) and cook for 20 to 25 minutes, basting twice during cooking.

Remove the chicken, place on a hot serving dish and cover with foil to keep it warm.

Blend the cornflour and cold water together and stir into the juices left in the roasting dish. Add the water chestnuts and cook on FULL (100%) for 1 to 1½ minutes or until the sauce thickens, stirring twice. Slice the chicken, pour the sauce over and serve garnished with the spring onions and tomato roses.
SERVES 4

PUNCHY HOT POT

METRIC/IMPERIAL
1 tablespoon vegetable oil
675 g/1½ lb turkey thigh meat, cubed, or turkey casserole meat
25 g/1 oz seasoned flour
1 large onion, sliced
1 clove garlic, crushed
100 g/4 oz carrots, sliced
200 ml/7 fl oz brown ale
200 ml/7 fl oz beef stock
1 teaspoon vinegar
1 teaspoon sugar
1½ teaspoons tomato purée
½ teaspoon Worcestershire sauce
1 bay leaf
salt
100 g/4 oz button mushrooms, halved

Place the oil in a large casserole and cook on FULL (100%) for 1 minute.

Toss the turkey in the flour. Add to the oil with the onion, garlic and carrots, blending well. Cover and cook on FULL (100%) for 10 minutes.

Add the brown ale, stock, vinegar, sugar, tomato purée, Worcestershire sauce, bay leaf and salt to taste, blending well. Cover and cook on FULL (100%) for 10 minutes. Reduce the setting to MEDIUM (50%) and cook for 20 minutes, stirring once.

Stir in the mushrooms, cover and cook on MEDIUM (50%) for a further 10 minutes. Remove and discard the bay leaf.
SERVES 4

TURKEY DIVAN

METRIC/IMPERIAL
75 g/3 oz butter
2 tablespoons chopped fresh parsley
100 g/4 oz fresh white breadcrumbs
225 g/8 oz button mushrooms, sliced
3 tablespoons plain flour
175 ml/6 fl oz milk
150 ml/¼ pint soured cream
salt
freshly ground black pepper
675 g/1½ lb turkey fillets, thinly sliced
2 × 250 g/9 oz packets frozen broccoli spears
grated Parmesan cheese

Place 50 g/2 oz of the butter in a bowl and heat on FULL (100%) for ½ minute or until melted. Add the parsley and breadcrumbs, blending well. Cook on FULL (100%) for 2 to 4 minutes, stirring frequently, until crisp and golden brown. Drain on absorbent kitchen paper.

Place the remaining butter in a bowl with the mushrooms. Cook on FULL (100%) for 1 minute. Stir in the flour and milk, blending well. Cook on FULL (100%) for 4 minutes, stirring twice. Blend in the soured cream, and salt and pepper to taste.

Add the turkey fillet slices to the sauce. Cover and cook on FULL (100%) for 13 to 15 minutes, stirring twice.

Place the frozen broccoli spears in a bowl. Cover and cook on FULL (100%) for 2 minutes. Separate the spears.

Place the broccoli in a single layer in the base of a heatproof serving dish. Spoon over the turkey mixture. Spoon the browned breadcrumbs around the edge of the dish and sprinkle with Parmesan cheese in the centre. Cook on FULL (100%) for 5 to 8 minutes until hot and bubbly, turning twice.

Serve hot with noodles or rice.
SERVES 6

TIPSY TURKEY

METRIC/IMPERIAL
4 turkey fillets or escalopes
salt
freshly ground black pepper
1 tablespoon vegetable oil
Sauce:
25 g/1 oz butter
1 onion, sliced

1 red pepper, cored, seeded and sliced
1 tablespoon plain flour
200 ml/7 fl oz lager or pale ale
150 ml/¼ pint chicken stock
½ teaspoon dried thyme
1 teaspoon sugar
4 tablespoons single cream
Garnish:
red pepper rings
parsley sprigs

To prepare the sauce, place the butter in a bowl and heat on FULL (100%) for ½ minute or until melted. Add the onion and red pepper, cover and cook on FULL (100%) for 4 minutes.

Stir the flour into the butter, blending well, then gradually add the lager or pale ale and stock. Stir in the thyme and sugar with salt and pepper to taste. Cover and cook on FULL (100%) for a further 4 to 6 minutes, stirring every 1 minute until boiling and thickened.

Meanwhile, split the turkey fillets or escalopes in half, through the centre, to give 8 thick slices. Sprinkle generously with salt and pepper.

Preheat a large browning dish on FULL (100%) for 5 minutes (or according to the manufacturer's instructions). Brush with the oil and cook on FULL (100%) for a further 1 minute. Add the turkey slices and turn quickly on all sides to brown evenly.

Spoon over the sauce and cook on FULL (100%) for 4 to 6 minutes. Stir in the cream, blending well. Garnish with pepper rings and parsley.
SERVES 4

ROAST TURKEY WITH CHESTNUT STUFFING

METRIC/IMPERIAL
1 × 3.5 kg/8 lb oven-ready turkey, weight excluding giblets
1 tablespoon vegetable oil
1 teaspoon paprika
1 tablespoon cornflour
2–3 tablespoons cold water
watercress sprigs, to garnish
bacon rolls (optional), to serve
Stuffing:
2 bacon rashers, derinded and diced
25 g/1 oz butter or margarine
225 g/8 oz unsweetened chestnut purée made from fresh or canned chestnuts
75 g/3 oz fresh white breadcrumbs

1 teaspoon chopped fresh parsley
grated rind of 1 lemon
salt
freshly ground black pepper
1 egg, beaten

To make the stuffing, put the bacon in a medium bowl and cook on FULL (100%) for 1 minute. Stir in the butter or margarine, then mix in all the remaining stuffing ingredients.

Press the stuffing into the neck end of the turkey, then fold over the flap and secure firmly with wooden cocktail sticks by putting the wings over the flap to hold it in place. Tie the legs together with string. Do not use metal skewers.

Put the turkey, breast side down, on to the largest shallow dish that will fit into the microwave oven. Cover with a large roasting bag slit lengthways and tucked under the sides of the dish to prevent the bag from blowing about.

Cook on FULL (100%) for 35 minutes, then leave the turkey to STAND for 30 minutes. Provided the oven is not required for anything else, it is hygienic to leave the turkey in the oven during this time.

Carefully pull back the roasting bag covering on one side and, if possible, spoon away any accumulated juices. Reserve for use in the gravy.

Turn the turkey over and rub the breast with the oil, paprika, salt and pepper. Shield any cooked parts with small pieces of foil, wrapping it firmly around the wing tips and legs, making sure that the foil is absolutely flat and does not protrude beyond the dish, where it might touch the metal sides or top of the microwave oven. Replace the roasting bag covering and cook on FULL (100%) for 25 minutes.

Remove any foil shielding, reduce the power to LOW (30%) and cook for 25 to 35 minutes or until the turkey is thoroughly cooked (when a thermometer inserted between the leg and the side, or in the thickest part of the breast, registers 85°C/185°F, or the juices run clear when the skin around the side is pierced with a sharp knife).

Transfer the turkey to a hot serving dish and cover completely with foil or put into a hot conventional oven to keep warm. Spoon away the fat from the dish and add the reserved juices. Blend the cornflour with the water and mix into the juices. Put the dish in the oven and cook on FULL (100%) for about 3 minutes, stirring every 1 minute until smooth and slightly thickened. To serve, garnish the turkey with watercress sprigs and serve with bacon rolls, if liked.
SERVES 6

Note: To thaw frozen turkey, allow about 32 to 50 minutes on MEDIUM (50%), turning over every 10 minutes and shielding wing tips and legs with foil after 20 minutes. Defrost only until icy, then leave to STAND until completely thawed.

Giblets should be removed as soon as it is possible to loosen them from the cavity and all metal clips must be cut away before the bird is put into the microwave oven. Frozen turkey may be left in the plastic package (which should be slit underneath) and placed in a shallow dish, in order to catch the juices.

Only the neck end of poultry should be stuffed and extra cooking time given if you prefer to use a sausage meat stuffing.

TURKEY CASSEROLE

METRIC/IMPERIAL
1 clove garlic, crushed
25 g/1 oz butter
1 large onion, finely chopped
½ green pepper, cored, seeded and finely chopped
½ red pepper, cored, seeded and finely chopped
½–1 teaspoon chilli powder
2 tablespoons tomato purée
1 chicken stock cube, crumbled
150 ml/¼ pint water
100 g/4 oz sweetcorn kernels
100 g/4 oz button mushrooms
1 teaspoon soy sauce
1 teaspoon brown sugar
450 g/1 lb cooked turkey, diced
salt
freshly ground black pepper
natural yogurt, to finish

Place the garlic, butter, onion, peppers, chilli powder and tomato purée in a large bowl. Cover and cook on FULL (100%) for 7 minutes or until tender, stirring halfway through cooking.

Stir in the crumbled stock cube, water, corn, mushrooms, soy sauce, brown sugar, turkey and salt and pepper to taste. Cover and cook on FULL (100%) for 8 minutes, stirring halfway through cooking. Transfer to a warm serving dish and spoon over the yogurt. Serve at once.
SERVES 4

Note: Chilli powders vary in their strength, so add a little at a time until the required degree of 'hotness' is obtained.

TURKEY WITH ORANGE AND ALMONDS

METRIC/IMPERIAL
4 turkey breasts (total weight about 675 g/1½ lb)
freshly ground black pepper
grated rind of 1 orange
50 g/2 oz flaked almonds, toasted
50 g/2 oz butter
125 ml/4 fl oz orange juice
1 tablespoon Grand Marnier
25 g/1 oz soft, dark brown sugar
1 orange, peeled and sliced, to garnish

Place the turkey breasts in a shallow casserole dish and sprinkle with pepper. Cover and cook on FULL (100%) for 6 minutes. Rearrange and turn over halfway through cooking. Set aside, covered.

Place the orange rind, almonds, butter, orange juice, Grand Marnier and sugar in a jug. Cook on FULL (100%) for 2 minutes.

Drain the juice off the turkey breasts. Pour over the hot sauce and cook on FULL (100%) for a further 2 minutes. Garnish with orange slices before serving.
SERVES 4

QUICK ROAST TURKEY WITH CRANBERRY STUFFING

METRIC/IMPERIAL
1 × 3.5 kg/8 lb oven-ready turkey, weight excluding giblets
25 g/1 oz butter
watercress sprigs, to garnish
Stuffing:
100 g/4 oz fresh white breadcrumbs
175 g/6 oz prunes, soaked overnight, stoned and chopped
2 dessert apples, peeled, cored and sliced
50 g/2 oz blanched almonds, chopped
3 tablespoons cranberry sauce
grated rind and juice of 1 lemon
salt
freshly ground black pepper
1 egg, beaten

To make the stuffing, mix the breadcrumbs with the prunes, apples, almonds, cranberry sauce, lemon rind, lemon juice and salt and pepper to taste, blending well. Bind together with the

beaten egg. Use to stuff the neck end of the turkey, securing with wooden cocktail sticks. Tie the legs together with string. Do not use metal skewers.

Rub the turkey skin with butter and protect the turkey wings with a little foil. Place, breast side down, on a roasting rack in a roasting bag, sealing the end with a piece of string or an elastic band. Place in a shallow dish, ensuring that the foil does not touch the sides of the oven. Cook on FULL (100%) for 30 minutes, turning the dish twice during cooking. Turn breast side up and cook on FULL (100%) for a further 30 to 35 minutes or until the juices run clear.

Wrap the turkey in foil, shiny side inside, and leave to STAND for 15 minutes.

Serve hot or cold, garnished with watercress sprigs.
SERVES 8

TURKEY AND HAM ROLLS

METRIC/IMPERIAL
4 small turkey escalopes
4 small slices lean ham
4 tablespoons chopped fresh herbs
2 tablespoons sunflower or grapeseed oil
1 onion, finely chopped
1 clove garlic, crushed
1 × 400 g/14 oz can tomatoes, chopped
2 teaspoons demerara sugar
1 tablespoon tomato purée
freshly ground black pepper

Place the escalopes between two sheets of grease-proof paper and beat them flat.

Lay half a slice of ham on each escalope. Top with 1 tablespoon of herbs. Roll up and secure with wooden cocktail sticks or string.

Preheat a large browning dish on FULL (100%) for 5 minutes (or according to the manufacturer's instructions). Without removing it from the oven, add the oil and the turkey rolls and cook on FULL (100%) for 2½ minutes on each side. Wrap in foil and set aside.

Place the remaining ingredients in a large bowl or casserole. Cover and cook on FULL (100%) for 6½ minutes, stirring several times during cooking. Lay the turkey rolls in the sauce, cover and cook on FULL (100%) for 3¼ minutes, stirring once during cooking. Leave to STAND, covered, for 5 minutes.
SERVES 4

DUCK WITH LYCHEES

METRIC/IMPERIAL
1 × 1.5 kg/3¼ lb oven-ready duck
1 teaspoon salt
1 × 400 g/14 oz can lychees
100 g/4 oz frozen petit pois
¼ teaspoon ground ginger
2 tablespoons chopped fresh parsley, to garnish

Rinse the duck and pat dry with absorbent kitchen paper. Shield the leg and wing tips with small pieces of foil. Place, breast side down, on a roasting rack in a large shallow dish, ensuring that the foil does not touch the oven walls. Cook on FULL (100%) for 15 minutes.

Remove the foil and turn the duck, breast side up. Prick the skin in several places to release the fat. Baste and cook on FULL (100%) for a further 10 to 13 minutes until the juices from the cavity run clear. Leave to STAND, covered, for 10 minutes.

Carefully lift the duck out of the dish and drain thoroughly. Remove all the flesh from the bone and cut into neat pieces. Sprinkle with salt.

Pour off the fat from the dish, leaving the residual duck juices. Add 150 ml/¼ pint juice from the lychees, and the peas. Sprinkle with the ginger, then cover and cook on FULL (100%) for 5 minutes, stirring once. Stir in the duck and cook on FULL (100%) for 2 to 3 minutes until thoroughly reheated.

Transfer to a hot serving dish. Surround with the lychees and sprinkle with parsley before serving.
SERVES 4

DUCK WITH APPLE SAUCE

METRIC/IMPERIAL
1 × 2 kg/4½ lb oven-ready duck
salt
freshly ground black pepper
Sauce:
450 g/1 lb cooking apples, peeled, cored and sliced
2 tablespoons water
25 g/1 oz butter
2 teaspoons sugar

Rinse the duck and pat dry with absorbent kitchen paper. Prick the skin and season with salt and pepper to taste. Shield the tail end, leg and wing tips with foil. Place in a roasting bag and secure loosely with an elastic band. Pierce the bag to allow any steam to escape.

Place the duck, breast side down, on a roasting rack or upturned saucer in a shallow cooking dish. Ensure that the foil does not touch the sides of the oven. Cook on MEDIUM (50%) for 25 minutes. Drain and discard the juices from the bag.

Lightly reseal the bag and return to the oven, breast side up. Cook on MEDIUM (50%) for a further 15 to 24 minutes, until cooked. Remove the duck from the roasting bag, wrap in foil and leave to STAND while preparing the sauce.

To prepare the sauce, place the apples and water in a bowl. Cover and cook on FULL (100%) for 6 to 8 minutes, stirring once. Leave to STAND, covered, for 4 minutes, then beat in the butter and sugar.

Crisp and brown the duck under a preheated hot grill, if liked. Serve hot with the apple sauce.
SERVES 4

DUCK IN MUSTARD SAUCE

METRIC/IMPERIAL
1 × 2 kg/4½ lb oven-ready duck
salt
freshly ground black pepper
Mustard sauce:
25 g/1 oz butter
1 duck's liver
1 onion, chopped
100 ml/4 fl oz red wine
1½ tablespoons lemon juice
grated rind of 1 small lemon
1–2 teaspoons Dijon mustard
Garnish:
watercress sprigs

Rinse the duck and pat dry with absorbent paper towels. Prick the skin of the duck and sprinkle with salt and pepper to taste. Shield the tips of the wings, tail end and legs of the duck with small pieces of foil, ensuring that they do not touch the sides of the oven. Place, breast side down, on a roasting rack or upturned saucer in a dish. Cook on FULL (100%) for 10 minutes.

Drain away any cooking juices and reserve 4 tablespoons in a bowl. Turn the duck over and cook on FULL (100%) for a further 20 to 25 minutes, until cooked. Remove from the oven and leave to STAND, wrapped in foil, for 10 minutes. Brown and crisp under a preheated hot grill, if liked.

Meanwhile, make the sauce. Place the butter in a bowl and heat on FULL (100%) for ½ minute or until melted. Add the duck's liver, cover and cook on FULL (100%) for ½ to 1 minute. Remove with a slotted spoon and mash to a smooth paste.

Add the onion to the reserved juices. Cover and cook on FULL (100%) for 3 minutes. Stir in the wine, lemon juice, lemon rind and mustard to taste. Cook on FULL (100%) for 2 to 3 minutes until boiling. Beat in the duck's liver to blend well.

Carve the duck into portions and serve coated with the sauce. Garnish with watercress sprigs.
SERVES 4

DUCK CASSEROLE

METRIC/IMPERIAL
½ green pepper, cored, seeded and diced
1 clove garlic, crushed
1 onion, chopped
1 carrot, sliced
1 celery stick, chopped
50 g/2 oz butter
1 tablespoon vegetable oil
4 duck legs (about 225 g/8 oz each)
225 g/8 oz tomatoes, skinned and chopped
50 g/2 oz mushrooms, sliced
2 teaspoons mixed dried herbs
150 ml/¼ pint hot chicken stock
50 ml/2 fl oz red wine
salt
freshly ground black pepper

Place the pepper, garlic, onion, carrot and celery in a large bowl. Cover and cook on FULL (100%) for 8 minutes, stirring once.

Meanwhile, melt the butter and oil in a frying pan on a *conventional hob* and fry the duck until golden brown. Drain on absorbent paper.

Add the duck to the vegetables in the bowl together with the tomatoes, mushrooms, herbs, stock, red wine and add salt and pepper to taste. Cover and cook on FULL (100%) for 15 minutes, then reduce the setting to LOW (30%) for 55 minutes, or until the duck is tender.

Remove the duck and vegetables with a slotted spoon and place on a warm serving dish. Skim the fat from the sauce and pour the sauce over the duck and vegetables. Serve hot with tagliatelle.
SERVES 4

DUCK WITH GRAPEFRUIT

METRIC/IMPERIAL
1 × 1.75 kg/4 lb oven-ready duck
1 tablespoon molasses sugar
2 apples, cored and sliced
1 clove garlic, crushed
8 peppercorns
salt
1 tablespoon clear honey
1 teaspoon soy sauce
1 grapefruit, peeled and cut into segments
Sauce:
2 tablespoons molasses sugar
1 tablespoon cornflour
150 ml/¼ pint grapefruit juice
1–2 tablespoons brandy
salt
freshly ground black pepper

Rinse the duck and pat dry with absorbent paper towels. Stuff the cavity with the sugar, apples, garlic, peppercorns and salt. Secure well to enclose with wooden cocktail sticks. Place in a roasting bag and secure loosely with an elastic band. Pierce the bag to allow any steam to escape.

Place the duck, breast side down, on an upturned sauce in a shallow cooking dish. Cook on FULL (100%) for 20 minutes.

Drain the juices from the bag and reserve. Mix the honey with the soy sauce, blending well. Baste the duck breast with the honey mixture. Lightly reseal the bag and return to the oven, breast side up.

Cook on MEDIUM (50%) for a further 20 minutes. Remove the duck from the roasting bag. Wrap in foil and leave to STAND while preparing the sauce.

To prepare the sauce, blend the sugar and cornflour with the grapefruit juice in a jug. Stir in 4 tablespoons of the reserved juices, blending well. Cook on FULL (100%) for 2 minutes, stirring every ½ minute until smooth and thickened. Stir in the brandy and season to taste with salt and pepper.

Place the grapefruit segments on a plate and cook on FULL (100%) for 1 minute.

Crisp and brown the duck under a preheated hot grill, if liked. Serve hot, garnished with the grapefruit segments and accompanied by the grapefruit sauce.
SERVES 4

RABBIT AND PRUNE PIE

METRIC/IMPERIAL
1 large onion, thinly sliced
1 clove garlic, crushed
1 carrot, thinly sliced
450 ml/¾ pint hot chicken or vegetable stock
1 teaspoon chopped fresh sage or ½ teaspoon
dried sage
1 teaspoon chopped fresh thyme or ½ teaspoon
dried thyme
4 rabbit joints, cut in half
1 tablespoon wholemeal flour
salt
freshly ground black pepper
100 g/4 oz 'no-soak' prunes (see note)
575 g/1¼ lb cooked potatoes
5 tablespoons skimmed milk
15 g/½ oz low-fat spread
1 tablespoon chopped fresh parsley or 1 teaspoon
dried mixed herbs

Place the onion, garlic and carrot in a deep baking dish with 3 tablespoons of the stock. Cover and cook on FULL (100%) for 4 minutes, stirring halfway through the cooking time.

Add the herbs and rabbit portions and stir. Cover and cook on FULL (100%) for 6½ minutes, stirring after 3 minutes. Remove the rabbit portions with a slotted spoon, wrap in foil and set aside.

Mix the flour with a little of the stock and stir into the vegetables in the baking dish. Gradually add the remaining stock and season with salt and pepper to taste. Cover the dish again and cook on FULL (100%) for 2½ minutes, stirring well halfway through the cooking time.

Return the rabbit joints to the sauce, replace the cover and cook on LOW (30%) for 16½ minutes (or on DEFROST/20% for 21 minutes), stirring several times during cooking. Add the prunes, cover again and cook on LOW (30%) for a further 6½ minutes. Leave to STAND, covered, while preparing the potato topping.

Mash the cooked potatoes with the milk, low-fat spread and parsley or herbs. Add plenty of black pepper to taste. Spoon the potato topping over the rabbit mixture and cook on FULL (100%) for 2½ minutes. Cook under a preheated hot grill until golden.
SERVES 4

Note: 'No-soak' prunes are now widely available from good supermarkets and can be used instead of ordinary prunes to save time.

HOT GAME TERRINE

METRIC/IMPERIAL
225 g/8 oz cold cooked mixed game (pheasant,
quail or hare, for example), finely chopped
50 g/2 oz cooked ham, chopped
50 g/2 oz mushrooms, finely chopped
2 cloves garlic, crushed
1 teaspoon mixed dried herbs
salt
freshly ground black pepper
2 eggs, lightly beaten
Garnish:
watercress sprigs
tomato slices

Mix the chopped game, ham, mushrooms, garlic and herbs in a bowl. Season to taste with salt and pepper and bind together with the beaten eggs.

Place a tall, straight-sided glass in the centre of a 16 cm/6½ inch soufflé dish lined with grease-proof paper to make a ring mould. Spoon in the game mixture and spread evenly.

Cover and cook on FULL (100%) for 5 to 6 minutes. Remove the cover and the glass, then turn out on to a warm serving dish and remove the greaseproof paper. Garnish with sprigs of watercress and tomato slices. Serve with hot toast.
SERVES 4

DUCK WITH CHERRIES

METRIC/IMPERIAL
1 × 1.75 kg/4 lb oven-ready duck
1 kg/2 lb Montmorency or Morello cherries
1 tablespoon red wine
3 tablespoons cherry brandy
1 tablespoon brandy
2 tablespoons cornflour
about 300 ml/½ pint hot chicken stock or
strained duck juices, skimmed
salt
freshly ground black pepper

Rinse the duck and pat dry with absorbent paper towels. Place the duck in a roasting bag, pierce the bag and secure with an elastic band. Place it, breast side down, on a trivet in a shallow dish and cook on FULL (100%) for 14 minutes. Turn the duck over and pour off any juices, then cook on FULL (100%) for a further 14 minutes. Remove the duck from the bag, wrap tightly in foil and leave to STAND for 15 to 20 minutes.

Cut the duck into serving pieces and place them on a plate. Cover tightly and stand the plate over a pan of hot water to keep the duck moist and hot.

Place the cherries and wine in a large bowl. Cover and cook on FULL (100%) for 9 minutes or until tender, stirring once. Stir in the cherry brandy and brandy and set aside, covered. Keep the sauce warm.

Mix the cornflour with a little water in a large jug to make a smooth paste. Stir in the hot chicken or duck stock and cook on FULL (100%) for 3 to 4 minutes, stirring every 1 minute. Taste and adjust the seasoning.

Arrange the duck on a warm serving dish. Remove the cherries from their sauce and spoon around the duck. Stir the sauce from the cherries into the duck stock sauce and spoon over the duck. Serve immediately with creamed potatoes and green beans.
SERVES 4

RABBIT WITH BLACK OLIVES

METRIC/IMPERIAL
1 × 1 kg/2 lb rabbit, skinned and jointed
2 tablespoons olive oil
2 cloves garlic, crushed
1 teaspoon dried rosemary
200 ml/7 fl oz red wine
50 ml/2 fl oz chicken stock
1 tablespoon tomato purée
2 tomatoes, skinned and chopped
salt
freshly ground black pepper
225 g/8 oz black olives, stoned and halved

Place the rabbit joints around the base and sides of a large bowl. Cover and cook on FULL (100%) for 6 minutes, rearranging once.

Stir in the oil, garlic, rosemary, wine, stock, tomato purée, tomatoes, and salt and pepper to taste. Cover and cook on FULL (100%) for 15 minutes, then rearrange and reduce the setting to LOW (30%). Cover and cook for 45 minutes or until tender, rearranging every 15 minutes. Add the olives 15 minutes before the end of cooking.

Arrange the rabbit and olives on a warm serving dish and pour over a little of the sauce. Serve immediately with boiled rice and braised fennel. Hand the remaining sauce separately.
SERVES 4

NORMANDY PHEASANT

METRIC/IMPERIAL
2 × 750 g/1¾ lb oven-ready pheasants
freshly ground black pepper
4 back bacon rashers, derinded
675 g/1½ lb potatoes, peeled and quartered
3 tablespoons water
4 tablespoons Calvados, warmed
50 g/2 oz butter
1 tablespoon vegetable oil
200 ml/7 fl oz dry cider
450 ml/¾ pint double cream

Sprinkle the inside of each pheasant with pepper. Place 2 rashers of bacon over the breast of each bird and secure with wooden cocktail sticks. Place the pheasants in roasting bags and secure with elastic bands, then prick the bags and place in a shallow dish. Cook on FULL (100%) for 19 minutes, turning over once.

Remove the pheasants from the bags and discard the bacon. Place the birds in a *conventional oven*, preheated to 200°C/400°F/Gas Mark 6, for 15 minutes until browned. Alternatively, wrap them tightly in foil and leave to STAND for 15 minutes.

Meanwhile, place the potatoes and water in a large bowl, cover and cook on FULL (100%) for 7 minutes. Leave to STAND, covered.

Heat 2 tablespoons of the Calvados in a small saucepan on a *conventional hob*. Using a long taper, set it alight and pour over the pheasants. When the flames have died down, cut the pheasants into even-sized serving pieces and keep pieces warm.

Drain the potatoes. Melt the butter and oil in a frying pan on a *conventional hob* and fry the potatoes until golden brown. Keep warm.

Meanwhile, pour the cider into a saucepan and boil vigorously on a *conventional hob* until reduced by half. Stir in the cream, a little at a time, then simmer, stirring constantly, until glossy and reduced by half. Adjust the seasoning.

Arrange the pheasant pieces in the centre of a warm serving dish, sprinkle with the remaining Calvados and pour over a little of the hot sauce. Serve the pheasant with the sauté potatoes and Braised Red Cabbage with Apples (see page 199). Hand the remaining sauce separately.
SERVES 4

Note: Under no circumstances can spirits be heated on their own in a microwave. Always heat them in a saucepan on a conventional hob.

BRAISED PHEASANT IN CREAM SAUCE

METRIC/IMPERIAL
75 g/3 oz butter
1 × 1.5 kg/3¼ lb oven-ready pheasant
1 teaspoon microwave browning seasoning
(optional)
1 onion, thinly sliced
300 ml/½ pint double cream
juice of ½ lemon
salt
freshly ground black pepper
watercress sprigs, to garnish

Place the butter in a roasting bag, loosely secure the end with a piece of string or an elastic band and cook on FULL (100%) for 1 to 1½ minutes until melted.

Place the pheasant in the roasting bag, turning in the butter to coat. Sprinkle with the seasoning, if using. Add the onion to the bag, loosely secure the end as before and place on a plate. Cook on FULL (100%) for 15 minutes, turning over once.

Meanwhile, mix the cream with the lemon juice and salt and pepper to taste. Add to the pheasant, re-tie the bag and cook on FULL (100%) for a further 8 minutes, turning over once. Leave to STAND for 10 minutes.

Carefully remove the pheasant from the bag and carve into serving portions. Place on a warmed serving plate and spoon over the creamy sauce.

Garnish with watercress sprigs and serve at once.
SERVES 4

DUCK WITH ORANGE

METRIC/IMPERIAL
1 × 2.5 kg/5½ lb oven-ready duck or 6 × 400 g/
14 oz duck joints
4 oranges
1 lemon
9 tablespoons caster sugar
6 tablespoons white wine vinegar
1½ tablespoons arrowroot
watercress sprigs, to garnish

Place the duck or joints on a roasting rack in a deep dish and cook on MEDIUM (50%) for 45 to 60 minutes or until the juices run clear when the flesh is pierced with a sharp knife. Reposition the pieces or turn the duck over three times during cooking. Halfway through, remove the surplus juices and fat to a jug. Brown and crisp the cooked duck under a preheated hot grill.

While the duck is cooking, squeeze the juice from 2 of the oranges and the lemon. Grate the zest of 1 orange, pare the lemon peel and cut into thin strips. Peel and thinly slice the remaining oranges, removing the pips, and reserve.

When the duck is ready, set aside while preparing the sauce. Put the lemon strips into a jug or bowl, barely cover with cold water and cook on FULL (100%) for about 2 minutes, until boiling. Cook on FULL (100%) for a further 1 minute. Drain and reserve.

Combine the sugar and vinegar in a bowl and cook on FULL (100%) for 2 minutes. Stir until the sugar has dissolved, then cook on FULL (100%) for about 7 minutes or until a purple-brown syrup forms.

Blend the arrowroot with 2 tablespoons of the duck juices and set aside.

Stir the remaining duck juices (about 300 ml/½ pint), the fruit juices (about 200 ml/7 fl oz), orange zest and lemon strips into the syrup.

Add the blended arrowroot and cook on FULL (100%) for 3½ minutes or until the sauce thickens, stirring once during cooking.

Arrange the duck on a bed of orange slices and garnish with watercress. Spoon half the sauce over the duck and serve the remaining sauce separately.
SERVES 6

QUAILS IN WHITE WINE

METRIC/IMPERIAL
75 g/3 oz butter
4 oven-ready quail
about 14 vine leaves
8 streaky bacon rashers, derinded
200 ml/7 fl oz dry white wine
1 tablespoon vegetable oil
4 slices white bread, crusts removed, cut into
triangles
1 tablespoon cornflour
salt
freshly ground black pepper

Place 15 g /½ oz of the butter inside each bird, then wrap them in the vine leaves. Stretch the bacon rashers with the back of a knife and wrap two rashers round each bird. Secure with wooden cocktail sticks.

Place the quails, breast side down, in a large bowl. Cover and cook on FULL (100%) for 5 minutes.

Pour over the wine, cover and cook on FULL (100%) for a further 5 minutes. Reduce the setting to LOW (30%), turn the birds over, cover and cook for 20 minutes or until tender, turning them over again after 10 minutes.

Meanwhile, melt the remaining butter with the oil in a frying pan on a *conventional hob* and fry the bread on both sides until golden brown. Keep warm.

Lift the quails from the cooking liquid and remove the cocktail sticks, bacon and vine leaves. Keep the quails and bacon warm and discard the vine leaves.

Mix the cornflour with a little water to make a smooth paste and stir into the sauce with salt and pepper to taste. Cook on FULL (100%) for 3 minutes, stirring every 1 minute.

Put the fried bread on a warm serving dish and place the quails on top. Spoon over a little sauce and arrange the bacon over the quails. Serve hot with sauté potatoes and Brussels sprouts. Hand the remaining sauce separately.
SERVES 2

PIGEONS IN RED WINE

METRIC/IMPERIAL
25 g/1 oz butter
1 tablespoon vegetable oil
2 pigeons, drawn and trussed
4 streaky bacon rashers, derinded
1 onion, finely chopped
1 tablespoon flour
2 tablespoons redcurrant jelly
150 ml/¼ pint red wine
150 ml/¼ pint stock
1 tablespoon tomato purée
salt
freshly ground black pepper
100 g/4 oz button mushrooms
50 g/2 oz stuffed olives
2 tablespoons chopped fresh parsley

Preheat a large browning dish on FULL (100%) for 5 minutes (or according to the manufacturer's instructions). Add the butter and oil, then place the pigeons, each wrapped in 2 rashers of bacon, in the heated dish. Cook on FULL (100%) for 3½ minutes, turning the birds frequently, so they are browned on all sides. Remove the birds and set aside.

Stir in the onion, cover and cook on FULL (100%) for 1½ to 2 minutes. Stir in the flour, redcurrant jelly, wine, stock, tomato purée and salt and pepper to taste. Return to the oven and cook on FULL (100%) for 1½ to 2 minutes.

Stir well and return the birds to the dish. Cover and cook on FULL (100%) for 6½ minutes, turning the dish and the birds after 3 minutes. Cook on FULL (100%) for a further 3½ minutes, then add the mushrooms, olives and parsley. Cook on FULL (100%) for a further 3½ minutes. Leave to STAND for 5 to 10 minutes before serving.
SERVES 4

Note: Timing of this dish may vary according to the age of the pigeons.

SPICED DUCK

METRIC/IMPERIAL
1 large onion, chopped
3 tablespoons dark, soft brown sugar
1½ teaspoons salt
2 tablespoons paprika
2 tablespoons tomato purée
2 tablespoons Worcestershire sauce
4 tablespoons white wine vinegar
4 tablespoons lemon juice
½ teaspoon dried rosemary
½ teaspoon dried chives
½ teaspoon grated nutmeg
900 ml/1½ pints cold water
freshly ground black pepper
1 × 2 kg/4½ lb duck, quartered
25 g/1 oz butter
25 g/1 oz plain flour
spring onions, to garnish

Place the onion, sugar, salt, paprika, tomato purée, Worcestershire sauce, vinegar, lemon juice, rosemary, chives, nutmeg, water, and pepper to taste in a large bowl. Add the duck and leave to marinate overnight.

Drain the duck, reserving the marinade. Place in a large bowl, cover and cook on FULL (100%) for 10 minutes. Halfway through cooking, drain off the juices, then rearrange the duck pieces.

Leave the duck to STAND, covered, for 10 minutes. Drain off the juices and cook, covered, on FULL (100%) for a further 8 minutes.

Place the duck on a grill pan and grill under a preheated conventional grill until the skin is crisp.

Meanwhile, place the butter in a large jug and heat on FULL (100%) for ½ minute or until melted. Stir in the flour. Measure out 600 ml/1 pint of the strained reserved marinade. Blend into the butter and flour mixture. Cook on FULL (100%) for 5 minutes, stirring every 1 minute.

Serve the duck with the sauce, garnished with spring onions.

SERVES 4

ROAST PHEASANT WITH BREAD SAUCE

METRIC/IMPERIAL
1 onion, peeled
6 cloves
150 ml/¼ pint milk
150 ml/¼ pint cold chicken stock
100 g/4 oz fresh white breadcrumbs
75 g/3 oz butter
salt
freshly ground black pepper
1 × 1 kg/2 lb oven-ready pheasant
3 streaky bacon rashers, derinded
1 tablespoon plain flour

To make the sauce, stud the onion with the cloves and place in a medium bowl. Add the milk, chicken stock, breadcrumbs, 50 g/2 oz of the butter, salt and pepper. Cook on FULL (100%) for 5½ minutes, stirring halfway through the cooking time.

Place the remaining butter inside the pheasant and secure the opening with trussing thread. Lay the bacon over the breast and secure.

Place the pheasant in a roasting bag and secure with an elastic band. Prick the bag and place in a shallow casserole. Cook on FULL (100%) for 7 minutes. Turn the pheasant over and cook on FULL (100%) for a further 7 minutes.

Remove the pheasant from the bag and discard the bacon. Wrap in foil and STAND for 10 minutes.

Place the pheasant in a grill pan. Sprinkle with flour and brown under a preheated grill.

Meanwhile, remove and discard the onion from the sauce. Cook on FULL (100%) for a further 3½ minutes, stirring halfway through to reheat. Serve the pheasant with the sauce handed separately.

SERVES 3

COUNTRY RABBIT CASSEROLE

METRIC/IMPERIAL
1 rabbit, cut into about 6 pieces
1 large onion, sliced
1 clove garlic, crushed
4 bacon rashers, derinded and chopped
3 carrots, sliced
1 celery stick, sliced
150 ml/¼ pint milk
150 ml/¼ pint light stock
¼ teaspoon dried mixed herbs
1 bay leaf
25 g/1 oz butter
25 g/1 oz plain flour
salt
freshly ground black pepper

Place the rabbit, onion, garlic, bacon, carrots, celery, milk, stock, herbs and bay leaf in a large casserole dish. Cover and cook on FULL (100%) for 12 minutes, stirring once. Leave to STAND, covered, for 10 minutes. Cook on FULL (100%) for a further 6 minutes.

Remove and discard the bay leaf. Strain the liquid from the casserole into a jug.

Place the butter in a bowl and heat on FULL (100%) for ½ minute or until melted. Stir in the flour and cook on FULL (100%) for 1 minute. Gradually add the strained liquid, and salt and pepper to taste, blending well. Cook on FULL (100%) for 3 minutes, stirring every 1 minute, until smooth and thickened.

Pour over the rabbit mixture and cook on FULL (100%) for a further 2 minutes.

SERVES 4 to 6

RABBIT CASSEROLE WITH DUMPLINGS

METRIC/IMPERIAL
1 teaspoon vegetable oil
675 g/1½ lb boneless rabbit or 4 large rabbit joints
2 tablespoons seasoned flour
1 onion, sliced
1 clove garlic, crushed
75 g/3 oz streaky bacon, derinded and chopped
4 celery sticks, chopped
2 leeks, sliced
2 carrots, sliced
400 ml/14 fl oz hot chicken stock

1 bouquet garni
salt
freshly ground black pepper
Dumplings:
25 g/1 oz streaky bacon, derinded and chopped
50 g/2 oz self-raising flour
25 g/1 oz shredded beef suet
1 tablespoon chopped fresh sage or 2 teaspoons dried sage
cold water to mix

Place the oil in a large casserole and heat on FULL (100%) for 1 minute.

Toss the rabbit in the flour. Add to the oil with the onion, garlic, bacon, celery, leeks and carrots. Cover and cook on FULL (100%) for 10 minutes. Add the stock, bouquet garni, salt and pepper. Cover and cook on FULL (100%) for 5 minutes.

Reduce the setting to MEDIUM (50%) and cook for 30 minutes, stirring twice.

Place all the dumpling ingredients in a bowl and mix to a soft dough. Turn on to a floured surface and form into 4 dumplings.

Stir the casserole and add the dumplings. Cover and cook on MEDIUM (50%) for 20 minutes. Leave to STAND for 5 minutes. Remove and discard the bouquet garni before serving.
SERVES 4

PHEASANT WITH WALNUTS AND GRAPES
METRIC/IMPERIAL
1 × 1 kg/2 lb oven-ready pheasant
salt
freshly ground black pepper
225 g/8 oz grapes, halved and seeded
50 g/2 oz walnuts, chopped
25 g/1 oz butter
150 ml/¼ pint dry white wine
150 ml/¼ pint double cream
2 egg yolks
watercress sprigs, to garnish

Preheat a large browning dish on FULL (100%) for 5 minutes (or according to the manufacturer's instructions).

Season the pheasant with salt and pepper and stuff with two-thirds of the grapes and walnuts. Secure the opening with wooden cocktail sticks.

Add the butter to the browning dish and swirl quickly to melt. Roll the pheasant in the melted butter. Cover and cook on MEDIUM (50%) for 12 minutes.

Turn the pheasant over, cover and cook on MEDIUM (50%) for a further 10 minutes.

Remove the pheasant with a slotted spoon and place on a warmed serving plate. Cover with foil, shiny side inside, and leave to STAND for 10 minutes.

Meanwhile, add the remaining grapes and walnuts to the dish juices with the wine. Blend the cream with the egg yolks and stir into the sauce, blending well.

Cook on FULL (100%) for 3 to 4 minutes, stirring twice, until lightly thickened.

Serve the pheasant hot and hand the sauce separately. Garnish with watercress sprigs, if liked, and serve with game chips.
SERVES 2

ROAST PHEASANTS WITH CRANBERRY SAUCE
METRIC/IMPERIAL
175 g/6 oz fresh cranberries
100 g/4 oz caster sugar
50 g/2 oz butter
2 × 1 kg/2 lb oven-ready pheasants
8 streaky bacon rashers, stretched
1 teaspoon cornflour
3 tablespoons sweet sherry
grated rind of 1 orange
Garnish:
pheasant tail feathers
watercress sprigs

Place the cranberries and sugar in a small bowl. Cover and cook on FULL (100%) for 4 minutes, stirring halfway through cooking.

Reduce the power to DEFROST (20%) and continue to cook for 10 minutes, stirring thoroughly halfway through cooking.

Place the cranberry mixture in a blender or food processor and purée until smooth. Set aside.

Place half of the butter inside each pheasant. Shield the thin ends of the legs with foil, ensuring that the foil does not touch the walls of the oven. Wrap the bacon around each bird and secure with wooden cocktail sticks. Truss the birds with string.

Place the birds, breast side down, in a shallow dish. Cover and cook on FULL (100%) for 10 minutes. Turn over, cover and cook on FULL (100%) for a further 10 to 12 minutes.

Remove the bacon, cocktail sticks and foil.

Place the birds under a preheated grill, breast side up, to crisp and brown the skin.

Meanwhile, blend together the cornflour, sherry and orange rind. Stir into the cranberry purée. Pour into a large jug and cook on FULL (100%) for 3 minutes, stirring every 1 minute.

Arrange the birds on a warm serving platter. Spoon over the cranberry sauce and garnish with the pheasant tail feathers and watercress.
SERVES 4 to 6

FRUIT-STUFFED DUCK

METRIC/IMPERIAL
175 g/6 oz fresh white breadcrumbs
350 g/12 oz prunes, soaked overnight, drained and stoned
grated rind of 1 orange
1 orange, peeled, segmented and pips removed
1 dessert apple, peeled, cored and chopped
salt
freshly ground black pepper
1 egg, lightly beaten
1 × 2.25 kg/5 lb duck, boned, but in one piece (the butcher should be asked in advance to do this)
Garnish:
strips of orange peel
orange slices

Mix together the breadcrumbs, prunes, orange rind, orange segments, apple and salt and pepper to taste. Bind together with the egg.

Stuff the cavity of the duck and close the end with string. Place the loose neck skin under the bird. Keeping the wings close to the bird, truss with string to make into the original shape of the bird.

Place the duck on a roasting rack, breast side down, in a shallow dish. Cook on FULL (100%) for about 35 to 40 minutes (see note below). Turn over after 10 minutes of cooking.

Leave to STAND, covered with foil, for 5 minutes before serving. Crisp the skin under a preheated hot grill, if liked. Remove the string and garnish with orange peel and orange slices.
SERVES 4

Note: Stuff the duck, then weigh it to calculate the microwave cooking time. Allow 7 to 8 minutes per 450 g/1 lb.

POT ROAST PHEASANT

METRIC/IMPERIAL
1 × 1 kg/2¼ lb pheasant
1 orange, peeled and divided into segments
2 tablespoons grapeseed or sunflower oil
1 onion, thinly sliced
50 ml/2 fl oz hot chicken stock
juice of 1 large orange or
50 ml/2 fl oz unsweetened orange juice
4 juniper berries, lightly crushed
6 thyme sprigs
pinch of salt
freshly ground black pepper
2 dessert apples
2 teaspoons cornflour, blended with 1 tablespoon water
1 tablespoon chopped fresh tarragon
1 tablespoon redcurrant jelly

Wipe the pheasant thoroughly inside and out with a piece of kitchen paper. Place the orange segments inside the cavity and secure with wooden cocktail sticks.

Heat a large browning dish for 5 minutes (or according to the manufacturer's instructions). Without removing it from the oven, add the oil and the pheasant, breast side down, and cook on FULL (100%) for 2 to 2½ minutes. Turn the pheasant and cook on FULL (100%) for a further 2 to 2½ minutes. Remove the bird and set aside.

Place the onion in a large bowl or casserole. Add 2 tablespoons of the hot stock and cook on FULL (100%) for 2 to 2½ minutes. Add the remaining stock and the orange juice, juniper berries, thyme and seasoning.

Add the pheasant, turning it over in the stock. Cover and cook on FULL (100%) for 3½ to 4 minutes. Baste with the juices, cover and continue cooking on LOW (30%) for 11½ minutes (or on DEFROST/20% for 15 minutes), basting several times during cooking. Place the pheasant on a warmed serving platter and wrap in foil.

Strain the cooking liquid through a fine sieve and return to the bowl or casserole, discarding the onion, juniper berries and thyme. Add the apple slices and cook on FULL (100%) for 1½ minutes, stirring halfway through. Remove the apple and arrange around the pheasant.

Mix the blended cornflour into the sauce. Cook on FULL (100%) for 1½ minutes, stirring well halfway through the cooking time. Stir in the tarragon and redcurrant jelly and pour into a warmed jug or sauce boat.
SERVES 4

VEGETABLES AND SALADS

FROZEN OVEN CHIPS

METRIC/IMPERIAL
15 g/½ oz lard or 1 tablespoon vegetable oil
175 g/6 oz frozen oven chips

Preheat a large browning dish on FULL (100%) for 5 minutes (or according to the manufacturer's instructions). Add the lard or oil and chips. Stir well and cook, uncovered, on FULL (100%) for 6 minutes, stirring once after 3 minutes. Leave to STAND for 1 minute, then drain on absorbent kitchen paper before serving.
SERVES 2

Note: To reheat cooked chips, put them into a dish lined with absorbent kitchen paper. Sprinkle with salt and pepper, if wished. Cook on FULL (100%) until very hot, stirring once during cooking. The time taken will depend on the quantity of chips to be reheated.

MANGETOUT

METRIC/IMPERIAL
350 g/12 oz fresh mangetout
6 tablespoons water
½ teaspoon salt
15 g/½ oz butter
mint sprigs, to garnish

Top and tail the mangetout and discard any stringy threads.
Combine the water and salt in a large shallow dish. Add the mangetout, cover and cook on FULL (100%) for 7 to 9 minutes, stirring occasionally.
Leave to STAND, covered, for 2 minutes. Drain, add the butter and toss well.
Serve garnished with sprigs of fresh mint.
SERVES 4

Note: Frozen mangetout may be used if fresh ones are unobtainable. They will take approximately half the above cooking time.

CABBAGE WITH CARAWAY

METRIC/IMPERIAL
3 tablespoons water
salt
350 g/12 oz cabbage, stalk removed, and finely shredded
1 tablespoon caraway seeds
15 g/½ oz butter

Place the water and salt in a large bowl and add the cabbage. Cover and cook on FULL (100%) for 8 minutes. Halfway through cooking, stir in the caraway seeds.
Stir the butter into the cabbage until melted.
SERVES 4

CREAMED POTATOES

METRIC/IMPERIAL
3 tablespoons water
pinch of salt
675 g/1½ lb potatoes, peeled and halved
25 g/1 oz butter, cut into pieces
2 tablespoons milk
1 tablespoon cream
pinch of grated nutmeg
salt
freshly ground white pepper
parsley sprigs, to garnish

Place the water and salt in a large bowl and add the potatoes. Cover and cook on FULL (100%) for 9 minutes, stirring halfway through cooking. Leave to STAND, covered, for 5 minutes.
Drain the potatoes and pass through a sieve or potato ricer. Set aside.
Place the butter and milk in a small bowl. Cook on FULL (100%) for 1 minute. Beat the butter, milk, cream, nutmeg and salt and pepper to taste into the potatoes. Reheat, if necessary.
Pile into a warm serving dish and garnish with the sprigs of parsley.
SERVES 6

BAKED POTATOES

METRIC/IMPERIAL
4 potatoes (about 175 g/6 oz each), scrubbed and
dried
15 g/½ oz butter
salt
freshly ground black pepper

Prick the potatoes thoroughly. Arrange, well spaced out, on a double thickness of absorbent kitchen paper, on the oven base or turntable. Cook on FULL (100%) for 6 minutes. Turn the potatoes over and cook on FULL (100%) for 6 to 9 minutes until tender but not soft.

Leave to STAND for 5 minutes, when the potatoes should be completely cooked. Split in half lengthways and top each half with butter, salt and pepper. Serve immediately.
SERVES 4

SPINACH

METRIC/IMPERIAL
675 g/1½ lb fresh leaf spinach
salt
freshly ground black pepper
15 g/½ oz butter

Wash the spinach and shake off surplus water. Discard the thick stems. Place in a dish, cover and cook on FULL (100%) for 8 to 9 minutes, stirring once.

Leave to STAND for 2 minutes. Sprinkle with salt and pepper to taste and dot with butter.
SERVES 4

STEAMED BRUSSELS SPROUTS

METRIC/IMPERIAL
675 g/1½ lb Brussels sprouts, trimmed
salt
6 tablespoons water

Place the sprouts in a large deep dish. Add the salt to the water and pour over the sprouts. Cover loosely and cook on FULL (100%) for 8 to 10 minutes, giving the dish a vigorous shake twice during cooking.

Leave to STAND for 5 minutes. Test for tenderness, then drain and serve hot.
SERVES 4 to 6

BROCCOLI SPEARS

METRIC/IMPERIAL
350 g/12 oz broccoli spears, trimmed
½ teaspoon salt
4 tablespoons water
freshly ground black pepper

Arrange the broccoli spears, with the stalks towards the outside edges, in a large shallow dish. Add the salt to the water and pour over the broccoli. Cover and cook on FULL (100%) for 7 minutes, giving the dish a half-turn after 4 minutes.

Leave to STAND, covered, for 2 to 4 minutes. Correct the seasoning, adding pepper to taste, before serving.
SERVES 4

BAVARIAN CABBAGE

METRIC/IMPERIAL
450 g/1 lb red cabbage, shredded
2 red dessert apples, cored and chopped
8 tablespoons water
1 teaspoon fresh lemon juice
2 tablespoons soured cream
salt
freshly ground black pepper

Mix the cabbage, apples, water and lemon juice in a large dish. Three-quarters cover and cook on FULL (100%) for 15 minutes, stirring every 5 minutes.

Carefully remove the cover, stir in the soured cream and add salt and pepper to taste.
SERVES 4

ONION RINGS

METRIC/IMPERIAL
1 large onion, cut into rings
25 g/1 oz butter
salt
freshly ground black pepper

Put the onion rings into a mixing bowl. Arrange the butter in the centre and season with salt and pepper. Cover and cook on FULL (100%) for 3 to 4 minutes.

Stir, then leave to STAND for 3 minutes before serving.
SERVES 4

SLIMMERS' RATATOUILLE

METRIC/IMPERIAL
225 g/8 oz courgettes, trimmed
450 g/1 lb aubergines, trimmed
salt
1 × 400 g/14 oz can tomatoes, chopped
½ teaspoon dried basil
salt
freshly ground black pepper
1 onion, finely chopped
grated Edam cheese, to garnish (optional)

Cut the courgettes and aubergines into 5 mm/
¼ inch slices. Arrange in a colander and sprinkle
with salt. Top with a plate and a weight, then
leave to STAND for 30 minutes. Rinse well
under cold, running water and shake off excess
water.

Layer the courgette and aubergine slices in a
casserole dish, with the tomatoes, basil, salt and
pepper and onion. Finish with a layer of tomatoes.

Cover and cook on FULL (100%) for 20
minutes, turning three times during cooking, if
necessary. Remove the cover for the last 7
minutes to allow some of the liquid to evaporate.
Serve hot or cold, sprinkled liberally with grated
Edam cheese, if liked.
SERVES 4

BROAD BEAN RAGOÛT

METRIC/IMPERIAL
1 onion, chopped
1 carrot, thinly sliced
2 cloves garlic, crushed
25 g/1 oz butter
50 g/2 oz bacon, derinded and chopped
salt
freshly ground black pepper
450 g/1 lb frozen broad beans

Place the onion, carrot, garlic, butter and bacon
in a large bowl. Cover and cook on FULL
(100%) for 8 minutes, stirring halfway through
cooking.

Stir in salt and pepper to taste and add the
frozen beans. Cover and cook on FULL (100%)
for 8 minutes, stirring halfway through cooking.
Leave to STAND, covered, for 5 minutes before
spooning into a warm serving dish. Serve with a
hot fish, meat or poultry dish.
SERVES 4

BRAISED ONIONS

METRIC/IMPERIAL
450 g/1 lb small, even-sized onions, peeled
15 g/½ oz butter
1 teaspoon yeast extract
salt
freshly ground black pepper

Score the onions round the middle with a sharp
knife. Put the butter and yeast extract in a large
shallow dish and cook on FULL (100%) for 1
minute until melted. Add the onions and toss to
coat with the savoury butter, then arrange
around the sides of the dish.

Cover loosely and cook on FULL (100%) for
10 to 12 minutes until just tender, giving the dish
a half-turn after 5 minutes. Leave to STAND,
covered, for 2 minutes. Season the onions with
salt and pepper to taste just before serving.
SERVES 4

GLAZED COURGETTES WITH NUTMEG

METRIC/IMPERIAL
12 small, even-shaped, firm courgettes
25 g/1 oz unsalted butter
1 teaspoon grated nutmeg
salt
freshly ground black pepper

Trim the courgettes and pierce each one in two
or three places with the tip of a sharp knife. Put
the butter and nutmeg in a large shallow dish and
cook on FULL (100%) for ½ minute or until
melted. Arrange the courgettes in a single layer
in the dish and cook on FULL (100%) for 3
minutes.

Transfer the courgettes in the centre of the dish
to the edges. Baste with the butter. Cover
loosely and cook on FULL (100%) for 4 minutes,
giving the dish a half-turn after 2 minutes.

Leave to STAND, covered, for 5 minutes.
Test by lightly pressing each courgette with a
finger. Those which just yield to this pressure are
cooked. Transfer any undercooked courgettes to
a small dish and cook on FULL (100%) for a
further ½ minute.

Transfer the courgettes to a heated serving
dish, season with salt and pepper to taste and
pour over the melted butter before serving.
SERVES 4

MUSHROOMS WITH BACON

METRIC/IMPERIAL
50 g/2 oz streaky bacon, derinded and chopped
1 onion, finely chopped
450 g/1 lb mushrooms, sliced
150 ml/¼ pint soured cream
salt
1–2 teaspoons lemon juice
1 teaspoon plain flour
2 teaspoons cold water
chopped fresh parsley, to garnish

Place the bacon and onion in a cooking dish. Cover and cook on FULL (100%) for 3 minutes.

Add the mushrooms, cover and cook on FULL (100%) for 10 minutes, stirring once. Add the soured cream, salt to taste and lemon juice, blending well.

Mix the flour and water to a smooth paste and stir into the mushroom mixture, blending well.

Cover and cook on FULL (100%) for 2 to 3 minutes, stirring twice. Serve hot, sprinkled with chopped parsley.

SERVES 4

DEVILLED MUSHROOMS

METRIC/IMPERIAL
225 g/8 oz button mushrooms, trimmed
25 g/1 oz butter
100 ml/4 fl oz double cream
1 tablespoon Worcestershire sauce
1 tablespoon tomato ketchup
½ teaspoon mustard powder
1 teaspoon vinegar
salt
freshly ground black pepper
pinch of grated nutmeg

Place the mushrooms in a dish with the butter. Cook on FULL (100%) for 3 minutes, stirring once.

Blend the cream with the Worcestershire sauce, tomato ketchup, mustard, vinegar, salt and pepper to taste and the nutmeg. Stir into the mushrooms, blending well.

Carefully divide between 4 ramekin dishes. Cover and cook on LOW (30%) for 3 minutes, rearranging once.

Stir each ramekin and serve with hot fingers of toast.

SERVES 4

CRUMBLY BUTTERED BRUSSELS

METRIC/IMPERIAL
450 g/1 lb Brussels sprouts, trimmed
4 tablespoons water
salt
75 g/3 oz butter
1 clove garlic, crushed (optional)
6 tablespoons toasted breadcrumbs
pinch of cayenne pepper

Place the sprouts in a dish with the water and a pinch of salt. Cover and cook on FULL (100%) for 7 to 9 minutes, stirring once. Drain thoroughly.

Place the butter in a bowl and heat on FULL (100%) for 1½ minutes or until melted. Add the garlic, if using, and the breadcrumbs, salt and cayenne pepper to taste, mixing well. Toss the cooked sprouts in the buttered crumbs. Cook on FULL (100%) for 3 minutes, stirring once. Serve hot.

SERVES 4

COURGETTE SHELLS WITH BACON

METRIC/IMPERIAL
4 courgettes, halved lengthways
1 bacon rasher, derinded and chopped
1 small onion, finely chopped
1 teaspoon dried mixed herbs
25–50 g/1–2 oz fresh white breadcrumbs
1 egg yolk
4 tablespoons stock
salt
freshly ground black pepper

Using a teaspoon, scoop the centres from the courgette halves. Set the shells aside and chop the scooped-out flesh (there should be about 25 g/1 oz).

Place the courgette flesh, bacon, onion and herbs in a small bowl. Cover and cook on FULL (100%) for 3 minutes. Stir in the breadcrumbs, egg yolk, stock and salt and pepper to taste.

Fill one half of each courgette shell with the stuffing. Replace the other half and secure with wooden cocktail sticks. Place in a shallow dish, cover and cook on FULL (100%) for 9 minutes, rearranging halfway through cooking. Leave to STAND for 3 to 4 minutes before serving.

SERVES 4

BROAD BEANS WITH HAM AND CREAM

METRIC/IMPERIAL
1 × 275 g/10 oz packet frozen broad beans
2 tablespoons water
2 tablespoons single cream
75 g/3 oz cooked ham, chopped
salt
freshly ground black pepper

Place the beans in a cooking dish with the water. Cover and cook on FULL (100%) for 8 minutes, stirring once. Drain thoroughly.

Stir in the cream, ham and salt and pepper to taste, blending well. Cook on FULL (100%) for 1 minute. Serve at once.
SERVES 4

RATATOUILLE NIÇOISE

METRIC/IMPERIAL
1 medium aubergine, thinly sliced
salt
1 courgette, sliced
6 tomatoes, skinned and chopped
1 green pepper, cored, seeded and finely chopped
1 onion, thinly sliced
1 tablespoon tomato purée
2 cloves garlic, crushed
6 tablespoons olive oil
1 thyme sprig
freshly ground black pepper
1 tablespoon chopped fresh basil
chopped fresh parsley, to garnish

Place the aubergine slices in a colander and sprinkle with salt. Leave to drain for 15 to 20 minutes to remove excess liquid, then rinse with cold water and pat dry with kitchen paper.

Place the aubergine, courgette, tomatoes, green pepper, onion, tomato purée, garlic, oil, thyme and salt and pepper to taste in a large bowl. Cover and cook on FULL (100%) for 15 minutes, stirring after 5 and 10 minutes.

Stir in the basil and adjust the seasoning, if necessary. Spoon on to a warm serving dish and garnish with the parsley.
SERVES 4

Note: Ratatouille is very versatile. It can be served hot or cold, made in small quantities for a starter or as a side dish to go with meat dishes, or in large quantities for a supper dish.

LEMON AND GARLIC POTATOES

METRIC/IMPERIAL
20 g/¾ oz butter
20 g/¾ oz plain flour
400 ml/14 fl oz milk
2 tablespoons lemon juice
grated rind of ½ lemon
1 clove garlic, crushed
salt
freshly ground black pepper
1 kg/2 lb potatoes, thinly sliced
snipped chives, to garnish

Place the butter in a jug and heat on FULL (100%) for ½ minute or until melted. Add the flour, blending well. Gradually add the milk and cook on FULL (100%) for 3 to 4 minutes, stirring every 1 minute until smooth and thickened. Stir in the lemon juice and rind, garlic, salt and pepper.

Place half the potato slices in a greased shallow dish. Pour over half the sauce. Top with the remaining potato slices and cover with the remaining sauce.

Partially cover and cook on FULL (100%) for 16 minutes, turning the dish twice. Leave to STAND for 5 minutes.

Cook under a preheated hot grill until golden, if wished. Garnish with chopped chives. Serve hot with chops, steak or chicken.
SERVES 4

Variation
Rosemary and lemon potatoes: prepare and cook as above but use 2 teaspoons chopped fresh rosemary instead of the garlic.

VICHY CARROTS

METRIC/IMPERIAL
3 tablespoons cold water
1 teaspoon caster sugar
450 g/1 lb carrots, thinly sliced
25 g/1 oz butter, cut into pieces
1 tablespoon chopped fresh parsley

Place the water, sugar and carrots in a medium bowl. Cover and cook on FULL (100%) for 6 to 9 minutes or until tender, stirring halfway through cooking. Drain and stir in the butter until melted. Fold in the parsley. Serve hot.
SERVES 4

MUSHROOMS IN SOURED CREAM SAUCE

METRIC/IMPERIAL
25 g/1 oz butter
1 tablespoon vegetable oil
350 g/12 oz button mushrooms, thickly sliced
salt
freshly ground black pepper
150 ml/¼ pint soured cream
paprika, to garnish

Preheat a large browning dish on FULL (100%) for 5 minutes (or according to the manufacturer's instructions).

Put the butter and oil into the hot dish, and stir in the mushrooms. Cover and cook on FULL (100%) for 3 minutes. Strain off the juice and, if wished, reserve for another dish (see note). Season well with salt and pepper, and stir in the soured cream. Cook on MEDIUM (50%) for 4 minutes. Serve hot or cold, sprinkled with paprika.
SERVES 4

Note: If Mushrooms in Soured Cream Sauce are to be served with meat or poultry, the juices from the mushrooms can be added to the gravy.

BRAISED CELERY

METRIC/IMPERIAL
3 tablespoons water
salt
450 g/1 lb head of celery, trimmed, and stalks halved
1 onion, thinly sliced
150 ml/¼ pint hot chicken stock
25 g/1 oz butter, cut into pieces
1 teaspoon chopped fresh parsley
freshly ground black pepper

Place the water and salt in an oblong or oval casserole dish. Place half the celery in the dish and spread the onion over the top. Cover the onion with the remaining celery. Cover and cook on FULL (100%) for 8 minutes. After 5 minutes of cooking, rearrange the vegetables.

Mix together the hot stock, butter, parsley and salt and pepper to taste. Pour over the celery, cover and cook on FULL (100%) for a further 3 minutes. Leave to STAND, covered, for 3 to 4 minutes before serving.
SERVES 4

ASPARAGUS WITH HERBED BUTTER SAUCE

METRIC/IMPERIAL
450 g/1 lb fresh asparagus
125 ml/4½ fl oz water
100 g/4 oz butter
4 tablespoons finely chopped fresh herbs (chives, parsley and tarragon, for example)

Trim the woody ends from the asparagus and thinly pare the outer tough skin from the stalk. Place in a cooking dish with half of the tips at each end. Add the water, cover and cook on FULL (100%) for 12 to 14 minutes, or until fork tender. Drain and place on a warmed serving dish.

Place the butter in a bowl. Cover and heat on FULL (100%) for 3 minutes, or until melted and bubbling hot. Stir in the herbs, blending well.

Spoon over the asparagus and serve at once.
SERVES 4

MUSHROOMS À LA GRECQUE

METRIC/IMPERIAL
1 tablespoon vegetable oil
1 small clove garlic, crushed
1 small onion, chopped
100 ml/4 fl oz dry white wine
2 tablespoons tomato purée
½ teaspoon dried mixed herbs
2 tomatoes, skinned, seeded and chopped
175 g/6 oz button mushrooms, trimmed
salt
freshly ground black pepper
chopped fresh parsley, to garnish
1 × 50 g/2 oz wholemeal bread roll, to serve (as a complete meal)

Place the oil, garlic and onion in a bowl. Cover and cook on FULL (100%) for 2 minutes, stirring once. Add the wine, tomato purée, herbs and tomatoes. Cook on FULL (100%) for 3 minutes, stirring once.

Add the mushrooms and cook on FULL (100%) for a further 3 minutes, stirring once. Leave to cool, then chill lightly.

Season with salt and pepper to taste and sprinkle with chopped parsley. Serve with a bread roll as a complete meal.
SERVES 1

BAKED AUBERGINES

METRIC/IMPERIAL
2 medium aubergines
salt
225 g/8 oz cooked, chopped chicken meat
1 tablespoon chopped fresh parsley
2 tablespoons cooked long-grain rice
25 g/1 oz raisins
salt
freshly ground black pepper
1 tablespoon cream cheese
2 tablespoons natural yogurt
50 g/2 oz Edam cheese, grated
fresh herbs, to garnish

Halve the aubergines lengthways and scoop out the flesh, leaving a shell 5 mm/¼ inch thick. Chop the flesh roughly.

Sprinkle the aubergine shells and the pulp with salt and leave to STAND for 30 minutes, to extract the excess moisture. Rinse the pulp and shell, and drain well.

Put the pulp into a mixing bowl and add the chicken, parsley, rice, raisins and salt and pepper. Combine with the cream cheese and yogurt. Pile the mixture back into the aubergine shells and top with the Edam cheese.

Arrange the shells in a round pie dish, around the outside edge. Cover and cook on FULL (100%) for 10 minutes. Give the dish a half-turn, twice, during cooking. Leave to STAND for 4 minutes and serve garnished with herbs.
SERVES 4

LYONNAISE POTATOES

METRIC/IMPERIAL
25 g/1 oz butter
100 g/4 oz onions, finely sliced
½ teaspoon salt
¼ teaspoon freshly ground black pepper
350 g/12 oz potatoes, peeled and rinsed
1 teaspoon chopped fresh parsley
parsley sprig, to garnish

Put the butter in an ovenproof or flameproof pie dish measuring about 15 cm/6 inches across the base. Cook on FULL (100%) for ½ minute or until melted.

Add the onions and season with salt and pepper. Cook on FULL (100%) for 4 minutes, stirring once during cooking, until the onions are golden brown.

Slice the potatoes and quickly shake dry in a clean cloth. Mix into the onions with the parsley, making sure that the potatoes are well coated with the butter mixture. Cover and cook on FULL (100%) for 7 minutes or until the potatoes are tender and a top slice breaks easily when pressed with the tip of a fork.

Carefully remove the cover and brown the potatoes under a preheated hot grill. Garnish with a sprig of parsley.
SERVES 2

Note: A plastic dish is not suitable for cooking the potatoes if they are to be grilled. When using an ovenproof pie dish, keep it well away from the flame or hot element of the grill.

FRENCH BEANS

METRIC/IMPERIAL
450 g/1 lb French beans, trimmed
6 tablespoons water
½ teaspoon salt
freshly ground black pepper

Slice the beans lengthways, as finely as possible. Combine the water and salt in a large shallow dish and add the beans. Make a well in the centre of the beans. Cover and cook on FULL (100%) for 8 to 12 minutes (depending upon size), giving the dish a half-turn once or twice during cooking, until tender.

Leave to STAND, covered, for 2 to 3 minutes before draining. Correct the seasoning, adding pepper to taste, before serving.
SERVES 4

COURGETTE AND TOMATO CASSEROLE

METRIC/IMPERIAL
450 g/1 lb courgettes, sliced
225 g/8 oz tomatoes, quartered
1 teaspoon dried basil
½ beef stock cube, crumbled
¼ teaspoon salt
¼ teaspoon freshly ground black pepper

Combine all the ingredients in a large deep dish. Cover and cook on FULL (100%) for 10 minutes, stirring occasionally, until the courgettes are tender.
SERVES 4

FENNEL WITH HAM AND CHEESE SAUCE

METRIC/IMPERIAL
450 g/1 lb fennel, halved
300 ml/½ pint water
salt
freshly ground black pepper
2 tablespoons plain flour
50 g/2 oz cooked ham, chopped
50 g/2 oz cheese, grated
2–3 tablespoons soured cream

Place the fennel, cut side down, in a cooking dish. Add the water and a pinch of salt. Cover and cook on FULL (100%) for 5 minutes. Turn the fennel over and cook on MEDIUM (50%) for a further 15 to 20 minutes until tender. Remove the fennel and set aside.

Mix the flour with a little water to a smooth paste and stir into the fennel stock. Stir in the ham, cheese and pepper to taste, blending well. Cook on FULL (100%) for 2 minutes, stirring twice.

Add the fennel and soured cream, tossing well so that the fennel is coated in the sauce. Cook on FULL (100%) for 2 minutes. Serve hot.
SERVES 2 to 3

STUFFED TOMATOES

METRIC/IMPERIAL
4 large tomatoes
25 g/1 oz butter
1 clove garlic, crushed
75 g/3 oz fresh soft breadcrumbs
50 g/2 oz grated Parmesan cheese
3 tablespoons finely chopped fresh parsley
salt
freshly ground black pepper

Remove the tops from the tomatoes, scoop out and discard the seeds. Stand upside down on absorbent kitchen paper to drain.

Place the butter in a bowl and heat on FULL (100%) for ½ minute or until melted. Add the garlic and cook on FULL (100%) for 1 minute.

Stir in the breadcrumbs, cheese, parsley and salt and pepper to taste. Spoon the mixture evenly into the tomato cases. Stand upright in a small baking dish. Cook on FULL (100%) for 2 minutes, turning the dish once, until just tender. Leave to STAND for 2 minutes before serving.
SERVES 4

CHEESE AND PINEAPPLE POTATOES

METRIC/IMPERIAL
4 large potatoes (about 225 g/8 oz each), scrubbed and dried
2 tablespoons cottage cheese
50 g/2 oz Cheddar cheese, grated
1 canned pineapple ring, chopped
salt
freshly ground black pepper

Prick each potato in several places. Arrange them on absorbent kitchen paper on the turntable or oven base. Cook on FULL (100%) for 7 minutes. Turn the potatoes over and cook on FULL (100%) for a further 8 to 10 minutes. Remove the potatoes from the oven, wrap each in foil and STAND, covered, for 5 minutes.

Mix together the cottage cheese, Cheddar cheese, pineapple, salt and pepper. Unwrap and mark a cross in the top of each potato, then push up from the base to form a waterlily shape. Divide the filling between each potato to serve.
SERVES 4

FRENCH-STYLE GREEN PEAS

METRIC/IMPERIAL
25 g/1 oz butter
2 streaky bacon rashers, derinded and chopped
6 spring onions, finely chopped
8 outside lettuce leaves, shredded
1 × 350 g/12 oz packet frozen peas
1 mint sprig
1 teaspoon sugar (optional)
salt
freshly ground black pepper
fresh mint leaves, to garnish

Place the butter in a cooking dish and heat on FULL (100%) for ½ minute or until melted. Add the bacon and spring onions, cover and cook on FULL (100%) for ½ minute.

Add the lettuce, peas, mint, sugar, if using, and salt and pepper to taste, blending well. Cover and cook on FULL (100%) for 3½ minutes, stirring twice. Stir well and cook for a further 1½ to 2 minutes.

Remove and discard the mint sprig and serve at once, garnished with fresh mint leaves.
SERVES 4

COURGETTE MEDLEY

METRIC/IMPERIAL
1 onion, sliced
2 cloves garlic, crushed
25 g/1 oz butter, cut into pieces
350 g/12 oz courgettes, trimmed and sliced
225 g/8 oz tomatoes, skinned and chopped
1 tablespoon tomato purée
1 teaspoon chopped fresh parsley
salt
freshly ground black pepper

Place the onion, garlic and butter in a large bowl. Cover and cook on FULL (100%) for 3 minutes.

Stir the courgettes, tomatoes, tomato purée, parsley and salt and pepper to taste into the onion mixture. Cover and cook on FULL (100%) for 8 minutes, stirring halfway through cooking.
SERVES 4

Variation
You can vary the vegetables used in this recipe. Replace the courgettes with aubergine slices or replace half the courgettes with slices of carrot.

NEW POTATOES WITH MINTED SAUCE

METRIC/IMPERIAL
675 g/1½ lb new potatoes, washed
3 tablespoons water
mint sprig
Sauce:
25 g/1 oz butter
25 g/1 oz plain flour
300 ml/½ pint milk
1 teaspoon finely chopped fresh mint
2 tablespoons cream
salt
freshly ground black pepper

Put the potatoes into a large casserole dish. Add the water and sprig of mint. Cover and cook on FULL (100%) for 10 minutes. Set aside, covered.

For the sauce, put the butter into a large jug and heat on FULL (100%) for 1 minute or until melted. Stir in the flour and milk, then cook on FULL (100%) for 3½ to 4 minutes, stirring every minute. Beat in the mint, cream and seasoning.

Drain the potatoes, arrange in a serving dish and pour over the sauce.
SERVES 4

DICED POTATO MAYONNAISE

METRIC/IMPERIAL
450 g/1 lb new potatoes, scraped and diced
3 spring onions, finely chopped
4 tablespoons water
½ teaspoon salt
4 tablespoons mayonnaise
1 tablespoon double cream
6 green olives, stoned and finely chopped
1 tablespoon chopped fresh parsley, to garnish

Combine the potatoes, spring onions, water and salt in a large shallow dish. Cover loosely and cook on FULL (100%) for 10 to 12 minutes, giving the dish a vigorous shake two or three times during cooking. Leave to STAND for 5 minutes. Drain the potatoes thoroughly.

Mix the mayonnaise, cream and olives together. Fold into the cooked potatoes and toss gently to coat with the sauce. Garnish with the chopped parsley and serve hot or cold.
SERVES 3 to 4

CAULIFLOWER CHEESE

METRIC/IMPERIAL
1 cauliflower (prepared weight 675 g/1½ lb)
Sauce:
25 g/1 oz butter
25 g/1 oz plain flour
300 ml/½ pint milk
salt
freshly ground black pepper
1 teaspoon made English mustard
50 g/2 oz Cheddar cheese, grated
chopped fresh parsley, to garnish

Rinse the cauliflower in water and place it in a medium bowl. Cover and cook on MEDIUM (50%) for 13 to 17 minutes, turning the cauliflower over halfway through cooking. Keep hot while making the sauce.

Place the butter in a jug and heat on FULL (100%) for ½ minute or until melted. Blend in the flour, milk, salt, pepper and mustard. Cook on FULL (100%) for 3½ to 4 minutes, stirring every 1 minute. Stir in the cheese and cook on FULL (100%) for a further 1 minute.

Pour the sauce over the cauliflower and garnish with the parsley.
SERVES 4

COURGETTES AU GRATIN

METRIC/IMPERIAL
575 g/1¼ lb courgettes, sliced diagonally
1 tablespoon olive oil
2 cloves garlic, crushed
salt
freshly ground black pepper
1 egg, lightly beaten
25 g/1 oz fresh white breadcrumbs
25 g/1 oz Gruyère cheese, grated

Place the courgettes, oil and garlic in a large bowl and add salt and pepper to taste. Cover and cook on FULL (100%) for 8 minutes, stirring halfway through cooking.

Using a fork, quickly stir in the beaten egg and then transfer the mixture to a warm flameproof dish.

Combine the breadcrumbs and cheese and sprinkle over the courgettes. Place under a preheated hot grill and cook until golden brown and bubbling.
SERVES 4

STUFFED AUBERGINE

METRIC/IMPERIAL
1 × 350 g/12 oz aubergine
1 small onion, finely chopped
½ green pepper, cored, seeded and finely chopped
225 g/8 oz tomatoes, skinned and finely chopped
50 g/2 oz mushrooms, chopped
50 g/2 oz butter or margarine
40 g/1½ oz fresh brown breadcrumbs
salt
freshly ground black pepper
100 g/4 oz Cheshire cheese, crumbled
chopped fresh parsley, to garnish

Remove the stalk and cut the aubergine in half lengthways. Scoop out the flesh, leaving a 5 mm/¼ inch wall. Chop the flesh finely.

Combine the aubergine pulp in a bowl with the onion, pepper, tomatoes and mushrooms, then add the butter or margarine cut into 4 pieces. Three-quarters cover the bowl and cook on FULL (100%) for 10 to 12 minutes, stirring occasionally during cooking, until the pulp is tender.

Stir in the breadcrumbs and salt and pepper to taste. Pile the mixture into the reserved shells. Transfer the shells to a shallow dish and cook on

FULL (100%) for 2 minutes to reheat the mixture.

Sprinkle the cheese on top of the filling and cook under a preheated hot grill until golden and bubbly. Serve hot, garnished with chopped parsley.
SERVES 2

Note: The aubergine shells make an attractive serving dish but are not meant to be eaten.

GREEN BEANS IN TANGY TOMATO SAUCE

METRIC/IMPERIAL
1 clove garlic, crushed
1 small onion, finely chopped
2 back bacon rashers, derinded and chopped
1 × 225 g/8 oz can tomatoes
1 teaspoon dried mixed herbs
pinch of sugar
1 × 275 g/10 oz packet frozen whole green beans

Place the garlic, onion and bacon in a cooking dish. Cook on FULL (100%) for 2 minutes, stirring once.

Add the tomatoes with their juice, herbs, sugar and beans, blending well. Cook on FULL (100%) for 10 minutes, stirring twice. Serve at once.
SERVES 4

THYME AND PARSLEY CARROTS

METRIC/IMPERIAL
3 tablespoons cold water
1 teaspoon demerara sugar
450 g/1 lb carrots, thinly sliced
25 g/1 oz butter, cut into pieces
1 teaspoon chopped fresh thyme
1 teaspoon chopped fresh parsley
thyme sprigs, to garnish

Place the water, sugar and carrots in a large bowl. Cover and cook on FULL (100%) for 8 minutes or until tender, stirring halfway through cooking.

Drain the liquid from the carrots and stir in the butter, thyme and parsley. Spoon into a warm serving dish and garnish with sprigs of fresh thyme.
SERVES 4

BEETROOT WITH SAVOURY CREAM

METRIC/IMPERIAL
450 g/1 lb beetroot
150 ml/¼ pint chicken stock
1 large onion, sliced
15 g/½ oz butter
150 ml/¼ pint double cream
salt
freshly ground black pepper

Place the beetroot and chicken stock in a shallow dish. Cover and cook on FULL (100%) for 10 to 12 minutes. Rearrange halfway through cooking. Set aside, covered.

Place the onion and butter in a medium bowl. Cover and cook on FULL (100%) for 3½ to 4 minutes.

Drain, peel and quarter the beetroot. Mix with the onion, cream, salt and pepper. Place in a warm serving dish and cook on FULL (100%) for a further 2 minutes or until hot. Do not let the cream boil.
SERVES 4

CREAMED MUSHROOMS

METRIC/IMPERIAL
450 g/1 lb field, oyster or cap mushrooms
25 g/1 oz butter
4 tablespoons plain flour
200 ml/7 fl oz milk
1 tablespoon chopped fresh parsley
25 g/1 oz grated cheese
salt
freshly ground black pepper
pinch of grated nutmeg
4 large slices buttered toast, to serve

Cut the mushrooms into bite-sized pieces if large, leave them whole if small.

Place the butter in a bowl and heat on FULL (100%) for ½ minute or until melted. Add the mushroom pieces, cover and cook on FULL (100%) for 4 minutes until tender, stirring once.

Stir the flour into the juices, blending well. Cook on FULL (100%) for ½ minute. Gradually add the milk and cook on FULL (100%) for a further 5 to 6 minutes, stirring every 1 minute until smooth and thickened. Stir in the parsley and the cheese until melted. Add salt, pepper and nutmeg to taste, then spoon on to slices of toast.
SERVES 4

STUFFED MARROW

METRIC/IMPERIAL
1 × 1 kg/2 lb marrow
40 g/1½ oz red lentils
50 ml/2 fl oz hot water
1 onion, finely chopped
1 clove garlic, crushed
2 tablespoons water
175 g/6 oz minced lean beef
1 tablespoon tomato purée
½ teaspoon yeast extract
1 tablespoon chopped fresh parsley, or
1 teaspoon dried mixed herbs
2 tablespoons fresh wholemeal breadcrumbs
pinch of salt
freshly ground black pepper

Trim the marrow and cut it in half lengthways. Scoop out some of the flesh, leaving a shell 1 cm/½ inch thick all round. Chop the scooped out flesh finely and reserve.

Place the lentils in a bowl and stir in the hot water. Cover and cook on FULL (100%) for 2 to 2½ minutes, stirring halfway through the cooking time.

Place the onion, garlic and water in a bowl or casserole. Cover and cook on FULL (100%) for 3 minutes, stirring once during cooking. Stir in the beef and cook on FULL (100%) for 1½ minutes. Stir with a fork to break up the meat and cook on FULL (100%) for a further 3½ to 4 minutes, stirring once during cooking.

Drain the lentils, if necessary, and stir into the beef. Add the chopped marrow flesh and the remaining ingredients, seasoning with salt and pepper to taste. Mix thoroughly and spoon into the marrow half-shells. Re-assemble the marrow halves and secure on either side with wooden cocktail sticks, or tie with string.

Place the marrow in a baking dish, cover and cook on FULL (100%) for 9 minutes, turning over two or three times during the cooking time. Wrap tightly in foil and leave to STAND for 8 minutes before serving, cut into thick slices.
SERVES 4 to 6

Note: This is an ideal dish to use up leftover cooked meat. There is no need, in this case, to cook the meat first. Simply mince it or chop it very finely and add it with the lentils. Use only 1 tablespoon of breadcrumbs as there will be less meat juices.

HERBY CARROTS IN ORANGE JUICE

METRIC/IMPERIAL
450 g/1 lb young carrots
6 tablespoons pure unsweetened orange juice
2 tablespoons water
2 tablespoons chopped fresh parsley
1 teaspoon chopped fresh mint
½ teaspoon salt
pinch of pepper
⅛ teaspoon sugar
1 teaspoon lemon juice
1 teaspoon corn oil
mint sprig, to garnish

Scrape the carrots, then slice diagonally. Combine all the remaining ingredients, except the corn oil, in a 2 litre/3½ pint bowl and stir in the carrots. Cover and cook on FULL (100%) for 10 to 12 minutes or until the carrots are tender.

Remove the carrots with a slotted spoon, replace the bowl of liquid in the oven and cook on FULL (100%) for 4 minutes or until only 3 tablespoons of liquid remain.

Stir in the corn oil and mix in the carrots. Transfer to a serving dish, cover and leave to cool. Chill until required. Garnish with mint before serving.
SERVES 4

POTATOES WITH PARMESAN CHEESE

METRIC/IMPERIAL
450 g/1 lb new potatoes, washed
50 g/2 oz butter
1 teaspoon salt
freshly ground black pepper
50 g/2 oz Parmesan cheese, grated
1 tablespoon chopped fresh parsley

Do not scrape the potatoes. Place the butter in a large shallow dish and heat on FULL (100%) for 1 minute until melted. Stir in the salt, pepper to taste and Parmesan cheese.

Using a fine cutter, grate the potato into the mixture and mix thoroughly. Cook on FULL (100%) for 10 minutes, stirring occasionally. Leave to STAND for 2 minutes, then garnish with the chopped parsley and serve hot.
SERVES 4

POMMES PARISIENNES

METRIC/IMPERIAL
1.5 kg/3 lb large potatoes, peeled
5 tablespoons water
1 teaspoon salt
1 tablespoon plain flour
25 g/1 oz butter

Cut out small even-shaped potato balls with a Parisienne cutter (potato baller).

Put the water and salt into a large roasting bag and shake well to dissolve the salt. Put the potatoes into the roasting bag and loosely seal with a large elastic band. Cook on FULL (100%) for 2½ minutes, then, using an oven glove, shake the bag gently to reposition. Cook on FULL (100%) for a further 2½ to 3 minutes, then drain thoroughly.

Sprinkle a clean teatowel with the flour and toss the potato balls until they are evenly coated.

Preheat a large browning dish on FULL (100%) for 5 minutes (or according to the manufacturer's instructions). Quickly add the butter and toss in the potato balls, stirring them once.

Cook on FULL (100%) for 3 minutes, stirring briefly halfway through cooking. Transfer to a heated serving dish.
SERVES 6 to 8

FENNEL AU GRATIN

METRIC/IMPERIAL
3 large heads of fennel
juice of 1 lemon
600 ml/1 pint boiling water
freshly ground black pepper
75 g/3 oz Edam cheese, grated
1 tablespoon chopped fresh parsley

Trim the fennel heads and cut into quarters. Place in a large bowl or casserole and sprinkle with the lemon juice. Add the boiling water, cover and cook on FULL (100%) for 10 minutes, stirring twice during the cooking time.

Drain the fennel and arrange in a lightly oiled, deep baking dish. Season with a little pepper and sprinkle over the grated cheese and parsley. Cook on FULL (100%) for 3¼ minutes or until the cheese has melted.

Leave to STAND for 4 minutes before serving.
SERVES 4 to 6

BUTTERED GINGER MARROW

METRIC/IMPERIAL
1 × 675 g/1½ lb marrow, peeled
25 g/1 oz butter
1 teaspoon salt
½ teaspoon freshly ground black pepper
½ teaspoon ground ginger

Cut the marrow in half lengthways and scoop out the seeds. Cut into even-sized chunks.

Put the butter in a large shallow dish and heat on FULL (100%) for ½ minute until melted. Stir in the salt, pepper and ginger.

Add the marrow and toss to coat with the melted butter. Cover loosely and cook on FULL (100%) for 8 to 10 minutes, giving the dish a thorough shake twice during cooking. Leave to STAND for 3 to 4 minutes before serving.
SERVES 4

MUSHROOMS WITH CHEESE TOPPING

METRIC/IMPERIAL
25 g/1 oz butter
75 g/3 oz fresh white breadcrumbs
1 clove garlic, crushed
225 g/8 oz mushrooms, trimmed
pinch of salt
freshly ground black pepper
1 small onion, finely chopped
2 tablespoons finely chopped fresh parsley
(optional)
50 g/2 oz strong Cheddar cheese, grated

Put the butter in an ovenproof glass jug and heat on FULL (100%) for 1 minute. Stir in the breadcrumbs and garlic. Cook on FULL (100%) for 3 minutes, stirring once, then set aside.

Remove the stalks from the mushrooms (use in a soup or sauce) and place the caps, dark side up, in a lightly greased dish. Sprinkle with salt, pepper, onion and parsley, if using.

Mix the cheese with the breadcrumbs and sprinkle over the mushrooms. Cook on FULL (100%) for 3 to 3½ minutes.
SERVES 3

Note: These mushrooms can be served as a starter or as an accompaniment to a meat dish; they are excellent served with steak.

CAPONATA

METRIC/IMPERIAL
4 tablespoons vegetable oil
4 celery sticks, finely chopped
2 large onions, sliced
4 small aubergines, diced
4 tablespoons tomato purée
1 tablespoon capers
50 g/2 oz green olives, stoned and chopped
2 tablespoons water
2 tablespoons red wine vinegar
1 teaspoon sugar
salt
freshly ground black pepper

Place the oil, celery and onions in a large bowl. Cover and cook on FULL (100%) for 4 minutes, stirring once.

Add the aubergines, blending well. Cover and cook on FULL (100%) for 4 minutes, stirring once.

Stir in the remaining ingredients. Cover and cook on FULL (100%) for a further 6 minutes, stirring once. Leave to STAND for 5 minutes.

Serve hot or cold with pork or chicken.
SERVES 4

CAULIFLOWER BAKE

METRIC/IMPERIAL
350 g/12 oz frozen cauliflower florets
Sauce:
25 g/1 oz butter
25 g/1 oz plain flour
100 g/4 oz curd cheese
salt
freshly ground black pepper
300 ml/½ pint milk
1 egg, beaten
Garnish:
25 g/1 oz ham, chopped
2 slices of toast, cut into triangles

Arrange the frozen cauliflower florets around the edge of a large shallow dish. Cover loosely with greaseproof paper and cook on FULL (100%) for 5 minutes, giving the dish a half-turn after 2 minutes. Leave to STAND, covered, while preparing the sauce.

Put the butter in a large bowl and heat on FULL (100%) for ½ minute to melt. Stir in the flour, then blend in the cheese and add salt and pepper to taste. Add the milk, a little at a time, stirring constantly. Cook on FULL (100%) for 2 minutes.

Whisk thoroughly until smooth, then cook on FULL (100%) for 1½ minutes. Add the egg gradually, stirring continuously, to yield a smooth, glossy sauce. Pour the sauce over the cauliflower and cook on FULL (100%) for 4 minutes, giving the dish a half-turn after 2 minutes.

Sprinkle with the chopped ham to garnish and arrange triangles of toast around the edge of the dish. Serve hot.
SERVES 2

Note: Left-over cooked cauliflower may be used for this dish; it can simply be reheated in the sauce.

CAULIFLOWER WITH CURRY SAUCE

METRIC/IMPERIAL
1 × 450 g/1 lb cauliflower
2 tablespoons water
Sauce:
25 g/1 oz butter
25 g/1 oz plain flour
1 teaspoon curry powder
1 tablespoon wine vinegar
salt
freshly ground black pepper
300 ml/½ pint milk
25 g/1 oz cheese, grated (optional)

Remove the outer leaves from the cauliflower and, using an apple corer, remove the centre of the stalk and discard. Wash the cauliflower and place in a large dish.

Add the water, cover and cook on FULL (100%) for 8 minutes, giving the dish a half-turn, halfway through cooking. Remove from the oven and STAND, covered, while preparing the sauce.

To make the sauce, place the butter in a large jug and heat on FULL (100%) for 1 minute. Add the flour, curry powder, wine vinegar and salt and pepper. Gradually stir in the milk. Cook on FULL (100%) for 3 to 4 minutes, stirring every minute.

Drain the cauliflower and place in a serving dish. Pour the sauce over the cauliflower. Sprinkle with cheese, if using, and serve immediately.
SERVES 3

SALSIFY IN PIQUANT SAUCE

METRIC/IMPERIAL
450 g/1 lb salsify, cut into 2.5 cm/1 inch pieces
juice of ½ lemon
25 g/1 oz butter
salt
1 tablespoon flour
1 tablespoon white wine
freshly ground black pepper
1 tablespoon soured cream

Place the salsify in a small deep dish. Immediately sprinkle with the lemon juice and stir well. Set aside for 10 minutes. Cover with cold water, then drain.

Add half of the butter and just enough salted water to cover the salsify. Cover the dish tightly and cook on FULL (100%) for 10 minutes, shaking occasionally. Drain the salsify, reserving 150 ml/¼ pint of the liquor. Arrange the salsify in a hot serving dish. Cover and keep warm.

To make the sauce, blend the remaining butter with the flour. Whisk into the reserved liquor, a little at a time, until thoroughly incorporated. Add the wine, season with pepper to taste, then cook on FULL (100%) for 2½ to 3 minutes until the sauce thickens, stirring every 1 minute. Stir in the soured cream.

Pour the sauce over the salsify and serve at once.
SERVES 4

PEPERONI

METRIC/IMPERIAL
15 g/½ oz butter
1 onion, chopped
¼ teaspoon garlic salt
2 large green peppers, cored, seeded and sliced
2 red peppers, cored, seeded and sliced
freshly ground black pepper

Combine the butter, onion and garlic salt in a large deep dish and cook on FULL (100%) for 3 minutes, stirring once. Add the pepper slices and season with black pepper to taste. Stir thoroughly.

Cover loosely and cook on FULL (100%) for 8 to 10 minutes or until the peppers are just tender, giving the dish a vigorous shake once or twice during cooking. Serve hot or cold.
SERVES 4

CELERY WITH LEMON AND ALMONDS

METRIC/IMPERIAL
25 g/1 oz butter
350 g/12 oz celery, cut into 7.5 cm/3 inch lengths
200 ml/7 fl oz chicken stock or water
100 ml/3½ fl oz lemon juice
1 tablespoon sugar
salt
freshly ground black pepper
50 g/2 oz flaked almonds
grated rind of 1 small lemon
celery leaves, to garnish

Place the butter in a shallow dish and heat on FULL (100%) for ½ minute or until melted. Add the celery, tossing well to coat. Cook on FULL (100%) for 3 minutes.

Add the stock or water, lemon juice, sugar and salt and pepper to taste. Cover and cook on FULL (100%) for 16 to 18 minutes, turning the dish twice.

Leave the celery to STAND while preparing the almonds. Place the almonds on a plate and cook on FULL (100%) for 4 to 5 minutes, stirring every 1 minute until golden.

Serve the celery sprinkled with the lemon rind and toasted almonds. Garnish with celery leaves.
SERVES 4

ONION AND POTATO BAKE

METRIC/IMPERIAL
450 g/1 lb onions, thinly sliced
575 g/1¼ lb potatoes, thinly sliced
salt
freshly ground black pepper
2 teaspoons dried mixed herbs
scant 75 ml/3 fl oz milk

Place the onions in a medium bowl, cover and cook on FULL (100%) for 5 minutes, stirring halfway through cooking.

Layer the potatoes and onions in a 1.2 litre/2 pint dish, sprinkling each layer with a little salt, pepper and herbs. Finish with a layer of neatly arranged potatoes. Pour in the milk and sprinkle on a few more mixed herbs.

Cover and cook on FULL (100%) for 9 minutes, giving the dish a half-turn halfway through cooking.
SERVES 4

SWEDE AND ORANGE PURÉE

METRIC/IMPERIAL
1 × 575 g/1¼ lb swede
150 ml/¼ pint water
4 tablespoons orange juice
salt
freshly ground black pepper
Garnish:
strips of orange peel
parsley sprigs

Scrub the swede and prick deeply in several places. Put into a roasting bag and add the water. Seal loosely with an elastic band, leaving a gap in the top, and cook on FULL (100%) for 10 minutes or until the swede feels soft when squeezed.

Carefully remove the elastic band, take out the swede and place it on a board. Using a sharp knife and a fork, peel the swede and cut into several pieces. Place in a blender or food processor with the orange juice and blend until smooth. Alternatively, press through a fine sieve. Add salt and pepper to taste.

Pour the purée into a suitable serving dish, cover and reheat on FULL (100%) for 2 to 3 minutes. Stir once before serving and garnish with the orange strips and parsley.
SERVES 6

CELERY WITH CARROTS

METRIC/IMPERIAL
6 sticks celery, cut into thin matchstick strips
225 g/8 oz carrots, cut into thin matchstick strips
25 g/1 oz butter
1 tablespoon snipped chives
1 teaspoon chopped fresh marjoram
salt
freshly ground black pepper
1 teaspoon chopped fresh parsley

The total weight of the vegetables should be about 350 g/12 oz.

Arrange the celery and carrots in a dish. Flake the butter over and sprinkle with chives and marjoram. Season well with salt and pepper.

Spoon over 2 tablespoons water. Cover and cook on FULL (100%) for 10 minutes, stirring once. Leave to STAND, covered, for 5 minutes. Sprinkle with parsley before serving.
SERVES 4

BROAD BEANS WITH WATER CHESTNUTS

METRIC/IMPERIAL
1 × 450 g/1 lb packet frozen broad beans
2 tablespoons cold water
50 g/2 oz butter
1 clove garlic, crushed (optional)
1 × 225 g/8 oz can water chestnuts, drained and sliced

Place the broad beans in a dish with the water. Cover and cook on FULL (100%) for 8 minutes, stirring once, halfway through cooking. Set aside.

Put the butter in a jug and heat on FULL (100%) for 1 minute. Add the garlic, if using.

Drain the beans and add the water chestnuts. Pour over the butter mixture and toss to coat. Cover and cook on FULL (100%) for 1 minute.
SERVES 4

CORN ON THE COB

METRIC/IMPERIAL
50 g/2 oz butter
4 × 175–225 g/6–8 oz fresh or frozen corn on the cob, thawed
salt
freshly ground black pepper

Place the butter in a large deep dish and heat on FULL (100%) for ½ minute until softened. Add the corn and turn to coat with the butter. Cover tightly and cook on FULL (100%) for 9 to 10 minutes, rearranging the corn halfway through cooking.

Leave to STAND, covered, for 3 to 5 minutes. Season with salt and pepper to taste and serve hot.
SERVES 4

CAULIFLOWER WITH TOMATO SAUCE

METRIC/IMPERIAL
1 × 675 g/1½ lb whole cauliflower, trimmed
1 onion, finely chopped
300 ml/½ pint water
salt
7 g/¼ oz butter
3 tomatoes, skinned, seeded and quartered
3 tablespoons tomato purée
1 bay leaf
2 tablespoons plain flour
4 tablespoons cold water
pinch of sugar
2 tablespoons double cream
2 tablespoons cheese, grated

Place the cauliflower, stalk side up, in a cooking dish with the onion, water, salt to taste and butter. Cover and cook on FULL (100%) for 5 minutes.

Turn the cauliflower stalk side down, cover and cook on MEDIUM (50%) for 10 minutes until tender. Remove the cauliflower with a slotted spoon and place on a serving plate.

Add the tomatoes, tomato purée and bay leaf to the cauliflower stock, blending well.

Mix the flour and 4 tablespoons water to a smooth paste and stir into the stock. Cook on FULL (100%) for 4 minutes, stirring twice.

Season to taste with salt and sugar. Remove and discard the bay leaf. Purée the sauce in a blender or food processor, or pass through a fine sieve. Stir in the cream with the cheese, blending well so that the cheese melts.

Pour the sauce over the cauliflower and cook on FULL (100%) for 2 minutes to reheat.
SERVES 4

BRAISED RED CABBAGE WITH APPLES

METRIC/IMPERIAL
25 g/1 oz butter
1 onion, chopped
450 g/1 lb red cabbage, coarsely shredded
2 cloves
250 ml/8 fl oz hot chicken stock
salt
freshly ground black pepper
2 cooking apples, peeled, cored and sliced

Place the butter and onion in a large bowl. Cover and cook on FULL (100%) for 3 minutes, stirring once.

Stir in the cabbage, cloves and hot stock and add salt and pepper to taste. Cover and cook on FULL (100%) for 4 minutes, stirring once.

Stir in the apples, cover and cook on FULL (100%) for 10 minutes, stirring halfway through cooking.

Leave to STAND, covered, for 5 minutes, then drain and spoon into a warm serving dish. Serve with hot meat, poultry or game dishes.
SERVES 4

WESTERN BAKED POTATOES

METRIC/IMPERIAL
4 potatoes (about 250 g/9 oz each), scrubbed and
dried
100 g/4 oz corned beef, cubed
1 × 450 g/1 lb can barbecue beans
salt
freshly ground black pepper
50 g/2 oz grated cheese

Prick the potatoes with a fork and arrange on
absorbent kitchen paper on the turntable or oven
base, spaced well apart. Cook on FULL (100%)
for 10 minutes. Turn over and rearrange, then
cook on FULL (100%) for a further 6 to 8
minutes. Wrap each potato in foil and leave to
STAND for 5 minutes.

Unwrap the potatoes. Split each potato in half
and scoop out the flesh. Mix the flesh with the
corned beef, beans and salt and pepper to taste,
blending well. Return the mixture to the potato
skins.

Sprinkle with the cheese and cook on FULL
(100%) for 3 to 4 minutes to reheat. Serve with
barbecued meats or sausages, or as a snack.
SERVES 4

DOLMAS

METRIC/IMPERIAL
8 large green cabbage leaves, stalks removed
1 onion, finely chopped
225 g/8 oz tomatoes, skinned and chopped
15 g/½ oz butter
4 tablespoons plain flour
300 ml/½ pint hot beef stock
½ teaspoon Worcestershire sauce
½ teaspoon dried oregano
salt
freshly ground black pepper
4 tablespoons cooked rice

Pour boiling water over the cabbage leaves and
allow them to soften for a minute or so. Drain.

Place the onion, tomatoes and butter in a
medium bowl. Cover and cook on FULL
(100%) for 4 minutes, stirring once.

Stir in the flour, then add the stock, Worcestershire sauce, oregano, salt and pepper to taste,
and the rice. Stir well, then cook on FULL
(100%) for 2 minutes.

Place a little of the vegetable mixture on each

cabbage leaf. Roll up the cabbage leaves to seal in
the filling and tie them with string. Arrange in a
shallow dish, cover and cook on FULL (100%)
for 7 minutes, giving the dish a half-turn halfway
through cooking. Leave the dolmas to STAND
for 5 minutes, then remove the string and serve.
SERVES 4

CREAMED SWEDE

METRIC/IMPERIAL
675 g/1½ lb swede, peeled and diced
3 tablespoons water
15 g/½ oz butter
1½ tablespoons double cream
salt
freshly ground black pepper
parsley sprig, to garnish

Place the diced swede and water in a large bowl.
Cover and cook on FULL (100%) for 14 to 15
minutes, stirring halfway through cooking.

Place the swede, water, butter, cream and salt
and pepper to taste in a blender or food processor
and purée until smooth. Reheat, if necessary, and
garnish with parsley to serve.
SERVES 6

MUSHROOMS IN TANGY CREAM SAUCE

METRIC/IMPERIAL
25 g/1 oz butter
1 onion, finely chopped
450 g/1 lb button mushrooms, trimmed
1 teaspoon plain flour
150 ml/¼ pint double cream
½ teaspoon grated nutmeg
1–2 teaspoons lemon juice
dash of Tabasco
salt
freshly ground black pepper

Place the butter and onion in a large dish. Cover
and cook on FULL (100%) for 3 minutes.

Add the mushrooms, blending well. Cover
and cook on FULL (100%) for 4 to 5 minutes,
stirring twice.

Add the flour, cream, nutmeg, lemon juice,
Tabasco and salt and pepper to taste, blending
well. Cook on FULL (100%) for 3 minutes,
stirring once. Serve at once with toast.
SERVES 4

LEMON-GLAZED LEEKS WITH CHEESE

METRIC/IMPERIAL
450 g/1 lb leeks, trimmed
25 g/1 oz butter
½ teaspoon salt
1 tablespoon lemon juice
1 tablespoon grated Parmesan cheese
freshly ground black pepper

Cut the leeks into 2.5 cm/1 inch slices and place in a shallow dish. Dot with the butter and sprinkle with the salt. Cover and cook on FULL (100%) for 8 minutes, stirring once, halfway through cooking.

Add the lemon juice and stir well. Cover and cook on FULL (100%) for 3 minutes, or until the leeks are tender. Sprinkle with the cheese and pepper to taste. Leave to STAND, covered, for 3 minutes before serving.
SERVES 4

ARTICHOKE MOUSSELINE

METRIC/IMPERIAL
6 globe artichokes
250 ml/8 fl oz half milk and half water, mixed
salt
1½ tablespoons lemon juice
3 tablespoons double cream
freshly ground black pepper
40 g/1½ oz butter, to serve

Remove the leaves from the artichokes, discarding the chokes but keeping the hearts. Trim away any woody or dry parts from the leaves.

Rinse, then place in a bowl with the water and milk, a pinch of salt and the lemon juice. Cover and cook on FULL (100%) for 16 to 18 minutes, stirring twice, until tender. Drain thoroughly, reserving the cooking juices.

Purée the artichokes (together with the trimmed leaves) in a blender or food processor until smooth. Add the cream and salt and pepper to taste, blending well. If necessary, add 2 to 3 tablespoons of the cooking juices to produce a smooth, creamy texture.

Spoon into a serving dish and fork attractively, or spoon into a piping bag fitted with a large star nozzle and pipe into a serving dish.

Cover and cook on FULL (100%) for 2 to 4 minutes to reheat. Dot with the butter to serve.
SERVES 4

BROAD BEANS IN HORSERADISH CREAM

METRIC/IMPERIAL
450 g/1 lb shelled broad beans
4 tablespoons water
salt
25 g/1 oz butter
2 tablespoons plain flour
300 ml/½ pint milk
4 tablespoons double cream
4 teaspoons horseradish sauce
pinch of caster sugar
freshly ground black pepper
chopped fresh parsley, to garnish

Place the broad beans in a bowl with the water and a little salt. Cover and cook on FULL (100%) for 6 to 8 minutes, shaking the dish once. Leave to STAND while preparing the sauce.

Place the butter in a bowl and heat on FULL (100%) for ½ minute or until melted. Stir in the flour, blending well. Gradually add the milk and cook on FULL (100%) for 4 to 4½ minutes, stirring every 1 minute until smooth and thickened.

Add the remaining ingredients, blending thoroughly. Fold in the drained, cooked beans, tossing well to coat.

Cook on FULL (100%) for 1 to 2 minutes to reheat. Sprinkle with chopped parsley and serve.
SERVES 4

BEETROOT WITH GINGER AND ORANGE

METRIC/IMPERIAL
450 g/1 lb cooked beetroot
1 onion, finely chopped
2.5 cm/1 inch piece fresh ginger, finely grated
grated rind and juice of 1 orange
pinch of salt
freshly ground black pepper

Peel the beetroot, cut into wedges and set aside.

Place the onion and ginger in a large bowl with the orange rind and juice. Cover and cook on FULL (100%) for 2½ minutes, stirring halfway through the cooking time. Stir in the prepared beetroot and season with salt and pepper. Cover as before and cook on FULL (100%) for a further 3¼ minutes, stirring after 2 minutes.

Serve this dish with baked ham or chicken.
SERVES 4

MIXED VEGETABLE PLATTER

METRIC/IMPERIAL
8 small new potatoes, scrubbed
6 tablespoons water
225 g/8 oz carrots, thinly sliced
225 g/8 oz green beans, sliced
1 tablespoon finely snipped chives, to garnish

Prick the skins of the potatoes. Place them in a large bowl and add 4 tablespoons of the water. Cover and cook on FULL (100%) for 8¾ minutes, stirring after 4 minutes. Using a slotted spoon, transfer the potatoes to a serving dish, cover with foil and keep warm.

Add the carrots to the water remaining in the bowl, cover and cook on FULL (100%) for 5 minutes, stirring halfway through the cooking time. Remove the carrots with a slotted spoon and arrange them beside the potatoes. Replace the foil cover and set aside.

Place the beans in the bowl. Add the remaining water and cover again. Cook on FULL (100%) for 6½ minutes, stirring halfway through the cooking time. With a slotted spoon, transfer the beans to the serving dish, arranging them next to the carrots and potatoes.

Discard the foil, cover and cook on FULL (100%) for 2½ minutes to heat through. Sprinkle with the chives and serve immediately.
SERVES 4

Note: If very small potatoes are unobtainable, substitute 4 medium potatoes, halved. You can vary the vegetables but check the individual cooking times.

MIXED VEGETABLE CURRY

METRIC/IMPERIAL
50 g/2 oz butter
1 large onion, chopped
2 cloves garlic, chopped
1 apple, peeled, cored and chopped
2 tablespoons curry powder
2 tablespoons plain flour
1 teaspoon ground allspice
salt
freshly ground black pepper
1 × 400 g/14 oz can tomatoes
1 × 400 g/14 oz can butter beans
1 vegetable stock cube, crumbled
boiling water (see method)
675–800 g/1½–1¾ lb prepared mixed vegetables (celery, cauliflower, carrots, aubergine and courgettes, for example)
2 tablespoons chutney
50 g/2 oz sultanas

Place the butter in a large casserole and heat on FULL (100%) for 1½ minutes or until melted. Add the onion, garlic and apple, blending well. Cook on FULL (100%) for 3 minutes, stirring once.

Add the curry powder, flour, allspice and salt and pepper to taste, blending well. Cook on FULL (100%) for 1 minute.

Meanwhile, drain the juice from the tomatoes and butter beans into a measuring jug. Add the crumbled stock cube and make up to 600 ml/1 pint with boiling water.

Gradually add the stock to the curry base, blending well. Cook on FULL (100%) for 6 minutes, stirring three times.

Add the prepared vegetables, chutney and sultanas, blending well. Cover and cook on FULL (100%) for 5 minutes. Reduce the setting and cook on MEDIUM (50%) for 30 minutes, stirring twice.

Add the tomatoes and butter beans, blending well. Cook on FULL (100%) for 5 minutes. Serve hot with boiled rice.
SERVES 6 to 8

BROAD BEANS À LA GRECQUE

METRIC/IMPERIAL
1 kg/2 lb fresh broad beans, shelled
300 ml/½ pint boiling water
1 onion, finely chopped
1 × 225 g/8 oz can tomatoes, chopped
2 tablespoons tomato purée
4 juniper berries, lightly crushed
1 bay leaf
½ teaspoon dried mixed herbs
1 tablespoon lemon juice
freshly ground black pepper
½ teaspoon paprika
chopped fresh parsley, to garnish

Place the broad beans in a large bowl or casserole and add the boiling water. Cover and cook on FULL (100%) for 8¼ minutes, stirring halfway through. Drain, then plunge the beans into cold water; drain again and set aside.

Put the onion in a bowl with 1 tablespoon of the juice from the tomatoes, and cook on FULL (100%) for 2½ minutes. Stir in the tomatoes and the remaining juice. Stir in the tomato purée and add the juniper berries, bay leaf and mixed herbs. Cover and cook on FULL (100%) for 5 minutes, stirring twice during the cooking time.

Stir in the broad beans, the lemon juice, pepper to taste and the paprika. Cover and cook on FULL (100%) for 3¼ minutes, stirring once. STAND, covered, for 5 minutes before serving. Remove the bay leaf and garnish with parsley before serving.

SERVES 4 to 6

GREEN BEANS IN SOURED CREAM

METRIC/IMPERIAL
450 g/1 lb young green or thin French beans, trimmed and cut into 2.5 cm/1 inch pieces
3 tablespoons water
150 ml/¼ pint soured cream
¼ teaspoon grated nutmeg
salt
freshly ground black pepper
40 g/1½ oz butter
40 g/1½ oz coarse fresh white breadcrumbs

Place the beans and water in a medium bowl. Cover and cook on FULL (100%) for 7 minutes, stirring halfway through cooking.

Drain the beans and stir in the soured cream, nutmeg and salt and pepper to taste. Cook on FULL (100%) for a further 3 minutes, stirring after 2 minutes. Do not allow the cream to boil.

Meanwhile, place the butter in a frying pan. Using the *conventional hob*, melt the butter and fry the breadcrumbs until golden brown.

Sprinkle the beans with the crumbs to serve.

SERVES 6

SPICED RED CABBAGE

METRIC/IMPERIAL
450 g/1 lb red cabbage, trimmed, cored and shredded
1 small onion, finely chopped
1 dessert apple, peeled, cored and chopped
25 g/1 oz butter
2 tablespoons wine vinegar
2 tablespoons brown sugar
1 teaspoon salt

½ teaspoon ground allspice
½ teaspoon grated nutmeg
1 teaspoon caraway seeds (optional)
freshly ground black pepper
150 ml/¼ pint boiling water

Combine all the ingredients in a deep dish and mix thoroughly. Cover the dish and cook on FULL (100%) for 9 to 11 minutes, until the cabbage is tender, stirring occasionally during cooking.

Leave to STAND, covered, for 3 minutes, then drain off excess liquid. Adjust the seasoning and serve hot.

SERVES 4

LEEKS IN WINE AND GARLIC SAUCE

METRIC/IMPERIAL
450 g/1 lb leeks, sliced
25 g/1 oz butter
25 g/1 oz plain flour
1 teaspoon French mustard
150 ml/¼ pint chicken stock
150 ml/¼ pint dry white wine
1 clove garlic, crushed
salt
freshly ground black pepper
Toasted Crumbs (see page 314)

Place the leeks in a casserole. Cover and cook on FULL (100%) for 8 minutes, stirring once. Set aside and prepare the sauce.

Place the butter in a large jug and heat on FULL (100%) for 1 minute. Stir in the flour, mustard, stock and wine. Add the garlic and salt and pepper.

Cook on FULL (100%) for 3½ to 4 minutes, stirring every 1 minute. Pour the sauce over the leeks and sprinkle the crumbs liberally over the surface. Reheat on FULL (100%) for 2 minutes.

SERVES 4

POTATO AND GREEN PEPPER RATATOUILLE

METRIC/IMPERIAL
225 g/8 oz potatoes, peeled
1 green pepper, cored and seeded
1 onion, peeled
½ teaspoon salt
½ teaspoon freshly ground black pepper
2 tablespoons vegetable oil
3 tablespoons soy sauce
about 1 tablespoon water

Slice the vegetables paper thin (use a food processor or mandoline if you have one). Combine all the ingredients in a large deep dish and make a well in the centre. Cover loosely and cook on FULL (100%) for 6 minutes.

Stir in a little more water if the ratatouille seems too dry. Cover loosely and cook on FULL (100%) for 6 to 10 minutes until the potatoes are just tender, stirring once. Leave to STAND, covered, for 5 minutes. Serve hot or cold.
SERVES 4

BROCCOLI WITH PIQUANT DRESSING

METRIC/IMPERIAL
450 g/1 lb fresh or frozen broccoli spears
4 tablespoons water
Dressing:
1 teaspoon tomato purée
2 teaspoons French mustard
150 ml/¼ pint single cream
1 teaspoon horseradish sauce
1 teaspoon salad cream
salt
freshly ground black pepper

Arrange the broccoli in a shallow oval or round dish, keeping the stalks towards the centre. Using a sharp knife, make two incisions in each stem.

Add the water. Cover and cook on FULL (100%) for 10 minutes, rearranging the broccoli once, halfway through cooking. Leave to STAND, covered, while preparing the dressing.

To prepare the dressing, mix together the tomato purée and mustard, then blend in the remaining ingredients. Drain the broccoli and return to the dish. Serve the dressing separately.
SERVES 4

WHOLEWHEAT SPINACH AND CHEESE QUICHE

METRIC/IMPERIAL
175 g/6 oz wholemeal flour
pinch of salt
40 g/1½ oz lard
40 g/1½ oz margarine
2 tablespoons iced water
Filling:
450 g/1 lb fresh spinach leaves or 1 × 225 g/8 oz
packet frozen leaf spinach
100 g/4 oz cottage cheese
2 eggs, beaten
75 ml/2½ fl oz single cream
4 tablespoons grated Parmesan cheese
salt
freshly ground black pepper

Mix the flour with the salt in a bowl. Rub in the lard and margarine with the fingertips until the mixture resembles fine breadcrumbs. Add the water and bind together to a firm but pliable dough. Turn on to a lightly floured surface and knead until smooth and free from cracks.

Roll out the pastry on a lightly floured surface to a round large enough to line a 20 cm/8 inch dish. Press in firmly, taking care not to stretch the pastry. Cut the pastry away, leaving a 5 mm/¼ inch 'collar' above the dish to allow for any shrinkage that may occur. Prick the base and sides well with a fork.

Place a double thickness of absorbent kitchen paper over the base, easing it into position round the edges. Cook on FULL (100%) for 3½ minutes, giving the dish a quarter-turn every 1 minute. Remove the paper and cook on FULL (100%) for a further 1½ minutes.

Place the fresh spinach in a bowl, cover and cook on FULL (100%) for 5 to 7 minutes. Drain thoroughly and chop coarsely. Alternatively, cook the frozen spinach on FULL (100%) for 6 to 7 minutes, breaking up the spinach after 3 minutes. Drain thoroughly and chop coarsely.

Mix together the cottage cheese, eggs, cream, Parmesan cheese and salt and pepper. Stir in the spinach, blending well. Spoon into the flan case and cook on LOW (30%) for 15 to 17 minutes, giving the dish a quarter-turn every 3 minutes. Allow to STAND for 10 to 15 minutes. The flan should set completely during this time.
SERVES 4

VEGETABLES RAJAH

METRIC/IMPERIAL
4 medium potatoes, sliced
4 large carrots, sliced
6 small turnips, sliced
1 × 425 g/15 oz can Madras hot curry cook-in-sauce
1 × 225 g/8 oz can tomatoes
3 onions, sliced
1 small green pepper, cored, seeded and sliced
1 clove garlic, finely chopped
1 tablespoon chopped stem ginger
100 g/4 oz frozen petits pois
100 ml/3½ fl oz natural yogurt
3 tablespoons chopped fresh mint

Place the potatoes, carrots, turnips, curry sauce and tomatoes with their juice in a large casserole, blending well. Cover and cook on FULL (100%) for 15 minutes, stirring once.

Add the onions, pepper, garlic, ginger and peas. Cover and cook on FULL (100%) for a further 10 minutes, stirring the vegetables once.

Cover and cook on MEDIUM (50%) for a further 20 minutes until the vegetables are just tender.

Stir in the yogurt and mint. Serve hot with boiled rice, poppadoms and chutneys as part of an Indian meal, or increase the quantities and serve with a simple green salad.
SERVES 4

SPINACH TERRINE

METRIC/IMPERIAL
20 large fresh spinach leaves
450 g/1 lb full-fat soft cheese
3 egg yolks
100 g/4 oz cooked ham, minced or finely chopped
2 teaspoons lemon juice
salt
freshly ground black pepper

Wash the spinach leaves well, shake thoroughly and place in a bowl. Cover and cook on FULL (100%) for 1½ minutes. Drain and rinse under cold running water.

Use about 8 spinach leaves to line a 20 × 10 cm/8 × 4 inch loaf dish.

Mix the cheese with the egg yolks, ham, lemon juice and salt and pepper to taste. Spoon one-third of the mixture into the base of the dish

and cover with 4 spinach leaves. Repeat twice, finishing with a layer of spinach leaves.

Partially cover and cook on MEDIUM (50%) for 5 minutes. Give the dish a half-turn and cook on FULL (100%) for 3 to 4 minutes or until just set. Allow to cool in the dish.

Chill lightly and serve in thin slices with a tomato sauce and crusty bread.
SERVES 6 to 8

VEGETARIAN FLAN WITH CELERIAC MOUSSELINE

METRIC/IMPERIAL
Celeriac mousseline:
350 g/12 oz celeriac, cut into chunks
150 ml/¼ pint hot skimmed milk and water, in equal parts
pinch of salt
2 tablespoons low-fat fromage blanc or Greek-style (strained) yogurt
chopped fresh parsley, to garnish
Flan:
1 onion, finely chopped
100 g/4 oz carrots, finely diced
300 ml/½ pint skimmed milk
100 g/4 oz turnip, finely diced
½ small red pepper, cored, seeded and finely diced
75 g/3 oz frozen peas
2 tablespoons finely chopped fresh sorrel or 2 tablespoons chopped fresh parsley
3 eggs
pinch of salt
freshly ground black pepper

First prepare the mousseline. Place the celeriac in a large bowl or casserole. Sprinkle with the milk and water mixture and season with salt. Cover and cook on FULL (100%) for 8 to 9 minutes, or until tender.

Transfer the celeriac, with the cooking liquid, to a blender or food processor and blend until smooth. Alternatively, rub the mixture through a sieve. Transfer the purée to a mixing bowl and beat in the fromage blanc or yogurt. Keep the mousseline warm while preparing the flan.

Place the onion and carrots in a large bowl or casserole. Add 4 tablespoons of the milk, cover and cook on FULL (100%) for 5 minutes, stirring halfway through the cooking time. Stir in the turnip and the red pepper, cover and cook on FULL (100%) for 4 minutes, stirring halfway through the cooking time. Stir in the peas, cover again and cook on FULL (100%) for a further 2½ minutes, stirring halfway through the cooking time. Stir in the chopped sorrel or parsley.

In a large bowl, beat the eggs and remaining milk together, season with salt and pepper and stir into the vegetable mixture. Pour into a lightly oiled 18 cm/7 inch flan dish. Cover lightly with greaseproof paper and cook on LOW (30%) for 8¼ minutes (or on DEFROST/20% for 11½ minutes), giving the dish a half-turn after 5 minutes.

Leave to STAND for 5 minutes before unmoulding on to a large serving dish. Spoon the celeriac mousseline into a warmed serving dish and garnish with the chopped fresh parsley before serving.

SERVES 4

Note: Sorrel is not readily available, unless you grow it yourself. Although parsley does not taste the same, it is the best substitute. You could also use fresh chives or chervil, or a mixture of the two. If celeriac is not available, serve the flan with tomato sauce.

VEGETABLE RISSOLES

METRIC/IMPERIAL
100 g/4 oz red lentils
600 ml/1 pint boiling chicken stock
1 large onion, finely chopped
1 celery stick, finely chopped
2 small carrots, grated
50 g/2 oz cooked green beans, finely chopped
50 g/2 oz fresh white breadcrumbs
3 eggs, beaten
1 teaspoon dried mixed herbs
salt
freshly ground black pepper
75 g/3 oz dry white breadcrumbs
2–3 tablespoons vegetable oil

Place the lentils and boiling stock in a bowl. Cover and cook on FULL (100%) for 15 to 20 minutes, stirring once, until tender. Drain, if necessary.

Mix the lentils with the onion, celery, carrots, beans, fresh breadcrumbs, two of the eggs, herbs and salt and pepper to taste. Leave to STAND for 30 minutes.

Shape the mixture into 8 rissoles. Dip each of these in the remaining beaten egg and then in the dry breadcrumbs to coat.

Preheat a large browning dish on FULL (100%) for 5 minutes (or according to the manufacturer's instructions). Brush with the oil and cook on FULL (100%) for a further 1 minute.

Add the rissoles and allow to brown on the underside, without cooking, for about 2 to 3 minutes. Turn over and cook on FULL (100%) for a further 4 to 5 minutes, rearranging them twice. Drain on absorbent kitchen paper and serve hot.

SERVES 4

MIXED VEGETABLES AU GRATIN

METRIC/IMPERIAL
350 g/12 oz cauliflower florets
2 tablespoons water
1 large onion, thinly sliced
1 large green pepper, cored, seeded and cut into rings
25 g/1 oz butter
2 medium beetroot, cooked and chopped
salt
freshly ground black pepper
150 ml/¼ pint double cream
¼ teaspoon lemon juice
1 clove garlic, crushed
100 g/4 oz mature Cheddar cheese, grated
50 g/2 oz fresh brown breadcrumbs
2 hard-boiled eggs, chopped
1 tablespoon chopped fresh parsley

Place the cauliflower and water in a bowl; cover and cook on FULL (100%) for 4 minutes. Drain the cauliflower with a slotted spoon and set aside. Place the onion and green pepper in the bowl with the butter. Cover and cook on FULL (100%) for 6½ minutes, stirring twice.

Place the beetroot in the base of a deep, oblong dish and arrange the onion and pepper on top, pouring over the butter from the bowl. Place the cauliflower florets on top and season well with salt and pepper.

Mix together the cream and lemon juice, add the garlic and pour evenly over the vegetables. Mix together the cheese and breadcrumbs and sprinkle over the top of the dish. Cook on FULL (100%) for 5 minutes, turning the dish three times during cooking.

Mix together the chopped hard-boiled eggs and parsley and spoon down the middle of the dish. Serve hot or cold.

SERVES 4 to 6

SPRING VEGETABLE MEDLEY

METRIC/IMPERIAL
25 g/1 oz butter
1 onion, finely sliced
1 small yellow pepper, cored, seeded and finely sliced
½ head fennel, sliced
1 potato, diced
1 small carrot, finely sliced
100 g/4 oz cauliflower florets
2 cloves garlic, crushed
1 teaspoon chopped fresh parsley
1 tablespoon tomato purée
25 g/1 oz plain flour
450 ml/¾ pint hot chicken or vegetable stock
salt
freshly ground black pepper
parsley sprigs, to garnish

Place the butter, onion, yellow pepper, fennel, potato, carrot, cauliflower, garlic, parsley and tomato purée in a large bowl. Cover and cook on FULL (100%) for 12 minutes, stirring after 4 and 8 minutes.

Sprinkle over the flour and stir it into the vegetables, then gradually stir in the hot stock and salt and pepper to taste. Cook on FULL (100%) for 5 minutes, stirring once, halfway through cooking. Garnish with parsley and serve as a supper dish.
SERVES 4

CARROT AND HERB RING

METRIC/IMPERIAL
4 large green cabbage leaves
1 onion, very finely chopped
1 clove garlic, crushed
175 ml/6 fl oz skimmed milk
450 g/1 lb carrots, grated
2 teaspoons brown sugar
50 g/2 oz Edam cheese, finely grated
freshly ground black pepper
2 eggs
2 tablespoons finely chopped fresh coriander
1 tablespoon finely chopped fresh parsley

Trim the cabbage leaves and remove the core of the stalk. Blanch the leaves in boiling water for 8 minutes. Plunge into cold water, drain and pat dry on absorbent kitchen paper. Set aside.

Place the onion and garlic in a large bowl with 4 tablespoons of the milk. Cover and cook on FULL (100%) for 3¼ minutes, stirring halfway through the cooking time. Stir in the carrots and sugar, cover and cook on FULL (100%) for 4 minutes, stirring halfway through the cooking time. Stir in the cheese and season with pepper. Beat the eggs in a bowl with the remaining milk and stir into the carrot mixture with the chopped herbs.

Line a lightly oiled 1 litre/1¾ pint ring mould with the cabbage leaves, allowing the tops of the leaves to overlap the top of the mould.

Pour the carrot mixture into the mould and fold over the overlapping leaves to form a lid. Cover with lightly oiled greaseproof paper and cook on FULL (100%) for 10 minutes, turning the mould around after 5 minutes. Leave to STAND, covered, for 10 minutes before un-moulding on to a serving dish.
SERVES 4

PIPÉRADE

METRIC/IMPERIAL
2 large green or red peppers, halved lengthways, cored and seeded
2 tablespoons olive oil
2 large onions, thinly sliced
½ red chilli, seeded and thinly sliced (optional)
2 cloves garlic, crushed
pinch of sugar
salt
freshly ground black pepper
450 g/1 lb tomatoes, skinned and chopped
4 eggs, lightly beaten
4 slices ham, chopped, to garnish

Grill the peppers under a preheated hot grill until the skins are charred, then slice them into thin strips.

Place the peppers, oil, onions, red chilli (if using), garlic, sugar and salt and pepper to taste in a medium bowl. Cover and cook on FULL (100%) for 10 minutes, stirring halfway through cooking.

Stir in the tomatoes, cover and cook on FULL (100%) for 6 minutes, stirring halfway through cooking.

Using a fork, stir in the eggs and cook on FULL (100%) for 2 minutes, stirring twice.

Pile the pipérade mixture on to a warm serving dish and sprinkle the ham around it. Serve as a supper dish or light lunch with hot toast.
SERVES 4

STIR-FRIED VEGETABLES

METRIC/IMPERIAL
50 g/2 oz butter or margarine
100 g/4 oz mangetout, trimmed
1 green pepper, cored, seeded and finely sliced
1 red pepper, cored, seeded and finely sliced
4 tablespoons soy sauce
1 teaspoon sherry
225 g/8 oz fresh beansprouts
1 tablespoon flaked almonds
salt
freshly ground black pepper
1 tablespoon sesame seeds

Preheat a large browning dish on FULL (100%) for 5 minutes (or according to the manufacturer's instructions). Immediately add the butter and stir in the mangetout and sliced peppers, continuing to stir until the heat dies down.

Stir in the soy sauce, sherry, beansprouts and almonds and cook on FULL (100%) for 5 minutes, stirring once or twice during cooking.

If necessary, add a little salt and a good shake of pepper. Sprinkle with sesame seeds and serve hot.

SERVES 6

MUSHROOM AND WALNUT QUICHE

METRIC/IMPERIAL
Pastry:
75 g/3 oz plain flour
pinch of salt
40 g/1½ oz soft margarine
1 tablespoon cold water
Filling:
15 g/½ oz butter
1 small onion, finely chopped
75 g/3 oz button mushrooms, sliced
15 g/½ oz walnuts, chopped
1 × 175 ml/6 fl oz can evaporated milk
3 eggs
salt
freshly ground black pepper

To make the pastry, sift the flour and salt together and rub in the margarine until the mixture resembles fine breadcrumbs. Stir in the water and mix to form a dough.

Roll out the pastry to fit an 18 cm/7 inch round flan dish. Place a piece of greaseproof paper in the pastry case, fill with dried beans and cook on FULL (100%) for 2 minutes. Remove the paper and beans, give the dish a half-turn and cook for a further 1 minute. (If using a conventional oven, bake blind at 200°C/400°F/Gas Mark 6 for 10 minutes.)

To make the filling, place the butter and onion in a bowl and cook on FULL (100%) for 1½ minutes. Stir, then cook for a further 1½ minutes or until the onion is soft. Drain and spread the onion in the flan case. Cover with the mushrooms and sprinkle the walnuts on top.

Put the evaporated milk in a jug and cook on FULL (100%) for ¾ minute or until warm. Beat in the eggs and season with salt and pepper to taste.

Pour the egg mixture into the flan case, reduce the setting to LOW (30%) and cook for 14 to 16 minutes or until the custard is set round the edges and just a little wobbly in the centre. Give the dish a quarter-turn every 3 minutes during cooking.

Leave to STAND for 10 minutes, during which time the custard will begin to set. If it is still wobbly, cook for a few minutes more. The custard should set completely by the time it is cold.

SERVES 2

SPINACH AND LEEK FLAN

METRIC/IMPERIAL
100 g/4 oz spinach, trimmed and blanched, defrosted if frozen
3 small leeks, thinly sliced
3 shallots or 1 onion, very finely chopped
1 tablespoon lemon juice
2 tablespoons water
pinch of salt
freshly ground black pepper
3 eggs
250 ml/8 fl oz skimmed milk
2 tablespoons fresh wholemeal breadcrumbs
1 tablespoon grated Parmesan cheese (see note)

Drain the spinach and squeeze to extract as much water as possible. Shred or chop finely and reserve.

Place the leeks and shallots or onion in a large bowl with the lemon juice and water. Cover and cook on FULL (100%) for 5¾ minutes, stirring halfway through the cooking time. Add the spinach, season with salt and pepper to taste, and mix well.

Beat the eggs in a bowl with the milk and stir into the spinach mixture. Pour the mixture into a lightly oiled, 23 cm/9 inch flan dish. Sprinkle on the breadcrumbs and cheese and cook on FULL (100%) for 10 minutes, turning the dish around halfway through the cooking time.

Leave to STAND for 10 minutes. Serve the flan hot or cold.
SERVES 4 to 6

Note: Rennet-free Cheddar cheese can be substituted for the Parmesan cheese, or omit the cheese and top with breadcrumbs only.

VEGETABLE CHEESE CRUMBLE

METRIC/IMPERIAL
Crumble topping:
150 g/5 oz plain flour
salt
freshly ground black pepper
50 g/2 oz butter
75 g/3 oz Cheddar cheese, grated
Filling:
50 g/2 oz butter
2 onions, sliced
2 celery sticks, chopped
3 carrots, sliced
25 g/1 oz plain flour
450 ml/¾ pint hot vegetable or chicken stock
225 g/8 oz cabbage, cored and shredded
225 g/8 oz tomatoes, skinned, seeded and chopped

Sift the flour into a bowl with salt and pepper to taste. Rub in the butter until the mixture resembles fine breadcrumbs. Stir in the cheese, blending well.

To make the filling, place the butter in a bowl and heat on FULL (100%) for 1 minute or until melted. Add the onions, celery and carrots, cover and cook on FULL (100%) for 6 minutes, stirring once. Stir in the flour, blending well. Gradually add the stock and cook on FULL (100%) for 5 minutes, stirring three times. Add the cabbage and tomatoes, blending well.

Carefully spoon the crumble mixture over the vegetables. Cook on FULL (100%) for 11 to 13 minutes, giving the dish a turn every 3 minutes. Leave to STAND for 5 minutes.

Brown under a preheated hot grill, if liked. Serve at once.
SERVES 4

GREEK CASSEROLE

METRIC/IMPERIAL
225 g/8 oz long-grain rice
600 ml/1 pint boiling water
2 × 275 g/10 oz packets frozen casserole vegetables
6 tablespoons cold water
1 tablespoon chopped fresh herbs
4 tablespoons tomato purée
1 × 275 g/10 oz packet frozen cut leaf spinach
250 ml/8 fl oz natural yogurt
2 egg yolks
1 tablespoon cornflour
1 tablespoon French mustard
200 g/7 oz feta or white Cheshire cheese, cubed
salt
freshly ground black pepper

Place the rice and boiling water in a bowl. Cover and cook on FULL (100%) for 10 minutes. Leave to STAND, covered, while preparing the vegetables.

Place the frozen casserole vegetables in a bowl with the cold water. Cover and cook on FULL (100%) for 10 minutes, stirring once. Drain well, then stir in the herbs and tomato purée, blending well.

Place the spinach in a bowl. Cover and cook on FULL (100%) for 8 minutes, stirring once. Drain well and stir into the rice.

Place the vegetable mixture in the base of a serving dish. Spoon the rice mixture over the top in an even layer.

Mix the yogurt with the egg yolks, cornflour and mustard, blending well. Fold in the cheese and season with salt and pepper to taste. Spoon over the rice and cook on FULL (100%) for 8 minutes, or until the egg mixture is just set around the edges. Leave to STAND for 5 minutes before serving.
SERVES 4 to 6

GARDEN VEGETABLE CASSEROLE

METRIC/IMPERIAL
40 g/1½ oz butter
1 onion, thinly sliced
3 tablespoons plain flour
1 teaspoon grated nutmeg
300 ml/½ pint milk
300 ml/½ pint hot chicken stock
salt

freshly ground black pepper
175 g/6 oz Cheddar cheese with ham and
mustard, grated
450 g/1 lb potatoes, peeled and thinly sliced
2 × 275 g/10 oz packets frozen sweetcorn, peas
and carrots
sliced tomatoes (optional)

Place the butter in a large bowl and heat on
FULL (100%) for ½ minute or until melted. Add
the onion and cook on FULL (100%) for 2
minutes.

Stir in the flour, nutmeg, milk, stock and salt
and pepper to taste, blending well. Cook on
FULL (100%) for 3½ to 4 minutes, stirring
every 1 minute until smooth and thickened. Add
the cheese, blending well.

Layer one-third of the potatoes in a cooking
dish. Top with one-third of the vegetables, then
one-third of the sauce. Repeat the layering twice,
finishing with a layer of sauce.

Top with the tomato slices, if using. Cook on
FULL (100%) for 30 minutes, turning the dish
twice, or until the potato is cooked in the centre
of the dish. Serve hot with a seasonal salad.
SERVES 4

NUTMEAL COURGETTES

METRIC/IMPERIAL
2 large courgettes
2 thick slices of bread, crusts removed
6 tablespoons milk
15 g/½ oz soft margarine
4 tablespoons finely chopped nuts
4 tablespoons grated cheese
1 egg
1 tablespoon chopped fresh parsley

Cut the courgettes in half lengthways. Place the
bread in a bowl and pour the milk over, then
turn the bread over and leave until the milk is
absorbed. Mash the bread, then stir in the
margarine, nuts, cheese and egg to form a soft
stuffing.

Pile the stuffing on top of the courgettes.
Arrange them, close together, in a dish in which
they fit snugly.

Cook on FULL (100%) for 4 to 5 minutes until
the courgettes are just tender, giving the dish a
half-turn after 3 minutes. Sprinkle with chopped
parsley before serving.
SERVES 2

SWISS TOMATO CASSEROLE

METRIC/IMPERIAL
40 g/1½ oz butter
40 g/1½ oz plain flour
450 ml/¾ pint milk
salt
freshly ground black pepper
100 g/4 oz Gruyère cheese, grated
4 tablespoons single cream
675 g/1½ lb ripe, firm tomatoes, skinned and
sliced
½ teaspoon dried basil
2 teaspoons caster sugar
25 g/1 oz grated Parmesan cheese

Place the butter, flour and milk in a bowl. Cook
on FULL (100%) for 5 to 6 minutes, stirring
every 1 minute until smooth and thickened.

Add salt and pepper to taste, the cheese and
cream, blending well.

Arrange a layer of sliced tomatoes in the base
of a casserole dish. Sprinkle with salt and pepper
to taste, a little basil and sugar, then cover with a
little sauce. Continue layering, finishing with a
layer of sauce. Sprinkle with the Parmesan
cheese.

Cover and cook on FULL (100%) for 10 to 12
minutes, turning the dish twice. Serve hot.
SERVES 4

SPINACH GNOCCHI

METRIC/IMPERIAL
225 g/8 oz frozen chopped spinach
175 g/6 oz Ricotta cheese
15 g/½ oz butter
2 eggs, lightly beaten
65 g/2½ oz plain flour
25 g/1 oz Parmesan cheese, finely grated
⅓ teaspoon grated nutmeg
salt
freshly ground black pepper

Place the frozen spinach in a small bowl and cook
on FULL (100%) for about 4 minutes or until
thawed, stirring twice. Then place the spinach in
a fine sieve and press to extract as much water as
possible; do not rub the spinach through the
sieve. Discard the water.

Return the spinach to the bowl and cook on
FULL (100%) for 3 minutes to draw off more
moisture. Stir in the Ricotta and butter and cook

on FULL (100%) for 2½ minutes, stirring once.

Stir in the eggs, flour, Parmesan and nutmeg. Add salt and pepper to taste, and set aside to chill for 2 hours or until firm.

Bring a large pan of lightly salted water to the boil on a *conventional hob*, then lower the heat to keep the water simmering.

Place spoonfuls of the gnocchi mixture on to a floured board. With floured hands, shape the mixture into small balls about the size of large walnuts. Drop the gnocchi into the simmering water and, as soon as they puff up and float on the surface, remove them with a slotted spoon. Each batch will take about 10 minutes.

Arrange the gnocchi on a warm, buttered serving dish and serve immediately. If desired, sprinkle extra Parmesan over the finished dish. Serve as a starter or as a vegetable with a hot fish, meat or poultry dish.
SERVES 2 to 4

Variation
Sieved cottage cheese can be used instead of Ricotta.

MUSHROOM AND BRAZIL NUT LOAF

METRIC/IMPERIAL
2 onions, finely chopped
2 cloves garlic, crushed
2 large carrots, finely diced
3 tablespoons water
450 g/1 lb mushrooms, finely chopped
50 g/2 oz shelled Brazil nuts, finely chopped
100 g/4 oz fresh wholemeal breadcrumbs
2 tablespoons chopped fresh parsley or
2 teaspoons dried mixed herbs
salt
freshly ground black pepper
2 eggs
120 ml/4 fl oz skimmed milk
6–8 large spinach leaves, trimmed and blanched

Place the onions, garlic and carrots in a large bowl with the water. Cover and cook on FULL (100%) for 3¼ minutes, stirring halfway through the cooking time. Stir in the mushrooms, cover and cook on FULL (100%) for a further 1½ to 2 minutes.

Stir in the nuts, breadcrumbs, herbs and salt and pepper to taste. Beat the eggs and milk together and stir into the mushroom mixture.

Drain the blanched spinach leaves thoroughly and pat them dry on absorbent kitchen paper. Reserve one of the leaves and use the remainder to line a lightly oiled 1.2 litre/2 pint loaf dish. Spoon in the mushroom mixture, pressing lightly to smooth the surface. Fold over any overlapping spinach leaves and top with the reserved spinach leaf. Cover loosely with lightly oiled greaseproof paper and cook on FULL (100%) for 16½ minutes, turning the dish around after 8 minutes.

Leave to STAND, covered, for 10 minutes before unmoulding on to a large platter. Serve hot or cold with Tomato Sauce (see page 307).

Note: If preferred, you can substitute cabbage leaves for the spinach. Alternatively, the loaf can be prepared without a spinach lining.

SPICY VEGETABLE CURRY

METRIC/IMPERIAL
1 onion, finely chopped
1 clove garlic, crushed
1 cm/½ inch piece of fresh root ginger, peeled and finely grated
300 ml/½ pint hot vegetable or chicken stock
1 teaspoon ground coriander
½ teaspoon chilli powder
2 teaspoons garam masala or curry powder
2 carrots, thinly sliced
1 potato, scrubbed and cut into 2.5 cm/1 inch cubes
175 g/6 oz small cauliflower florets
2 tablespoons sultanas
2 tablespoons tomato purée
1 dessert apple, cored and cubed but not peeled
100 g/4 oz fresh okra, washed and drained (optional)
pinch of salt
freshly ground black pepper
1 tomato, cut into wedges

Place the onion, garlic and ginger in a large bowl or casserole. Add 4 tablespoons of the stock and stir in the spices. Cover and cook on FULL (100%) for 2½ minutes, stirring halfway through the cooking time. Stir in the carrots, cover and cook on FULL (100%) for 5¾ minutes, stirring twice during cooking.

Stir in the potato, cauliflower and sultanas. Add the remaining stock and the tomato purée. Cover again and cook on FULL (100%) for a further 6½ minutes, or until the vegetables are tender, stirring two or three times during cooking.

Stir in the apple, okra, if using, and season with salt and pepper. Replace the cover and cook on FULL (100%) for 4 minutes, stirring halfway through the cooking time. Add the tomato, cover again and cook on FULL (100%) for a further 2½ minutes.

Leave to STAND, covered, for 8 minutes before serving.

SERVES 4

STUFFED ONIONS

METRIC/IMPERIAL
2 tablespoons bulgar wheat
7 tablespoons boiling water
4 large onions, peeled
1 small courgette, finely chopped
1 tablespoon chopped fresh parsley, or
1 teaspoon dried mixed herbs
1 teaspoon soy sauce
pinch of salt
freshly ground black pepper

Place the bulgar wheat in a small bowl, add 4 tablespoons of the boiling water and leave to soak while preparing the onions.

Cut a slice off the top of each onion and, using a sharp knife, remove the centres, leaving shells about 5 mm/¼ inch thick all round. Place the onions in a circle on a plate and set aside.

Chop the onion centres very finely and place them in a large bowl with the remaining boiling water. Cover and cook on FULL (100%) for 2 to 2½ minutes, stirring halfway through the cooking time.

Add the courgette, parsley or herbs, soy sauce, salt, pepper and soaked bulgar wheat. Mix thoroughly and spoon into the reserved onion shells.

Cook the stuffed onions on FULL (100%) for 11½ minutes, rearranging them halfway through the cooking time. Allow to STAND for 5 minutes before serving.

SERVES 4

Note: Bulgar wheat (cracked wheat or burghul wheat) is a partially cooked wheat product with a delicious nutty flavour. It can be soaked and used in salads or used instead of rice in pilaff dishes. It is available from health food stores.

STUFFED CABBAGE IN CHILLI SAUCE

METRIC/IMPERIAL
1 small Savoy cabbage, weighing about 1 kg/2 lb
1 onion, finely chopped
1 egg
350 g/12 oz minced lean beef
1 tablespoon easy-cook long-grain rice
5 tablespoons beef stock
1 teaspoon fresh lemon juice
2 teaspoons salt
½ teaspoon freshly ground black pepper
300 ml/½ pint water
Sauce:
5 tablespoons tomato purée
¼ teaspoon hot chilli powder
¼ teaspoon Worcestershire sauce
salt
freshly ground black pepper
1 tablespoon instant potato powder

Wash the cabbage and remove any damaged outer leaves. Trim the base and remove part of the centre core with a sharp knife. Pull the leaves open and scoop out the centre, reserving this part for use in another recipe.

To make the filling, mix together the onion, egg, minced beef, rice, stock, lemon juice and salt and pepper to taste. Spoon into the hollow of the cabbage, pressing the mixture down firmly. Fold the outer leaves over the top to cover.

Pour the water into a large bowl and put in the cabbage. Cover and cook on FULL (100%) for 20 minutes, giving the cabbage a quarter-turn every 5 minutes. Carefully transfer the cabbage to a serving dish (reserving the liquid) and cover. Leave to STAND while making the sauce.

To make the sauce, stir the tomato purée, chilli powder and seasoning into the liquid remaining in the bowl, then mix in the dried potato. Cover and cook on FULL (100%) for 3 minutes or until the sauce boils and thickens. Stir vigorously. Hand the hot sauce separately.

SERVES 2

GOLDEN VEGETABLE CURRY

METRIC/IMPERIAL
1 tablespoon vegetable oil
1 small green pepper, cored, seeded and finely chopped
2 carrots, finely sliced
1 celery stick, finely chopped
2 large onions, finely chopped
3 tomatoes, skinned and chopped
1 tablespoon lemon juice
1 large eating apple, peeled, cored and chopped
25 g/1 oz dark brown sugar
2 tablespoons curry powder
2 teaspoons turmeric
2 tablespoons desiccated coconut
25 g/1 oz plain flour
300 ml/½ pint hot vegetable stock
2 tablespoons sultanas
25 g/1 oz peanuts
salt
freshly ground black pepper

Place the oil, green pepper, carrots and celery in a bowl. Cover and cook on FULL (100%) for 5 minutes.

Stir in the onions, tomatoes, lemon juice, apple, sugar, curry powder, turmeric and coconut. Cover and cook on FULL (100%) for 10 minutes, stirring halfway through cooking.

Stir in the flour, hot stock, sultanas, peanuts, salt and pepper. Cover and cook on FULL (100%) for a further 4 minutes, stirring halfway through cooking. Serve with brown rice.
SERVES 4

CAULIFLOWER AND GREEN BEAN SALAD

METRIC/IMPERIAL
350 g/12 oz fresh cauliflower, divided into florets
5 tablespoons water
225 g/8 oz frozen whole green beans
120 ml/4 fl oz French dressing
a little red and green pepper, chopped (optional)
finely chopped hard-boiled egg, to garnish (optional)

Place the cauliflower florets in a shallow oval dish, keeping the stems to the centre. Add 3 tablespoons of the water. Cover tightly and cook on FULL (100%) for 5 to 6 minutes. Stir and set aside.

Put the beans into a shallow oval dish and add 2 tablespoons of water. Cover tightly and cook on FULL (100%) for 6 minutes, stirring once during cooking.

Drain the cauliflower and beans. Combine in a bowl and pour over the French dressing. Add the peppers and toss to coat. Cool and then refrigerate. Pile into a serving dish and, if liked, garnish with chopped egg.
SERVES 4

FLASH-COOKED SALAD

METRIC/IMPERIAL
1 cucumber, cut into 3 mm/⅛ inch slices
6 celery sticks, finely sliced
100 g/4 oz cauliflower florets, broken into sprigs
100 g/4 oz carrots, cut into thin matchstick strips
6 tablespoons medium red wine
4 tablespoons corn or sunflower oil
1 teaspoon freshly ground black pepper
½ teaspoon salt
1 teaspoon sugar

Combine all the ingredients in a large bowl. Cover and cook on FULL (100%) for 2 minutes. Stir thoroughly, then cover and cook on FULL (100%) for a further 2 minutes. Stir once more.

Leave to cool, but do not chill. Spoon the mixture into a salad bowl before serving.
SERVES 6

POTATO SALAD WITH CHIVES

METRIC/IMPERIAL
450 g/1 lb new potatoes, scrubbed and sliced
1 small onion, chopped
4 tablespoons water
salt
freshly ground black pepper
5 tablespoons mayonnaise
1 tablespoon snipped chives

Place the potatoes, onion, water and a pinch of salt in a cooking dish. Cover and cook on FULL (100%) for 8 to 10 minutes, stirring twice. Leave to STAND, covered, for 5 minutes. Drain well.

Add the mayonnaise, chives and salt and pepper to taste. Toss the potatoes lightly in the mixture to coat.

Serve warm or cold.
SERVES 3 to 4

GERMAN POTATO SALAD

METRIC/IMPERIAL
675 g/1½ lb potatoes, peeled and cut into chunks
4 tablespoons water
4 streaky bacon rashers, derinded and chopped
½ bunch spring onions, finely sliced
25 g/1 oz butter
1 tablespoon flour
100 g/4 oz garlic sausage, cubed
150 ml/¼ pint single cream
salt
freshly ground black pepper
Garnish:
poppy seeds
snipped chives

Place the chunks of potato and water in a bowl. Cover loosely and cook on FULL (100%) for 8 to 10 minutes, stirring once, until tender. Leave to STAND, covered, while cooking the bacon mixture.

Place the bacon, onions and butter in a dish and cook on FULL (100%) for 4 minutes. Stir in the flour, garlic sausage, cream and salt and pepper to taste. Cook on FULL (100%) for 1 minute. Stir in the drained, cooked potatoes and sprinkle with poppy seeds and chopped chives.
SERVES 4

VEGETABLE RICE SALAD

METRIC/IMPERIAL
½ onion, finely chopped
1 tablespoon vegetable oil
1 teaspoon curry powder
½ teaspoon paprika
1 teaspoon tomato purée
150 ml/¼ pint cold water
1 teaspoon lemon juice
2 tablespoons salad oil
1 tablespoon white wine vinegar
225 g/8 oz long-grain rice
600 ml/1 pint boiling water
1 teaspoon salt
2 tomatoes, skinned, seeded and coarsely chopped
¼ cucumber, cubed
3 celery sticks, sliced

Place the onion, vegetable oil, curry powder and paprika in a bowl and cook on FULL (100%) for 1 minute. Add the tomato purée, cold water and lemon juice. Cover and cook on FULL (100%)

for 3 minutes. Add the salad oil and vinegar and mix well to blend. Set aside.

Place the rice, boiling water and salt in a bowl. Cover and cook on FULL (100%) for 3 minutes. Reduce the power setting to MEDIUM (50%) and cook for a further 12 minutes, stirring twice.

Stir in the curry dressing and leave to STAND, covered, for 5 minutes. Allow to cool.

Fold the tomatoes, cucumber and celery into the curried rice mixture. Serve lightly chilled.
SERVES 4

LEMONY SALAD APPETIZER

METRIC/IMPERIAL
2 tablespoons vegetable oil
1 clove garlic, crushed
1 small onion, peeled
finely grated rind and juice of 1 large lemon
150 ml/¼ pint dry vermouth
2 tablespoons soft brown sugar
3 tablespoons chopped fresh parsley
salt
freshly ground black pepper
225 g/8 oz young carrots, cut into matchstick strips
225 g/8 oz shelled broad beans

Place the oil, garlic and onion in a bowl. Cook on FULL (100%) for 2 minutes, stirring once.

Add the lemon rind and juice, vermouth, sugar, parsley and salt and pepper to taste, blending well. Add the vegetables and stir well to coat in the marinade. Cover and cook on FULL (100%) for 5 minutes, stirring once.

Allow to cool, then chill thoroughly. Serve chilled as part of a salad.
SERVES 4

STIR-FRY SALAD

METRIC/IMPERIAL
225 g/8 oz long-grain rice
600 ml/1 pint boiling water
5 tablespoons vegetable oil
1 onion, chopped
3 celery sticks, thinly sliced
1 × 100 g/4 oz packet frozen sliced green beans
1 × 100 g/4 oz packet frozen peas
1 × 275 g/10 oz packet frozen sweetcorn kernels

4 tablespoons soy sauce
½ teaspoon mustard powder
2 tablespoons white wine vinegar
2 teaspoons soft brown sugar
salt
freshly ground black pepper
2–3 tablespoons chopped almonds

Place the rice in a casserole dish with the boiling water. Cover and cook on FULL (100%) for 3 minutes. Reduce the power setting to MEDIUM (50%) and cook for a further 12 minutes. Leave to STAND while cooking the vegetables.

Place 1 tablespoon of the oil in a casserole with the onion and celery. Cover and cook on FULL (100%) for 2 minutes. Stir in the beans, peas and sweetcorn. Cover and cook on FULL (100%) for 5 minutes, stirring once.

Meanwhile, place the remaining oil, soy sauce, mustard powder, vinegar, sugar and salt and pepper to taste in a screw-topped jar and shake well to mix.

Gently fold the rice and dressing into the vegetable mixture and leave to cool at room temperature. Chill, then serve topped with the almonds.
SERVES 6 to 8

VEGETABLE VINAIGRETTE
METRIC/IMPERIAL
100 g/4 oz young green beans, trimmed
3 tablespoons cold water
salt
freshly ground black pepper
100 g/4 oz courgettes, thickly sliced
100 g/4 oz button mushrooms, trimmed
2 hard-boiled eggs, quartered
2 tablespoons olive oil
juice of ½ lemon
chopped fresh herbs (parsley, chives, marjoram, oregano, for example)
1 lemon, quartered, to garnish

Place the beans in a bowl with 2 tablespoons of the water and a pinch of salt. Cover and cook on FULL (100%) for 2 minutes. Drain and refresh under cold running water. Drain and pat dry.

Place the courgettes in a bowl. Cover and cook on FULL (100%) for 2 minutes. Refresh under cold running water. Drain well and pat dry.

Place the mushrooms in a bowl with the remaining water. Cover and cook on FULL

(100%) for 1½ to 2 minutes, stirring once. Drain and refresh under cold running water. Drain well and pat dry.

Arrange the vegetables on a plate with the eggs. Combine the oil and lemon juice, season with salt and pepper to taste and beat with a whisk or fork until thick and creamy.

Spoon over the vegetables and sprinkle with herbs to taste. Garnish with lemon wedges and serve at room temperature.
SERVES 2

CARROT AND PARSNIP CROQUETTES
METRIC/IMPERIAL
350 g/12 oz carrots, thinly sliced
350 g/12 oz parsnips, thinly sliced
6 tablespoons water
pinch of salt
freshly ground black pepper
25 g/1 oz polyunsaturated margarine
50 g/2 oz fresh wholemeal breadcrumbs, toasted
50 g/2 oz hazelnuts, toasted and finely chopped
1 egg, lightly beaten

Place the carrots and parsnips in a large bowl or casserole. Add the water, cover and cook on FULL (100%) for 11 to 12 minutes, stirring two or three times during cooking. Allow to STAND, covered, for 5 minutes before draining.

Mash the vegetables with a fork or press through a coarse sieve and mix well. Transfer to a bowl. Add a pinch of salt, if required, together with some pepper and beat in the margarine. Cover and leave to cool.

When the mixture is cool enough to handle, roll it into 8 to 12 cylinder-shaped croquettes. Place them in a single layer on a lightly floured plate and refrigerate for 1 hour or until the croquettes are firm.

Mix the breadcrumbs and hazelnuts and spread them on a plate or a sheet of greaseproof paper. Dip the croquettes in the beaten egg and roll in the breadcrumb mixture. Arrange them in a circle on a large shallow dish or plate, lined with absorbent kitchen paper. Cook on FULL (100%) for 3 minutes, rearranging the croquettes half-way through the cooking time. Serve at once.
MAKES 8 to 12

PASTA, RICE AND PULSES

VEGETABLE LASAGNE

METRIC/IMPERIAL
2 courgettes, thinly sliced
175 g/6 oz button mushrooms, thinly sliced
pinch of salt
freshly ground black pepper
175 g/6 oz dried lasagne verdi
2 tablespoons grated Parmesan cheese
Tomato sauce:
2 onions, thinly sliced
1 clove garlic, crushed
1 green pepper, cored, seeded and thinly sliced
2 tablespoons water
1 × 400 g/14 oz can tomatoes, chopped
2 tablespoons tomato purée
1 teaspoon dried mixed herbs
1 tablespoon wholemeal flour, blended with
2 tablespoons water
Cheese sauce:
25 g/1 oz polyunsaturated margarine
2 tablespoons wholemeal flour
450 ml/¾ pint skimmed milk
50 g/2 oz Edam cheese, grated
1 teaspoon French or German mustard
freshly ground black pepper

First prepare the tomato sauce. Place the onions, garlic and green pepper in a large bowl with the water and cook on FULL (100%) for 2½ minutes, stirring halfway through the cooking time. Stir in the chopped tomatoes, with their juice, and the tomato purée and herbs. Cover and cook on FULL (100%) for 4 minutes, stirring halfway through the cooking time. Stir in the wholemeal flour mixture, cover as before and cook on FULL (100%) for 2½ minutes, stirring well after each minute.

Stir the courgettes and mushrooms into the tomato sauce. Season with salt and pepper to taste, cover again and cook on FULL (100%) for 4 minutes. Set aside while making the cheese sauce.

Place the margarine in a large jug and heat on FULL (100%) for ½ minute to melt. Add the flour and gradually stir in the milk. Cook on FULL (100%) for 2½ minutes, stirring thoroughly every 1 minute until smooth and thickened. Stir in the cheese and mustard and season with black pepper. Leave to STAND, covered, for 5 minutes.

To assemble the dish, spread a layer of tomato sauce on the base of a baking dish. Arrange a layer of uncooked lasagne on top. Spoon over half the remaining tomato sauce and top with more lasagne. Add a final layer of tomato sauce and cover with the remaining lasagne. Spoon the cheese sauce over the top and sprinkle with the Parmesan cheese. Cook on FULL (100%) for 10 minutes, giving the dish a half-turn after 5 minutes.

If liked, cook under a preheated hot grill until golden. Leave to STAND for 5 minutes.
SERVES 4

Note: You can also use fresh lasagne – if you do so, reduce the cooking time on FULL (100%) to 6½ minutes.

SPAGHETTI ALL'UOVA

METRIC/IMPERIAL
salt
1 tablespoon vegetable oil
1.75 litres/3 pints boiling water
225 g/8 oz dried spaghetti
3 eggs, lightly beaten
100 g/4 oz butter, cut into pieces
50 g/2 oz pecorino cheese, grated

Place the salt, oil and water in a large bowl. Soften the spaghetti in the water until completely immersed. Cover and cook on FULL (100%) for 8 minutes, checking during cooking that all the spaghetti is covered with water.

Leave to STAND, covered, for 10 minutes. Drain and toss in the beaten eggs until set.

Place half the butter in a serving bowl. Pile in the spaghetti and dot with the remaining butter. Serve sprinkled with the grated cheese.
SERVES 4

NOODLES

METRIC/IMPERIAL
225 g/8 oz dried noodles
1.2 litres/2 pints boiling water
1 teaspoon salt
1 teaspoon vegetable oil

Place the noodles in a large deep dish. Add the boiling water and salt, then stir in the oil. Cook on FULL (100%) for 6 minutes, stirring once. Cover tightly and leave to STAND for 5 minutes until the noodles are just tender. Drain and serve at once.
SERVES 4 to 6

NOODLES WITH PEA AND BACON SAUCE

METRIC/IMPERIAL
225 g/8 oz smoked back bacon, derinded and chopped
1 onion, chopped
1 tablespoon chopped mixed fresh herbs
450 g/1 lb frozen peas
100 ml/4 fl oz chicken stock
225 g/8 oz dried egg noodles
600 ml/1 pint boiling water
1 tablespoon vegetable oil
salt
freshly ground black pepper
150 ml/¼ pint single cream

Place the bacon in a casserole dish. Cover and cook on FULL (100%) for 7 minutes, stirring once. Remove the bacon with a slotted spoon and drain on absorbent kitchen paper.

Stir the onion and herbs into the bacon fat, blending well. Cover and cook on FULL (100%) for 3 minutes, stirring once. Add the peas and stock, blending well. Cover and cook on FULL (100%) for 10 minutes, stirring once. Set aside.

Place the noodles in a bowl with the boiling water, oil and a pinch of salt. Cover and cook on FULL (100%) for 6 minutes, stirring once. Leave to STAND while preparing the sauce.

Purée the pea mixture in a blender or food processor, or pass through a fine sieve. Add the cream and salt and pepper to taste, blending well. Cook on FULL (100%) for 1 to 2 minutes.

Drain the noodles and place on a warmed serving dish. Spoon over the sauce and sprinkle with the bacon to serve.
SERVES 4

GARLIC CHEESE AND HERB PASTA

METRIC/IMPERIAL
225 g/8 oz dried wholewheat tagliatelle
1.2 litres/2 pints hot water
1 teaspoon sunflower oil
pinch of salt
100 g/4 oz low-fat soft cheese
2 tablespoons skimmed milk
2 cloves garlic, crushed
1 tablespoon finely chopped fresh basil, or
1 teaspoon dried basil
freshly ground black pepper
50 g/2 oz Brazil nuts, finely chopped
fresh basil, shredded, to garnish

Place the pasta, hot water, oil and salt in a large bowl. Cover and cook on FULL (100%) for 6 minutes, or until the pasta is just tender, stirring twice during cooking. Leave to STAND, covered, for 5 minutes.

Meanwhile, mix the low-fat soft cheese, milk, garlic and basil together in a bowl.

Drain the pasta and return to the bowl. While it is still hot, stir in the cheese mixture, and mix well. Add plenty of black pepper to taste and sprinkle with the chopped nuts. Serve immediately, garnished with the shredded basil.
SERVES 4

STUFFED CANNELLONI

METRIC/IMPERIAL
1 small onion, finely chopped
1 tablespoon vegetable oil
175 g/6 oz chicken livers, chopped
1 × 225 g/8 oz can tomatoes, drained
225 g/8 oz mushrooms, finely chopped
8 tubes dried cannelloni
900 ml/1½ pints boiling water
Tomato Sauce (see page 307)
grated Parmesan cheese

Place the onion and oil in a large dish and cook on FULL (100%) for 2½ minutes, until the onion is soft. Stir in the chicken livers and cook on FULL (100%) for 2½ minutes, stirring once. Add the tomatoes and mushrooms and cook on FULL (100%) for a further 1½ to 2 minutes.

Place the cannelloni tubes in a 1.5 litre/2½ pint oval dish and pour over the boiling water, making sure the cannelloni are totally covered. Cook on FULL (100%) for 8 to 10 minutes, rearranging the cannelloni halfway through the cooking time. Drain and stuff each tube with the filling, using a teaspoon.

Return the cannelloni to the oval dish. Pour over the tomato sauce, making sure the cannelloni are covered. Sprinkle with Parmesan cheese and reheat on FULL (100%) for 1 minute.
SERVES 4

PASTA SHELLS WITH BOLOGNESE SAUCE

METRIC/IMPERIAL
175 g/6 oz dried pasta shells
900 ml/1½ pints boiling water
1 teaspoon salt
1 tablespoon vegetable oil
Bolognese sauce:
1 tablespoon oil
4 streaky bacon rashers, derinded and chopped
1 onion, finely chopped
450 g/1 lb minced lean beef
50 g/2 oz mushrooms, chopped
1 teaspoon chopped fresh parsley
1 beef stock cube, crumbled
1 teaspoon French mustard
1 teaspoon dried oregano
1 × 225 g/8 oz can tomatoes, chopped
3 tablespoons tomato purée
1 wine glass red wine
salt
freshly ground black pepper
grated Parmesan cheese for sprinkling

Place the pasta in a deep bowl and pour over the boiling water. Add the salt and oil, then cover and cook on FULL (100%) for 10 to 12 minutes, stirring once.

Remove from the oven and stir. Leave to STAND, covered with a clean tea towel, for 5 minutes, then drain.

Preheat a large browning dish on FULL (100%) for 5 minutes (or according to the manufacturer's instructions). Stir in the oil, bacon and onion. Cover and cook on FULL (100%) for 3 minutes. Stir in the minced beef and cook on FULL (100%) for 3 minutes.

Add all the remaining ingredients and stir well. Cover and cook on MEDIUM (50%) for 16 minutes. Arrange the drained pasta on a serving dish and pour the sauce over. Sprinkle with grated cheese and serve.
SERVES 4

NOODLE AND HAM BAKE

METRIC/IMPERIAL
225 g/8 oz cooked ham, chopped
1 onion, finely chopped
3 tablespoons chopped fresh parsley
225 g/8 oz cooked noodles
300 ml/½ pint milk
2 eggs, beaten
½ teaspoon salt
pinch of grated nutmeg
50 g/2 oz Cheddar cheese, grated
25 g/1 oz butter
1 teaspoon ground paprika

Place the ham, onion and parsley in a dish. Cover and cook on FULL (100%) for 5 minutes, stirring once.

Place half of the noodles in a greased cooking dish. Top with the ham mixture, then the remaining noodles.

Mix the milk with the eggs, salt and nutmeg, blending well. Pour over the noodles. Sprinkle with the cheese and dot with the butter. Sprinkle with paprika and cook on FULL (100%) for 10 minutes, turning the dish once.

Reduce the power setting to MEDIUM (50%) and cook for 18 to 20 minutes, turning the dish twice. Leave to STAND for 5 to 10 minutes before serving.
SERVES 4

NOODLES WITH CHEESY LEEKS

METRIC/IMPERIAL
350 g/12 oz dried egg noodles
900 ml/1½ pints boiling water
1 tablespoon vegetable oil
675 g/1½ lb leeks, sliced
4 tablespoons cold water
salt
freshly ground black pepper
25 g/1 oz butter
25 g/1 oz plain flour
450 ml/¾ pint milk
1 teaspoon made mustard
100 g/4 oz cheese, grated

Place the noodles, boiling water and oil in a bowl. Cover and cook on FULL (100%) for 6 minutes. Leave to STAND while cooking the leeks.

Place the leeks in a bowl with the water and a

pinch of salt. Cover and cook on FULL (100%) for 12 minutes, stirring once.

Place the butter in a bowl and heat on FULL (100%) for ½ minute or until melted. Stir in the flour, then gradually add the milk, blending well. Cook on FULL (100%) for 3½ to 4 minutes, stirring every 1 minute until smooth and thickened. Add the mustard, salt and pepper to taste and half of the cheese, blending well.

Drain the noodles and place in a serving dish. Drain the leeks and place on top of the noodles. Pour over the cheese sauce and sprinkle with the remaining cheese. Serve at once.
SERVES 4

SPAGHETTI WITH NEAPOLITAN SAUCE

METRIC/IMPERIAL
350 g/12 oz dried spaghetti
1.5 litres/2½ pints boiling water
1 tablespoon vegetable oil
Sauce:
2 tablespoons olive oil
1 large onion, chopped
1 clove garlic, crushed
450 g/1 lb tomatoes, skinned, seeded and chopped
1 tablespoon chopped mixed fresh herbs (thyme, oregano, parsley, for example)
salt
freshly ground black pepper
15 g/½ oz butter
grated Parmesan cheese for sprinkling

Hold the spaghetti in a deep bowl with the boiling water and vegetable oil, until softened and completely immersed. Cover and cook on FULL (100%) for 10 to 12 minutes. Leave to STAND, covered, while preparing the sauce.

Place the olive oil, onion and garlic in a bowl. Cover and cook on FULL (100%) for 3 minutes. Add the tomatoes, blending well. Cover and cook on FULL (100%) for 3 minutes, stirring once.

Add the herbs and salt and pepper to taste, blending well. Cover and cook on FULL (100%) for a further 2 minutes.

Drain the spaghetti and toss with the butter. Arrange around the outside of a heated serving dish. Pour the sauce into the centre and serve at once, sprinkled with Parmesan cheese.
SERVES 4

TORTELLINI IN CREAMY PESTO SAUCE

METRIC/IMPERIAL
175 g/6 oz dried tortellini
900 ml/1½ pints boiling water
1 tablespoon vegetable oil
salt
freshly ground black pepper
150 ml/¼ pint single cream
1 tablespoon canned or bottled pesto sauce
grated Parmesan cheese for sprinkling

Place the tortellini in a bowl with the boiling water, oil and a pinch of salt. Cover and cook on FULL (100%) for 12 to 14 minutes. Leave to STAND, covered, while preparing the sauce.

Place the cream in a bowl and cook on FULL (100%) for 1½ minutes. Add the pesto sauce and pepper to taste, blending well.

Drain the tortellini and add to the sauce. Toss well to mix. Sprinkle with Parmesan cheese and serve with a crisp green salad.
SERVES 2

TAGLIATELLE WITH MUSHROOM SAUCE

METRIC/IMPERIAL
50 g/2 oz butter
225 g/8 oz bacon, derinded and chopped
100 g/4 oz mushrooms, sliced
25 g/1 oz plain flour
300 ml/½ pint milk
salt
freshly ground black pepper
350 g/12 oz dried tagliatelle verdi
600 ml/1 pint boiling water
1 tablespoon vegetable oil

Place half the butter in a bowl and heat on FULL (100%) for ½ minute or until melted. Add the bacon, cover and cook on FULL (100%) for 6 minutes, stirring once. Remove with a slotted spoon and drain on absorbent kitchen paper.

Add the mushrooms to the bacon fat, blending well. Cover and cook on FULL (100%) for 2 minutes. Set aside.

Place the remaining butter in a bowl and heat on FULL (100%) for ½ minute or until melted. Add the flour, blending well. Gradually add the milk and cook on FULL (100%) for 3½ to 4 minutes, stirring every 1 minute until smooth and thickened. Stir in the bacon, mushrooms with their juice, and salt and pepper to taste, blending well. Set aside.

Place the tagliatelle in a bowl with the boiling water and oil. Cover and cook on FULL (100%) for 6 minutes, stirring once. Leave to STAND, covered, for 3 minutes. Drain thoroughly and place in a heated serving dish.

Meanwhile, reheat the sauce on FULL (100%) for 2 minutes, stirring once. Spoon over the tagliatelle and serve at once.

SERVES 4

LASAGNE AL FORNO

METRIC/IMPERIAL
2 tablespoons vegetable oil
1 onion, finely chopped
1 clove garlic, crushed
350 g/12 oz minced lean beef
1 × 225 g/8 oz can tomatoes
50 g/2 oz mushrooms, chopped
1 beef stock cube, crumbled
½ teaspoon dried oregano
2 tablespoons tomato purée
salt
freshly ground black pepper
12 sheets of quick-cooking lasagne
Toasted Crumbs (see page 314)
grated Parmesan cheese
Sauce:
50 g/2 oz butter
50 g/2 oz plain flour
600 ml/1 pint milk
1 teaspoon made mustard
salt
freshly ground black pepper
75–100 g/3–4 oz Mozzarella cheese, grated

Preheat a large browning dish on FULL (100%) for 5 minutes (or according to the manufacturer's instructions). If a browning dish is not available, use a large mixing bowl, but *do not* preheat.

Place the oil in the dish or bowl and cook on FULL (100%) for ½ minute. Add the onion, garlic and meat and stir well. Cook on FULL (100%) for 2 minutes.

Stir in the tomatoes, mushrooms, stock cube, oregano and tomato purée. Season well with salt and pepper. Cover and cook on MEDIUM (50%) for 26 minutes. Leave to STAND.

To make the sauce, place the butter in a 2 litre/ 3½ pint jug or mixing bowl, and cook on FULL (100%) for 1½ minutes. Stir in the flour and half the milk to form a roux. Gradually stir in the

remaining milk, the mustard and salt and pepper. At this stage the sauce will appear very lumpy.

Cook on FULL (100%) for 5 minutes, stirring twice. Beat well, then cook on FULL (100%) for a further 3 minutes. Beat in the cheese.

To assemble the dish, grease an ovenproof glass dish with some melted butter. Cover the base with a little cheese sauce. Arrange three sheets of lasagne over the cheese, cover with a layer of meat and then a layer of cheese sauce. Continue layering in this way until all the ingredients have been used, finishing with a layer of cheese sauce.

Sprinkle the top with a few toasted crumbs and a little Parmesan cheese. Cover and cook on FULL (100%) for 18 minutes. Serve with a green salad.

SERVES 4

HAM AND CHICKEN LASAGNE

METRIC/IMPERIAL
1 × 350 g/12 oz chicken portion
175 g/6 oz dried lasagne verdi
½ teaspoon vegetable oil
900 ml/1½ pints boiling water
salt
1 onion, finely chopped
1 small green pepper, cored, seeded and finely chopped
40 g/1½ oz butter
40 g/1½ oz plain flour
300 ml/½ pint milk
150 ml/¼ pint hot chicken stock
50 g/2 oz cooked ham, finely chopped
freshly ground black pepper
40 g/1½ oz Cheddar cheese, finely grated

Place the chicken in a shallow dish. Cover and cook on FULL (100%) for 6 minutes. Leave to STAND, covered, for 5 minutes. Discard the skin and bones, and chop the flesh. Set aside.

Place the lasagne in a 5 cm/2 inch deep, oblong casserole dish. Pour over the oil, boiling water and salt, completely covering the lasagne with water. Cover and cook on FULL (100%) for 9 minutes.

Leave to STAND, covered, for 15 minutes. Drain the lasagne and place it on a separate plate.

Place the onion, green pepper and butter in a medium bowl. Cover and cook on FULL (100%) for 7 minutes.

Sprinkle in the flour and gradually stir in the milk. Cook on FULL (100%) for 4 minutes, then blend in the hot stock. Stir in the chicken, ham, salt and pepper. Cook on FULL (100%) for a further 2 minutes.

Place half the drained lasagne in a layer at the bottom of a casserole dish. Pour over half the sauce. Place the remaining lasagne over the sauce and cover with the remaining sauce. Sprinkle the cheese on top and cook on FULL (100%) for 1¼ minutes or until the cheese has melted.

Brown under a preheated conventional grill.
SERVES 4

SEAFOOD SPAGHETTI

METRIC/IMPERIAL
1.75 litres/3 pints boiling water
½ teaspoon salt
1 tablespoon oil
225 g/8 oz dried spaghetti
1 × 400 g/14 oz can tomatoes
1 tablespoon tomato purée
100 g/4 oz peeled prawns
1 × 225 g/8 oz can crabmeat, drained
12 pimiento-stuffed olives, drained
salt
freshly ground black pepper
3 teaspoons cornflour (optional)
Garnish:
grated Parmesan cheese
12 extra pimiento-stuffed olives

Pour the boiling water into a large heatproof mixing bowl. Add the salt and oil, then hold the spaghetti in the water, curling it round as it softens, until it is completely immersed. Cover and cook on FULL (100%) for 10 to 12 minutes. Set aside, covered, while preparing the sauce.

In a large jug put the tomatoes, tomato purée, prawns, crabmeat, olives and salt and pepper to taste. Cover and cook on FULL (100%) for 6 minutes, stirring once, halfway through cooking.

Cream the cornflour to a smooth paste with a little cold water and stir into the hot seafood sauce. Return to the oven and cook on FULL (100%) for 1 minute. Stir.

Drain the spaghetti, arrange it on a serving dish and pour over the seafood sauce. Sprinkle liberally with Parmesan cheese and garnish with olives. Serve with a mixed salad.
SERVES 4

SPAGHETTI WITH HAM AND MUSHROOMS

METRIC/IMPERIAL
15 g/½ oz butter
50 g/2 oz mushrooms, thinly sliced
2 tomatoes, sliced
175 g/6 oz cooked ham, diced
1 tablespoon sweet pickle (optional)
225 g/8 oz cold cooked spaghetti
salt
freshly ground black pepper

Put the butter and mushrooms in a shallow dish and cook on FULL (100%) for 2 minutes. Add the tomatoes, turning them over so they are evenly coated with butter. Cook on FULL (100%) for 2 minutes.

Add the diced ham and sweet pickle, if using, and arrange the cold spaghetti on top. Cover loosely and cook on FULL (100%) for 2 to 3 minutes until the spaghetti is hot, giving the dish a half-turn once during cooking. Add salt and pepper to taste and serve immediately, accompanied by a crisp green salad, if liked.
SERVES 1 to 2

SEAFOOD PASTA SALAD

METRIC/IMPERIAL
225 g/8 oz dried pasta shells
1.2 litres/2 pints boiling water
450 g/1 lb firm white fish (cod or haddock, for example)
2 tablespoons cold water
100 g/4 oz peeled shrimps
1 red or green pepper, cored, seeded and chopped
Green onion dressing:
5 tablespoons vegetable oil
2 tablespoons lemon juice
1 clove garlic, crushed
2 tablespoons chopped fresh parsley
3 spring onions, sliced
3 tablespoons grated Parmesan cheese
salt
freshly ground black pepper
few radishes, sliced, to garnish

Place the pasta shells and boiling water in a bowl, stirring well. Cover and cook on FULL (100%) for 6 minutes, stirring once. Leave to STAND while cooking the fish.

Place the fish in a cooking dish with the cold

water. Cover and cook on FULL (100%) for **4** minutes, turning the fish once. Drain, remove any skin and bones and flake into bite-sized chunks.

Mix the pasta with the fish, shrimps and pepper, blending well. Leave to cool.

Meanwhile, place the oil, lemon juice, garlic, parsley, spring onions, Parmesan cheese and salt and pepper to taste in a blender or food processor and blend until thoroughly combined.

Pour the dressing over the pasta salad and toss to coat. Chill lightly before serving garnished with sliced radishes.

SERVES 4 to 6

PASTA SLAW

METRIC/IMPERIAL
100 g/4 oz dried wholewheat spaghetti rings
450 ml/¾ pint boiling water
salt
freshly ground black pepper
100 g/4 oz white cabbage, shredded
4 celery sticks, finely chopped
100 g/4 oz carrots, grated
1 onion, finely chopped
175 ml/6 fl oz low-fat natural yogurt

Place the spaghetti rings in a bowl with the boiling water and a pinch of salt. Cover and cook on FULL (100%) for 10 to 12 minutes, stirring once. Leave to STAND, covered, for 5 minutes, then cool under running water.

Mix the pasta with the cabbage, celery, carrots and onion, blending well. Mix the yogurt with salt and pepper to taste and pour over the salad. Toss well to mix. Chill lightly before serving.

SERVES 4

CRUNCHY PASTA SALAD WITH AVOCADO

METRIC/IMPERIAL
175 g/6 oz dried pasta spirals
1 litre/1¾ pints boiling water
1 tablespoon vegetable oil
salt
freshly ground black pepper
¼ teaspoon dry mustard
3 tablespoons olive oil
1 tablespoon wine vinegar
1 celery stick, finely chopped
1 carrot, finely grated

½ green pepper, cored, seeded and diced
½ red pepper, cored, seeded and diced
2 cloves garlic, crushed
1 teaspoon chopped fresh herbs of your choice
1 tablespoon toasted almonds
2 avocados, peeled, stoned and cut into pieces

Place the pasta, boiling water and vegetable oil in a large bowl. Cover and cook on FULL (100%) for 10 to 12 minutes.

Check during cooking to be sure that the pasta remains immersed in the water. Leave to STAND, covered, for 5 minutes, then drain. Rinse the pasta under cold running water. Drain thoroughly and set aside.

Place the salt, pepper and mustard in a mixing bowl. Add the olive oil and mix together. Whisk in the vinegar.

Add the celery, carrot, peppers, garlic, herbs and almonds. Toss in the pasta. Gently fold in the avocado pieces just before serving.

SERVES 4

CURRIED CHICKEN PASTA SALAD

METRIC/IMPERIAL
175 g/6 oz dried pasta shells
900 ml/1½ pints boiling water
1 tablespoon vegetable oil
salt
freshly ground black pepper
150 ml/¼ pint mayonnaise
2 tablespoons single cream
2 teaspoons mild curry powder
225 g/8 oz cooked chicken, skinned and chopped into bite-sized pieces
2 celery sticks, chopped
lettuce leaves, to serve

Place the pasta in a bowl with the boiling water, oil and a pinch of salt. Cover and cook on FULL (100%) for 12 to 14 minutes, stirring once. Leave to STAND for 5 to 10 minutes, until tender. Drain and cool under running water.

Meanwhile, mix the mayonnaise with the cream, curry powder and salt and pepper to taste, blending well.

Add the chicken, celery and the cool, drained pasta shells to the dressing and toss gently to coat.

Line a serving dish with lettuce leaves and top with the curried chicken pasta salad.

SERVES 4

PASTA SHELLS WITH AVOCADO DRESSING

METRIC/IMPERIAL
350 g/12 oz dried pasta shells
1.5 litres/2½ pints boiling water
1 teaspoon vegetable oil
salt
freshly ground black pepper
4 spring onions, chopped
2 tablespoons chopped fresh parsley
Dressing:
1 ripe avocado, halved and stoned
juice of 1 lemon
1 clove garlic, crushed
1 teaspoon caster sugar
150 ml/¼ pint single cream

Place the pasta, boiling water, oil and a pinch of salt in a bowl. Cover and cook on FULL (100%) for 12 minutes, stirring once. Leave to STAND for 5 minutes, then drain and allow to cool.

To make the dressing, scoop the avocado flesh out of the skins and place in a blender or food processor with the lemon juice, garlic, sugar and cream. Purée until smooth, then season to taste with salt and pepper.

Add the avocado dressing to the pasta shells with the spring onions and parsley. Toss well to mix. Serve lightly chilled.
SERVES 4

PASTA AND TUNA SALAD

METRIC/IMPERIAL
225 g/8 oz dried pasta bows or shells
900 ml/1½ pints boiling water
1 tablespoon vegetable oil
salt
1 × 200 g/7 oz can tuna in oil
1 green pepper, cored, seeded and chopped
4 celery sticks, chopped
100 g/4 oz black olives, stoned
Dressing:
2 tablespoons chive mustard
2 tablespoons white wine vinegar
2 tablespoons single cream
freshly ground black pepper
Garnish:
radish slices

Place the pasta in a deep dish with the water, oil and salt to taste. Cover and cook on FULL (100%) for 12 to 14 minutes. Leave to STAND

for 5 minutes. Drain well, rinse with cold water and drain again.

Drain the oil from the tuna and reserve. Flake the tuna into chunks and add to the pasta with the pepper, celery and olives, tossing well to mix.

Blend the reserved tuna oil with the chive mustard, vinegar, cream and salt and pepper to taste. Toss with the salad ingredients. Serve at once, garnished with a circle of radish slices.
SERVES 4

TAGLIATELLE WITH CHEESE AND NUTS

METRIC/IMPERIAL
25 g/1 oz butter
350 g/12 oz cream cheese
50 g/2 oz grated Parmesan cheese
100 g/4 oz walnuts, chopped
1 tablespoon chopped fresh parsley
450 g/1 lb dried tagliatelle
1.75 litres/3 pints boiling water
1 tablespoon vegetable oil
salt
freshly ground black pepper

Place the butter in a bowl and heat on FULL (100%) for ½ minute or until melted. Add the cream cheese, Parmesan cheese, walnuts and parsley. Cook on FULL (100%) for 1½ minutes, stirring once. Leave to STAND, covered, while cooking the tagliatelle.

Place the tagliatelle, boiling water and oil in a bowl. Cover and cook on FULL (100%) for 6 minutes. Leave to STAND, covered, for 3 minutes.

Drain the tagliatelle and place in a warmed serving dish. Reheat the cheese mixture on FULL (100%) for 1 minute, stirring once. Pour over the tagliatelle and toss well to coat. Season to taste with salt and pepper and serve at once.
SERVES 6

FLUFFY WHITE RICE

METRIC/IMPERIAL
225 g/8 oz easy-cook rice
½ teaspoon salt
15 g/½ oz butter
550 ml/18 fl oz boiling water

Put the rice, salt and butter in a large mixing bowl. Pour over the boiling water. Cover and cook on FULL (100%) for 3 minutes. Reduce the power setting to MEDIUM (50%) and cook for a further 12 minutes, stirring once. STAND, covered, for 15 minutes. Fluff up with a fork and serve.
SERVES 4

Note: Rice cooks beautifully in the microwave oven. It can be stored in the freezer and reheats well.

BROWN RICE

METRIC/IMPERIAL
225 g/8 oz brown rice
pinch of salt
550 ml/18 fl oz boiling water

Combine the rice, salt and water in a large bowl. Cover loosely and cook on FULL (100%) for 3 minutes. Reduce the power setting to MEDIUM (50%) and cook for a further 25 minutes, stirring twice. Leave to STAND, covered, for 5 minutes. Fluff the rice with a fork to serve.
SERVES 4

MONTANA RICE

METRIC/IMPERIAL
1 small onion, chopped
2 tablespoons vegetable oil
50 g/2 oz cooked pork, finely chopped
175 g/6 oz cooked rice
2 eggs, beaten
1½ tablespoons soy sauce
freshly ground black pepper

Combine the onion and the oil in a shallow dish and cook on FULL (100%) for 2 minutes until the onion is soft, stirring once during cooking. Add the pork and rice and mix thoroughly.

Beat the eggs and soy sauce together with a light sprinkling of pepper. Pour evenly over the rice mixture and cook on FULL (100%) for 3 to 4 minutes, until the egg has set and the mixture is thoroughly heated. Serve hot, either alone or accompanied by peas, French beans or other vegetables of your choice.
SERVES 1 to 2

Note: The cooking time for the dish will depend on the temperature of the rice. If freshly cooked, warm rice is used, the dish will cook more quickly than if cold leftover rice is used.

SAVOURY RICE RING

METRIC/IMPERIAL
100 g/4 oz butter
1 small onion, chopped
½ green pepper, cored, seeded and chopped
grated rind of 1 orange
225 g/8 oz long-grain rice
600 ml/1 pint boiling stock
225 g/8 oz pork fillet, sliced
1 onion, sliced
juice of ½ orange
2 tablespoons sherry
2 teaspoons cornflour
2 tablespoons water
orange slices, to garnish

Place half the butter in a bowl and heat on FULL (100%) for 1 minute or until melted. Add the chopped onion and pepper, blending well. Cover and cook on FULL (100%) for 2 minutes.

Add the orange rind, rice and boiling stock, blending well. Cover and cook on FULL (100%) for 3 minutes. Reduce the power setting to MEDIUM (50%) and cook for a further 12 minutes, stirring once. Leave to STAND for 5 minutes.

Spoon the rice into a large, greased, glass ring mould, pressing down well.

Meanwhile, place the remaining butter in a bowl and heat on FULL (100%) for 1 minute or until melted. Add the pork and onion. Cover and cook on FULL (100%) for 2 minutes. Add the orange juice and sherry, blending well.

Blend the cornflour with the water and stir into the pork mixture. Cover and cook on FULL (100%) for 1 minute, stirring once.

Reheat the rice mould by cooking on FULL (100%) for 2 to 4 minutes. Invert on to a warmed serving plate. Fill with the pork mixture and garnish with the orange slices.
SERVES 4

MUSHROOM BROWN RICE RISOTTO

METRIC/IMPERIAL
75 g/3 oz butter
1 onion, sliced
225 g/8 oz brown rice
150 ml/¼ pint dry white wine
600 ml/1 pint boiling vegetable stock
225 g/8 oz mushrooms, sliced
1½ teaspoons dried basil
salt
freshly ground black pepper
3 tablespoons grated Parmesan cheese

Place the butter, onion and rice in a large bowl. Cook on FULL (100%) for 5 minutes, stirring once.

Add the wine, boiling stock, mushrooms, basil and salt and pepper to taste. Cover and cook on FULL (100%) for 3 minutes. Reduce the power setting to MEDIUM (50%) and cook for a further 25 minutes, stirring twice. Leave to STAND, covered, for 5 minutes.

Sprinkle with the Parmesan cheese and serve while still hot.
SERVES 4

BRAISED BROWN RICE WITH GARLIC

METRIC/IMPERIAL
50 g/2 oz butter
1 large onion, finely chopped
2 cloves garlic, crushed
salt
freshly ground black pepper
400 g/14 oz brown rice
900 ml/1½ pints hot chicken stock
150 ml/¼ pint dry white wine
chopped fresh parsley, to garnish

Place the butter, onion, garlic and salt and pepper to taste in a large bowl. Cover and cook on FULL (100%) for 5 minutes, stirring halfway through cooking.

Stir in the rice, hot chicken stock and wine. Cover and cook on FULL (100%) for 3 minutes. Reduce the power to MEDIUM (50%) and cook for a further 25 minutes, stirring two to three times. Leave to STAND, covered, for 5 minutes. Sprinkle with chopped parsley and fluff to separate the rice before serving.
SERVES 4

CASSEROLED RICE WITH SPINACH

METRIC/IMPERIAL
50 g/2 oz butter
450 g/1 lb long-grain Italian rice
600 ml/1 pint boiling chicken stock
225 g/8 oz fresh spinach, trimmed
50 g/2 oz walnuts, coarsely chopped
salt
freshly ground black pepper

Place the butter in a casserole dish and heat on FULL (100%) for 1 minute or until melted. Add the rice and boiling stock, blending well. Cover and cook on FULL (100%) for 3 minutes. Reduce the power setting to MEDIUM (50%) and cook for a further 12 minutes, stirring twice. Leave to STAND, covered, for 10 minutes.

Meanwhile, place the spinach in a bowl with just the water clinging to the leaves. Cover and cook on FULL (100%) for 2 minutes or until just soft.

Drain the spinach and stir into the rice with the walnuts and salt and pepper to taste. Toss lightly with two forks to mix. Serve at once as a main meal accompaniment.
SERVES 4

TURKEY RISOTTO

METRIC/IMPERIAL
25 g/1 oz butter
1 large onion, sliced
175 g/6 oz long-grain rice
2 carrots, cut into thin strips
100 g/4 oz frozen peas
225 g/8 oz cooked turkey, skinned and chopped
3 tablespoons sage and onion mustard
350 ml/12 fl oz boiling chicken stock
salt
freshly ground black pepper

Place the butter in a large bowl with the onion. Cover and cook on FULL (100%) for 3 minutes, stirring once.

Add the rice, carrots, peas, turkey, mustard, boiling stock and salt and pepper to taste, blending well. Cover and cook on FULL (100%) for 20 minutes, stirring twice. Leave to STAND, covered, for 5 minutes.

Serve hot with a crisp green salad.
SERVES 4

RICE SALAD RING

METRIC/IMPERIAL
225 g/8 oz Fluffy White Rice (see page 224)
1 × 225 g/8 oz packet mixed frozen vegetables
salt
freshly ground black pepper

Prepare the rice according to the recipe. Immediately after STANDING time, place in a sieve and run under cold running water, turning the rice with a fork to separate and cool all the grains. Shake off as much water as possible and place the rice in a large mixing bowl.

Place the vegetables, in their packet, on a plate. Pierce the packet and cook on FULL (100%) for 4 minutes. Drain and rinse under cold running water, until cold.

Add the vegetables to the cooked and cooled rice. Toss to mix and add salt and pepper to taste. Press into a ring mould and refrigerate until required.
SERVES 6

Variation
Mixed rice salad: add 25 g/1 oz raisins, 3 slices of drained, chopped pineapple and 25 g/1 oz roughly chopped walnuts to the cooled rice mixture. Pile on to a bed of lettuce and top with 40 g/1½ oz peanuts to serve.

SAFFRON AND PAPRIKA RICE

METRIC/IMPERIAL
3 tablespoons dry white wine
¼ teaspoon ground cumin
¼ teaspoon saffron powder
175 g/6 oz long-grain rice
1 onion, finely chopped
1 small green pepper, cored, seeded and chopped
½ teaspoon salt
450 ml/¾ pint hot chicken stock
½ teaspoon paprika
few drops of red food colouring
2 teaspoons water

Combine the wine, cumin and saffron in a large deep dish. Cook on FULL (100%) for 2 minutes until boiling. Stir in the rice, onion, green pepper, salt and stock. Cover and cook on FULL (100%) for 3 minutes. Reduce the power to MEDIUM (50%) and cook for a further 12 minutes until the rice is tender and the stock has

been absorbed, stirring two or three times during cooking. Leave to STAND, covered, for 5 minutes.

Transfer 3 to 4 tablespoons of the rice mixture to a separate dish and mix in the paprika, food colouring and water. Continue stirring until all the rice grains are red. Return to the saffron rice mixture and fold in gently. Serve hot.
SERVES 3 to 4

PERSIAN RICE PILAFF

METRIC/IMPERIAL
225 g/8 oz long-grain rice
50 g/2 oz butter
50 g/2 oz hazelnuts, finely chopped
600 ml/1 pint hot chicken or beef stock
1 teaspoon salt
1 teaspoon powdered cardamom
½ teaspoon turmeric
25 g/1 oz sultanas

Rinse the rice and drain thoroughly. Put the butter in a large deep casserole and cook on FULL (100%) for 1 minute until melted. Stir in the rice. Cook on FULL (100%) for 3 minutes, stirring once during cooking. Add the hazelnuts and cook on FULL (100%) for 2 minutes.

Stir in the stock, salt, cardamom, turmeric and sultanas. Cover and cook on FULL (100%) for 3 minutes. Reduce the power to MEDIUM (50%) and cook for a further 12 minutes, stirring twice during cooking. Stir, then cover tightly and leave to STAND for 5 minutes before serving.
SERVES 4 to 6

Note: Serve as a curry accompaniment, or simply with a mixed salad, or sprinkled with chopped hard-boiled egg.

VEGETABLE AND HAM RISOTTO

METRIC/IMPERIAL
50 g/2 oz butter
1 large onion, finely chopped
¼ green pepper, cored, seeded and finely diced
¼ red pepper, cored, seeded and finely diced
1 tablespoon tomato purée
1 clove garlic, crushed
1 teaspoon dried mixed herbs
50 g/2 oz mushrooms, finely chopped
400 g/14 oz long-grain rice

750 ml/1¼ pints hot chicken stock
100 g/4 oz ham, finely chopped
¼ teaspoon vegetable oil
salt
freshly ground black pepper
1 tablespoon chopped fresh parsley, to garnish
Parmesan cheese, to serve

Place the butter, onion, peppers, tomato purée, garlic, herbs and mushrooms in a large bowl. Cover and cook on FULL (100%) for 8 minutes, stirring halfway through cooking.

Stir in the rice, stock, ham, oil, salt and pepper. Cover and cook on FULL (100%) for 3 minutes. Reduce the power setting to MEDIUM (50%) and cook for a further 12 minutes, stirring twice. Remove from the oven and leave to STAND, covered, for 8 minutes.

Stir the risotto with a fork and sprinkle with chopped parsley. Hand grated Parmesan cheese separately, and serve with a mixed green salad.
SERVES 4

FESTIVE CHICKEN WITH RICE

METRIC/IMPERIAL
4 chicken breasts, skinned
25 g/1 oz seasoned flour
75 g/3 oz butter
2 tablespoons vegetable oil
1 × 175 g/6 oz jar cranberry sauce
25 g/1 oz sugar
1 onion, sliced
grated rind and juice of 1 orange
½ teaspoon ground cinnamon
½ teaspoon ground ginger
225 g/8 oz long-grain rice
600 ml/1 pint boiling water
1 teaspoon salt

Preheat a large browning dish on FULL (100%) for 5 minutes (or according to the manufacturer's instructions). Dip the chicken in the seasoned flour to coat.

Add the butter and oil to the browning dish and swirl to coat. Add the chicken and cook on FULL (100%) for 2 minutes, turning over once. Set aside.

Place the cranberry sauce in a casserole dish. Cook on FULL (100%) for 1 to 2 minutes, stirring once, until hot, smooth and bubbly. Add the sugar, onion, orange rind and juice, cinnamon and ginger, blending well. Add the chicken

and toss well to coat in the sauce. Cover and cook on FULL (100%) for 10 minutes, stirring once. Leave to STAND while cooking the rice.

Place the rice, boiling water and salt in a bowl. Cover and cook on FULL (100%) for 3 minutes. Reduce the power setting to MEDIUM (50%) and cook for a further 12 minutes, stirring twice. Leave to STAND, covered, for 5 minutes.

Spoon the rice on to a warmed serving dish and top with the festive chicken.
SERVES 4

VEGETABLE AND CASHEW RICE

METRIC/IMPERIAL
50 g/2 oz butter
1 onion, chopped
1 clove garlic, crushed
225 g/8 oz brown rice
600 ml/1 pint boiling water
½ teaspoon ground turmeric
1 teaspoon sea salt
1 large carrot, cut into thin strips
225 g/8 oz French beans, cut into 5 cm/2 inch pieces
1 small red pepper, cored, seeded and chopped
3 tablespoons water
4 tomatoes, skinned and quartered
freshly ground black pepper
175 g/6 oz toasted cashew nuts

Place the butter in a large casserole and heat on FULL (100%) for 1 minute or until melted. Add the onion, garlic, rice, water, turmeric and salt, blending well. Cover and cook on FULL (100%) for 3 minutes. Reduce the power to MEDIUM (50%) and cook for a further 25 minutes or until tender. Leave to STAND for 5 minutes, then drain thoroughly, if necessary.

Meanwhile, place the carrot, beans and red pepper in a bowl with the cold water. Cover and cook on FULL (100%) for 4 to 5 minutes, until tender.

Drain the vegetables, then fold into the rice mixture with the tomatoes, pepper to taste and half the cashew nuts.

Cook on FULL (100%) for a further 2 to 3 minutes to reheat. Serve sprinkled with the remaining cashew nuts.
SERVES 4

HERBED RICE SALAD

METRIC/IMPERIAL
450 g/1 lb long-grain rice
900 ml/1½ pints boiling water
1 onion, thinly sliced
6 tablespoons chopped fresh herbs (basil, parsley and chives, for example)
6 tablespoons French dressing

Place the rice in a large bowl with the boiling water, stirring well. Cover and cook on FULL (100%) for 3 minutes. Reduce the power setting to MEDIUM (50%) and cook for a further 12 minutes, stirring once. Leave to STAND, covered, for 10 minutes.

Stir in the onion, herbs and dressing, blending well. Leave to cool, then chill until required.

Stir just before serving to blend.

SERVES 6 to 8

BROWN RICE SALAD

METRIC/IMPERIAL
900 ml/1½ pints boiling water
175 g/6 oz brown rice
salt
freshly ground black pepper
½ cucumber, chopped
4 spring onions, sliced
¼ green pepper, cored, seeded and chopped
¼ red pepper, cored, seeded and chopped
50 g/2 oz green olives
450 g/1 lb cooked meat or fish, chopped or flaked
Dressing:
2 tablespoons olive oil
1 tablespoon lemon juice
1 teaspoon chopped fresh parsley
pinch of garlic salt

Place the boiling water in a bowl with the rice and a pinch of salt. Cover and cook on FULL (100%) for 3 minutes. Reduce the power setting to MEDIUM (50%) and cook for a further 25 minutes, stirring twice, until tender. Leave to STAND, covered, for 5 to 10 minutes. Rinse under cold running water until cool, then drain thoroughly.

Place the rice in a bowl with the cucumber, spring onions, peppers, olives and meat or fish. Add salt and pepper to taste and mix well.

Beat the oil with the lemon juice, parsley and garlic salt. Stir into the salad just before serving.

SERVES 4 to 6

CHICKEN RISOTTO

METRIC/IMPERIAL
400 g/14 oz cooked chicken, cut into bite-sized pieces
225 g/8 oz long-grain rice
1 large onion, chopped
2 cloves garlic, crushed
50 g/2 oz butter
550 ml/18 fl oz boiling chicken stock
½ green pepper, cored, seeded and chopped
1 teaspoon dried mixed herbs
50 g/2 oz mushrooms, sliced
salt
freshly ground black pepper

Place the chicken, rice, onion, garlic and butter in a large bowl. Cook on FULL (100%) for 5 minutes, stirring once.

Add the boiling stock, pepper and herbs, blending well. Cover and cook on FULL (100%) for 3 minutes. Reduce the power setting to MEDIUM (50%) and cook for a further 12 minutes, stirring twice. Add the mushrooms and salt and pepper, blending well. Cover and leave to STAND for 5 minutes before serving.

SERVES 4

RICE WITH RAISINS AND ORANGE

METRIC/IMPERIAL
175 g/6 oz brown rice
2 onions, finely chopped
600 ml/1 pint hot chicken stock
pinch of salt
50 g/2 oz raisins
2 oranges

Rinse the rice in cold water, drain well and place in a large bowl with the onion. Stir in the hot stock, cover and cook on FULL (100%) for 3 minutes. Add a pinch of salt and stir in the raisins. Cover as before and cook on MEDIUM (50%) for a further 25 minutes. Stir and leave to STAND, covered, for 5 minutes.

Meanwhile, grate one of the oranges and reserve the rind. With a sharp knife, remove all the pith from both oranges and divide them into segments, discarding any pips.

On completion of the standing time, stir the orange segments into the rice with a fork, fluffing up the grains. Garnish with orange rind.

SERVES 4

EGG FRIED RICE

METRIC/IMPERIAL
2 tablespoons corn or sunflower oil
1 large onion, finely chopped
350 g/12 oz cold, cooked, long-grain rice
2 eggs
1 tablespoon soy sauce
salt
freshly ground black pepper
25 g/1 oz butter or margarine

Put the oil in a 2 litre/3½ pint bowl and stir in the onion. Cook on FULL (100%) for 5 minutes, stirring once, until the onion is soft.

Stir the cold rice into the onion mixture and cook on FULL (100%) for 5 minutes, stirring occasionally, until the mixture is hot.

Beat the eggs and soy sauce together. Stir into the hot rice and cook on FULL (100%) for 1 minute or until the egg is cooked, stirring once.

Sprinkle the rice mixture with salt and pepper to taste, then stir in the butter or margarine. Serve hot.

If the egg fried rice is to be reheated, add an extra 15 g/½ oz butter before serving.
SERVES 6

SAUSAGE RISOTTO

METRIC/IMPERIAL
450 g/1 lb pork sausages
100 g/4 oz streaky bacon, derinded and chopped
1 onion, chopped
2 celery sticks, thinly sliced
2 courgettes, cut into thin strips
350 g/12 oz long-grain rice
2 tablespoons tomato purée
600 ml/1 pint boiling chicken stock
½ teaspoon dried oregano
salt
freshly ground black pepper
1 tablespoon chopped fresh parsley

Place the sausages on a plate or microwave grill rack and prick thoroughly with a fork. Cook on FULL (100%) for 5 to 6 minutes, turning and rearranging the sausages once.

Place the bacon in a large bowl and cook on FULL (100%) for 3 minutes, stirring once. Add the onion and celery. Cover and cook on FULL (100%) for 4 minutes, stirring once.

Add the courgettes, rice, tomato purée, chicken stock, oregano and salt and pepper to taste, blending well. Cover and cook on FULL (100%) for a further 13 minutes, stirring twice. Leave to STAND for 10 minutes.

Meanwhile, cut the sausages into bite-sized pieces. Stir into the risotto mixture with the parsley. Serve at once.
SERVES 4

SPECKLED BROWN RICE WITH PINE NUTS

METRIC/IMPERIAL
40 g/1½ oz butter
1 onion, finely chopped
1 small red pepper, cored, seeded and finely chopped
1 clove garlic, crushed
175 g/6 oz brown rice
25 g/1 oz pine nuts
2 tomatoes, skinned and chopped
900 ml/1½ pints hot water
1–1½ teaspoons salt
½ teaspoon freshly ground black pepper

Put the butter in a 1.75 litre/3 pint casserole and heat on FULL (100%) for about 1 minute or until melted.

Stir in the onion, red pepper, garlic and rice and cook on FULL (100%) for 5 minutes, stirring once during cooking, until the rice grains are golden and the onions translucent.

Add the pine nuts, tomatoes, hot water, salt and pepper and stir well. Cover and cook on FULL (100%) for 35 minutes, stirring once during cooking.

Stir once at the end of the cooking period, cover immediately and leave to STAND for 10 minutes for the rice to absorb all the liquid fully. Fluff the rice with a fork before serving.
SERVES 6

PILAU RICE

METRIC/IMPERIAL
175 g/6 oz easy-cook long-grain rice
40 g/1½ oz butter
1 clove garlic, crushed (optional)
25 g/1 oz flaked almonds
450 ml/¾ pint nearly boiling water
¼ chicken stock cube, crumbled
pinch of ground ginger
½ teaspoon salt
¼ teaspoon ground cardamom

½ teaspoon ground turmeric
¼ teaspoon ground coriander
2 tablespoons sweetcorn kernels
2 tablespoons frozen peas
2 tablespoons sultanas

Rinse the rice in a sieve under hot running water and shake dry. Rest the sieve on a pad of absorbent kitchen paper to prevent dripping and absorb any residual liquid.

Put the butter in a 1.5 litre/2½ pint deep casserole or bowl and heat on FULL (100%) for 1 minute or until melted. Stir in the garlic, if using, add the rice and almonds and cook on FULL (100%) for 3 minutes, stirring once during cooking.

Add all the remaining ingredients, making sure that the stock cube is dissolved in the hot water. (Although the water can be boiled in the microwave, it is simpler and quicker to boil it in a kettle.) Stir thoroughly, then cook without covering on FULL (100%) for a further 12 minutes until the rice is tender and most of the liquid has been absorbed. Immediately cover and leave to STAND for 10 minutes before serving.
SERVES 4

CURRIED BLACK-EYED BEANS
METRIC/IMPERIAL
350 g/12 oz dried black-eyed beans, soaked overnight in cold water
1.5 litres/2½ pints cold chicken stock
25 g/1 oz butter
2 carrots, cut into thin strips
1 onion, finely chopped
1 celery stick, finely chopped
2–3 teaspoons curry powder
2 tablespoons plain flour
4 tablespoons tomato purée
300 ml/½ pint beef stock
2 tablespoons Worcestershire sauce
50 g/2 oz sultanas
salt
freshly ground black pepper

Place the drained beans in a large casserole with the cold chicken stock. Cover and cook on FULL (100%) for 10 minutes.

Stir, re-cover and cook on MEDIUM (50%) for 10 to 15 minutes until tender, stirring occasionally. Drain thoroughly.

Place the butter in a bowl and heat on FULL

(100%) for ½ minute or until melted. Add the carrots, onion and celery, blending well. Cover and cook on FULL (100%) for 4 minutes, stirring once.

Stir in the curry powder and cook on FULL (100%) for 1 minute. Blend in the flour. Gradually add the tomato purée, beef stock, Worcestershire sauce, sultanas, salt and pepper to taste. Cook on FULL (100%) for 5 to 7 minutes, stirring every 2 minutes until thickened.

Stir in the beans. Cook on FULL (100%) for 1 to 2 minutes. Serve with an Indian meal.
SERVES 4

DHAL
METRIC/IMPERIAL
150 g/5 oz dried lentils
2 tablespoons vegetable oil
1 small onion, chopped
1 clove garlic, crushed
1 teaspoon curry powder
¼ teaspoon ground ginger
¼ teaspoon chilli powder
1 teaspoon salt
1 litre/1¾ pints boiling water

Rinse and drain the lentils. Combine the oil, onion, garlic, curry powder, ginger and chilli powder in a large deep dish and cook on FULL (100%) for 4 minutes, until the onions are lightly browned.

Stir in the lentils, salt and boiling water. Cover and cook on FULL (100%) for 20 to 25 minutes until the lentils are tender, stirring two or three times during cooking.

Using a potato masher, mash the lentils thoroughly to form a thick purée. Continue cooking on FULL (100%) for a further 3 to 5 minutes if the lentils are not soft enough to mash. Serve as a curry accompaniment or vegetable.
SERVES 4

CHICKPEA CURRY
METRIC/IMPERIAL
1 large onion, finely chopped
1 carrot, thinly sliced
1 clove garlic, crushed
1 teaspoon ground coriander
½ teaspoon turmeric
½ teaspoon chilli powder
1 teaspoon garam masala or curry powder

600 ml/1 pint hot chicken or vegetable stock
175 g/6 oz chickpeas, covered in boiling water
and soaked overnight
1 tablespoon tomato purée
½ small green pepper, seeded and thinly sliced
2 tablespoons raisins or sultanas
pinch of salt
fresh coriander leaves, to garnish (optional)

Place the onion, carrot and garlic in a large bowl. Add the spices, stir in 4 tablespoons of the hot stock and cook on FULL (100%) for 4 minutes, stirring halfway through the cooking time.

Drain the chickpeas and stir into the bowl with the remainder of the hot stock and the tomato purée.

Cover and cook on FULL (100%) for 34 to 35 minutes, stirring several times during cooking.

Stir in the raisins or sultanas and season with salt. Cover as before and cook on FULL (100%) for a further 6½ minutes, stirring two or three times during cooking. Leave to STAND, covered, for 10 minutes before serving. Garnish with fresh coriander leaves, if using.
SERVES 4

Serving suggestions
Made with vegetable stock, this is an ideal vegetarian main meal dish. Serve it with brown rice, wholemeal bread or poppadoms. It could also be served as an accompaniment to a meat or fish curry.

Variation
For a quick curry, use 1 × 425 g/15 oz can of chickpeas, drained. Reduce the stock to 250 ml/8 fl oz. Follow the method above but change all the cooking times to 4 minutes and STAND for 6 minutes.

LENTIL AND TOFU LOAF

METRIC/IMPERIAL
200 g/7 oz red lentils
600 ml/1 pint very hot water
100 g/4 oz Cheddar cheese, grated
1 onion, finely chopped
1 tablespoon chopped fresh parsley
1 tablespoon Worcestershire sauce
¼ teaspoon chilli powder
freshly ground black pepper
1 egg, lightly beaten
150 g/5 oz tofu, chopped

Rinse the lentils in cold water and drain. Place in a large bowl with the hot water. Cover and cook on FULL (100%) for 8¾ minutes or until the lentils have formed a stiff purée.

Stir in the cheese, onion, parsley, Worcestershire sauce and chilli. Season with plenty of black pepper. Beat the egg and tofu together until smooth, and stir into the lentil mixture.

Lightly oil a 450 g/1 lb loaf dish and spoon in the lentil mixture. Cover loosely with grease-proof paper and cook for 12½ minutes on FULL (100%), turning the dish twice during cooking. Leave to STAND for 10 minutes before turning it out on to a serving dish.

Serve the loaf in slices, either hot with a tomato sauce or cold with a mixed green salad or tomato and fresh basil salad.
SERVES 4 to 6

GREEN LENTIL CASSEROLE

METRIC/IMPERIAL
275 g/10 oz green lentils
900 ml/1½ pints hot water
1 onion, finely chopped
3 bacon rashers, rind and fat removed, and chopped
2 carrots, thinly sliced
2 small celery sticks, thinly sliced
900 ml/1½ pints hot vegetable stock
1 leek, thinly sliced
2 tablespoons wholemeal flour
freshly ground black pepper

Rinse the lentils in cold water and drain. Place them in a large bowl or casserole, stir in the hot water, cover and cook on FULL (100%) for 7½ minutes, stirring two or three times during cooking. Drain the lentils.

Place the onion, bacon, carrots and celery in a large bowl with 4 tablespoons of the stock, cover and cook on FULL (100%) for 6 minutes, stirring after 3 minutes. Add the leek, cover and cook on FULL (100%) for 1½ minutes.

Blend the flour with 6 tablespoons of the stock and stir into the vegetables. Gradually stir in the remaining stock and lentils. Season, recover and cook on FULL (100%) for 9 minutes, stirring several times. Allow to STAND for 10 minutes.
SERVES 4 to 6

DESSERTS AND CONFECTIONERY

STEWED PLUMS

METRIC/IMPERIAL
675 g/1½ lb firm dessert plums
75–100 g/3–4 oz demerara sugar
¼ teaspoon almond essence

Combine the plums and sugar in a large deep dish. Cover loosely and cook on FULL (100%) for 3 minutes.

Add the almond essence and stir well. Cover and cook on FULL (100%) for 3 to 4 minutes until the plums are soft. Leave to STAND, covered, for 3 minutes before serving.
SERVES 4

CARAMELIZED ORANGES

METRIC/IMPERIAL
4 large oranges
25 g/1 oz unsalted butter
50 g/2 oz demerara sugar
1 tablespoon chopped fresh mint
20 cloves
mint sprigs, to decorate
Syrup:
100 g/4 oz sugar
4 tablespoons water

Grate the rind from the oranges and set aside. Remove all of the pith with a sharp knife and cut each orange horizontally into 4 or 5 slices.

Blend the butter, half of the sugar and chopped mint together. Spread a little of the mixture over each orange slice, then reassemble the slices to form whole oranges. Spread the rest of the mixture over the outside of the oranges and sprinkle with the remaining sugar and grated orange rind. Insert a wooden cocktail stick through the centre of each orange to secure. Press 5 or 6 cloves into each orange.

To prepare the syrup, spread the sugar in a large shallow dish and sprinkle with the water. Cook on FULL (100%) for 1 minute until dissolved. Stir, then cook on FULL (100%) for 1 minute until a thick syrup is formed.

Place the oranges in the syrup and cook on FULL (100%) for 1 minute. Baste the oranges with the syrup and give the dish a half-turn. Cook on FULL (100%) for 3 minutes. Baste again. Leave until cold to allow the oranges to fully absorb the flavours of the spices.

To reheat for serving, cook on FULL (100%) for 2 to 3 minutes. Decorate with sprigs of mint.
SERVES 4

GOLDEN BAKED APPLES

METRIC/IMPERIAL
4 large Bramley apples
4 teaspoons mincemeat
½ teaspoon mixed spice
4 tablespoons golden syrup or thin honey
4 tablespoons pure orange juice
glacé cherries or a few toasted almonds, to decorate (optional)

Core the apples and then use a small piece of each core to fill the base of each apple. Score a cut around the middle of each apple to prevent bursting.

Mix the mincemeat with the spice and use to fill each apple cavity. Place the apples in a shallow dish and pour 1 tablespoon of syrup or honey over each one.

Pour the orange juice around the apples; cover and cook on FULL (100%) for 9 to 10 minutes. Leave to STAND for 3 minutes.

Spoon the orange juice over the apples. Decorate with glacé cherries or a few toasted almonds, if liked, and serve with vanilla ice cream.
SERVES 4

APPLE CRUNCH WITH YOGURT TOPPING

METRIC/IMPERIAL
675 g/1½ lb cooking apples, peeled, cored and thinly sliced
175 g/6 oz soft, dark brown sugar
125 g/4½ oz digestive wheatmeal biscuits
75 g/3 oz butter or margarine
150 ml/¼ pint natural yogurt
1 teaspoon cornflour
demerara sugar, to decorate

Place the apples in a 900 ml/1½ pint pie dish. Cook on FULL (100%) for 3 minutes until the apples soften.

While the apples are cooking, put the sugar in a bowl, add the biscuits and coarsely crush with the head of a rolling pin. Spread the mixture on top of the apples.

Put the butter or margarine in the bowl and heat on FULL (100%) for ½ to ¾ minute until melted. Pour evenly over the biscuit mixture. Cook on FULL (100%) for 3 minutes, then give the dish a quarter-turn and cook on FULL (100%) for a further 3 minutes. Leave to STAND while preparing the topping.

To make the topping, mix the yogurt and cornflour in a small bowl and stir until well blended. Reduce the setting to LOW (30%) and cook for 8 to 9 minutes, stirring frequently, until the mixture thickens to the consistency of half-whipped cream.

Pour the yogurt topping over the apple pudding, sprinkle over the demerara sugar and serve hot or cold.
SERVES 6

PINEAPPLE DELIGHTS

METRIC/IMPERIAL
4 pineapple rings
175 g/6 oz fresh raspberries
3 large egg whites (size 1 or 2)
175 g/6 oz caster sugar
50 g/2 oz ground almonds

Put one pineapple ring in each of 4 fairly deep ovenproof or heatproof sundae dishes. Divide the raspberries equally between the dishes.

To make the meringue, place the egg whites in a large grease-free bowl and beat them until they are very stiff. Beat in the sugar, 1 tablespoon at a time, and continue beating until all the sugar has been incorporated. The mixture will be very thick and glossy. Using a metal spoon, fold in the ground almonds.

Stand each sundae dish on a small plate and divide the meringue mixture between them. Cook all four together on FULL (100%) for 3 minutes, rearranging once. Serve at once.
SERVES 4

Note: For a crisp brown top, finish this dessert by cooking under a preheated very hot grill for a few seconds.

PEACHES AND CURAÇAO

METRIC/IMPERIAL
2 fresh peaches, skinned, stoned and sliced
1 tablespoon Curaçao liqueur

Place the peach slices in a serving dish. Cover and cook on FULL (100%) for 1 minute.

Add the Curaçao, blending well. Serve at once while the peaches are still hot.
SERVES 1

SUNFLOWER BAKED APPLES

METRIC/IMPERIAL
4 cooking apples (about 275 g/10 oz each)
Stuffing:
4 tablespoons sultanas
2 tablespoons unsweetened apple juice
1 teaspoon ground cinnamon
1 tablespoon clear honey
50 g/2 oz shelled walnuts, finely chopped
25 g/1 oz sunflower seeds

First make the stuffing. Place the sultanas and apple juice in a small bowl and cook on FULL (100%) for 1 minute. Stir in the cinnamon, honey, walnuts and sunflower seeds and leave to STAND while preparing the apples.

Core, but do not peel, the apples. With the point of a sharp knife, score the skin around the middle of each fruit. Arrange the apples in a circle in a shallow baking dish. Spoon the stuffing into the cavities and cook on FULL (100%) for 5 minutes. Give the dish a half-turn and cook on FULL (100%) for a further 4 to 5 minutes or until the apples are just tender. Leave to STAND for 5 minutes.
SERVES 4

BUTTERSCOTCH BANANAS

METRIC/IMPERIAL
15 g/½ oz butter
25 g/1 oz soft brown sugar
1 tablespoon golden syrup
300 ml/½ pint milk
3 teaspoons cornflour
3 medium bananas
juice of half a lemon (optional)
40 g/1½ oz walnuts, roughly chopped, or
40 g/1½ oz grated chocolate, to decorate

To make the sauce, put the butter, sugar and syrup into an ovenproof glass jug, and cook on FULL (100%) for 2½ minutes, stirring once.

Stir in the milk, reserving 1 tablespoonful. Cook on FULL (100%) for 2½ minutes.

Cream the cornflour with the remaining milk. Pour the heated liquid on to the mixed cornflour and beat well. Cook on FULL (100%) for 1 minute or until boiling. Beat well until smooth.

Slice the bananas, arrange them in a dish and sprinkle with lemon juice, if using. Pour the sauce over to coat and cook on FULL (100%) for 1½ minutes. Serve immediately, sprinkled with nuts or chocolate.
SERVES 4

Note: When the cold milk is added the caramel will harden, but as the milk warms it will melt again and blend into the sauce to give the butterscotch flavour.

SHERRIED ALMOND PEARS

METRIC/IMPERIAL
2 large ripe pears, halved, peeled and cored
50 g/2 oz butter
25 g/1 oz soft brown sugar
50 g/2 oz ground almonds (for economy use half cake crumbs, half ground almonds)
2 drops of almond essence
1 tablespoon sherry
120 ml/4 fl oz white wine or pure orange juice
2 glacé cherries, halved
whipped cream, to decorate

Arrange the pear halves, hollow sides uppermost, in a shallow serving dish.

Place the butter in a large jug and cook on DEFROST (20%) for 2 minutes. Beat in the

sugar, ground almonds, almond essence and sherry, a little at a time. Use to fill the four pear hollows.

Pour the wine or orange juice around the pears. Cover and cook on FULL (100%) for 2 to 3 minutes. (The length of time will depend on the size and ripeness of the pear halves.)

Spoon the wine or juice over the pears. Serve hot or cold, decorated with half a cherry and whipped cream.
SERVES 2 to 4

JAMAICAN BANANA, PINEAPPLE AND FIGS

METRIC/IMPERIAL
1 × 150 g/5 oz banana, thickly sliced
1 × 50 g/2 oz slice fresh pineapple, chopped
15 g/½ oz dried figs, chopped
7 g/¼ oz low-fat spread
¼ teaspoon mixed spice
1 tablespoon dark rum

Place the banana, pineapple and figs in a small serving dish. Dot with the spread, sprinkle with the spice and pour over the rum.

Cover and cook on FULL (100%) for 1½ minutes. Serve at once.
SERVES 1

APRICOT COMPOTE

METRIC/IMPERIAL
250 g/9 oz dried apricots
600 ml/1 pint boiling water
1 slice fresh lemon
75 g/3 oz caster sugar
25 g/1 oz raisins
50 g/2 oz flaked almonds, toasted (optional)
whipped cream, to decorate

Place the apricots in a mixing bowl and pour over the boiling water. Add the lemon and sugar and stir well.

Cover and cook on FULL (100%) for 12 minutes, stirring once after 6 minutes. Stir in the raisins, then allow to cool completely. If possible, chill overnight.

Sprinkle with toasted almonds, if using, and serve with whipped cream.
SERVES 4

HOT FRUIT COMPOTE

METRIC/IMPERIAL
450 g/1 lb mixed dried fruits (pineapple, pears,
peaches, for example)
250 ml/8 fl oz cold tea
200 ml/7 fl oz water
4 tablespoons clear honey
juice of ½ lemon
1 cinnamon stick
3–4 cloves
2 tablespoons brandy or Madeira

Mix the fruit with the tea, water, honey, lemon
juice, cinnamon and cloves in a large deep dish.
Leave to STAND for 2 hours.
Cover loosely with greaseproof paper and
cook on FULL (100%) for 12 to 14 minutes, or
until the fruit is tender, stirring twice.
Remove and discard the cinnamon stick and
cloves. Stir in the brandy or Madeira, blending
well.
Serve hot or chilled with yogurt, soured
cream, whipped cream or ice cream.
SERVES 4

CRUNCHY FRUIT MUESLI

METRIC/IMPERIAL
1 tablespoon safflower oil
2 tablespoons clear honey
100 g/4 oz rolled oats
2 tablespoons wheatgerm
2 teaspoons bran
25 g/1 oz flaked almonds
25 g/1 oz hazelnuts, chopped
25 g/1 oz dried pears, chopped
25 g/1 oz dried apricots, chopped
25 g/1 oz raisins
natural yogurt, to serve

Place the oil and honey in a large bowl and cook
on FULL (100%) for ½ minute. Add the oats,
wheatgerm, bran and almonds, blending well.
Spread on to a large plate or microwave
baking tray and cook on FULL (100%) for 3
minutes, stirring every ½ minute so that the
muesli browns evenly.
Add the hazelnuts, pears, apricots and raisins,
blending well. Cover and leave to STAND for 1
minute.
Serve while still warm with natural yogurt.
SERVES 6 to 8

POIRES BELLE HÉLÈNE

METRIC/IMPERIAL
4 dessert pears (total weight 450 g/1 lb), peeled,
with stalks left on
Sauce:
100 g/4 oz plain chocolate
3 tablespoons golden syrup
2 tablespoons double cream
1 tablespoon sherry
1–2 tablespoons single cream or milk (optional)

Stand the pears on a plate and cook on FULL
(100%) for 5 minutes or until tender, rearranging
once. Set aside to cool.
Break the chocolate into pieces and place in a
small jug. Cook on MEDIUM (50%) for 2½ to
3 minutes or until it is soft and melted, stirring
twice. Stir well until smooth, then stir in the
golden syrup, the double cream and the sherry.
Set aside until cool.
Transfer the pears to a serving dish and spoon
the chocolate sauce over them just before serving. Should the sauce require thinning, stir in 1
to 2 tablespoons of single cream or milk.
SERVES 4

ORANGE SEMOLINA

METRIC/IMPERIAL
600 ml/1 pint milk
75 g/3 oz semolina
25 g/1 oz caster sugar
1 egg, lightly beaten
grated rind of 1 large orange
2 tablespoons double cream
2 oranges, peeled, cut into small pieces and pips
removed
orange rind, shredded with a zester, to decorate

Place the milk in a very large bowl. Cook on
FULL (100%) for 5 minutes or until boiling.
Whisk in the semolina and sugar. Partially
cover and cook on FULL (100%) for 4½ minutes, whisking halfway through cooking. Check
frequently to ensure the mixture does not boil
over.
Beat in the egg and orange rind, then the
cream. Divide the orange pieces between 4
dessert glasses and pour over the semolina mixture. Refrigerate to chill.
Serve decorated with shredded orange rind.
SERVES 4

FRUIT CONDÉ

METRIC/IMPERIAL
50 g/2 oz pudding or round-grain rice
600 ml/1 pint skimmed milk
25 g/1 oz sugar
450 g/1 lb fresh fruit (kiwi, mandarins, grapes,
bananas and apples, for example), peeled and
segmented

Place the rice and milk in a large deep dish. Cover and cook on FULL (100%) for 10 minutes, stirring once.

Stir in the sugar, blending well. Cover and cook on DEFROST (20%) for 20 minutes, stirring four times. Leave to STAND, covered, for 5 minutes.

Spoon the rice into 4 sundae glasses in alternate layers with the mixed fruit. Finish with a decoration of fruit. Serve warm or cold.
SERVES 4

POACHED FRUITS WITH CRUNCHY TOPPING

METRIC/IMPERIAL
Plums:
300 ml/½ pint sweet red vermouth
2 tablespoons sugar
675 g/1½ lb plums
Apricots:
300 ml/½ pint water
100 g/4 oz sugar
1 teaspoon almond essence
675 g/1½ lb apricots
Crunchy topping:
about 100 g/4 oz cake crumbs
4 tablespoons sugar
50 g/2 oz flaked almonds
Zabaglione sauce:
4 egg yolks
50 g/2 oz caster sugar
100 ml/4 fl oz sweet white wine, sherry or
Marsala
150 ml/¼ pint whipping cream, lightly whipped

To prepare the plums, place the vermouth and sugar in a bowl. Cook on FULL (100%) for 8 minutes. Add the plums, blending well. Cover and cook on FULL (100%) for 10 minutes, stirring once. Leave to cool, then chill slightly.

To prepare the apricots, place the water, sugar and almond essence in a bowl. Cook on FULL (100%) for 8 minutes. Add the apricots, blending

well. Cover and cook on FULL (100%) for 10 minutes, stirring once. Leave to cool, then chill lightly.

To make the topping, place the cake crumbs, sugar and almonds on a flat dish and stir together to mix. Cook on FULL (100%) for 6 minutes, stirring every 1 minute, until brown and crisp. Leave to cool, then sprinkle over the poached fruits.

To make the sauce, whisk the egg yolks and sugar until pale and creamy. Whisk in the wine, blending well. Cook on FULL (100%) for 2 to 3 minutes, whisking every 1 minute until thickened. Remove from the oven and continue to whisk for 3 to 4 minutes, until very thick and creamy. Gradually whisk in the cream, then chill lightly.

Serve the poached fruits with their crispy topping, and hand the sauce separately.
SERVES 6 to 8

RICE PUDDING

METRIC/IMPERIAL
50 g/2 oz long-grain rice
600 ml/1 pint milk
25 g/1 oz sugar
25 g/1 oz butter, flaked
2 tablespoons single cream or 'top of the milk'
a little grated nutmeg

Put the rice, milk and sugar in a mixing bowl and stir well. Put the butter on the top. Cover and cook on FULL (100%) for 4 minutes, then stir.

Cook on MEDIUM (50%) for 20 to 25 minutes, stirring once. Leave to STAND for 5 minutes, then stir in the cream and sprinkle with nutmeg.
SERVES 3 to 4

PLUMS WITH PORT

METRIC/IMPERIAL
1 kg/2 lb dessert plums, halved and stoned
75–100 g/3–4 oz brown sugar
100 ml/4 fl oz port wine

Place the plums in a cooking dish. Sprinkle over the sugar and pour over the port wine.

Cover and cook on FULL (100%) for 7 to 8 minutes, stirring twice, until tender.

Serve warm or lightly chilled with whipped cream.
SERVES 4

COMPOTE OF MIXED DRIED FRUIT

METRIC/IMPERIAL
100 g/4 oz dried apricots
100 g/4 oz dried prunes
100 g/4 oz dried figs
about 450 ml/¾ pint cold water
1 tablespoon lemon juice
4 tablespoons orange juice
100 g/4 oz dried apple rings
75–100 g/3–4 oz brown sugar
natural yogurt or soured cream, to serve
(optional)

Combine the apricots, prunes and figs in a large deep dish. Add sufficient water to cover, then stir in the lemon and orange juice. Cover with a lid and leave to stand for 2 hours.

Mix in the apple rings and brown sugar. Cover loosely and cook on FULL (100%) for 12 minutes until the figs are tender, giving the dish a shake occasionally during cooking.

Serve either hot or chilled, topped with a spoonful of yogurt, or soured cream, if preferred.
SERVES 6

RUBY PEARS

METRIC/IMPERIAL
150 g/5 oz sugar
150 ml/¼ pint water
4 ripe dessert pears, peeled but stalks left on
grated rind and juice of 1 lemon
4 cloves
red food colouring

Place the sugar and water in a deep cooking dish. Cook on FULL (100%) for 4 minutes, stirring twice.

Add the pears, lemon rind, lemon juice and cloves. Cook on FULL (100%) for 5 minutes, turning the dish once.

Using a slotted spoon, carefully remove the pears and set aside. Add sufficient red food colouring to the syrup to produce a bright pink colour.

Return the pears to the syrup and turn in the syrup until an even colour is achieved. Serve hot or cold with cream.
SERVES 4

ORANGE AND APPLE FOOL

METRIC/IMPERIAL
1 apple, peeled, cored and sliced
grated rind and juice of 1 small orange
sugar or artificial sweetener to taste
1 egg white
1 teaspoon natural yogurt
½ teaspoon soft brown sugar

Place the apple, orange rind and juice in a bowl. Cover and cook on FULL (100%) for 3 minutes.

Allow to cool, then purée in a blender or food processor. Sweeten to taste with sugar or artificial sweetener.

Whisk the egg white until it stands in stiff peaks. Using a metal spoon, fold into the apple mixture. Spoon into a serving dish and chill thoroughly.

Just before serving, top with the yogurt and sprinkle with the brown sugar.
SERVES 1

SEMOLINA PUDDING

METRIC/IMPERIAL
1 rounded tablespoon custard powder
25 g/1 oz semolina
50 g/2 oz caster sugar
2 eggs, separated
600 ml/1 pint milk

Mix the custard powder with the semolina, caster sugar, egg yolks and milk in a cooking dish. Cook on FULL (100%) for 8 minutes, stirring twice.

Reduce the setting and cook on LOW (30%) for 8 to 10 minutes, stirring twice.

Whisk the egg whites until they stand in stiff peaks. Using a metal spoon, fold into the hot semolina pudding.

Serve hot or cold with stewed or fresh fruit.
SERVES 4

APPLE FOOL

METRIC/IMPERIAL
1 kg/2 lb cooking apples, peeled, cored and sliced
100 g/4 oz sugar
300 ml/½ pint double cream
green food colouring

Mix the apples with the sugar in a cooking dish. Cover and cook on FULL (100%) for 13 minutes, stirring twice.

Allow to cool, then purée in a blender or food processor until smooth.

Whip the cream until it stands in soft peaks. Using a metal spoon, fold into the apple mixture.

Divide the mixture in half and colour one half with green food colouring. Layer the plain and coloured apple fool in 4 dessert glasses. Chill slightly before serving with crisp dessert biscuits.
SERVES 5 to 6

BANANAS RIO

METRIC/IMPERIAL
4 ripe bananas, peeled
6 tablespoons orange juice
2 tablespoons lemon juice
4 tablespoons brown sugar
pinch of salt
25 g/1 oz butter
2 tablespoons desiccated coconut
whipped cream, to serve

Place the bananas in a greased shallow serving dish. Mix the orange juice with the lemon juice, sugar and salt, blending well. Spoon over the bananas.

Dot with the butter and cover loosely with greaseproof paper. Cook on FULL (100%) for 4 to 4½ minutes, turning the dish once.

Serve hot or warm, sprinkled with the coconut and topped with whipped cream.
SERVES 4

BAKED BANANAS WITH MARMALADE SAUCE

METRIC/IMPERIAL
1 teaspoon lemon juice
4 tablespoons cold water
½ teaspoon cornflour
6 tablespoons orange marmalade
25 g/1 oz unsalted butter
4 firm bananas, peeled

Combine the lemon juice, water and cornflour in a large shallow dish and cook on FULL (100%) for 1 minute, stirring twice. Stir in the orange marmalade and cook on FULL (100%) for 2 to 3

minutes, until the mixture boils, stirring twice. Stir in the butter to melt.

Place the bananas in the dish and spoon the sauce over them. Cook on FULL (100%) for 1 to 2 minutes, moving the outside bananas to the centre after ¾ minute.
SERVES 4

FRESH APPLE AND ORANGE COMPOTE

METRIC/IMPERIAL
2 dessert apples, peeled, cored and cut into rings
1 tablespoon lemon juice
2 oranges
4 tablespoons thick honey
2 tablespoons wheatgerm

Arrange the apples in a large shallow dish and sprinkle with lemon juice. Grate the orange rind over the apples.

Peel the oranges, removing all pith, and slice the flesh, removing the pips. Place the oranges on top of the apples and add the honey and wheatgerm.

Cover and cook on FULL (100%) for 2 minutes, until the honey has melted, giving the dish a half-turn after 1 minute. Serve hot or chilled.
SERVES 4

HUNGARIAN WITCHES FROTH

METRIC/IMPERIAL
6 cooking apples, peeled, cored and sliced
150 ml/¼ pint lemon juice
225 g/8 oz caster sugar
1½ tablespoons brandy
3 egg whites
25 g/1 oz walnuts, chopped

Place the apples in a cooking dish with the lemon juice. Cover and cook on FULL (100%) for 10 to 12 minutes, until cooked and soft.

Stir in the sugar, blending well to dissolve. Place in a blender or food processor and blend until smooth. Add the brandy and chill.

Whisk the egg whites until they stand in stiff peaks. Using a metal spoon, fold into the apple purée. Spoon into individual glass dishes and sprinkle with chopped walnuts. Serve chilled.
SERVES 6

RICH CHOCOLATE MOUSSE

METRIC/IMPERIAL
225 g/8 oz milk or plain chocolate
4 large eggs (size 1 or 2), separated
Decoration:
whipped cream
toasted almonds (see note)

Break the chocolate into pieces and place in a mixing bowl. Cook on MEDIUM (50%) for 3½ to 4 minutes, until the chocolate has melted, stirring twice. Allow to cool slightly, then beat in the egg yolks, one at a time.

Whisk the egg whites until they stand in soft peaks. Using a metal spoon, fold into the chocolate mixture.

Divide the mixture between 4 sundae dishes and refrigerate until set (about 1 hour). Decorate with whipped cream and toasted nuts.
SERVES 4

Note: To toast nuts, place a double thickness of absorbent kitchen paper on a plate and arrange about 25 g/1 oz flaked almonds in a ring around the edge. Cook on FULL (100%) for 1 minute. Rearrange the nuts and cook on FULL (100%) for 1 minute. Cool completely before using.

APRICOT CHIFFON

METRIC/IMPERIAL
1 × 135 g/4¼ oz packet lemon jelly
100 ml/4 fl oz water
2 × 220 g/7¾ oz cans apricots in water or low-calorie syrup
300 ml/½ pint low-fat natural yogurt

Place the jelly in a jug with the water. Cook on FULL (100%) for 2 to 3 minutes until the jelly has dissolved.

Drain the water or syrup from the apricots and add to the jelly to make up to 300 ml/½ pint. Chill until just beginning to set.

Reserve 5 apricot halves and chop the remainder into quarters.

Whisk the setting jelly until foamy, then whisk in the yogurt. Fold in the chopped apricots and turn into a 450 g/1 lb loaf tin. Chill until set.

To serve, dip the loaf tin briefly into hot water, then invert on to a serving dish. Decorate with the reserved apricot halves.
SERVES 4

ORANGE CREAMS

METRIC/IMPERIAL
4 large firm oranges
300–450 ml/½–¾ pint milk
25 g/1 oz cornflour
50 g/2 oz sugar
50 g/2 oz chocolate chips
25 g/1 oz sweet biscuits, crushed

Cut the oranges in half and carefully scoop out the flesh, without breaking the skins. Press the flesh through a strainer to squeeze out the juice. Make the juice up to 600 ml/1 pint with milk. Scrape away the pith from the orange shells and set them aside.

In a large bowl, blend the cornflour and sugar with a little of the milk. Add the orange milk and stir well. Cook on FULL (100%) for 4 to 5 minutes until the mixture is smooth and thick, beating every 1 minute.

Leave to cool for 10 minutes, then stir in the chocolate chips. Spoon into the reserved orange shells and sprinkle with the biscuit crumbs.
SERVES 4 to 6

EASY CHOCOLATE MOUSSE

METRIC/IMPERIAL
150 ml/¼ pint water
50 g/2 oz caster sugar
1 tablespoon cocoa powder
½ teaspoon vanilla essence
3 teaspoons powdered gelatine
2 egg whites
200 ml/7 fl oz evaporated milk, chilled
Decoration:
whipped cream
flaked chocolate

Place the water in a jug and cook on FULL (100%) for 1½ minutes. Stir in the sugar, cocoa powder and vanilla essence, beating well. Stir in the gelatine until dissolved. Set aside.

Whisk the egg whites until they stand in stiff peaks. Whisk the evaporated milk until thick and creamy. Beat the evaporated milk into the gelatine mixture. Using a metal spoon, fold in the egg whites, blending well.

Pour into a 900 ml/1½ pint soufflé dish and chill until set. Serve decorated with whipped cream and flaked chocolate.
SERVES 6

CRÈME BRÛLÉE

METRIC/IMPERIAL
300 ml/½ pint double cream
300 ml/½ pint milk
1 tablespoon granulated sugar
1 tablespoon vanilla essence
4 egg yolks, beaten
4 tablespoons brown sugar

Combine the cream, milk, granulated sugar and vanilla. Strain in the egg yolks and beat thoroughly. Divide the mixture between 4 or 6 individual ramekin dishes.

Half-fill a 600 ml/1 pint jug with cold water and place in the back of the microwave oven. Arrange the ramekin dishes, well spaced out, on the oven base or turntable. Cook on LOW (30%) for 12 to 16 minutes, rearranging the dishes every 3 minutes and removing each one as soon as it is cooked. Test by inserting a knife into the centre; the crème is cooked when the knife comes out clean.

Leave to cool, then chill in the refrigerator for at least 4 hours before serving. Sprinkle the brown sugar over the chilled crème. Press lightly, then place under a preheated hot grill until the sugar melts and caramelizes.

Chill thoroughly in the refrigerator before serving.
SERVES 4 to 6

BAKED EGG CUSTARD

METRIC/IMPERIAL
5 eggs
750 ml/1¼ pints skimmed milk, warmed
few drops of vanilla essence
1 tablespoon soft, light brown sugar
1 tablespoon clear honey
pinch of grated nutmeg

Beat the eggs thoroughly in a large bowl. While still beating, slowly add the warmed milk. Stir in the vanilla essence, sugar and honey. Pour into a large baking dish, cover loosely with greaseproof paper and cook on FULL (100%) for 1½ to 2 minutes. Sprinkle with nutmeg, cover as before and cook on LOW (30%) for 10 minutes (or on DEFROST/20% for 12½ minutes).

Leave to STAND, covered, for 6 to 8 minutes or until set.
SERVES 6

ZABAGLIONE

METRIC/IMPERIAL
1 large egg (size 1 or 2)
2 large egg yolks (size 1 or 2)
50 g/2 oz caster sugar
150 ml/¼ pint sweet sherry or Marsala
To serve:
4 sponge fingers

Place the whole egg and egg yolks in a large bowl; remove the threads, then whisk until creamy. Add the sugar and continue whisking until the mixture is light and the consistency of half-whipped cream.

Pour the sherry or Marsala into a jug and cook on FULL (100%) for 1½ to 2 minutes until just boiling. Pour on to the eggs, in a thin stream, whisking continually. As soon as the mixture thickens, cook on LOW (30%) for 1 to 1½ minutes until the sides of the bowl feel warm.

Beat vigorously with an electric mixer, on high speed, for 4 to 5 minutes until the zabaglione is thick. Spoon into warmed stemmed glasses and serve at once, decorated with sponge fingers.
SERVES 4

SUMMER FRUIT MOUSSE

METRIC/IMPERIAL
450 g/1 lb mixed summer fruits, such as blackcurrants, strawberries and raspberries, hulled
1 tablespoon water
100 g/4 oz caster sugar
1 envelope or 3 teaspoons powdered gelatine, dissolved in 7 tablespoons hot water
150 ml/¼ pint whipping cream
2 egg whites
whipped cream, to decorate (optional)

Layer the fruit in a bowl and add the water. Cover and cook on FULL (100%) for 5 minutes. Immediately stir in the sugar so that it dissolves. Sieve the fruit and fold the prepared gelatine into the purée. Cover and set aside in a refrigerator for 40 minutes, or until almost set.

Half-whip the cream and fold it into the fruit mixture. In a clean bowl, whip the egg whites until they stand in peaks; then fold into the fruit mixture, using a metal spoon.

Pour into sundae dishes and chill to set. Decorate with whipped cream, if required.
SERVES 3 to 4

CRÈME CARAMEL

METRIC/IMPERIAL
Caramel:
100 g/4 oz granulated sugar
4 tablespoons water
Custard:
600 ml/1 pint milk less 2 tablespoons
4 eggs, lightly beaten
25 g/1 oz caster sugar
2 tablespoons double cream

Place the sugar and water in a small bowl. Cook on FULL (100%) for 2½ minutes. Stir until the sugar has dissolved. Cook on FULL (100%) for a further 5 minutes, or until the caramel is a golden colour.

Divide the caramel between 6 ramekins or small bowls, and swirl around to coat the bottom and sides evenly. Set aside.

To make the custard, place the milk in a large jug and cook on FULL (100%) for 4 minutes. Whisk in the eggs, sugar and cream. Strain into the ramekins.

Arrange the ramekins in a circle in the microwave. Reduce the power to DEFROST (20%) and cook for 14 to 17 minutes or until just set. Rearrange halfway through cooking. Set aside to cool, then chill. Unmould on to individual serving plates to serve.
SERVES 6

Note: The actual cooking time will vary depending upon the temperature of the heated milk. Check after 14 minutes and remove any custards as soon as they are cooked.

CHOCOLATE POTS WITH PRALINE

METRIC/IMPERIAL
175 g/6 oz plain cooking chocolate
4 tablespoons cold, strong black coffee
25 g/1 oz butter, softened
1 tablespoon sugar
1 teaspoon brandy
75 g/3 oz finely crushed Praline (see page 273)
175 g/6 oz double cream
little grated chocolate, to decorate
few boudoir biscuits or ratafias, to serve

Break the chocolate into pieces and place in a bowl with the coffee. Cook on FULL (100%) for 3 minutes until the chocolate is melted, stirring

once. Beat thoroughly, then add the butter, sugar, brandy and praline. Leave to cool slightly.

Whip the cream until it forms soft peaks. Fold most of the cream into the chocolate mixture, reserving the remainder for decoration. Divide the chocolate cream between 4 or 6 ramekin dishes and chill in the refrigerator for at least 1 hour before serving.

Whip the remaining cream until stiff and use to pipe a rosette on each serving. Sprinkle with grated chocolate to decorate. Serve with boudoir biscuits or ratafias.
SERVES 4 to 6

CHOCOLATE BRANDY MOUSSE

METRIC/IMPERIAL
2–3 tablespoons sugar
2 tablespoons custard powder
600 ml/1 pint milk
few drops of vanilla essence
100 g/4 oz plain chocolate
7 g/¼ oz powdered gelatine
2 tablespoons water
2 tablespoons brandy
150 ml/¼ pint double or whipping cream
Decoration:
whipped cream
chocolate curls

In a large jug or bowl, mix sugar to taste with the custard powder and a little of the milk. Gradually add the remaining milk and cook on FULL (100%) for 5 to 6 minutes, stirring every 1 minute, until smooth and thick. Add a few drops of vanilla essence, blending well. Allow the mixture to cool.

Break the chocolate into squares and place in a bowl. Cook on MEDIUM (50%) for 2½ to 3 minutes, stirring twice, until melted.

Meanwhile, mix the gelatine with the water in a small jug and leave until the liquid is absorbed.

Cook on FULL (100%) for ½ minute until dissolved. Stir the melted chocolate, dissolved gelatine and brandy into the custard, blending well.

Whip the cream until it stands in soft peaks. Fold into the custard mixture with a metal spoon. Spoon into a serving dish or individual glasses and chill to set.

Decorate with swirls of whipped cream and chocolate curls.
SERVES 4

LIME JELLY MOUSSE

METRIC/IMPERIAL
1 × 135 g/4¾ oz packet lime jelly
grated rind and juice of 1 lime
100 g/4 oz full-fat soft cheese
2 egg whites
1 bar flake chocolate (optional)

Put the jelly into a measuring jug and add water to make up to 450 ml/¾ pint. Cook on FULL (100%) for 3 minutes or until the water is nearly boiling. Stir to dissolve the jelly thoroughly, then leave until cool but not set.

In a large bowl, beat the grated rind, lime juice and cheese together. Add the dissolved jelly and beat thoroughly. Leave in a cool place until the mixture is just beginning to set.

Whisk the egg whites until stiff. Stir one generous spoonful of the beaten whites into the jelly mixture, then fold in the remainder.

Spoon the mousse into individual ramekins or glasses and chill until set. Decorate with crushed flake chocolate, if liked.
SERVES 4

APRICOT PARFAIT

METRIC/IMPERIAL
about 100 g/4 oz cooking chocolate
150 ml/¼ pint milk
25 g/1 oz sugar
2 egg yolks
few drops of almond essence
1 × 400 g/14 oz can apricots, well drained
300 ml/½ pint double cream, beaten until peaks form
1 tablespoon Apricot Brandy or Orange Curaçao

Chill a 900 ml/1½ pint pudding basin until it is cold to the touch.

Break up the chocolate, place in a small jug and cook on FULL (100%) for 1 minute. Stir, then cook on FULL (100%) for a further ½ minute or until the chocolate is shiny on top. Stir until evenly melted.

Pour the melted chocolate into the chilled basin and swirl so that the bowl is completely coated. Make sure that the chocolate comes right to the top of the basin. Replace the basin in the refrigerator. (If the chocolate begins to roll away from the top of the basin, add a second coat when the first is set. This may require the melting of a little more chocolate.)

Place the milk and sugar in a bowl and cook on FULL (100%) for 1 minute, stirring once.

Beat the egg yolks and almond essence together, and stir into the warm milk. Cook on FULL (100%) for about ½ minute, then stir and cook for a further 30 to 40 seconds until the custard is hot but not boiling (or curdling will occur). Cover and leave until cold.

Purée the apricots in a blender or food processor until smooth. Beat in the cream, then beat in the cooled custard and the liqueur.

Pour the mixture into the chocolate-lined pudding basin and place in the freezer for a minimum of 2 hours.

To turn out, dip the basin into a bowl of very hot water for 15 to 20 seconds, then dry and turn out on to a serving dish. Leave to STAND for 10 minutes before cutting and serving.
SERVES 6

Note: For a special occasion the parfait can be decorated with piped cream and apricot slices.

RASPBERRY MOUSSE

METRIC/IMPERIAL
450 g/1 lb raspberries
100 g/4 oz cream cheese
50 g/2 oz caster sugar
4 tablespoons water
3 teaspoons powdered gelatine
2 egg whites
150 ml/¼ pint double cream, whipped
Decoration:
whipped cream
raspberries

Purée the raspberries in a blender or food processor. Beat the cheese with the sugar until soft and smooth. Stir in the raspberry purée and set aside.

Place the water in a small jug and heat on FULL (100%) for ½ minute. Stir in the gelatine until dissolved. Gradually stir the gelatine into the raspberry purée, blending well.

Whisk the egg whites until they stand in stiff peaks. Fold the cream into the raspberry mixture, blending well. Using a metal spoon, fold in the egg whites. Pour into a 900 ml/1½ pint soufflé dish and chill until set.

Serve decorated with whipped cream and raspberries.
SERVES 6

APRICOT CREAM

METRIC/IMPERIAL
450 g/1 lb apricots, stoned and quartered
3 tablespoons water
75 g/3 oz caster sugar
20 g/¾ oz powdered gelatine
300 ml/½ pint double cream, stiffly whipped
Decoration:
whipped cream (optional)
thin slices of fresh apricot

Place the apricots (reserve two for decoration), water and sugar in a medium bowl. Cover and cook on FULL (100%) for 4 to 5 minutes, stirring halfway through cooking. Leave to STAND, covered, for 3 minutes.

Pour the mixture into a blender or food processor and sprinkle in the gelatine. Purée until smooth and the gelatine has dissolved. Set aside to cool.

Gently fold the whipped cream into the purée and pour into a glass serving dish. Chill until set. Serve decorated with whipped cream and thin slices of fresh apricot.
SERVES 2 to 4

Note: If wished, divide the mixture into 4 individual serving dishes.

LEMON SOUFFLÉ

METRIC/IMPERIAL
165 g/5½ oz caster sugar
3 teaspoons powdered gelatine, dissolved in 2 tablespoons hot water
pinch of salt
200 ml/7 fl oz water
3 eggs, separated
grated rind and juice of 1 lemon
200 ml/7 fl oz double cream
Decoration:
whipped cream
lemon butterflies

Lightly grease a 600 ml/1 pint soufflé dish. Cut a double strip of greaseproof paper, equal in width to the height of the dish plus 5 cm/2 inches, and long enough to go right round the outside of the dish. Lightly grease the top 5 cm/2 inches and tie securely with string around the outside of the dish, greased side inside.

Mix 100 g/4 oz of the sugar with the dissolved gelatine, salt, water and egg yolks in a cooking dish, blending well. Cook on LOW (30%) for 6 minutes or until the mixture *almost* reaches boiling point, stirring twice. *Do not allow to boil.*

Add the lemon rind and juice, blending well. Leave to cool and thicken but not set.

Whisk the egg whites until they stand in stiff peaks. Whisk in the remaining caster sugar until firm and shiny.

Whip the cream until it stands in soft peaks. Using a metal spoon, fold into the lemon mixture with the egg white mixture. Pour into the prepared soufflé dish and chill until set.

Using the back of a knife, carefully ease the greaseproof paper away from the soufflé. Decorate with whipped cream and lemon butterflies.
SERVES 4 to 6

Variation

Gooseberry soufflé: prepare and cook as above but use 120 ml/4 fl oz unsweetened gooseberry purée instead of the lemon rind and juice. Tint the mixture pale green with food colouring, if liked.

CHOCOLATE MOUSSE WITH GRAND MARNIER

METRIC/IMPERIAL
225 g/8 oz plain chocolate
25 g/1 oz butter
2 tablespoons Grand Marnier
4 egg yolks
4 egg whites, stiffly whisked
Decoration:
150 ml/¼ pint double cream
2 tablespoons Grand Marnier

Break the chocolate into pieces and place in a medium bowl. Cook on MEDIUM (50%) for 3 to 3½ minutes or until melted, stirring twice.

Add the butter, Grand Marnier and egg yolks and beat them together until the mixture is smooth.

Using a metal spoon, gently fold in the egg whites and spoon into a 1 litre/1¾ pint serving dish. Chill in the refrigerator until set.

Whip the cream until it is thick, then gently fold in the Grand Marnier. Pipe the cream on to the mousse to decorate.
SERVES 4 to 6

Variations
Use another orange-flavoured liqueur, brandy or strong black coffee instead of the Grand Marnier.

BRAMBLE SYLLABUB

METRIC/IMPERIAL
450 g/1 lb blackberries, hulled
1½ tablespoons sugar
¾ teaspoon ground mace
3 egg whites
150 g/5 oz caster sugar
2 tablespoons lemon juice
150 ml/¼ pint dry white wine
300 ml/½ pint double cream, whipped
a few whole blackberries, to decorate

Place the blackberries in a cooking dish with the sugar and mace. Cook on FULL (100%) for 3 to 4 minutes, until soft but still whole, stirring once. Leave to cool.

When cool, spoon the fruit into the bases of 8 stemmed dessert glasses.

Whisk the egg whites until they stand in stiff peaks. Using a metal spoon, fold in the sugar, lemon juice, wine and whipped cream.

Carefully spoon over the fruit mixture, then chill for 1 hour. Serve lightly chilled and decorated with a few whole blackberries.
SERVES 8

MANGO MOUSSE

METRIC/IMPERIAL
1 × 175 g/6 oz can evaporated milk
4 tablespoons water
2 teaspoons powdered gelatine
1 × 450 g/1 lb can sweetened mango pulp
1 tablespoon sugar (optional)
whipped cream or grated dark chocolate, to decorate

Chill the can of evaporated milk in the freezer for 30 minutes.

During the last 15 minutes, put the water in a jug and cook on FULL (100%) for ¾ minute or until boiling. Sprinkle the gelatine over the surface and stir into the water, then cook on FULL (100%) for ¼ minute until the mixture is clear and dissolved. Stir, then leave to STAND for 10 to 15 minutes to cool slightly.

In a large bowl, whip the evaporated milk until it is thick.

Fold the mango pulp into the whipped evaporated milk, then pour the dissolved gelatine in from a height, and mix thoroughly (to achieve greatest volume, fold rather than stir in the dissolved gelatine).

Add sugar, if needed, then pour into a serving dish and chill until set.

Decorate with whipped cream or grated chocolate before serving.
SERVES 4

Note: A squeeze of fresh lime juice sprinkled over the mousse at the time of serving greatly enhances the flavour.

APPLE AND BLACKBERRY SNOW

METRIC/IMPERIAL
450 g/1 lb Bramley apples, peeled and thinly sliced
225 g/8 oz fresh blackberries
75 g/3 oz caster sugar
2 egg whites

Put the apples and blackberries into a mixing bowl. Cover and cook on FULL (100%) for 6½ minutes, stirring once.

Leave to STAND for 2 minutes, then beat in the sugar. Purée in a blender or pass through a fine sieve into a mixing bowl, and leave to cool.

Beat the egg whites until they stand in soft peaks. Using a metal tablespoon, fold into the fruit mixture. Pile into sundae glasses and chill before serving.
SERVES 4

APRICOT FOOL

METRIC/IMPERIAL
350 g/12 oz dried apricots
350 ml/12 fl oz water
450 ml/¾ pint Custard Sauce (see page 311)
2 tablespoons double cream
sugar to taste
1 egg white

Rinse the apricots and combine with the water in a large deep dish. Cover loosely and cook on FULL (100%) for 12 minutes, stirring once. Allow to cool, then purée in a blender or food processor, or press through a sieve.

Beat the custard and cream into the apricot purée and add sugar to taste. Beat the egg white until stiff, then fold into the mixture. Spoon into a serving dish and chill to set. If wished, decorate with whipped cream.
SERVES 6

COFFEE CREAMS

METRIC/IMPERIAL
300 ml/½ pint milk
2 large egg yolks (size 1), lightly beaten
50 ml/2 fl oz water
25 g/1 oz powdered gelatine
65 g/2½ oz caster sugar
150 ml/¼ pint double cream
150 ml/¼ pint whipping cream
1½ tablespoons coffee essence
Decoration:
75 ml/3 fl oz whipping cream, whipped
cocoa, coffee or chocolate powder

Place the milk in a large jug and cook on FULL (100%) for 3 minutes or until very hot. Beat in the egg yolks and cook on FULL (100%) for 1 minute or until the mixture starts to thicken. Beat halfway through cooking and be careful not to let the mixture curdle.

Place the water in a small jug and cook on FULL (100%) for 1½ minutes or until very hot. Stir in the gelatine until it has completely dissolved.

Beat the gelatine liquid and the sugar into the milk custard. Set aside until cool, stirring occasionally.

Beat the double and whipping creams together until thick and fold in the coffee essence. Check the flavour, adding more coffee essence if desired. Fold the cream into the cooled custard and pour into stemmed glasses. Chill in the refrigerator.

Pipe a decoration on each glass with the whipped cream and sprinkle over a little cocoa, coffee or chocolate powder. Serve with langue de chat biscuits.
SERVES 4 to 6

INDIVIDUAL CHOCOLATE MOUSSE

METRIC/IMPERIAL
25 g/1 oz plain chocolate
small knob of butter
1 egg, separated
15 g/½ oz white chocolate
rose leaves, to decorate

Place the plain chocolate in a bowl and heat on FULL (100%) for ½ to 1 minute or until melted. Stir in the butter, blending well.

Add the egg yolk and mix well to blend.

Whisk the egg white until it stands in stiff peaks. Fold through the chocolate mixture with a metal spoon. Pour into a small serving dish and chill to set, about 2 to 4 hours.

Meanwhile, place the white chocolate in a bowl and heat on FULL (100%) for ½ minute or until melted. Very lightly oil the undersides of a few washed rose leaves. Dip the underside of each leaf in the white chocolate to coat. Leave to harden and set, then carefully peel away the leaf from the chocolate.

Serve the chocolate mousse prettily decorated with the white chocolate leaves.
SERVES 1

ORANGE JELLY

METRIC/IMPERIAL
300 ml/½ pint water
3 tablespoons sugar
3 rounded teaspoons powdered gelatine
300 ml/½ pint orange juice

Place the water in a jug and cook on FULL (100%) for 2 minutes or until hot. Stir in the sugar, beating well. Stir in the gelatine until dissolved.

Add the orange juice and stir well to blend. Pour into a 600 ml/1 pint mould or bowl and chill to set.

If using a mould, dip briefly into hot water and invert on to a plate to serve.
SERVES 4

LOGANBERRY CHEESE MOUSSE

METRIC/IMPERIAL
100 g/4 oz cream cheese
50 g/2 oz caster sugar
450 g/1 lb fresh loganberries, puréed
2 tablespoons water
2 tablespoons white wine
3 teaspoons powdered gelatine
150 ml/¼ pint double cream
2 egg whites
langue de chat biscuits, to serve
Decoration:
150 ml/¼ pint double cream, whipped
few fresh loganberries

Beat together the cheese and sugar until soft and smooth. Stir in the fruit purée and set aside.

Place the water and wine in a small jug. Cook on FULL (100%) for ½ minute or until the liquid is very hot. Sprinkle the gelatine over and stir well until dissolved. Cool slightly, then stir into the cheese mixture, ensuring that it is well incorporated. Set aside.

Whip the cream until firm but not very stiff and gently fold into the purée. Whisk the egg whites until stiff, then gently fold into the mixture. Pour into a 900 ml/1½ pint glass serving dish and refrigerate until set.

Decorate with the whipped cream and fresh loganberries. Serve with langue de chat biscuits.
SERVES 4

Note: Any puréed, canned or frozen fruit can be used in place of the loganberries.

BREAD AND BUTTER PUDDING

METRIC/IMPERIAL
12 thin slices white bread with crusts removed, well buttered and cut into quarters
100 g/4 oz seedless raisins
½ teaspoon mixed spice
1½ tablespoons soft brown sugar
4 eggs
600 ml/1 pint milk
4 tablespoons caster sugar
½ teaspoon vanilla essence
50 g/2 oz demerara sugar

Cover the base of a greased ovenproof dish with a layer of the bread, buttered side up. Sprinkle with half the raisins, half the spice and half the brown sugar. Add a second layer of bread and sprinkle on the remaining raisins, spice and brown sugar. Top with a final layer of bread, buttered side up.

To make the egg custard, beat the eggs in a large heatproof jug. Put the milk, caster sugar and vanilla in another jug and cook on FULL (100%) for 3½ minutes. Pour the hot milk mixture on to the eggs, beating well.

Strain the mixture on to the bread and leave to STAND for 15 minutes to allow the bread to absorb most of the liquid. Do not cover.

Cook on MEDIUM (50%) for 12 to 15 minutes. Leave to STAND for 5 minutes until set. Before serving, sprinkle with demerara sugar and, if liked, cook under a preheated hot grill to crisp the top.
SERVES 6 to 8

SPICED APPLE CRUMBLE WITH DEVONSHIRE CREAM

METRIC/IMPERIAL
67. -/1½ lb cooking apples, peeled, cored and finely sliced
¼ teaspoon ground cloves
¼ teaspoon ground cinnamon
75 g/3 oz caster sugar
300 ml/½ pint Devonshire cream, to serve
Crumble topping:
50 g/2 oz self-raising flour
175 g/6 oz wholemeal flour
100 g/4 oz butter or soft margarine
75 g/3 oz demerara sugar

Combine the flours in a mixing bowl and rub in the butter or margarine until the mixture resembles fine breadcrumbs. Stir in 50 g/2 oz of the demerara sugar.

Put the apples into a 1.2 litre/2 pint oval pie dish. Stir in the ground cloves, cinnamon and caster sugar and mix thoroughly.

Spoon the crumble topping over the fruit and press down firmly. Sprinkle the remaining demerara sugar on top.

Cook on FULL (100%) for 6 minutes. Give the dish a half-turn and cook on FULL (100%) for a further 5 minutes, or until a round-bladed knife inserted into the topping comes out clean.

If liked, cook the crumble under a preheated hot grill until golden. Serve hot with Devonshire cream.
SERVES 6

RHUBARB AND GINGER CRUMBLE

METRIC/IMPERIAL
575 g/1¼ lb fresh rhubarb, cut into chunks, or 450 g/1 lb frozen rhubarb chunks, thawed
2 tablespoons water
½ × 100 g/4 oz jar ginger in syrup
50 g/2 oz almonds, chopped
Crumble topping:
75 g/3 oz butter or margarine
175 g/6 oz wholemeal or plain flour
100 g/4 oz demerara sugar

Put the rhubarb and water into a deep 1.2 litre/2 pint oval pie dish. Three-quarters cover and cook on FULL (100%) for 5 minutes. Stir so that the harder pieces are moved towards the centre.

Add 2 tablespoons of the ginger syrup, 4 pieces of the ginger, sliced finely, and 25 g/1 oz of the chopped almonds and stir to mix. Three-quarters cover and cook on FULL (100%) for a further 2 minutes.

Rub the butter or margarine into the flour until the mixture resembles fine breadcrumbs. Stir in the remaining almonds and the demerara sugar.

Spoon the crumble mixture evenly over the rhubarb, pressing the topping down lightly. Cook on FULL (100%) for 6 to 7 minutes until the crumble is set and a round-bladed knife, inserted through the topping only, comes out clean.

Leave to STAND for 5 minutes, then cook at a distance of 15 cm/6 inches under a preheated hot grill until golden. If wished, serve decorated with slices of orange.
SERVES 6

PINEAPPLE AND KIRSCH UPSIDE-DOWN PUDDING

METRIC/IMPERIAL
Fruit base:
2–3 slices fresh pineapple, 5 mm/¼ inch thick, 1 slice left whole, the others quartered
5 tablespoons Kirsch
40 g/1½ oz butter
25 g/1 oz soft brown sugar
3 glacé cherries, quartered
Cake mixture:
100 g/4 oz butter
100 g/4 oz caster sugar
2 eggs, lightly beaten
100 g/4 oz self-raising flour
2 tablespoons Kirsch

Place the pineapple on a plate and sprinkle over 3 tablespoons of the Kirsch. Leave to marinate for 3 hours.

Place the butter in a 1.2 litre/2 pint soufflé dish. Sprinkle over the brown sugar, then cook on FULL (100%) for 1 minute. Arrange the pineapple and cherries over the base in a decorative pattern.

To prepare the cake mixture, beat together the butter and caster sugar until light and fluffy. Beat in the eggs, a little at a time. Fold in the flour and then the Kirsch. Gently spread the cake mixture over the pineapple base, being careful not to disturb the pattern.

Cook on FULL (100%) for 6½ minutes,

turning the dish round halfway through cooking. Remove from the oven and STAND for 3 minutes before turning out. During the standing time, prick the cake mixture with a skewer and sprinkle over the remaining Kirsch.

Turn out on to a warm serving dish and serve hot or warm with cream.
SERVES 4

Note: Serve this pudding as soon as it is cooked as it tends to harden on cooling.

MARMALADE ROLY POLY

METRIC/IMPERIAL
225 g/8 oz self-raising flour
pinch of salt
100 g/4 oz shredded suet
150 ml/¼ pint cold water
Filling:
100 g/4 oz marmalade
1 teaspoon lemon juice
1 tablespoon raisins
Topping:
2 tablespoons caster sugar
pinch of grated nutmeg
pinch of ground cinnamon

Sift the flour and salt into a bowl. Stir in the suet, blending well. Add the cold water and mix to a soft dough. Roll out on a lightly floured surface until 23 cm/9 inches square.

Mix the marmalade with the lemon juice and raisins in a small bowl. Cook on FULL (100%) for ½ minute. Spread evenly over the suet pastry square, leaving a 1 cm/½ inch border around the edge. Carefully roll up like a Swiss roll.

Place, seam side down, on a large piece of greaseproof paper and roll the greaseproof up loosely around the pastry roll, allowing plenty of space for the pudding to rise. Tie the ends of the paper with string or secure with elastic bands. Place on a large plate and loosely cover with greaseproof paper.

Cook on FULL (100%) for 8 minutes, turning the plate once, or until well risen and cooked through. Test by inserting a skewer into the centre of the pudding – if it comes out clean the pastry dough is cooked.

Mix the sugar with the nutmeg and cinnamon. Remove all wrappings and place the roly poly on a warmed serving dish. Sprinkle with the sugar mixture. Serve hot with custard.
SERVES 6

APRICOT SPONGE PUDDING

METRIC/IMPERIAL
1 × 575 g/1¼ lb can apricot halves
1 teaspoon cornflour
1 tablespoon cold water
2 eggs, beaten
4 tablespoons sugar
½ teaspoon vanilla essence
50 g/2 oz plain flour, sifted
2 tablespoons vegetable oil

Drain the apricots, reserving the juice, and place in the centre of a large shallow dish. Pour the apricot juice into a large jug and cook on FULL (100%) for 5 minutes. Blend the cornflour with the water, then stir in the apricot syrup and cook on FULL (100%) for 2 minutes, stirring twice. Set aside.

Beat the eggs, sugar and vanilla essence together until thick and creamy. Fold in the flour, a little at a time, then gradually fold in the oil.

Place spoonfuls of the mixture around the apricots to form a border. Cook on LOW (30%) for 3 minutes, then cook on FULL (100%) for 5 minutes or until the sponge is just dry on top, giving the dish a half-turn after 2½ minutes. Place under a preheated medium grill to brown the top.

Serve hot, accompanied by the sauce which can be reheated on FULL (100%) for 1 minute, if necessary.
SERVES 4

HONEY CRUNCH CRUMBLE

METRIC/IMPERIAL
675 g/1½ lb cooking apples, peeled, cored and sliced
6 tablespoons clear honey
75 g/3 oz butter
175 g/6 oz muesli-style breakfast cereal

Put the apples in a serving dish and drizzle over half the honey.

Place the butter in a bowl and heat on FULL (100%) for 1½ to 2 minutes or until melted.

Stir in the remaining honey and the cereal, mixing well to coat. Spoon on top of the apples. Cook on FULL (100%) for 11 to 13 minutes, giving the dish a quarter-turn every 3 minutes.
SERVES 4

FAMILY APPLE AMBER

METRIC/IMPERIAL
100 g/4 oz butter
100 g/4 oz fresh white or brown breadcrumbs
100 g/4 oz rolled oats
1 kg/2 lb apples (a mixture of cookers and eaters), peeled and cored
50 g/2 oz caster sugar
a few raisins
75 g/3 oz demerara sugar
2 teaspoons mixed spice
50 g/2 oz chopped walnuts (optional)
cream or Custard Sauce (see page 311), to serve

Place the butter in a mixing bowl and heat on FULL (100%) for 1½ minutes or until melted. Stir in the breadcrumbs and oats, coating with the butter. Cook on FULL (100%) for 5 minutes, stirring once.

Slice the apples into a 19 cm/7½ inch deep soufflé dish or casserole and layer with caster sugar and raisins.

Add the demerara sugar, spice and walnuts (if using) to the breadcrumb mixture. Sprinkle the crumble over the prepared fruit and cook on FULL (100%) for 5 minutes.

Leave to STAND for 3 minutes. Serve with cream or Custard Sauce.
SERVES 4 to 6

CREAMY RICE PUDDING

METRIC/IMPERIAL
50 g/2 oz round-grain pudding rice
¼ teaspoon grated nutmeg
450 ml/¾ pint boiling water
25 g/1 oz sugar
1 × 175 ml/6 fl oz can evaporated milk
1 teaspoon butter

Combine the rice, nutmeg and boiling water in a large deep dish. Cover and cook on FULL (100%) for 8 minutes, stirring occasionally. Add the sugar and the evaporated milk and cook on LOW (30%) for 20 to 25 minutes, stirring occasionally, until the rice is just tender.

Stir in the butter. Leave to STAND, covered, for 5 minutes before serving.
SERVES 3 to 4

Note: As rice pudding cools, it tends to thicken. Add a little fresh milk or cream to thin it and reheat, if desired.

LEMON MERINGUE PIE

METRIC/IMPERIAL
Filling:
225 g/8 oz sugar
4 tablespoons cornflour
pinch of salt
250 ml/8 fl oz cold water
3 egg yolks
120 ml/4 fl oz lemon juice
2 teaspoons grated lemon rind
40 g/1½ oz butter
Crumb base:
50 g/2 oz butter
6 digestive biscuits, crushed
25 g/1 oz sugar
Meringue topping:
3 egg whites
pinch of cream of tartar
100 g/4 oz sugar
½ teaspoon vanilla essence

To prepare the filling, mix the sugar, cornflour and salt together. Put the water in a large bowl and cook on FULL (100%) for 3 minutes until boiling. Toss in the sugar mixture and beat vigorously until a smooth sauce is obtained. Cook on FULL (100%) for 3 minutes, stirring frequently.

Beat the egg yolks and lemon juice together and blend with a few spoonfuls of the sauce. Add to the sauce and mix thoroughly. Cook on FULL (100%) for 1 minute, stirring once. Stir in the lemon rind and butter, then leave to cool.

For the crumb base, put the butter in a 20 cm/8 inch round pie dish and heat on FULL (100%) for 1 minute until melted. Add the biscuits and sugar, mix thoroughly and press firmly into the base of the dish. Spoon the filling over the top.

To make the meringue topping, whisk the egg whites and cream of tartar together until stiff. Add half the sugar and the vanilla essence and whisk until the mixture is stiff once more; then fold in the remaining sugar. Spread the meringue evenly over the filling to the edge of the dish.

Cook on FULL (100%) for 4 minutes, giving the dish a quarter-turn every 1 minute. Flash briefly under a preheated hot grill until lightly browned. Serve hot or cold.
SERVES 6

Note: If the meringue topping cracks during cooking, coax it back into position with a palette knife before browning.

JULY FRUIT MERINGUE PUDDING

METRIC/IMPERIAL
1 banana, sliced
1 sharp dessert apple, cored and sliced
1 large peach, stoned and sliced
1 tablespoon lemon juice
3 egg whites
175 g/6 oz caster sugar

Combine the fruit in a large shallow dish and sprinkle with the lemon juice.

Beat the egg whites until stiff. Add half of the sugar and continue beating until stiff peaks form. Fold in the remaining sugar.

Spread the meringue over the fruit with a spatula, making sure it reaches the edges of the dish. Cook on MEDIUM (50%) for 8 minutes until the meringue is firm, giving the dish a half-turn after 4 minutes.

Place under a preheated hot grill for ½ minute to brown the top. Serve hot or cold.
SERVES 6

APPLE AND COCONUT CHARLOTTE

METRIC/IMPERIAL
100 g/4 oz butter
225 g/8 oz fresh soft breadcrumbs
50 g/2 oz desiccated coconut
150 g/5 oz brown sugar
450 g/1 lb cooking apples, peeled, cored and thinly sliced
grated rind and juice of 1 lemon

Put the butter in a deep pie dish and heat on FULL (100%) for 2 minutes until melted. Stir in the breadcrumbs and cook on FULL (100%) for 3 minutes, stirring once.

Stir in the coconut and cook on FULL (100%) for 1 minute. Remove half of this mixture and set aside. Press the remainder into the base of the dish and sprinkle half of the sugar on top.

Arrange the apple slices on top of the mixture. Sprinkle with the lemon rind, juice and the remaining sugar. Top with the rest of the coconut and crumb mixture. Cook on FULL (100%) for 4 to 5 minutes until the apple is soft. Place under a preheated grill to brown the top, if desired.
SERVES 4

CHOCOLATE WALNUT CRÊPES

METRIC/IMPERIAL
Batter:
1 egg
1 egg yolk
300 ml/½ pint milk
pinch of salt
100 g/4 oz plain flour
Sauce:
1 tablespoon cocoa powder
25 g/1 oz butter
1½ tablespoons golden syrup
2 tablespoons chopped walnuts

Place all the ingredients for the crêpe batter in a blender or food processor and blend until the mixture is smooth. Set aside for at least 30 minutes before using.

Using the *conventional hob*, heat a little oil in a 15 cm/6 inch frying pan. Pour in sufficient crêpe batter to just cover the base of the pan. Cook until golden brown on one side. Flip the crêpe over and cook until the other side is golden. Transfer to a plate; cover and keep warm. Continue until you have made 8 crêpes.

To make the sauce, place the cocoa powder, butter and syrup in a large jug. Cook on FULL (100%) for 1½ minutes or until the mixture is melted and hot, stirring once.

Fold each crêpe in half, then half again, to make a fan shape, and arrange on a serving dish. Cook on FULL (100%) for 1 to 1½ minutes.

Pour the sauce over the crêpes and sprinkle them with the chopped walnuts. Serve with cream or vanilla ice cream.
SERVES 4

MARSHMALLOW AND ALMOND RASPBERRIES

METRIC/IMPERIAL
175 g/6 oz plain cooking chocolate
1 × 100 g/4 oz packet marshmallows
3 tablespoons milk
6 tablespoons double cream
350 g/12 oz fresh raspberries
50 g/2 oz flaked almonds, toasted

Line a 23 cm/9 inch shallow dish with microwave cling film. Break up the chocolate and cook on MEDIUM (50%) for 4½ to 5 minutes until melted, stirring twice.

Using a pastry brush, spread the chocolate evenly over the base and sides of the dish, then chill in the refrigerator until set.

Combine the marshmallows and milk in a large bowl and cook on FULL (100%) for 1½ to 2 minutes or until the marshmallows puff up. Stir until the mixture is smooth.

Chill for 30 to 40 minutes or until just beginning to thicken. Lightly whip the cream, then fold into the marshmallow mixture.

Carefully transfer the chocolate case to a serving dish. Fill with the raspberries and pile the marshmallow cream on top. Sprinkle with the toasted almonds.

Chill in the refrigerator for 5 hours, or until the topping has set, before serving.
SERVES 6

APFELROMTOPF

METRIC/IMPERIAL
4 large, even-sized cooking apples
1 banana, peeled
2 teaspoons lemon juice
25 g/1 oz blanched almonds, finely grated
1 teaspoon chopped angelica
6 glacé cherries, chopped
¼ teaspoon ground cinnamon
100 g/4 oz soft brown sugar
4 tablespoons double cream
1 tablespoon rum

Using a sharp knife or apple corer, remove the cores from the apples. Trim a thin slice from the top of each one. Arrange the apples in a shallow round dish and cook on FULL (100%) for 3 to 4 minutes or until the sides yield under gentle pressure. Leave to STAND for 2 to 3 minutes.

Mash the banana with the lemon juice, then stir in the almonds, angelica, cherries, cinnamon and half of the sugar.

Scoop out about three-quarters of the pulp from the centre of each apple, leaving a thick shell. Stir the apple pulp into the banana mixture, then pile back into the apple shells.

Return to the dish and cook on FULL (100%) for 3½ to 4 minutes until the apples are tender, giving the dish a half-turn once during cooking. Transfer the apples to individual serving dishes.

Stir the cream, rum and remaining sugar into the residual juice in the dish and cook on FULL (100%) for 1½ to 2 minutes until the sauce boils. Spoon this syrup over the apples and serve hot.
SERVES 4

DATE AND HAZELNUT PUDDING

METRIC/IMPERIAL
4 eggs, separated
50 g/2 oz brown sugar
50 g/2 oz fresh soft breadcrumbs
50 g/2 oz hazelnuts, grated
100 g/4 oz block cooking dates

Well grease a 2.25 litre/4 pint ring mould. In a mixing bowl, beat the egg yolks until frothy. Add the sugar and continue beating until the mixture is very thick. Mix in the breadcrumbs and hazelnuts.

Put the block of dates in the oven and cook on FULL (100%) for ¼ to ½ minute until soft. Mash the dates and stir into the pudding mixture. Beat the egg whites until stiff, then fold into the mixture until completely incorporated.

Turn into the greased mould and cook on FULL (100%) for 4 minutes, giving the dish a quarter-turn every 1 minute, until just dry on top. Turn out on to a heated plate and serve at once.

SERVES 6 to 8

Note: This pudding tends to sink slightly in the centre on turning out.

CHOCOLATE AND BRANDY DESSERT CAKE

METRIC/IMPERIAL
175 g/6 oz soft margarine
175 g/6 oz caster sugar
40 g/1½ oz cocoa powder
1 teaspoon baking powder
150 g/5 oz self-raising flour
1 tablespoon brandy
2 tablespoons milk
3 large eggs (size 1)
Decoration:
300 ml/½ pint double or whipping cream, whipped
1 tablespoon brandy (optional)
75 g/3 oz chocolate, grated or shaved

Place all the ingredients for the cake in a large bowl. Beat well until the mixture is smooth, but do not overbeat.

Lightly grease an 18 cm/7 inch round cake dish, 9 cm/3½ inches deep and line the base with lightly greased greaseproof paper. Spoon the mixture into the dish and stand it on an upturned plate. Cook on FULL (100%) for 7 minutes, turning it round once or twice during cooking.

Leave the cake to STAND for 5 minutes before turning it out, upside down (so that the bottom is now the top) on to a wire tray. Leave it to cool.

When the cake is completely cold, whip the cream and stir in the brandy, if using. Split the cake in half and spread some of the cream over the bottom half. Replace the top and decorate with more whipped cream and grated chocolate shavings or shapes.

MAKES one 18 cm/7 inch cake

BREAD PUDDING

METRIC/IMPERIAL
8 thick slices slightly stale bread, including crusts, cut into small pieces
2 eggs, beaten
350 ml/12 fl oz milk
1 medium, ripe banana, sliced
350 g/12 oz mixed dried fruit (raisins, currants, sultanas, peel)
50 g/2 oz glacé cherries, chopped
75 g/3 oz soft, dark brown sugar
2 teaspoons gravy browning
1 tablespoon black treacle
1 tablespoon apricot jam or marmalade
40 g/1½ oz self-raising flour
1 teaspoon lemon juice
1 teaspoon ground cinnamon
2 teaspoons mixed spice
50 g/2 oz butter, melted
25 g/1 oz mixed nuts, chopped (optional)
a little caster sugar, to finish

Place the bread pieces in a large mixing bowl. Beat together the eggs and milk. Pour over the bread and leave to soak for 20 minutes.

Beat well with a fork. Add all the remaining ingredients, except the caster sugar, and beat well with a wooden spoon to combine. Divide between two 1 kg/2 lb plastic loaf dishes.

Cook each container separately on MEDIUM (50%) for 22 to 24 minutes, giving the dish a half-turn, twice, during cooking. Leave in the container and STAND, covered, for 20 minutes.

Turn out and, when quite cold, sprinkle with caster sugar and serve with custard or cream.

SERVES 6 to 8

APPLE AND SULTANA SUET PUDDING

METRIC/IMPERIAL
150 g/5 oz shredded suet
½ teaspoon baking powder
250 g/9 oz self-raising flour
150 ml/¼ pint water
25 g/1 oz fresh brown breadcrumbs
100 g/4 oz soft, dark brown sugar
2 teaspoons ground cinnamon
100 g/4 oz sultanas
600 g/1¼ lb cooking apples, peeled, cored and thinly sliced

Place the suet, baking powder and flour in a bowl and mix together. Gradually add water to make pastry. Roll out two thirds of the pastry until 3 mm/⅛ inch thick and line a greased 1.5 litre/2½ pint basin.

Mix together the breadcrumbs, sugar, cinnamon and sultanas. Starting and ending with the apples, make alternate layers with the breadcrumb mixture.

Roll out the remaining pastry and cover the filling, making sure the pastry lid is well sealed. Make 2 cuts in the lid. Cover with greaseproof paper, allowing sufficient room for rising. Cook on FULL (100%) for 5 minutes. Turn the basin round and cook for a further 6 minutes. Leave to STAND, covered, for 5 minutes.
SERVES 4 to 6

CHOCOLATE UPSIDE-DOWN PUDDING

METRIC/IMPERIAL
caster sugar for coating
1 × 225 g/8 oz can pineapple slices, drained
5 glacé cherries, halved
200 g/7 oz self-raising flour
pinch of salt
3 tablespoons drinking chocolate
100 g/4 oz soft margarine
100 g/4 oz caster sugar
100 g/4 oz soft, dark brown sugar
2 eggs, beaten
5 tablespoons evaporated milk, mixed with 5 tablespoons water

Prepare a 19 cm/7½ inch soufflé dish by lightly brushing the base and sides with oil. Fit a circle of greaseproof paper in the base and use a little sugar to coat the sides. Tap out any surplus.

Arrange the pineapple and cherries in an attractive pattern on the base of the dish.

Sift together the flour, salt and drinking chocolate into a bowl. Rub in the margarine until the mixture resembles fine breadcrumbs; then stir in the sugars.

Make a well in the centre of the dry ingredients and, using an electric whisk, beat in the eggs, then the milk and water mixture. Beat well for 1 minute. Pour the mixture on to the pineapple and cherries and level the surface.

Cook on FULL (100%) for 10½ to 11 minutes, giving the dish a half-turn three times during cooking, if necessary. The pudding is cooked when a wooden cocktail stick inserted into the centre comes out clean.

Let the pudding STAND, covered, for 5 minutes, before turning out.
SERVES 6

Note: As a speedy alternative, a good quality packet sponge mix can be used instead of the recipe given here. Make up as directed on the packet, but add 2 extra tablespoons of water. Cook on FULL (100%) for 5 minutes.

MANDARIN PUDDING

METRIC/IMPERIAL
50 g/2 oz butter
3 slices of bread, crusts removed
50 g/2 oz brown sugar
1 × 225 g/8 oz can mandarin oranges, drained
25 g/1 oz sultanas
2 eggs, beaten
300 ml/½ pint milk

Put the butter in a deep round flameproof dish and heat on FULL (100%) for 1 minute until melted. Cut the bread into triangles and place in the dish, turning the pieces over so that they are completely coated with butter; then arrange them neatly. Sprinkle with all but 2 tablespoons of the brown sugar. Arrange the mandarin oranges and sultanas on top.

Beat the eggs and milk together and pour over the fruit. Cook on MEDIUM (50%) for 10 to 12 minutes, until the custard has set at the edges but is still slightly wet in the centre, giving the dish a quarter-turn every 4 minutes during cooking.

Leave to STAND for 5 minutes, then sprinkle with the remaining sugar and place under a preheated hot grill to brown the top. Serve hot.
SERVES 4

HOT BRAZIL SUNDAES

METRIC/IMPERIAL
7 g/¼ oz butter
25 g/1 oz Brazil or cashew nuts, coarsely
chopped
4 tablespoons single cream
25 g/1 oz brown sugar
1 banana, sliced
coffee ice cream, to serve

Place the butter and nuts in a bowl. Cook on
FULL (100%) for 1 to 1½ minutes or until just
golden. Add the cream and sugar, blending well.
Cover and cook on FULL (100%) for ½ to 1
minute, until boiling, stirring twice.

Arrange the banana slices and scoops of coffee
ice cream on 2 serving plates. Spoon over the hot
sauce and serve at once.
SERVES 2

STEAMED TREACLE PUDDING

METRIC/IMPERIAL
75 g/3 oz plain flour
75 g/3 oz fresh soft white breadcrumbs, sieved
50 g/2 oz sugar
50 g/2 oz shredded suet
1 egg
1 tablespoon golden syrup
1 tablespoon black treacle
3–4 tablespoons milk
¼ teaspoon bicarbonate of soda
3–4 tablespoons golden syrup, warmed

Combine the flour, breadcrumbs, sugar and suet
in a mixing bowl and make a well in the
centre.

In another bowl beat the egg, syrup, treacle, 3
tablespoons milk and the bicarbonate of soda
together. Pour into the dry ingredients and mix
well, adding more milk, if necessary, to obtain a
consistency which drops easily from a spoon.

Turn the mixture into a well-greased 1 litre/
1¾ pint glass pudding basin. Cover with a large
piece of greaseproof paper or microwave cling
film pleated across the middle.

Cook on FULL (100%) for 3½ to 4 minutes
until the pudding is just dry on top, giving a
quarter-turn every 1 minute.

Turn out on to a warm serving dish and pour
the syrup over the top.
SERVES 4 to 5

APPLE CURD PUDDING

METRIC/IMPERIAL
3 large cooking apples, peeled, cored and
quartered
lemon juice for sprinkling
1½ tablespoons cornflour
few drops of vanilla essence
6 tablespoons soft brown sugar
4 tablespoons undiluted orange squash
40 g/1½ oz butter
8 digestive biscuits, finely crushed

Slice the apples thinly and sprinkle with lemon
juice. Combine the cornflour, vanilla essence,
sugar and orange squash in a large shallow dish.
Add the apples and mix thoroughly. Cook on
FULL (100%) for 5 minutes, stirring once during
cooking.

Put the butter in a bowl and heat on FULL
(100%) for 1 minute until melted. Stir in the
biscuit crumbs. Spread over the apples and cook
on FULL (100%) for 4 to 5 minutes, giving the
dish a half-turn halfway through cooking. Leave
to STAND for 2 minutes. Serve hot.
SERVES 4

JAM-CAPPED SUET PUDDING

METRIC/IMPERIAL
3 tablespoons raspberry jam
175 g/6 oz self-raising flour
75 g/3 oz caster sugar
75 g/3 oz shredded suet
2 large eggs (size 1 or 2)
5 tablespoons milk

Lightly brush a 900 ml/1½ pint pudding basin
with a little oil. Spread the jam over the base and
sides of the basin.

Sift the flour into a mixing bowl, and stir in
the sugar and suet. Beat together the eggs and
milk and mix into the dry ingredients. Stir to
combine.

Spoon into the prepared pudding basin and
level the top. Cook on MEDIUM (50%) for 10
to 12 minutes, giving the dish a half-turn, twice,
during cooking. The top should still be just
moist.

Leave to STAND, covered, for 5 minutes
before turning out. Serve with Custard Sauce
(see page 311).
SERVES 6

APRICOT UPSIDE-DOWN PUDDING

METRIC/IMPERIAL
25 g/1 oz demerara sugar
1 × 375 g/13 oz can apricot halves, drained
4 blanched almonds, halved
2 tablespoons frozen concentrated orange juice, thawed
100 g/4 oz soft margarine
100 g/4 oz caster sugar
2 eggs, beaten
1 teaspoon almond essence
100 g/4 oz self-raising flour
1 teaspoon baking powder
2 tablespoons milk

Line a 1.75 litre/3 pint soufflé dish with greaseproof paper. Sprinkle the base with demerara sugar and top with the apricot halves and almonds, arranged attractively. Carefully spoon the orange juice over the top.

Cream the margarine and sugar until light and fluffy. Gradually beat in the eggs and almond essence. Fold in the flour and baking powder with a metal spoon and stir in the milk.

Spoon the sponge mixture over the prepared base. Loosely cover with greaseproof paper and cook on FULL (100%) for 6½ to 7 minutes, turning the dish every 1½ minutes.

To serve, invert the pudding on to a warmed serving dish. Serve cut into wedges with custard or single cream.
SERVES 6

CHOCOLATE SAUCE

METRIC/IMPERIAL
100 g/4 oz milk or plain chocolate
25 g/1 oz butter
150 ml/¼ pint water or milk
1½ teaspoons cornflour

Break the chocolate into pieces and place in a jug with the butter and water or milk. Cook on MEDIUM (50%) for 3 to 4 minutes, stirring twice.

Put the cornflour into a bowl and mix to a smooth paste with a little water. Pour the hot chocolate mixture on to the cornflour, stirring all the time. Return to the oven and cook on FULL (100%) for 1 minute before serving. Serve with Rich Chocolate Pudding (see page 255).
SERVES 4

TOPSY TURVY CHERRY PUDDING

METRIC/IMPERIAL
1 × 400 g/14 oz can cherry pie filling
1 packet chocolate sponge cake mix
eggs, as directed by packet instructions
custard or cream, to serve

Spread the pie filling over the base of a 19 cm/7½ inch soufflé dish, 10 cm/4 inches deep.

Make up the cake mix according to directions, adding the eggs and 1 tablespoon of water. Spread the sponge mixture evenly over the pie filling.

Cook on FULL (100%) for 5½ minutes. Remove from the oven, cover and leave to STAND for 2 minutes.

Turn out on to a plate and serve with custard or cream.
SERVES 6

GINGER SPONGE WITH GRENADINE SAUCE

METRIC/IMPERIAL
25 g/1 oz butter
25 g/1 oz caster sugar
½ egg, beaten
25 g/1 oz self-raising flour
½ teaspoon ground ginger
40 ml/1½ fl oz Grenadine syrup
½ teaspoon arrowroot powder
40 ml/1½ fl oz water

Cream the butter with the sugar until light and fluffy. Gradually beat in the egg, blending well. Using a metal spoon, fold in the flour and ginger. Stir in 2 teaspoons of the Grenadine syrup.

Lightly grease a small individual pudding bowl or measuring jug and add the sponge mixture. Cover loosely and cook on FULL (100%) for 1½ to 2 minutes, until well risen and cooked. Allow to STAND for 2 minutes.

Meanwhile, mix the arrowroot with the water in a small jug. Stir in the remaining Grenadine syrup. Cook on FULL (100%) for ½ to 1 minute, stirring twice, until the sauce is clear and thickened.

Turn the pudding out on to a serving plate and spoon over the sauce.
SERVES 1

ORANGE BAVAROIS

METRIC/IMPERIAL
2 tablespoons Cointreau
1 tablespoon powdered gelatine
300 ml/½ pint fresh orange juice
2 egg yolks
25 g/1 oz sugar
grated rind of 1 orange
200 ml/7 fl oz double cream, stiffly whipped
thin strands of orange rind, to decorate

Place the Cointreau in a small cup, sprinkle over the gelatine and set aside to soak.

Place the orange juice in a small jug and cook on FULL (100%) for 3 minutes.

Place the egg yolks in a medium bowl, add the sugar and beat until thick and creamy.

Gradually beat the hot orange juice and the grated orange rind into the egg mixture. Cook on FULL (100%) for 2½ minutes or until it has thickened slightly, beating every ½ minute.

Beat in the gelatine and stir until dissolved. Set aside until it begins to set, stirring occasionally.

Fold in the cream, pour the mixture into a 600 ml/1 pint mould and chill in the refrigerator until set. Turn out and decorate with the orange strands.
SERVES 4

RICH CHOCOLATE PUDDING

METRIC/IMPERIAL
2 large eggs
50 g/2 oz caster sugar
25 g/1 oz plain flour
25 g/1 oz cocoa
Chocolate Sauce (see page 254), to serve

Using an electric whisk or rotary beater, beat the eggs and sugar together in a mixing bowl until thick and pale (about 4 minutes). Sift together the flour and cocoa, put on a plate and cook on FULL (100%) for 5 seconds just to warm.

Using a metal tablespoon, lightly fold the warmed cocoa and flour into the egg mixture. Pour into an ungreased 1.2 litre/2 pint ovenproof pudding basin and cook on FULL (100%) for 3½ minutes.

Leave to STAND for 3 minutes before turning out. Serve with hot Chocolate Sauce.
SERVES 4

GOLDEN AUTUMN PUDDING

METRIC/IMPERIAL
100 g/4 oz butter
100 g/4 oz soft brown sugar
40 g/1½ oz raisins
15 g/½ oz walnut pieces
1 small banana, finely chopped
1 dessert apple, peeled, cored and finely chopped
grated rind and juice of 1 small orange
1 egg, beaten
150 g/5 oz self-raising flour
1 teaspoon ground cinnamon
1 tablespoon milk
2 tablespoons brown rum

Place 40 g/1½ oz of the butter in a bowl and heat on FULL (100%) for ½ minute or until melted. Stir in 40 g/1½ oz of the sugar with the raisins, walnut pieces, banana and apple.

Cream the remaining butter with the remaining sugar and the orange rind until light and fluffy. Gradually beat in the egg.

Sift the flour with the cinnamon and fold into the creamed mixture with the orange juice. Add the milk and rum, blending well to give a mixture with a soft, dropping consistency.

Spoon one-third of the apple mixture on to the base of a greased pudding basin or ring mould and top with one-third of the cake mixture. Repeat twice, finishing with a layer of cake mixture.

Cook on LOW (30%) for 4 to 5 minutes. Raise the power setting and cook on FULL (100%) for 3 to 4 minutes, turning the dish twice. Leave to STAND for 5 minutes.

To serve, invert the pudding on to a warmed serving plate. Serve hot with cream or custard.
SERVES 4

GOOSEBERRY AND MINT PUDDING

METRIC/IMPERIAL
Sponge pudding:
100 g/4 oz butter
100 g/4 oz caster sugar
2 eggs, beaten
100 g/4 oz self-raising flour
pinch of salt
1–2 tablespoons hot water
4–5 tablespoons gooseberry jam
½ teaspoon chopped fresh mint

Custard:
300 ml/½ pint milk
2 eggs
1 tablespoon caster sugar
1 teaspoon cornflour
2–3 drops of vanilla essence

Grease a 900 ml/1½ pint pudding basin well.

Cream the butter with the sugar until light and fluffy. Add the eggs, blending well. Sift the flour with the salt and fold into the mixture with a metal spoon. Add enough water to make a soft, dropping consistency.

Mix the jam with the mint and place in the bottom of the basin. Spoon the sponge mixture on top. Partially cover and cook on FULL (100%) for 6 to 7 minutes, turning the basin once. Leave to STAND for 5 to 10 minutes.

Place the milk in a jug and cook on FULL (100%) for about 3 minutes or until almost boiling. Lightly beat the eggs, sugar, cornflour and vanilla essence together. Pour the milk on to this mixture, stir well to blend and strain back into the jug.

Stand the jug in a deep dish containing hand-hot water to come halfway up the sides and cook on FULL (100%) for 4 minutes, stirring every 1 minute to keep the sauce smooth. The custard is cooked when it lightly coats the back of the spoon. Serve with the turned-out sponge pudding.
SERVES 4

HONEY APPLE SAUCE

METRIC/IMPERIAL
1½ teaspoons cornflour
150 ml/¼ pint apple juice plus a few drops of lemon juice
1 tablespoon runny honey
25 g/1 oz raisins

Blend the cornflour with a little apple juice to a smooth consistency.

Place the remaining apple juice, honey and raisins in a jug and cook on FULL (100%) for 2 minutes.

Whisk in the blended cornflour and cook on FULL (100%) for 1 minute. Serve with Fruity Apple Pudding.
MAKES 150 ml/¼ pint

MARIE LOUISE CUPS

METRIC/IMPERIAL
100 g/4 oz plain chocolate
50 g/2 oz chocolate sponge cake, crumbled
75 g/3 oz prepared soft fruit (raspberries, strawberries or cherries, for example), sliced
2–3 tablespoons sherry
300 ml/½ pint double cream
chocolate curls, to decorate

Break the chocolate into pieces and place in a bowl. Cook on MEDIUM (50%) for 2½ to 3 minutes, stirring twice, or until melted. Use the melted chocolate to coat the insides of 7 paper bun cases, then turn the cases upside down so that the chocolate edges remain thicker than the base. Chill until set, about 1 to 2 hours.

Mix the sponge cake with the fruit and enough sherry to moisten.

Carefully peel away the paper cases from the chocolate. Fill each chocolate cup with an equal quantity of the sponge mixture.

Whip the cream until it stands in soft peaks. Spoon into a piping bag fitted with a large star nozzle and pipe generously, in swirls, on top of the sponge mixture. Decorate with chocolate curls and serve lightly chilled.
SERVES 7

FRUITY APPLE PUDDING

METRIC/IMPERIAL
1 small egg
150 ml/¼ pint milk
1 large cooking apple, peeled, cored and grated
100 g/4 oz fresh brown or white breadcrumbs
50 g/2 oz shredded suet
175 g/6 oz dried mixed fruit
1 tablespoon honey
1 teaspoon mixed spice
grated rind and juice of 1 orange
Honey Apple Sauce (see left), to serve

Beat together the egg and the milk. Add all the remaining ingredients and mix well.

Pour into an ungreased medium mixing bowl. Cover and cook on MEDIUM (50%) for 6 to 7 minutes, then on FULL (100%) for 2 minutes.

Leave to STAND while making the Honey Apple Sauce. Turn the pudding on to a plate and pour over the hot sauce.
SERVES 6

QUEEN OF PUDDINGS

METRIC/IMPERIAL
3 egg yolks
50 g/2 oz caster sugar
600 ml/1 pint milk
2 drops of vanilla essence
175 g/6 oz fresh white breadcrumbs
grated rind of ½ lemon
2 tablespoons jam
Topping:
175 g/6 oz caster sugar
3 egg whites, stiffly whisked

Place the egg yolks, caster sugar, milk and vanilla essence in a jug and whisk together. Cook on FULL (100%) for 4 minutes.

Place the breadcrumbs and grated lemon rind in a 1.2 litre/2 pint casserole and stir in the milk mixture. Cook on FULL (100%) for 5½ minutes, stirring halfway through cooking. Set aside.

Place the jam in a small dish and cook on FULL (100%) for 1 minute. Gently spread the jam over the cooked breadcrumb and milk mixture.

For the topping, fold the sugar into the whisked egg whites. Spread the meringue over the jam and swirl into decorative peaks.

Brown the pudding under a preheated hot grill.
SERVES 4

APPLE PANCAKES

METRIC/IMPERIAL
1 large egg (size 1)
1 egg yolk
300 ml/½ pint milk
100 g/4 oz plain flour
150 ml/¼ pint double cream
cream, to serve (optional)
Filling:
675 g/1½ lb eating apples, peeled, cored and chopped
25 g/1 oz sultanas
25 g/1 oz butter
½ teaspoon ground cinnamon
50 g/2 oz demerara sugar

Beat together the egg, egg yolk and milk. Put the flour in a mixing bowl and whisk in the egg mixture. Set aside.

Place the apples, sultanas, butter, cinnamon and 25 g/1 oz of the sugar in a large bowl. Cover and cook on FULL (100%) for 7 minutes, stirring halfway through cooking. Set aside, covered.

Using a small frying pan on a *conventional hob*, make 8 thin pancakes. Fold each pancake in half and half again to form a fan shape.

Fill a pocket of each pancake with a spoonful of the apple mixture and arrange the filled pancakes in a shallow flameproof dish. Pour over the cream and sprinkle with the remaining sugar. Place under a preheated moderate grill and cook until the sugar has melted and the topping is brown and bubbling. Serve with extra cream, if wished.
MAKES 8

BUTTERSCOTCH FLAN

METRIC/IMPERIAL
Pastry case:
175 g/6 oz plain flour, sifted
pinch of salt
75 g/3 oz butter or hard margarine
1 × 50 g/2 oz piece of banana
1 tablespoon cold water
Filling:
75 g/3 oz unsalted butter
100 g/4 oz dark, soft brown sugar
½ teaspoon vanilla essence
50 g/2 oz cornflour
100 ml/3½ fl oz single cream
2 large (size 2) egg yolks
Topping:
2 large (size 2) egg whites
75 g/3 oz caster sugar

Mix the flour and salt in a large bowl and rub in the butter or margarine.

Mash the banana with the water, stir into the flour mixture, then knead lightly (the pastry can be made successfully in a food processor). Roll out the dough and use to line a 21 cm/8½ inch greased flan dish.

Leave to STAND at room temperature for 10 to 15 minutes, then line with greaseproof paper and baking beans and bake 'blind' in a preheated *conventional oven* on 200°C/400°F/Gas Mark 6 for 15 minutes. Remove the paper and beans, reduce the oven temperature to 190°C/375°F/Gas Mark 5 and bake for a further 5 to 10 minutes until the pastry is cooked through.

While the pastry is baking, make the filling. Put the butter in a 1.2 litre/2 pint bowl and cook on FULL (100%) for 1½ minutes or until melted. Add the sugar, stirring until it is dissolved, then cook on FULL (100%) for a further 1 minute or until the mixture is bubbling. At this stage the sugar will appear to separate from the butter.

Combine the vanilla essence, cornflour, cream and egg yolks thoroughly. Pour into the sugar mixture, reduce the setting to LOW (30%) and cook for 9 to 10 minutes, stirring frequently, until the filling is thickened and creamy. Pour into the baked pastry shell.

To make the topping, whisk the egg whites until they stand in stiff peaks. Whisk in just under half of the sugar, beating until the mixture regains its stiffness. Sprinkle the remaining sugar over the surface and, using a metal spoon, fold into the meringue.

Spread the meringue over the flan, lifting peaks with a fork or knife and making sure that the meringue reaches right to the edges of the pastry. Return the flan, still in its dish, to the *conventional oven* and bake at the lower temperature for 10 to 15 minutes, until the meringue topping is light brown. Serve warm or cold.
SERVES 4

SCANDINAVIAN LAYER PUDDING

METRIC/IMPERIAL
100 g/4 oz soft margarine
200 g/7 oz caster sugar
100 g/4 oz hazelnuts, finely chopped
100 g/4 oz flour
½ teaspoon almond essence
675 g/1½ lb cooking apples, peeled, cored and sliced
juice of ½ lemon
2 tablespoons water
300 ml/½ pint double cream
4 peaches, stoned and peeled

Beat the margarine and 100 g/4 oz sugar until soft and fluffy, then beat in the hazelnuts, flour and almond essence. Place the mixture in a deep dish and cook on FULL (100%) for 5 minutes, stirring well every 2 minutes. Set aside to cool.

Place the apples in a mixing bowl with the lemon juice and the remaining sugar. Toss well, add the water and cook on FULL (100%) for 6 to 8 minutes or until the apples are soft. Stir twice during cooking.

Whip the cream until fairly stiff and reserve a little for decoration. Slice the peaches and reserve a few slices for decoration. Crumble the cooked nut mixture (if necessary this may be placed in a plastic bag and crushed with a rolling pin).

Arrange layers of the crumble, apples, peaches and cream in a 1.2 litre/2 pint glass serving bowl, ending with a layer of crumble. Decorate with the reserved whipped cream and peach slices. Serve warm.
SERVES 4 to 6

APPLE, APRICOT AND ALMOND SPONGE

METRIC/IMPERIAL
225 g/8 oz dried apricots
600 ml/1 pint cold water
450 g/1 lb cooking apples, peeled, cored and sliced
25 g/1 oz caster sugar
50 g/2 oz toasted flaked almonds, to decorate
Sponge:
50 g/2 oz soft margarine
50 g/2 oz caster sugar
1 egg
25 g/1 oz self-raising flour
½ teaspoon baking powder
25 g/1 oz ground almonds

Place the dried apricots with half the water in a bowl and cook on FULL (100%) for 15 to 16 minutes, stirring three times. Add the remaining water and continue to cook on FULL (100%) for a further 10 minutes, stirring twice.

Add the apples and sugar to the drained apricots in a mixing bowl and cook on FULL (100%) for 4 minutes, stirring once. Transfer to a 1.2 litre/2 pint dish.

To make the sponge, place the margarine, sugar, egg, flour, baking powder and ground almonds in a mixing bowl and whisk thoroughly to give a light, fluffy consistency. Spread this mixture over the fruit in the dish and sprinkle the toasted almonds over the top. Cook on FULL (100%) for 5 minutes, turning the dish three times during cooking. Serve with whipped cream.
SERVES 4 to 6

Note: For a quicker alternative, used drained, canned apricots and omit the first 25 to 26 minutes cooking time.

PINEAPPLE RICE PUDDING

METRIC/IMPERIAL
50 g/2 oz round-grain pudding rice
¼ teaspoon grated nutmeg
7 g/¼ oz butter
900 ml/1½ pints boiling water
25 g/1 oz caster sugar
1 × 175 g/6 oz can evaporated milk
1 × 375 g/13 oz can pineapple tidbits in natural juice

Place the rice, nutmeg, butter and boiling water in a 900 ml/1½ pint oval pie dish. Stir gently to mix, then half cover and cook on FULL (100%) for 20 minutes, stirring occasionally.

Stir in the sugar and evaporated milk and cook on FULL (100%) for 9 minutes, or until the pudding is creamy and the rice is tender, stirring once. Cover completely and leave to STAND for 5 minutes.

Stir in the pineapple and its juice, blending well. Cook on FULL (100%) for a further 2 minutes. Serve at once.
SERVES 4

ORANGE BREAD AND BUTTER PUDDING

METRIC/IMPERIAL
3 slices bread from a large cut loaf, buttered
300 ml/½ pint milk
2 tablespoons sultanas
1 tablespoon currants
2 tablespoons grated orange rind
1 tablespoon chopped mixed peel
3 tablespoons demerara sugar
2 eggs
orange quarters, to decorate

Cut each slice of bread into 4 triangles and arrange 10 of these around the base and sides of a 1 litre/1½ pint pie dish, buttered side against the dish. Place the extra 2 triangles, buttered side up, in the centre of the dish. The crusts should form a border around the edge of the dish.

Combine the milk, sultanas, currants, grated orange rind and chopped peel and 1 tablespoon of the sugar in a bowl or jug. Cook on FULL (100%) for 2½ minutes or until the milk is hot but not boiling.

Beat the eggs in a separate small bowl. Add 2 tablespoons of the hot milk mixture, stir thoroughly, then pour into the milk mixture.

Stir, then pour into the pie dish. Leave to STAND for 10 minutes.

Reduce the setting to LOW (30%) and cook for 10 minutes. Turn the dish round, sprinkle the remaining sugar over the pudding and cook on LOW (30%) for a further 3 minutes or until the custard is just set. The 2 triangles of bread placed in the base of the dish may rise to the top during cooking and the custard may not be quite set in the middle, but do not cook any longer or the mixture may curdle.

For a more attractive finish, cook the pudding under a preheated hot grill at a distance of 15 to 20 cm/6 to 8 inches until golden. Serve hot or cold, decorated with the orange quarters.
SERVES 4

APPLE AND BLACKBERRY CRUMBLE

METRIC/IMPERIAL
450 g/1 lb fresh or frozen blackberries
450 g/1 lb apples, peeled, cored and sliced
75 g/3 oz demerara sugar
Crumble topping:
175 g/6 oz plain flour
½ teaspoon mixed spice
40 g/1½ oz butter
40 g/1½ oz lard
25 g/1 oz sugar
50 g/2 oz fresh breadcrumbs

Place the blackberries in a large deep dish and, if frozen, cook on DEFROST (20%) for 5 minutes to thaw. Add the sliced apples and two-thirds of the sugar and mix thoroughly.

To prepare the topping, sift the flour and spice into a bowl. Rub in the butter and lard until the mixture resembles coarse breadcrumbs. Stir in the sugar and breadcrumbs.

Spread evenly over the fruit and flatten gently with a spatula. Sprinkle the remaining demerara sugar on top.

Cook on FULL (100%) for 14 to 16 minutes, giving the dish a quarter-turn every 3 to 4 minutes, until a skewer inserted into the topping comes out clean. Leave to STAND for 5 minutes before serving.

If a crisp brown topping is preferred, place under a preheated hot grill until lightly browned.
SERVES 6

TREACLE PUDDING

METRIC/IMPERIAL
3 tablespoons golden syrup
100 g/4 oz self-raising flour
50 g/2 oz shredded suet
50 g/2 oz caster sugar
1 egg
2 tablespoons water
4 tablespoons milk
2 drops of vanilla essence

Place the golden syrup in the bottom of a lightly greased 900 ml/1½ pint basin.

Mix the flour, suet and sugar together. Beat in the egg, water, milk and vanilla essence. Spoon the mixture on to the syrup in the basin.

Cover the basin with greaseproof paper and cook on FULL (100%) for 2 minutes. Remove the paper and turn the basin round. Cook on FULL (100%) for a further 2 minutes.

Leave the pudding to STAND for 2 minutes before turning out and serving.
SERVES 4

RHUBARB AND ORANGE CRUMBLE

METRIC/IMPERIAL
75 g/3 oz butter
225 g/8 oz muesli
675 g/1½ lb rhubarb, sliced
50 g/2 oz caster sugar
grated rind of 1 orange
1 tablespoon orange juice
orange slices, to decorate (optional)

Place the butter in a jug and heat on FULL (100%) for 1 to 1½ minutes until melted. Stir in the muesli and mix well to coat with butter.

Layer the rhubarb with sugar, orange rind and orange juice in an ovenproof glass dish.

Sprinkle the muesli mixture on top and cook on FULL (100%) for 8 to 12 minutes.

Leave to STAND for 3 minutes before serving hot with fresh cream. Alternatively, serve cold, decorated with slices of fresh orange.
SERVES 4

JAMAICAN SAVARIN

METRIC/IMPERIAL
150 ml/¼ pint milk
2 teaspoons sugar
2 teaspoons dried yeast
225 g/8 oz plain flour
pinch of salt
150 g/5 oz butter
4 eggs, beaten
Syrup:
175 g/6 oz sugar
5 tablespoons water
2 tablespoons rum
Glaze:
6 tablespoons apricot jam
25 g/1 oz chopped mixed candied peel
Decoration:
fresh fruit to taste

Pour the milk into a jug and cook on FULL (100%) for ½ minute until warm. Whisk in the sugar and yeast with a fork. Set aside for 10 to 15 minutes until frothy.

Sift the flour and salt into a mixing bowl and cook on FULL (100%) for ¼ minute. Make a well in the centre and pour in the yeast liquid. Draw some of the flour over the top. Cover and set aside for 40 minutes until the mixture is spongy.

Cut the butter into small pieces and add to the mixture with the beaten eggs. Beat thoroughly for at least 5 minutes until the mixture is smooth and elastic. Turn into a well-greased 2.2 litre/ 4 pint ring mould. Cover and leave until doubled in size. Cook on FULL (100%) for 5 seconds every 10 minutes to hasten rising, if wished.

When the mixture has risen halfway up the mould, cook on FULL (100%) for 3 to 3½ minutes, until just dry on top, giving the dish a quarter-turn every 1 minute. Turn out on to a wire tray and allow to cool slightly.

To make the syrup, place the sugar and water in a large jug and cook on FULL (100%) for 7 minutes. Stir in the rum. Spoon the syrup over the savarin and allow it to soak in.

Place the apricot jam in a jug and cook on FULL (100%) for ¼ minute. Spread over the top and sides of the savarin. Sprinkle the sides with chopped peel.

Transfer carefully to a serving plate and allow to cool. Fill the centre of the savarin with chopped fresh fruit to taste and serve with fresh cream.
SERVES 8

SHERRY TRIFLE

METRIC/IMPERIAL
750 ml/1¼ pints Egg Custard (see page 312)
Cake base:
½ teaspoon baking powder
50 g/2 oz self-raising flour
50 g/2 oz sugar
50 g/2 oz soft margarine
1 large egg (size 1 or 2)
½ teaspoon vanilla essence
Filling:
1 × 400 g/14 oz can raspberries
2 tablespoons sweet sherry
Decoration:
150 ml/¼ pint double cream, whipped
few glacé cherries
few angelica leaves

Prepare the custard and allow to cool slightly.

Beat together all the ingredients for the cake base in a large bowl for 1 to 2 minutes. Cook on FULL (100%) for 1 minute. Give the bowl a half-turn and cook on FULL (100%) for 1 minute, until the cake base is just dry on top. Leave to STAND for 2 minutes.

Using a spoon, break the cake into pieces, and turn into a serving bowl. Spread the raspberries and their juice over the cake and sprinkle with the sherry. Pour the custard over the top and chill until firm.

Decorate with whipped cream, glacé cherries and angelica leaves before serving.
SERVES 4 to 6

BLACKCURRANT BAKED CHEESECAKE

METRIC/IMPERIAL
Base:
50 g/2 oz butter
175 g/6 oz digestive biscuits, crushed
Filling:
50 g/2 oz butter
50 g/2 oz sugar
225 g/8 oz cream cheese
150 ml/¼ pint soured cream
2 eggs, separated
1 × 400 g/14 oz can blackcurrant pie filling

Line a 23 cm/9 inch deep flan dish with grease-proof paper.

To make the base, place the butter in a bowl and heat on FULL (100%) for ½ minute or until melted. Stir in the biscuit crumbs, stirring well to coat. Spoon into the base of the dish, pressing down well.

To make the filling, cream the butter and sugar until light and fluffy. Gradually beat in the cream cheese, soured cream and egg yolks, blending well.

Whisk the egg whites until they stand in stiff peaks. Using a metal spoon, fold the beaten egg white into the cream mixture. Spoon on top of the biscuit base. Cook on FULL (100%) for 8 minutes, turning the dish twice. Leave to STAND until cool.

When cool, top the cheesecake with the pie filling. Serve lightly chilled.
SERVES 8

GINGERED WALNUT FLAN

METRIC/IMPERIAL
Pastry:
225 g/8 oz plain flour
pinch of salt
50 g/2 oz lard
50 g/2 oz butter
1 tablespoon caster sugar
2–3 tablespoons iced water
Filling:
50 g/2 oz butter
3 eggs, beaten
175 g/6 oz soft, dark brown sugar
1 teaspoon ground ginger
5 tablespoons golden syrup
175 g/6 oz walnuts, coarsely chopped
whipped cream, to serve

Sift the flour with the salt into a bowl. Rub in the lard and butter until the mixture resembles fine breadcrumbs. Stir in the sugar and water and bind together to a firm but pliable dough. Turn on to a lightly floured surface and knead until smooth and free from cracks.

Roll out the pastry on a lightly floured surface to a round large enough to line a 23 cm/9 inch flan dish. Press in firmly, taking care not to stretch the pastry. Cut the pastry away, leaving a 5 mm/¼ inch 'collar' above the dish to allow for any shrinkage that may occur. Prick the base and sides well with a fork.

Place a double thickness of absorbent kitchen paper over the base, easing into position around the edges.

Cook on FULL (100%) for 3½ minutes, giving the dish a quarter-turn every 1 minute.

Remove the paper and cook on FULL (100%) for a further 1½ minutes.

Prepare the filling by placing the butter in a bowl. Heat on FULL (100%) for ¾ to 1 minute or until melted. Stir in the eggs, sugar, ginger, syrup and walnuts, blending well.

Spoon into the flan case and cook on MEDIUM (50%) for 18 to 20 minutes, giving the dish a quarter-turn every 4½ minutes, until set. Allow to cool.

Serve cut into wedges, topped with swirls of whipped cream.

MAKES one 23 cm/9 inch flan

LEMON ALMOND CHEESECAKE

METRIC/IMPERIAL
Base:
50 g/2 oz butter
100 g/4 oz digestive biscuits, crushed
50 g/2 oz flaked almonds
Filling:
100 g/4 oz cream cheese
100 g/4 oz curd cheese
50 g/2 oz caster sugar
1 egg, beaten
2 teaspoons lemon juice
½ teaspoon vanilla essence
½ teaspoon cornflour
300 ml/½ pint double cream

Place the butter in a bowl and heat on FULL (100%) for 1 minute or until melted. Stir in the biscuit crumbs and almonds, blending well. Press the mixture evenly into the base and sides of a 21.5 cm/8½ inch diameter shallow glass cake dish. Cook on FULL (100%) for 1 minute.

To make the filling, mix the cream cheese with the curd cheese, sugar, egg, lemon juice, vanilla essence and cornflour, blending well. Pour into the crumb crust. Cook on LOW (30%) for 8 to 10 minutes, turning the dish three times. When cooked, the filling will be set around the outside of the dish but the centre will still be slightly soft. Leave to STAND for 10 minutes.

Spoon 2 to 3 tablespoons of the cream over the surface of the cheesecake and cook on FULL (100%) for 1 minute. Leave to cool, then chill the cheesecake for 2 to 4 hours.

Just before serving, whip the remaining cream until it stands in soft peaks. Pipe over the top of the cheesecake in an attractive design.

SERVES 5 to 6

CHESTNUT CHARLOTTE RUSSE

METRIC/IMPERIAL
150 ml/¼ pint lemon jelly, made up but not set
5 candied lemon slices, halved
a few strips of angelica
24 sponge fingers
300 ml/½ pint milk
2 eggs
1 tablespoon caster sugar
2–3 drops of vanilla essence
150 ml/¼ pint canned sweetened chestnut purée
7 g/¼ oz powdered gelatine
1 tablespoon water
1 tablespoon lemon juice
300 ml/½ pint double or whipping cream
Decoration:
whipped cream
marrons glacés

Lightly oil the base of a 1 litre/1¾ pint charlotte mould. Pour in a very thin layer of the lemon jelly and chill to set.

Place the lemon slices and strips of angelica in a decorative pattern on top of the jelly and pour over the remaining jelly, taking care not to disturb the lemon slices and angelica from their position. Chill to set.

Arrange the sponge fingers around the sides of the charlotte mould, sugared sides outwards.

Place the milk in a jug and cook on FULL (100%) for about 3 minutes or until almost boiling. Lightly beat the eggs, sugar and vanilla essence together. Pour on the milk, stir well to blend and strain back into the jug.

Place the jug in a water bath containing hand-hot water that comes halfway up the sides, and cook on FULL (100%) for 4 minutes, stirring every 1 minute to keep the sauce smooth. The custard is cooked when it lightly coats the back of the spoon. Allow to cool slightly, then whisk in the chestnut purée until well blended.

Soften the gelatine in the water and lemon juice. Cook on FULL (100%) for ½ to 1 minute until clear and dissolved. Stir into the custard mixture, blending well. Chill until almost set.

Whip the cream until it stands in soft peaks. Fold the cream into the custard mixture and pour into the charlotte mould. Chill until set.

To serve, trim the sponge fingers, then dip the mould briefly into hot water and invert the charlotte on to a serving dish. Decorate with whipped cream and marrons glacés.

SERVES 6

PEACH CRUNCH PIE

METRIC/IMPERIAL
50 g/2 oz butter
175 g/6 oz sweet digestive biscuits (including
some chocolate digestives), crushed
1 × 400 g/14 oz can sliced or halved peaches
25 g/1 oz icing sugar, sifted
2 teaspoons arrowroot
yellow food colouring

Put the butter in an 18 cm/7 inch round pie dish
and heat on FULL (100%) for 1 minute or until
melted.

Add the biscuit crumbs and mix thoroughly.
Press into the base and sides of the dish to form a
flan case. Cook on FULL (100%) for 2 minutes,
giving the dish a half-turn after 1 minute.

Drain the juice from the peaches and reserve
150 ml/¼ pint. Arrange the peaches in the flan
case. Combine the icing sugar, arrowroot and a
few drops of yellow colouring in a jug. Gradually blend in the reserved peach juice. Cook on
FULL (100%) for 2 minutes until the glaze
thickens, stirring occasionally.

Pour the glaze over the fruit and leave to cool.
Serve cold, with fresh cream, if liked.
SERVES 4

Note: To loosen the crust when cold, dip the
base of the dish in hot water.

BLACK CHERRY CREAM PIE

METRIC/IMPERIAL
Base:
100 g/4 oz butter
165 g/5½ oz bran flakes
1½ tablespoons soft brown sugar
Filling:
1 × 425 g/15 oz can black cherries in syrup
1 × 135 g/4¾ oz packet black cherry jelly
300 ml/½ pint black cherry yogurt
300 ml/½ pint double cream, whipped

Place the butter in a large bowl and heat on
FULL (100%) for 1½ to 2 minutes or until
melted. Stir in the bran flakes and sugar, tossing
well to coat. Press on to the base and sides of a
deep 23 cm/9 inch flan tin with a removable base.
Chill for about 30 minutes until set.

Drain the juice from the cherries into a bowl.
Add the jelly and cook on FULL (100%) for 2½

to 3½ minutes, stirring once, to dissolve completely. Chill until just beginning to set.

Whisk the jelly with the yogurt until foamy.
Fold in half the cream with a metal spoon. Pour
into the pie case. Chill to set.

Pipe or swirl the remaining cream on top of
the pie and decorate with the black cherries.
Serve chilled.
MAKES one 23 cm/9 inch pie

APRICOT TRIFLE

METRIC/IMPERIAL
1 tablespoon caster sugar
1 packet sponge mix, made up as directed but
add 2 extra tablespoons milk
about 2 tablespoons cherry jam
Apricot Compote (see page 234), refrigerated
overnight
4 tablespoons sherry
few drops of almond essence
Custard Sauce (see page 311)
1 egg yolk
300 ml/½ pint whipping cream
Decoration:
angelica
glacé cherries

To cook the sponge, first prepare a 19 cm/
7½ inch soufflé dish by lightly brushing the base
and sides with oil. Put a circle of greaseproof
paper on the base and coat the sides with sugar.
Tap out any surplus sugar.

Pour the prepared sponge mixture into the
soufflé dish and cook on FULL (100%) for 4
minutes. Leave to STAND, covered, for 4
minutes, before turning out on to a cooling rack.

Split the cooled sponge cake in half and spread
with jam. Sandwich together and cut into
chunks. Use the sponge chunks to line a large,
deep glass serving dish.

Drain the juice from the apricots and mix with
the sherry. Spoon over the sponge and press
down with the back of a metal spoon. Mix the
apricots with the almond essence and pile evenly
on to the sponge.

Cool the custard sauce slightly and beat in the
egg yolk. Pour the custard over the apricots to
cover. Cool and refrigerate to set.

Whisk the cream until it stands in soft peaks,
then spread over the custard to cover. Using a
fork, make a pattern on the cream and decorate
with glacé cherries and angelica.
SERVES 6

CHOCOLATE REFRIGERATOR CAKE

METRIC/IMPERIAL
100 g/4 oz plain cooking chocolate
150 g/5 oz unsalted butter
2 tablespoons golden syrup
225 g/8 oz semi-sweet biscuits, crushed
25 g/1 oz nuts, chopped
25 g/1 oz glacé cherries, chopped
25 g/1 oz raisins

Break the chocolate into pieces and place in a bowl with the butter and golden syrup. Cook on FULL (100%) for 4 minutes, stirring once.

Add the biscuit crumbs, nuts, cherries and raisins, blending well. Spoon into a greased 23 cm/9 inch cake tin and freeze for 2 to 4 hours to set.

Cut into 16 pieces for serving. Top with a little whipped cream, if liked. Store in the refrigerator for up to 2 weeks.

MAKES 16 pieces

CREAMY APPLE FLAN

METRIC/IMPERIAL
Flan case:
100 g/4 oz butter
1 tablespoon golden syrup
200 g/7 oz ginger biscuits, crushed
50 g/2 oz hazelnuts, finely chopped
Filling:
575 g/1¼ lb dessert apples, peeled, cored and sliced
2 tablespoons lemon juice
75 ml/3 fl oz double or whipping cream
2 large eggs (size 1)
50 g/2 oz caster sugar
¼ teaspoon ground cinnamon
Decoration:
1 red apple, cored, sliced and dipped in lemon juice
whipped cream (optional)

Place the butter in a large jug and heat on FULL (100%) for 1½ to 2 minutes or until melted. Stir in the syrup until well blended, then mix in the crushed biscuits and nuts. Place the mixture in a shallow 20 cm/8 inch round cake tin or deep flan tin with a removable base. Using the back of a spoon, press the biscuit mixture over the base and sides of the tin.

Place the apples and lemon juice in a large bowl. Cover and cook on FULL (100%) for 7 minutes, stirring halfway through cooking.

Beat together the cream, eggs, sugar and cinnamon. Mix with the apples and purée in a blender or food processor.

Return the apple and cream mixture to the bowl and cook on FULL (100%) for 2½ minutes, stirring every ½ minute to avoid curdling.

Pour the mixture into the flan case and chill in the refrigerator. Decorate with slices of apple and serve with whipped cream, if wished.

SERVES 4

HONEY CHEESECAKE

METRIC/IMPERIAL
Base:
1 tablespoon golden syrup
100 g/4 oz butter
225 g/8 oz digestive biscuits, crushed
Filling:
350 g/12 oz full-fat soft cheese
½ teaspoon ground cinnamon
1 tablespoon lemon juice
2 tablespoons water
1 tablespoon powdered gelatine
4 tablespoons clear honey
150 ml/¼ pint double or whipping cream, whipped
Decoration:
150 ml/¼ pint double or whipping cream, whipped
walnut halves

Place the syrup and butter in a medium bowl. Cook on FULL (100%) for 1¼ minutes. Stir in the crushed biscuits and mix well. Use this mixture to line a 20 cm/8 inch flan dish.

Beat the cheese and cinnamon together until smooth.

Place the lemon juice and water in a jug and stir in the gelatine. Cook on FULL (100%) for ¼ minute. Stir well to make sure the gelatine has dissolved.

Place the honey in another jug. Cook on FULL (100%) for ½ minute, then pour the honey into the first jug containing the gelatine and mix well together. Allow to cool slightly.

Beat the honey mixture into the cheese mixture and fold in the whipped cream. Spoon into the flan case and chill until set.

Decorate the cheesecake with the whipped cream and walnut halves.

SERVES 6

PEACHY CHEESECAKE

METRIC/IMPERIAL
Base:
75 g/3 oz butter
175 g/6 oz digestive biscuits, crushed
100 g/4 oz caster sugar
Filling:
3 tablespoons raspberry jam
1 × 400 g/14 oz can sliced peaches, drained
225 g/8 oz cream cheese
150 ml/¼ pint soured cream
2 eggs, separated
½ teaspoon almond essence
3 teaspoons cornflour, blended with a little water
toasted almonds, to decorate

Place the butter in a large mixing bowl and heat on FULL (100%) for 1½ to 2 minutes or until melted. Mix in the biscuit crumbs with 25 g/1 oz sugar. Press over the base of a large soufflé dish or a 25 cm/10 inch flan dish.

To make the jam easy to spread, place in a small dish and cook on FULL (100%) for 10 to 15 seconds. Spread over the biscuit base.

Chop the peaches, reserving 6 slices for decoration. Arrange the chopped peaches over the jam and refrigerate.

Place the cream cheese in a large mixing bowl and cook on MEDIUM (50%) for 2 minutes. Beat in the remaining sugar, soured cream, egg yolks, almond essence and blended cornflour, mixing well.

Whisk the egg whites until stiff. Using a metal spoon, fold into the cheese mixture. Pour over the peaches to cover evenly.

Cook on MEDIUM (50%) for 10 minutes. Give the dish a half-turn. Cook on FULL (100%) for 2 minutes.

Leave until quite cold. Decorate with the reserved, drained peach slices and a few toasted almonds.
SERVES 8

GRAPEFRUIT CHEESECAKE

METRIC/IMPERIAL
Base:
50 g/2 oz butter
100 g/4 oz digestive biscuits, crushed
Filling:
175 g/6 oz cream cheese
2 eggs, lightly whisked

pinch of salt
75 g/3 oz caster sugar
3 tablespoons undiluted grapefruit juice
vanilla essence
almond essence
100 ml/4 fl oz soured cream
Decoration:
150 ml/¼ pint double cream, whipped
grapefruit segments

Place the butter in a bowl and heat on FULL (100%) for ½ to 1 minute or until melted. Stir in the crushed biscuit crumbs and mix well. Press into a 20 cm/8 inch flan dish, lining the base and sides evenly.

Lightly whisk the filling ingredients together until well blended and smooth. Pour into the flan dish and cook on FULL (100%) for 1½ to 2 minutes, turning the dish after 1 minute. Cook on FULL (100%) for a further 1 minute, turning after ½ minute.

Leave to STAND for 1 minute, then return to the oven and cook on FULL (100%) for a further 1 minute, turning after ½ minute. Allow to cool, then chill in the refrigerator.

Decorate with whipped cream and grapefruit segments.
SERVES 4 to 6

CHERRY CHEESECAKE

METRIC/IMPERIAL
Base:
75 g/3 oz butter
175 g/6 oz crunchy sweet biscuits, finely crushed
Filling:
450 g/1 lb cream cheese
100 g/4 oz caster sugar
3 eggs, beaten
2 teaspoons vanilla essence
150 ml/¼ pint soured cream
3 tablespoons clear honey
Decoration:
½ can cherry pie filling
150 ml/¼ pint double cream, whipped

Put the butter in a bowl and heat on FULL (100%) for 1 minute or until melted. Add the biscuit crumbs and stir well. Cook on FULL (100%) for 1 minute.

Line the base of a 20 cm/8 inch round flan dish with greaseproof paper. Press the crumbs into the base and sides of the dish to form a flan case.

Beat the cream cheese, sugar, eggs and vanilla

gether until smooth. Pour this filling into the prepared flan case. Cook on LOW (30%) for 20 to 25 minutes until the centre is almost set, giving the dish a quarter-turn every 5 minutes during cooking.

Stir the soured cream into the honey, then pour over the top of the cheesecake. Cook on FULL (100%) for 1 minute. Allow to cool, then chill in the refrigerator for 1 hour.

Pile the cherry filling on top of the cake and decorate the edge with rosettes of whipped cream.

SERVES 6

PECAN AND MAPLE SYRUP CHEESECAKE

METRIC/IMPERIAL
Base:
75 g/3 oz butter
175 g/6 oz digestive biscuits, crushed
25 g/1 oz golden granulated sugar
Filling:
65 g/2½ oz caster sugar
1 tablespoon water
65 g/2½ oz shelled pecan nuts or 225 g/8 oz whole pecan nuts
350 g/12 oz full-fat soft cheese
2 eggs, lightly beaten
25 g/1 oz cornflour
75 ml/3 fl oz maple syrup
Decoration:
150 ml/¼ pint double or whipping cream
shelled pecan nuts

Place the butter in a small jug and heat on FULL (100%) for 1½ to 2 minutes or until melted. Stir into the crushed biscuits and granulated sugar and spread over the base of a 23 cm/9 inch flan dish, pressing down well with the back of a spoon until it is smooth.

Place the caster sugar and water in a large jug and cook on FULL (100%) for 2 minutes, stirring after 1 minute.

Stir in the nuts and cook on FULL (100%) for 1½ minutes, stirring every ½ minute. Spread the nut mixture over a piece of greaseproof paper and leave it to cool. Then cover with another piece of greaseproof paper and, with a rolling pin, crush the nuts thoroughly. Set aside.

Place the cheese, eggs and cornflour in a medium bowl and beat well. Cook on FULL (100%) for 4 minutes, beating well every 1 minute.

Slowly beat in the maple syrup, then cook on FULL (100%) for 2 minutes, beating well every ½ minute.

Stir in the crushed nut mixture and spread over the biscuit base. Chill thoroughly.

To serve, decorate with double cream and pecan nuts.

SERVES 6 to 8

SULTANA CHEESECAKE WITH RUM

METRIC/IMPERIAL
Base:
50 g/2 oz butter
2 teaspoons golden syrup
100 g/4 oz malted milk biscuits, finely crushed
Filling:
225 g/8 oz curd cheese
100 g/4 oz full-fat soft cheese
100 g/4 oz cottage cheese, sieved
15 g/½ oz powdered gelatine
2 tablespoons rum
50 g/2 oz sugar
2 large eggs (size 1 or 2), lightly beaten
25 g/1 oz sultanas
2 tablespoons soured cream
Decoration:
whipped cream
sultanas

Place the butter and syrup in a small jug and heat on FULL (100%) for 1 minute or until melted. Mix with the biscuit crumbs and spread over the bottom of a 21 cm/8½ inch loose-bottomed fluted flan or quiche dish. Use the back of a spoon to press down the crust and smooth it over.

Beat together the cheeses in a very large jug. Cook on FULL (100%) for 1½ minutes, stirring after 1 minute.

Sprinkle the gelatine over the rum and leave for 5 minutes. Cook on FULL (100%) for ¼ minute to dissolve. Beat the dissolved gelatine, sugar and eggs into the cheese mixture. Cook on FULL (100%) for 3 minutes, beating every 1 minute.

Stir in the sultanas and cook on FULL (100%) for a further ½ minute. Stir in the soured cream, then spread over the prepared crust. Chill until set.

Decorate with rosettes of whipped cream and a few sultanas.

SERVES 6

PLUM CHEESECAKE

METRIC/IMPERIAL
Base:
100 g/4 oz butter
1 tablespoon golden syrup
225 g/8 oz digestive biscuits, crushed
Filling:
225 g/8 oz plum purée
25 g/1 oz caster sugar
1 tablespoon powdered gelatine
300 g/11 oz full-fat soft cheese
6 tablespoons double cream
Decoration:
150 ml/¼ pint double or whipping cream, stiffly
whipped
2 fresh plums, stoned and quartered

To make the base, put the butter in a large jug and heat on FULL (100%) for 1½ to 2 minutes or until melted. Stir in the syrup until it is well blended, then mix in the crushed biscuits. Place the mixture in a shallow 20 cm/8 inch round cake or deep flan tin with a removable base. Using the back of a spoon, press the biscuit mixture over the base and sides of the tin.

Place the plum purée and the sugar in a large jug and cook on FULL (100%) for 3 minutes or until very hot. Sprinkle the gelatine over and stir well until it has dissolved. Set aside to cool.

Beat the cheese and cream together until smooth, then gradually beat in the plum mixture. Spoon the mixture into the biscuit crumb case and smooth over. Chill in the refrigerator.

Remove the cheesecake from the tin and decorate with swirls of cream and quartered plums.
SERVES 6 to 8

OLDE ENGLISH
CHRISTMAS PUDDING

METRIC/IMPERIAL
50 g/2 oz currants
75 g/3 oz raisins
75 g/3 oz sultanas
5 glacé cherries, chopped
1 small cooking apple, peeled, cored and
chopped
25 g/1 oz candied peel, chopped
40 g/1½ oz shelled almonds, skinned and
chopped
grated rind of 1 lemon
grated rind and juice of 1 small orange

50 g/2 oz flour
¼ teaspoon salt
¼ teaspoon mixed spice
¼ teaspoon ground cinnamon
¼ teaspoon grated nutmeg
50 g/2 oz dark brown sugar
25 g/1 oz fresh breadcrumbs
50 g/2 oz shredded suet
3 tablespoons stout
2 tablespoons brandy
1 tablespoon black treacle
2 eggs, beaten
milk (as necessary)

In a large bowl, mix together all of the fruit, peel, nuts, grated rind and juice. Sift the flour, salt and spices together. Add to the fruit with the sugar, breadcrumbs and suet. Mix well.

Stir in the remaining ingredients, adding just enough milk to form a mixture which will easily drop from a spoon. Cover and leave in a cool place overnight.

Turn into a greased 1 litre/1¾ pint pudding basin. Cover loosely and cook on FULL (100%) for 8 minutes, giving the basin a quarter-turn every 2 minutes. Leave to STAND for a few hours, then cook on FULL (100%) for 2 to 3 minutes to reheat.

Alternatively, cook on LOW (30%) for 16 to 24 minutes, then STAND for 10 minutes.

Serve with custard, cream or brandy butter.
SERVES 4 to 6

RASPBERRY GÂTEAU

METRIC/IMPERIAL
4 eggs, separated
175 g/6 oz sugar
grated rind and juice of 1 lemon
75 g/3 oz fine semolina
1 tablespoon ground almonds
2 tablespoons sweet sherry
450 g/1 lb raspberries
sugar (optional)
300 ml/½ pint double cream, whipped
100 g/4 oz flaked almonds, toasted

Place the egg yolks and sugar in a bowl and whisk together until thick and creamy. Add the lemon rind, juice, semolina and ground almonds. Stiffly beat the egg whites and fold them into the mixture.

Grease two 18 cm/7 inch flan dishes or line with microwave cling film. Spoon half the gâteau mixture into each dish and spread evenly. Cook the cakes, one at a time, on MEDIUM (50%) for 5 to 6 minutes until dry on top, giving the dish a half-turn after 2½ minutes.

Leave the cakes in the dishes until cold, then invert one cake on to a serving plate. Sprinkle with the sherry, then cover with the raspberries, reserving a few for decoration. Add sugar to taste, if desired.

Invert the other cake on top. Spread two-thirds of the cream over the sides and top of the cake. Press the almonds around the sides and decorate the top with piped cream rosettes and the reserved raspberries.

MAKES one 18 cm/7 inch gâteau

MOCHA HONEY GÂTEAU

METRIC/IMPERIAL
Cake:
175 g/6 oz butter
75 g/3 oz demerara sugar
2 tablespoons clear honey
3 eggs, beaten
120 g/4½ oz self-raising flour
40 g/1½ oz cocoa powder
1 teaspoon instant coffee granules
4 tablespoons hot water
few drops of vanilla essence
Filling and topping:
40 g/1½ oz cornflour
450 ml/¾ pint milk
2 tablespoons instant coffee granules
215 g/7½ oz light, soft brown sugar
350 g/12 oz butter
65 g/2½ oz walnuts, finely chopped
Decoration:
chocolate curls or crumbled chocolate flake

Lightly grease a 20 cm/8 inch cake dish or soufflé dish and line the base with lightly greased, greaseproof paper.

Cream the butter with the sugar and honey until light and fluffy. Add the eggs, one at a time, beating well.

Sift the flour with the cocoa powder and fold into the butter mixture with a metal spoon.

Dissolve the coffee in the water and stir in the vanilla essence. Fold into the cake mixture with a metal spoon. Spoon into the prepared dish and cook on FULL (100%) for 5½ to 6½ minutes, giving the dish a quarter-turn every 1½ minutes. Leave to STAND for 5 to 10 minutes before turning out on to a wire tray to cool.

When cold, carefully cut the cake horizontally into 3 equal layers.

Make the filling and topping by blending the cornflour with a little of the milk in a bowl to form a smooth paste. Place the remaining milk in a jug with the coffee and sugar. Cook on FULL (100%) for 1½ minutes. Add the blended cornflour, stirring well to mix. Cook on FULL (100%) for 5 to 6 minutes, stirring twice, until smooth and thick. Cover the surface with grease-proof paper dampened on the top side and leave to cool completely.

Beat the butter until creamy. Gradually add the cold coffee sauce, beating well to form a smooth mixture.

Mix one-third of the coffee filling with 25 g/ 1 oz of the walnuts. Sandwich the cake layers together with this filling. Spread the top and sides of the cake with about half of the remaining coffee mixture. Press the remaining walnuts on to the sides of the cake. Place the remaining coffee mixture in a piping bag fitted with a large star nozzle and pipe swirls on top of the cake.

Decorate with chocolate curls or crumbled chocolate flake. Cut into wedges to serve.

MAKES one 20 cm/8 inch gâteau

RASPBERRY MOUSSE CAKE

METRIC/IMPERIAL
175 g/6 oz butter
175 g/6 oz caster sugar
3 eggs, beaten
finely grated rind and juice of 1 lemon
175 g/6 oz self-raising flour
1 teaspoon baking powder
350 g/12 oz raspberries
2 tablespoons icing sugar
2 tablespoons Cointreau
3 tablespoons orange juice
1½ teaspoons powdered gelatine
1 egg white
150 ml/¼ pint double cream
150 ml/¼ pint extra thick natural yogurt
toasted flaked almonds, to decorate

Cream the butter and sugar until light and fluffy. Gradually beat in the eggs, lemon rind and lemon juice.

Sift the flour and baking powder together and fold into the cake mixture with a metal spoon. Spoon into a large microwave baking ring. Cook on FULL (100%) for 7 minutes, turning the ring twice – the top will still be moist when cooked but will dry out after standing. Leave to STAND for 10 minutes, then turn out to cool on a wire rack.

When cold, slice a thin layer from the top of the cake and set aside.

Return the rest of the cake to the clean ring mould. Using a grapefruit knife, cut out the cake to leave a 1 cm/½ inch thick shell. (Use the cake crumbs for another recipe.)

Purée 225 g/8 oz of the raspberries in a blender or food processor with the icing sugar and Cointreau. Sieve to remove the seeds.

Place the orange juice in a bowl and heat on FULL (100%) for ½ minute until hot. Briskly stir in the gelatine to dissolve. Stir into the fruit purée, blending well.

Whisk the egg white until it stands in stiff peaks and lightly whip the cream until it stands in soft peaks. Using a metal spoon, fold the egg white, the remaining raspberries and half of the cream into the fruit purée.

Spoon into the sponge shell and cover with the reserved top slice. Cover and chill overnight or for at least 6 to 8 hours.

To serve, unmould the mousse cake on to a serving dish. Whisk the yogurt into the remaining cream and spoon over the cake. Sprinkle with almonds to decorate. Cut into wedges to serve.

SERVES 6 to 8

COFFEE AND WALNUT GÂTEAU WITH BRANDY SAUCE

METRIC/IMPERIAL
40 g/1½ oz self-raising flour
15 g/½ oz cornflour
½ teaspoon baking powder
50 g/2 oz soft margarine
50 g/2 oz soft, dark brown sugar
1 teaspoon coffee essence
1 egg
40 g/1½ oz walnuts, finely chopped
Filling and topping:
2 tablespoons apricot jam
1 × 300 g/11 oz can mandarin segments, drained
1 walnut half
Sauce:
35 g/1¼ oz butter, softened
15 g/½ oz flour
9 tablespoons hot water

1 egg yolk
120 ml/4 fl oz whipping cream
2 teaspoons rum
2 teaspoons brandy
25 g/1 oz icing sugar, sifted
¼ teaspoon vanilla essence

Grease a 600 ml/1 pint, 12.5 cm/5 inch diameter soufflé dish or round cake dish and line the base and sides with greased greaseproof paper, so that the paper stands 2.5 cm/1 inch higher than the dish.

To make the cake, sift the flour, cornflour and baking powder together into a mixing bowl. Add the margarine, brown sugar, coffee essence, egg and walnuts and beat for 1 minute until the mixture is smooth.

Spoon into the prepared dish and cook on FULL (100%) for 1 minute. Turn the dish and cook for a further 1 to 2 minutes, then leave to STAND for 3 to 4 minutes. Carefully turn out the cake, then reverse again, so that the cake is the right way up. Leave to cool.

Split the cake horizontally into 3 pieces and sandwich with layers of jam and mandarin segments. Spread a border of jam around the top of the cake and decorate with a circle of mandarin segments and the walnut half. Transfer carefully to a serving plate.

To make the sauce, combine 15 g/½ oz of the butter and the flour in a small bowl and beat until smooth.

Put the water into a medium bowl and cook on FULL (100%) for 2 minutes or until steaming. Whisk in the butter mixture a little at a time. Cook on FULL (100%) for a further 1 minute, stirring once.

Beat the egg yolk with 2 tablespoons of the sauce and gradually beat into the remaining sauce. Reduce the setting to LOW (30%) and cook for ½ to 2 minutes, beating after 1 minute and at the end until thickened.

Remove the bowl and beat in the remaining butter a little at a time. Leave to cool.

Half-whip the cream, then add the rum, brandy, icing sugar and vanilla essence and beat until thick. Gradually beat the sauce into the flavoured cream. Serve with the gâteau.
SERVES 2

CHOCOLATE MOUNTAIN

METRIC/IMPERIAL
100 g/4 oz margarine, softened
100 g/4 oz caster sugar
25 g/1 oz cocoa powder
90 g/3½ oz self-raising flour
1 teaspoon baking powder
2 drops of vanilla essence
2 tablespoons milk
2 large eggs (size 1 or 2), lightly beaten
8 large marshmallows, diced
150 ml/¼ pint warm coffee
sugar to taste
3 tablespoons medium sherry
Decoration:
250 ml/8 fl oz double cream, whipped
flaked chocolate
2–3 sparklers (optional)

Place the margarine, caster sugar, cocoa, flour, baking powder, vanilla, milk and eggs into a large bowl. Using an electric mixer, beat together until smooth. Do not overbeat.

Grease a 1.2 litre/2 pint bowl (or line with microwave cling film). Spoon the mixture into the bowl and cover. Place in the oven on an upturned pie dish and cook on FULL (100%) for 4½ to 5 minutes or until the base of the pudding is cooked. Leave to STAND, covered, for 10 minutes.

Leaving the pudding in the bowl, use a small sharp knife to cut a circle about 10 cm/4 inches in diameter. Scoop out the mixture from the pudding to form a well.

Leave the pudding to cool completely, then fill the well with the diced marshmallows. Cut a lid from the pudding mixture and cover the marshmallows. Prick the pudding.

Mix the warm coffee with sugar to taste and the sherry. Pour it over the pudding and refrigerate, uncovered, for about 2 hours.

Turn the pudding out on to a serving plate and remove the lining, if necessary. Cover with whipped cream and sprinkle with flaked chocolate.

For special occasions, push sparklers into the top of the pudding and set alight just before serving.
SERVES 4

BLACKBERRY AND HONEY SORBET

METRIC/IMPERIAL
1 kg/2 lb blackberries, hulled
4 tablespoons clear honey
225 g/8 oz sugar
300 ml/½ pint water
2 egg whites

Place the blackberries, honey, sugar and water in a cooking dish. Cover and cook on FULL (100%) for 6 to 8 minutes until tender, stirring once. Allow to cool, then rub through a fine nylon sieve.

Spoon into a freezer tray and freeze until almost solid. Spoon into a bowl and whisk until the ice crystals have been broken down and the mixture is smooth.

Whisk the egg whites until they stand in stiff peaks. Using a metal spoon, fold into the blackberry mixture. Return the mixture to the freezer tray and freeze until firm.

About 30 minutes before serving, transfer to the refrigerator and leave to soften slightly.

Serve scooped into dessert glasses with crisp dessert biscuits or wafers.
SERVES 4 to 6

TOASTED ALMOND ICE CREAM

METRIC/IMPERIAL
300 ml/½ pint milk
1 large egg (size 1)
2 large egg yolks (size 1)
300 ml/½ pint double cream, stiffly whipped
1 teaspoon almond essence
50 g/2 oz toasted split almonds, chopped
25 g/1 oz toasted split almonds, cut into slivers, to decorate

Place the milk in a small jug and cook on FULL (100%) for 3 minutes or until boiling. Set aside for 10 minutes.

Place the egg and the yolks in a medium bowl and beat until pale and creamy. Stir in the milk and cook on FULL (100%) for 2½ minutes or until the custard has thickened, beating every ½ minute to avoid curdling.

Whisk the custard well, then set it aside to cool, whisking occasionally while it is cooling. Fold the cream into the cooled custard and stir in the almond essence. Transfer to a freezer container and chill in the freezer for about 1 to 1½ hours until it is partially frozen.

Whisk the ice cream mixture until it is smooth. Fold in the chopped almonds and return to the freezer until frozen.

About 30 minutes before serving, transfer to the refrigerator to soften slightly. Serve the ice cream in scoops in individual bowls, decorated with slivers of almond.

SERVES 4 to 6

LEMON SORBET

METRIC/IMPERIAL
3 large lemons, washed
225 g/8 oz caster sugar
600 ml/1 pint water
1 egg white
Decoration (optional):
mint sprigs
finely grated lemon rind

Place the lemons on a plate and cook on FULL (100%) for 1 minute. (This will improve the juice yield.) Grate the rind from 2 lemons, very finely, avoiding any pith.

Squeeze the juice from the fruit and strain into a large mixing bowl.

Put the sugar and water into a very large bowl (see note) and stir. Cook on FULL (100%) for 4 minutes, stirring once during cooking. Stir again to ensure that the sugar has dissolved.

Add the grated lemon rind. Cover and cook on FULL (100%) for 4 minutes or until boiling point is reached. Stir again, return to the oven and cook on FULL (100%) for 8 minutes.

Strain the boiled syrup very carefully into the lemon juice. Pour the mixture into ice trays and cool.

When cold, freeze until mushy (this will take about 1 hour). Turn into a large cold bowl and beat until the mixture is almost white.

Quickly beat the egg white until it stands in soft peaks, then fold into the sorbet, using a metal spoon. Freeze until firm (3 to 4 hours).

About 1 hour before serving, transfer the sorbet to the refrigerator to soften. Scoop into chilled glasses and serve decorated with a mint sprig and a little grated lemon rind.

SERVES 4

Note: The bowl will become very hot when the sugar syrup is boiled, so be sure to use oven gloves when removing it from the oven.

ORANGE AND APRICOT ICE CREAM

METRIC/IMPERIAL
1 × 175 ml/6 fl oz can frozen concentrated orange juice
225 g/8 oz dried apricots
2 eggs
450 ml/¾ pint milk
175 g/6 oz sugar
300 ml/½ pint double cream

Place the orange juice in a jug and cook on FULL (100%) for 1 to 2 minutes, until melted. Add sufficient water to make up to 600 ml/1 pint. Pour into a mixing bowl with the apricots and leave to soak for 1 hour.

Whisk the eggs, milk and sugar together in another bowl and cook on FULL (100%) for 4 minutes, stirring every 1 minute. Allow to cool.

Cook the orange juice and apricots on FULL (100%) for 6½ minutes, stirring once, then allow to cool. Stir the cream into the egg mixture, pour into a shallow rigid container and partially freeze.

Place the orange juice and apricots in a blender or food processor and purée until smooth. Stir into the partially frozen ice cream. Freeze for 1 hour, whisk thoroughly and then freeze until solid. Allow to thaw slightly at room temperature before serving.

SERVES 6 to 8

COFFEE ICE CREAM

METRIC/IMPERIAL
300 ml/½ pint double cream
300 ml/½ pint single cream
50 g/2 oz caster sugar
1½ teaspoons coffee essence
4 egg yolks
3 teaspoons cornflour

Put 1.2 litre/2 pint plastic ice cream container in the freezer.

Whip the double cream to the very soft peak stage. Refrigerate to chill.

Put the single cream into a jug and cook on FULL (100%) for 3 minutes or until boiling.

Meanwhile, beat together the sugar, coffee essence and egg yolks in a large bowl. Blend in the cornflour.

Pour the heated cream on to the egg yolk mixture, beating well. Cook on FULL (100%)

for 1 to 2 minutes, until boiling point is reached. Remove from the oven, then beat again. Leave to STAND for 10 minutes.

Place the bowl in a large mixing bowl containing ice cubes. Leave, beating occasionally, until quite cold.

Beat the refrigerated whipped cream into the custard. Put the bowl into the freezer until the ice cream reaches setting point (about 35 minutes). Beat well with an electric hand whisk or rotary whisk.

Put the mixture into the ice cream container and freeze until firm (about 2 hours). About 30 minutes before serving, transfer the ice cream to the refrigerator to soften. Serve with Chocolate Sauce, if liked (see page 311).

SERVES 4 to 6

RICH CHOCOLATE CHIP ICE CREAM

METRIC/IMPERIAL
300 ml/½ pint single cream
3 eggs, beaten
40 g/1½ oz caster sugar
2 teaspoons vanilla essence
150 ml/¼ pint double cream
100 g/4 oz plain chocolate, grated, or 100 g/4 oz chocolate polka dots (chocolate drops)

Mix the single cream with the eggs and sugar in a heatproof bowl. Cook on FULL (100%) for 4 to 6 minutes, stirring every 1 minute, until slightly thickened. Stir in the vanilla essence and allow to cool.

When cool, pour the custard into freezer trays and freeze until half frozen.

Meanwhile, whip the double cream until it stands in soft peaks. Whisk the half-frozen custard until smooth. Using a metal spoon, fold in the whipped cream and chocolate. Return to the freezer trays and freeze until firm.

About 30 minutes before serving, transfer the ice cream to the refrigerator and leave to soften slightly.

Serve scooped into dessert glasses with wafers or crisp dessert biscuits.

SERVES 4 to 6

CREAMY VANILLA ICE CREAM

METRIC/IMPERIAL
2 eggs, beaten
450 ml/¾ pint milk
175 g/6 oz sugar
3 teaspoons vanilla essence
300 ml/½ pint double cream

Mix the eggs with the milk and sugar in a heatproof bowl. Cook on FULL (100%) for 6 minutes, stirring every 2 minutes, until slightly thickened. Allow to cool.

Add the vanilla essence and cream, blending well. Pour into a freezer tray and freeze until almost firm.

Remove from the freezer, turn into a bowl and whisk until smooth and creamy. Return to the freezer tray and freeze until firm.

About 30 minutes before serving, transfer the ice cream to the refrigerator and leave to soften slightly.

Serve scooped into dessert glasses with crisp dessert biscuits or wafers.

SERVES 4 to 6

CREAMY SQUARES

METRIC/IMPERIAL
200 g/7 oz cooking chocolate
50 g/2 oz ground almonds
50 g/2 oz mixed dried fruit
50 g/2 oz glacé cherries, chopped
25 g/1 oz desiccated coconut
50 g/2 oz caster sugar
1 large egg (size 1 or 2), beaten

Break up the chocolate and put into the base of a 2.25 litre/4 pint ice cream container. Cook on MEDIUM (50%) for 4½ to 5 minutes, stirring twice during cooking. Spread over the base of the container to coat. Refrigerate for 10 minutes until set.

Mix all the dry ingredients together in a mixing bowl and bind with the beaten egg. Spread the mixture in an even layer over the set chocolate, pressing down with the back of a tablespoon.

Cook on LOW (30%) for 11 minutes. Leave to cool in the container, then refrigerate. When chilled and firm, turn out and cut into tiny squares.

MAKES 40

CANDIED APPLES

METRIC/IMPERIAL
175 g/6 oz soft brown sugar
50 g/2 oz caster sugar
25 g/1 oz margarine
5 tablespoons water
1 teaspoon vinegar
1 tablespoon golden syrup
4 firm, ripe eating apples, well washed and dried

Put the sugars, margarine, water, vinegar and syrup into a mixing bowl and stir well to mix. Cook on FULL (100%) for 1 minute. Stir well for a few minutes to ensure that all the sugar has dissolved.

Return the bowl to the oven and cook on FULL (100%) for 10 minutes, or until a little toffee dropped into cold water hardens and cracks or breaks cleanly. A sugar thermometer should read 143°C/290°F (but it must be used outside the microwave oven).

Insert wooden skewers into the apples and dip each apple into the toffee, swirling it round until it is completely coated. Immediately plunge into cold water.

Leave the apples on a greased tray to set. When set and cold, wrap each apple in cling film.
MAKES 4

PRALINE

METRIC/IMPERIAL
100 g/4 oz whole almonds
225 g/8 oz granulated sugar

Cut a double sheet of greaseproof paper to fit the oven base or turntable. Mix the almonds and sugar on the paper. Cook on FULL (100%) for 11 to 13 minutes, until the sugar melts to form a dark brown syrup. Stir frequently and turn the mixture with a wooden spoon during cooking.

Leave to cool in the oven, then remove the praline from the oven and crush with a rolling pin or pulverise in a blender.

Use crushed praline in confectionery, and to decorate cakes and desserts.
MAKES 275 g/10 oz

Note: Mixtures with a high sugar content reach very high temperatures during cooking. The praline will continue to cook rapidly after the oven is switched off. Take care not to overcook, as this will give the praline a bitter flavour.

ALMOND AND PEANUT BRITTLE

METRIC/IMPERIAL
225 g/8 oz sugar
6 tablespoons golden syrup
100 g/4 oz salted peanuts
100 g/4 oz flaked almonds
7 g/¼ oz butter
1 teaspoon vanilla essence
1 teaspoon baking powder

Place the sugar and golden syrup in a large heatproof bowl. Cook on FULL (100%) for 4 minutes, stirring twice.

Add the peanuts and almonds, blending well. Cook on FULL (100%) for 3 to 5 minutes or until a rich golden colour.

Add the butter and vanilla essence, blending well. Cook on FULL (100%) for 1 to 2 minutes. Stir in the baking powder and stir gently until light and foamy. Pour on to a lightly greased baking tray and leave to set.

To serve, break the brittle up into small pieces. Store it in an airtight tin until required.
MAKES 450 g/1 lb

FUDGE

METRIC/IMPERIAL
225 g/8 oz granulated sugar
225 g/8 oz caster sugar
50 g/2 oz butter
300 ml/½ pint whipping cream
150 ml/¼ pint milk
1 teaspoon vanilla essence

Put all the ingredients into an ovenproof mixing bowl and stir well.

Cook on MEDIUM (50%) for 10 minutes. Stir well to ensure that the sugar has dissolved. If the mixture still appears to be gritty, cook on MEDIUM (50%) for a further 2 to 3 minutes.

Return to the oven and cook on FULL (100%), until the mixture reaches 115°C/240°F when tested with a sugar thermometer – this should occur within a minute or two. (Use the thermometer *outside* the microwave oven.) Beat with a wooden spoon until the mixture becomes dull.

Pour into a well-greased 19 × 19 × 2.5 cm/ 7½ × 7½ × 1 inch cake tin. Leave to cool and refrigerate overnight to set. Cut into squares.
MAKES about 50

COCONUT ICE

METRIC/IMPERIAL
450 g/1 lb caster sugar
150 ml/¼ pint milk
75 g/3 oz desiccated coconut
few drops of pink food colouring

Lightly grease an 18 × 23 × 2.5 cm/7 × 9 × 1 inch shallow dish or tray.

Place the sugar and milk in a large heatproof bowl. Cook on FULL (100%) for 4 to 5 minutes, stirring twice.

Continue cooking on FULL (100%) until the soft ball stage is reached or until a sugar thermometer registers 115°C/240°F, about 4 to 6 minutes. (Use the thermometer *outside* the oven.)

Add the coconut, blending well. Pour half of the mixture into the prepared tray. Colour the remainder pink with food colouring and pour over the white layer. Leave to harden and set. Cut into squares to serve.

MAKES about 575 g/1¼ lb

GLACÉ GRAPES

METRIC/IMPERIAL
175 g/6 oz bunch of large grapes
100 g/4 oz granulated sugar
1 teaspoon powdered glucose
5 tablespoons water

Prepare glacé fruit no longer than 1 hour before serving. Wash and dry the grapes thoroughly and separate into pairs. Brush a baking tray with oil or line with greaseproof paper.

Place the sugar, glucose and water in a large heatproof jug. Stir once, then cook on FULL (100%) for 5 to 6½ minutes until a sugar thermometer registers 155°C/310°F (when the crack stage is reached and a little of the syrup poured into cold water forms brittle strands). Do not stir during cooking.

Using a fork, quickly dip the grapes, one pair at a time, into the syrup to coat completely. Place on the prepared tray and leave for 5 minutes until set.

MAKES about 12 pairs

Note: Other fresh fruit, such as cherries and orange segments, may be glacéd in the same way with similar success, provided they are completely dry before dipping in the syrup.

CHOCOLATE MARZIPAN CHERRIES

METRIC/IMPERIAL
1 × 225 g/8 oz packet marzipan
few drops of pink food colouring
16 to 20 glacé cherries
175 g/6 oz plain cooking chocolate

Knead the marzipan lightly, then pour on the pink food colouring and knead until an even colour is obtained. Divide into 16 to 20 even-sized pieces. Roll each one into a ball, then flatten to form a circle. Place a cherry in the centre of each, draw up the sides and roll gently between the palms of the hands until no joins are visible.

Arrange the marzipan cherries on a tray and chill in the refrigerator for 30 minutes. Break the chocolate into pieces and place in a small bowl. Cook on MEDIUM (50%) for 4½ to 5 minutes, stirring twice, until melted but still holding its shape. Dip the cherry balls into the chocolate, one at a time, to coat thoroughly. Leave until the chocolate has set. Serve chilled, if preferred.

MAKES 16 to 20

MARZIPAN CHOCOLATES

METRIC/IMPERIAL
100 g/4 oz marzipan
225 g/8 oz plain or milk chocolate
few flaked almonds, crystallized violets or sugar flowers, to decorate

Using your hands, work the marzipan until pliable. Shape into small balls and small cigar shapes.

Break the chocolate into pieces and place in a mixing bowl. Cook on MEDIUM (50%) for 3 to 4 minutes, stirring twice. Beat until smooth.

Put a small amount of chocolate on the end of a round-bladed knife or palette knife. Position one piece of shaped marzipan on the chocolate, which will hold it in place. Spoon over the melted chocolate until coated. Alternatively, spear with a skewer and dip in the chocolate to coat. Place on a plate to set, and repeat until all the shapes have been coated.

Just before setting point is reached, decorate each marzipan chocolate with a piece of flaked almond, crystallized violet or sugar flower.

MAKES about 12

MARRONS GLACÉS

METRIC/IMPERIAL
675 g/1½ lb large chestnuts
350 g/12 oz granulated sugar
350 g/12 oz powdered glucose
300 ml/½ pint water
1 teaspoon vanilla essence

Start preparing marrons glacés at least 3 days before you intend to serve them.

Slit the chestnuts and place 10 on the oven shelf. Cook on FULL (100%) for 2 to 3 minutes, stirring frequently, until the chestnuts are soft. Quickly remove the skins. Repeat with the remaining chestnuts.

Combine the sugar, glucose, water and vanilla in a large bowl. Mix thoroughly, then set aside for 15 minutes. Stir again, then cook on FULL (100%) for 5 minutes or until the mixture is boiling. Cook on FULL (100%) for 2 minutes. Add the chestnuts and cook on FULL (100%) for 2 minutes. Cover and set aside for 24 hours.

Cook on FULL (100%) for 5 minutes or until boiling, then cook on FULL (100%) for 2 minutes. Cover and set aside for a further 24 hours. Repeat the process once more.

Carefully remove the chestnuts from the syrup and leave on a wire rack to drain and cool. When cold, wrap each chestnut in waxed or non-stick paper.
MAKES 20 to 30

ALMOND AND GINGER CLUSTERS

METRIC/IMPERIAL
50 g/2 oz flaked almonds
75 g/3 oz plain chocolate
25 g/1 oz crystallized ginger, chopped
finely chopped crystallized ginger, to decorate

Place the almonds on a plate and cook on FULL (100%) for 2 minutes. Stir to rearrange and cook for a further 2 minutes or until lightly browned. Leave to cool, then cut into thin slivers.

Break the chocolate into pieces and place in a bowl. Cook on MEDIUM (50%) for 2 to 2½ minutes, stirring twice, until melted. Add the almonds and ginger, blending well.

Spoon into 12 paper sweet cases. Sprinkle with the chopped ginger to decorate and leave to set.
MAKES 12

TIPSY TRUFFLES

METRIC/IMPERIAL
100 g/4 oz plain chocolate
1 egg yolk
15 g/½ oz butter
2 teaspoons sherry or rum
1 tablespoon single cream
50 g/2 oz ground almonds
50 g/2 oz toasted almond nibs or chocolate vermicelli

Break the chocolate into pieces and place in a mixing bowl. Cook on MEDIUM (50%) for 2½ to 3 minutes, stirring twice, until smooth.

Beat in the egg yolk, butter, sherry or rum, cream and ground almonds. Refrigerate for 10 minutes.

Shape into 12 balls, each the size of a walnut, and roll in the almonds or vermicelli. Put the truffles into sweet paper cases and refrigerate.
MAKES 12

COLETTES

METRIC/IMPERIAL
275 g/10 oz plain chocolate
150 ml/¼ pint double cream
1 tablespoon brandy
20 whole hazelnuts, skinned

Break the chocolate into pieces and place 100 g/ 4 oz in a bowl. Cook on MEDIUM (50%) for 2½ to 3 minutes, stirring twice, until melted. Use to coat the insides of 20 round *petit four* cases, then turn the cases upside down so that the chocolate edges remain thicker than the base. Chill until set, about 1 to 2 hours.

Place the cream in a bowl and cook on FULL (100%) for 1 to 1½ minutes or until just to the boil. Add the remaining chocolate, stirring well to melt completely. Cook on FULL (100%) for 1 to 1½ minutes or until just to the boil. Stir in the brandy, blending well.

Allow to cool, then chill until the mixture is just beginning to set. Spoon into a piping bag fitted with a star nozzle and pipe equal quantities of the chocolate truffle mixture into the chocolate cases. Chill to set.

Carefully peel away the paper cases from the chocolate colettes and decorate each with a hazelnut. Return to new *petit four* cases and serve lightly chilled.
MAKES 20

TRIO TRUFFLES

METRIC/IMPERIAL
200 ml / 7 fl oz double cream
few drops of vanilla essence
450 g / 1 lb plain chocolate
40 g / 1½ oz butter
½ Jamaica ginger cake
about 50 g / 2 oz chocolate vermicelli
about 50 g / 2 oz long-thread coconut
about 75 g / 3 oz chopped nuts

Place the cream in a bowl and cook on FULL (100%) for 2 to 3 minutes until hot but not boiling. Stir in a few drops of vanilla essence.

Break the chocolate into pieces, place in a bowl and cook on MEDIUM (50%) for 5 to 7 minutes until melted, stirring and checking regularly. Blend with the cream.

Chill the mixture until beginning to set, then beat in the butter until the mixture is light and fluffy.

Rub the ginger cake through a coarse sieve and beat into the cool truffle mixture. Allow the mixture to set a little, then divide into small walnut-sized pieces and roll into small balls.

Divide the truffles into 3 portions and roll one portion in chocolate vermicelli, the second in coconut and the third in nuts. Place in paper sweet cases and serve as an after-dinner treat.
MAKES 40 to 45

CHOCOLATE BOURBON BALLS

METRIC/IMPERIAL
100 g / 4 oz pecans or walnuts, finely chopped
3 tablespoons bourbon whisky
100 g / 4 oz butter
500 g / 1 lb 2 oz icing sugar, sifted
675 g / 1½ lb plain chocolate chips

Combine the nuts with the bourbon. Cover and refrigerate overnight. Put the butter in a small heatproof bowl and heat on FULL (100%) for 1½ to 2 minutes or until melted. Gradually stir in the sugar and then add the nuts and whisky, mixing well. Refrigerate until the mixture is firm enough to hold its shape for dipping. Add more sugar if the mixture is not stiff enough. Put the chocolate into a heat-resistant bowl and cook on FULL (100%) for 4 to 5 minutes, until melted.

While the chocolate is melting, shape the mixture into balls. Arrange the balls on a tray lined with waxed paper and return to the refrigerator to harden. Spear each ball with a wooden cocktail stick and dip into the melted chocolate. Replace on the paper and refrigerate.

Only dip a few bourbon balls at a time, leaving the remainder in the refrigerator. If the balls become too soft, put them back in the refrigerator to harden. Should the chocolate become too stiff, cook on FULL (100%) for 1 minute to soften.
MAKES 18

CHOCOLATE CRACKLES

METRIC/IMPERIAL
2 tablespoons clear honey
75 g / 3 oz butter
2 teaspoons drinking chocolate powder
175 g / 6 oz icing sugar
100 g / 4 oz chocolate rice cereal

Place the honey and butter in a large bowl and heat on FULL (100%) for 2 to 2½ minutes or until melted.

Add the chocolate powder, icing sugar and rice cereal, blending well.

Spoon equally into about 30 paper cake cases and leave to set. Store in an airtight tin and eat within 2 days of making.
MAKES 30

FRENCH CHOCOLATES

METRIC/IMPERIAL
12 oz plain chocolate chips
100 g / 4 oz walnuts, ground
generous 150 ml / ¼ pint sweetened condensed milk
1 teaspoon vanilla essence
pinch of salt
chocolate vermicelli
shredded coconut
chopped nuts

Put the chocolate into a heatproof bowl and cook on FULL (100%) for 3 to 3½ minutes until melted.

Stir in the nuts, milk, vanilla essence and salt. Leave to cool for 5 minutes. Roll into balls and coat with chocolate strands, coconut or nuts, as desired. Place on a greased baking sheet and refrigerate until set.
MAKES 40 to 50

MERRY MINTS

METRIC/IMPERIAL
40 g/1½ oz butter
2 tablespoons milk
440 g/15½ oz icing sugar
pinch of cream of tartar
½ teaspoon peppermint extract
pink and green food colouring

Put the butter and milk in a medium heatproof bowl. Heat on FULL (100%) for 1 minute until the butter melts. Stir in the frosting mix. Cook on FULL (100%) for 2 to 3 minutes until the mixture bubbles. Stir frequently.

Add the peppermint. Divide the mixture in two, colouring one half green and the other pink.

Place teaspoonfuls of the mixture on waxed paper and leave until set.
MAKES 40

DIVINITY

METRIC/IMPERIAL
675 g/1½ lb granulated sugar
50 g/2 oz glucose syrup
¼ teaspoon salt
2 egg whites
¼ teaspoon vanilla essence
100 g/4 oz nuts, chopped

Put the sugar, syrup and 150 ml/¼ pint water in a large heatproof bowl and cook on FULL (100%) for 10½ to 11½ minutes until a sugar thermometer reads 155°C/310°F or a teaspoonful of mixture separates into hard brittle threads when dropped into cold water.

Add the salt to the egg whites and whisk until stiff. Slowly pour the syrup in a thin stream into the egg whites, beating constantly until the mixture loses its shine and thickens.

Stir in the vanilla and nuts. Drop teaspoonfuls of the mixture at once on to waxed paper.
MAKES 30

CHOCOLATE AND WALNUT FUDGE

METRIC/IMPERIAL
900 g/2 lb granulated sugar
400 g/14 oz can evaporated milk
225 g/8 oz butter
350 g/12 oz plain chocolate chips
200 g/7 oz jar marshmallow cream
1 teaspoon vanilla essence
100 g/4 oz walnuts, chopped
walnut halves, to decorate

Combine the sugar, milk and butter in a large heatproof bowl. Cook on FULL (100%) for 15 to 18 minutes until a sugar thermometer registers 115°C/240°F or a teaspoonful of the mixture dropped into cold water forms a soft ball. Stir frequently during cooking and watch carefully to avoid the mixture boiling over.

Mix in the chocolate and marshmallow cream. Stir until well blended. Add the vanilla and chopped nuts. Pour into a buttered 23 cm/9 inch square dish. Cool and cut into squares. Decorate with walnut halves.
MAKES 25 to 35

Note: If marshmallow cream is not available, halve the quantity of sugar and add 16 marshmallows cut in half when cooking the sugar, milk and butter.

FLUFFY MARSHMALLOW

METRIC/IMPERIAL
7 g/¼ oz powdered gelatine
4 tablespoons cold water
100 g/4 oz sugar
90 g/3½ oz glucose syrup
½ teaspoon vanilla essence
icing sugar

Sprinkle the gelatine over the cold water in a large heatproof bowl. Cook on FULL (100%) for 30 to 45 seconds until the gelatine dissolves.

Stir in the sugar and heat briefly until dissolved, then add the syrup and vanilla essence. Beat with an electric mixer for about 15 minutes or until the mixture is very thick and resembles marshmallow.

Turn into a 20 cm/8 inch square tin, generously coated with icing sugar. Leave to stand at room temperature for about 1 hour until set.

Turn on to a board, sprinkled with plenty of icing sugar, and cut into 2.5 cm/1 inch squares with a knife dipped in cold water. Toss the marshmallows in icing sugar.
MAKES 64

CAKES, BISCUITS AND BREADS

VICTORIA SANDWICH

METRIC/IMPERIAL
175 g/6 oz butter
175 g/6 oz caster sugar
3 eggs, beaten
175 g/6 oz plain flour
2 teaspoons baking powder
pinch of salt
2 tablespoons hot water
5 tablespoons raspberry jam
icing sugar for dusting

Line a 20 cm/8 inch cake or soufflé dish with greaseproof paper.

Cream the butter and sugar until light and fluffy. Add the eggs, a little at a time, beating well to blend.

Sift the flour with the baking powder and salt and fold into the creamed mixture with the hot water.

Spoon into the prepared dish and level the surface carefully. Cook on FULL (100%) for 6½ to 7½ minutes, giving the dish a quarter-turn every 2 minutes. The cake will still be slightly sticky and moist on the surface at this stage but will dry out with the residual heat in the cake. Allow to STAND for 5 minutes before turning out on to a wire rack to cool.

To serve, split the cake in half and sandwich together with the jam. Dust the top with sifted icing sugar.
MAKES one 20 cm/8 inch round cake

GENOESE SPONGE

METRIC/IMPERIAL
4 eggs
100 g/4 oz caster sugar
100 g/4 oz plain flour
pinch of salt
50 g/2 oz butter
5 tablespoons jam
150 ml/¼ pint whipped cream
icing sugar for dusting

Line a 20 cm/8 inch cake or soufflé dish with greaseproof paper.

Whisk the eggs and sugar together until they are very thick and pale and have trebled in volume. Sift the flour and salt together and, using a metal spoon, carefully fold into the whisked mixture.

Place the butter in a bowl and heat on FULL (100%) for 1 to 1½ minutes or until melted. Using a metal spoon, gently fold into the whisked mixture.

Pour into the prepared dish and cook on FULL (100%) for 4½ to 5 minutes, giving the dish a quarter-turn every 1½ to 2 minutes. Leave to STAND for 5 to 10 minutes before turning out on to a wire rack to cool.

To serve, split the cake in half and sandwich together again with the jam and cream. Dust the top with icing sugar and serve cut into wedges.
MAKES one 20 cm/8 inch round cake

COFFEE ALMOND TORTE

METRIC/IMPERIAL
1 Genoese Sponge (see above)
300 ml/½ pint whipping cream
2 tablespoons strong black coffee
2 tablespoons sifted icing sugar
100 g/4 oz flaked almonds

Prepare and cook the Genoese Sponge as described above. Allow to cool, then split into two layers.

Whip the cream with the coffee and icing sugar until it stands in soft peaks. Sandwich the cake layers together with some of the coffee cream. Use the remainder to cover the top and sides of the cake.

Press the flaked almonds against the sides of the cake to coat. Serve while very fresh, cut into wedges.
MAKES one 20 cm/8 inch round cake

278

QUICK VIENNA SPONGE

METRIC/IMPERIAL
75 g/3 oz self-raising flour
2 teaspoons cornflour
pinch of salt
75 g/3 oz caster sugar
50 g/2 oz butter
2 teaspoons cocoa powder, sifted
3 eggs, beaten

Line the base of a 20 cm/8 inch deep round glass dish with greaseproof paper. Do not grease the sides of the dish.

Sift the flour, cornflour and salt into a bowl. Add the sugar, blending well.

Place the butter in a bowl and heat on FULL (100%) for 1 to 1½ minutes or until melted. Add the cocoa powder, blending well.

Add to the flour mixture with the eggs and beat well to blend. Pour into the prepared dish and cook on LOW (30%) for 5½ to 7 minutes until cooked, turning the dish twice. Leave to STAND for 5 minutes, then loosen with a knife and turn out on to a wire rack to cool.

Serve cut into wedges.
MAKES one 20 cm/8 inch round cake

CAKE MIX SANDWICH CAKE

METRIC/IMPERIAL
1 × 350 g/12 oz packet plain cake mix
4 tablespoons jam

Prepare the cake mix according to the instructions on the packet, adding the required amount of eggs and liquid.

Line the bases of two 18 cm/7 inch round shallow dishes with greaseproof paper and grease the sides. Divide the mixture evenly between the dishes.

Cook the cakes separately. Cook on LOW (30%) for 4 to 6 minutes or cook on FULL (100%) for 2 minutes, until the top is just dry, giving the dish a quarter-turn every 1 minute. Leave to STAND in the dishes for 5 minutes, then run a knife round the edge of each cake and turn out on to a wire rack. When cool, carefully remove the greaseproof paper.

Place one cake under a preheated grill to brown the top. Spread the other cake layer with the jam and place the browned cake layer on top.
MAKES one 18 cm/7 inch round cake

SUPREME CHOCOLATE CAKE

METRIC/IMPERIAL
50 g/2 oz flaked almonds
175 g/6 oz butter, softened
175 g/6 oz dark brown sugar
3 large eggs (size 1 or 2)
5 tablespoons clear honey
150 ml/¼ pint soured cream
175 g/6 oz self-raising flour
6 tablespoons cocoa powder
6 tablespoons ground almonds
3 tablespoons granulated sugar
3 tablespoons cold water
Sauce:
175 g/6 oz plain chocolate
40 g/1½ oz butter
6 tablespoons brown rum

Grease and line the base of a 2 litre/3½ pint round straight-sided casserole dish.

Arrange the almonds in a single layer on a plate. Cook on FULL (100%) for 5 minutes, stirring once or twice until golden, checking frequently. Allow to cool on absorbent kitchen paper.

Cream the butter and brown sugar until pale and fluffy. Beat in the eggs, one at a time, then the honey and soured cream.

Sift the flour and cocoa together. Using a metal spoon, fold lightly into the cake mixture, then fold in the ground almonds. Spoon the mixture into the prepared cooking dish and cook on FULL (100%) for 10 minutes until cooked, turning the dish twice. Sprinkle at once with the flaked almonds.

Place the sugar and water in a small bowl and cook on FULL (100%) for 3 to 4 minutes or until just beginning to caramelize. Very quickly drizzle over the almonds on the cake surface. Leave to STAND for 10 minutes. Invert on to a baking sheet, then on to a wire rack to cool.

The cake may be served plain at this stage or with chocolate rum sauce. To make the sauce, break the chocolate into pieces and place in a bowl with the butter. Cook on FULL (100%) for 3 minutes, stirring twice, or until melted. Whisk in the rum and serve at once. This sauce hardens quickly on cooling but can be melted again using DEFROST (20%).
SERVES 4 to 6

CHOCOLATE AND COFFEE CROWN CAKE

METRIC/IMPERIAL
175 g/6 oz butter
150 g/5 oz dark, soft brown sugar
3 eggs, beaten
175 g/6 oz plain flour, sifted
2 teaspoons coffee and chicory essence
4 tablespoons cocoa powder
½ teaspoon baking powder
¼ teaspoon grated nutmeg
¼ teaspoon vanilla essence
1 tablespoon milk
Butter icing:
175 g/6 oz unsalted butter
¼ teaspoon coffee and chicory essence
175 g/6 oz icing sugar, sifted

Grease a 23 cm/9 inch ring mould and line the base with greaseproof paper.

To make the cake, beat the butter and sugar together until light and fluffy. Beat in the eggs, a little at a time, until well blended. Using a metal spoon, fold in the flour.

Place one-quarter of the mixture in a small bowl and flavour with the coffee and chicory essence. Set aside.

Add the cocoa powder, baking powder and nutmeg to the remaining mixture, blending well. Stir in the vanilla essence and milk. Pour into the prepared ring mould and cook on FULL (100%) for 5 minutes, giving the dish a quarter-turn three times during cooking. Leave to STAND for 5 minutes, then loosen with a knife and turn out on to a wire rack to cool.

Reverse the mould, grease well and line the base with greaseproof paper. Spoon in the coffee-flavoured batter mixture and cook on FULL (100%) for 2 minutes. Leave to STAND for 4 minutes then loosen with a knife, turn out and leave to cool on a wire rack.

To make the butter icing, beat the butter and coffee and chicory essence together. Gradually work in the icing sugar to make a soft icing.

Generously spread the butter icing around the sides and narrower end of the coffee cake, then insert the cake, smooth side up, into the up-turned chocolate ring.

Pipe butter icing in a circle on top of the cake where the two sections meet. Serve cut into wedges.

MAKES one 23 cm/9 inch cake

STRAWBERRY GÂTEAU

METRIC/IMPERIAL
175 g/6 oz caster sugar
175 g/6 oz self-raising flour, sifted
175 g/6 oz soft margarine
3 large eggs (size 1 or 2)
3 tablespoons milk
2 tablespoons strawberry jam
300 ml/½ pint double cream, whipped and chilled
50 g/2 oz flaked almonds, toasted
225 g/8 oz fresh strawberries
strips of angelica, to decorate

Prepare a 19 cm/7½ inch soufflé or cake dish by lightly brushing the sides and base with oil. Line the base with a circle of greaseproof paper. Coat the sides with a little extra sugar and tap out any surplus.

Put the sugar, flour, margarine, eggs and milk into a mixing bowl and beat until smooth. Continue beating for 2 minutes by hand or for 1 minute if using an electric mixer.

Pour the mixture into the prepared dish and cook on FULL (100%) for about 7 to 9 minutes (giving the dish a half-turn twice during cooking, if necessary), until a wooden cocktail stick inserted into the centre comes out clean.

Leave to STAND for 5 minutes, then turn out on to a cooling rack which has been covered with a clean tea towel. Remove the paper and leave to cool.

When cold, cut the cake in half. Fill with the jam and sandwich the two halves together again. Coat the sides of the cake with some of the whipped cream, then roll the sides in the nuts.

Spread some of the remaining cream on the top to cover. Decorate with strawberries, angelica and rosettes of cream.

MAKES one 19 cm/7½ inch round cake

CHOCOLATE GÂTEAU

METRIC/IMPERIAL
3 large eggs (size 1 or 2)
2 tablespoons milk
1 tablespoon golden syrup
150 g/5 oz self-raising flour
25 g/1 oz cocoa powder
175 g/6 oz soft margarine
175 g/6 oz caster sugar
3 tablespoons lemon curd
Decoration:
75 g/3 oz plain chocolate
150 ml/¼ pint cream, whipped

Grease the base of a soufflé or cake dish, 19 cm/
7½ inches in diameter, 10 cm/4 inches deep. Cut
a circle of greaseproof paper and line the base of
the dish. Do not apply more oil on the base or
sides.

Put the eggs, milk, syrup, flour, cocoa, margarine and sugar in a bowl. Using an electric
whisk, beat well to combine and then beat for a
further 1 minute. Alternatively, mix by hand and
beat vigorously for 2 minutes with a wooden
spoon.

Put the mixture into the prepared dish and
level the top. Cook on FULL (100%) for 7 to 9
minutes, until a wooden cocktail stick inserted
into the centre comes out clean.

Remove from the oven and leave to STAND
for 5 minutes, covered with a clean tea towel.
Turn on to a cooling rack and, when cold, split
and fill with lemon curd.

Break up the chocolate and heat on MEDIUM
(50%) for 2 to 2¼ minutes. Beat well until
smooth. Pour the melted chocolate over the
cake. Allow to cool, then decorate the gâteau
with rosettes of whipped cream.

MAKES one 19 cm/7½ inch gâteau

CHOCOLATE YOGURT CAKE

METRIC/IMPERIAL
150 ml/5 fl oz vegetable oil
150 ml/5 fl oz natural yogurt
4 tablespoons golden syrup
175 g/6 oz caster sugar
3 eggs
3 tablespoons cocoa powder
½ teaspoon bicarbonate of soda
225 g/8 oz self-raising flour
pinch of salt

Grease a 20 cm/8 inch cake or soufflé dish.

Place the oil, yogurt, golden syrup, sugar and
eggs in a bowl. Beat well with a wooden spoon
until well blended. Add the cocoa powder,
bicarbonate of soda, flour and salt and mix well.

Spoon into the prepared dish and level the
surface. Cook on FULL (100%) for 9 minutes,
giving the dish a quarter-turn every 2 minutes.

Leave to STAND for 6 minutes before turning
out on to a wire rack to cool.

MAKES one 20 cm/8 inch round cake

CHOCOLATE CHERRY CAKE

METRIC/IMPERIAL
100 g/4 oz butter
100 g/4 oz sugar
2 eggs, beaten
100 g/4 oz self-raising flour
50 g/2 oz cocoa powder
50 g/2 oz ground almonds
4 tablespoons clear honey
4 tablespoons milk
8 to 10 glacé cherries, halved
Icing:
2 tablespoons milk
50 g/2 oz unsalted butter
1 tablespoon cocoa powder
½ teaspoon vanilla essence
200 g/7 oz icing sugar, sifted

Grease a 15 cm/6 inch deep round cake dish (or
line with microwave cling film).

Cream the butter and sugar together in a bowl
until light and fluffy. Beat in the eggs, a little at a
time. Sift the flour and cocoa on to the mixture,
then fold into the mixture with the ground
almonds, honey and sufficient milk to form a
consistency which easily shakes from a spoon.

Turn the mixture into the prepared cake dish
and smooth the top with a palette knife. Cook on
FULL (100%) for 5 to 6 minutes until just dry on
top, giving the dish a quarter-turn every 1½
minutes during cooking. Turn out on to a wire
rack set over a tray. Cover the top of the cake
with the glacé cherries, then leave to cool.

To make the icing, place the milk, butter,
cocoa and vanilla in a bowl and cook on FULL
(100%) for 1½ minutes. Stir in the icing sugar
and beat until smooth. Pour the icing over the
cake, spreading it over the top and sides. Leave
to set before transferring to a serving plate.

MAKES one 15 cm/6 inch round cake

WALNUT CAKE

METRIC/IMPERIAL
175 g/6 oz margarine
175 g/6 oz soft brown sugar
3 eggs, beaten
225 g/8 oz plain flour
1½ teaspoons baking powder
½ teaspoon salt
2 tablespoons milk
1 teaspoon vanilla essence
75 g/3 oz walnuts, chopped

Grease an 18 cm/7 inch deep round cake dish and line the base with greaseproof paper.

Cream the margarine and sugar until light and fluffy. Add the eggs, a little at a time, beating well to blend.

Sift the flour with the baking powder and salt. Using a metal spoon, fold into the creamed mixture with the milk and vanilla essence. Fold in the walnuts.

Spoon into the prepared dish and level the surface. Cook on FULL (100%) for 6 to 7 minutes, turning the dish every 1½ minutes. Leave to STAND for 5 minutes before turning out on to a wire rack to cool.

MAKES one 18 cm/7 inch round cake

LIGHTNING COFFEE CAKE

METRIC/IMPERIAL
50 g/2 oz soft margarine
50 g/2 oz soft brown sugar
75 g/3 oz self-raising flour
1 large egg (size 1 or 2)
2 teaspoons instant coffee powder, dissolved in 2 teaspoons milk
Decoration:
whipped cream
demerara sugar

Lightly grease a 0.75 litre/1¼ pint Pyrex soufflé dish.

Place the margarine, sugar, flour, egg and coffee-flavoured milk in a bowl. Stir only enough to make a smooth, soft mixture.

Spread evenly into the prepared dish and cook on FULL (100%) for 4 minutes or until the top of the cake is dry to the touch. Allow to cool in the dish. When cool, top with whipped cream and sprinkle with demerara sugar. Serve straight from the dish while fresh.

SERVES 6 to 8

DEVIL'S FOOD CAKE

METRIC/IMPERIAL
75 g/3 oz plain flour
35 g/1¼ oz cocoa powder
¼ teaspoon bicarbonate of soda
75 ml/3 fl oz milk
75 g/3 oz butter or margarine, softened
75 g/3 oz caster sugar
2 large eggs (size 1 or 2)
75 g/3 oz golden syrup
25 g/1 oz ground almonds
American frosting:
175 g/6 oz granulated sugar
100 ml/3½ fl oz cold water
1 egg white
¼ teaspoon cream of tartar

To make the cake, lightly grease a 1 litre/1¾ pint plastic ring mould. Alternatively, put a glass in the middle of an ordinary dish.

Sift the plain flour and cocoa powder together in a mixing bowl. Blend the bicarbonate of soda with the milk and add to the flour. Add the butter or margarine, caster sugar, eggs, syrup and almonds, beating for 1 to 2 minutes until smooth.

Pour the cake mixture into the prepared ring and cook on FULL (100%) for 2 minutes. Give the dish a half-turn and cook on FULL (100%) for a further 2 minutes or until the cake is just dry on top. Leave to STAND for 4 to 5 minutes before turning on to a wire rack. Place the wire rack over another tray and leave the cake until cool but not cold.

Meanwhile, make the American frosting. Mix the sugar and water together in a medium ovenproof bowl. Cook on FULL (100%) for 3 minutes, then remove the bowl and stir until the sugar has completely dissolved.

Return the bowl to the oven and cook on FULL (100%) for 5 minutes, without stirring, until the soft ball stage is reached – 115°C/240°F. (A few drops of the syrup should form a soft ball when dropped into ice-cold water. When the ball is removed from the water, it should immediately lose its shape.) Remove the bowl and beat the mixture with a wooden spoon until cloudy.

Whisk the egg white until stiff peaks form. Add the cream of tartar, then pour the hot syrup into the beaten white. Continue whisking as the mixture cools. Pour or spoon the frosting over the cake and leave uncovered until the icing crisps on the surface.

MAKES one ring cake

APPLE RING CAKE

METRIC/IMPERIAL
1 × 350 g/12 oz packet plain cake mix
175 g/6 oz cooking apple, peeled, cored and chopped
3 heaped tablespoons apricot jam, sieved
2 tablespoons water
1 red-skinned dessert apple, cored and sliced

Make up the cake mixture according to the directions on the packet. Add the chopped cooking apple and mix well. Turn into a greased 750 ml/1¼ pint ring mould, suitable for use in the microwave oven.

Cook on FULL (100%) for 4 to 5 minutes until the cake is just dry on top and a skewer, inserted into the centre, comes out clean. Turn on to a sheet of greaseproof paper and leave to cool.

Combine the jam and water in a bowl. Cook on FULL (100%) for 1½ minutes until boiling briskly. Spread half the jam over the top and sides of the cake.

Arrange the apple slices, overlapping, on the top of the cake. Coat with the remaining jam. Allow to cool, then transfer the cake to a serving plate.

MAKES one ring cake

CHOCOLATE AND ORANGE CHEQUERED CAKE

METRIC/IMPERIAL
1 × 350 g/12 oz packet plain cake mix
2 teaspoons water
2 tablespoons cocoa powder, sifted
2 teaspoons orange juice
few drops of orange food colouring
1 × 200 g/7 oz can apricot pie filling
100 g/4 oz plain cooking chocolate
orange jelly slices, to decorate

Grease two 18 cm/7 inch straight-sided round dishes and line the bases with greased greaseproof paper.

Prepare the cake mix according to the directions on the packet. Divide the mixture in half. Add the water and cocoa to one half, and the orange juice and colouring to the other.

Place alternate even spoonfuls of chocolate and orange mixture in each dish. Cook the cakes one at a time. Cook on FULL (100%) for 2 minutes, giving the dish a quarter-turn every ¼ minute.

Leave to STAND for 5 minutes before turning out on to a wire rack to cool. When cold, sandwich the cakes together with the pie filling.

Break the chocolate into a bowl and cook on MEDIUM (50%) for 4 to 4¼ minutes, stirring twice, until melted but still holding its shape. Pour over the cake and smooth over the top and sides with a palette knife. Allow to set, then decorate with orange jelly slices.

MAKES one 18 cm/7 inch round cake

ORANGE STREUSEL CAKE

METRIC/IMPERIAL
Streusel topping:
25 g/1 oz plain flour
1 teaspoon ground cinnamon
2 teaspoons cocoa powder
50 g/2 oz butter, chilled
75 g/3 oz brown sugar
Cake base:
50 g/2 oz butter
150 g/5 oz sugar
175 g/6 oz plain flour
2 teaspoons baking powder
pinch of salt
grated rind and juice of 1 orange
about 5 tablespoons milk
1 egg, beaten

To prepare the streusel topping, sift the flour, cinnamon and cocoa into a bowl. Cut the butter into small pieces and lightly rub into the dry ingredients. Stir in the sugar.

To make the cake base, cream the butter and sugar together in a mixing bowl until light and fluffy. Sift the flour with the baking powder and salt over the creamed mixture and add the grated orange rind. Make up the orange juice to 150 ml/¼ pint with milk, then add to the mixture, together with the beaten egg. Beat for 2 minutes until smooth.

Turn the mixture into a greased 18 cm/7 inch deep round cake dish. Cook on FULL (100%) for 3 minutes, giving the dish a quarter-turn every ¾ minute.

Sprinkle the streusel evenly over the top. Cook on FULL (100%) for 3 minutes, giving the dish a half-turn every 1½ minutes. When a skewer inserted into the centre of the cake comes out clean, the cake is ready. Turn out on to a wire rack to cool.

MAKES one 18 cm/7 inch round cake

CHOCOLATE-TOPPED SPONGE RING

METRIC/IMPERIAL
100 g/4 oz soft margarine
100 g/4 oz caster sugar
100 g/4 oz self-raising flour
2 large eggs (size 1 or 2)
50 g/2 oz chocolate, grated

Lightly grease a 22 cm/8½ inch Pyrex savarin dish. Place the margarine, sugar, flour and eggs in a bowl and stir only enough to make a smooth, soft mixture.

Spread evenly into the prepared dish and cook on FULL (100%) for 5 to 5½ minutes or until the top of the cake is dry to the touch. Sprinkle immediately with the chocolate and leave to cool. Serve while fresh straight from the dish.
MAKES one 22 cm/8½ inch ring cake

MADEIRA CAKE

METRIC/IMPERIAL
175 g/6 oz butter
50 g/2 oz lard
225 g/8 oz sugar
3 large eggs (size 1 or 2), beaten
175 g/6 oz self-raising flour
50 g/2 oz plain flour
3–4 tablespoons evaporated milk
Glaze:
1 tablespoon evaporated milk
1 tablespoon dark brown sugar
½ teaspoon arrowroot

Grease the sides of an 18 cm/7 inch deep round dish and line the base with greaseproof paper.

Cream the butter, lard and sugar together until light and fluffy. Beat in the eggs, a little at a time. Sift the flours together, then fold into the mixture, together with the evaporated milk.

Turn the mixture into the prepared dish and smooth the top with a palette knife. Cook on FULL (100%) for 5 to 6 minutes until just dry on top, giving the dish a quarter-turn every 1 minute. Leave the cake in the dish for 2 minutes, then turn out and cool on a wire rack.

To make the glaze, blend the evaporated milk, sugar and arrowroot together. Brush over the top of the cake. Place under a preheated moderate grill to lightly brown the top.
MAKES one 18 cm/7 inch round cake

ORANGE TIPSY CAKE

METRIC/IMPERIAL
175 g/6 oz butter
175 g/6 oz caster sugar
175 g/6 oz self-raising flour
1 teaspoon baking powder
3 large eggs (size 1 or 2)
finely grated rind of 2 oranges
Tipsy syrup:
75 g/3 oz caster sugar
juice of 2 oranges
1 teaspoon Cointreau
Topping:
225 g/8 oz plain chocolate-flavoured cake covering
1 teaspoon vegetable oil

Grease an 18 cm/7 inch deep round cake dish and line the base with greaseproof paper. Using string, fix a double thickness 'collar' of greaseproof paper round the sides of the dish, protruding 2.5 cm/1 inch above the rim.

Place the butter in a large bowl and cook on FULL (100%) for 1 minute or until melted. Add the remaining cake ingredients and beat well until smooth and blended. Spoon into the prepared dish and level the surface.

Cook on FULL (100%) for 6 minutes, giving the dish a half-turn once. Leave to STAND for 5 minutes, then loosen the cake with a knife, remove the paper collar and turn out on to a wire rack set over a tray. Peel away any paper on the base of the cake.

To make the tipsy syrup, mix the sugar and orange juice in a bowl. Cook on FULL (100%) for 2 minutes or until boiling. Cook for a further 2 minutes or until the syrup thickens slightly. Stir in the Cointreau, blending well.

Using a sharp pointed knife, pierce deeply through the warm cake in several places. Gradually pour the syrup over the cake until it is all absorbed.

To make the topping, break up the chocolate and place in a bowl. Cook on MEDIUM (50%) for 4 to 5 minutes until just beginning to melt, stirring twice. Stir in the oil until well blended. Pour over the top and sides of the cake. Leave until slightly set, then swirl with a fork to give a raised effect.

Leave in a cool place until the chocolate is completely set. Cut into wedges to serve.
MAKES one 18 cm/7 inch round cake

COFFEE ICE CREAM CAKE

METRIC/IMPERIAL
2 eggs, separated
2 tablespoons coffee essence
50 g/2 oz icing sugar, sifted
150 ml/¼ pint double cream
1 Genoese Sponge (see page 278)
icing sugar for dusting

Beat the egg yolks and coffee essence together. Whisk the egg whites until they stand in soft peaks, then gradually whisk in the icing sugar until thick and glossy. Using a metal spoon, fold the egg yolks into the egg white mixture.

Whip the cream until it stands in soft peaks. Using a metal spoon, fold into the coffee mixture. Pour the mixture into a freezer tray and freeze until firm, about 2 to 4 hours.

Meanwhile, prepare and cook the Genoese Sponge as described on page 278. Allow to cool. Carefully split the cake into three layers. Sandwich together with the coffee ice cream.

Place on a serving plate and dust with icing sugar. Serve at once, cut into wedges.
SERVES 4 to 6

CARROT CAKE WITH SOFT CHEESE FROSTING

METRIC/IMPERIAL
3 eggs
75 g/3 oz demerara sugar
1½ teaspoons mixed spice
3 tablespoons clear honey
150 ml/¼ pint grapeseed or sunflower oil
225 g/8 oz wholemeal flour
2 teaspoons baking powder
3 tablespoons skimmed milk
225 g/8 oz carrots, finely grated
Frosting:
275 g/10 oz low-fat soft cheese
2 tablespoons soft, light brown sugar
100 g/4 oz mixed chopped nuts, toasted

Lightly oil a 15 cm/6 inch diameter soufflé dish. In a large bowl, beat the eggs, sugar, spice, honey and oil together thoroughly. Fold in the flour, a little at a time, and mix in the baking powder and milk.

Stir in the grated carrots and pour into the prepared dish. Cook on FULL (100%) for 5 to 6½ minutes. Leave to STAND for 10 minutes and test the cake by inserting a clean skewer into the centre. If it comes out clean, the cake is done. If not, return to the oven for a further 1 to 2 minutes and test again.

Turn the cake out on to a wire rack; cover loosely with absorbent kitchen paper and leave to cool completely while preparing the frosting.

To make the frosting, place the low-fat cheese and sugar in a bowl and beat together thoroughly. Transfer the cooled cake to a plate and spread the frosting all over it.

Coat the top and sides of the cake with the chopped, toasted nuts.
MAKES one 15 cm/6 inch round cake

CHERRY OAT CAKE

METRIC/IMPERIAL
1 tablespoon caster sugar
225 g/8 oz soft brown sugar
175 g/6 oz soft margarine
50 g/2 oz glacé cherries, chopped
100 g/4 oz raisins
50 g/2 oz rolled oats
1 teaspoon baking powder
pinch of salt
50 g/2 oz mixed nuts, chopped
175 g/6 oz strong flour (wholemeal or white)
1 large egg (size 1 or 2)
Decoration (optional):
100 g/4 oz cooking chocolate, melted
4 glacé cherries, halved

Prepare an 18 cm/7 inch soufflé or cake dish by brushing the sides and base lightly with oil. Cut a circle of greaseproof paper to fit the base and use a tablespoon of caster sugar to coat the sides. Do *not* apply more oil to the base. Tap out any surplus sugar.

Place the brown sugar and margarine in a mixing bowl. Cook on MEDIUM (50%) for 4 to 4½ minutes, until the margarine has melted. Stir well.

Stir in the prepared cherries, raisins, rolled oats, baking powder, salt, mixed nuts and flour. Mix well, then add the egg to combine the ingredients.

Pile the mixture into the prepared dish and level the top. Cook on MEDIUM (50%) for 15 minutes. Leave to STAND in the container for 5 minutes before turning out on to a rack to cool.

When cool, spread the top with melted chocolate and decorate with cherries, if wished.
MAKES one 18 cm/7 inch round cake

WALNUT STREUSEL CAKE

METRIC/IMPERIAL
Streusel topping:
25 g/1 oz butter
75 g/3 oz soft brown sugar
25 g/1 oz self-raising flour
50 g/2 oz walnuts, chopped
1 teaspoon ground cinnamon
Cake:
75 g/3 oz butter
175 g/6 oz caster sugar
1 egg, beaten
175 g/6 oz self-raising flour
pinch of salt
150 ml/¼ pint milk

Lightly grease a 19 cm/7½ inch round deep dish and line the base with greaseproof paper.

Prepare the topping by beating the butter and sugar until light and fluffy. Add the flour, walnuts and cinnamon and mix until a light crumb mixture is obtained.

To make the cake, cream the butter and sugar until light and fluffy. Beat in the egg, blending well. Add the flour, salt and milk and beat well to blend. Spoon into the prepared dish and carefully level the top. Cook on FULL (100%) for 4 to 5 minutes, turning the dish twice. Sprinkle the topping over the cake and cook on FULL (100%) for a further 1½ minutes.

Allow to cool slightly, then turn out on to a wire rack to cool. Cut into wedges to serve.
MAKES one 19 cm/7½ inch round cake

ORANGE AND APPLE CAKE

METRIC/IMPERIAL
1½ tablespoons soft, dark brown sugar
25 g/1 oz whole blanched almonds, toasted
3 eggs
75 g/3 oz demerara sugar
150 ml/¼ pint grapeseed or sunflower oil
175 g/6 oz wholemeal flour
1½ teaspoons baking powder
1 small orange
2 eating apples, peeled, cored and grated

Lightly oil a 15 cm/6 inch diameter soufflé dish. Sprinkle the dark brown sugar all over the base and arrange the toasted almonds on top.

In a large bowl, beat the eggs, demerara sugar and oil together thoroughly. Fold in the flour, a little at a time; add the baking powder and mix well.

Grate the rind of the orange finely and reserve. Remove all the pith from the orange and chop the flesh finely. Stir into the cake mixture with the rind and the apples.

Spoon the mixture into the dish on top of the almonds. Cover and cook on FULL (100%) for 5 minutes, turning the dish around halfway through the cooking time. Leave to STAND, covered, for 8 minutes and test the cake by inserting a clean skewer into the centre. If it comes out clean, the cake is done. If not, return to the oven for a further 1 to 2 minutes.

Turn out on to a wire rack, cover loosely with absorbent kitchen paper and leave to cool.
MAKES one 15 cm/6 inch round cake

CHOCOLATE BANANA RING

METRIC/IMPERIAL
2 eggs
4 tablespoons milk
150 g/5 oz soft brown sugar
100 g/4 oz soft margarine
450 g/1 lb bananas, chopped
225 g/8 oz self-raising flour
½ teaspoon baking powder
40 g/1½ oz drinking chocolate powder
Icing:
50 g/2 oz icing sugar, sifted
40 g/1½ oz drinking chocolate
1 tablespoon water

Place the eggs, milk, sugar, margarine and bananas in a blender or food processor and blend until smooth.

Sift the flour, baking powder and drinking chocolate into a large bowl. Stir in the banana mixture and mix thoroughly until well combined. Spoon the mixture into a 2.25 litre/4 pint greased microwave baking ring. Cook on FULL (100%) for 6 minutes.

Gently spread any uncooked cake mixture over the surface. Turn round and cook on FULL (100%) for a further 3 minutes. Leave the ring to STAND for 5 minutes before turning it out. Leave to cool completely.

Mix the sifted icing sugar and drinking chocolate together. Quickly stir in the water. Spread the glacé icing over the top of the cake, drizzling some down the sides of the cake.
MAKES one ring cake

NUTTY GINGERBREAD

METRIC/IMPERIAL
a little caster sugar
225 g/8 oz plain flour
½ teaspoon salt
1 teaspoon bicarbonate of soda
½ teaspoon mixed spice
2 teaspoons ground ginger
100 g/4 oz brown sugar
100 g/4 oz black treacle
100 g/4 oz margarine
100 g/4 oz golden syrup
1 large egg (size 1 or 2), beaten
150 ml/¼ pint milk
25 g/1 oz mixed nuts, finely chopped

First prepare a 23 cm/9 inch ring mould. Brush the mould with a little melted butter and sprinkle with caster sugar; tap out any surplus.

Sift together the flour, salt, soda, spice and ginger. Put the sugar, treacle, margarine and syrup in a large mixing bowl and cook on MEDIUM (50%) for 4 to 4½ minutes. Stir well, then leave to cool slightly for 2 to 3 minutes.

Beat the egg and milk together, and add to the syrup mixture. Make a well in the centre of the dry ingredients and add the liquid ingredients gradually, beating well to form a smooth batter.

Sprinkle the chopped nuts evenly over the base of the prepared mould, then pour in the cake batter. Cook on MEDIUM (50%) for 15 to 16 minutes, giving the dish a half-turn twice during cooking, if necessary. Leave to STAND in the dish for 10 minutes, then turn out and leave to cool completely.

MAKES one 23 cm/9 inch ring cake

LEMON SPONGE CAKE

METRIC/IMPERIAL
225 g/8 oz self-raising flour
¼ teaspoon baking powder
100 g/4 oz butter
100 g/4 oz soft, dark brown sugar
2 eggs
2 teaspoons grated lemon rind
1 tablespoon milk
2 tablespoons lemon juice
3 tablespoons lemon curd
225 g/8 oz icing sugar, sifted
2 tablespoons water
yellow food colouring
8 sugared lemon slices, to decorate

Sift the flour and baking powder into a large bowl. Rub in the butter until the mixture resembles breadcrumbs, then stir in the sugar. Beat in the eggs, one at time, then stir in the lemon rind, milk and lemon juice.

Spoon the mixture into a greased and lined 18 cm/7 inch round, 9 cm/3½ inch deep container. Stand on an upturned plate and cook on FULL (100%) for 2 minutes.

Turn the container round and cook on FULL (100%) for a further 2 minutes. Turn round again and cook on FULL (100%) for a further 1 minute. Leave the sponge to STAND for 5 minutes before turning it out, upside down, on to a serving plate. Leave to cool completely.

Split the cake into 2 layers. Spread one layer with the lemon curd and replace the other layer on top.

Mix the icing sugar with the water and yellow food colouring. Pour over the cake and decorate with lemon slices.

MAKES one 18 cm/7 inch round cake

MIXED FRUIT AND WALNUT CAKE

METRIC/IMPERIAL
175 g/6 oz self-raising flour
2 teaspoons mixed spice
175 g/6 oz soft margarine
3 large eggs (size 1 or 2)
1 tablespoon milk
1 teaspoon liquid gravy browning
175 g/6 oz soft brown sugar
1 tablespoon black treacle
100 g/4 oz mixed dried fruit
25 g/1 oz walnuts, chopped
a little caster sugar for sprinkling

First, prepare a soufflé or cake dish, 19 cm/7½ inches in diameter, 10 cm/4 inches deep. Lightly oil the base of the dish and line with a circle of greaseproof paper. Do not apply any more oil.

Put all the ingredients, except the fruit, nuts and caster sugar, into a large mixing bowl. Mix to combine and beat for 2 minutes with a wooden spoon. Alternatively, use an electric mixer and beat for 1 minute.

Lightly fold in the fruit and nuts, then turn into the prepared dish. Cook on FULL (100%) for 7 to 8 minutes. Leave to STAND, covered, for 5 minutes. Turn out and, when quite cold, sprinkle the top with caster sugar.

MAKES one 19 cm/7½ inch round cake

RICH FRUIT CAKE

METRIC/IMPERIAL
150 g/5 oz butter
2 eggs
150 g/5 oz soft brown sugar
2 tablespoons black treacle
1 tablespoon brandy
75 g/3 oz plain flour
75 g/3 oz self-raising flour
3 tablespoons milk
2 teaspoons ground mixed spice
25 g/1 oz nuts, chopped
25 g/1 oz glacé cherries, chopped
450 g/1 lb mixed dried fruit

Place the butter in a large mixing bowl. Cook on FULL (100%) for 1½ minutes. Add the eggs, sugar, treacle and brandy, blending well.

Using a metal spoon, fold in the flours. Add the milk, spice, nuts, cherries and mixed dried fruit and stir well to blend.

Spoon into a 1.5 litre/2½ pint soufflé dish and level the surface. Cook on LOW (30%) for 40 to 45 minutes, turning the dish twice.

Allow to STAND for 30 minutes before turning out on to a wire rack to cool. Serve when cold, cut into wedges.
MAKES one round cake

DATE CAKE

METRIC/IMPERIAL
a little caster sugar
175 g/6 oz self-raising flour, sifted
½ teaspoon mixed spice
100 g/4 oz soft margarine
75 g/3 oz soft, dark brown sugar
100 g/4 oz stoned chopped dates
2 large eggs (size 1 or 2)
4 tablespoons milk
1 tablespoon black treacle
1 teaspoon gravy browning

Lightly brush a 19 cm/7½ inch soufflé or cake dish with oil and coat the base and sides with a sprinkling of sugar; tap out any surplus. Sift the flour and spice into a mixing bowl and rub in the fat. Add the sugar and dates, and mix well.

Beat together the eggs, milk, treacle and gravy browning. Stir into the dry ingredients and mix well to combine.

Pour the cake mixture into the prepared dish. Level the top and cook on FULL (100%) for 5½ minutes, giving the dish a half-turn, halfway through cooking, if necessary.

Leave to STAND, covered with a clean tea towel, for 6 minutes. Turn out on to a cooling rack and allow to cool completely.

Before serving, sprinkle with a little caster sugar.
MAKES one 19 cm/7½ inch round cake

FRUIT LOAF

METRIC/IMPERIAL
175 g/6 oz plain flour
2 teaspoons baking powder
½ teaspoon salt
25 g/1 oz butter
2 tablespoons brown sugar
1 egg, beaten
150 ml/¼ pint natural yogurt
¼ teaspoon bicarbonate of soda
50 g/2 oz raisins
25 g/1 oz currants
Caramel Colouring (see page 314)

Sift the flour, baking powder and salt into a mixing bowl. Rub in the butter until the mixture resembles fine breadcrumbs. Add the sugar, egg, yogurt and bicarbonate of soda and mix to form a smooth, soft dough. Mix in the raisins and currants.

Line the base of an 18 × 10 cm/7 × 4 inch loaf-shaped dish with greaseproof paper. Spoon in the mixture and smooth the top with a palette knife. Cook on FULL (100%) for 4 to 4½ minutes until just dry on top, giving the dish a quarter-turn every 1 minute.

Turn out and place, top side down, on a grill rack. Brown under a preheated grill. Turn over and brush the top with caramel before serving. Serve warm or cold, sliced and buttered.
MAKES one loaf cake

LIGHT FRUIT CAKE

METRIC/IMPERIAL
100 g/4 oz butter
100 g/4 oz soft brown sugar
3 eggs, beaten
175 g/6 oz plain flour
2½ teaspoons baking powder
2 teaspoons mixed spice
25 g/1 oz currants
25 g/1 oz raisins

100 g/4 oz sultanas
25 g/1 oz chopped mixed peel
5 glacé cherries, chopped
40 g/1½ oz ground almonds
1 teaspoon Caramel Colouring (see page 314), or gravy browning
3–4 tablespoons milk
2 tablespoons sieved apricot jam, warmed
4 tablespoons toasted flaked almonds

Grease the sides of an 18 cm/7 inch deep round cake dish and line the base with greaseproof paper.

Cream the butter and sugar together in a bowl until light and fluffy. Add the beaten eggs, a little at a time, beating thoroughly between each addition.

Sift the flour, baking powder and mixed spice together over the mixture. Add the dried fruit, peel, cherries and ground almonds and lightly fold into the mixture, adding the caramel and sufficient milk to give a firm, dropping consistency.

Turn the mixture into the prepared dish and smooth the top with a palette knife. Cook on FULL (100%) for 6 to 8 minutes until the cake is just dry on top, giving the dish a quarter-turn every 1½ minutes.

Leave to cool in the dish, then turn out and brush the top with warmed apricot jam to glaze. Sprinkle with the almonds.
MAKES one 18 cm/7 inch round cake

LEMON TEABREAD

METRIC/IMPERIAL
grated rind of 1 lemon
about 3 tablespoons lemon juice
75 g/3 oz currants
100 g/4 oz raisins
25 g/1 oz sultanas
225 g/8 oz plain wholemeal flour
½ teaspoon baking powder
pinch of salt
75 g/3 oz butter
100 g/4 oz soft, dark brown sugar
1 egg, beaten
3 tablespoons milk
¼ teaspoon bicarbonate of soda
15 g/½ oz mixed peel

Combine the lemon rind, juice, currants, raisins and sultanas in a basin and cook on FULL (100%) for 1½ minutes or until the mixture

boils. Leave standing, covered, until all the juice is absorbed. Leave for a few minutes to cool down.

Sift the flour with the baking powder and salt into a mixing bowl and rub in the butter until the mixture resembles fine breadcrumbs. Stir in the sugar.

Beat the egg, milk and bicarbonate of soda together and pour into the flour mixture. Mix thoroughly, then fold in the mixed peel and the fruit mixture.

Put the mixture into a loaf-shaped container about 20 × 13 × 10½ cm/8 × 5 × 3 inches. Reduce the setting to MEDIUM (50%) and cook for 11 minutes or until the mixture is just dry on top.

Leave the teabread in the cooking container to STAND for 5 minutes before turning out on to non-stick silicone paper. Immediately reverse to prevent the top of the cake from being damaged. Serve warm, slicing with a sharp knife.
MAKES one loaf cake

Note: If you prefer to eat the teabread cold, it should be wrapped tightly in cling film immediately after its standing time. To eat hot, it may be reheated on FULL (100%) for about ½ minute.

CHRISTMAS CAKE

METRIC/IMPERIAL
225 g/8 oz butter
175 g/6 oz dark brown sugar
4 eggs, beaten
225 g/8 oz plain flour
pinch of salt
1 teaspoon mixed spice
25 g/1 oz ground almonds
75 g/3 oz mixed almonds and walnuts, chopped
10 glacé cherries, quartered
50 g/2 oz candied peel, finely chopped
225 g/8 oz currants
100 g/4 oz raisins
175 g/6 oz sultanas
50 g/2 oz stoned dates, chopped
grated rind and juice of 1 large orange
1 teaspoon Caramel Colouring (see page 314)
3 tablespoons brandy
To finish:
450 g/1 lb almond paste
575 g/1¼ lb royal icing

Grease the sides of a 20 cm/8 inch deep round dish and line the base with greaseproof paper.

Cream the butter and sugar together in a large bowl until fluffy. Add the beaten egg, a little at a time, beating well between each addition. Sift the flour, salt and spice into the mixture and stir well.

Add the ground almonds, chopped nuts, cherries, peel, dried fruit, orange rind and juice. Fold into the mixture gently. Stir in the caramel and brandy.

Cook on LOW (30%) for 5 minutes. Draw the mixture in from the sides to the middle with a fork. Cook on LOW (30%) for 15 minutes, giving the dish a half-turn every 5 minutes. Leave to STAND for 15 minutes, then cook on LOW (30%) for 15 to 20 minutes, giving the dish a half-turn every 5 minutes, until the cake is just dry on top.

If the cake seems to be cooking too fast around the edge, cut out a circular piece of foil, about 2.5 cm/1 inch wide. Place over the edge of the cake to shield for the final 5 minutes. This will enable the middle of the cake to 'catch up' on cooking.

Slide a knife around the edge of the cake and leave in the dish to cool slightly before turning out on to a wire rack. When completely cold, wrap in foil, seal tightly and store in a cool place until a few weeks before Christmas.

Cover with almond paste, leave to dry for 3 to 4 days, then cover with royal icing.
MAKES one 20 cm/8 inch round cake

RAISIN AND WALNUT LOAF

METRIC/IMPERIAL
150 ml/¼ pint orange juice
1 teaspoon bicarbonate of soda
25 g/1 oz butter
½ teaspoon vanilla essence
75 g/3 oz raisins
75 g/3 oz soft brown sugar
1 large egg (size 1 or 2), beaten
175 g/6 oz plain flour
1 teaspoon baking powder
¼ teaspoon salt
75 g/3 oz walnuts, chopped

Grease the sides of a 23 × 10 cm/9 × 4 inch loaf dish and line the base with greaseproof paper.

Put the orange juice in a mixing bowl and cook on FULL (100%) for 1 to 1½ minutes until hot. Stir in the bicarbonate of soda and butter, then add the vanilla, raisins and sugar. Stir in the

beaten egg, a little at a time, and beat well. Sift the flour, baking powder and salt together over the top. Stir gently, then fold in the nuts.

Turn the mixture into the prepared dish and smooth the top. Cook on FULL (100%) for 6 to 8 minutes until just dry on top, giving the dish a quarter-turn every 2 minutes. Transfer to a wire rack to cool.

Serve sliced and buttered, preferably soon after cooling.
MAKES one loaf cake

STRAWBERRY SHORTCAKE

METRIC/IMPERIAL
225 g/8 oz plain flour
50 g/2 oz icing sugar
150 g/5 oz unsalted butter, softened
¼ teaspoon vanilla essence
450 g/1 lb fresh strawberries
300 ml/½ pint double cream, whipped
25 g/1 oz granulated sugar

Sift the flour and icing sugar together in a bowl. Add the butter and vanilla and mix with a table knife until the butter is completely incorporated and the mixture resembles fine breadcrumbs.

Line the base of a 23 cm/9 inch round shallow dish with greaseproof paper. Spoon in the shortcake mixture and spread evenly. Press down with the back of a spoon to smooth the top. Cook on LOW (30%) for 8 minutes or until a skewer inserted into the centre of the shortcake comes out clean. Give the dish a quarter-turn every 2 minutes during cooking. Leave to cool in the dish for at least 1 hour.

Carefully turn out the shortcake on to a serving plate, or leave in the dish, if preferred. Slice half the strawberries and arrange them, overlapping, over the shortcake. Cover with a thick layer of cream, then pile the remaining strawberries on top. Pipe the remaining whipped cream on top to decorate the edges. Sprinkle generously with granulated sugar just before serving.
MAKES one 23 cm/9 inch cake

Variation
Frozen strawberries are not recommended for this recipe but frozen blackberries, carefully thawed and drained, may be substituted if fresh soft fruit is unobtainable.

WALNUT BISCUITS

METRIC/IMPERIAL
75 g/3 oz soft margarine
50 g/2 oz soft brown sugar
100 g/4 oz self-raising flour, sifted
½ teaspoon mixed spice
½ egg, beaten
12 walnut halves

Beat together the margarine and sugar until light and fluffy. Using a metal spoon, fold in the flour and spice with the egg. Mix well.

Turn on to a lightly floured board and knead until smooth. Roll into 12 even-sized balls and arrange 6 on an ungreased 30 × 20 × 5 cm/ 12 × 8 × 2 inch ovenproof glass dish (3 down each side).

Press half a walnut on top of each one, and cook on MEDIUM (50%) for 5 to 6 minutes. Remove from the oven and allow to cool slightly before transferring to a cooling rack. Repeat with the remaining 6 biscuits.
MAKES 12

Note: These biscuits will harden on cooling; store in an airtight tin.

CHOCOLATE QUICKIES

METRIC/IMPERIAL
100 g/4 oz butter
2 tablespoons cocoa powder
1 tablespoon demerara sugar
2 tablespoons golden syrup
225 g/8 oz semi-sweet biscuits, crushed
100 g/4 oz plain or milk chocolate

Place the butter in a bowl with the cocoa, demerara sugar and golden syrup. Cook on FULL (100%) for 3 to 4 minutes, stirring once until boiling and bubbly.

Stir in the biscuit crumbs, blending well. Pour into a greased 18 cm/7 inch square cake dish and press out evenly.

Break the chocolate into pieces and place in a bowl. Cook on MEDIUM (50%) for 2½ to 3 minutes or until melted, stirring twice. Pour over the biscuit mixture. As the chocolate sets, mark it into swirls with a knife.

Chill until set, then cut into about 12 to 16 squares or bars.
MAKES 12 to 16

GENOESE ICED FANCIES

METRIC/IMPERIAL
4 eggs
100 g/4 oz sugar
50 g/2 oz butter
100 g/4 oz plain flour
1 teaspoon baking powder
Icing:
5 tablespoons orange juice
50 g/2 oz butter
450 g/1 lb icing sugar, sifted
orange and yellow food colouring
Decoration:
crystallized orange and lemon slices

Grease two 20 cm/8 inch square dishes (or line with microwave cling film).

Using an electric beater or rotary whisk, whisk the eggs and sugar together in a large mixing bowl until very thick and creamy. The mixture is beaten sufficiently when a fork drawn through the top leaves a channel.

Put the butter in a jug and heat on FULL (100%) for ¾ to 1 minute or until just melted. Sift the flour and baking powder together over the creamed mixture and pour the melted butter round the edge of the bowl. Using a metal spoon, gently fold in the flour and butter, using a figure-of-eight movement, until thoroughly incorporated.

Divide the mixture between the lined dishes, tilting them so the batter spreads evenly and reaches the corners.

Cook the cakes one at a time. Cook on FULL (100%) for 3½ to 4 minutes until spongy and just dry on top, giving the dish a half-turn once during cooking. Leave to stand until cold before turning out and decorating.

To make the icing, put the orange juice and butter in a large bowl and cook on FULL (100%) for 1½ minutes. Add the icing sugar and beat thoroughly until smooth. Divide the icing in half. Beat the orange colouring into one portion and the yellow colouring into the other.

Spread the orange icing over one cake and the yellow icing over the other cake. Leave until set, then cut the cakes into 5 cm/2 inch squares. Decorate each one with orange and lemon slices.
MAKES 32

Note: These cakes should be stored in an airtight container in a cool place. They may also be frozen successfully.

SPICE AND NUT BISCUITS

METRIC/IMPERIAL
75 g/3 oz polyunsaturated margarine
2 tablespoons dark brown sugar
50 g/2 oz walnuts, chopped
150 g/5 oz wholemeal flour
1½ teaspoons mixed spice
½ tablespoon skimmed milk
2 tablespoons clear honey
50 g/2 oz chopped nuts, toasted

In a large bowl, beat the margarine with the sugar until creamy. Stir in the walnuts.

Mix together the flour and spice and add to the creamed mixture, stirring until well combined. Add the milk and work the mixture to a firm dough. Knead lightly into a ball.

Roll out the dough on a lightly floured surface until 5 mm/¼ inch thick. Cut out twelve to fifteen 5 cm/2 inch rounds.

Line the oven turntable or base with a double layer of lightly oiled greaseproof paper and arrange the biscuits in a circle on the paper. Cook on FULL (100%) for 3¼ minutes, rearranging the biscuits halfway through the cooking time. Brush the biscuits with honey and sprinkle with chopped nuts, then allow to cool.
MAKES 12 to 15

BUTTERSCOTCH SLICES

METRIC/IMPERIAL
50 g/2 oz butter
175 g/6 oz brown sugar
75 g/3 oz plain flour
1 teaspoon baking powder
1 egg, beaten
½ teaspoon vanilla essence
25 g/1 oz chopped nuts

Put the butter in a large bowl and heat on FULL (100%) for 1 minute until melted. Stir in the sugar and cook on FULL (100%) for 2 minutes. Leave to cool.

Sift the flour and baking powder on to the mixture, then add the egg, vanilla and nuts. Beat well to mix thoroughly.

Grease a 20 cm/8 inch square dish and spread the mixture over the base. Cook on FULL (100%) for 2½ to 3½ minutes until the cake is just dry on top. Leave to cool, then cut into slices.
MAKES 12 to 16

OAT FINGERS

METRIC/IMPERIAL
75 g/3 oz soft margarine
75 g/3 oz soft, dark brown sugar
1 tablespoon golden syrup
150 g/5 oz rolled oats

Put the margarine, sugar and syrup into an ovenproof mixing bowl. Cook on FULL (100%) for 1½ minutes. Add the oats, stirring until well coated.

Press the oat mixture into a greased 20 cm/8 inch pie dish. Cook on MEDIUM (50%) for 8 minutes, giving the dish a half-turn, twice, during cooking. Leave to STAND for 10 minutes, then mark into fingers. When cold, remove from the dish.
MAKES 10

SHORTBREAD FINGERS

METRIC/IMPERIAL
100 g/4 oz cold butter
50 g/2 oz caster sugar
175 g/6 oz plain flour
½ teaspoon salt
caster sugar for sprinkling or 50 g/2 oz
milk chocolate to coat

Lightly grease a 23 × 13 × 5 cm/9 × 5 × 2 inch shallow dish and sprinkle with caster sugar, tapping out any surplus.

Combine the butter (straight from the refrigerator) and sugar. Gradually work in the flour and salt to form a pliable dough.

Press the dough into the prepared dish, using your hands. If possible, refrigerate for 20 minutes or freeze for 5 minutes. Prick well all over.

Cook on FULL (100%) for 4 to 4½ minutes, giving the dish a half-turn, twice, during cooking.

Leave to STAND in the dish for 10 minutes, then turn out on to a board. Cut into fingers and, when quite cold, sprinkle with caster sugar.

Alternatively, while the shortbread is cooling, break the chocolate into pieces and place in a small ovenproof jug. Cook on MEDIUM (50%) for 1¾ to 2¾ minutes, stirring twice. When fully melted, spread over the shortbread. Allow to cool and set, then cut into fingers with a warm knife.
SERVES 6 to 8

JAM TARTS

METRIC/IMPERIAL
1 × 175 g/6 oz packet frozen shortcrust pastry, thawed
Caramel Colouring (see page 314)
6 tablespoons jam

Roll out the pastry thinly and cut out six 6 cm/ 3½ inch circles, using a pastry cutter. Carefully place the pastry circles in a 6-holed bun or muffin dish. Lightly press the pastry into the base and sides of each mould to form tartlet cases. Prick the base of the pastry tartlets with a fork.

Cook on FULL (100%) for 4 to 4½ minutes until the pastry is puffed and just firm. Brush each tartlet case with caramel and half-fill with jam. Cook on FULL (100%) for ½ minute. Allow to cool before serving.
MAKES 6

APRICOT TARTINES

METRIC/IMPERIAL
50 g/2 oz butter or margarine, softened
50 g/2 oz caster sugar
50 g/2 oz stale cake crumbs
50 g/2 oz ground almonds
2 large eggs (size 1 or 2)
½ teaspoon almond essence
½ teaspoon lemon juice
Streusel:
50 g/2 oz butter or hard margarine
100 g/4 oz self-raising flour
4 teaspoons demerara sugar
Decoration:
12 teaspoons apricot jam
150 ml/¼ pint double cream, whipped
12 apricot halves, canned or fresh, skinned
pieces of glacé cherry and apricot

Prepare 12 individual paper cake cases, using a double or triple thickness of paper for each tartlet to ensure a good shape. The outer case can be re-used.

Beat the butter or margarine and sugar together until light and fluffy. Stir in the cake crumbs and ground almonds and beat in the eggs, almond essence and lemon juice.

To make the streusel, rub the butter or margarine into the flour in a mixing bowl, until the mixture resembles fine breadcrumbs. Stir in the sugar.

Half-fill each cake case with the frangipan mixture and arrange in batches of 6 in a circle on the microwave base or turntable. Cook each batch on FULL (100%) for 1 minute, then remove and press the streusel on top to reach to the top of the paper case. Cook each batch on FULL (100%) for a further 1 minute.

Leave the cakes to STAND for 5 minutes, then remove from the paper cases and place upside down on a wire tray.

Spread a spoonful of apricot jam on the top of each cake and spread the cream around the sides.

Drain the apricots thoroughly and place 1 apricot half, cut side down, on top of the jam. Arrange on a serving platter, decorated with cherry and apricot pieces.
MAKES 12

CHOCOLATE BISCUITS

METRIC/IMPERIAL
50 g/2 oz wholemeal flour
50 g/2 oz self-raising flour
100 g/4 oz porridge oats
25 g/1 oz dark brown sugar
½ teaspoon salt
½ teaspoon bicarbonate of soda
100 g/4 oz butter, softened
4 tablespoons milk
350 g/12 oz plain chocolate

Combine all the ingredients, except the chocolate, in a large bowl. Mix thoroughly and knead to form a soft dough. Roll out on a floured surface to a thickness of 5 mm/¼ inch and cut out 5 cm/2 inch rounds. Re-roll the trimmings and cut out again.

Line a tray or the oven base or turntable with greaseproof paper or a folded roasting bag. Arrange 9 biscuits in a circle around the edges. Cook on FULL (100%) for 4 minutes, turning the tray occasionally.

The biscuits are ready when they can be removed from the tray easily without breaking. Transfer each one to a wire cooling rack as soon as it is cooked. Repeat with the remaining biscuits.

Break the chocolate into a bowl and cook on MEDIUM (50%) for 5½ to 6½ minutes, stirring twice, until just melting. Dip the biscuits into the chocolate one at a time, to coat completely. Lift out with a fork and place on greaseproof paper.

Chill in the refrigerator until the chocolate has set, then trim the edges to neaten. Store in an airtight container in a cool place until required.
MAKES 18

CHOCOLATE OATIES

METRIC/IMPERIAL
100 g/4 oz plain chocolate
100 g/4 oz butter
175 g/6 oz brown sugar
2 eggs, beaten
100 g/4 oz plain flour
1 teaspoon salt
1 teaspoon baking powder
75 g/3 oz walnuts, chopped
175 g/6 oz rolled oats
2 teaspoons vanilla essence

Break the chocolate into pieces and place in a bowl. Cook on MEDIUM (50%) for 2½ to 3 minutes or until melted, stirring once.

Meanwhile, cream the butter and sugar together until light and fluffy. Beat in the eggs and cooked chocolate, blending well.

Sift the flour with the salt and baking powder. Add to the chocolate mixture with the walnuts, oats and vanilla essence. Beat well to blend.

Place in walnut-sized pieces on a lightly greased microwave baking tray, about 15 at a time. Cook on FULL (100%) for 3 minutes, turning the tray once.

Allow to cool on a wire rack.
MAKES about 60

CORNFLAKE CRUNCHIES

METRIC/IMPERIAL
1 egg white
½ teaspoon vanilla essence
65 g/2½ oz sugar
40 g/1½ oz ground almonds
25 g/1 oz cornflakes, lightly crushed
2–3 sheets rice paper

Whisk the egg white until stiff, then fold in the vanilla, sugar, ground almonds and cornflakes. Divide the mixture into 12 pieces, each about the size of a walnut. Roll each piece into a ball.

Line the oven base or turntable with rice paper and arrange the crunchies on top, spacing them well apart. Cook on MEDIUM (50%) for 5 to 6 minutes, giving the sheets a half-turn after 2½ minutes. To test the crunchies, insert a skewer into the centre of each one; if it comes out clean the crunchie is cooked.

Transfer to a wire rack and allow to cool before serving.
MAKES 12

LEMON AND HONEY CRISPIES

METRIC/IMPERIAL
100 g/4 oz margarine
50 g/2 oz caster sugar
2 tablespoons runny honey or golden syrup
2 teaspoons lemon juice
25 g/1 oz raisins
100 g/4 oz cornflakes
a little chocolate vermicelli or coloured sugar strands, to decorate

Put the margarine, sugar and honey or syrup into a mixing bowl. Cook on FULL (100%) for 1 minute. Stir well, reduce the power setting to MEDIUM (50%) and cook for 3 minutes.

Stir to ensure that the sugar has dissolved. Stir in the lemon juice, raisins and cornflakes.

Arrange 20 paper cake cases on a cooling tray and pile a small amount of the cornflake mixture into each case. Leave to set.

Just before the crispies have set, sprinkle some chocolate vermicelli or coloured sugar strands on top of each.
MAKES 20

FLORENTINES

METRIC/IMPERIAL
50 g/2 oz butter
50 g/2 oz demerara sugar
1 tablespoon golden syrup
50 g/2 oz glacé cherries, chopped
75 g/3 oz walnuts, chopped
25 g/1 oz sultanas
25 g/1 oz blanched almonds, chopped
25 g/1 oz mixed peel, chopped
25 g/1 oz plain flour

Place the butter, sugar and golden syrup in a bowl. Cook on FULL (100%) for 1 to 1½ minutes or until melted.

Add the cherries, walnuts, sultanas, almonds, peel and flour. Mix well to blend.

Cook the florentines in about three batches by placing teaspoonfuls of the mixture, spaced well apart, on greaseproof paper. Cook each batch on FULL (100%) for 1½ minutes. Remove from the oven and shape the edges neatly with a knife.

When slightly cooled, lift carefully with a palette knife on to a cooling rack. Serve plain or coat one side with melted chocolate, if liked.
MAKES 12 to 15

FLAPJACKS

METRIC/IMPERIAL
100 g/4 oz butter
25 g/1 oz caster sugar
40 g/1½ oz soft brown sugar
4 tablespoons golden syrup
pinch of salt
200 g/7 oz rolled oats
50 g/2 oz grapenuts

Lightly grease a 23 cm/9 inch square shallow glass dish.

Place the butter and sugars in a bowl. Cook on FULL (100%) for 1½ minutes. Add the syrup, salt, oats and grapenuts, blending well. Press the mixture evenly into the prepared dish.

Cook on FULL (100%) for 5 minutes, turning the dish twice. Leave to cool in the dish and cut into squares to serve.
MAKES about 16

BAKEWELL TART

METRIC/IMPERIAL
Pastry:
100 g/4 oz plain flour
50 g/2 oz butter
25 g/1 oz sugar
2 egg yolks, beaten
Filling:
50 g/2 oz butter
50 g/2 oz sugar
25 g/1 oz ground almonds
50 g/2 oz cake crumbs
few drops of vanilla essence
1 teaspoon lemon juice
2 tablespoons raspberry jam
Topping:
100 g/4 oz icing sugar, sifted
1 tablespoon water
red food colouring

Sift the flour into a bowl. Rub in the butter until the mixture resembles fine breadcrumbs, then stir in the sugar. Add the egg yolks and knead lightly until the mixture forms a ball. Put into a polythene bag and chill in the refrigerator for at least 30 minutes.

Roll out the pastry thinly and use to line a 20 cm/8 inch fluted flan dish. Prick the base and sides of the pastry with a fork and cook on MEDIUM (50%) for 6 minutes until dry on top.

To prepare the filling, cream the butter and sugar together in a bowl until light and fluffy. Stir in the almonds, cake crumbs, vanilla and lemon juice.

Spread a thin layer of jam over the base of the pastry, cover with the filling and cook on LOW (30%) for 6½ to 7 minutes until the filling has set in the middle. Blend the icing sugar with the water to form a thin paste. Transfer 1 tablespoon of the icing to a separate bowl and beat in the red food colouring.

Pour the white icing over the flan, then quickly pipe thin straight lines of red icing on top, about 2.5 cm/1 inch apart. Quickly draw a skewer across the lines, at right angles and at similar intervals, to create a feathered pattern.
MAKES one 20 cm/8 inch tart

SHORTBREAD FANS

METRIC/IMPERIAL
100 g/4 oz softened butter or soft margarine
25 g/1 oz caster sugar
1 egg yolk, beaten
175 g/6 oz self-raising flour, sifted
caster sugar, to decorate

Put all the ingredients together in a mixing bowl and work with the hands until a soft dough is formed. Shape into a 20 cm/8 inch round between 2 sheets of greaseproof paper. Remove the top sheet of greaseproof paper but leave the dough in position on the lower sheet.

Using a 5 cm/2 inch cutter, remove a round from the centre of the dough and cut this round into 8 triangles.

Mark the large circle into 8 wedges and prick thoroughly with a fork. Place one of the small triangles on the outer edge of each section.

Carefully lift the greaseproof paper and dough into the microwave oven, making sure that the paper does not impede the process if the oven is fitted with a turntable.

Fill an individual paper cake case with baking beans and insert into the centre of the dough. Cook on FULL (100%) for 4 minutes or until the shortbread is just dry on top. Test with a cocktail stick to make sure that it is set. Leave for a few minutes before removing the paper and shortbread from the oven.

Remove the paper case and baking beans and sprinkle the top of the shortbread with caster sugar. Cut into sections before the shortbread is quite cold.
MAKES 8

CUP CAKES

METRIC/IMPERIAL
2 large eggs (size 1 or 2)
100 g/4 oz caster sugar
100 g/4 oz self-raising flour
100 g/4 oz soft margarine
2 tablespoons milk
2 tablespoons warm water
175 g/6 oz icing sugar, sifted
few drops of food colouring
25 g/1 oz butter
coloured sugar strands, to decorate

Put the eggs, sugar, flour, margarine and milk in a mixing bowl. Beat for 2 minutes with a wooden spoon to combine. Alternatively, use an electric mixer and beat for 1 minute.

Arrange 6 double thickness paper cake cases in a ring on a plate, leaving a gap in the centre. (This means using 2 cases for each cake. An alternative is to use a special microwave 6-holed bun or muffin dish which gives sufficient support, so that only one cake case needs to be used for each cake.)

Put 1 tablespoon of the mixture into each case and cook on FULL (100%) for 2 minutes. Leave the cakes to STAND for 1 minute, then turn on to a rack to cool. Continue with this method until all the mixture has been used.

To make the icing, beat the water into the icing sugar. Beat in the colouring and butter, and use immediately to ice the cakes. Decorate with coloured sugar strands.
MAKES 18

GINGERBREAD SQUARES

METRIC/IMPERIAL
50 g/2 oz butter or margarine
50 g/2 oz dark, soft brown sugar
3 tablespoons black treacle
75 g/3 oz plain flour
1 teaspoon ground ginger
1 teaspoon cinnamon
1 egg
5 tablespoons milk
½ teaspoon bicarbonate of soda
crystallized ginger, to decorate

Combine the butter or margarine, sugar and treacle in a 1.5 litre/2½ pint mixing bowl and cook on FULL (100%) for ¾ minute or until the butter is melted. Stir to dissolve the sugar. Sift in the flour, ginger and cinnamon. Stir the mixture, then mix in the egg.

Put the milk in a cup or glass and cook on FULL (100%) for ½ minute, until steaming but not boiling. Stir in the bicarbonate of soda. Pour the milk into the flour mixture and beat thoroughly to the consistency of a thin batter.

Grease and line the base of a plastic rectangular container about 18 × 15 × 5 cm/7 × 6 × 2 inches deep. Pour in the batter, reduce the setting to MEDIUM (50%) and cook for 3½ minutes. Give the dish a half-turn and cook on MEDIUM (50%) for a further 3½ minutes or until just dry on top. Leave to cool.

Turn out on to a sheet of non-stick silicone paper and immediately reverse to ensure that the top is undamaged. Leave whole, wrap in cling film and store for a few days for an even better flavour.

Alternatively, cut into about 12 squares, top with a piece of crystallized ginger and serve at once.
MAKES about 12

CHOCOLATE COOKIES

METRIC/IMPERIAL
225 g/8 oz butter
100 g/4 oz muscovado sugar
1 teaspoon vanilla essence
225 g/8 oz self-raising flour
50 g/2 oz powdered chocolate

Cream the butter with the sugar and vanilla essence until light and fluffy.

Sift the flour with the chocolate and gradually add to the butter mixture to make a smooth dough. Form teaspoons of the mixture into 24 small balls about the size of a walnut. Flatten each ball with a fork.

Place 6 at a time on a microwave baking tray or lightly greased greaseproof paper and cook on FULL (100%) for 1¾ to 2¼ minutes, depending upon size. Give the tray or paper a half-turn halfway through the cooking time.

Allow to cool on a wire tray. Repeat with the remaining mixture.
MAKES 24

Variation
Chocolate chip cookies: prepare and cook the biscuits as above but use 50 g/2 oz chocolate polka dots instead of powdered chocolate.

COCONUT COOKIES

METRIC/IMPERIAL
50 g/2 oz soft margarine
65 g/2½ oz sugar
1 small egg, beaten
few drops of vanilla essence
75 g/3 oz plain flour
25 g/1 oz desiccated coconut
pinch of salt
1 tablespoon raspberry or strawberry jam

Beat the margarine and sugar together until light and fluffy. Stir in the egg and vanilla, then add the flour, coconut and salt; mix thoroughly. Knead until a smooth, pliable dough is formed.

Divide the dough into 16 pieces. Roll each piece into a ball and press the end of a table knife handle into the centre of each one, to make a hollow. Arrange half of the cookies in a circle on a large greased plate (or plate lined with micro-wave cling film). Cook on FULL (100%) for 3½ to 4½ minutes, giving the plate a quarter-turn every minute, until the cookies are just firm.

Carefully transfer the cookies to a wire cooling rack and spoon a little jam into the centre of each one. Repeat with the remaining cookies. Allow to cool before serving.
MAKES 16

DATE AND RAISIN BARS

METRIC/IMPERIAL
175 g/6 oz self-raising flour
175 g/6 oz ground rice
75 g/3 oz brown sugar
175 g/6 oz butter
100 g/4 oz block stoned dates
100 g/4 oz sultanas
2 tablespoons honey
1 tablespoon lemon juice
2 tablespoons water
¼ teaspoon grated nutmeg
¼ teaspoon ground cinnamon

Combine the flour, ground rice and sugar in a large bowl, then rub in the butter until the mixture forms large crumbs. Put the dates, sultanas, honey, lemon juice and water in a shallow dish and cook on FULL (100%) for 1 minute.

Break up the dates and mash lightly with a fork, adding a few drops of water to moisten, if necessary. Stir in the nutmeg and cinnamon.

Cook on FULL (100%) for 1 to 1½ minutes until the mixture thickens.

Grease a shallow 20 cm/8 inch square dish. Spread half of the crumble mixture evenly over the base. Cover with the date spread, then top with the remaining crumbs. Press the mixture down firmly, then cook on FULL (100%) for 5½ to 6½ minutes, giving the dish a half-turn after 3 minutes. To test the mixture, insert a skewer into the centre; if it comes out clean, the mixture is cooked.

Allow to cool slightly, then mark into bars. Cool completely before serving.
MAKES 15

Note: The crumble mixture may seem very soft immediately after removing from the oven, but it becomes firm during cooling.

VIENNESE CHERRY CAKES

METRIC/IMPERIAL
225 g/8 oz plain flour
3 tablespoons custard powder
65 g/2½ oz sugar
175 g/6 oz butter
Decoration:
150 ml/¼ pint double cream, whipped
12 glacé cherries

Sift the flour and custard powder together into a mixing bowl. Add the sugar, then rub in the butter until the mixture clings together. Knead until smooth. Divide the mixture between 12 paper cake cases, pressing the mixture down with the back of a teaspoon.

Place half of the cakes in a 6-holed bun or muffin dish. Cook on FULL (100%) for 2 to 2½ minutes, giving the dish a half-turn after 1 minute. Test each cake before removing from the oven by inserting a skewer into the centre; if it comes out clean the cake is cooked. Transfer to a wire rack to cool. Cook the remaining cakes in the same way.

Leave the cakes until cold. Unwrap to show the fluted edges or serve in the paper cases. Before serving, decorate each cake with a piped swirl of whipped cream and top with a glacé cherry.
MAKES 12

Note: When fresh cherries are in season, use stoned ones in place of glacé cherries.

FIG AND WALNUT WEDGES

METRIC/IMPERIAL
75 g/3 oz polyunsaturated margarine
75 g/3 oz soft, dark brown sugar
2 eggs
175 g/6 oz wholemeal flour
75 g/3 oz dried figs, finely chopped
½ teaspoon ground cinnamon
½ teaspoon ground ginger
1 tablespoon skimmed milk
150 g/5 oz walnuts, chopped

In a large bowl, beat the margarine and sugar until creamy. Beat in the eggs, one at a time.

Place 2 tablespoons of the flour in a plastic bag; add the figs and shake thoroughly.

Mix the remaining flour with the spices and gradually add this to the egg mixture with the milk. Fold in the floured figs and 75 g/3 oz of the walnuts. Spoon the cake mixture into a lightly oiled 23 cm/9 inch flan dish. Sprinkle on the remaining walnuts and cook on FULL (100%) for 4½ minutes, turning the dish halfway through the cooking time. Allow to STAND until firm, then cut into 12 wedges and transfer to a wire rack to cool completely.
MAKES 12

SULTANA SQUARES

METRIC/IMPERIAL
225 g/8 oz self-raising flour
pinch of salt
100 g/4 oz butter
100 g/4 oz light muscovado or soft brown sugar
¼ teaspoon ground cinnamon
150 g/5 oz sultanas
2 eggs, beaten
4 to 6 tablespoons milk

Lightly grease an 18 cm/7 inch square cake dish and line the base with greased greaseproof paper.

Sift the flour and salt into a bowl. Rub in the butter until the mixture resembles fine breadcrumbs. Stir in the sugar, cinnamon and sultanas, blending well. Add the eggs and sufficient milk to make a soft dropping consistency.

Spoon into the prepared dish and cook on FULL (100%) for 5½ to 7 minutes, giving the dish a quarter-turn every 1½ minutes. Cool slightly, then turn out and cut into squares.
MAKES 8

SPICY CURRANT BISCUITS

METRIC/IMPERIAL
225 g/8 oz plain flour
½ teaspoon ground mixed spice
¼ teaspoon grated nutmeg
175 g/6 oz butter, softened
75 g/3 oz currants
150 g/5 oz demerara sugar

Sift the flour with the mixed spice and nutmeg. Add the butter, currants and 100 g/4 oz of the demerara sugar. Knead to make a firm dough.

Divide the mixture into 2 pieces and form each into a 15 cm/6 inch long roll. Roll in the remaining sugar to coat. Using a sharp knife, cut each roll into 15 slices. Place 5 at a time on a microwave baking sheet or lightly greased greaseproof paper and cook on FULL (100%) for 1¾ to 2¼ minutes. Give the baking sheet or paper a half-turn halfway through the cooking time. Allow to cool on a wire tray. Repeat with the remaining mixture.
MAKES 30

CHOCOLATE OAT CHEWS

METRIC/IMPERIAL
75 g/3 oz butter
50 g/2 oz caster sugar
2 tablespoons golden syrup
225 g/8 oz quick-cook oats
3 tablespoons cocoa powder
1 teaspoon vanilla or rum essence
25 g/1 oz walnuts, chopped
50 g/2 oz raisins, chopped

Grease a 20 cm/8 inch square cake dish.

Place the butter, sugar and golden syrup in a bowl. Cook on FULL (100%) for 3 to 4 minutes or until boiling and bubbly, stirring once.

Add the oats, cocoa powder, vanilla or rum essence, walnuts and raisins, blending well. Spoon into the prepared cake dish, levelling the surface. Allow to cool then chill until set. Cut into 5 cm/2 inch squares to serve.
MAKES 16

BROWNIES

METRIC/IMPERIAL
75 g/3 oz plain chocolate
100 g/4 oz butter
2 eggs
225 g/8 oz sugar
1 teaspoon vanilla essence
100 g/4 oz plain flour, sifted
100 g/4 oz mixed nuts, chopped

Grease a 20 cm/8 inch square dish (or line with microwave cling film).

Break the chocolate into pieces and place in a bowl with the butter. Cook on FULL (100%) for 1½ to 2 minutes until the chocolate has melted.

In another bowl, beat the eggs, sugar and vanilla together until thick and creamy. Fold in the flour and chocolate mixture in alternate spoonfuls. Fold in the nuts.

Turn the mixture into the prepared dish and spread smoothly. Cook on FULL (100%) for 5 to 6 minutes until a skewer inserted into the centre comes out clean. Give the dish a quarter-turn every 1 minute during cooking.

Leave in the dish until cold, then turn out and cut into squares.
MAKES 16 to 20

TREACLE AND SPICE SQUARES

METRIC/IMPERIAL
1½ teaspoons vinegar
4 tablespoons milk
100 g/4 oz plain flour
1 teaspoon baking powder
¼ teaspoon bicarbonate of soda
pinch of salt
¼ teaspoon ground ginger
½ teaspoon ground cinnamon
¼ teaspoon ground allspice
50 g/2 oz butter
50 g/2 oz brown sugar
1 egg, beaten
175 g/6 oz black treacle
whipped cream, to decorate (optional)

Mix the vinegar and milk together and set aside. Sift the flour, baking powder, bicarbonate of soda, salt, ginger, cinnamon and allspice together.

Cream the butter with the sugar until light and fluffy. Add the beaten egg, a little at a time,

beating thoroughly after each addition. Fold the sifted dry ingredients into the mixture, together with the black treacle and vinegar and milk mixture.

Turn the batter into a greased 20 cm/8 inch square dish. Cover and cook on FULL (100%) for 4 to 5 minutes until the colour deepens and the cake is just dry on top. Give the dish a quarter-turn every 1½ minutes during cooking.

Leave to STAND for 10 minutes before turning out. Cut into squares and serve while still slightly warm, or store uncut in an airtight tin until required. Before serving, top each square with a spoonful of whipped cream, if desired.
MAKES 16

WHOLEMEAL LOAF

METRIC/IMPERIAL
1 teaspoon caster sugar
1 teaspoon dried yeast
300 ml/½ pint warm water
450 g/1 lb plain wholemeal flour
½ teaspoon salt
15 g/½ oz butter
1 tablespoon bran for sprinkling

Mix the sugar with the yeast and half of the water in a jug. Leave in a warm place for 10 to 15 minutes until well risen and frothy.

Place the flour and salt in a bowl and cook on FULL (100%) for ½ minute to warm. Rub in the butter, then add the yeast liquid and the remaining water. Mix to a firm but pliable dough.

Knead on a lightly floured surface for about 5 minutes until smooth and elastic. Return to the bowl, cover and leave in a warm place until doubled in size. This process may be hastened by using the microwave: cook on FULL (100%) for 5 seconds, then leave to STAND for 10 to 15 minutes. Repeat as necessary.

Knead for a further 2 to 3 minutes, then shape and place in a greased 450 g/1 lb loaf dish. Cover and leave to rise until the dough reaches the top of the dish. Use the microwave hastening process again, if liked.

Sprinkle with the bran and cook on FULL (100%) for 6 minutes, giving the dish a quarter-turn every 2 minutes. Remove from the dish and allow to cool on a wire rack.

For a crisp brown crust, place the bread under a preheated hot grill until golden.
MAKES one 450 g/1 lb loaf

SODA BREAD

METRIC/IMPERIAL
100 g/4 oz plain flour
225 g/8 oz plain wholemeal flour
1 teaspoon bicarbonate of soda
1 teaspoon baking powder
1 teaspoon salt
1 tablespoon salad oil
150 ml/¼ pint natural yogurt
150 ml/¼ pint water
1 teaspoon molasses (optional)
1 teaspoon milk (optional)

Mix together the flours, bicarbonate of soda, baking powder and salt in a bowl.

Add the oil, yogurt and water and mix to form a soft dough. Shape the dough into a 15 cm/6 inch round on a well-floured surface. Using a long-bladed knife, make two deep cuts cross-ways, cutting almost through the dough.

Lift the dough carefully on to a sheet of absorbent kitchen paper and cook on FULL (100%) for 5 minutes.

Mix together the molasses and milk, if using, then brush over the surface. Cook on FULL (100%) for a further 1 minute.

Remove the bread, peel off the paper and leave to STAND for 5 minutes before slicing and serving.
SERVES 4

CHEESY SODA BREAD

METRIC/IMPERIAL
450 g/1 lb plain wholemeal or white flour
2 teaspoons mustard powder
2 teaspoons bicarbonate of soda
2 teaspoons cream of tartar
1 teaspoon salt
25 g/1 oz lard
1 teaspoon dried sage
100 g/4 oz Cheddar cheese, grated
300 ml/½ pint milk
1 tablespoon lemon juice
25 g/1 oz porridge oats

Mix the flour with the mustard powder, bicarbonate of soda, cream of tartar and salt. Rub in the lard until the mixture resembles fine bread-crumbs. Stir in the sage and cheese, blending well.

Mix the milk with the lemon juice and mix into the dry ingredients, blending well to make a soft dough. Knead on a lightly floured surface until smooth and elastic. Shape into a round and sprinkle the oats over it.

Place on a large plate or microwave baking tray and mark into 4 sections with a sharp knife. Cook on MEDIUM (50%) for 5 minutes, turning the dish once.

Cook on FULL (100%) for a further 3 minutes. Leave to STAND for 10 minutes before transferring to a wire rack to cool.
SERVES 4

FARMHOUSE ORCHARD SCONES

METRIC/IMPERIAL
175 g/6 oz plain wholemeal flour
50 g/2 oz plain flour
½ teaspoon salt
4 teaspoons baking powder
50 g/2 oz butter
1 egg, beaten
4–6 tablespoons milk
cracked wheat, for sprinkling (optional)
Filling:
2 red-skinned apples
2 tablespoons lemon juice
100–175 g/4–6 oz full-fat soft cheese

Sift the flours, salt and baking powder into a bowl. Rub in the butter until the mixture resembles fine breadcrumbs. Stir in the egg and sufficient milk to form a soft dough. Knead on a lightly floured surface until smooth.

Grease an 18 cm/7 inch flan dish and line the base with lightly greased greaseproof paper. Shape the dough into an 18 cm/7 inch round and place in the dish. Mark into 8 wedges with a sharp knife. Sprinkle the top with cracked wheat, if using.

Cook on FULL (100%) for 2 minutes, then give the dish a half-turn and cook on FULL (100%) for a further 2 to 2¼ minutes. Allow to cool slightly before turning on to a wire tray to cool.

Core both apples and cut one into 8 slices. Toss in half of the lemon juice. Finely chop the remaining apple and toss in the remaining lemon juice. Fold the chopped apple into the cheese, blending well.

Break the scones in half, fill with the cheese mixture and with the apple slices.
MAKES 8

YEAST PANCAKES

METRIC/IMPERIAL
5 tablespoons milk
1 teaspoon sugar
1 teaspoon dried yeast
100 g/4 oz plain flour
pinch of salt
65 g/2½ oz butter, at room temperature
2 eggs, beaten

Put the milk in a jug and cook on FULL (100%) for ¼ minute until just warm to the touch. Add the sugar and yeast and beat with a fork until thoroughly blended. Set aside for 10 to 15 minutes until frothy.

Sift the flour and salt into a mixing bowl and cook on FULL (100%) for ¼ minute. Make a well in the centre and pour in the yeast liquid. Flick some of the flour over the top of the liquid. Cover and set aside for 30 minutes until the yeast mixture is spongy.

Cut the butter into small pieces and add to the mixture with the beaten eggs. Beat thoroughly for 5 minutes until the batter is smooth and elastic.

Line the oven base with greased greaseproof paper. Place spoonfuls of the yeast batter well apart on the paper and cook on FULL (100%), allowing ¼ to ½ minute for each pancake. Transfer the pancakes to a wire rack as soon as they are dry on top. Serve while still warm, spread with butter and jam.
MAKES 16 to 20

CHELSEA BUNS

METRIC/IMPERIAL
450 g/1 lb White Bread dough (see page 302)
25 g/1 oz butter
150 g/5 oz currants
50 g/2 oz soft brown sugar
soft brown sugar for sprinkling
pinch of ground cinnamon
2 tablespoons sieved apricot jam

Lightly grease a large shallow dish.

Follow the instructions and method for the white bread dough until the end of the first proving.

Knead the dough on a lightly floured surface until smooth and elastic. Roll out to a rectangle measuring about 30 × 23 cm/12 × 9 inches.

Place the butter in a bowl and heat on FULL (100%) for 1 minute or until melted. Brush over the dough and sprinkle with the currants and 50 g/2 oz soft brown sugar. Roll up from one of the long ends like a Swiss roll.

Cut across the roll to make 8 slices and place, side by side, in the cooking dish. Cover and leave in a warm place until doubled in size.

Sprinkle the top with a little sugar and cinnamon. Cook on FULL (100%) for 4 to 5 minutes, turning the dish once. Leave to STAND for 5 to 10 minutes before cooling on a wire rack.

Place the jam in a bowl and cook on FULL (100%) for ½ minute. While still hot, brush the jam over the Chelsea buns.
MAKES 8

BROWN ROLLS

METRIC/IMPERIAL
300 ml/½ pint milk
2 teaspoons dried yeast
1 teaspoon sugar
350 g/12 oz plain wholemeal flour
100 g/4 oz plain flour
1 teaspoon salt
2 teaspoons malt extract
2 tablespoons vegetable oil
Topping:
beaten egg, to glaze
sesame seeds for sprinkling

Put the milk in a jug and cook on FULL (100%) for ½ to ¾ minute until just hot to the touch. Add the yeast and sugar and beat with a fork until thoroughly blended. Set aside for 10 to 15 minutes until frothy.

Sift the flours and salt into a mixing bowl and cook on FULL (100%) for ½ minute. Make a well in the centre and pour in the yeast liquid, malt extract and 1 tablespoon oil. Work the dough mixture with one hand until it leaves the sides of the bowl clean.

Turn on to a lightly floured surface and knead until the dough is smooth and no longer sticky. Add a little more liquid if it is too dry. Place in a large bowl, cover and leave until doubled in size. To hasten the rising process, cook on FULL (100%) for 5 seconds occasionally.

Turn the dough on to a lightly floured surface and knead lightly, then divide into 16 equal-sized pieces. Shape each one into a roll. Brush with the remaining oil and leave to rise for 20 to 30 minutes until the dough springs back when lightly pressed with the fingertip.

Arrange half the rolls, well spaced out, on a large greased plate or on the oven base lined with greased greaseproof paper. Cook on FULL (100%) for 3 to 3½ minutes, turning the rolls over once during cooking. Cook the remaining rolls in the same way.

While the rolls are still hot, brush the tops with beaten egg to glaze and sprinkle with sesame seeds. Brown under a preheated hot grill.
MAKES 16

BASIC WHITE BREAD

METRIC/IMPERIAL
1 teaspoon caster sugar
1 teaspoon dried yeast
300 ml/½ pint warm water
450 g/1 lb plain flour
½ teaspoon salt
40 g/1½ oz butter
2 teaspoons vegetable oil
1 tablespoon cracked wheat for sprinkling

Mix the sugar with the yeast and half of the water in a jug. Leave to STAND in a warm place until well risen and frothy.

Sift the flour and salt into a mixing bowl and cook on FULL (100%) for ½ minute or until warm. Rub in the butter; add the yeast liquid and remaining water, and mix to a pliable dough.

Knead on a lightly floured surface for about 5 minutes until smooth and elastic. Return to the bowl, cover and leave in a warm place until the dough has doubled in size. This process can be hastened by using the microwave: cook on FULL (100%) for 5 seconds, then leave to stand for 10 to 15 minutes and repeat.

Knead the dough for a further 2 to 3 minutes, then shape and place in a greased 1 kg/2 lb loaf dish. Leave in a warm place until doubled in size, repeating the microwave hastening process, if liked.

Lightly brush the bread with the oil and sprinkle with the cracked wheat. Cook on FULL (100%) for 1 minute; reduce the setting and cook on MEDIUM (50%) for 7 to 9 minutes, giving the dish a half-turn three times during cooking. Alternatively, the bread may be cooked on FULL (100%) for 5 minutes, turning twice.

Leave to STAND for 5 minutes before turning out on to a wire rack to cool.

Brown under a preheated hot grill, if a crispy brown crust is liked.
MAKES one 1 kg/2 lb loaf

GLAZED SAVARIN

METRIC/IMPERIAL
150 ml/¼ pint water
1 teaspoon sugar
15 g/½ oz dried yeast
250 g/9 oz plain flour
½ teaspoon salt
few blanched almonds
50 g/2 oz butter
2 eggs, beaten
Syrup:
100 g/4 oz caster sugar
150 ml/¼ pint water
few drops of lemon juice
Apricot glaze:
4 tablespoons sieved apricot jam
2–3 tablespoons hot water

Place the water and sugar in a small jug and cook on FULL (100%) for ¼ to ½ minute until warm. Stir in the yeast, then leave in a warm place for 10 to 15 minutes until well risen and frothy.

Sift the flour and salt into a bowl. Stir in the yeast liquid, mixing well. Knead to a soft dough. Return the dough to the bowl, cover and cook on FULL (100%) for ¼ minute. Leave to STAND for 5 minutes. Repeat three to four times or until the dough has doubled in size.

Meanwhile, grease a 23 cm/9 inch microwave savarin mould and arrange a few blanched almonds in the base.

Place the butter in a bowl and heat on FULL (100%) for 1½ to 2 minutes. Gradually beat the melted butter and beaten eggs into the dough to make a rich, smooth batter.

Pour the batter into the mould. Cover and cook on FULL (100%) for ¼ to ½ minute; give a quarter-turn and leave to STAND for 5 minutes. Repeat this procedure until the mixture has risen to the top of the mould.

Cook on FULL (100%) for 10 minutes, turning twice. Leave to STAND for 2 to 3 minutes before turning out to cool on a wire rack.

To make the syrup, place the sugar and water in a heatproof bowl. Cook on FULL (100%) for 8 minutes until a thick syrup forms. Stir in the lemon juice and carefully spoon over the still warm savarin. Allow to cool completely.

Place the savarin on a large serving plate. Mix the apricot jam with the hot water and brush over the savarin.
SERVES 6 to 8

HONEY BREAD

METRIC/IMPERIAL
350 g/12 oz plain flour
1 teaspoon bicarbonate of soda
1 teaspoon baking powder
¼ teaspoon salt
½ teaspoon ground ginger
½ teaspoon mixed spice
6 tablespoons clear honey
175 ml/6 fl oz milk
2 tablespoons vegetable oil
1 egg

Sift the dry ingredients into a mixing bowl. Combine the honey and milk in a jug and cook on FULL (100%) for ½ minute. Beat in the oil and egg. Pour on to the flour mixture and beat vigorously for at least 3 minutes.

Turn the mixture into a greased 18 × 10 cm/7 × 4 inch loaf-shaped dish and cook on LOW (30%) for 8 to 10 minutes until just dry on top, giving the dish a quarter-turn occasionally. Remove the loaf from the dish and place under a preheated hot grill to brown the top.

Slice and serve warm, generously spread with butter. Alternatively, leave to cool, then slice and serve toasted.
MAKES one tea loaf

MALT LOAF

METRIC/IMPERIAL
2 teaspoons dried yeast
1 teaspoon sugar
120 ml/4 fl oz warm water
2 teaspoons black treacle
2 tablespoons malt extract
15 g/½ oz butter
100 g/4 oz plain wholemeal flour
100 g/4 oz strong plain white flour, sifted
½ teaspoon salt
25 g/1 oz sultanas
1 tablespoon clear honey

Mix the yeast, sugar and water together in a small bowl. Set aside for 10 to 15 minutes until frothy.

Put the treacle, malt extract and butter in a small bowl and cook on FULL (100%) for 1 minute until melted.

Place the flours and salt in a large mixing bowl and cook on FULL (100%) for ½ minute. Stir in the yeast liquid and the syrup mixture, then add the sultanas. Mix to a sticky dough, adding a little more warm water, if necessary.

Turn on to a lightly floured surface and knead until smooth. Roll into a ball and replace in the mixing bowl. Cover and leave until doubled in size. To hasten the rising process, cook on FULL (100%) for 5 seconds occasionally.

Grease a 23 × 10 cm/9 × 4 inch loaf-shaped dish or similar-sized box and line the base with greaseproof paper. Press the dough evenly into the dish. Cover and leave to STAND for 10 minutes. Cook on FULL (100%) for 5 seconds. Leave to rise for a further 10 minutes.

Remove the cover and cook on FULL (100%) for 1 minute. Give the dish a half-turn and cook on LOW (30%) for 4 to 5 minutes until well risen and just dry on top.

Transfer the loaf to a wire cooling rack and, while still hot, brush the top with clear honey to glaze. Serve spread with butter.
MAKES one loaf

WHOLEMEAL SCONES

METRIC/IMPERIAL
175 g/6 oz plain wholemeal flour
2 teaspoons baking powder
½ teaspoon cream of tartar
40 g/1½ oz polyunsaturated margarine
50 g/2 oz sultanas
about 6 tablespoons skimmed milk
milk for brushing
bran for sprinkling

In a large bowl combine the flour, baking powder and cream of tartar. Add the margarine and rub in until the mixture forms fine crumbs. Stir in the sultanas and add enough milk to form a soft dough.

Place the dough on a floured surface and knead lightly. Roll out until 2 cm/¾ inch thick and cut out 5 cm/2 inch rounds with a fluted cutter. Knead the trimmings together and repeat this process until all the dough has been used. Brush the scones with milk and sprinkle with bran.

Line the oven turntable or base with a lightly oiled double layer of greaseproof paper and arrange the scones in a circle on the paper. Cook on FULL (100%) for 1½ to 2 minutes. Rearrange the scones and cook on FULL (100%) for a further 1½ to 2 minutes. Leave to STAND for 5 minutes. Serve the scones while still warm, with Greek-style yogurt and strawberries.
MAKES 6

CORN BREAD

METRIC/IMPERIAL
100 g/4 oz coarse yellow cornmeal
100 g/4 oz plain flour
2 tablespoons baking powder
½ teaspoon salt
1 tablespoon sugar
50 g/2 oz soft margarine
1 egg, beaten
250 ml/8 fl oz milk

Sift the cornmeal, flour, baking powder and salt together into a mixing bowl. Stir in the sugar, then mix in the margarine with a fork until thoroughly blended. Add the egg and milk and beat to form a smooth dough which has a soft, dropping consistency.

Grease a 23 × 10 cm/9 × 4 inch loaf-shaped dish (or line with microwave cling film). Spoon the dough into the dish and spread evenly. Cook on FULL (100%) for 4 minutes until just dry on top, giving the dish a quarter-turn every 1 minute, until cooked.

Brown the bread on all sides under a preheated hot grill before serving, if desired.
MAKES one loaf

BRAN AND APRICOT BUNS

METRIC/IMPERIAL
50 g/2 oz dried apricots
175 g/6 oz wholemeal flour
2 teaspoons baking powder
2 tablespoons bran
2 eggs, beaten
120 ml/4 fl oz skimmed milk
4 tablespoons soft, dark brown sugar
85 ml/3 fl oz grapeseed or sunflower oil
bran for sprinkling

Place the apricots in a bowl, cover with hot water and leave to soak for 30 minutes. Drain well and chop finely. Set aside.

In a large bowl mix together the flour, baking powder and bran. Stir the eggs, milk, sugar and oil together throughly and beat into the dry ingredients, mixing well.

Stir in the reserved apricots and spoon into a lightly oiled microwave bun tray, filling each cup no more than half full. Sprinkle each bun with a little bran and cook on FULL (100%) for 3 minutes, turning the tray around halfway through the cooking time. Allow to STAND for

5 minutes. Turn the buns out on to a wire rack, cover with an absorbent paper towel and leave to cool. Serve split and buttered.
MAKES 8

CORNISH WHOLEWHEAT SCONES

METRIC/IMPERIAL
100 g/4 oz plain wholemeal flour
100 g/4 oz self-raising flour
pinch of salt
1 teaspoon sugar
50 g/2 oz butter
½ teaspoon bicarbonate of soda
1 teaspoon cream of tartar
2 tablespoons natural yogurt
1 egg, beaten
4–6 tablespoons milk
To serve:
raspberry or strawberry jam
whipped cream or butter

Place the flours, salt and sugar in a mixing bowl. Rub in the butter until the mixture resembles fine breadcrumbs. Mix the bicarbonate of soda and cream of tartar with the yogurt, then stir into the flour mixture, together with the beaten egg. Add sufficient milk to form a soft dough which easily drops from a spoon.

Grease a 6-holed bun or muffin dish. Two-thirds fill each hollow with the scone mixture. Cook on FULL (100%) for 2½ to 3 minutes until the scones are well-risen, giving the dish a quarter-turn every ¾ minute. Insert a skewer into the centre of each one; if it comes out clean the scones are cooked. Return any uncooked scones to the oven and cook on FULL (100%) for a further ½ minute or until cooked.

Place the scones upside down on a grill rack. Brown under a preheated hot grill. Turn over and brown the tops.

Serve warm with jam and whipped cream or butter.
MAKES 6 to 8

Note: Refill the bun or muffin dish with any remaining mixture. Microwave on FULL (100%), allowing ½ minute for each scone.

CHEESY FLOWERPOT LOAVES

METRIC/IMPERIAL
175 g/6 oz plain wholemeal flour
25 g/1 oz wheat bran
½ teaspoon salt
½ teaspoon dry mustard
50 g/2 oz Farmhouse English Cheddar cheese, finely grated
1½ teaspoons dried yeast
1 teaspoon sugar
300 ml/½ pint warm water
1 egg, beaten

In a mixing bowl, mix together the flour, bran, salt, mustard and cheese. Dissolve the dried yeast with the sugar in the water and leave in a warm place until it becomes frothy. Whisk in the beaten egg.

Mix the yeast liquid into the dry ingredients and beat well to form a soft mixture. Place a small round of greaseproof paper in the base of six 7.5 cm/3 inch clay flowerpots to cover the hole. Divide the mixture between the 6 flowerpots and cover with a piece of cling film. Leave in a warm place until the mixture has almost doubled in size.

Uncover the pots and cook, two at a time, on FULL (100%), allowing 2½ minutes for each pair. When cooked, slide a knife between the bread and the flowerpot and turn out on to a wire rack to cool. Remove the greaseproof paper from the base of the breads. Serve on the day they are made with butter and cheese.
MAKES 6

Variations
Herby cheese flowerpot loaves: add 2 teaspoons dried herbs to the dry ingredients.
Nutty cheese flowerpot loaves: add 50 g/2 oz roughly chopped walnuts to the dry ingredients.

TEA SCONES

METRIC/IMPERIAL
225 g/8 oz plain flour
pinch of salt
2 teaspoons baking powder
50 g/2 oz butter
25 g/1 oz sugar
25 g/1 oz currants
1 egg, beaten
4–6 tablespoons milk

Sift the flour, salt and baking powder into a mixing bowl and rub in the butter until the mixture resembles breadcrumbs. Add the sugar and currants. Stir in the beaten egg and sufficient milk to form a smooth, soft dough which drops from a spoon.

Shape the dough into a ball, then flatten to form a round, about 1 cm/½ inch thick. Cut into 4 cm/1½ inch rounds. Place on a piece of greased greaseproof paper in the oven, spacing them well apart.

Cook on FULL (100%) for 2½ to 3 minutes, moving the scones around from time to time. Insert a skewer into the centre of each scone; if it comes out clean, the scones are cooked. Return any uncooked scones to the oven and cook on FULL (100%) for a further ½ minute or until cooked.

Place the scones upside down on a grill rack. Brown under a preheated hot grill. Turn over and brown the tops. Serve warm, split and buttered.
MAKES 6 to 8

OATCAKES

METRIC/IMPERIAL
100 g/4 oz wholemeal flour
50 g/2 oz rolled oats
pinch of salt
50 g/2 oz vegetable fat
1 egg, lightly beaten
1 tablespoon soft, light brown sugar

In a large bowl, mix together the flour, rolled oats and salt. Rub in the vegetable fat, add the egg and sugar and mix to a firm dough, suitable for rolling.

Roll out on a lightly floured surface to 5 mm/¼ inch thick. Cut out ten 7.5 cm/3 inch rounds. Line the base of the microwave cooker with a double layer of lightly oiled greaseproof paper and arrange the oatcakes in a circle on the paper. Cook on FULL (100%) for 1½ minutes. Rearrange the cakes and cook on FULL (100%) for a further 1½ minutes. Transfer to a wire rack to cool. Serve with a selection of cheeses or a chickpea dip.
MAKES 10

Note: Medium or coarse oatmeal may be used instead of rolled oats.

SAUCES, STUFFINGS AND ACCOMPANIMENTS

GRAVY I

METRIC/IMPERIAL
juices from the roasting dish
1–2 tablespoons plain flour
300 ml/½ pint hot stock
1 stock cube, crumbled
salt
freshly ground black pepper

Pour away the surplus dripping from the roasting dish and stir in enough flour to absorb the remaining fat. Cook on FULL (100%) for 2 to 3 minutes, stirring twice, until the flour browns.

Gradually stir in the stock and stock cube. Cook on FULL (100%) for 2 to 3 minutes until the gravy boils, stirring every 1 minute. Add salt and pepper to taste.
MAKES 300 ml/½ pint

WHITE POURING SAUCE

METRIC/IMPERIAL
25 g/1 oz butter
25 g/1 oz plain flour
300 ml/½ pint milk
salt
freshly ground black or white pepper

Place the butter in a large heatproof jug and heat on FULL (100%) for ½ minute or until melted. Add the flour, blending well. Gradually add the milk and salt and pepper to taste.

Cook on FULL (100%) for 3½ to 4 minutes, stirring every 1 minute until smooth and thickened. Use as required.
MAKES 300 ml/½ pint

Variations
Basic white coating sauce: prepare as above but use 50 g/2 oz butter, 50 g/2 oz plain flour.

Cheese sauce: prepare as above but stir 75 g/3 oz grated cheese and 1 teaspoon made mustard into the finished sauce.
Mushroom sauce: prepare as above but stir 50–100 g/2–4 oz lightly cooked and thinly sliced mushrooms into the finished sauce.
Parsley sauce: prepare as above but stir 1 to 2 tablespoons chopped fresh parsley into the finished sauce.
Onion sauce: prepare as above but stir 1 large chopped and cooked onion into the finished sauce.
Egg sauce: prepare as above but stir in 1 finely chopped hard-boiled egg.
Sweet white sauce: prepare as above but omit the salt and pepper. Stir sugar to taste into the finished sauce.

GRAVY II

METRIC/IMPERIAL
40 g/1½ oz butter
40 g/1½ oz wholemeal flour
salt
freshly ground black pepper
1 tablespoon tomato purée
600 ml/1 pint hot, well-flavoured stock
1 bay leaf
½ teaspoon dried mixed herbs
juices from the roasting dish

Place the butter in a large jug or mixing bowl and heat on FULL (100%) for 1 minute.

Stir in the flour, salt and pepper and mix well. Cook on FULL (100%) for ½ minute.

Gradually mix in the tomato purée and then all the stock and the herbs. Cook on FULL (100%) for 7 minutes, stirring every 1½ to 2 minutes during cooking, until boiling. Beat in the meat juices, discard the bay leaf, and serve at once.
MAKES 600 ml/1 pint

HOLLANDAISE SAUCE

METRIC/IMPERIAL
50 g/2 oz butter
50 g/2 oz savoury butter with black pepper
2 egg yolks
2 tablespoons wine vinegar or lemon juice

Place the butter and savoury butter in a bowl. Heat on FULL (100%) for 1½ minutes or until melted.

Gradually whisk in the egg yolks and vinegar or lemon juice, blending well. Cook on FULL (100%) for ½ minute, whisking three times to prevent curdling.

Whisk for a further ½ minute, then pour into a warmed sauceboat to serve.

Serve hot with poached fish, especially salmon, globe artichokes or other cooked vegetables.
SERVES 4

Variation
Sauce mousseline: fold 120 ml/4 fl oz lightly whipped double cream into the sauce just before serving. Serve with shellfish and chicken.

CHUNKY TOMATO SAUCE

METRIC/IMPERIAL
2 streaky bacon rashers, derinded and chopped
1 large carrot, sliced
1 large onion, chopped
2 celery sticks, sliced
1 × 400 g/14 oz can tomatoes
2 tablespoons tomato purée
½ teaspoon dried basil
1 tablespoon chopped fresh parsley
salt
freshly ground black pepper

Place the bacon in a dish and cook on FULL (100%) for 2 minutes, stirring once. Add the carrot, onion and celery, blending well. Cover and cook on FULL (100%) for 6 minutes, stirring once.

Add the tomatoes with their juice, tomato purée, basil, parsley and salt and pepper to taste, blending well. Cover and cook on FULL (100%) for 6 minutes, stirring once.

Serve chunky, or purée in a blender or food processor until smooth. Use as required.
MAKES 450 ml/¾ pint

FRESH TOMATO SAUCE

METRIC/IMPERIAL
25 g/1 oz butter
1 onion, finely chopped
1 clove garlic, crushed
salt
1 teaspoon caster sugar
1 teaspoon dried oregano
2 tablespoons tomato purée
25 g/1 oz plain flour
575 g/1¼ lb tomatoes, skinned and chopped
freshly ground black pepper
150 ml/¼ pint hot chicken stock

Place the butter, onion, garlic, salt, sugar, oregano and tomato purée in a large bowl. Cover and cook on FULL (100%) for 5 minutes.

Stir in the flour, tomatoes and pepper to taste, then cover and cook on FULL (100%) for a further 5 minutes. Stir in the hot stock. Cool the sauce slightly, then pour into a blender or food processor and blend until smooth.

Sieve the sauce. Return to the bowl and reheat on FULL (100%) for 3 minutes before serving.

Serve with hamburgers, chops, sausages and fish.
MAKES 600 ml/1 pint

PIZZAIOLA SAUCE

METRIC/IMPERIAL
1 tablespoon vegetable oil
2 onions, very finely chopped or minced
2 cloves garlic, crushed
2 small green peppers, cored, seeded and sliced
50 g/2 oz mushrooms, sliced
1 × 400 g/14 oz can tomatoes
2 teaspoons dried marjoram or oregano
dash of chilli sauce
salt
freshly ground black pepper

Place the oil in a bowl and cook on FULL (100%) for 1 minute. Add the onion, garlic and peppers, blending well. Cover and cook on FULL (100%) for 5 minutes, stirring once.

Add the mushrooms, tomatoes with their juice, herbs, chilli sauce and salt and pepper to taste, blending well. Cover and cook on FULL (100%) for 5 minutes, stirring once.

Serve hot with hamburgers, chops and chicken pieces.
SERVES 4

HOT BARBECUE SAUCE

METRIC/IMPERIAL
1 small onion, grated
4 tablespoons tomato purée
150 ml/¼ pint water
1 tablespoon wine vinegar
1 tablespoon Worcestershire sauce
2 teaspoons brown sugar
salt
freshly ground black pepper
2 tablespoons redcurrant jelly

Place all the ingredients in a bowl and cook on FULL (100%) for 7½ minutes, stirring three times during cooking.

This sauce is delicious served with pork or lamb dishes.
MAKES 200 ml/7 fl oz

BÉCHAMEL SAUCE

METRIC/IMPERIAL
1 small onion, peeled
1 carrot, sliced
1 bay leaf
blade of mace
12 peppercorns
few parsley sprigs
300 ml/½ pint milk
25 g/1 oz butter
25 g/1 oz plain flour
salt
freshly ground black pepper

Place the onion, carrot, bay leaf, mace, peppercorns, parsley and milk in a large jug. Cook on LOW (30%) for 10 to 11 minutes until hot. Strain and discard the flavourings.

Place the butter in another jug and heat on FULL (100%) for 1 minute or until melted. Stir in the flour and salt and pepper to taste.

Gradually add the strained milk, blending well. Cook on FULL (100%) for 1½ to 2 minutes until smooth and thickened, stirring twice. Use as required.
MAKES 300 ml/½ pint

Variations

Mornay sauce: prepare and cook as above but add 1 egg yolk mixed with 2 tablespoons double cream and 50 g/2 oz grated cheese to the hot sauce. Whisk until the cheese melts and the sauce is smooth.

Fish sauce: prepare as above but stir 2 tablespoons cooked, peeled prawns, ½ teaspoon lemon juice or anchovy essence and a pinch of paprika into the finished sauce.

Caper sauce: prepare as above but stir 1 tablespoon chopped capers and 1 tablespoon caper juice into the finished sauce.

Chaud-froid sauce: prepare and cook as above. Dissolve 1 tablespoon powdered gelatine in 150 ml/¼ pint hot water. Cook on FULL (100%) for 1 minute, then stir into the sauce, blending well. Use when cold.

CURRY SAUCE I

METRIC/IMPERIAL
50 g/2 oz savoury butter with black pepper
1 onion, chopped
1 apple, peeled, cored and chopped
1 tablespoon ground coriander
½ teaspoon ground cumin
½ teaspoon ground ginger
25 g/1 oz sultanas
2 tablespoons plain flour
2 teaspoons curry powder
pinch of salt
450 ml/¾ pint hot stock
1 teaspoon black treacle

Place the butter, onion, apple, coriander, cumin, ginger and sultanas in a bowl. Cover loosely and cook on FULL (100%) for 10 minutes, stirring once.

Add the flour, curry powder and salt, blending well. Gradually add the stock and treacle. Cover and cook on FULL (100%) for 10 minutes, stirring once. Use as required.
SERVES 4

CURRY SAUCE II

METRIC/IMPERIAL
1 onion, chopped
1 clove garlic, crushed
1 apple, peeled, cored and chopped
1 tablespoon ground coriander
1 teaspoon turmeric
½ teaspoon ground cumin
¼ teaspoon chilli powder
¼ teaspoon ground cinnamon
¼ teaspoon ground ginger
¼ teaspoon grated nutmeg
1½ tablespoons plain flour

1 tablespoon tomato purée
1 teaspoon lemon juice
¼ teaspoon meat extract
2 teaspoons curry paste
450 ml/¾ pint hot stock
salt
freshly ground black pepper

Place the onion, garlic, apple, coriander, turmeric, cumin, chilli powder, cinnamon, ginger and nutmeg in a medium bowl. Cover and cook on FULL (100%) for 4½ minutes, stirring halfway through cooking.

Stir in the flour, tomato purée, lemon juice, meat extract, curry paste, hot stock and salt and pepper to taste. Cover and cook on FULL (100%) for 8 to 10 minutes, stirring three times during cooking.
SERVES 4

QUICK TOMATO SAUCE

METRIC/IMPERIAL
1 × 400 g/14 oz can tomatoes
1 large onion, finely chopped
2 cloves garlic, crushed
2 tablespoons tomato purée
1 tablespoon clear honey or 2 teaspoons brown sugar
120 ml/4 fl oz hot vegetable or chicken stock or water
1 bouquet garni or 1 teaspoon dried mixed herbs
pinch of salt
freshly ground black pepper

Place all the ingredients in a large bowl or casserole and stir well. Cover and cook on FULL (100%) for 10 minutes, stirring several times during cooking. Leave to STAND, covered, for 5 minutes. Remove the bouquet garni, if using, before serving.
MAKES 600 ml/1 pint

Variation
Tomato coulis: prepare as above but omit the honey or sugar from the recipe. Discard the bouquet garni, if using, pour the sauce into a blender or food processor and blend until smooth. Finally, push through a sieve. This type of sauce can be used hot or cold.

CRANBERRY WINE SAUCE

METRIC/IMPERIAL
450 g/1 lb fresh cranberries
6 tablespoons port wine
grated rind of 1 small orange
grated rind of ½ small lemon
350 g/12 oz granulated sugar

Place the cranberries, wine, orange rind, lemon rind and sugar in a bowl, blending well. Cover and cook on FULL (100%) for 18 to 20 minutes, stirring every 6 minutes, until pulpy.

Serve warm or cold with roast game or poultry.
MAKES 750–900 ml/1¼–1½ pints

GOOSEBERRY SAUCE

METRIC/IMPERIAL
400 g/14 oz gooseberries, topped and tailed
150 ml/¼ pint water
25 g/1 oz cornflour
50 g/2 oz caster sugar

Place the gooseberries and 120 ml/4 fl oz of the water in a large bowl. Cover and cook on FULL (100%) for 6 minutes, stirring halfway through cooking. Rub through a sieve or purée in a blender or food processor until smooth.

Blend together the cornflour and remaining water. Stir into the gooseberries. Stir in the sugar and cook on FULL (100%) for 3 minutes, stirring halfway through cooking.

This is the classic accompaniment to grilled mackerel.
MAKES 450 ml/¾ pint

APPLE SAUCE

METRIC/IMPERIAL
450 g/1 lb cooking apples, peeled, cored and sliced
2 tablespoons water
25 g/1 oz butter

Place all the ingredients in a bowl and cook on FULL (100%) for 6 to 8 minutes, stirring once during cooking. Sieve or beat the sauce until smooth.

Serve with pork dishes and roast duck.
MAKES 300 ml/½ pint

SWEET AND SOUR SAUCE

METRIC/IMPERIAL
1 × 400 g/14 oz can pineapple pieces in natural
juice
150 ml/¼ pint chicken stock
1½ tablespoons brown sugar
3 tablespoons wine vinegar
2 teaspoons soy sauce
1 teaspoon tomato ketchup
pinch of Chinese 5-spice powder
1½ tablespoons cornflour
50 g/2 oz spring onions, chopped
1 small red pepper, cored, seeded and chopped
1 small green pepper, cored, seeded and chopped

Drain the juice from the pineapple into a bowl.
Add the stock, sugar, vinegar, soy sauce, ketch-
up, 5-spice powder and cornflour, blending well.
Cook on FULL (100%) for 5 to 7 minutes,
stirring three times, until clear and thickened.
 Add the pineapple pieces, spring onions and
peppers, blending well. Cook on FULL (100%)
for 2 minutes, stirring once. Cover and leave to
STAND for 5 minutes.
 Serve hot with pork, chicken or shellfish.
MAKES 750 ml/1¼ pints

BREAD SAUCE

METRIC/IMPERIAL
1 onion, peeled and studded with 4 cloves
300 ml/½ pint milk
½ small bay leaf
6 white peppercorns
1 small blade of mace or pinch of grated nutmeg
65 g/2½ oz fresh white breadcrumbs
15 g/½ oz butter
2 tablespoons single cream
salt
freshly ground black pepper

Place the onion, milk, bay leaf, peppercorns,
mace or nutmeg in a bowl. Cook on FULL
(100%) for 4 minutes. Cover and leave to
STAND for 10 minutes.
 Strain the milk into a bowl and stir in the
breadcrumbs. Cook on FULL (100%) for 2
minutes.
 Add the butter, cream and salt and pepper to
taste, blending well. Cook on FULL (100%) for
1 minute, stirring once.
 Serve hot with poultry or game.
MAKES 450 ml/¾ pint

CUMBERLAND SAUCE

METRIC/IMPERIAL
2 tablespoons soft brown sugar
pinch of cayenne pepper
150 ml/¼ pint hot chicken stock
150 ml/¼ pint red wine
1 tablespoon cornflour
3 tablespoons redcurrant jelly
grated rind of ½ small orange
2 tablespoons orange juice
salt
freshly ground black pepper

Place the sugar, cayenne, chicken stock and wine
in a large bowl or jug and cook on FULL (100%)
for 2½ minutes. Blend the cornflour with a little
cold water and stir into the sauce. Add the
remaining ingredients and cook on FULL
(100%) for 2 minutes, stirring twice.
 This sauce makes an excellent accompaniment
to gammon or pork dishes.
MAKES 450 ml/¾ pint

SAVOURY EGG SAUCE

METRIC/IMPERIAL
50 g/2 oz butter
25 g/1 oz plain flour
salt
freshly ground black pepper
300 ml/½ pint milk
1 egg yolk
2 tablespoons single cream
1 teaspoon lemon juice

Place 25 g/1 oz butter in a jug and cook on FULL
(100%) for about 1 minute, until very hot. Stir in
the flour and salt and pepper to taste. Stir in the
milk.
 Cook on FULL (100%) for 3½ minutes. Beat
very well with a balloon whisk, then set aside. (It
is important to allow the sauce to STAND for a
short while before adding the egg yolk and
cream as the sauce may curdle if it is too hot.)
 Beat together the egg yolk and cream, then
beat into the slightly cooled sauce. Beat in the
remaining butter, a little at a time, and finally stir
in the lemon juice.
SERVES 3

Note: This sauce can be used as an alternative to
Hollandaise sauce.

BRANDY SAUCE

METRIC/IMPERIAL
1½ tablespoons cornflour
300 ml/½ pint milk
25 g/1 oz caster sugar
2 tablespoons brandy
25 g/1 oz butter

Mix the cornflour with a little of the milk in a bowl until smooth.

Put the remaining milk into a large jug and heat on FULL (100%) for 2 minutes. Pour the heated milk on to the blended cornflour, stirring all the time.

Return to the jug and cook on FULL (100%) for 1 to 2 minutes, stirring twice, until boiling, smooth and thickened.

Beat in the sugar, brandy and butter until well blended. Serve hot.
SERVES 4

HOT FUDGE SAUCE

METRIC/IMPERIAL
25 g/1 oz plain chocolate
15 g/½ oz butter
2 tablespoons milk
100 g/4 oz soft brown sugar
1 tablespoon golden syrup

Break the chocolate into small pieces and place in a bowl with the butter. Cook on FULL (100%) for 1 minute, stirring once.

Add the milk, sugar and golden syrup, blending well. Cook on FULL (100%) for 3 to 4 minutes, stirring every 1 minute. Serve hot over ice cream or mousse.
SERVES 2

BUTTERSCOTCH SAUCE

METRIC/IMPERIAL
250 g/9 oz light brown sugar
40 g/1½ oz butter
6 tablespoons evaporated milk

Place the sugar and butter in a large heatproof jug. Cook on FULL (100%) for 1 minute.

Add the evaporated milk, blending well. Cook on FULL (100%) for 1¼ minutes, stirring once. Serve at once.
MAKES 300 ml/½ pint

CHOCOLATE SAUCE

METRIC/IMPERIAL
100 g/4 oz plain cooking chocolate
5 tablespoons golden syrup
3 tablespoons cocoa powder
3 tablespoons warm water
25 g/1 oz butter, melted

Break the chocolate into pieces and place in a large bowl with the syrup. Cook on FULL (100%) for 2 minutes or until melted.

In a separate basin, blend the cocoa powder with the warm water and melted butter. Add to the chocolate mixture and cook on FULL (100%) for a further ½ to 1 minute.
MAKES 300 ml/½ pint

CUSTARD SAUCE

METRIC/IMPERIAL
1 large egg (size 1 or 2)
40 g/1½ oz plain flour
25 g/1 oz soft brown sugar
¼ teaspoon vanilla essence
600 ml/1 pint milk

Beat the egg, flour, sugar and vanilla essence together. Pour the milk into a large bowl and cook on FULL (100%) for 4 minutes until steaming. Pour on to the egg mixture, whisking continuously.

Strain the custard back into the bowl and cook on LOW (30%) for 6 minutes until the sauce thickens, whisking two or three times during cooking.
MAKES 750 ml/1¼ pints

QUICK CUSTARD SAUCE

METRIC/IMPERIAL
2 tablespoons custard powder
1–2 tablespoons sugar
600 ml/1 pint milk

Place the custard powder and sugar to taste in a bowl. Mix with about 2 tablespoons of the milk to make a smooth paste. Gradually add the rest of the milk, blending well.

Cook on FULL (100%) for 6 minutes, stirring the mixture every 2 minutes, until smooth and thickened.
MAKES 600 ml/1 pint

CHOCOLATE MINT SAUCE

METRIC/IMPERIAL
75 g/3 oz plain cooking chocolate
50 ml/2 fl oz water
200 g/7 oz sugar
150 g/5 oz golden syrup
pinch of salt
75 ml/3 fl oz single cream or evaporated milk
⅛ teaspoon peppermint essence

Break up the chocolate and place in large heat-proof bowl with the water. Cook on FULL (100%) for ¾ minute, stirring once.

Add the sugar, syrup and salt, blending well. Cook on FULL (100%) for 9 minutes, stirring every 1 minute, or until a preserving thermometer reaches 115°C/240°F or a small drop of the mixture forms a soft ball when dropped into a glass of cold water (test with the thermometer *outside* the oven).

Gradually add the cream or evaporated milk and peppermint essence, blending well. Use as required.
MAKES 450 ml/¾ pint

EGG CUSTARD

METRIC/IMPERIAL
300 ml/½ pint milk
2 drops of vanilla essence
1 egg
1 egg yolk
50 g/2 oz caster sugar
25 g/1 oz plain flour

Place the milk and vanilla essence in a large jug and cook on FULL (100%) for 2 minutes.

Place the egg, egg yolk and sugar in a bowl and beat together. Add the flour and beat until smooth. Gradually stir in the milk.

Cook the custard on FULL (100%) for 2 minutes, whisking every ½ minute, until smooth and thickened. Serve with steamed sponge pudding.
MAKES 400 ml/14 fl oz

CHOCOLATE CUSTARD

METRIC/IMPERIAL
15 g/½ oz cornflour
15 g/½ oz cocoa powder
25 g/1 oz caster sugar
300 ml/½ pint milk
15 g/½ oz butter

Place the cornflour, cocoa powder and sugar in a 600 ml/1 pint jug. Gradually blend in the milk. Cook the custard on FULL (100%) for 2½ minutes, stirring every 1 minute, until thick and smooth. Beat in the butter and serve.
MAKES 300 ml/½ pint

MELBA SAUCE

METRIC/IMPERIAL
350 g/12 oz raspberries, sieved
3 tablespoons caster sugar
2 teaspoons cornflour
1 tablespoon water
½ teaspoon lemon juice

Place the raspberries and sugar in a 600 ml/1 pint jug. Blend the cornflour with the water and stir into the raspberries. Cook on FULL (100%) for 2½ minutes, stirring every 1 minute.

Stir in the lemon juice, and allow to cool.
MAKES 250 ml/8 fl oz

ORANGE SAUCE

METRIC/IMPERIAL
75 g/3 oz butter
175 g/6 oz icing sugar, sifted
175 ml/6 fl oz concentrated orange juice
15 g/½ oz cornflour
grated rind of 1 orange
1 egg, separated

Place the butter in a medium bowl and heat on FULL (100%) for 1 minute or until melted. Beat the icing sugar into the melted butter.

Blend the orange juice and cornflour together and stir into the sugar mixture. Beat in the orange rind and egg yolk. Cook on FULL (100%) for 2½ minutes or until thickened, stirring every ½ minute.

Whisk the egg white into the orange sauce. Serve with sponge pudding.
MAKES 400 ml/14 fl oz

MUSHROOM STUFFING

METRIC/IMPERIAL
25 g/1 oz butter
75 g/3 oz mushrooms, chopped
50 g/2 oz fresh white breadcrumbs
grated rind of 1 lemon
1 teaspoon dried tarragon
salt
freshly ground black pepper
1 small egg, beaten

Put the butter into a small bowl and heat on FULL (100%) for 1 minute. Stir in the mushrooms, breadcrumbs, lemon rind, tarragon, and salt and pepper to taste.

Add the beaten egg, stir to combine, and use to stuff the neck end of the bird.
MAKES sufficient stuffing for a 1.5 kg/3½ lb chicken

CHESTNUT STUFFING

METRIC/IMPERIAL
100 g/4 oz streaky bacon, derinded and chopped
1 × 575 g/1¼ lb can whole, peeled chestnuts, drained
salt
freshly ground black pepper
100 g/4 oz fresh brown breadcrumbs
25 g/1 oz butter, melted
1 teaspoon dried thyme
1 egg, beaten

Put the bacon into a small mixing bowl and cook on FULL (100%) for 2 minutes.

Place the chestnuts in a large bowl and mash with a fork. Add the bacon and bacon fat, salt and pepper, breadcrumbs, butter and thyme to the chestnuts. Mix well. Add the beaten egg, stir to combine and use to stuff the neck end of the bird.
MAKES sufficient stuffing for a 3 kg/7 lb turkey

MOCK GOOSE STUFFING

METRIC/IMPERIAL
15 g/½ oz butter
1 small onion, chopped
100 g/4 oz fresh white breadcrumbs
225 g/8 oz cooking apples, peeled, cored and chopped
75 g/3 oz prunes, soaked, stoned and sliced
¼ teaspoon ground ginger
salt
freshly ground black pepper
1 egg, beaten

Place the butter in a bowl with the onion. Cover and cook on FULL (100%) for 2 minutes, stirring once.

Add the breadcrumbs, apples, prunes, ginger and salt and pepper to taste, blending well. Bind together with the beaten egg. Use as required.
MAKES sufficient stuffing for a boned leg of lamb

SAVOURY ONION STUFFING

METRIC/IMPERIAL
2 Spanish onions, finely chopped
25 g/1 oz butter
150 ml/¼ pint chicken stock
50 g/2 oz fresh white breadcrumbs
2 teaspoons dried sage, thyme or parsley
¼ teaspoon salt
¼ teaspoon freshly ground black pepper

Combine the onion and butter in a bowl and cook on FULL (100%) for 3 minutes. Add the stock, cover and cook on FULL (100%) for 5 minutes.

Stir in the breadcrumbs, herbs and salt and pepper to taste. Cook on FULL (100%) for 1 minute. Allow to cool thoroughly before using to stuff chicken or any other type of poultry.
MAKES sufficient stuffing for a 1.5 kg/3½ lb chicken

TURKEY STUFFING

METRIC/IMPERIAL
50 g/2 oz butter
1 onion, finely chopped
1 turkey heart, chopped
1 turkey liver, chopped
175 g/6 oz mushrooms, sliced
50 g/2 oz liver pâté
225 g/8 oz chestnut purée
1 celery stick, chopped
100 g/4 oz smoked bacon, derinded and chopped
1 tablespoon chopped fresh parsley
salt
freshly ground black pepper
25–50 g/1–2 oz fresh white breadcrumbs

Place the butter in a large bowl and heat on FULL (100%) for ½ minute or until melted. Add the onion, turkey heart, turkey liver and mushrooms, blending well. Cover and cook on FULL (100%) for 3 minutes, stirring once.

Add the liver pâté, chestnut purée, celery, bacon, parsley and salt and pepper to taste, blending well. Add sufficient breadcrumbs to bind the stuffing ingredients together. Use as required.

MAKES sufficient stuffing for a 5.5 kg/12 lb turkey

PEANUT STUFFING

METRIC/IMPERIAL
40 g/1½ oz butter
1 small onion, finely chopped
50 g/2 oz salted peanuts, chopped
½ teaspoon dried sage
50 g/2 oz fresh white breadcrumbs
1 cooking apple, peeled, cored and sliced
2 teaspoons chopped fresh parsley
1 tablespoon water
freshly ground black pepper
lemon juice

Place the butter in a large bowl and heat on FULL (100%) for 1 minute or until melted. Add the onion and peanuts, blending well. Cook on FULL (100%) for 2½ minutes, stirring once.

Add the sage, breadcrumbs, apple, parsley and water, blending well. Cover and cook on FULL (100%) for 5 minutes, stirring once.

Season to taste with pepper and lemon juice. Use as required.

MAKES sufficient stuffing for a 1.5 kg/3½ lb chicken

CROÛTONS

METRIC/IMPERIAL
50 g/2 oz butter
1 tablespoon oil
4 slices from a sliced loaf, crusts removed

Place the butter and oil in a medium shallow dish and heat on FULL (100%) for 1½ minutes to melt.

Cut the bread into small cubes and toss into the hot butter and oil until coated. Cook on FULL (100%) for 4 minutes, stirring twice. Allow to STAND for 2 minutes before serving. Drain on absorbent kitchen paper.

SERVES 4

TOASTED CRUMBS

METRIC/IMPERIAL
50 g/2 oz butter
100 g/4 oz fresh white or brown breadcrumbs

Put the butter in a jug and heat on FULL (100%) for 1½ minutes. Stir in the breadcrumbs until coated with the butter, then cook on FULL (100%) for 2 minutes. Stir well, breaking down any lumps.

Cook on FULL (100%) for 2 minutes. Stir again, then cook on FULL (100%) for 1½ minutes. Stir and set aside.

During a brief standing time the crumbs will crisp up. Cool completely before storing.

Note: This recipe is useful for savoury dishes. The crumbs keep well and can be prepared in bulk and frozen or refrigerated in an airtight container.

CARAMEL COLOURING

METRIC/IMPERIAL
100 g/4 oz sugar
4 tablespoons water
1 teaspoon vegetable oil

Combine the sugar and water in a 600 ml/1 pint heat-resistant jug. Cook on FULL (100%) for 6 minutes, without stirring.

Pour 3 tablespoons of water into a glass or cup and put in the microwave oven beside the syrup. Cook on FULL (100%) for 1½ to 2 minutes until the water is boiling and the syrup is a very dark brown colour.

Protecting the hands with oven gloves, gradually add the boiling water to the syrup, then stir in the oil. Leave to cool, then pour into a screw-top bottle. Use as required.

MAKES 100 g/¼ lb

Note: Caramel colouring may be added in small quantities to fruit cakes, sauces, stews or other dishes which require more depth of colour.

PRESERVES AND DRINKS

QUICK AND EASY MARMALADE

METRIC/IMPERIAL
1 × 875 g/1 lb 13 oz can prepared Seville oranges
water (as directed on can)
2 kg/4 lb granulated sugar
15 g/½ oz butter

Empty the contents of the can of oranges into a 2.25 litre/4 pint ovenproof mixing bowl and stir in the water and sugar. Cook on FULL (100%) for 4 minutes and stir well.

Cook on FULL (100%) for 5 to 7 minutes, stirring with a wooden spoon every 2 minutes, until the sugar has dissolved.

Cook on MEDIUM (50%) for 28 to 30 minutes, stirring twice during cooking. When stirring for the first time, stir in the butter.

To test for setting, put a teaspoon of marmalade on a cold saucer. Allow to STAND for 2 minutes, then push the surface with a finger. If the skin wrinkles, then the marmalade is ready; if not, cook on FULL (100%) for a further 1 to 2 minutes, then test again. When setting point is reached, bottle in warm sterilized jars. Allow to cool, then cover with waxed paper, seal and label.

MAKES 2.5 kg/5½ lb

PLUM JAM

METRIC/IMPERIAL
1 kg/2 lb juicy plums
150 ml/¼ pint water
¼ teaspoon almond essence
1 kg/2 lb sugar

Put the plums in a large bowl with the water and almond essence. Cover and cook on FULL (100%) for 15 minutes, stirring occasionally. Remove as many of the stones as possible with a slotted spoon.

Stir in the sugar and leave to stand for 30 minutes, stirring occasionally, until dissolved.

Cook on FULL (100%) for 30 to 40 minutes, stirring occasionally, until a spoonful of the syrup wrinkles when placed on a cold plate. (Remove and discard any remaining stones.)

Leave to cool slightly, then pour into hot sterilized jars. Cover with microwave cling film. Return to the oven and cook on FULL (100%) for 1 to 1½ minutes until the cling film bubbles up. Using oven gloves, remove from the oven. Allow to cool, then cover with waxed paper and seal. Store in a cool place until required.

MAKES 1.5 kg/3 lb

MICROWAVE STRAWBERRY JAM

METRIC/IMPERIAL
1.2 kg/2½ lb strawberries, hulled
juice of 1 lemon
1.5 kg/3 lb sugar
7 g/¼ oz butter
½ bottle pectin

Place the strawberries in a large heatproof bowl and crush thoroughly. Add the lemon juice and sugar, blending well.

Cook on FULL (100%) for 15 minutes, stirring every 5 minutes. Add the butter and stir well to blend. Cook on FULL (100%) for a further 10 minutes, stirring twice. Remove from the oven and stir in the pectin. Allow to cool until syrupy so that the fruit does not float.

Ladle into warm sterilized jars. Allow to cool, then cover with waxed paper, seal and label. Store in a cool dark place until required.

MAKES about 2.25 kg/5 lb

STRAWBERRY PRESERVE

METRIC/IMPERIAL
1 kg/2 lb large strawberries, hulled
1.5 kg/3 lb sugar
3 tablespoons lemon juice

Rinse the strawberries and dry thoroughly. Put the strawberries and sugar into a large bowl. Toss gently, then cover and leave for 24 hours.

Add the lemon juice and stir thoroughly. Cook on FULL (100%) for 10 to 15 minutes, stirring two or three times during cooking, until the mixture reaches a full rolling boil. Cook on FULL (100%) for 5 to 10 minutes, stirring occasionally, until the syrup is thick.

Leave to cool slightly, then pour into warm sterilized jars. Allow to cool, then cover with waxed paper and seal. Store in a cool place until required.
MAKES about 1.75 kg/4 lb

Note: This recipe produces a preserve of whole strawberries in a thick syrup, not a thick jam.

BERRY AND APPLE JAM

METRIC/IMPERIAL
100 g/4 oz blackcurrants or blueberries
100 g/4 oz redcurrants
225 g/8 oz gooseberries
225 g/8 oz cooking apples
150 ml/¼ pint water
1 kg/2 lb sugar

Wash, top and tail the soft fruit. Peel, core and slice the apples. Combine all the fruit in a large bowl and stir in the water. Cover loosely and cook on FULL (100%) for 7 to 8 minutes. Leave to STAND for 30 minutes.

Add the sugar to the fruit and stir until dissolved. Cover and cook on FULL (100%) for 15 to 20 minutes, stirring occasionally, until a spoonful of the syrup wrinkles when placed on a cold plate.

Leave to cool for a few minutes, then pour into hot sterilized jars, leaving 2.5 cm/1 inch space at the top. Cover loosely with microwave cling film and cook on FULL (100%) for ½ to 1 minute until the cling film bubbles up. Using oven gloves, remove the jars from the oven. Allow to cool, then cover with waxed paper and seal. Store in a cool place until required.
MAKES 1.25 kg/2½ lb

MICROWAVE MINT JELLY

METRIC/IMPERIAL
50 g/2 oz fresh mint, washed
450 g/1 lb sugar
300 ml/½ pint distilled vinegar
1 bottle pectin
few drops of green food colouring

Finely chop half of the mint and set aside. Place the remaining mint in a large heatproof bowl with the sugar and vinegar. Cook on FULL (100%) for 8 minutes, stirring twice.

Remove the mint with a slotted spoon. Cook the sugar mixture on FULL (100%) until boiling, about 2 minutes, then cook for a further 1 minute.

Strain the liquid through muslin, then stir in the liquid pectin and a few drops of green colouring, blending well. Return to the bowl and cook on FULL (100%) for 4 minutes, stirring once.

Stir in the remaining chopped mint. Cool slightly, then stir again. Ladle into warm sterilized jars. Allow to cool, then seal and label. Store until required.
MAKES 900 g/2 lb

APPLE JELLY

METRIC/IMPERIAL
750 ml/1¼ pints apple juice
1 kg/1¼ lb sugar
1 teaspoon lemon juice
150 ml/¼ pint pectin
few drops of green food colouring

Combine the apple juice, sugar and lemon juice in a large bowl. Cover and cook on FULL (100%) for 10 minutes, stirring occasionally. Stir in the pectin. Without covering, cook on FULL (100%) for 7 to 10 minutes until a drop of the syrup forms a thread when suspended from a wooden spoon.

Stir in the green colouring and allow to cool slightly. Pour into hot sterilized jars, leaving a 2.5 cm/1 inch space at the top. Cover loosely with microwave cling film and cook on FULL (100%) for ½ to 1 minute until the cling film bubbles up. Using oven gloves, remove the jars from the oven.

Allow to cool, then cover with waxed paper and seal. Store in a cool place until required.
MAKES 1–1.25 kg/2–2½ lb

ORANGE AND REDCURRANT JELLY

METRIC/IMPERIAL
1 kg/2 lb redcurrants, topped and tailed
5 tablespoons water
5 tablespoons unsweetened orange juice
675 g/1½ lb sugar
¼ bottle pectin

Place the redcurrants in a bowl and crush with a wooden spoon. Add the water and orange juice, blending well. Cook on FULL (100%) for 10 minutes, stirring once.

Strain the mixture through a jelly bag into a bowl. If necessary, make up to 600 ml/1 pint with water.

Add the sugar, blending well. Cook on FULL (100%) for 8 minutes, stirring twice. Cook the mixture on FULL (100%) until boiling, about 2 minutes, then cook for a further 1 minute.

Stir in the liquid pectin, blending well. Cook on FULL (100%) for 4 minutes, stirring once.

Cool slightly, then ladle into warm sterilized jars. Allow to cool, then cover with waxed paper, seal and label. Store until required.

MAKES 1.5 kg/3 lb

STRAWBERRY AND GRAND MARNIER PRESERVE

METRIC/IMPERIAL
575 g/1¼ lb strawberries, hulled
900 g/2 lb caster sugar
2–3 tablespoons Grand Marnier
½ bottle pectin
2 tablespoons lemon juice

Crush the strawberries with the sugar and Grand Marnier in a bowl. Cook on FULL (100%) for 1 minute. Stir well and leave the mixture to stand for 30 minutes.

Stir and cook on FULL (100%) for ½ minute. Leave to stand for a further 30 minutes.

Add the pectin and lemon juice, blending well. Pour into 3 to 4 small clean jars, leaving 1 cm/½ inch headspace. Cover with foil and leave to stand in a warm kitchen for 48 hours.

Serve with scones and teabreads, or use as a sponge cake filling. Store in the refrigerator for up to 1 week.

MAKES about 1.6 kg/3½ lb

DAMSON PRESERVE

METRIC/IMPERIAL
2.25 kg/5 lb damsons
150 ml/¼ pint plus 2 tablespoons water
1 kg/2 lb sugar

Wash the fruit, dry thoroughly and place in a large bowl. Add the water. Cover loosely and cook on FULL (100%) for 15 minutes. Press through a sieve to remove the stones. Stir in the sugar.

Partially cover and cook on FULL (100%) for 20 to 25 minutes, stirring occasionally, until the preserve is thick enough to leave a channel when stirred with a wooden spoon.

Leave to cool slightly, then pour into hot sterilized jars. Cover loosely with microwave cling film. Return to the oven and cook on FULL (100%) for 1 to 1½ minutes until the cling film bubbles up. Remove from the oven with oven gloves. Allow to cool, then cover with waxed paper, seal and label. Store in a cool place until required.

MAKES 1.75 kg/4 lb

ORANGE PRESERVE

METRIC/IMPERIAL
2 large oranges, scrubbed
1 lemon
300 ml/½ pint water
450 g/1 lb sugar

Wash the oranges and lemon and cut them in half. Place in a large bowl with the water. Cover loosely and cook on FULL (100%) for 10 minutes. Remove the fruit carefully and leave to STAND for 5 minutes.

Discard the pips, shred the oranges finely and squeeze the juice from the lemon. Return to the bowl, stir in the sugar and leave for 10 minutes until completely dissolved. Cook on FULL (100%) for 20 to 25 minutes, stirring occasionally, until a spoonful of the syrup wrinkles when dropped on to a cold plate.

Pour into hot sterilized jars, leaving a 2.5 cm/1 inch space at the top. Cover loosely with microwave cling film and cook on FULL (100%) for 1 minute until the cling film bubbles up. Using oven gloves, remove from the oven. Allow to cool, then cover with waxed paper and seal. Store in a cool place.

MAKES 750 g/1½ lb

ORANGE AND LEMON CURD

METRIC/IMPERIAL
2 medium lemons
2 medium oranges
225 g/8 oz unsalted butter, cut into pieces
450 g/1 lb sugar
5 eggs, lightly beaten

Wash the fruit and arrange on a plate. Cook on FULL (100%) for 1½ minutes.

Finely grate the rind from the fruit and put it into a mixing bowl. Halve the fruits and squeeze and strain the juice into the bowl. Add the butter and the sugar.

Cook on MEDIUM (50%) for 8 minutes, stirring twice during cooking. Stir well to ensure the sugar has dissolved.

Strain the eggs into the bowl and beat well with a wooden spoon. Return the bowl to the oven and cook on MEDIUM (50%) for about 15 minutes, stirring every 2 minutes during cooking, until the mixture coats the back of the spoon. Pour into warm sterilized jars. Allow to cool, then cover with waxed paper, seal and label. Keeps for up to 3 weeks if stored in a cool place.
MAKES about 1.25 kg/2½ lb

RASPBERRY PRESERVE

METRIC/IMPERIAL
1 kg/2 lb raspberries, hulled
1 kg/2 lb caster sugar

Do not wash the fruit. Place the raspberries in a mixing bowl and crush them with the back of a wooden spoon.

Add the sugar. Cover the bowl with cling film and leave in a cool place overnight.

Remove the cling film. Cover and cook on FULL (100%) for 5 minutes, then stir.

Reduce the power setting to MEDIUM (50%) and cook for 32 to 35 minutes, stirring twice during cooking.

To test for setting, put a little jam on to a cold saucer. Leave to cool for a minute or two and then push the jam with your finger. If the jam is ready, it will crinkle slightly. If not, return to the oven and cook a little longer. Put in warm sterilized jars. Allow to cool, then cover with waxed paper, seal and label.
MAKES 1.6 kg/3½ lb

RASPBERRY JAM

METRIC/IMPERIAL
800 g/1¾ lb raspberries, hulled
7 g/¼ oz citric acid
625 g/1 lb 6 oz preserving sugar
15 g/½ oz unsalted butter

Place the raspberries in a large heatproof bowl and sprinkle with the citric acid. Cook on FULL (100%) for 10 minutes until soft.

Add the sugar and butter, blending well. Cook on FULL (100%) for 40 to 45 minutes, stirring every 5 minutes, until setting point is reached (see Raspberry Preserve).

Leave to STAND for 20 minutes. Ladle into warm sterilized jars. Allow to cool, then cover with waxed paper, seal and label. Store in a cool dark place until required.
MAKES 1 kg/2 lb

LEMON CURD

METRIC/IMPERIAL
grated rind and juice of 3 lemons
75 g/3 oz unsalted butter
225 g/8 oz sugar
3 large eggs (size 1 or 2), beaten

Put the lemon rind, juice and butter in a large bowl and cook on FULL (100%) for 3 minutes until the butter has melted.

Stir in the sugar and cook on FULL (100%) for 2 minutes. Stir until the sugar has dissolved, then strain in the eggs, stirring constantly.

Cook on LOW (30%) for 12 to 14 minutes, stirring occasionally, until the mixture is thick enough to coat the back of a spoon. Spoon into dry sterilized jars. Allow to cool, then seal and store in a cool place for up to 3 weeks.
MAKES 750 g/1½ lb

FRESH APRICOT JAM

METRIC/IMPERIAL
1.4 kg/3 lb apricots, halved and stoned
7 g/¼ oz citric acid
200 ml/7 fl oz water
1.6 kg/3½ lb granulated or preserving sugar

Place the apricots in a large heatproof bowl. Mix the citric acid with the water and pour over the apricots. Cover and cook on FULL (100%) for

20 minutes or until the apricots are soft, stirring twice.

Stir in the sugar, blending well. Cook on FULL (100%) for 45 to 50 minutes, or until setting point is reached, stirring every 10 minutes.

Ladle into warm sterilized jars. Allow to cool, then cover with waxed paper, seal and label.
MAKES about 2.75 kg/6 lb

REDCURRANT AND APPLE JAM

METRIC/IMPERIAL
450 g/1 lb redcurrants, topped and tailed
300 ml/½ pint water
350 g/12 oz cooking apples, peeled, cored and sliced
1 kg/2 lb caster sugar

Place the redcurrants and water in a mixing bowl and cook on FULL (100%) for 2½ minutes. Stir in the apples and continue to cook on FULL (100%) for 4 minutes.

Add the sugar and stir until dissolved. Return to the oven and cook on FULL (100%) for a further 17 to 21 minutes, stirring occasionally during cooking, until the jam has reached setting point. To test for setting, put a little jam on a cold saucer. Leave to cool for a minute or two and then push the jam with your finger. If the jam is ready, it will crinkle slightly. If not, return to the oven and cook a little longer.

Bottle in warm sterilized jars. Allow to cool, then cover with waxed paper, seal and label. Store in a cool place.
MAKES about 1.25 kg/2½ lb

THREE FRUIT MARMALADE

METRIC/IMPERIAL
1½ medium lemons
1½ medium oranges
1½ medium grapefruit
600 ml/1 pint boiling water
1.6 kg/3½ lb granulated or preserving sugar

Wash the fruit, cut into quarters and slice thinly. Retain the pips and tie them in a piece of muslin.

Place the fruit and the pips in a large heatproof bowl. Add 150 ml/¼ pint of the boiling water. Leave to stand overnight.

Add the remaining boiling water, cover and cook on FULL (100%) for 25 minutes. Remove and discard the muslin. Add the sugar and stir until dissolved. Cook on FULL (100%) for 20 to 30 minutes or until setting point is reached, stirring every 5 minutes.

To test for setting, put a teaspoon of marmalade on a cold saucer. Allow to stand for 2 minutes, then push the surface with a finger. If the skin wrinkles, then the marmalade is ready. If not, cook on FULL (100%) for a further 1 to 2 minutes, then test again.

Ladle into warm, sterilized jars. Allow to cool, then cover with waxed paper, seal and label.

Store until required.
MAKES 2.25–2.75 kg/5–6 lb

CIDER AND SAGE JELLY

METRIC/IMPERIAL
150 ml/¼ pint boiling water
4 tablespoons chopped fresh sage
900 g/2 lb sugar
450 ml/¾ pint sweet cider
150 ml/¼ pint liquid pectin

Mix the water with the sage and leave to stand for 15 minutes.

Place the sugar and cider in a large heatproof bowl. Cook on FULL (100%) for 8½ minutes, stirring once.

Strain the herbs and add the water to the syrup mixture. Cook on FULL (100%) for 6 minutes or until boiling. Stir in the liquid pectin, blending well. Cook on FULL (100%) for 3 minutes. Stir well, then leave to STAND for 1 minute.

Ladle into warm sterilized jars. Allow to cool, then cover with waxed paper, seal and label. Store in a cool place until required.
MAKES about 1.25 kg/2½ lb

TANGY CHOCOLATE SPREAD

METRIC/IMPERIAL
50 g/2 oz butter
225 g/8 oz sugar
juice of 1 lemon
25 g/1 oz cocoa powder
1 tablespoon evaporated milk
1 large egg (size 1 or 2), beaten

Put the butter and sugar in a large jug and cook on FULL (100%) for 2 minutes. Beat thoroughly, then stir in the lemon juice, cocoa powder and evaporated milk. Beat thoroughly, strain in the beaten egg and beat again.

Cook on LOW (30%) for 4 minutes, stirring once during cooking, then cook on FULL (100%) for 2 minutes until the mixture boils.

Leave to cool, then pour into small pots. Seal with jam pot covers or cling film and leave until cold. Store in the refrigerator until required.

Serve as a spread or use as a cake filling.
MAKES 225 g/½ lb

BOTTLED DAMSONS

METRIC/IMPERIAL
450 g/1 lb caster sugar
300 ml/½ pint boiling water
1 kg/2 lb damsons, halved and stoned

Place the sugar and boiling water in a 1.75 kg/4 lb preserving jar. Cook on FULL (100%) for 4 minutes, stirring once.

Add the damsons to the jar, packing down well. Partially cover to allow any steam to escape. Cook on FULL (100%) for 5 minutes.

Reduce the setting and cook on MEDIUM (50%) for 5 minutes.

Cover, seal, label and leave until cold. Wipe any stickiness from the jar and check that the seal is good. Store the damsons until required.
MAKES one 1.75 kg/4 lb jar

ROSY PEARS

METRIC/IMPERIAL
175 g/6 oz caster sugar
450 ml/¾ pint dry red or rosé wine
6 large pears, peeled
2 tablespoons lemon juice

Place the sugar and wine in a 1.75 kg/4 lb preserving jar. Cook on FULL (100%) for 4 to 5 minutes, stirring the mixture once.

Brush the pears with the lemon juice and add to the jar. Partially cover to allow steam to escape. Cook on FULL (100%) for 4 minutes.

Reduce the setting and cook on MEDIUM (50%) for 4 minutes.

Seal, label and leave until cold. Wipe any stickiness from the jar and check that the seal is good. Store the pears until required.
MAKES one 1.75 kg/4 lb jar

SWEETCORN RELISH

METRIC/IMPERIAL
250 ml/8 fl oz malt vinegar
few strands of saffron
1 red pepper, cored, seeded and chopped
1 green pepper, cored, seeded and chopped
1 celery stick, chopped
1 onion, finely chopped
1 clove garlic, chopped
225 g/8 oz sugar
675 g/1½ lb sweetcorn kernels
15 g/½ oz salt
pinch of mustard powder
pinch of ground mace
pinch of dried tarragon
2 tablespoons arrowroot powder, blended with a little cold water

Mix the vinegar with the saffron and leave to turn yellow.

Place the peppers, celery, onion and garlic in a bowl. Strain in the vinegar, blending well. Cover and cook on FULL (100%) for 5 minutes.

Add the sugar, sweetcorn, salt, mustard, mace and tarragon, blending well. Cook on FULL (100%) for 5 minutes, stirring once.

Stir the arrowroot liquid into the vegetable mixture, blending well. Cook on FULL (100%) for 8 minutes, stirring once. Leave to STAND for 5 minutes. Ladle into warm sterilized jars. Seal, label and store until required.
MAKES 1.5 kg/3 lb

MEDITERRANEAN CHUTNEY

METRIC/IMPERIAL
1 kg/2 lb tomatoes, skinned and chopped
450 g/1 lb Spanish onions, chopped
450 g/1 lb courgettes, thinly sliced
1 large green pepper, cored, seeded and chopped
1 large red pepper, cored, seeded and chopped
225 g/8 oz aubergine, chopped
2 large cloves garlic, crushed
1 tablespoon cayenne pepper
1 tablespoon ground paprika
1 tablespoon ground coriander
300 ml/½ pint malt vinegar
350 g/12 oz sugar

Place the tomatoes in a large heatproof bowl with the onions, courgettes, peppers, aubergine, garlic, cayenne pepper, paprika and coriander. Cook on FULL (100%) for 15 minutes, stirring twice.

Add the vinegar and sugar, blending well. Cook on FULL (100%) for 15 minutes, stirring twice. Leave to STAND for 5 minutes.

Ladle into warm sterilized jars. Seal, label and store until required.
MAKES 2.75 kg/6 lb

TOMATO CHUTNEY

METRIC/IMPERIAL
350 g/12 oz tomatoes, skinned and chopped
350 g/12 oz cooking apples, peeled, cored and sliced
1 onion, finely chopped
350 g/12 oz raisins
2 tablespoons salt
2 teaspoons mixed spice
1 clove garlic, crushed
225 g/8 oz molasses sugar
450 ml/¾ pint malt vinegar

Place the tomatoes, apples and onion in a large bowl. Cover and cook on FULL (100%) for 10 minutes, stirring halfway through cooking.

Stir in the raisins, salt, mixed spice, garlic, sugar and vinegar. Cook on FULL (100%) for 24 minutes, stirring the chutney several times during cooking.

Allow the chutney to cool before spooning into warm sterilized jars. Seal and label.
MAKES about 1.5 kg/3 lb

RHUBARB CHUTNEY

METRIC/IMPERIAL
450 g/1 lb rhubarb, sliced
50 g/2 oz raisins
50 g/2 oz sultanas
few cloves
4 onions
150 g/5 oz soft brown sugar
pinch of mustard
pinch of salt
grated rind of 1 orange
450 ml/¾ pint malt vinegar

Place all the ingredients in a large dish and cook on FULL (100%) for 25 minutes, stirring every 5 minutes.

Bottle the chutney while still hot in warm sterilized jars. Cover with waxed paper, seal and label.
MAKES about 1 kg/2 lb

PICCALILLI

METRIC/IMPERIAL
225 g/8 oz cucumber, cubed
225 g/8 oz green tomatoes, chopped
225 g/8 oz onions, sliced
225 g/8 oz shallots, peeled and left whole
225 g/8 oz cauliflower florets
225 g/8 oz celery, chopped
generous 1 litre/2 pints water
25 g/1 oz salt
25 g/1 oz flour
2 teaspoons dry mustard
¼ teaspoon turmeric
75 g/3 oz sugar
Spiced vinegar:
600 ml/1 pint malt vinegar
blade of mace
few peppercorns
few cloves
pinch of ground allspice
pinch of ground cinnamon
pinch of chilli powder

Place all the vegetables in a large bowl and cover with the water and salt. Cover the bowl and leave overnight.

For the spiced vinegar, place the vinegar and all the spices in a bowl and cook on FULL (100%) for 6½ minutes, stirring once. Allow to cool.

Drain and rinse the vegetables and place in a

bowl. Cover and cook on FULL (100%) for 4 minutes.

Mix the flour, mustard, turmeric and sugar with a little of the spiced vinegar to a smooth paste. Pour the remaining spiced vinegar into a jug and cook on FULL (100%) for 1½ to 2 minutes, until hot. Pour on to the blended flour, stir and return to the jug. Cook on FULL (100%) for a further 1½ to 2 minutes, stirring twice.

Pour the vinegar mixture over the vegetables. Cook on FULL (100%) for 10 minutes, stirring twice during cooking. Leave to STAND for 5 minutes before bottling in warm sterilized jars. Cover with waxed paper, seal and label.
MAKES about 1.5 kg/3 lb

JAPANESE PUNCH

METRIC/IMPERIAL
300 ml/½ pint brewed tea, strained
4 cloves
1 cinnamon stick
½ teaspoon ground ginger
small mint sprig
1.2 litres/2 pints lemonade

Place the tea, cloves, cinnamon, ginger and mint in a large heatproof bowl. Cook on FULL (100%) for 3 minutes. Leave to STAND until cool.

Strain the tea mixture into a jug and top up with the lemonade. Mix well to blend. Serve lightly chilled.
SERVES 6 to 8

REAL OLD-FASHIONED LEMONADE

METRIC/IMPERIAL
finely grated rind of 2 lemons
juice of 4 lemons
3 tablespoons water
225 g/8 oz sugar
iced water, to serve

Place the lemon rind, lemon juice, water and sugar in a large heatproof jug, blending well. Cook on FULL (100%) for 4 minutes, stirring twice. Leave to STAND, covered, until cool.

Chill thoroughly, then dilute to taste with iced water (about 300 ml/½ pint iced water to 50 ml/ 2 fl oz lemonade concentrate).
SERVES 6 to 8

SPICY APPLE JUICE

METRIC/IMPERIAL
450 g/1 lb cooking apples, peeled, cored and sliced
2 tablespoons water
sugar to taste
150 ml/¼ pint dry white wine
¼ teaspoon ground cinnamon
300 ml/½ pint sparkling cider

Place the apples in a bowl with the water and sugar to taste. Cover and cook on FULL (100%) for 5 minutes.

Pour the mixture into a blender or food processor with the wine and cinnamon. Blend until smooth. Allow to cool or keep warm. Stir in the cider and serve at once, either warm or cold.
SERVES 6

IRISH COFFEE

METRIC/IMPERIAL
175 ml/6 fl oz cold black coffee
2–3 tablespoons Irish whiskey
1–2 teaspoons sugar
1–2 tablespoons double cream

Place the coffee, whiskey and sugar to taste in an Irish coffee goblet or heatproof glass. Cook on FULL (100%) for 1½ to 2 minutes until very hot but not boiling. Stir well to blend.

Whip the cream lightly until slightly thickened. Pour over the back of a teaspoon on to the coffee so that it forms a distinctive layer. Serve at once.
SERVES 1

ORANGE AND LEMON TEA

METRIC/IMPERIAL
750 ml/1¼ pints cold weak tea, strained
1 lemon, washed and sliced
1 orange, washed and sliced

Pour the tea into a large serving jug and cook on FULL (100%) for 4¾ to 5¼ minutes until boiling. Add the fruit, then cover tightly. Leave to infuse for 5 minutes before pouring into heated glasses, adding a lemon and orange slice to each glass.
SERVES 4

FOAMING MOCHA

METRIC/IMPERIAL
4 teaspoons drinking chocolate
3 teaspoons instant coffee granules
1 teaspoon sugar
600 ml/1 pint milk
1 egg white
ground cinnamon for sprinkling

Blend the drinking chocolate, coffee, sugar and milk in a large heatproof jug. Cook on FULL (100%) for 4 to 5 minutes until very hot but not boiling. Pour into mugs or heatproof glass tumblers.

Whisk the egg white until it stands in stiff peaks. Spoon on top of the mocha drink and sprinkle with ground cinnamon. Serve at once.
SERVES 2

CREAMY COCOA

METRIC/IMPERIAL
3 tablespoons cocoa powder
50 g/2 oz sugar
900 ml/1½ pints milk

Blend the cocoa, sugar and milk in a large heatproof jug. Cook on FULL (100%) for 4 to 5 minutes until very hot but not boiling.

Whisk well until hot, steaming and frothy. Pour into mugs and serve at once.
SERVES 4

HONEYED POSSET

METRIC/IMPERIAL
3 egg yolks
2 rounded tablespoons clear honey
150 ml/¼ pint medium white wine
grated rind of 1 orange

Place the egg yolks and honey in a bowl and whisk well to blend.

Place the wine and orange rind in a jug and cook on FULL (100%) for 1½ minutes until just boiling. Pour on to the egg mixture, whisking continuously.

Return the bowl to the oven and cook on LOW (30%) for 1 to 1½ minutes. Whisk until very thick and frothy, about 3 to 5 minutes.

Serve at once in warmed glasses.
SERVES 4

FRESH TOMATO JUICE

METRIC/IMPERIAL
12 ripe tomatoes, skinned and chopped
100 ml/4 fl oz water
1 onion, sliced
2 celery sticks (with leaves), sliced
1 bay leaf
3 parsley sprigs
1 teaspoon Worcestershire sauce
1 teaspoon sugar
salt
freshly ground black pepper

Place the tomatoes in a bowl with the water, onion, celery, bay leaf and parsley, blending well. Cover and cook on FULL (100%) for 3 minutes, stirring once.

Reduce the setting and cook on MEDIUM (50%) for 4 minutes, stirring once.

Strain the mixture and add the Worcestershire sauce, sugar and salt and pepper to taste, blending well. Cool and chill before serving.
SERVES 2

TOM AND JERRYS

METRIC/IMPERIAL
150 ml/¼ pint milk
20 g/¾ oz butter
2 eggs, separated
1 tablespoon sugar
¼ teaspoon vanilla essence
75 ml/3 fl oz brandy
75 ml/3 fl oz brown rum
grated nutmeg for sprinkling

Place the milk and butter in a large heatproof jug and cook on FULL (100%) for 1½ minutes, stirring once.

Whisk the egg whites until they stand in stiff peaks. Add the sugar and whisk until stiff and glossy. Fold in the egg yolks and vanilla essence, blending well.

Slowly pour the milk mixture into the egg mixture, whisking constantly. Whisk in the brandy and rum. Cook on FULL (100%) for 1 minute.

Whisk the mixture until it becomes frothy. Serve at once, with a little nutmeg sprinkled on top.
SERVES 3

ORANGE TEA

METRIC/IMPERIAL
250 ml/8 fl oz orange juice
600 ml/1 pint water
1 tablespoon caster sugar
2 tea bags
Decoration:
4 orange slices
4 mint sprigs

Place the orange juice, water and sugar in a large jug. Cook on FULL (100%) for 8 minutes, stirring halfway through cooking.

Stir in the tea bags, cover and leave to STAND for 4 minutes.

Stir the orange tea, remove the tea bags, then pour into 4 glasses and float a slice of orange on the top. Decorate each glass with a sprig of mint.
SERVES 4

ICELANDIC COFFEE

METRIC/IMPERIAL
600 ml/1 pint cold strong black coffee
150 ml/¼ pint Grand Marnier
4 tablespoons demerara sugar
120 ml/4 fl oz double cream, whipped

Put the coffee in a large jug and cook on FULL (100%) for 4½ to 5 minutes until steaming. Cover and set aside.

Divide the Grand Marnier between 4 drinking glasses. Arrange on the oven base or turntable and cook on FULL (100%) for ½ minute. Remove from the oven, ignite and add the sugar and coffee while still flaming.

Top each glass with a generous spoonful of whipped cream and serve immediately.
SERVES 4

FROSTY NIGHT PUNCH

METRIC/IMPERIAL
250 ml/8 fl oz water
1 tea bag
1 small orange, cut into pieces
4 cloves
½ teaspoon lemon juice
½ cinnamon stick
60 ml/2 fl oz whisky
60 ml/2 fl oz dry cider

60 ml/2 fl oz orange juice
25 g/1 oz brown sugar
2 cinnamon sticks, to decorate

Place the water in a large jug. Cook on FULL (100%) until boiling. Place the tea bag in a small bowl. Add the boiling water, orange, cloves, lemon juice and cinnamon. Stir, cover and stand for 3 to 4 minutes.

Strain into a large jug. Stir in the remaining ingredients and cook on FULL (100%) for 3 minutes or until warm; do not boil. Pour into 2 heatproof tumblers. Add a cinnamon stick to each tumbler before serving.
SERVES 2

MULLED WINE

METRIC/IMPERIAL
750 ml/1¼ pints red wine
12 cloves
2 small pieces of cinnamon stick
grated rind and juice of 1 lemon
grated rind and juice of 1 orange
2–3 tablespoons brown sugar

Combine the wine, cloves, cinnamon, lemon and orange rinds and juice in a large bowl and cook on FULL (100%) for 5 minutes until nearly boiling. Strain into a heated bowl, add sugar to taste and serve warm.
SERVES 6

Note: Take care not to over-sweeten. More sugar may be added to the wine when serving.

HOT WHISKY EGG NOG

METRIC/IMPERIAL
750 ml/1¼ pints milk
65 ml/2½ fl oz whisky
50 g/2 oz caster sugar
2 eggs, lightly beaten
grated nutmeg for sprinkling

Place the milk, whisky and sugar in a large jug. Cook on FULL (100%) for 6 minutes, stirring halfway through cooking.

Beat the eggs into the hot milk mixture. Strain into 4 heatproof or warmed tumblers. Sprinkle grated nutmeg over each and serve immediately.
SERVES 4

RUSSIAN CHOCOLATE

METRIC/IMPERIAL
300 ml/½ pint milk
5 teaspoons drinking chocolate
1 measure brandy
1 tablespoon double cream
grated chocolate, to decorate

Place the milk in a heatproof mug and cook on
FULL (100%) for 1¼ minutes. Stir in the
drinking chocolate, blending well.

Add the brandy, blending well. Cook on
FULL (100%) for ½ minute. Pour the cream on
top of the chocolate mixture and sprinkle with
grated chocolate. Serve at once.
SERVES 1

ORANGEADE

METRIC/IMPERIAL
4 oranges
1 lemon
900 ml/1½ pints cold water
75 g/3 oz sugar

Thinly pare the rind from the oranges and lemon
and place in a bowl with the water. Cook on
FULL (100%) for 6 to 7 minutes until very hot.
Add the sugar and stir to dissolve. Cover and
leave until cold.

Strain the mixture into a jug and add the juice
from the oranges and lemon, blending well.
Serve cold.
MAKES 1.2 litres/2 pints

RICH HOT CHOCOLATE

METRIC/IMPERIAL
50 g/2 oz plain chocolate, broken into pieces
5 tablespoons hot water
450 ml/¾ pint milk
whipped cream for topping

Place the chocolate in a large jug. Cook on FULL
(100%) for 3½ minutes or until the chocolate has
melted.

Stir in the water and then the milk, blending
well. Cook on MEDIUM (50%) for 2 to 2½
minutes stirring once. Pour into 4 warmed cups
and top each with a spoonful of whipped cream.
Serve at once.
SERVES 4

AFTER EIGHT COFFEE

METRIC/IMPERIAL
1 tablespoon Crème de Menthe
1 rounded teaspoon demerara sugar
175 ml/6 fl oz cold black coffee
1–2 tablespoons double cream

Place the Crème de Menthe, sugar and coffee in a
stemmed, heatproof glass. Cook on FULL
(100%) for 1½ to 2 minutes until very hot but
not boiling. Stir well to dissolve the sugar
completely.

Whip the cream lightly, then pour over the
back of a spoon on to the coffee so that it forms a
layer on the surface. Serve the coffee at once.
SERVES 1

SUMMER FRUIT PUNCH

METRIC/IMPERIAL
50 g/2 oz caster sugar
150 ml/¼ pint water
60 ml/2 fl oz orange juice
60 ml/2 fl oz lemon squash
60 ml/2 fl oz pineapple juice
60 ml/2 fl oz grape juice
300 ml/½ pint cold tea
orange and apple slices
mint, to decorate

Place the sugar and water in a jug. Cover and
cook on FULL (100%) for 3 minutes. Stir well to
dissolve the sugar. Set aside to cool.

Mix together the orange juice, lemon squash,
pineapple juice, grape juice, cold tea and cooled
syrup. Place slices of fruit in a bowl. Add the
punch and chill. Serve in tall glasses decorated
with mint.
SERVES 4

BASIC FOOD DEFROSTING CHART

Food	Quantity	Power setting	Time in minutes	Instructions
Meat				
Beef–joints	per 450 g/1 lb	DEFROST	10	Turn over at least once. Leave to stand for 10–15 minutes.
–steaks (large)	per 450 g/1 lb	DEFROST	6–8	Leave to stand for 10–15 minutes.
–steaks (small)	per 450 g/1 lb	DEFROST	4–6	Leave to stand for 10–15 minutes.
–minced beef	per 450 g/1 lb	DEFROST	9–10	Break up with a fork during defrosting time. Leave to stand for 10–15 minutes.
–burgers	2 × 100 g/4 oz	DEFROST	4–6	Leave to stand for 2 minutes.
	4 × 100 g/4 oz	DEFROST	10–12	Leave to stand for 5 minutes.
Lamb–joints	per 450 g/1 lb	DEFROST	5–6	Turn over at least once. Leave to stand for 10–15 minutes.
–chops	per 450 g/1 lb	DEFROST	6–8	Turn and rearrange halfway through defrosting time. Leave to stand for 5 minutes.
Pork–joints	per 450 g/1 lb	DEFROST	7–8	Turn over at least once. Leave to stand for 10–15 minutes.
–chops	per 450 g/1 lb	DEFROST	7–9	Turn and rearrange halfway through defrosting time. Leave to stand for 5 minutes.
Veal–joints	per 450 g/1 lb	DEFROST	8–9	Turn over at least once. Leave to stand for 10–15 minutes.
–chops	per 450 g/1 lb	DEFROST	7–9	Turn and rearrange halfway through defrosting time. Stand for 5 minutes.
Kidney	per 450 g/1 lb	DEFROST	9–10	Turn over at least once. Leave to stand for 5 minutes.
Liver	per 450 g/1 lb	DEFROST	8–9	Turn over at least once. Stand for 5 minutes.

Food	Quantity	Power setting	Time in minutes	Instructions
Bacon–joint	450 g/1 lb	DEFROST	8	Turn over at least once. Leave to stand for 20-30 minutes.
—rashers	1 × 225 g/ 8 oz pkt	DEFROST	2-3	Turn over halfway through defrosting time. Leave to stand for 5 minutes.
Sausages–thin	450 g/1 lb	DEFROST	5	Turn over and rearrange halfway through defrosting time. Leave to stand for 5 minutes.
—thick	450 g/1 lb	DEFROST	5-6	Turn over and rearrange halfway through defrosting time. Leave to stand for 5 minutes.
Sausagemeat	per 450 g/1 lb	DEFROST	6-8	Break up with a fork during defrosting time. Leave to stand for 10-15 minutes.
Stewing or braising meat–cubed	675 g/1½ lb	DEFROST	12	Separate pieces of meat during defrosting time. Stand for 10-15 minutes
Made-up meat products —casserole with vegetables	4 portions	FULL	14-16	Stir twice during recommended defrosting and reheating time.
shepherd's pie	1 × 400 g/14 oz	FULL	5 + 6	Allow to stand 2 minutes between defrosting and reheating time.
—roast meat and gravy	350 g/12 oz	FULL	3 + 3½	Allow to stand 3 minutes between defrosting and reheating times.
Poultry and Game Chicken–whole	per 450 g/1 lb	DEFROST	6-7	Shield the wing tips with foil. Give the dish a quarter-turn occasionally. Leave to stand 10-15 minutes, then remove giblets.
—pieces	per 450 g/1 lb	LOW	8	Place the meatiest part of the chicken pieces to the outside of the dish. Turn over halfway through defrosting time. Leave to stand 5-10 minutes.

BASIC FOOD DEFROSTING CHART (continued)

Food	Quantity	Power setting	Time in minutes	Instructions
Turkey–whole	per 450 g/1 lb	DEFROST	10–12	Shield the tips of the wings and legs with foil. Turn over twice during the defrosting time and give the dish a quarter-turn occasionally. Shield any warm spots with foil during defrosting time. Stand 15–20 minutes, remove giblets.
Duck–whole	per 450 g/1 lb	DEFROST	5–6	Shield the wings, tail-end and legs with foil. Give the dish a quarter-turn occasionally. Stand 10–15 minutes, remove giblets.
Grouse, Guinea fowl, Partridge, Pheasant, Pigeon, Poussin, Quail and Woodcock	per 450 g/1 lb	DEFROST	6–7	Shield the tips of the wings and legs with foil. Turn over halfway through the defrosting time and give the dish a quarter-turn occasionally. Leave to stand 10 minutes.
Poultry stew or braising meat–cubed	675 g/1½ lb	DEFROST	10–12	Separate pieces of poultry during defrosting time. Stand for 10–15 minutes.
Poultry casserole with vegetables	4 portions	FULL	12–14	Stir twice during defrosting and reheating time.
Fish and Shellfish Fish fillets	per 450 g/1 lb	DEFROST	7–8	Arrange thinner tail ends to centre of dish. Leave to stand for 5–10 minutes.
Fish steaks (cod, salmon and coley for example)	1 × 175 g/6 oz 2 × 175 g/6 oz	DEFROST DEFROST	2 3–4	Leave to stand for 10 minutes. Stand for 10 minutes.
Whole fish (herrings, trout and mackerel for example)	1 × 225-275 g/ 8-10 oz 2 × 225-275 g/ 8-10 oz	DEFROST DEFROST	4–6 9–11	Turn over halfway through defrosting time.

Food	Quantity	Power setting	Time in minutes	Instructions
Crabmeat	per 225 g/8 oz	DEFROST	4	Break up with a fork during defrosting time. Leave to stand for 10-15 minutes.
Lobster–whole	1 × 450 g/1 lb 1 × 675 g/1½ lb	DEFROST DEFROST	12-15 14-16	Turn over halfway through defrosting time. Leave to stand 10 minutes.
Prawns, scampi and shrimps	per 450 g/1 lb	DEFROST	7-8	Separate pieces during defrosting time. Leave to stand for 5-10 minutes.
Scallops	per 450 g/1 lb	DEFROST	7½-10	Separate pieces during defrosting time. Leave to stand for 5-10 minutes.
Kippers–fillets	per 450 g/1 lb	DEFROST	5-7	Arrange tail ends to centre of dish. Stand for 3 minutes.
Fish cakes	4 × 75 g/3 oz	DEFROST	5-6½	After defrosting allow to stand 3 minutes.
Rice and Pasta Cooked long-grain rice	per 225 g/8 oz	DEFROST	5-6	Stir twice. Leave to stand for 2 minutes.
Cooked brown rice	per 225 g/8 oz	DEFROST	6-7	Stir twice. Leave to stand for 2 minutes.
Cooked egg noodles	per 225 g/8 oz	DEFROST	6	Stir twice. Leave to stand for 2 minutes.
Cooked spaghetti	per 225 g/8 oz	DEFROST	6½	Stir twice. Leave to stand for 2 minutes.
Cooked pasta shells	per 225 g/8 oz	DEFROST	7	Stir twice. Leave to stand for 2 minutes.
Cooked macaroni	per 225 g/8 oz	DEFROST	7	Stir twice. Leave to stand for 2 minutes.
Cooked lasagne	per 225 g/8 oz	DEFROST	6	Turn over once. Leave to stand for 3 minutes.

BASIC FOOD DEFROSTING CHART (continued)

Food	Quantity	Power setting	Time in minutes	Instructions
Sauces	per 300 ml/ ½ pint	FULL	4–5	Stir twice and whisk at end of recommended defrosting and reheating time.
Stock	per 300 ml/ ½ pint	FULL	2½–3	Break down frozen block during defrosting time. Stand for 5 minutes.
Fruit Fruit dry-packed with sugar	per 450 g/1 lb	FULL	4–8	Gently shake or stir twice during defrosting time. Leave to stand for 5–10 minutes.
Fruit packed with sugar syrup	per 450 g/1 lb	FULL	8–12	Gently shake or stir twice during defrosting time. Stand for 5–10 minutes.
Open frozen or free-flow fruit	per 450 g/1 lb	DEFROST	4–8	Gently shake or stir twice during defrosting time. Stand for 5–10 minutes.
Butter	1 × 250 g/9 oz	DEFROST	2–3	Turn once and leave to stand for 5 minutes.
Eggs–white only	2	DEFROST	1½–2	Leave to stand for 5 minutes.
Yogurt	1 × 150 ml/ 5 fl oz carton	FULL	1	Remove lid. Stir for 1 minute after defrosting to mix.

CONVENIENCE FOOD DEFROSTING AND COOKING CHART

Food	Quantity	Power setting	Time in minutes	Instructions
Meat and Meat Products Shepherd's pie	1 × 400 g/14 oz	FULL	5+6	Allow to stand for 2 minutes between defrosting and cooking.

Food	Quantity	Power setting	Time in minutes	Instructions
Beefburgers	4	FULL	3-4	Place on absorbent kitchen paper. Turn over once.
Meat pie	1 × 100 g/4 oz	DEFROST then FULL	3/2 + 2	Allow to stand for 2 minutes between all defrosting and cooking times.
	1 × 450 g/1 lb	DEFROST then FULL	12-15/ 3 + 4	Allow to stand for 10 minutes after defrosting and 4 minutes between and after cooking times.
Lasagne	1 × 450 g/1 lb	DEFROST then FULL	8-10 + 4/9	Cover to cook. Allow to stand for 6 minutes between defrosting times.
Steak and kidney pudding	1 × 125 g/4 oz	DEFROST then FULL	2 + 3/2½	Allow to stand for 5 minutes between defrosting times and for 2 minutes after cooking.
Individual 'boil-in-bag' ready meals	1 × 170 g/6 oz	DEFROST	11-12	Pierce bag. Allow to stand for 2 minutes before serving.
Fish and Fish Products				
Fish steak in sauce	1 × 170 g/6 oz	DEFROST	11-12	Pierce bags and turn once or twice during cooking.
	2 × 170 g/6 oz	MEDIUM	11-12	
	4 × 170 g/6 oz	FULL	16-17	
Cook-in-bag smoked haddock or buttered kippers	1 × 198 g/7 oz	FULL	6	Pierce bag and turn once during cooking.
Fish fingers	10	DEFROST then FULL	6/1½ + 1	Place in a circle on a plate and dot with butter. Allow to stand for 4 minutes between defrosting times. Turn over halfway through cooking times.
Soups	300 ml/½ pint	FULL	3	Break down solid block during cooking.
	600 ml/1 pint	FULL	6	
Savoury Snacks Pâté	1 × 198 g/7 oz pack	DEFROST	3-4	Allow to stand for 15 minutes.

Food	Quantity	Power setting	Time in minutes	Instructions
Pizza	1 individual	FULL	1½–2	Place on absorbent kitchen paper.
	1 family size	FULL	3–4	
Pancakes	8 stacked	DEFROST	4–6	Rearrange twice. Allow to stand for 5 minutes.
Filled flan or quiche	1 family size	FULL	4–5	Turn once. Allow to stand for 3 minutes.
Bread	1 large unsliced loaf	DEFROST	4	Turn twice. Allow to stand for 5–10 minutes.
	1 small unsliced loaf	DEFROST	3	Turn twice. Allow to stand for 10 minutes.
	1 large sliced loaf.	DEFROST	4	Turn several times. Allow to stand for 10–15 minutes.
	1 slice bread	DEFROST	¼–½	Check constantly.
	2 bread rolls	DEFROST	½–1	Place on absorbent kitchen paper. Allow to stand for 2–3 minutes.
	4 bread rolls	DEFROST	1½–2	Place on absorbent kitchen paper.
	2 pitta breads	DEFROST	1½–2	Place on absorbent kitchen paper.
	2 croissants	DEFROST	½–1	Place on absorbent kitchen paper.
	2 crumpets	FULL	½–¾	Place on absorbent kitchen paper.
	2 teacakes	FULL	¾	Place on absorbent kitchen paper.
	450 g/1 lb bread dough	DEFROST	5+3	Place on absorbent kitchen paper. Allow to stand for 8 minutes between defrosting times and for 5 minutes after defrosting. To *defrost only*.
Cakes and Biscuits				
Biscuits	225 g/8 oz	DEFROST	1–1½	Turn once and allow to stand for 5 minutes.
Small light fruit cake	1	DEFROST	5–6	Turn once. Allow to stand for 10 minutes.
Buns/rock cakes	2	DEFROST	1–1½	Stand for 5 minutes.
Small cream-filled sponge	1	FULL	¾	Allow to stand for 10–15 minutes.
Small jam-filled sponge	1	DEFROST	3	Allow to stand for 5 minutes.

GUIDE TO REHEATING

Food	Quantity	Time in minutes	Power setting
Meats			
Main dishes with sauce	1 serving	3	FULL
	2 servings	6	FULL
	4 servings	10	FULL
Plated meals – meat and two vegetables	1 serving	6	FULL
Hamburgers	1 serving	1	FULL
	2 servings	1½–2	FULL
	4 servings	2½–3	FULL
Hot dogs and frankfurters	1 serving	½	FULL
	2 servings	1	FULL
	4 servings	1½	FULL
Sliced meat or chicken	1 serving	1½–2	MEDIUM
	2 servings	2½–3½	MEDIUM
Soups	1 serving	2	FULL
	2 servings	3–4	FULL
Fish			
Fish in sauce	1 serving	2	FULL
	2 servings	3–3½	FULL
Vegetables	1 serving	1	FULL
	2 servings	2	FULL
	4 servings	4	FULL
Stewed Fruit	1 serving	1	FULL
	2 servings	1½–2	FULL
	4 servings	3–4	FULL
Puddings and Desserts			
Sponge pudding	1 serving	½	FULL
Milk pudding	1 serving	1	FULL

Food	Quantity	Time in minutes	Power setting
Fruit pie	1 serving	½	FULL
Miscellaneous			
Rice and pasta	1 serving	½–1	FULL
	2 servings	1–2	FULL
Porridge	1 serving	1–2	FULL
	2 servings	2–3	FULL
Baked beans	1 serving	1½–2	FULL
	2 servings	2½–3	FULL
Sauces	300 ml/ ½ pint	2–3	FULL

GUIDE TO REHEATING BOILED SHELLFISH

Shellfish	Quantity	Time in minutes on FULL
Lobster–tails	450 g/1 lb	5–6

Turn tails over halfway through the cooking time.

Lobster–whole	450 g/1 lb	6–8

Allow to stand for 5 minutes before serving. Turn over halfway through the cooking time.

Prawns/scampi	450 g/1 lb	5–6

Arrange the peeled shellfish in a ring in a shallow dish and cover with cling film, snipping two holes in the top to allow the steam to escape.

Shrimps	450 g/1 lb	5–6

Arrange the peeled shrimps in a ring in a shallow dish and cover with cling film, snipping two holes in the top to allow the steam to escape.

GUIDE TO COOKING FISH

Fish		Quantity	Time in minutes on FULL	Preparation
Bass	whole	450 g/1 lb	5–7	Shield the head and tail with foil. Cut the skin in two or three places to prevent it from bursting.
Cod	fillets	450 g/1 lb	5–7	Place the fillet tails in the centre of the dish or shield with foil. Cut the skin in two or three places to prevent it from bursting.
	steaks	450 g/1 lb	4–5	Cover with greaseproof paper before cooking.
Haddock	fillets	450 g/1 lb	5–7	Place the fillet tails to the centre of the dish or shield with foil. Cut the skin in two or three places to prevent it from bursting.
	steaks	450 g/1 lb	4–5	Cover with greaseproof paper before cooking.
Halibut	steaks	450 g/1 lb	4–5	Cover with greaseproof paper before cooking.
Kippers	whole	1	1–2	Cover with cling film and snip two holes in the top to allow the steam to escape.
Red mullet and red snapper	whole	450 g/1 lb	5–7	Shield the head and tail with foil. Cut the skin in two or three places to prevent it from bursting.
Salmon	steaks	450 g/1 lb	4–5	Cover with greaseproof paper before cooking.
Salmon trout	whole	450 g/1 lb	6–8	Shield the head and tail with foil. Cut the skin in two or three places to prevent it from bursting.
Scallops		450 g/1 lb	4–6	Cover with dampened absorbent kitchen paper.
Smoked haddock	whole	450 g/1 lb	4–5	Cover with cling film, snipping two holes in the top to allow the steam to escape.

Fish		Quantity	Time in minutes on FULL	Preparation
Trout	whole	450 g/1 lb	4–6	Place in the centre of the dish. Shield the head and tail with strips of foil attached with wooden cocktail sticks, cut the skin in two or three places to prevent it from bursting. Allow to stand for 5–10 minutes.

GUIDE TO COOKING MEAT, POULTRY AND GAME
Cooking time is per 450 g/1 lb or for quantity given.

Type and cut of meat, poultry or game		Time in minutes on MEDIUM	Time in minutes on FULL	Preparation
BEEF				
topside	rare	12	5–6	Choose a good quality joint with an even covering of fat and a neat shape. Turn over once during cooking. After cooking remove from the microwave and allow to stand for 15–20 minutes, wrapped in foil, before carving and serving.
	medium	14	6½–7½	
	well done	16	8½–9½	
sirloin	rare	12	5–6	Bone and roll, wrap in foil and stand for 15–30 minutes before cooking.
	medium	14	6½–7½	
	well done	16	8½–9½	
rib	rare	12–13	5½–6½	Ideally, bone and roll the joint before cooking. Allow to stand for 15–30 minutes, wrapped in foil, before cooking for the recommended time.
	medium	14–15	7–8	
	well done	16–17	8–10	
minced beef		14–16	10–12	Cook in a covered dish. Stir during cooking time. Leave to stand for 2 minutes.
rump steak	rare		2	Preheat a browning dish according to the manufacturer's instructions. Add the meat and brown. Turn over halfway through the recommended time for cooking the meat.
	medium		3–4	
	well done		4	

Cooking time is per 450 g/1 lb or for quantity given.

Type and cut of meat, poultry or game		Time in minutes on MEDIUM	Time in minutes on FULL	Preparation
fillet steak	rare		2	Ideally, cook on MEDIUM. If
	medium		2-3	using FULL, leave to rest for 10
	well done		3	minutes halfway through the
braising steak		16-17	10	recommended cooking time.
hamburgers	1 (100g/4oz)		2-3	Preheat a browning dish
	2 (100 g/4 oz)		3-4	according to the
	3 (100 g/4 oz)		4-5	manufacturer's instructions.
	4 (100 g/4 oz)		5-6	Add the hamburgers and cook
	1 (225 g/8 oz)		2½-3½	for the recommended time,
	2 (225 g/8 oz)		6-7	turning the 100 g/4 oz burgers over halfway through the cooking time, and turning the 225 g/8 oz burgers over twice during the cooking time.
LAMB				
leg	on bone	11-13	8-10	Choose a good quality joint.
	off bone	12-13	9-10	Roll the meat into a neat shape if it is off the bone. Cover the pointed end with foil to protect it if on the bone. Allow to stand for 25-30 minutes, wrapped in foil, before carving.
breast		14-16	12	Roll and stuff, if liked, before cooking. Allow to stand for 30 minutes, wrapped in foil, before cooking.
crown roast			5	Cover tips of bone with foil during cooking.
loin of lamb		11-13	8-10	Choose a good quality joint. Roll into a neat shape if off the bone. Allow to stand, in foil, for 25-30 minutes before carving.
chops	loin or 2 chump		6-7	Preheat the browning dish in the microwave oven according
	4		7-9	to the manufacturer's
	6		15-17	instructions. Add the lamb chops to the dish and cook for the recommended time, turning over halfway through cooking time to ensure even treatment.

Type and cut of meat, poultry or game		Time in minutes on MEDIUM	Time in minutes on FULL	Preparation
PORK leg		13–15	10	Choose a good quality joint. Cover the pointed end with foil to protect from over-cooking. Score fat with a sharp knife and sprinkle liberally with salt to get a crisp crackling. Allow to stand for 20 minutes, wrapped in foil, before carving. Brown under a hot grill if liked.
loin		14–16	10–13	Roll into a neat shape before cooking. Stand for 20 minutes in foil, before carving.
fillet chops	loin or 2 chump	14–18	7	Preheat the browning dish. Add the chops and cook for the recommended time, turning over halfway through cooking.
	3	19–24		
	4	26–32		
	6	33–37		
Bacon or gammon joint Gammon steaks (each) Bacon		11–12 14		Cook in a browning dish if liked (observing preheating times) or cover with cling film. Turn halfway through the cooking time.
	4 slices 450 g/1 lb		3½–4 12–14	Place on a plate or bacon rack and cover with absorbent kitchen paper. Turn rashers over halfway through cooking.
Liver Kidney Sausages			5–6 7–8	Prick sausages thoroughly and arrange on a rack or plate. Cover with absorbent kitchen paper and turn halfway through the cooking time.
	2		1½–2	
	4		3–3½	
CHICKEN	whole	6–8	9–10	Shield the tips of the wings and legs with foil. Place in a roasting bag in a dish with 2-3 tablespoons stock. Give the dish a half turn halfway through the cooking time. Place the meatiest part of the chicken piece to the outside of the dish. Cover with greaseproof paper.
	pieces 1	2–4		
	2	4–6		
	3	5–7		
	4	6½–10		
	5	7½–12		
	6	8–14		

Type and cut of meat, poultry or game		Time in minutes on MEDIUM	Time in minutes on FULL	Preparation
DUCK	whole	7–8	9–11	Shield the tips of the wings, tail end and legs with foil. Prick the skin thoroughly to help release the fat. Place in a dish in a roasting bag on a trivet and turn over halfway through the cooking time.
Grouse, Guinea fowl, Partridge, Pheasant, Quail, Pigeon and Poussin		6–8	9–11	Shield the tips of the wings and legs with foil. Smear the breast with a little butter and place in a roasting bag in a dish. Turn the dish halfway through the cooking time.
TURKEY		9–11	11–13	Shield wing tips and legs with foil. Put in roasting bag in dish with stock. Turn over at least once.

MEAT BROWNING AIDS

There are many browning agents and aids which can be used to add colour and flavour to those foods which do not brown readily in the microwave oven:

Browning agent	Food	Preparation
Soy sauce	Beef, lamb, pork, poultry and game.	Brush on to meat or rub into poultry and game.
Tomato ketchup/Brown sauce	Beef, hamburgers, poultry	Brush on to meat and poultry.
Crushed crisps	Poultry joints	Roll in the crisps to coat.
Colourful dry soup mix	Poultry and game	Sprinkle on or roll in to coat.
Melted butter and ground paprika	Poultry and game	Brush on butter and sprinkle with paprika.
Worcestershire sauce	Hamburgers, beef, lamb or pork	Brush on item.
Toasted breadcrumbs	Poultry	Brush with butter and roll in crumbs to coat.
Jams, jellies, glazes	Poultry, ham and game	Glaze for last 10 minutes of cooking time.
Microwave seasoning	All meats, poultry and game	Sprinkle on item.
Browning dish	All meats, poultry and game	Turn on all sides to brown.

GUIDE TO COOKING FRESH VEGETABLES

Vegetables	Quantity	Water/salt	Preparation	Time in minutes on FULL	Cooking notes
Artichokes, globe	1	8 tablespoons/ ½ teaspoon	Discard the tough, outer leaves. Snip the tips off the remaining leaves and cut off the stems. Cover to cook.	5–6	To test if cooked, at the minimum time, try to pull a leaf from the whole artichoke. If it comes away freely, the artichoke is cooked. Drain upside down before serving.
	2	8 tablespoons/ ½ teaspoon		7–8	
	4	250 ml/8 fl oz/ 1 teaspoon		14–15	
Asparagus	450 g/1 lb	6 tablespoons/ ½ teaspoon	Place in a dish, arranging any thicker stems to the outside of the dish and tender tips to the centre. Cover to cook.	6–7	Give the dish a half turn after 3 minutes' cooking time.
Aubergines	2 medium, halved	2 tablespoons/ ½ teaspoon	Cover to cook.	7–9	Scoop out the cooked flesh from the halved aubergines and use as required.
	1 peeled and cubed	2 tablespoons/ ¼ tablespoon		5–6	Stir the cubed aubergine after 3 minutes' cooking time.
Beans, all except thin French beans.	450 g/1 lb	8 tablespoons/ ½ teaspoon	Cover to cook.	14–16	Stir the beans twice during cooking. Test after the minimum time to see if cooked.
French beans	450 g/1 lb	8 tablespoons/ ½ teaspoon	Cover to cook.	5–7	
Beetroot	2 medium	8 tablespoons/ ½ teaspoon	Cover to cook.	12–16	Stir or rearrange halfway through the cooking time. Stand for 10 minutes.
	5 medium	8 tablespoons/ ½ teaspoon		22–25	
Broccoli	450 g/1 lb	8 tablespoons/ ½ teaspoon	Place in a dish with the stalks to the outside. Cook covered.	10–12	Stir or give the dish a half turn after 6 minutes.

Vegetables	Quantity	Water/salt	Preparation	Time in minutes on FULL	Cooking notes
Brussels sprouts	450 g/1 lb	4 tablespoons/ ½ teaspoon	Trim damaged or coarse leaves; cut large sprouts in half. Cover to cook.	7-9	Stir the sprouts after 4 minutes' cooking time.
Cabbage, shredded	450 g/1 lb	8 tablespoons/ ½ teaspoon	Use a large dish and fit cabbage loosely. Cover to cook.	8-9	Stir or rearrange halfway through the cooking time.
Carrots, whole sliced	450 g/1 lb 1 kg/2 lb 450 g/2 lb	8 tablespoons/ ½ teaspoon 8 tablespoons/ ½ teaspoon	Cut carrots into 1 cm/½ inch thick slices. Slicing diagonally reduces the cooking time by 2 minutes. Cover.	12-14 18-20 12-14	Stir or rearrange halfway through the cooking time.
Cauliflower, whole florets	1 medium about 675 g/ 1½ lb 450 g/1 lb	8 tablespoons/ ½ teaspoon 8 tablespoons/ ½ teaspoon	Cover to cook	13-17 10-12	Turn a whole cauliflower or florets halfway through the cooking time. Allow whole cauliflower to stand for 5 minutes after cooking.
Celery, whole or sliced	450 g/1 lb	4 tablespoons/ ¼ teaspoon	Cover to cook	14-16	Turn or stir halfway through the cooking.
Chicory, whole	4 medium	4 tablespoons	Cover to cook and add salt after cooking.	5-8	Rearrange halfway through the cooking.
Corn on the cob	1 2 4 6	3 tablespoons 3 tablespoons 5 tablespoons 5 tablespoons	Cover to cook	4-5 7-8 13-15 17-20	Cook the corn in the husk with no extra water. Rearrange cobs halfway through cooking.
Courgettes, sliced whole	450 g/1 lb 6 small		Cover to cook.	5-6 7	Dot lightly with 25 g/1 oz butter before cooking. Stir halfway through the cooking time.

Vegetables	Quantity	Water/salt	Preparation	Time in minutes on FULL	Cooking notes
Leeks, sliced	450 g/1 lb	4 tablespoons/ ½ teaspoon	Cover to cook.	10–12	Stir halfway through the cooking time.
Marrow, sliced	450 g/1 lb		Cover with greaseproof paper before cooking. Add salt after cooking.	8–10	Stir halfway through the cooking time.
Mushrooms, whole or sliced	225 g/8 oz 450 g/1 lb	2 tablespoons water or butter	Cover to cook. Add salt, if liked, after cooking.	2–4 4–6	Stir halfway through the cooking time.
Onions, whole or quartered	4 medium 8 medium	4 tablespoons/ ½ teaspoon	Cover to cook.	10–12 14–16	Stir halfway through the cooking time.
Parsnips, cubed	450 g/1 lb	8 tablespoons/ ½ teaspoon	Cover to cook.	8–10	Stir halfway through the cooking time.
Peas, shelled	450 g/1 lb 1 kg/2 lb	8 tablespoons/ ½ teaspoon	Cover to cook.	9–11 12–14	Stir halfway through the cooking time. Add 15–25 g/½–1 oz butter after cooking and allow to stand for 5 minutes.
Potatoes, peeled and quartered	450 g/1 lb	8 tablespoons/ ½ teaspoon	Cover to cook	10–14	Stir twice during cooking.
baked in skins	1 2 3 4		Prick thoroughly and cook on absorbent kitchen paper.	4–6 6–8 8–12 12–16	Potatoes may still feel firm when cooked. Stand for 3–4 minutes.
Spinach	450 g/1 lb		Wash but do not dry before cooking. Place in a roasting bag and secure loosely with string.	6–8	Drain if necessary before serving.
Tomatoes, halved	2	salt to taste	Add a knob of butter and a little pepper to each half before cooking. Cover to cook.	1–1½	

Vegetables	Quantity	Water/salt	Preparation	Time in minutes on FULL	Cooking notes
Turnips, cubed	450 g/1 lb (2–3 medium turnips)	8 tablespoons/ ¼ teaspoon	Cover to cook	12–14	Stir twice during cooking.

GUIDE TO COOKING FROZEN VEGETABLES

Generally, no extra water is required for cooking frozen vegetables but 2–3 tablespoons may be added if liked.

Vegetable	Quantity	Time in minutes on FULL
Asparagus	225 g/8 oz 450 g/1 lb	6–7 11
Beans, broad	225 g/8 oz 450 g/1 lb	8 10
Beans, French or runner	225 g/8 oz 450 g/1 lb	7 10
Broccoli	225 g/8 oz 450 g/1 lb	6–8 8–10
Cabbage	225 g/8 oz 450 g/1 lb	6–7 10–11
Carrots	225 g/8 oz 450 g/1 lb	7 10
Cauliflower florets	225 g/8 oz 450 g/1 lb	5 8
Corn kernels	225 g/8 oz 450 g/1 lb	4 7–8
Corn on the cob	1 2	4–5 7–8

Vegetable	Quantity	Time in minutes on FULL
Courgettes	225 g/8 oz 450 g/1 lb	4 7
Diced and mixed vegetables	225 g/8 oz 450 g/1 lb	5–6 7–9
Peas	225 g/8 oz 450 g/1 lb	4 8
Spinach, chopped, or still in leaf	225 g/8 oz 450 g/1 lb	7–8 10–11
Root vegetable stewpack (mixed)	225 g/8 oz 450 g/1 lb	7 10
Swedes	225 g/8 oz 450 g/1 lb	7 11
Turnips	225 g/8 oz 450 g/1 lb	8 12

GUIDE TO COOKING RICE

Rice	Quantity	Preparation	Time in minutes on FULL then MEDIUM	Standing time
Brown rice	225 g/8 oz	Place in a deep, covered container with 600 ml/1 pint boiling salted water.	3/25	5–10
American easy-cook rice	225 g/8 oz	Place in a deep, covered container with 600 ml/1 pint boiling salted water.	3/12	5–10

GUIDE TO COOKING PASTA

Pasta	Quantity	Preparation	Time in minutes on FULL	Standing time
Egg noodles and tagliatelle	225 g/8 oz	Place in a deep, covered container with 600 ml/1 pint boiling salted water and 1 tablespoon oil.	6	3
Pasta shells and shapes	225 g/8 oz	Place in a deep, covered container with 900 ml/1½ pints boiling salted water and 1 tablespoon oil.	12–14	5–10
Spaghetti	225 g/8 oz	Hold in a deep, covered container with 1 litre/1¾ pints boiling salted water to soften, then submerge or break in half and add 1 tablespoon oil.	10	5–10

GUIDE TO COOKING FRUIT

Fruit–type and quantity	Preparation	Time in minutes on FULL
450 g/1 lb cooking apples	Peel, core and slice, then sprinkle with 100 g/4 oz sugar.	6–8
450 g/1 lb plums, cherries, damsons or greengages	Stone and wash. Sprinkle with 100 g/4 oz sugar and the grated rind of ½ lemon.	4–5
450 g/1 lb soft berries	Top and tail or hull. Wash and add 100 g/4 oz sugar.	3–5

INDEX